Collaborating, Consulting, and Working in Teams for Students with Special Needs

ANN KNACKENDOFFEL

Kansas State University

PEGGY DETTMER

Kansas State University

LINDA P. THURSTON

Kansas State University

 **Pearson**

New York, NY

Director and Portfolio Manager: *Kevin Davis*
Content Producer: *Janelle Rogers*
Senior Development Editor: *Christina Robb*
Media Project Manager: *Lauren Carlson*
Portfolio Management Assistant: *Anne McAlpine*
Executive Field Marketing Manager: *Krista Clark*
Executive Product Marketing Manager: *Christopher Barry*
Procurement Specialist: *Carol Melville*
Full Service Project Management: *Thistle Hill Publishing Services, LLC*
Cover Designer: *Carie Keller*
Cover Image: *Rido/Shutterstock*
Composition: Cenveo® Publisher Services

Credits and acknowledgments borrowed from other sources and reproduced, with permission, in this textbook appear below and on the appropriate page within text.

Pen-and-Ink Illustrations: Jane More Loeb

Library of Congress Cataloging-in-Publication Data
Names: Knackendoffel, Ann, author. | Knackendoffel, Ann. | Dettmer, Peggy. |
 Thurston, Linda P.
Title: Collaborating, consulting, and working in teams for students with special
 needs / Ann Knackendoffel, Kansas State University, Peggy Dettmer, Kansas
 State University, Linda P. Thurston, Kansas State University.
Description: Eighth edition. | New York, NY : Pearson, [2018] | Includes
 bibliographical references and index.
Identifiers: LCCN 2017004094| ISBN 9780134672588 (pbk.) | ISBN 0134672585
 (pbk.)
Subjects: LCSH: Children with disabilities—Education—United States. |
 Special education—United States. | Educational consultants—United
 States. | Teaching teams—United States.
Classification: LCC LC4031 .D47 2018 | DDC 371.9—dc23
LC record available at https://lccn.loc.gov/2017004094

1   17

ISBN-10   0-13-467258-5
ISBN-13: 978-0-13-467258-8

ABOUT THE AUTHORS

Ann Knackendoffel, assistant professor in special education at Kansas State University, earned a Ph.D. from the University of Kansas in special education and school administration. She co-authored a book on collaborative problem solving between general educators and special educators and created online alternative course materials for general education majors focusing on students with special needs. Dr. Knackendoffel has taught students at elementary and secondary levels and students with high incidence disabilities. She teaches a graduate-level course in consultation and collaboration for special educators at Kansas State University and has conducted numerous workshops and conference presentations on collaborative school consultation. She teaches courses in the areas of special education academic interventions and assistive technology. Her particular interests are collaborative problem solving, use of technology in education, and supervision of paraeducators.

Peggy Dettmer is professor emeritus of education at Kansas State University, where she earned an M.S. in special education and Ph.D. in educational psychology. Her forty-two years of teaching experience were divided somewhat evenly between K–8 public schools and the teacher education program at Kansas State University, where her areas of emphasis were educational psychology, assessment for effective teaching, education of gifted and talented students, collaborative school consultation, creativity, and professional development. She chaired the Educational Psychology and Counseling Department and directed the College of Education honors program for several years. She was senior author of the first seven editions of this book and co-authored a book on classroom assessment as well as numerous articles for refereed journals. She has conducted many professional development activities in her main areas of professional interest.

Linda P. Thurston is a professor in the Department of Special Education, Counseling and Student Affairs, Associate Dean for Research and Graduate Studies, and Lydia E. Skeen Endowed Chair in Education at Kansas State University. In addition to teaching research and evaluation courses at the graduate level in the College of Education, she founded a university-based evaluation center and led the planning of a graduate certificate in social justice education. Thurston has published and taught in the areas of disabilities, gender, family, and issues related to social justice in evaluation and education. She served as a program officer in the Education and Human Resources Directorate at the National Science Foundation for several years.

BRIEF TABLE OF CONTENTS

CONTENTS

■■■■■

3   Structuring Foundations for Collaboration, Consultation, and Teamwork   70

4   Communicating Effectively for Collaboration and Teaming   108

5   Using the Problem-Solving Process in Collaborative School Consultation and Teamwork   144

6   Using Tools for Organizing, Managing, and Evaluating Collaboration   179

7   Collaborating as Instructional Partners and Teams   223

8   Building Collaborative Relationships with Team Members from Diverse Populations and Contexts   279

9 Engaging Families in Home-School Collaborations and Partnerships   313

10 Working in Collaborative Teams with Paraeducators   345

11 Collaborating Through Leadership, Advocacy, and Community Partnerships   385

12 Charting Your Course for Collaborative School Consultation   413

PREFACE

From the first edition in 1993 through the eight editions to date, the purpose of this book has been to promote school collaboration, consultation, and teamwork in order to transform school learning environments into settings where education is special for every student and all educators can be successful in their complex, demanding roles.

NEW TO THIS EDITION

The eighth edition is available as an enhanced Pearson eText,[1] emphasizing student-centered learning, with the following features:

- **Embedded Video Examples:** Our new digital format allows us to directly link to short, accessible, informative videos introducing students to education professionals, educational challenges, diverse teams, and strategies for collaboration.
- **Application Exercises:** Each chapter concludes with an opportunity for students to apply their understanding of chapter concepts via a brief short-answer assessment. Relevant feedback is provided by the authors to scaffold student understanding.

As with every revision of this text, the content and references from the previous edition were carefully edited and updated. Beyond that, however, revisions in this eighth edition of the book have been guided by feedback from students, input from colleagues in education, suggestions from editors and reviewers and other users of the book, and our own teaching and studies. The major revisions include:

- Reorganization of chapters and content within chapters to reflect changing times with new educational policies and teaching tools, as well as continued exploration for ways to help students with very special needs achieve success in school.
- Updates on educational designs and models such as Response to Intervention, Universal Design for Learning, Professional Learning Communities, teamwork for data-based decision making, collaborative consultation models, techniques and practices for educating collaboratively, and expanded content for working with para-educators and co-teachers.
- More opportunities to put collaborative school consultation theories and methods into practice with activities and expanded resources that personalize learning and promote concepts presented.
- Application exercises that conclude each chapter with the opportunity to summarize the content, construct a brief application to a hypothetical situation, and read feedback in the form of a sample response from the text's authors.

---

[1]*Please note that eText enhancements are only available in the Pearson eText, and are not available in third-party eTexts such as VitalSource and Kindle.*

- Attention to expanded technology tools for collaboration and communication, especially social media for communication and consultation, resource sharing, observation, planning and management, and evaluation.

We aspire to have users of the book become knowledgeable, caring, ethical, and wise decision-making professionals. Educators in an increasingly complex and interconnected world need much more than basic knowledge and practical application in their classrooms. Their challenging instructional roles will call for more complex and sophisticated skills in problem identification and problem solving, communication and collaboration, thinking critically and creatively, planning for special needs of their students, and assessing and evaluating their progress. General education teachers and administrators, special education teachers and directors, early childhood education teachers, school psychologists, school counselors, related services and support personnel, professional development and curriculum development staff, and community leaders, including those in medical and social fields, must become co-educators with students and their families in planful, purposeful ways.

Teacher education programs in the past did not stress development of interpersonal skills among colleagues. Now educators collaborate with their co-educators, and in doing so they become wiser, more insightful, and more skilled instructional partners. This book intends to be a vehicle for developing such skills. It has been constructed to bridge *principles* of collaboration, consultation, and teamwork in the school context and *practices* of processes and content to address and serve students' special needs.

Each of the twelve chapters begins with instructional objectives and a brief list of key terms. Short situations set the stage for chapter content. Activities within the text provide opportunities to practice, discuss topics with others, agree and disagree, dig deeper, and even have some fun along the way. Lists of tips at the ends of each chapter offer practical suggestions and reminders for putting the content to use.

INSTRUCTOR SUPPLEMENTS

The following, author-created, resources are available for instructors to download at **www.pearsonhighered.com/educators**. Instructors enter the authors or title of this book, select the 8th edition, and then click on the "Resources" tab to log in and download instructor resources.

- The **Instructor's Resource Manual** (013445863X / 9780134458632) provides an objective- and subjective-item test bank and additional activities beyond those presented in the book.
- **PowerPoint Slides** (0134447638 / 9780134447636) are available to download for each chapter. Presentations include key concept summaries and other aids to help students understand, organize, and remember core concepts and ideas.

ACKNOWLEDGMENTS

We are pleased to recognize individuals who have contributed to the thinking, teaching, and writing of this book. In a collaborative process it is not easy to tell where the contribution of one appears, another interfaces, and yet another goes on from there. This demonstrates once again the complexity and the beauty of working together toward lofty aims.

We thank our editors and assistants for their guidance and oversight in the development of this project: Ann Davis, Christina Robb, Kevin Davis, Janelle Rogers, and Anne McAlpine. We also extend our appreciation to the reviewers: Dr. Jane Leatherman, Indiana–Purdue University, Fort Wayne; Nancy Glomb, Utah State University; Rita Brusca-Vega, Purdue University Calumet; Deborah S. Reed, University of North Florida; and Cindy Topdemir, University of South Florida. Once again we extend posthumous recognition to Jane More Loeb for her pen-and-ink drawings. As teacher, director of mentorships for gifted and talented middle school students, curriculum specialist for children with learning and behavioral disorders, devoted wife and dedicated mother, Jane influenced school and home co-educators with her instruction, special education curriculum, photography, and artwork.

Conceptualizing, planning, writing, editing, and organizing material for this book takes months of work and requires understanding and patience from family. We acknowledge and appreciate the understanding and support they provided during the production of this manuscript. Even Paisley the dog spent many late nights by the computer waiting patiently for bedtime to come at last.

We trust that the material presented in this enhanced eText, the accompanying *Instructor's Manual with Test Bank*, and the *PowerPoint* package, all available online, will be helpful and inspirational to those who use them. The suggestions and contributions of students, families, teaching colleagues, reviewers, and editorial staff have been an important part of the process and the product. That is what collaborative school consultation and teamwork are all about.

CHAPTER 1

WORKING TOGETHER IN COLLABORATION, CONSULTATION, AND TEAMS

"Why did you choose education as a career?" That question has been posed over the course of many years to experienced teachers, graduate students studying for advanced degrees in education, and undergraduate students just beginning their teacher education programs. Responses from all groups are amazingly similar:

- *"I want to make a difference in children's lives."*
- *"I want to help kids reach their potential."*
- *"I want to make the world a better place."*

Some teachers speak of their passion for a particular curricular area and the desire to share that enthusiasm with students. But other factors—respect and gratitude from the public, wanting to emulate a favorite teacher, plentiful job opportunities, steady salary, anticipation of summer vacations, are further down on teachers' lists as reasons for choosing a career in education.

Goals to mold younger generations and make the world a better place are lofty ones indeed. In the past such goals were built on expectations of being in "my classroom," with "my students," using "the teaching ideas I have been assembling and can put into practice." But these goals no longer fit neatly into twenty-first century environments. Now educators are being called on to work in more interactive ways by collaborating with colleagues as school co-educators for learning of all *students in* inclusive *school environments, in partnerships with families as home co-educators of students, in planning differentiated instruction for diverse needs, and as models for the teamwork that will be required in careers and community life of the future.*

CHAPTER OBJECTIVES

On completing this chapter, the reader should be able to:

1. Define processes of collaboration, consultation, and teamwork in the school environment.
2. Illustrate factors that motivate educators to collaborate and work as teams.
3. Describe roles and responsibilities inherent in collaborative school consultation endeavors.
4. Identify historical events in education that have led to collaborative school consultation.

5. Discuss benefits for students and educators from collaboration and teamwork.

6. Give examples of competencies needed for educators to be effective collaborators and team members.

KEY TERMS

client	consult	home co-educator
co-educator	consultant	network
collaboration	consultation	school co-educator
collaborative ethic	consultee	teamwork
collaborative school consultation	co-teaching	

■ ■ ■ ■ ■ ■

SITUATION 1.A[1]

The setting is the faculty room of a typical high school where four faculty members are sharing school news and airing their concerns.

English Teacher: I'm getting another student with intellectual disability next week—more outcomes of the legislation for special education, I guess. I'll have him in my English class, along with the student who has behavior disorders.

Math Teacher: [with a chuckle] Must be because you're doing such a great job with that one. [serious tone] But I know what you mean. Our special ed teachers don't seem to be providing as much direct service for these students as they did when I first started teaching. But that was before we'd ever heard the words "inclusion" or "collaboration" or "co-teaching."

Music Teacher: And before we were introduced to mainstreaming in least restrictive environments (remember that one?) and inclusionary classrooms.

English Teacher: Well, a "collaborative school consulting teacher" (now that's a mouthful!) is coming to our next departmental meeting to talk about our roles in helping students with their special needs. I understand we're going to be asked to collaborate with her, along with all the other things we do, of course. We may even be encouraged to try some co-teaching with the special education staff.

Physical Education Teacher/Coach: Hmmm, don't those two words cancel each other out? "Consult" and "collaborate," that is. I believe you English teachers call that an oxymoron.

Music Teacher: I guess I'd be inclined to consult a tax accountant for some expert advice and think of collaboration as where everyone works together to accomplish some common goals they've agreed on. As for co-teaching, I can tell you what a difficult process that is when you have a group of independent thinkers and free spirits who like to do things their own way and all want to be the star!

English Teacher: Well, frankly I'm not interested in word plays right now. I'm more concerned about finding out where the time is going to come from to do all the planning and coordinating this will require. My schedule is packed, and my few minutes of free time don't jibe with anyone else's except for this brief lunch period. Furthermore, I want to know who will have the bottom-line responsibility for which students, and when, where, and how that will happen.

Math Teacher: Right. I've had some concerns about expectations for student achievement in my courses, not to mention all the testing we're required to do and what the test results will show. I think we need more information and then more help to accomplish all of this. I hope we get it.

[1]We recommend that persons using this book with a group take parts to read each of the situations aloud, contributing in conversational tone and style. In this way, the situations will seem relevant rather than artificial.

Teachers in earlier times worked alone in their classrooms for the most part. They marked the attendance forms, took lunch counts, completed other required daily procedures, and then closed their classroom doors to teach. They tried to handle each learning and behavioral situation with minimal assistance. Asking for help would have been tantamount to showing insecurity or demonstrating incompetence. After all, capable teachers in the past had managed eight grades in one-room schoolhouses without assistance, hadn't they?

But now schools are multi–dimensional centers of activity in which teachers and students are challenged in many different ways to prepare for the escalating demands of an increasingly complex future. Legislation, educational reform movements, business and industry demands, and parent pressures have spawned programs such as charter schools, voucher systems, dual-language classrooms, block scheduling, professional learning communities, and the rising incidence of homeschooling. Various configurations of school settings have been tried where students move between classrooms, or stay put while teachers move, or receive part of the day's instruction from co-teachers and sometimes from special education teachers. Classrooms have been designed with half-walls, no walls, multi-grade students, or combined-subjects students. In the midst of this, the individual teacher, with myriad responsibilities and widely diverse groups of students, can still feel stranded and alone in a crowded setting. In spite of all the comings and goings, the typical school environment is devoid of stimulating interaction with adults. Teachers may be just next-door or down the hall from other adults, yet paradoxically somewhat insulated from each other during the school day. Tight schedules, dictated by bells and passing routines, discourage meaningful discussion about the day's activities that sometimes extend into evening responsibilities, so school personnel teach and lead and supervise students autonomously for the most part. This makes teaching a lonely occupation in a very public place. (See Figure 1.1.)

Many teachers, especially those just beginning their teaching careers, have been reluctant to discuss their concerns or ask for assistance from support personnel, lest their competency be questioned and their confidence waver. Lack of dialogue with peers contributes to feelings of isolation and inhibits opportunities to learn from them

FIGURE 1.1   "I Feel So Alone!"

(Johnson & Pugach, 1996). In the meantime, other educators, including resource teachers, related services personnel and support personnel, and family caregivers, have waited in the wings until called on for counsel and assistance. Too often the potential sources of help become involved only after situations reach crisis level—when they could have been more helpful in initial stages of problem identification and early intervention.

As the teacher's list of responsibilities grows and the time available for instruction diminishes, the burden of trying to serve exceptional learning needs (ELN) of all students becomes heavier. Adding to the complexity of the school day with its array of curricular and extra-curricular activities is the growing awareness by educators that <u>all</u> students, not just those identified for placement in special education, have individual needs that require special attention. Furthermore, every student has unique abilities and talents to be nurtured. So the challenge of developing student potential and serving special needs of all students to prepare them for extended education, fields of work, and citizenship roles can seem overwhelming.

WHY WORK TOGETHER AS EDUCATORS?

In our increasingly interdependent and specialized world, it is unlikely that one person will have enough knowledge and ability in any field of endeavor for every circumstance. This is especially relevant in education where populations are diverse, the developmental stages range from preschool to postsecondary, and students' life choices are broad palettes of possibility. Teaching is a multidimensional activity. An educator's role has never been easy, and it is becoming more challenging each year. School personnel are bombarded with more and more responsibilities. Legislators, community leaders, and the general public are raising expectations for student achievement and measurable yearly progress, yet not sure what is best for their schools and communities. However, one thing is certain. Existing programs and practices will not be enough to address the complex issues and multiple concerns of the future.

Expectations for education have escalated and expanded well beyond the one-room schoolhouse or isolated classroom where a teacher was the be-all and end-all for students. Teams and networks of personnel are needed to address issues of instruction, management of the learning environment, assessment of student achievement, professional development activity for educators, partnerships with parents, and communication with community leaders. So if educators expect to "make the world a better place, make a difference in children's lives, and help others reach their potential," it is reasonable that they consult, collaborate, and work as teams in partnership with others to achieve their lofty goals.

Collaborative school consultation in the teaching profession is not out of line with other professions. It is becoming more and more routine in fields as varied as business, medicine, law, industry, fashion, sports, construction, scientific research, journalism, decorating, finance—the list is endless. Some consultants even have their own consultants! Teamwork is emphasized frequently across a wide range of work settings, from service professions to trades to government to community leadership. In fields where networking is encouraged with others who have similar yet helpfully different perspectives, results have been dramatic. Sharing expertise stimulates productivity and growth as colleagues collaborate and consult with peers in their areas of special abilities.

ACTIVITY 1.1

What Are a Teacher's Responsibilities?

What does a teacher do in the course of a day, a week, a school year? With one or two colleagues, in short phrases, list all the specific responsibilities you can think of that a teacher typically performs during the course of the school year. Draw upon recollections from your student days, college coursework, student teaching, and any teaching experiences that you have had. Remember to include not only responsibilities for instruction and curriculum preparation but also for assessment, classroom management, extracurricular duties, supervision, maintenance of learning environments, preparation of materials, and professional development activities. Expect to come up with dozens and dozens.

If you do this with several educators representing various grade levels, content areas, and specialized roles, your combined lists will be an impressive and perhaps surprising collection of teaching responsibilities. Engaging in the process itself will be an example of collaboration, with every participant contributing ideas from personal viewpoints and experiences.

DESCRIBING COLLABORATION, CONSULTATION, AND TEAMWORK

Practical definitions of "collaboration," "consultation," and "teamwork" in school settings must be general enough for application in a wide range of school structures and circumstances, yet flexible enough for adaptation to many types of schools and communities. Defining terms is difficult due to the challenges of drawing meaningful boundaries and the risks of being too limiting or too broad (John-Steiner, Weber, & Minnis, 1998). Drawing from sources that include *Webster's Third New International Dictionary*, unabridged (1976), *Webster's New Collegiate Dictionary*, 8th edition (1996), and *World Book Dictionary, Volumes 1 and 2* (2003), several shades of meaning and a number of synonyms emerge that can be applied to schools and education. The words and synonyms complement each other to form a conceptual foundation for collaboration, consultation, and teamwork in contemporary teaching and learning environments.

The process of forming definitions or descriptions requires careful attention to semantics because meanings can vary from user to user and from context to context. People who say "Oh, it's just semantics; so it's no big deal," are overlooking the importance of appropriate word selection for verbal, written, or sign-language communication. Consider the responsibilities of a foreign diplomat in applying delicate nuances of meaning to complex ideas about key issues on the world stage. It is quite likely that much communication and interaction among diverse populations and nations worldwide gets twisted in translation. Discussions of abstract concepts such as motivation, respect, effort, expectations and fairness, or concepts that elude definitive assessment such as differentiation, ability, and achievement are particularly vulnerable to distortion and erosion in the process of translation.

Careful selection of words and thoughtful construction of definitions are a start toward effective communication and collaboration. Words make the trip through a person's nervous system before they can be referred outward to the real thing (Sondel, 1958). A person should not assume that everyone responds to words in precisely the same way. Consider the word "chair." It might signal "time out" to a misbehaving toddler or become a place for a tired parent to relax. A dentist may see a chair as a special piece of equipment for professional work, while to a college professor it might mean a coveted position, and to a convicted murderer it might portend death (Sondel, 1958). Perusing synonyms for a particular word can uncover shades of meaning available for diverse settings. A well-known example is the number and variety of meanings that people native to the Arctic regions have for the concept of "snow."

Definitions that will be helpful to continue the analysis and application of collaborative school consultation and teamwork, as drawn and condensed from several sources, are:

co-educator: An educator who collaborates, consults, teams with, co-teaches, networks with other educator(s) to address students' needs for learning and doing. May be a school educator, home educator (parent or other caregiver), or community resource person.

collaboration: To labor together, or to work jointly in cooperative interaction to achieve a shared goal.

collaborative ethic: A philosophy of shared purpose and interdependent practices among co-educators in working together for best interests of students and schools.

teamwork: Joint action in which each person participates cooperatively and collaboratively to contribute to the goal and subordinates personal prominence to enhance the effectiveness of the group.

consult: To advise or seek advice; to confer, consider, examine, refer to, communicate in order to decide or plan something, seek an opinion as a guide to one's own judgment, request information or facts, or talk over a situation with someone.

consultation: Advisement, counsel, a conference; formal or informal deliberation to provide direct services to students or to work with co-educators in addressing special needs.

consultant: One who provides professional input or renders services in a field of special knowledge and training, or more simply, one who consults with another for a common purpose.

client: An individual, a group, an agency, or other entity receiving consulting services in order to learn (know the material) and do (apply that learning) in school and beyond, who is often but not always the student.

consultee: As described in social science literature, a mediator between consultant and client (Tharp, 1975); one who confers with a consultant to gather and exchange information and advice and apply it for the client's needs. The consultee is often, but by no means always, the general education or classroom teacher, and in some cases the consultee can be advisor to the consultant.

co-teaching: When two or more teachers plan and implement instruction, and monitor and assess student achievement, typically in an inclusive, collaborative classroom environment.

network: A system of connections among individuals or groups having similar purposes who interact and collaborate to accomplish shared goals.

Drawing upon words just defined, the following description will frame major concepts presented in this material:

Collaborative school consultation is an interactive process in which school co-educators, home co-educators, students, and resource and support personnel combine their knowledge and expertise to determine the student's educational needs, plan learning and behavioral goals, implement the plan, assess outcomes, and follow up as needed.

In Situation 1.A presented earlier, the client is the new student with an intellectual disability. The special education teacher for the school district will serve that student directly for part of the school day and indirectly by collaborating with the classroom teacher of English. The student may receive some direct service from the special education teacher as special education consultant, but for the most part, the direct service comes to the student from the classroom teacher as a general education consultee.

Co-educators in a consultant role do not hold claim to all the expertise. Competent consultants also listen and learn. They help consultees discover and apply what they already know. They help them recognize their talents and trust their own skills. Consultation helps consultees develop skills to solve current problems and generalize those skills to other problems. It is an interactive process requiring active participation of the consultee, not imposition of the process. Consultants should engage in self-analysis and reflection about the impact they will have on the consultative process.

Co-teaching and other teaming and networking interactions are examples of collaboration. The collaborative consultation relationship requires mutual trust and behaviors that allow joint exploration of ways to help students. Johnson and Donaldson (2007) present collaboration as a way of overcoming the triple-threat norms of autonomy, egalitarianism, and deference to authority that have long characterized schools. Effective collaborative school consultation and teamwork will mean having co-educators who are more capable and more confident in their capabilities when addressing students' special needs than they were in autonomous teaching environments.

Goals and objectives for special education services are based on identification of needs as outlined in the Individual Education Plans (IEPs) developed collaboratively by **school co-educators** and **home co-educators**. This identification is contingent on defining the disability, disabilities, or exceptional ability, but it is not a label to be "put upon" a student. Special education teachers make it clear that, "Labels are for file folders or plastic totes, not children." Furthermore, it is important to note that most disabilities are "invisible disabilities" such as attention deficit, learning disability, hearing impairment, autism spectrum disorder, and some psychological and mental health issues.

Lists of terms used in special education to identify needs may vary among federal, state, and local agencies, but typically include: autism spectrum disorder, emotional/behavioral disorder, speech and language impairment, deafness or hearing impairment, dual sensory impairment, intellectual disability, specific learning disability, multiple disabilities, orthopedic impairments, traumatic brain injury, and visual impairment or blindness. More than half of states in the United States also include gifted and talented as a part of special education because of their exceptional learning needs.

■ ■ ■ ■ ■ ▬▬▬▬▬▬▬▬▬▬▬

ACTIVITY 1.2
How Can Teachers Work Together?

With your collaborating participants, if possible, sort the list of teacher responsibilities you compiled in Activity 1.1 into categories of tasks, such as: 1) instructional, 2) curricular, 3) managerial, 4) evaluative, 5) supportive, and 6) professional-growth related categories. Then decide which tasks might be carried out productively and enjoyably when working with others to accomplish them. As an example, if the responsibility for ordering books and supplies is classified as managerial, teams of teachers might collaborate to pool their library allocations and make decisions about materials that could be shared or used for team teaching. Such a collaborative activity could spark a co-educator's interest in co-teaching with those materials, or borrowing them to extend that curriculum and instruction to another grade level, or loaning out materials to the co-educator who plans to order them.

Then mark with an asterisk (*) other responsibilities you and your group listed that you think have collaborative potential. As an example (one that involves high levels of trust and communication), two co-educators might exchange assessment of students' portfolios. The positive outcomes of this collaboration could be substantial, while less-than-positive outcomes could be used for productive discussions about rubric development and feedback methods.

Areas of responsibility might emerge that have been overlooked, such as "organizing cross-grade tutors and study-buddies" or "involving families in preparing notebooks of potential community resources." Think of these as springboards for future collaborations among school co-educators or in partnerships with home and community co-educators.

Video Example
from
YouTube

ENHANCEDetext
Video Example 1.1.

This video explains what
collaboration is and why it
important to collaborate.
(https://www.youtube.com/
watch?v=Po40I4c94R0&
index=1&listd=
PLdzGKRHkB_h2udsSEOiNjq-
m09pjYfA00)

When compared and contrasted with practices in business, industry, and numerous other professions, collaboration on a regular basis in school settings tends to be more occasional and happenstance than frequent and planned. Available and congruent time blocks are necessary for productive interaction with colleagues, but these opportunities are few in the course of a busy school day. Then, too, practical structures for working together and training for these less familiar roles have been minimal. It follows that careful assessment of collaborative outcomes has been the exception, not the routine. However, the growing complexities of teaching and escalating demands for student achievement and accountability of schools underscore the strong need for working together in many dimensions.

MOTIVATION FOR WORKING TOGETHER

In a school context, all three processes—collaboration, consultation, and teamwork—involve interaction among school personnel, families and students, and community to achieve common goals. However, there are subtle distinctions. In school consultation, the consultant contributes specialized expertise toward an educational problem and the consultee delivers direct service utilizing that expertise. Consultants and consultees begin to collaborate when they assume equal ownership of the problem and solutions. It is a way of working in which power struggles and ineffectual politeness can be detrimental to team goals. Collaborative consultation must be voluntary, and it should be noted that successful consultants use different styles of interaction under different circumstances for different situations (Friend & Cook, 1992).

While true consultation is voluntary, that doesn't mean you have to throw up your hands and give up if you meet resistance. Think of opportunities to collaborate as a door being in varying degrees of openness. Whether the door is shut, cracked open, or fully open, your goal is to move the "door" or collaborative relationship to the next level. If the door is shut—the person doesn't want to collaborate—then you should begin with simply building a cordial relationship—making a point to acknowledge the person when you pass in the hall and maybe start up a conversation about something casual, not necessarily work-related. If the proverbial door is open slightly to collaboration, your goal is to move the relationship to the next step from primarily social interactions to education-related discussions. Solicit the person's opinion about a district initiative or share something you read in a recent professional journal or from an education online newsletter or blog and ask for their thoughts on the topic. Use this opportunity to share something about co-planning or co-teaching while thinking aloud and posing questions around the topic and how it might work in your school. Finally, if you have faculty with whom you have successful collaborative relationships, think about how you can take those one step further in having them help bring along those on the fence or share your joint success with others. It's all about pushing the door open just a little more.

Collaborating as a teaching team can fuel group spirit and develop process skills that help teachers interact in more productive ways (Maeroff, 1993). One of the best examples of working together is a musical ensemble. Whether one is accompanying, performing with a small group, or playing with an orchestra, band, or choir, it is the united effort that creates the musical experience. Musicians of many instruments are not brought together to play the same note! Doing so would only make the music louder, not richer and more harmonious. In similar fashion, co-educators work in concert, not usually in perfect unison, to create an effective learning experience for all students in the class. Consultation, collaboration, and teaming up to co-teach or partner in learning activities will create many opportunities to engage in a strengths-type interaction so that each person is learning from and building on the strengths of the others.

ACTIVITY 1.3
Collaboration in Many Venues

The word "collaboration" is popping up with increasing frequency in newscasts, speeches, documentaries, sports reviews, entertainment and media discussions, political panels, organizational reports, blogs, casual conversations, science breakthroughs, community meetings, and many other arenas of our daily lives. It is a frequent topic in professional journals, articles, books, and the popular TED Talks. For one week, listen and watch for appearance of the word. Then make note of each time you see or hear the word and the context in which it appeared. If tallying is not convenient, just make a mental note, "There it is. I did hear or see 'collaborate' mentioned X times today." Then consolidate your findings with those of others and discuss when, where, and why it appeared.

What Collaborative Consultation *Is*

As illustrated by Pugach and Johnson (2002), collaboration is a way of being, not a set of isolated actions. The collaborative process reframes how educators interact in school contexts, including special education teachers with regular education teachers, public schools with institutions of higher education, and agencies with schools and families. Welch (1998) deconstructs the term "collaboration" and comes up with a unique concept of working together for mutual benefit. It is different from "cooperation" in which all come to agreement, but perhaps not all are benefiting. He contends that schools tend to be more cooperative than collaborative, explaining it as parallel but sometimes uneasy co-existence of general and special education. He further notes that coordination is more characteristic of interagency involvement such as in the Individual Family Service Plan (IFSP) than of the school-managed Individual Educational Plan (IEP). Welch faults the

IEP process as often involving little or no collaboration during development and implementation; it tends to be drafted before a meeting using a generalized template, then quickly reviewed and hastily approved by the team, thus "essentially negating the 'I' in the IEP process" (Welch, 1998, p. 128.). One way to improve the process would be for the classroom teacher, who is required by IDEA 2004 to participate, to participate very actively rather than as a relatively passive observer.

Wesley and Buysse (2006) distinguish consultation as operating on two planes simultaneously; that is, consulting co-educators manage consultation components while concentrating on interpersonal aspects of trusting relationships with consultees. These early childhood special educators propose that critical elements in the consultative process are having the best research findings available, using family and professional wisdom, and drawing on family and professional values. The collaborating consultant must first do no harm and then deliver services that are academically and ethically sound.

When educators—special education teachers, classroom teachers, school administrators, related services and support personnel, as well as families and community agencies, are consulting and collaborating as members of an educational team, what specific kinds of things are they doing? A summary list typically includes one or more of these:

- Discussing students' needs and ways of addressing those needs
- Listening to colleagues' concerns about a teaching situation
- Identifying learning and behavior problems and engaging in Functional Behavior Assessment (FBA) and Positive Behavior Intervention Plans (PBIP)
- Assisting families in transition periods—from early childhood education programs to kindergarten, elementary to middle school, middle school to high school, and high school to work or postsecondary education
- Differentiating instruction for all learners using principles of universal design for learning (UDL)
- Recommending classroom alternatives as first interventions for students with special learning and behavior needs
- Adapting lessons and assignments based on learner needs
- Serving as a medium for student referrals
- Demonstrating instructional techniques to help with special needs or abilities
- Providing direct assistance to colleagues in assessing the learning and behavioral needs of students
- Leading or participating in professional development activities
- Designing and implementing Individual Education Programs (IEPs)
- Sharing resources, instructional materials, and teaching ideas
- Utilizing technology for efficient and productive interactions among students as well as among co-educators
- Participating in co-teaching or demonstration teaching
- Engaging in observation, assessment, and evaluation activities
- Serving on curriculum committees, textbook committees, extracurricular activities committees, and school advisory councils

- Following through and following up on educational issues and concerns with co-educators, students and their families, and communities
- Networking with other educational professionals and other agencies who can be resources for students' needs

What Collaborative Consultation Is *Not*

School consultation is *not* therapy, counseling, or supervision. West and Idol (1987), and Morsink, Thomas, and Correa (1991) distinguish consultation as being focused on issues, in contrast with counseling that is focused on individuals. The focus must be upon educational concerns relevant to the welfare of the client and not on problems of consultees. Conoley and Conoley (1982) caution that the consultant must collaborate for issues and needs of the client, typically the student, not on the consultee who typically is the teacher.

Consulting specialists have to work diligently to shed the "expert" image held by many teachers toward consultants or specialists (Pugach & Johnson, 1989). So it is important for classroom teachers to be recognized as having expertise and resourcefulness to contribute. Collaborative consultation can emanate from any role pertinent to the case if the participants are well informed. As a professional in the medical field commented, patients collaborate with their doctors because patients are so well informed about their own conditions. This approach could be applied productively to collaborative school consultation. No consultant is the be-all, end-all expert. Any co-educator can be in a consultant role when circumstances dictate. Collaboration among professional colleagues is *not* talk or discussion for its own sake. It is important for busy, multitasking educators to have high quality think time in order to plan, sort, and prepare their professional agenda in personal ways. Furthermore, collaboration must not be hierarchical or judgmental but voluntary and entered into with parity among the teaching partners.

It is very important that collaborative services *not* be perceived as a money-saving strategy in inclusive settings to eliminate or reduce the number of school personnel or as a solution to special education teacher shortages. Even more importantly, consultative and collaborative structures providing indirect service must not be regarded as substitutes for cases where there is a strong need for direct services. School administrators and members of the local school boards must plan carefully to avoid setting up hierarchical climates that could encourage inappropriate consultative practices. Collaborative school consultation and co-teaching cannot be forced upon educators. As emphasized earlier, the process *must* be voluntary.

Another important consideration is to protect the rights of teachers to have some ideas that are theirs alone. Most teachers are willing, even eager, to share ideas and lend help to colleagues; however, they should not be asked to give up their specialties any more than chefs should be expected to relinquish their most prized recipes. Such altruistic behavior would result in giving up practices that are individually special and personally satisfying. That is not the purpose of collaboration, nor should it be a presumed condition of co-teaching. There will be times when teachers need to be autonomous in their work. At such times, collaborators will want to encourage colleagues to develop personal skills and strengths, but then step aside.

ROLE OPPORTUNITIES AND RESPONSIBILITIES IN COLLABORATIVE ENDEAVORS

When contemplating collaborative and consultative roles, educators often express their concerns by asking questions such as these:

- Who am I in this role?
- How do I carry out the responsibilities of this role?
- How will I know whether or not I am succeeding?
- How can I prepare for the role?

First, it is essential that central administrators and policy-makers such as school boards explain the importance of consultative, collaborative, and co-teaching roles. Then building-level administrators must reiterate the value of these practices to the school, staff, and students. Parity, voluntary participation, and collegial interdependence should be emphasized. A key factor for success is allocating sufficient time and suitable places for interactions to take place.

Teachers will need encouragement to enthusiastically share the responsibilities for all students in collaborative environments. Related services personnel and support personnel will need to be integrated into a collaborative context. Families must receive information about the purposes and benefits of collaborative roles and partnered teaching. They will need to be assured that these services are right for their child. Students should be an integral part of the planning process and have opportunities to participate as young collaborators intensely involved in their own educational process.

SITUATION 1.B

In your mind's eye, return to the school district where Situation 1.A took place. Listen to four special education teachers who are talking in the district's main conference room before the special education director arrives for a planning meeting.

Secondary High Incidence Special Education Teacher: I understand we're here to decide how we're going to inform staff and parents about the consultation and collaboration and perhaps co-teaching practices we'll be implementing soon. But I think we'd better figure out first just what it is we'll be doing in these roles.

Behavioral Disorders Teacher Specialist: Definitely. I have a really basic question that I've been thinking about a lot. What am I going to do the first week, even the first day, as a consulting teacher? I understand a few people on our staff have had some experience in collaboration and consulting in former positions, but this is new to the rest of us.

Gifted Education Teacher: I agree. I've been thinking about all those different teaching styles and methods of doing things that will surface as we work closely together. Teachers won't all like or want the same things for their classrooms and their students.

Elementary High Incidence Special Education Teacher: And remember, we are supposed to say, "<u>Our</u> students." Yes, I doubt this is something we can become experts about very quickly. But from what little I've had a chance to read and ask others about collaborative processes, the key to success is using good communication skills and problem-solving techniques.

Gifted Education Teacher: Yes, and at the same time we have to take into account the amount of resources it will take to provide the materials and methods each student needs. I'm a bit apprehensive about it all, but I'm willing to try it.

Behavioral Disorders Teacher Specialist: I guess I am, too. I've been thinking for some time now that our current methods of dealing with learning and behavior problems are not as effective and efficient as they should be. And I realize really bright kids are being kept on hold in the classroom much of the time. Changing the way we do things can be energizing, you know. I think we have to be optimistic about the possible benefits for both students <u>and</u> teachers, including us.

Secondary High Incidence Special Education Teacher: Well, I for one happen to feel a sense of urgency because my first experience of being a collaborative consultant is coming up soon. I'll be doing some observation and perhaps co-teaching with an English teacher at the high school next week. She already has a student with severe learning and behavioral disability in one of her classrooms. We'll be organizing a plan for this new student with intellectual disability who's enrolling in that school. That's why I'd like to talk it over and arrive at some consensus about the collaborative consultation process and also about co-teaching.

Elementary High Incidence Special Education Teacher: I'll be interested both professionally and personally in how you get along with that. As I think you all know, I have a son at the high school who is placed on the autism spectrum. It's been a struggle for him and his teachers in many of his high school classes. In my family, we are concerned about his eventual transition to either getting more education or going to the job market. From what I've read and heard about resource consultation and interagency networking, I'm very interested in having more collaborative efforts in our schools to help him develop his potential and give our family a positive outlook down the road.

Interchangeable Roles and Responsibilities

Educators are becoming more and more aware that collaboration to achieve a common goal often produces more beneficial results than isolated efforts made by an individual. As the familiar homily reminds us, two heads are better than one, and several heads are better yet. The collaborative consultation process channels each individual's strengths and talents toward serving the client's needs.

Any person who consults in one situation may be a consultee or even a client in another. In each of these instances, consultant and consultee would share responsibility for working out a plan to help the client. A special education teacher might be a consultant for one situation and a consultee in another. The student is typically a client (recipient of the intervention), but in some cases could be a consultee or even a consultant. Consultation might be initiated by the social worker, special reading teacher, or general classroom teacher. Consultation where several educators collaborate could also be requested by a parent or a school counselor. The combinations of roles participating in school collaboration and consultation to help students and teachers are virtually limitless. In Figure 1.2, each role, depending on circumstance, could be a consultant, a consultee, or a client. Although roles and responsibilities may vary among individuals and across situations, if there is understanding about the nature of the role and appreciation for its possibilities, a collaborative and facilitative spirit will prevail.

FIGURE 1.2   Collaborators in the Consultant, Consultee, or Client Role

Special education teacher	Student with learning disability
General classroom teacher	Student with behavioral disorder
School psychologist	Preschool student
School counselor	Student with an intellectual disability
Reading specialist	Student with high aptitude/talent
Building administrator	Student with attention deficit disorder
Gifted program facilitator	Student with physical disability
School nurse	Parent of student with disability
Media specialist	Parent of student with high aptitude/talent
Technology specialist	Community-based mentor
Resource room teacher	Student on the autism spectrum
School cafeteria personnel	Medical doctor/dentist
School bus driver	University professor in special education
School custodian	Speech and language pathologist
Special education director	University professor in general education
Early childhood teacher	Probation officer
Curriculum specialist	Head Start personnel
Professional development personnel	State Department of Education personnel
Student (preservice) teacher	Paraeducator
Social worker	Minister/priest/rabbi/imam
School advisory council member	School board member
School district administrator	Other?

■ ■ ■ ■ ■

ACTIVITY 1.4
Interchangeable Roles for Consultant, Consultee, and Client

When we think about collaboration with special education, the typical image that comes to mind involves the special educator serving as the consultant, with the general education teacher being the consultee, and the student as the client. In fact, those roles are very common. This activity is designed to broaden your perspective. Write each of the persons/positions listed in Figure 1.2 on three different color slips of paper. For example, red slips could represent the consultant role, blue slips the consultee, and green the client. Put all the slips of the same color in separate containers to draw from or spread them out face down on a table. Next, have each person draw one slip of paper from each color category and then create a scenario where the person/position might be in each of the roles. For example, you might have a student on the autism spectrum in the consultant role when she visits with the special education teacher (consultee) about the bus driver (client) not allowing her to sit in the same seat on the bus each morning. Join together with others to share your scenarios and/or collaborate to come up with situations that may not be apparent to you on your own. Doing this will help you realize that anyone could potentially be in any one of these three roles.

School improvement issues and legislative mandates may have convinced educators that the concept of collaborative school consultation is a promising method for helping students with special needs. But conversion of concepts to practice is not so simple. Questions in Situation 1.B above were raised in the school district conference room by four special educators about practical concerns that hinted at even more issues:

- Where do I begin as a collaborating school consultant?
- What do I do the first day on the job? The first week?
- Let me see a sample schedule for the first week, and the first month also.
- Where am I to be headed by the end of the year?

Other questions and concerns that are likely to surface sooner or later include:

- Will I have opportunity to work with students? After all, that's the reason I chose teaching as a career.
- Where's my room? Will I have office space and supplies?
- Will I have a space and time in the schedule for group work with students?
- Will I be regarded as an important part of the teaching staff and welcomed?
- If I need some special preparation for this role, how do I get that?
- How will I be evaluated in this role, and by whom?
- As a collaborating consultant who helps consultees meet special needs, will I be working myself out of a job?

In addition to these concerns, special education teachers may be thinking:

- Will participating in collaboration and consultation make me appear incompetent?
- How much of my classroom time with students will be needed to do this method of service?
- How do I go about allocating that time?
- When will I have time and space to interact like this with other teachers?

Participants in consultation and collaboration will want to voice their concerns and work through their feelings of insecurity as they sort out the dynamics of their new roles. School administrators have the responsibility of initiating open, candid expressions of concerns, providing assurance of support, and encouraging candid discussions about issues before they escalate into problems.

HISTORICAL BACKGROUND OF COLLABORATIVE SCHOOL CONSULTATION

At this point, it will be constructive to take a fresh look at the background of social movements, educational reforms, and legislative actions that have elevated collaboration, consultation, co-teaching, and teamwork to the forefront of effective teaching for special needs. Although this background material is familiar to most special education teachers and many general education teachers, reviewing it for the purpose of noting the frequent emphasis on collaboration in recent years will be instructive.

The origin of special education in public schools dates back to the mid-nineteenth century, when state followed state (Rhode Island in 1840, Massachusetts in 1852, and eventually all others) in passing compulsory school attendance laws that mandated formal education for every school-age child regardless of disability, giftedness, or other special need. Now, in the twenty-first century, up to one-third of all school-age children are experiencing difficulties in school because of special learning and behavioral needs. If the exceptional learning needs of gifted students were included, this figure would increase substantially.

These realities, along with various social issues of the times, have spurred interest in school consultation, collaboration, and other forms of teamwork such as co-teaching, mentoring, cooperative learning, and peer tutoring. The result has been an escalating number of conferences, publications, research studies, pilot programs, federal and state grants, training projects, as well as development of several teacher preparation courses and programs for understanding and applying collaborative practices in schools. State and national organizations have formed to focus on special needs and recommend practices for addressing those needs. A brief look at educational history from the past several decades will highlight significant events in the merger of special education and general education philosophies and practices that have led to the call for collaborative school consultation.

Collaborative School Consultation in Historical Perspective

School consultation probably originated in mental health and management fields (Reynolds & Birch, 1988). Gerald Caplan (1970) had developed consultation programs to train staff members for working with troubled adolescents in Israel at the close of World War II. Building upon this Caplanian mental health consultation concept (Caplan, Caplan, & Erchul, 1995), mental health services escalated and moved into school settings, where consultation services of school psychologists produced promising results. The role of consultation in school psychology was broadened to encourage collaborative relationships (Gallessich, 1974; Pryzwansky, 1974). Such relationships were nurtured to help teachers, administrators, and parents deal with future problems as well as immediate concerns.

Intensive special education advocacy, federal policy-making for exceptional students, and technological advancements influenced special education practices for students who were at that time described as being handicapped (Nazzaro, 1977). Examples of consulting in the areas of speech and language therapy, and in hearing-impaired and visually-impaired programs, date from the late 1950s. Emphasis on teacher consultation for students with learning disabilities and behavior disorders appears in the literature as early as the mid-1960s. At that time, consultants for the most part were not special educators but clinical psychologists and psychiatric social workers.

By the mid-1960s the term "school consultation" was listed in *Psychological Abstracts* (Friend, 1988). School counselors began to promote the concept of proactive service, so that by the early 1970s consultation was being recommended as an integral part of contemporary counseling service. This interest in collaborative relationships on the part of counselors and psychologists reflected a desire to influence the individuals, groups, and systems that most profoundly affect students (Brown, Wyne, Blackburn, & Powell, 1979).

The behavioral movement had been gaining momentum in the late 1960s and it fueled interest in alternative models for intervention and the efficient use of time and other resources. This interest sparked development of a text by Tharp and Wetzel (1969) in which they presented a triadic consultation model using behavioral principles in school settings. The triadic model is the basic pattern upon which many subsequent models and methods for consultation have been constructed. In the 1960s advocates representing special needs pressed for the right of those with mental retardation (now termed "intellectual disability") to have opportunities as similar as possible to those in mainstream society. Passage of the Elementary and Secondary Education (ESEA) in 1965 authorized funding and made specific provisions for students with disabilities (Talley & Schrag, 1999). Reauthorizations of that legislation in 1988 and 1994 mandated parent involvement and coordination in early childhood programs such as Head Start, encouraging school and community-linked services through the Community Schools Partnership Act. Consultation and collaboration became essential factors in coordinating the array of services provided for students with special needs.

The decade of the 1970s was a very busy time in the field of special education. By 1970 the special education literature contained references to a method of training consulting teachers to serve students in special education at the elementary level (McKenzie, Egner, Knight, Perelman, Schneider, & Garvin, 1970). The first direct explication of a consulting teacher service delivery model for students with mild disabilities was by McKenzie, Enger, Knight, Perelman, Schneider, and Garvin in 1970. This group described a program at the University of Vermont for preparation of consulting teachers and a plan for implementing a consulting teacher model in the state (Lilly & Givens-Ogle, 1981). The

Education for All Handicapped Children's Act (EHA) was passed in 1975 and signed by President Gerald Ford, reauthorized in 1990 as the Individuals with Disabilities Education Act (IDEA), amended as IDEA 1997, and reauthorized in 2004. These legislative actions contained national guidelines on service delivery of education for students with disabilities (Talley & Schrag, 1999). One of the many guidelines was prescription of multidisciplinary and multidimensional services to be coordinated for maximizing student learning and development. By the mid-1970s consultation was being regarded as a significant factor in serving students with special needs. Special education became a major catalyst for promoting consultation and collaboration in schools (Friend, 1988). Consultation became one of the most significant educational trends by the mid-1980s for serving students with special needs

As interest in school consultation escalated in the 1980s, the National Task Force on Collaborative School Consultation, sponsored by the Teacher Education Division (TED) of the Council for Exceptional Children (CEC), sent a publication to state departments of education with recommendations for teacher consultation services in a special education services continuum (Heron & Kimball, 1988). Several guidelines were presented for: development of consultative assistance options; definition of a consulting teacher role and recommended pupil–teacher ratio; requirements for pre-service, in-service, and certification preparation programs. The report included a list of education professionals skilled in school consultation and a list of publications featuring school consultation.

By 1990 a new journal focusing on school consultation, *Journal of Educational and Psychological Consultation*, (JEPC), was available. A preconvention workshop, sponsored by the Teacher Education Division of the Council for Exceptional Children, on school consultation and collaboration programs and practices was a featured event at the 1990 annual CEC conference in Toronto. Early leaders in school consultation conceptualized models to fit more appropriately with inclusive schools and expanded roles of school personnel. Caplan's mental health consultation model evolved into mental health collaboration as a better choice of practice for school-based professionals (Caplan, Caplan, & Erchul, 1995). Bergan (1995) similarly described an evolution from the school psychologist's behavioral consultation focus on assessment, labeling, and placement activities to an expanded role of consultative and collaborative problem solving for students' needs. The framework for behavioral consultation was revised to become a case-centered, problem-solving approach that could be teacher-based, parent-based, or conjoint-based (parent-teacher) consultation in which the consultee's involvement is critical to success of positive client outcomes (Kratochwill & Pittman, 2002).

During the 1970s, 1980s, 1990s, and 2000s, educators witnessed an explosion of interest and wave after wave of reports, proposals, and legislative mandates calling for educational reform. The 1970s was a decade of monumental litigation and legislation that changed the education landscape for students with disabilities. In 1970, only one in five children with disabilities was educated, and many states had laws excluding certain students with disabilities from school. Landmark court decisions in the early 1970s leading up to the passage of P.L. 94-142 in 1975 paved the way for educational opportunities for children with disabilities. For example, the *Pennsylvania Association for Retarded Citizens (PARC) v. Commonwealth of Pennsylvania* (1971) and *Mills v. Board of Education of the District of Columbia* (1972) established the responsibility of states and localities to educate children with disabilities. The Rehabilitation Act of 1973 guaranteed civil rights to all persons with disabilities and required accommodations for students with disabilities in schools. The Rehabilitation Act of 1973 set the stage for the Education for All Handicapped Children Act (EHA) also known as P.L. 94-142. When it was passed in 1975, P.L. 94-142 guaranteed a free appropriate public education to every child with a disability. This law had a dramatic, positive impact on millions of children with disabilities in every state and local community across the country. Students with disabilities were to be educated in the least restrictive environment (LRE) and the mainstreaming movement began. After that legislation was passed, educators could no longer arbitrarily place individuals with disabilities in a special school or self-contained classroom. A continuum of service options was to be available and the type of service or placement was to be as close to the normal environment as possible, with general education teachers responsible for the success of those students. In order to meet this new responsibility, general education teachers were to receive help from special education personnel. This was an important provision.

The 1980s saw an increasing national concern for young children with disabilities and their families. The 1986 amendments to EHA (P.L. 99-457) mandated free and appropriate public education (FAPE) for preschool children ages 3–5, with disabilities and incentive monies to states to provide programs and services to children with disabilities from birth. An Individualized Family Service Plan (IFSP) was required for each child served, thus extending the concept of the IEP to provide support for the child and the family (Smith, 1998). Early intervention programs for infants and toddlers with disabilities proliferated following the legislation. Because disabilities of children in early intervention programs often are severe, services of parents, other caregivers, and specialists from several disciplines were deemed essential. Families are described in a broad sense, not necessarily as a father-and-mother unit, to include parents, grandparents, older siblings, aunts and uncles, or others functioning in a caregiver role. Families would have an integral part in the therapy through home-based programs. The IFSP would be developed by a multidisciplinary team having family members as active participants. Children would be served according to family needs, allowing for a wide range of services with parent training as one of those services, with family choices considered in all decisions.

During this same time period, many were calling for the dismantling of a separate special education system. The Regular Education Initiative (REI), introduced by Madeleine Will of the Office of Special Education and Rehabilitative Services, U.S. Department of Education, called for rethinking how services were provided to students with disabilities. In a position paper issued by Will (1986), she stated that too many children were being inappropriately identified and placed in learning disabilities programs. In that paper, Will called for collaboration between special education personnel and general education personnel to provide special services within the general education classroom. Will suggested merging special and regular education into a unified system where the resources of both regular and special education would be merged to provide all students with the benefits of general education programming with individualized instruction provided to students. Many advocates of students with severe disabilities supported REI as a way of serving all students within the general education classroom.

In 1990, early in the third wave of reform, Public Law 94–142 was amended with the passage of Public Law 101–476, the Individuals with Disabilities Education Act (IDEA). That legislation's primary elements were:

- All references to children as handicapped were changed to children with disabilities.
- New categories of autism and traumatic brain injury (TBI) were added, to be served with increased collaboration among all special education teachers, classroom teachers, and related services personnel.
- More emphasis was placed on requirements to provide transition services for students 16 years of age and older.

Two distinct groups emerged to advocate for REI—the high incidence group (many cases) that included learning disabilities, behavioral disorders, and mild/moderate mental retardation, and the low-incidence group (fewer cases) that included students with severe intellectual disabilities. Both groups shared three goals:

- To merge special and general education into one inclusive system
- To increase dramatically the number of children with disabilities who would be in mainstream classrooms
- To strengthen academic achievement of students with mild and moderate disabilities and underachievers without disabilities

The Americans with Disabilities Act (ADA) also was passed in 1990, prohibiting discrimination against people of all ages having disabilities in matters of transportation, public access, local government, and telecommunications. It required schools to make all reasonable accommodations for access by students and it extended provisions concerning fairness in employment to employers who do not receive federal funds (Smith, 1998).

In 1997, after much study and discussion nationwide, reauthorization and amendments for IDEA were approved by Congress and signed into law by President Clinton. One part of the legislation, known as IDEA '97, was provision for improved parent/professional partnerships and another part included the requirement that states would have paraeducator training for their roles. A third important feature was emphasis on collaboration among general educators and special educators, parents, related services personnel, and other service providers. This inclusion meant that general educators in particular must be actively engaged in selecting program modifications and supports, alternative-grading procedures, and assistive technology devices (Williams & Martin, 2001). Transition services and interagency linkages also were noted as being vital areas of assistance from collaborating consultants.

In 2002, the Elementary and Secondary Education Act of 1965 was reauthorized by enactment of the No Child Left Behind Act (NCLB), with sweeping implications for schools' testing programs. Unfortunately, NCLB increased pressure on educators to teach objectives of the tests assess rather than design assessments that test objectives of the curriculum (Hanna & Dettmer, 2004). Schools that failed to demonstrate "adequate yearly progress" on the high-stakes accountability tests were to be penalized. Such mandates put pressures on school personnel to ensure that children served by IDEA would not be left behind.

In 2004, the U.S. Congress reauthorized IDEA 1997 with passage of IDEA 2004. A few of the areas targeted for improvement or change were:

- High expectations for students with disabilities, to increase abilities for employment and independent living
- Professional development and training of all pre-service and school personnel who work with children having disabilities, including skills and knowledge and use of scientifically-based (research-based) instructional processes to the maximum extent possible
- Compatibility with No Child Left Behind performance goals for adequate yearly progress
- Stipulation of roles to attend IEP conferences, including parents, not fewer than one regular education teacher, not fewer than one special education teacher, an individual who can interpret instructional implications of evaluations, and a representative of the school district who has supervisory responsibilities and is knowledgeable about the general education curriculum and outside agency resources

In June 2010 the Council of Chief State School Officers and National Governors Association Center for Best Practices released the Common Core State Standards (CCS) for instruction. The Council for Exceptional Children and other national disability organizations contributed an introductory statement on how to implement the standards appropriately for students with disabilities. Goals for the standards specified key knowledge and skills in a format that was to make clear what the focus of teachers and assessments should be (Conley, 2011). The standards for grades K–12 were developed in collaboration with content experts, teachers, school administrators, states personnel, and parents to establish goals for learning that prepared students for success in college and the work world. Along with language arts and math standards were standards for literacy, numeracy, cross-disciplinary skills, communication collaboration, critical thinking, and use of technology. The CCS allowed for the widest possible range of students to participate fully, along with appropriate accommodations for maximum participation of students with special education needs (*CEC Today*, 2011).

The NCLB legislation was overdue for reauthorization in 2007, but that did not happen despite politicians threatening to overhaul or remove NCLB. In 2007, five years after President George W. Bush reauthorized the Elementary and Secondary Education Act (ESEA) as NCLB, Congress did not reauthorize the ESEA due to lack of bipartisan cooperation. This resulted in NCLB/ESEA being unchanged. It was replaced by the 2010 Race to the Top agenda, an initiative focusing on test scores as ultimate measures of educational quality (Ravitch, 2011) and requiring adoption of the Common Core Standards for applications to receive Race to the Top funding. In July 2015, both the House and the Senate made their own changes to ESEA, eventually merging the two bills into a single bill, known as the Every Student Succeeds Act. In December 2015, the newest version of the Elementary and Secondary Education Act (ESEA), known as the Every Student Succeeds Act (ESSA), was signed into law by President Barack Obama, to go into effect fully in the 2017–2018 school year. But before implementation, further clarification on certain provisions would be necessary.

The law made significant changes to the role of tests and requires states to include other factors in school accountability systems rather than just test scores. The new provisions greatly reduce the stakes of state tests for schools and teachers. The Every Student Succeeds Act also gives states substantially more autonomy over how and when they administer tests and how they define success. States and local districts will be able to determine if student test scores will be considered in teacher performance reviews. President Obama gave states that adopted Common Core standards competitive federal grants. Initially forty-two states and the District of Columbia adopted Common Core standards. Since 2009, several states have repealed Common Core. The Every Student Succeeds Act specifies that the federal government may not mandate or give states incentives to adopt or use a particular set of academic standards. Only time will tell how many states that adopted the Common Core will continue using these standards. Bottom line, ESSA limits the federal government's role in education and gives more power to the states and local districts.

The concepts of inclusion and collaborative school consultation that have swept the nation in recent years did not suddenly emerge out of a vacuum. They emanated from the long line of special education movements and mandates briefly described above and summarized in Figure 1.3. The merger was intended to modify many aspects of the rigidly compartmentalized, often stigmatizing, and very expensive special education structure. Furthermore, proponents of inclusive schools made the case that all students are unique individuals with special needs requiring differentiated individual attention; therefore, practices used effectively for exceptional students should be made available to all students (McLeskey & Henry, 1998; McLeskey, Henry, & Hodges, 1998).

All educators share responsibility for student achievement and behavior. There must be total commitment from principal to school custodian (Federico, Herrold, & Venn, 1999). Every inclusive school looks different, but all inclusive schools are characterized by a sense of community, high standards, *collaboration and cooperation, partnership with families* [italics added], changing roles and an array of services, flexible learning environments, strategies based on research, new forms of accountability, and ongoing professional development (Federico, Herold, & Venn, 1999; Working Forum on Inclusive Schools, 1994).

The general public in the new millennium is aware that teaching is not just the responsibility of professional educators within the school's walls. Community members and resource personnel beyond school campuses are needed as collaborators and team members who can help plan and direct rich, authentic learning experiences for students.

Also gaining prominence is an awareness of the need for collaboration among general and special education teachers that will give students opportunities for learning and practicing skills related to standards set forth by governing bodies of each area. The practice of teaming across classrooms is being utilized by many dedicated teachers as an approach that can bring students closer to achieving the standards (Kluth & Straut, 2001).

The next several decades of this millennium are critical for professional educators as they learn to work together and to *enjoy* doing it. It will be very important for them to model such behaviors because their students also will be expected to work collaboratively as adults in their careers and community roles. Strong partnerships between home and school educators will be an increasingly essential part of helping students become capable, ethical leaders for the future.

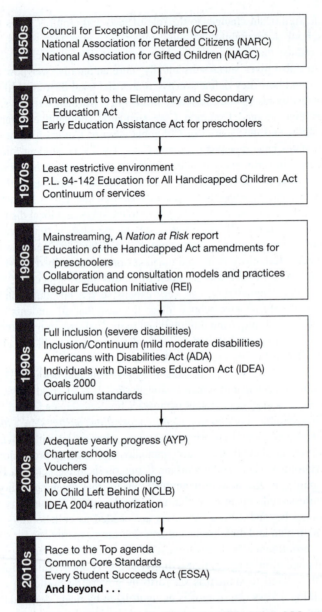

1950s
Council for Exceptional Children (CEC)
National Association for Retarded Citizens (NARC)
National Association for Gifted Children (NAGC)

1960s
Amendment to the Elementary and Secondary
  Education Act
Early Education Assistance Act for preschoolers

1970s
Least restrictive environment
P.L. 94-142 Education for All Handicapped Children Act
Continuum of services

1980s
Mainstreaming, *A Nation at Risk* report
Education of the Handicapped Act amendments for
  preschoolers
Collaboration and consultation models and practices
Regular Education Initiative (REI)

1990s
Full inclusion (severe disabilities)
Inclusion/Continuum (mild moderate disabilities)
Americans with Disabilities Act (ADA)
Individuals with Disabilities Education Act (IDEA)
Goals 2000
Curriculum standards

2000s
Adequate yearly progress (AYP)
Charter schools
Vouchers
Increased homeschooling
No Child Left Behind (NCLB)
IDEA 2004 reauthorization

2010s
Race to the Top agenda
Common Core Standards
Every Student Succeeds Act (ESSA)
And beyond . . .

FIGURE 1.3   Historic Path of Important Educational Movements

BENEFITS OF COLLABORATIVE SCHOOL CONSULTATION

School environments that promote collaborative consultation tend to involve all school personnel in the teaching and learning processes. Information is shared and knowledge levels about student characteristics and needs, and strategies for meeting those needs, are

Video Example
from
YouTube

▶

ENHANCEDetext
Video Example 1.2.

Watch this video to see how one district was able to achieve meaningful student gains when they changed their interaction approach between teachers, administrators, and stakeholders. (https://www.youtube.com/watch?v=RSdjoegcY2I)

broadened. Importantly, many of the strategies are helpful with other students who have similar but less severe needs. A number of specific benefits of school consultation and collaboration can result from successful collaborative school consultation and team efforts.

First is the much-needed support and assistance for students in the inclusive classroom. Consulting special education teachers help classroom teachers develop repertoires of materials and instructional strategies. Many find this more efficient than racing from one student to another in a resource room as all work on individual assignments. As one special education teacher succinctly put it, "In my resource room, by the time I get to the last student, I find that the first student is stuck and has made no progress. So I frantically run through the whole cycle again. Running shoes are a must for my job!" They also find ways of helping classroom teachers to be confident and successful with students with special needs. At times they can assume an instructional role in the classroom, which frees the classroom teacher to study student progress, set up arrangements for special projects, or work intensively with a small group of students.

When general classroom and special education teachers collaborate, each has ownership and involvement in serving special needs. General education teachers learn from special education teachers, and the special education consulting teachers learn from the classroom teachers. Each can often use the knowledge gained for other students with similar needs. Fewer students may need to be taken from the classroom for individual services and when they are "pulled out," the service is addressed by need rather than by special education "label."

Collegial interaction is effective in reducing the isolation and feelings of burnout among teachers, bringing satisfaction toward the work and stimulating enthusiasm. Inger makes an interesting case for working together:

> Over time, teachers who work closely together on matters of curriculum and instruction find themselves better equipped for classroom work. They take considerable satisfaction from professional relationships that withstand differences in viewpoints and occasional conflict (Inger, 1993, p. 1).

Interestingly, when working together, teachers seem better prepared to support one another's strengths and accommodate weaknesses. They are organized in ways that ease strain of personnel turnover, providing assistance to beginners and newcomers including veteran teachers, and awareness of school values, traditions, and resources (Inger, 1993).

Another benefit of collaboration that serves students in heterogeneous settings is reduction in stigmatizing effects of labels such as "delayed," "disordered," "disabled," "having disabilities," "exceptional," or even "gifted." Collaboration can also reduce referrals to remedial programs. In a study of special education in an inclusionary middle school, Knowles (1997) found that collaboration and teamwork decreased special education referrals and grade-level retention of students. Fewer referrals for special education services means reduced expenditures for costly and time-consuming psychological assessments and special education interventions. Educators can focus more time and energy on teaching and facilitating and less time on testing, labeling, and qualifying students. In addition, a ripple effect extends services to students by encouraging modifications and alternatives for their special needs. Collaboration also increases teachers' job satisfaction when teachers can be free to reflect, collaborate, and design their own professional growth (Morel, 2014). A successful consultation process becomes a supportive tool that teachers increasingly value and use. As inclusive school systems become more prevalent, collaborative consultation will be integral to school program success.

Administrators can benefit from eased loads of pressure and planning when classroom teachers are efficient in working with a wide range of student needs. Principals find it stimulating to visit and observe in classrooms as team participants, collaborating on ways of helping every student succeed and reinforcing teacher successes with all of their students. This is, for many administrators, a welcome change from the typical classroom visitations they make for purposes of teacher evaluation.

A collaborative consultation approach is a natural system for nurturing harmonious staff interactions. Teachers who have become isolated or autonomous in their teaching styles and instructional philosophy often discover that working with other adults for common goals is quite stimulating. Sharing ideas can add to creativity, open-endedness, and flexibility in developing educational programs for students with special needs. In addition, more emphasis and coordination can be given to cross-school and long-range planning, with an increased use of outside resources for student needs. Collaborative consultants can be catalysts for professional development, pinpointing areas in which to create staff development sessions and informational materials for helping co-educators learn specific techniques for special needs.

Parents or caregivers of the exceptional student often become extremely frustrated with labeling, fragmented curriculum, and isolation from peers endured by their children. So they respond enthusiastically when they learn that several educators are functioning as a team for the student. Their attitudes toward school improve, and they are more likely to become more involved in planning and carrying through with the interventions (Idol, 1988), more eager to share their ideas, and helpful in monitoring their child's learning. They are especially supportive when consulting services allow students in special education programs to remain in their neighborhood schools and to receive more assistance from interagency sources for their child's special needs.

Another benefit, frequently overlooked, is the maintenance of continuity in learning programs as students progress through their K–12 school experiences. This, too, is a savings in time, energy, and resources of the educational staff and often the parents as well. Last, but certainly not least, is the opportunity to be an example for students in developing the collaborative and interactive skills they will need for their future.

Why It Can Be Difficult to Work Together

Teachers may wish for more small-group meetings that are focused on mutual interests and more grade-level meetings that address common concerns. They may want more opportunities to observe other teachers and other schools. They may seek richer professional development experiences. But that does not mean they are keen on engaging in collaboration and consultation activities. Stumbling blocks of resistance formed by attitudes, traditions, misconceptions, and misunderstandings can impede smooth travel on the road to successful collaboration and teamwork. Some teachers comment candidly that they did not choose teaching as a career to work all that much with adults. Others feel that teaming up with co-teachers or consulting teachers will be perceived as a flag calling attention to their weaker areas or a no-confidence vote in their abilities. They could argue that already there is too little time for the careful planning and concentrated effort that productive interaction would require. Furthermore, opportunities may be rare and hard to arrange for meaningful observation of educators in other school venues. One aspect that troubles special education teachers and families is the possibility that collaboration time may siphon off precious time previously allocated for direct services to students.

When teachers do have time and opportunity to interact with colleagues for learning new ideas and revitalizing their professional enthusiasm, it is likely to be during professional development sessions. Sometimes this happens, but unfortunately these activities often are too highly structured (and perhaps on inappropriate topics) and too brief for productive interaction. Many are scheduled at the end of the school day, when teachers are tired and wanting to reflect a bit on their teaching day, set the stage for the next day, and then turn their attention toward home or community activities. Even more undesirable to some is being scheduled on Saturday, when they must compete with family and community activities that beckon. Now and then teachers have visits to their classrooms by other teachers, supervisors, administrators, student teachers, and sometimes parents. However, if not prepared for properly and followed up appropriately, these occasions can trigger feelings of anxiety and defensiveness more than support and collegiality.

Proposals to adopt merit pay for teachers whose classes perform exceptionally well have been faulted as weakening school-based collaboration because teaching is a collaborative art with no one teacher responsible for student success or failure (Carpenter, 2016). Merit systems that reward certain teachers may fail to recognize contributions of previous teachers to students' success at later grade levels.

Another stumbling block to effective collaboration, more subtle in nature, is the contrived collegiality that is based on quick fixes with neglect of fundamental supports. This false collegiality leads to proliferation of unwanted meetings and paperwork and disillusionment over the value of collaboration (Brownell, Yeager, Rennells, & Riley, 1997). Teachers may go through the more visible motions of collaboration but then quietly go about their teaching in ways to which they have become accustomed.

Some school systems promote co-teaching as a way of allowing teachers to support and learn from each other and broaden their teaching repertoires. But these, too, must be well-planned and managed, or even if well intended, they can result in turn-teaching— "You teach this part of the lesson and then take a break or make the copies we need for next hour, while I handle the part coming up."

Sometimes there is confusion or lack of clarity about the meanings of "collaboration," "compromise," and "cooperation." Compromise usually entails giving up part of, or conceding, something, and cooperation requires coming together to agree so the work can proceed. Collaboration, on the other hand, is shared responsibility and decision-making for planning, implementation, and evaluation. Professionals cannot be coerced into collegiality and collaboration. Teachers who are accustomed to being in charge and making virtually all the day-to-day decisions in their classrooms cannot be directed to just go out and collaborate with each other or co-teach to any significant degree. They need incentives of time, structure, practice, encouragement, and positive feedback about effectiveness in order to perform these sophisticated and demanding functions successfully. DuFour (2004) finds that educators may equate collaboration with congeniality and camaraderie, but a viable learning community must have the right structures to build a culture of collaboration. This includes shared goals, strategies, materials, and expected outcomes of collaborative ethics that are public and well accepted by all.

COMPETENCIES FOR EFFECTIVE COLLABORATIVE SCHOOL CONSULTANTS

Competencies for collaborating, consulting, co-teaching, and working in teams as co-educators are centered in several categories of skills and attitudes:

- Knowledge and awareness of collaborative processes
- Communication skills
- Problem-solving techniques
- Organization and management of collaborative processes
- Partnerships with co-educators in schools, homes, and communities
- Appreciation and respect for human diversity
- Change agentry
- Adherence to principles of ethics for collaborative school consultation

Effective co-educators are knowledgeable about both special education and general education curriculum and instruction. They are interested in current trends and topics, and innovative in generating new ideas. They respect and value differences in professional perspectives and personal preferences among their colleagues. They strive to understand how schools function and aim for a panoramic view of the educational scene. They are flexible and resilient along with being practical and realistic. This requires that they be assertive and risk-taking when need be but diplomatic at all times. They work for success of their school and home co-educators to ensure that all students will be successful learners.

The concept of teamwork is receiving increased attention and enthusiasm among school professionals. Teamwork as co-educators means striving for the good of the whole—where individual preferences are subtended or set aside for the larger cause. Many heads and hearts are better than one, and the pooled experiences, talents, knowledge, and ideas of a group are even better than the sum of the individual parts.

Welch and Sheridan (1995) suggest that team-taught instruction can be micro-level staff development when each teacher models instruction for the other. Commercial companies offer activities, games, puzzles, and outdoor gaming equipment for team building. They purport to develop rapport and team spirit by energizing members to work together harmoniously. Some seem glitzy and merely playful, but others have potential for building awareness and trust through cohesion-building activities. Professional development consultants should observe in schools and query school personnel to determine if such techniques would be a turn-on or a turn-off for that group. Simple, straightforward collaborative structures, with explanation of benefits they provide for helping students with their special needs, may be the most time efficient and acceptable to busy teachers.

Successful collaborators relate well to teacher colleagues and other staff members, administrators, parents, and, by all means, students. They develop mature, objective viewpoints toward all aspects of education. While working to help students learn, they seek to have a positive outlook on the entire school context. They link people with resources and refer people to other sources when needed. Collaborative school consultants are self-confident, but if running low on resources or ideas, they do not hesitate in finding a consultant for themselves!

Perhaps most of all, the consultant is a change agent. As one very experienced, collaborating school consultant put it, "You have to be abrasive enough to create change, but pleasant enough to be asked back so you will do it some more," (M.O. Bradley, personal communication, 1987). Each section of this book will elaborate on components of collaborative school consultation competencies, and in the concluding section a rubric will be provided to assess and evaluate development of the competencies.

The Collaborative School Consultation Ethic

A collaborative ethic is a set of values or principles that supports collegial styles of interaction among co-equal individuals engaging voluntarily in making decisions or solving problems (Phillips & McCullough, 1990; Friend & Cook, 1990; Welch, Sheridan, Fuhriman, Hart, Connell, & Stoddart, 1992). Why do educators need to focus on ethical principles and practices when their professional aims and aspirations are already built on principled attitudes and behaviors? A practical response would be that as models for students who will be leaders of tomorrow, educators are conveying the importance of ethical behavior in <u>every</u> field addressed by the curriculum. They can model the interrelationships and teamwork with their professional colleagues that will be keys to success in virtually any work role their students may have in the future.

■ ■ ■ ■ ■ ■ ■

ACTIVITY 1.5
School Philosophies That Feature a Collaborative Ethic

With a small group (3–6) of interested co-educators, discuss the topic of collaborative school consultation ethics. Focus on key words such as "excellence," "achievement," "trust," "respect," "fairness," "caring attitudes," "effective communication," and "confidentiality." Compose a description of a collaborative ethical climate for educators that you would like to have for your school environment.

Then seek out and collect several attendance center or school district handbooks and other promotional materials for education in that area. Look for phrases in the school philosophy or mission statement to find phrases that feature high ideals and lofty goals for every learner and educator in a collaborative environment. If no school philosophy has been developed and presented to the public, then interview the school administrators, school board members, and parent groups about the need to do that. Be prepared to recommend ways in which ethical behaviors can be encouraged and modeled.

Reports from school districts throughout the United States identify collaboration as a key variable in the successful implementation of inclusive education (Villa & Thousand, 2003, p. 22). In collaboration, the differentiated tasks can be allocated among individuals having various skills to contribute. Sometimes collaboration means recognizing differences and finding ways to accommodate those differences. The collaborative process is enriched by diversity among collaborators—diversity of experience, perspectives, values, skills, and interests. Individual differences among adults who consult and collaborate are rich ingredients for successful collaborations. The great need to acknowledge adult differences and use them constructively in collaborative enterprises will be the focus of another chapter.

 ENHANCEDetext **Application Exercise 1.1.** Click to apply your understanding of a collaborative school ethic.

TIPS FOR WORKING TOGETHER IN SCHOOLS

1. Value, and find ways to demonstrate beyond token lip service, the value of consultation, collaboration, and teamwork as tools for planning and coordinating instruction.
2. Do not wait to be approached for opportunities to consult, collaborate, and co-teach.
3. Strive for using collaborative efforts to problem-solve together, even if it means giving up some of your own agenda.
4. Refrain from assuming that colleagues are waiting around to be "saved."
5. Find, or develop if need be, good examples of school philosophies emphasizing a collaborative ethic and working in partnerships with co-educators.
6. Ask for help when you are facing a problem because it has a humanizing, rapport–building effect.
7. Interact with every co-educator in your attendance center(s) regularly.
8. Learn all you can about various methods of consulting, collaborating, co-teaching, and engaging in other kinds of collegial teamwork, determining what worked and what didn't work that would apply to your school environment.
9. Leave the door open, both figuratively and literally, for future partnerships and collaborations.
10. Encourage each member of a collaborative group to share knowledge and perceptions about an issue, in order to establish a solid framework in which to discuss the issue.

■■■■■

CHAPTER 2

WORKING TOGETHER WITH DIFFERING PERSPECTIVES AND PREFERENCES

Picture a patchwork quilt made of many colors, textures, prints, and patterns. The patches have been assembled with care and joined together skillfully. Each piece is unique and contributes to the whole in its own way. Some colors and patterns might seem to clash, but without these variations the quilt would be drab and dull. All together they form a collage in which each area contributes to the beauty and function of the whole.

A school is like a patchwork quilt. Each person is unique, differing from the others in personality, attitudes, values, interests, and skills but blending to form a human montage. Every individual within the school environment contributes special qualities to enrich the whole. People may differ markedly and even take serious issue with one another on occasion because of their differences. But the array of individuals who come together in the school environment each day will provide unlimited opportunities for collaborating as teachers and learners.

Educators are attuned to the need for recognizing and accommodating individual differences of students as they plan for learning needs, but too often they overlook or do not understand the individual differences among adults with whom they work. Why are such distinctions so important? They are meaningful because the synergy created by diversity among adults in the school environment, if recognized, respected, and used in constructive ways, can provide co-educators with many ways of teaching effectively and helping students learn successfully.

CHAPTER OBJECTIVES

On completing this chapter, the reader should be able to:

1. Differentiate between professional perspectives and personal preferences that can affect the abilities and inclinations of co-educators to collaborate, consult, and co-teach.

2. Explain the effects that professional perspectives can have on collaborative school consultation and teamwork.

3. Explain ways that differences in personal preferences can affect the abilities and inclinations of co-educators to collaborate, consult, and co-teach.

4. Analyze your professional perspectives and personal preferences in order to facilitate collegiality and teamwork among co-educators.

5. Describe ways that school co-educators and home co-educators can respect their differences.

6. Utilize adult differences to facilitate collaboration.

KEY TERMS

hidden curriculum   personal preference   professional perspective
onedownsmanship   personality   taxonomic domains
persona

SITUATION 2.A

The morning after a professional development day for faculty in a rural-consolidated middle school, teachers could be heard commenting on that experience as they prepared to take up instruction where they had left off two days earlier. The theme for the professional development event had been introduction to and exploration of an idea to implement a district-wide mentoring program for students that school administrators had learned about during their last statewide conference. Several teachers voiced their opinions about the all-day event and the proposed program:

"I'm eager to try that teaching strategy in our school. Why don't we give it a chance? It's been working so well in other schools."

"Here we go again. Another change that will probably spin us around for our latest ride on the school improvement merry-go-round."

"Why are some people so negative toward new ideas before they even try them out? We could at least wait to see what happens when others use them."

"We seem to see eye-to-eye on everything important in our department. What a great group of colleagues I have."

"I say let's take some risks and do something innovative for a change."

"Another meeting on 'school improvement' issues. They drag on and on, and we have nothing to show for the time wasted."

"I like the direction our school is heading to try out some new ideas that can involve outstanding people in our community."

"Seems like we just get settled into some new program and it's going pretty well, but then we're pulled into something entirely different."

"This was my first 'inservice' and I picked up every handout, but I don't know when I'll have time to study them."

"What a drag yesterday was! I won't support any such program and I didn't come away with a single thing I could use in my classroom. Besides that, the box lunch was terrible."

"Wasn't that a great workshop? I learned a lot more about middle-school students and things they need for development in all domains of learning."

If a person views the world and reacts to it in ways unlike another, it is because that person processes information differently and sees the situation in a very different light. It would be convenient but myopic to expect that the viewpoints of colleagues will

FIGURE 2.1   Sharing Perspectives and Preferences

mirror one's own views and leave one wondering why everyone is not agreeable enough to fall into step and like the same things. Similarly, it would be pleasant and comfortable although unrealistic to seek out only colleagues whose likes and dislikes matched one's own. Different viewpoints contribute diverse insights that help broaden understanding of issues and problems. Expanded outlooks on educational perspectives and variations of personality and temperament among co-educators will lead to opportunities for productive planning and problem solving. If such opportunities are to reap benefits, they must be treated as assets, analyzed, and put to good use. (See Figure 2.1.)

DIFFERENTIATING BETWEEN PROFESSIONAL PERSPECTIVES AND PERSONAL PREFERENCES

People in all walks of life bring their own perspectives and preferences to their work. A perspective is a mental view of facts and ideas, seeing the relevant data in meaningful relationships. Perspectives are philosophical in nature—such as reasons for choosing one's profession, one's work ethics, views on what one's role is for that work and what it should be, opinions about how the work should be done, outlook on its value, and much more. They need not remain static; perspectives can change with time and experience.

A preference is a selection or choice to which one gives priority. Preferences emanate from one's **personality** (disposition or temperament) and **persona** (the public role a person assumes or is perceived to assume). Preferences indicate what a person likes better and holds higher than other things. An example would be preferences for making decisions. Will they be based on facts or on possibilities? Another would be a penchant for functioning. Will it be planned and orderly or spontaneous and flexible? When working in groups, will each person be very aware of others' feelings and wishes or more analytical and impersonal toward the task? Preferences are not changed easily, so individuals tend to make adjustments, if needed, in their interactions with others.

People sometimes set aside their own perspectives and preferences for the good of the order. In the case of teachers, this may be for fostering unanimity or focusing on the general interests of students, schools, or communities, or bolstering their own confidence levels. Examples of deferring to other perspectives and preferences appear in matters of grading systems, school rules, test adaptations, family conferences, and much more. However, individuals tend to use their own preferred ways of setting up their classroom, or teaching a favorite unit, or providing feedback on student work.

Which should be addressed first when studying variables that affect collaborative consultation and working in teams—professional perspectives or personal preferences? The proverbial chicken, when asked a "what's first?" question, responded that "chicken" comes before the proverbial egg because chicken is listed first in the dictionary. The decision to begin here with professional perspectives assumes that much teaching philosophy comes first from prior school experiences and then from teacher preparation programs. Preservice educators may be forming their perspectives and preferences as they learn from others and complete their preparation programs.

A note of caution is needed pertaining to interpretation of perspectives and preferences. This kind of information often is obtained informally and typically shared as a self-report. So there is always the possibility that such information is more self-serving than candid. But when this caution is kept in mind and the information is solicited in a professional manner as a helpful and positive activity, it need not be regarded as a major hindrance to studying perspectives and preferences.

DIFFERENCES IN PROFESSIONAL PERSPECTIVES ON TRADITION, AND MUCH MORE

Professional perspectives tend to be framed within factors of traditions, time, territory (or turf), taxonomies, talents, and trust. Some of the differences are minor and easily ignored or just accepted but others are major enough to be potential impediments to collegiality and collaboration. Each of these areas bears examination as a key component of collaborative school consultation and teamwork.

The Tradition Factor

Traditions in the school environment include customs and conventions that are carried out through habit or convenience. They pop into the limelight with words to the effect that "We've always done it that way." Traditions begun long ago by legislative and administrative edict sometimes continue on and on due to disinterest and neglect. They may solidify into conventions that are hard to set aside even when they no longer serve educators and learners well. Educators may dislike some traditions and a few may have negative consequences. Examples of traditions are:

- Considering special education a place where students who need special help are to be
- Labeling children and placing them in special services for an unspecified length of time
- Referring to students in special education classes as "your" kids rather than as "our" kids
- Designating students for special education services when in reality there is a misfit between their abilities and the demands of inflexible school structures and undifferentiated curriculum and instruction
- Describing secondary schools as institutions that teach subjects and elementary-level schools as establishments that teach children
- Looking on families of students at risk as problems rather than as integral parts of the solution
- Looking on general education services and support services as "boats passing in the stream" rather than as integral components collaborating for exceptional needs
- Relating to consulting teachers as experts with all the answers rather than as colleagues collaborating with teachers who are experts in their own right
- Framing processes of teaching and learning in negatively nuanced metaphors that are patterned on disease, military, business, or industrial models.

Examples of semantics that can be damaging are "target" (a word used sparingly in this book and replaced with words such as "focus" or "client"), "training" (also to be avoided and replaced with "preparation" or "instruction"), "intervention," "remediation," and others that infer sickness, such as "diagnostic," "prescriptive," "treatment," "impaired," "monitor," "referral," "disability," "adaptive," and "label." Ill-chosen words and terms erect barriers to understanding. When words with more constructive and positive tones can be used, they should be. Other inappropriate metaphors and more helpful ones for framing education will appear in another chapter.

Outmoded and undesirable traditions can be altered or overturned in climates that cultivate sensitivity and clear reasoning. One example of tradition breaking that has been successful is replacement of the unacceptable term "the handicapped" with "those who have special needs."

The Time Factor

Time is the most problematic aspect of trying to collaborate and engage in teamwork within a traditional school setting. "Where will I find the time to get together with my colleagues?" says an overscheduled teacher who already feels the strain of an overextended caseload. But the reality is that time has not gone missing; it is not lost, but has just been used for other things. Time is an unredeemable resource that everyone gets in the same amount. As for how it is used—that's the challenge. It is determined by a combination of choice, necessity, fate, and a little luck.

Co-educators who want to collaborate and teachers who would like to co-teach must choose to "spend" some of their limited time in that way while attending to whatever their designated responsibilities are. They know that fate may deal them even less time if they are called on to do bus duty for a sick colleague, or more time if a meeting is canceled, each situation being outside their control. Teachers never have enough time, and if they do manage to carve out a bit here and there to collaborate with co-educators, families of their students, or related services personnel, they are fortunate if those minutes match up with available minutes of their intended collaborators.

A factor often overlooked is the time needed for just thinking about curriculum, instruction, resources, and assessments. A teacher may spend hours upon hours conceptualizing a unit, revising and redoing until the perfect plan finally forms in a clear perspective. Next come gathering of materials and lesson preparation. Much of this effort, contrary to effort demanded in many other work roles, is carried out on the teacher's own personal and family time. Differentiating curriculum and instruction for students with special needs typically requires even more time and effort beyond conventional preparations.

Some time and opportunity for gathering new ideas and revitalizing professional enthusiasm through interaction with co-educators might occur during professional development sessions, but these activities are often too ill timed, highly structured, and short-lived to allow for productive interaction. Then, too, some sessions are scheduled unwisely for the end of the day, when teachers are tired, want to reflect a bit on their teaching day, set things up for next day, and then turn their attention toward family or community activities.

Educators may wish they could have more small-group meetings to address teaching concerns, but that does not necessarily signal a desire to collaborate or co-teach. They may appreciate the value of conferring with students' families beyond the expected parent-teacher conference but feel apprehensive about making a home- or neutral-site visit or asking a parent to come to school for a daytime or evening visit. Opportunities to observe other teachers and visit other schools are hard to arrange; they may have appeal, but teachers are conflicted by frustrations of leaving their classrooms in the care of others. Some school systems encourage co-teaching as a way of allowing teachers to interact with and observe other teachers in a collegial way. But well-intentioned efforts to set up co-teaching environments can be less than collaborative if not planned carefully. The outcome of poor or minimal planning could be simply turn teaching—"You teach this part of the lesson and then take a break or go online to gather resources for an upcoming lesson, while I handle the part coming up." Effective co-teaching is based on much planning and organizing, and that takes time. Even so, hard-working and time-challenged educators may relish the thought of team teaching, or otherwise interacting with other adults during the school day, or venting frustrations to a sympathetic ear, or bouncing new teaching ideas off interested colleagues for their reactions.

On the other hand, some may state their perspective candidly on collaboration and teamwork by saying that they did not choose teaching as a career to work all that much with adults. Others feel that teaming up with co-teachers or consulting teachers could be perceived as a red flag signaling their weaker areas or expressing a no-confidence vote in their abilities. Still another aspect that troubles special education teachers, as well as parents, is the possibility that collaboration may siphon off precious minutes needed for direct services to students. Teachers could argue convincingly there is just too little time for the careful planning and concentrated effort that productive collaboration requires, picking up on the familiar complaint that "It will just be a waste of precious time."

So where is time to be begged, borrowed, or found for collaborating, teaming, and networking? A section of a later chapter will focus on this need. For every element in the school day and every structure for the school year, time is a defining feature with the potential for posing problems or creating benefits for school personnel.

The Territory (Turf) Factor

Issues of territory, or "turf," arise in areas of school life that are as varied as curriculum development, selection of materials, allocation of academic time, scheduling, shared classrooms and equipment, shared paraeducators, noise levels, discipline procedures, grading policies, homework policies, incentives to encourage student effort, and much, much more. These kinds of concerns stem from a number of realities and practicalities emanating from differences among educators in their professional perspectives.

Educators cannot be coerced into being collegial and working together closely. Teachers who are accustomed to being in charge and making virtually all the day-to-day decisions in their classrooms cannot be directed to just go out and collaborate with each other or co-teach to any great degree. Likewise, teachers who have favorite subjects, preferred ways of planning and instructing, and definite ideas about teaching and assessment will not give them up lightly. Some are displeased when teaching partners are selected for them. They would prefer to choose their own collaborator or to continue in partnerships that are established. However, this may not be an option if it is a case of general education and special education personnel. Special educator services in many districts are stretched thin and must be shared among several buildings and classrooms.

Some teachers speak out to say that they just need their "space." They acknowledge that they don't like others looking over their shoulders while they teach or breathing down their necks when they sort through materials or critique student work. Dealing with differences in professional perspectives is a challenging task because even in a collaborative, sharing environment, having one's place and routines—one's turf—continues to be important to the educator. Turf and ownership issues can be problematic for novice teachers who are settling into their first teaching positions. They want to get off to a good start with colleagues, but they also have ideas for setting up the dream classrooms that they have preparing for and designing in their minds for years. Striking out to do things one's own way as a novice teacher is a bit scary but also invigorating; this is what teacher education students work hard for in their classes and student teaching experiences. Collaboration for them must be an opportunity to learn but also a chance to share *their* often new and bold ideas, and veteran teachers must make sure they can do so.

Astute building administrators will recognize that the issue of territory can be a threat to successful interactions, so they will watch for signs of discord. If there is evidence that tension is brewing, possibilities to alleviate the pressures include having individual conferences with co-educators to solicit support, distributing material to promote collaborative enterprises, setting up an inservice session, having bulletin boards posted that feature staff working together as a team, arranging an agenda-specific departmental meeting, or in extreme cases, rearranging teaching assignments with agreement by the individuals involved.

Another aspect of the school environment that is linked to territory but not talked about much is the **hidden curriculum** (Dettmer, 2006). It is taught and learned covertly in venues such as hallways, lunchrooms, restrooms, playgrounds, schedules and bells and public address systems, bulletin boards, trophy showcases, assemblies, informal conversation groups, conferences, meetings, and general attitudes and behaviors of students and adults when they share space and form groups. The hidden curriculum extends and embellishes the teaching and learning arena, with much of its activity and influence happening paradoxically in the social domain.

One other aspect of space bears mentioning—territoriality within the classroom. Sometimes teachers carve out a space and stay there until they are reminded, or come to realize it themselves, that they are slighting certain areas of the room and perhaps the students or resource personnel who choose to be located there or are assigned to be there. It is to collaborating teachers' advantage to move about, sharing enthusiasm and encouraging participation, yet taking care not to intimidate or close in on students in a domineering manner. If two or more teachers are team teaching, the "teacher wealth" can be spread around to cover all "turf" and have more engagement with students.

ACTIVITY 2.1

To Share or Not to Share? That Is the Question!

Should teachers share their best instructional strategies with other teachers? In small groups, explore feelings when asked to share a favorite recipe with someone who probably will go to some of the same meal events you will be attending. Then discuss feelings and reactions to sharing one's favorite curriculum and instruction techniques with co-educators. Should there be limits to generosity? Or is everything in a teacher's repertoire of ideas and strategies "fair game" for use by collaborators and co-teachers? How should this question be addressed for the benefit of all, especially the students?

The Taxonomy Factor

Taxonomies in education are organizational tools that guide educators in developing instructional objectives and planning strategies for the instruction. One of the most frequently cited works in educational literature is the *Taxonomy of Educational Objectives, Handbook I: Cognitive Domain* (Bloom, Engelhart, Furst, Hill, & Krathwohl, 1956). It was developed with an aim toward improving tests, but the developers soon realized that they needed first to develop a classification system for instructional objectives that would guide curriculum development and instructional strategies. People learn facts and comprehend material; then they apply their knowledge and understanding to accomplish what they need and want to do. A taxonomy structure is useful for these purposes.

Learning and doing occur within four **taxonomic domains**—the cognitive domain of thinking, the affective domain of feeling, the physical (designated herein as sensorimotor) domain of absorbing and performing, and the social domain of relating to others. Activity in each of these domains can range from simple to complex, with potential for low-road transfer (using the learning in similar material and situations) or opportunity for high-road transfer (applying and adapting the material to problem solving and novel situations). Integrated domains of thinking, feeling, doing, and interacting provide a fertile field for co-educators to co-plan, co-instruct, and co-evaluate student learning.

Understanding the hierarchical levels inherent in taxonomies is requisite for designing differentiated curriculum for all students, particularly those with exceptional learning needs. So they are addressed here in abbreviated form and with some expansions. The cognitive domain and affective domain will be extended by two and three levels respectively, the physical domain revised to be a sensorimotor domain, and a newly developed taxonomy presented for the social domain.

Taxonomy of the Cognitive Domain.   The six categories of the very familiar cognitive domain are described briefly here as (Hanna & Dettmer, 2004):

- **Knowledge:** Recalling or recognizing facts, principles, methods, and the like. This area of learning is essential, of course; but unfortunately, recall is overemphasized in most classroom instruction.
- **Comprehension:** Understanding of meaning as demonstrated by explaining or paraphrasing. Comprehension is necessary but does not cultivate deep understanding and tends to receive an inappropriately large proportion of instructional time.
- **Application:** Using ideas, rules, or principles in new situations and to facilitate real-life problem solving.
- **Analysis:** Taking apart components of a concept to find the relationships among those parts.
- **Synthesis:** Putting elements together in new ways within limits set by a given framework.
- **Evaluation:** Assessing and judging purposefully the goals, ideas, methods, products, or materials learned.

Bloom's taxonomy for the cognitive domain has been helpful in making educators aware that a great proportion of instruction is directed toward simple recall of facts and explaining or restating learned material. Surprisingly, this is more characteristic of secondary schools than elementary schools. As much as 80 percent to 90 percent of high school learning can be classified as thinking at the very basic knowledge or comprehension levels, while content that has rich potential for transfer of learning such as application, analysis, synthesis, and evaluation, is neglected in favor of more simplistic and more easily assessed drill, practice, and regurgitation (Hanna & Dettmer, 2004). This emphasis on lower-level learning hampers development of complex thinking and doing skills and stifles potential for creative thinking and production.

FIGURE 2.2   Four Domains for Thinking and Doing

DOMAIN	Cognitive	Affective	Sensorimotor	Social
PROCESS	Thinking	Feeling	Sensing, moving	**Interacting**
CONTENT	Mental	Emotional	Physical	**Sociocultural**
PURPOSE	Expand thinking	Enhance feeling	Cultivate senses and movement	**Enrich relationships**
BASIC LEARNING	Know Understand	Receive Respond	Observe React	**Relate Communicate**
APPLIED LEARNING	Apply Analyze Evaluate	Value Organize Internalize	Act Adapt Authenticate	**Participate Negotiate Adjudicate**
IDEATIONAL LEARNING	Synthesize Imagine Create	Characterize Wonder Aspire	Harmonize Improvise Innovate	**Collaborate Initiate Convert**

All students, regardless of disabilities or aptitudes, are entitled to be taught and must be encouraged to learn at levels of analysis and evaluation, and beyond that to synthesis and innovation. Co-educators should have high expectations for all students whether in general education, education of gifted students, or special education for students with disabilities and developmental delays. (See Figure 2.2.)

Taxonomy of the Affective Domain.   In 1964, Krathwohl, Bloom, and Masia directed the development of the *Taxonomy of Educational Objectives, Handbook II: Affective Domain*. The original committee in 1956 had recognized the need for addressing affective functions, but had been discouraged by the difficulty of designing ways to measure them.

It is logical that cognitive and affective domains are components of learning and doing. The classification scheme's five categories for the affective domain (Krathwohl et al., 1964) are again ordered from simplest to most complex. Briefly described, they are (Hanna & Dettmer, 2004):

- **Receiving:** Being aware of something or someone in the environment and attending at least passively.
- **Responding:** Reacting to the environment and responding to elements within that environment.
- **Valuing:** Showing commitment by responding voluntarily and seeking out ways to respond.
- **Organization:** Integrating knowledge and applying information to something regarded as important.
- **Characterization by a Value or Value Complex:** Organizing values into a whole and acting in accordance with newly acquired values or beliefs.

Extending the Cognitive and Affective Taxonomies. Developers of the cognitive domain taxonomy did not promote their work as the be-all and end-all for processes of thinking and doing. They frowned on fragmentation of educational purposes and aimed to set the taxonomy at a level of generality that allowed for flexibility and growth. They thought of the taxonomies as fluid and unfinished, and encouraged more thought and development of the concepts They hoped not to abort teachers' thinking and development of curriculum, and they did not want the taxonomies to be used as recipes, which, unfortunately, some teachers have been prone to do.

Rereading the original works and pondering significances of their profoundly important ideas can be a rewarding professional development exercise or collaborative experience for educators that may lead to new ideas about teaching and learning. For example, since the original cognitive and affective domains were conceptualized, interest in creativity has expanded, generating increased research on creative thinking and development of original products as an important part of school curriculum. Imagination is a cognitive and affective tool with which students explore how the world works in wonderful and mysterious ways (Dettmer, 2006). Therefore, stimulating the imagination should not be treated as a recreational activity left for that bit of extra time before the dismissal bell or as a reward for getting the "real work" done, but it should be regarded as a means of enhancing the educational value of any lesson.

Co-educators who collaborate in curriculum development can do much to dispel this misconception. The cognitive taxonomy can be expanded to include categories for imagination and creativity. Then, because cognitive activities of imagination and creativity are accompanied by affective components, categories of wonder (in using one's imagination) and aspire (aiming for and accepting risks in order to create) fit well into the affective domain. Finally, the affective domain calls for a parallel to evaluation in the cognitive domain, and internalize is a good fit.

Taxonomic levels need not be rigid step stones. However, a line of demarcation is called for to distinguish low-road thinking and feeling (knowledge and comprehension, receiving and responding) from high-road thinking (everything beyond that). Here is a brief listing of key words for categories in both domains as altered to include the enhancements.

- **Cognitive:** Know, Comprehend, Apply, Analyze, Synthesize, Evaluate, Imagine, Create
- **Affective:** Receive, Respond, Value, Organize, Characterize, Internalize, Wonder, Aspire

Taxonomy of the Sensorimotor Domain. When Bloom et al. (1956) presented the cognitive taxonomy and later on the affective taxonomy, they made little mention of physical development. But in the years since that time there has been increasing attention to motor skills needed for areas such as athletics, art, industry, and technology and to the sensing elements that are critical to the learning process. Therefore, several psychomotor taxonomies have appeared, including those developed by Simpson (1972) and Harrow (1972). However, such taxonomies did not emphasize the senses as integral components of motor skills. Senses are especially important to teachers of students who are challenged because of disabilities in hearing, seeing, smelling, touching, tasting, speaking, feeling, moving, being still, staying in balance, having highly elevated sensitivities and movements, and having difficulties with other sensorimotor-based activities. Then, too, some sensorimotor functions are supportive or compensatory attributes for those with disabilities and special needs. As just one simple example, a visually impaired person may develop a very keen sense of hearing or smell. Therefore, taxonomy for the physical realm must not be limited to motor activity. In the school curriculum, the physical perspective should include sensory input, with attention to sight, sound, touch, taste, and smell, and perhaps other elements not yet included, such as balance and sensitivity, in the school curriculum. Many teachers, particularly at the primary levels, do this already because they realize the importance of sensory input for learning. A taxonomic structure that moves beyond the psychomotor realm in order to include sensorimotor functions can be organized into eight levels. These are (Dettmer, 2006):

- **Observe:** Using the senses to notice.
- **React:** Showing recognition with senses and/or movement.
- **Act:** Becoming involved by demonstrating physical and sensory response.
- **Adapt:** Adjusting sensorimotor activity to fit unfamiliar situations.
- **Authenticate:** Assessing validity of particular sensorimotor processes for conditions and purposes.
- **Harmonize:** Integrating sensorimotor activities into existing situations.
- **Improvise:** Developing new aspects of sensorimotor response for problem solving.
- **Innovate:** Constructing new, self-expressive sensorimotor actions and solutions.

Taxonomy of the Social Domain.   The social realm is an aspect of learning and doing that has been neglected even more than the sensorimotor domain. However, teachers and students relate to each other continuously in sociocultural settings. They develop networks of relationships in richly interactive within-school and after-school or extracurricular environments. Some of the most serious student behavioral and relational problems occur in this area.

Layers of relationship are somewhat hierarchical; they can be arranged into an eight-category taxonomy for a social domain. The categories, described in more detail here than the previous three because they are new and they apply significantly to consultation, collaboration, and teamwork, are (Hanna & Dettmer, 2004; Dettmer, 2006):

- **Relating:** Acknowledging the presence of others, making eye contact, attending to their words or actions, showing acceptance of others.
- **Communicating:** Sending or receiving messages from others to speak, gesture, call, sing, signal, listen. The most overlooked aspect of the communication process, to be discussed in an upcoming chapter, is listening. Messages are sent verbally and nonverbally, with body language often being the more powerful of these two types.
- **Participating:** Joining in, volunteering for, going along with, or actively and willingly taking part in grouped activities. Much of school life previews later life and careers where belonging to and taking part in groups is a vital function.

- **Negotiating:** Negotiating often takes place informally. Mediating and arbitrating are extensions of negotiation and a means of setting aside singularly personal preferences to accommodate and assimilate those of others.
- **Collaborating:** Working together for the success of the group or the project. Teamwork conducted in a collaborative climate is a necessary quality in family, career, and community life for the twenty-first century.
- **Adjudicating:** Conciliating to settle differences as they arise. Conciliation is an outcome of effective mediation and arbitration efforts. Those who communicate and negotiate effectively in social settings are more able to mediate differences to the benefit of all.
- **Initiating:** Creating opportunities and processes for interactions, even if social risks are involved, in order to catalyze social action and change.
- **Converting:** Managing social transitions smoothly and fairly, convincing others to join in for social aims that can benefit all.

Taxonomies guide the assessment process so as to be facilitative, not punitive. When teaching a concept at the basic (knowledge and comprehension) levels (for example, the times tables) and expecting students to attend to the lesson (by receiving it and responding to it), instructors will allow sufficient time for learning the material at preestablished, announced competency levels. If the material cannot be mastered and learners must move on, reteaching and correctives are employed. In this event, extending activities must be made available for those who do not need to "mark time" or as one student described it, "rev my motor with my brakes on." Collaborative consultation among teachers and resource personnel is invaluable in situations that call for curriculum differentiation.

As collaborating teachers plan together, they should discuss how to enhance student growth in critical thinking and creative thinking skills and help students develop tolerance for differing points of view. When lesson objectives are aimed at higher-order thinking, instructors should designate a level of achievement that is reasonable for open-ended, never-ending learning—for example, second-graders keeping logs of interesting words to use in creative writing activities, or high-school students' evaluation of benefits of various power sources for an energy-hungry nation, or middle-school students' comparisons of the needs for harvesting raw materials such as tree logs with the need to protect endangered species such as fish or owls. Then they need to stipulate the point in time at which the class must move on, thereby accepting the reality of varying levels of achievement among the group.

When objectives for learning are focusing on creativity and innovation, with wonder and risk-taking as affective components, teachers, mentors, and content-area specialists will need to provide flexible time limits and suspend expectations for specific levels of achievement. If they feel inadequate to critique students' work and present constructive feedback in specialized areas, they will want to call in experts and outside resources personnel to consult and collaborate with them and with the students. Students will be major participants in planning the curriculum and assessing their performance at this level, with collaborative team effort taking place among all.

▪ ▪ ▪ ▪ ▪

ACTIVITY 2.2
Addressing All Domains

Select a favorite unit you would like to teach or have taught and examine your lesson plans for doing that. Look for inclusion of activities that provide learning experiences in each of four domains—cognitive, affective, sensorimotor, and social. If any of the four has not been addressed, think of ways the unit could be extended to include domains that have been neglected.

For further challenge, after analyzing your plan for that favorite unit, take part in a small-group interaction where all persons describe what their lesson-plan analysis revealed. Then collaborate to offer ideas for activities that could be added to include missing domains.

The Talents Factor

The word "talent" as applied to adults is an important component of the educational environment. A pool of educators will contain many talents and skills. This deep and wide pool is one of the best resources that schools can provide to the curriculum and the hidden curriculum as well. Talent even has the potential for defusing turf tension because when every individual's talents are recognized and encouraged to shine, protecting one's place becomes less important, perhaps even inconsequential.

Some talent is group talent—as in the case of a Final Four basketball team, a renowned acting troupe, a debate team, or a team of widely acclaimed surgeons. Other talent is individual—such as that of a stand-up comedian, an award-winning chef, or a master teacher—that could become an aspect of team talent if shared in partnerships and mentorships. Schools are filled with budding talents of students at all grade levels. However, teacher talent may stay hidden under heavy caseloads and unforgiving time clocks. Latent talents are opportunities for constructing teams of talented individuals. Once formed, they can work together for student growth, faculty development, and school improvement.

Talent is a fine vehicle through which to diversify instruction for students with developmental disabilities and showcase the results. One classroom for teenage students with developmental delays discovered cooking talent in their midst. They began to make healthful snacks and treats, first for themselves and then for students and teachers in their building. With the money left over after buying ingredients, they expanded their operation to include other attendance centers. After several months of success, and a few trials and setbacks from which they learned much, they developed a catering service that reached beyond school walls into the community with its excellent reputation and products. A number of consultants and collaborators, including district and building administrators, were involved in this exceedingly successful venture, but the kudos and recognitions were theirs to relish. Students in special education classes have much to contribute, and will learn many things as they are doing so, when they and their teachers are given opportunities to develop and use their talents.

The Trust Factor

Trust is an enigmatic and elusive construct when applied to the work setting. Although daily news reports from national media trumpet instance upon instance of failed trust in areas such as finance, government, business, industry, sports, and the like, educators who have been entrusted with the public's most precious commodity of all—children and youth—are expected to function in trustworthy fashion at all times to prepare their students for an honorable future among others who may be trustworthy or not.

Building trust in young students requires careful instruction and modeling by caring educators. Expecting to find trust in others is in and of itself an act of trust and respect. The example of the successful catering service built and operated by teenage students with developmental delays was a case of talent and expertise built on a mountain of trust. Numerous national reports have laid out the competencies that young people will need for their future roles, emphasizing the ability to work with others, trust in them, and rely on them during problem-finding and problem-solving activities. Trust emanates from the collaborative ethic that must be present with every interaction in and for schools, whether between classroom teacher and student, administrator and parent, paraeducator and special education teacher, or school board members and community members.

Trust is demonstrated when teachers observe educators in other school settings and look over co-teachers' shoulders in the classroom. It is solidified by courteous exits and respectful post-observation discussions where, just as teachers do in a parent-teacher conference, visiting and observing teachers will want to begin and end with positive things to say about their visits. Trust is needed most when educators are keepers of confidential information about students that must be handled in a discreet but constructive way.

Co-educators can recommend that faculty meetings be rotated among classrooms, labs, and athletic sites, stepping into colleagues' shoes and space for that short period of time. This change of venue and perspective could add insight to future collaborations. A sign-up sheet where each one signs for a preferred time would be a good way to initiate the arrangement. It would be especially constructive when the group is a mix of general and special education staff, or elementary and secondary staff, or vocational and academic department teachers. During these times of visitation and follow-up discussions, colleagues must make a strong effort to listen and learn. The listening should be long enough to find areas of agreements and disagreements, and the learning intense enough to feel the pull of others' convictions.

Areas of Differences in Teacher Practices

A challenge was issued in an earlier chapter to list 100 or more responsibilities that school personnel perform in their roles. What if that challenge was extended to compile a list of how many different ways educators go about carrying out these responsibilities? For example, some arrive early in the morning to prepare for classes; others stay late and prepare for the next day. Some plan curriculum by the week and others by the month. Some use cooperative learning techniques. Others like to have peer tutors or volunteer aides. Some arrange student seating in rows or groups; a few have removed the seats from their classrooms! Differences in a wide array of teaching practices can set co-educators apart from one another when they set out to collaborate for instruction and classroom management.

■ ■ ■ ■ ■ ▬▬▬▬▬▬▬▬▬▬▬▬▬▬▬▬▬▬▬▬▬▬▬▬▬▬▬▬▬▬▬▬▬▬▬▬▬▬▬

ACTIVITY 2.3
Identifying Areas of Difference

What factors could partition educator characteristics into categories? Begin with the obvious ones—for example, age or generation, years of teaching experience, curriculum areas taught, age or grade levels taught, geographic location of school (urban, suburban, consolidated, small rural), teacher education program attended, and so forth. As suggested in the initial challenge, if this activity is done in collaboration with teachers from other grade levels, content areas, school sizes, and locations, the list that is generated will be even richer.

Discuss what effects these differences could have on teaching and classroom management. For example, do teachers of the baby-boomer generation differ in perspectives on discipline from those of generation X? What about gender of teachers? If that is not considered important as a category of difference, then why do elementary schools often seek out male applicants for lower-grade teaching levels? In analyzing the problem-solving capacities of groups engaged in various team endeavors, Page (2007) finds that cognitive diversity is at least as important as intelligence in dealing with complex, multidimensional issues. Page further notes that those with different types of disciplinary training bring different tools and diverse understandings to the task. Conoley (1994) states:

> It requires courage to detail differences from the accepted ways of seeing, knowing, and doing . . . . If I say I am interested in learning about the world, but wish to do so in a way that puts a focus on connections, I hope that can be understood as another way. If you say you are interested in learning about the world, but wish to do so in a way that puts a focus on isolated events, I hope that can be understood as just another way. There are many ways to a truth with many faces. (p. 49)

In the previous challenge, readers were asked to think of and record a hundred or more responsibilities that school personnel perform in their roles of duty. Any lists that were compiled most likely included tasks as varied as making lesson plans, helping individual students, attending staff meetings, conferencing with parents, ordering supplies, and much, much more. What if the challenge were to compile a list of ways in which teachers and all other school personnel might differ as they go about these tasks? A place to begin is to consider the plethora of variables that might set educators apart from one another, such as grade levels of students taught, size of school, credentials required, and so forth. An important variable for launching and perfecting the practice of collaborative school consultation is the demarcation between general education and special education.

▬▬▬▬▬▬▬▬▬▬▬▬▬▬▬▬▬▬▬▬▬▬▬▬▬▬▬▬▬▬▬▬▬▬▬▬▬▬▬

General Education and Special Education

Traditions, time, turf, taxonomies, talent, and trust are variables that shape all aspects of teaching and learning every day, year in and year out. But other variables need to be taken into account for having significant influence on collaboration, consultation, and teamwork. Those would include comparison of general education with special education.

Ongoing dialogue among special education teachers and regular classroom teachers is essential. As brought out in the section on traditions, the days of "them" versus "us" are over, just as the term "my students" has been overridden by newer language focusing on our students in our classrooms. Even so, it is not clear that general educators and special educators understand each other all that well yet. More than three decades ago Stainback and Stainback (1985) noted unique differences between regular and special education teachers, and they attributed the differences to preparation received for teaching roles. They felt that variations in teachers' specializations could be used to provide optimal opportunities for every student within one unified educational system. But now general educators have become an integral part of education in inclusive schools for students with disabilities, and many have reported that they still feel unprepared for these responsibilities (Brownell, Adams, Sindelar, Waldron, & Vanhover, 2006). Collaboration is being more widely recognized, promoted, and accepted as an essential component in enhancing the ability of both general and special co-educators to function in their roles in inclusive schools. However, teachers whose perspectives differ most significantly are least likely to collaborate (Brownell et al., 2006). This underscores the importance of having co-educators understand what their colleagues are thinking and feeling in the school environment to provide instruction for all students.

Mismatches between teachers, whether between general education and special education, or elementary and secondary, or fine arts and vocational programs, or even secondary and postsecondary, can create discord and insensitive independent thinking rather than shared problem solving. So every educator needs to have a "big picture" of both general and special education curriculum, along with state and local standards, instructional approaches for diverse learning needs, ways of aligning goals with curriculum, teaching and behavioral management strategies for special needs, and assessment methods for grading and reporting on outcomes (McDonnell, McLaughlin, & Morrison, 1997; Walsh, 2001). A particularly volatile area is evaluation, or assessment and grading of student achievement, and this has a domino effect on selection and development of curriculum.

Learning and behavioral goals and assessments are issues yet to be resolved in the backwash of No Child Left Behind (NCLB) and the ensuing controversies surrounding development and implementation of the Common Core Standards. But such issues must not be allowed to discourage co-educators from collaborating and co-teaching. It is up to school administrators, counselors, school psychologists, experienced teachers, and parents to increase their own understandings of valid learning goals, assessment processes, and scoring reasons. These understandings can be built through staff development activities, ongoing collaborative endeavors, and informal consultative dialogues. Walsh (2001) asserts that one major decision to be made by both general and special education teachers is what is not absolutely necessary for all students to learn in order to meet high content standards. The foundation for such understanding should be laid in teacher preparation programs before new teachers enter the hustle-bustle of school life and their first classroom where they will have immediate responsibilities for making decisions relevant to curriculum and assessment and working hard to carry them out.

Novice teachers bring many assets to their first professional assignments. They are enthusiastic and eager to put into practice the ideas they have been accumulating for months. They have been exposed to the most recent educational theories, methods, and materials. Many completed their student teaching assignments under the supervision of master teachers in excellent schools. But knowledge does not become wisdom without experience. A major difference between the novice and the veteran teacher, whether in general education or special education, is the experience that informs wisely so that one can make decisions such as, "Yes, this is a promising plan," or "No, we don't want to try it with that student."

Grade Levels and Curriculum Areas

Grade level differences among elementary and secondary teachers may be less likely than general and special education differences to interfere with collaborative enterprises; however, there are times that district-wide groups do come together for the purposes of aligning curriculum to state standards or Common Core Standards, or adopting a district-wide textbook series. Professional perspectives among preschool, elementary, middle school, and high school teachers also can vary considerably in regard to classroom organization and management of learning and behavior.

One cliché discussed earlier as a tradition is revealed when elementary and secondary teaching are distinguished one from the other with the phrase "secondary teachers teach content and elementary teachers teach kids." This is a flawed, overstated assumption that needs rethinking because young children are very curious about the world and they hunger for interesting subject matter, while teens crave interaction with peers and especially their friends. Professional development experiences and collaborative activities could be designed for curricular emphasis on richer content for elementary-age children and more creative use of social structures for adolescent learning.

Curricular-area differences also affect schedules in ways that impinge on collaboration and professional development experiences. Physical education teachers may request to be excused from much of the staff development because of their coaching duties and supervision of sports events. Vocational teacher classrooms and shops often are housed apart from the other classrooms. Athletic coaches are away from their assigned classes for many hours, depending on the sports season. Science projects and needed monitoring may spill over into other class periods, causing schedules and patience levels to fray. Music, debate, and academic competition groups are away several times during the year to take part in competitions and performances. Such realities make the scheduling of collaborative consultation and professional development activities especially difficult at the secondary level.

More Differences Influencing Professional Perspectives

Other areas where co-educators may differ, especially when they plan co-teaching strategies, include:

- Homework—how much, how often, what kind, how critiqued and how graded
- Pull-out or pull-in sessions for students that deviate from normal classroom procedures
- Requirements for making up work missed during pull-out sessions
- Test accommodations and modifications for students with disabilities
- Grading policies
- Whether or not to allow do-over work for full or partial credit
- Time out, positive and negative reinforcement, and contract contingencies

- Frequency and type of parent involvement in the classroom
- Noise and activity levels within the classroom
- Appearance and upkeep of classrooms, especially shared learning areas
- How much group and collaborative work students may (or are required to) do
- Being the only teacher who is not a parent, or vice versa
- Observation of teachers in other classrooms or schools
- Using student portfolios as a means of authentic assessment with involvement of students in development of the portfolio rubrics
- Spending personal money for classroom teaching supplies, and to what limits (a practice looked on with disfavor by some teachers who cannot or will not do it, and requests of some parents to have their child placed with the teacher who will supplement with personal resources. A report released in July of 2013 by the National School Supply and Equipment Association carried the headline, "K–12 Teachers Out of Pocket $1.6 billion on Classroom Tools," with 99.5 percent of all public school teachers spending some of their own money to enrich the curriculum (Nagel, 2013). National average was $485 among teachers surveyed, and 10 percent spent $1,000 or more out of pocket.

What should be done toward sorting out and managing differences in professional perspectives to form a suitable plan for working together? First and foremost, there must be understanding and acceptance among co-educators, including administrators, and students' families concerning two broad realities:

- Variation in achievement among students cannot be eliminated. This could only be done by speeding up less able students through artificial, unethical means, or slowing down very able students, again unethically, by withholding opportunities to learn. Both of these options are, of course, totally unacceptable. But there is no Lake Wobegon where all students are above average. No federal mandates, preschool programs, master plans for parent involvement, or rigorous teaching programs can erase the reality of differences in achievement.
- Second, good teaching will **increase** individual differences in achievement among students. This is because students with less ability and those with disabilities will learn, while those with more ability will learn even more if not held back by teaching practices and school policies that pull performance expectations to the middle.

When educators make peace with these two realities, they are empowered to move on in constructive ways that will benefit all students (Hanna & Dettmer, 2004). If collaborating educators are not in congruence with these two principles, their efforts toward working together will be uncomfortably and awkwardly off balance from the start. Educators must internalize, reflect on, accept, and teach so that differences in achievement cannot be ignored or eliminated, and good teaching will be expected to increase the differences.

As in constructing a building, several areas are requisite to development of an educator's professional perspectives. All eight include both stumbling blocks and steppingstones to effective consultation and collaboration:

- Types of learning theory
- Kinds of subject matter
- Types of instructional goals
- Orientations in time and achievement levels
- Kinds of tests
- Types of scores
- Interpretations of scores
- Domains for learning and doing, with transfer of the learning

If co-educators differ markedly in these areas and do not work through their differences, well-meaning efforts to collaborate and co-teach will indeed cause them to stumble. On the other hand, if collaboration and teamwork are healthy and enjoyable, the processes will provide stepping-stones to success for teachers and learners.

Types of Learning Theory

Learning theory frames expectations for achievement, construction of instructional objectives, and methods of assessment. For purposes here, a brief look will be on three predominant types of learning theory—cognitive, behavioral, and social. Each of these types is appropriate in some contexts and not so well suited for others (Hanna & Dettmer, 2004). Special education teachers have learned and practiced many behavioral principles. So have some general education teachers. However, many of the latter still prefer the cognitive theory or social cognitive theory approach to instruction for most students.

Preservice teachers may have been swayed into an either/or outlook on learning theory to the extent that they profess they are a "behaviorist" or a "cognitivist." But when they collaborate with other educators to identify student needs and plan instruction for the needs, they may find that their "language" is not being used, or perhaps two "languages" are being spoken. One co-educator might focus on observation, reinforcement conditions for modifying behaviors, responses, prerequisite skills, instructional sequencing, and observable criteria for measurement as in behavioral theory. Another may feature mental constructs, active processing of information, reinforcement as a means of providing information, and construction of knowledge. A third may speak in terms of a co-constructed process in which people interact and negotiate to understand, apply, and problem-solve. The dissonance among these three perspectives (behavioral, cognitive, and social) can put even an experienced teacher off balance and may be especially confusing to a novice teacher who erroneously thinks the choice must be either/or.

Three Kinds of Subject Matter

Subject matter can be channeled into one of three kinds—essential, developmental, or ideational. Each kind has its place in a well-designed curriculum at all age and ability levels and in all content areas. The distinctions among the three will mold teacher expectations for student achievement, and the goal setting, instructional strategies, and assessment methods to help fulfill those expectations. They also will influence markedly the teacher-student, teacher-teacher, and teacher-family interactions. Here again, differences of perspective are molded to some extent by educators' affiliations with general or special education focus, their grade levels, curricular areas, preferred school of learning theory, teaching styles, and preferred assessment methods.

Essential subject matter is that which is at the most basic and clear-cut level within a closed, fixed sphere for learning. The objectives can be described with specificity and the material is to be mastered by students. This content is the basis for further learning; it can be used in similar situations through low-road transfer. Teachers instruct with well-defined material, and students are to learn the material in its entirety. Time is allocated for mastery; if the material is not learned, compensatory activities are provided to help. Examples of essential content to be mastered would be:

- Toilet training, recognition of colors for the preschool set
- Letters of the alphabet, simple sight words for kindergarten/primary grades
- Times tables, assigned spelling words for intermediate grades
- Traffic signs and symbols, standard keyboard position, procedure for setting up a microscope, music symbols and notation, target of completing a lap in a relay, or rules for baseball as examples for continuation of essential learning.

Teachers of students with learning disabilities or developmental disability formulate many goals using this type of curriculum material. It is taught and learned for mastery.

The second kind of subject matter is developmental. It is specifiable but expansive to the extent that it either cannot be fully mastered or it need not be fully mastered in order to continue to learn and do. With developmental material, varying levels of achievement among students are to be expected. All students must have opportunities to learn many things at the developmental level. Examples of developmental content would be naming the capitals of all countries of the world (possible but is it essential?), listing all vice-presidents of the United States (again, possible, but does it really need to be transferred to any other situation?), learning volleyball techniques (when can all possibilities ever be learned?), welding a metal joint (what is perfection?) or baking a soufflé (and who among the best chefs attains mastery for this?). This material is taught for only as much achievement as possible or deemed reasonable and necessary.

Lastly, some subject matter is neither specifiable nor easily mastered. This ideational sphere of learning is broad, open-ended, and novel. Diverse outcomes and wide ranges of achievement among students are expected. Transfer of learning is at a high level; ideational material can be transferred to new situations calling for complex problem solving and innovation. Only a representation of the immense range of material is taught, and only some of what was taught is tested. In addition, some instructed content is not tested, and some content that was not taught but is related to the topic is tested to find out if there is transfer of learning to more complex problems or new situations. Educators with an orientation toward cognitive theory are quite comfortable with ideational subject matter, and teachers of students with high aptitude "live here" when planning instruction for students' needs as dictated by their advanced abilities. The classrooms of such teachers are likely to provide learning centers and encourage independent studies. Group discussions with no predetermined outcomes are a vehicle for stimulating the learning. Examples of ideational content would be to show in picture format how addition and multiplication are related, or to collect and record data from a square yard of ground in an outdoor area, or to illustrate an infringement on human rights that are provided by a particular amendment to the United States Constitution, or to plan a nutritional menu for a month on a given budget, or to apply principles of energy production and conservation to the concept of global warming. Material here is never masterable and learning is ongoing.

Differences in professional perspective emanating from general education and special education, grade levels, learning theory orientations, and subject matter realms can have significant effects on collaboration, consultation, and teamwork, and especially co-teaching teams. These effects may be deleterious or, when addressed head-on with respect, understanding, and accommodation, they can invigorate teaching and stimulate student efforts as well.

Annual Goals and Instructional Objectives

Principles related to learning theories and subject-matter contexts will frame the kinds of goals and objectives that are formulated. They direct teachers in lesson planning and inevitably surface in arenas such as textbook selection meetings and IEP conferences, creating another distinct difference in professional perspective between special education and general education teachers.

Special education teachers are well schooled in Mager-type behavioral objectives that indicate explicitly how attainment of goals and objectives will be sought and assessed, so they construct annual goals that outline the behaviors, conditions, and achievement levels to be met. The goals include: 1) an observable student behavior, 2) conditions for demonstrating the behavior, and 3) minimal level of attainment expected. General education teachers may have been exposed to Mager-based principles, and they are required under reauthorized IDEA legislation to attend some IEP conferences where this process for annual goal development is put into practice. But many prefer to use Gronlund-based instructional objectives for instruction in developmental and ideational subject matter—those large, expansive bodies of content with no endpoint achievement levels. Because such goals are not easily measured, several indicants are provided for each instructional objective that have measurable verbs to sample behaviors for determining student progress. This distinction between goal types—Mager-based and Gronlund-based—has been sharpened by legislation such as P.L. 94-142 and by methods emphasized in teacher preparation programs and teacher education literature. Much of the special education curriculum calls for mastery-type learning of essential subject matter, if only to ensure measurability of progress on IEP goals. This disadvantages students with disabilities unless they also have opportunities to learn and to do with developmental and ideational subject matter as well. Effective teachers, both general education and special education, will make sure they provide those opportunities, *and setting instructional objectives collaboratively will be a key factor.*

Achievement of broad instructional objectives with measurable indicants and measurable goals as called for in IEPs must be assessed by reliable and valid means to show progress. But ideational goals and most developmental goals are not strictly measurable by efficient means such as paper-pencil tests. Evidence of achievement must be determined by authentic assessments carefully designed to demonstrate that progress has been made toward meeting the goals. Only basic, essential goals that can be met by recognition and recall of learned information are objectively measurable in reliable and practical ways. The rub in all of this is that to determine progress toward measurable annual goals, the curriculum needs to be simplistically masterable. Building curriculum only on easily-measured goals will short-change students in special education programs who need and are entitled to opportunities for learning broad, open-ended, interesting, novel content.

What to do? As a start, to buy the needed instructional time for students who must learn apart from the class or leave the classroom periodically for remedial or practice sessions in a resource room, some IEP goals should be embedded into general education curriculum. Then some broad, high-road transfer goals for students should be incorporated into both general education and special education curriculum. If this does not happen, there will not be enough time in the school day to provide all the learning opportunities to which students with special needs are entitled. This reality makes collaboration between special education and general education teachers even more imperative. All students must have opportunities to achieve at deep levels regardless of disability or cultural or linguistic diversity; instructional objectives must be interpreted as minimal statements of expectations and not the outer limits of the learning (Hanna & Dettmer, 2004).

Students who learn differently or happen to have learning difficulties must not be left behind, and students with high aptitude should not be held back. Consultation and collaboration, with links to other educational resources, can help ensure that all students have opportunity to learn, to develop their potential, and to explore their unique interests. Discussions among collaborative school consultants about this issue could have profound motivational influences and positive effects on higher-order learning by students with disabilities and behavioral problems. Collaboration becomes more valued and sought when co-educators see that it is working to the benefit of students.

Time and Achievement Dimensions

As teachers make decisions about the complexity of the subject matter to be taught and develop annual goals or instructional objectives for student learning, they must determine whether the instruction will be set in a time dimension or an achievement dimension. In other words, will students be given all the time they need to master the goals, or will there be a level of achievement they must reach before they can move on to other materials? Here again, differences among collaborating and co-teaching teachers can have a divisive effect on collaborative efforts. But it need not be that way. They must talk it through and come to consensus in students' best interests.

Essential material typically is framed in a time dimension, with correctives provided if and when students cannot master the material in the time allowed. In the past, this has often been the point at which the special education teacher assists with interventions in anticipation that the student can and must learn the material in order to move on with the class.

Conversely, developmental subject matter and most assuredly ideational material should be set in the achievement dimension. Students will not need to stay with that material until it is mastered because mastery is not sought, and variance in student achievement is to be expected. This is a critical juncture for co-educators to meet and plan learning opportunities for all students in developmental and ideational subject matter. Put another way and reiterating previous statements, no student with disabilities should be denied access to higher levels of thinking and doing; in fact, a case could be made that they need such instruction more than students who can function successfully in a more or less self-directed fashion when provided with resources for doing so. Collaborators must take such concerns into account when they plan instruction for students who have been achieving slowly or at low levels. Their collective aim must not be to expect students of lesser and greater ability to "come together at the middle," but rather to have high expectations for all students. Then they should design curriculum that helps all students master what is truly essential and move on to opportunities for learning at more complex levels to the greatest extent of which they are capable.

Assessment and Evaluation Processes

The next three types of professional perspectives are intertwined and therefore are grouped for discussion. They are purposes of tests, types of scores, and interpretations of scores. Professional differences within these components of assessment, along with political pressures from inside and outside the schools, are extremely important factors for working together successfully, and they can be among the most divisive factors that thwart the best of intentions toward collaborative school consultation. One compelling reason for their importance is that they include high-stakes involvement of school co-educators, home co-educators, and students profoundly and passionately.

Tests are administered to students for one of two purposes—either to ascertain level of achievement on stated criteria or to determine achievement in relation to others. So tests are either mastery tests or differentiating tests, yielding scores that are criterion referenced or domain referenced. Criterion-referenced scores relate to specifiable content learned for mastery, while domain-referenced scores relate to broad, open-ended spheres of learning and are compared with scores obtained by well-identified and relevant reference groups.

Teachers do teach to the test for mastery testing; in fact, they should inform students precisely what they will be tested on and then provide appropriate instruction so that every student has every opportunity to master the material and be prepared to "ace" the test. Students need to know what they will be accountable for and then they need to know whether they succeeded. Parents need to know that this is the function of such tests.

Conversely, for a differentiating or discriminatory test, teachers do not teach explicit content. They teach for learning, and doing that extends beyond recall and comprehension (low-road transfer) so that students can apply broad, open-ended content (with high-road transfer to new problems and novel situations). For discriminatory tests, the instruction must be excellent and expectations for student achievement must be held high. But co-educators should acknowledge that the tests are intended to differentiate between students who have learned (or, it must be said, in many instances already knew) the material, and those who have not, and then compare their achievement with that of others in an appropriate reference group. Comparisons are sought so that useful decisions can be made, such as to determine class rankings, or to facilitate entry to advanced programs or higher education, or to award scholarships. But in a more immediate and practical vein, important decisions can be made about planning and pacing instruction, grouping or not grouping students, referring students to testing for special education programs, selecting appropriate materials for continued learning, and much more that could not be obtained from the limited information provided by mastery tests over specified material in closed content domains.

Interpretation of test scores can expose important professional differences among educators. In reality, many educators are not well enough acquainted with methods of score interpretation. Too many have never had formal instruction in measurement and testing; unfortunately, this is especially true among preservice teachers who do not even have experience on which to rely for making their decisions.

Scores fall into two main types: First, there are raw scores and the closely-related percentage scores that are suitable for interpreting scores on domain-referenced material where content is clear-cut and is to be mastered. Meaning can be ascribed to progress on such material by noting a raw score such as 8 out of 10 words spelled correctly, for example, or 90 percent of the twenty assigned arithmetic problems worked correctly.

The second type, derived scores, compare student achievement with that of others. They are discriminatory by design, to discriminate between those who have learned the material and those who have not. (Note that "discriminate" is a psychometric term referring to comparisons of scores and is not to be confused with the odious use of the word in stereotype or prejudice toward people.) Scores on discriminatory, norm-referenced tests can be reported by several means, some more satisfactory than others: Grade (G.E.) equivalents or age (A-E) equivalents; ranks and percentile ranks; and standard scores such as deviation IQs, stanines, z-scores, T-scores, and normal curve equivalencies (NCEs).

Professional differences about scores and their interpretations can cause serious friction among co-educators because scores are used for evaluations, placements, grades, school reports to the public, communications with parents, and even assessments of teaching. Most school administrators would not look favorably on teachers who awarded all "A" grades for every student, nor would they do so on teachers whose composite of student grades never rose above "D." They would begin to look at the teacher's planning and instruction as too limited or too demanding. Unfortunately, score interpretations are often arrived at in a flawed manner and can result in quite misleading information. Just a few of the more flawed and sensitivity-laden issues are:

- Using percentages to score nonmasterable material. The folly of this practice can be challenged by asking, "Let's see. That score is 70 percent of what?" which is of course unanswerable for open-ended subject matter. A score of 70 percent on the week's spelling list makes sense, but a score of 70 percent on a test asking for important, globe-encircling causes and effects of World War II does not. A rigid system of percentage grading would lock content into the mastery mode where only simple, essential material is taught.
- Confusing percentile scores with percentages. Percentiles put scores into rank file for comparison with others in a group selected for the comparison. That could be last year's similar classes, this year's multiple sections of the same class, district-wide classes of the same subject and grade level, national averages, and so forth. Percentiles are easily understood by students and their parents, but because they do represent ranks, they cannot be summed and averaged in grade books.

- Using grade (G.E.) and age (A-E) equivalencies. Most uses of G.E.s and A-Es are ill advised because they lead to serious misinterpretations by parents and sometimes even by teachers and administrators. As just one example, a parent might ask, "If my 5th grader scored at the 8th-grade level in both math and reading, shouldn't she be advanced to the 8th grade, or at least elevated to 8th-grade math and reading curriculum?" This requires back-pedaling by the teacher and searching for reasonable explanations to parents, so this score type is better avoided.
- "Grading on the curve." Some teachers cling to this very questionable but frequently employed practice for assigning letter grades, and alas, some school district policies dictate that it be used. Many school handbooks can attest to this practice, although it is a misuse of student evaluation and an abuse of the learning process. The policy is harshly inappropriate because learning is not a zero-sum game with just so much learning to go around. When teachers announce before testing, and sometimes even before their instruction, that grade distributions will contain one or two As, for example, and X number of Bs, Cs, Ds, and perhaps Fs, effects on student learning will be many and mostly negative.

Achievement cannot be packaged into tidy, preordained "amounts" if students are to be interested and motivated to learn. Where there is "grading on the curve," they will concentrate instead on competing and "taking away" from others. Some will withdraw from even trying to learn. The resultant peer pressure, not to mention the damper on learning, will be debilitating to motivation and interpersonal relations among students who feel they must compete to "bump" others for the few top grades and stay away from the inevitable bottom of the distribution. No clearer message for not collaborating and working together could be sent. Collaborating teachers can forget about demonstrating collegiality and shared effort if they adopt this evaluation perspective. Furthermore, students will be ill prepared for the teamwork and collaborations expected of them in their careers and communities.

So again, what to do? Collaborating educators must address the issue head on and talk it through! One reasonable option is use of a system such as modified percentage grading that does not link grades to the top student, but employs a covert kind of norm referencing system instead. This process would anchor a class's scores to other groups as explained earlier in regard to percentiles, and allow for adjustments to be made by the teacher so grade distributions come out as experienced teachers sense that they should. Pre-service teachers typically have little background of assessment experience, and they have no former reference groups to draw upon, but they can learn much when in collaboration with veteran teachers to guide their novitiate grading processes. Furthermore, the entire teaching staff and perhaps even parents would welcome an opportunity for consultation and professional development sessions directed toward the extremely important teaching responsibility of student assessment and evaluation. Some of the assessment issues to be addressed by special education and general education teachers in collaborative consultations include accommodation and adaptation for students with disabilities. Adaptations are made through accommodations or modifications of testing procedures. Accommodations are changes in regular test conditions, and modifications are techniques that change the test to make it different from others in the group. These special education practices have important educational, social, and legal ramifications that must be understood by school administrators and general classroom teachers as well as special education and resource personnel. Collaborative consultation is a fitting process for examining all aspects of these complex issues and potential adaptations of professional perspective in order to make right decisions.

Portfolios have special appeal for collaborating teachers who can use authentic data drawn from across a wide variety of curricular and behavioral areas. Some are especially keen on having student involvement in the portfolio assessment process. One could say that portfolios are evidence of what the student did learn and do, rather than what they did not do correctly on a test. However, some educators are not so enthusiastic about this method of assessment for several reasons. A major concern is the need for well-designed rubrics to measure progress or goal attainment. As Bloom and associates found when working to develop good tests, they first needed to design good learning goals. In similar fashion, co-educators would find that development of rubrics and goal setting could be complementary processes in IEP conferences. It also would be good cause for having students involved in at least a portion of the IEP conference that is, after all, about them and their interests and needs.

To briefly summarize professional perspectives presented up to this point, eight main topics have been presented: Taxonomies in cognitive, affective, sensorimotor, and social domains; learning theories; subject matter; goals and objectives; time and achievement orientations; and tests, scores, and score interpretations. The process of co-educators talking about differing professional perspectives can be stimulating and enlightening, and oftentimes discussants feel they have become more united in teaching and learning principles that really matter. That said, there will be times during collaboration when colleagues must simply agree to disagree on one or more topics. Then they can move on with confidence in the knowledge that their decisions have been made together after much thought and discussion, and are the very best ones that could be made at that time under those circumstances for their students. This would not mean that collaboration and consultation failed, and it should not discourage co-educators from seeking out other ways of coming together in the future to revisit the issues or address new ones. Indeed, follow-through and follow-up processes, to be discussed in a later chapter, may result in movement from extreme positions toward more collaborative perspective with the passage of time and perhaps some focused professional development activity.

■ ■ ■ ■ ■ ▬▬▬▬▬▬▬▬▬▬▬▬▬▬▬▬▬▬▬▬▬▬▬▬▬▬▬▬▬▬▬▬

ACTIVITY 2.4
Examining Your Professional Perspectives

In groups of three or four persons, allow three minutes to discuss each of these questions. (All should expect to participate, but occasionally a person may opt out of a turn.)

Would you rather teach a general education classroom or a special education resource room, and why?

In order to improve behavior, do you favor positive reinforcement techniques with contingencies, or talking and reasoning with students to improve behavior?

Do you think students should be allowed to redo work and receive full credit or partial credit for the redo, or not be allowed to redo work?

Assuming both teachers would grade fairly, do you want to be perceived by students as "a tough grader" or as "an easy grader?"

What is your perspective on teaming up a student with disabilities and a student with advanced aptitude as study-buddies or tutor-tutee, or as members of a cooperative learning group?

Do you think teachers should supplement teaching materials with their own resources?

Then the whole group shares some interesting and helpful things they learned from the discussion. They may even generate more either/or questions to discuss.

Today's youth will be leaders in a global community that is shrinking, so to speak. A sense of urgency propels educators to prepare students for functioning successfully in societies that are increasingly diverse and multicultural. It is important to demonstrate and model such skills and attitudes for students every day within the school context. Collaborative consultation and co-teaching are natural and appropriate vehicles for demonstrating the value of using individual differences in professional perspectives both constructively and ethically.

DIFFERENCES IN PERSONAL PREFERENCES THAT AFFECT COLLABORATION AMONG CO-EDUCATORS

The previous section emphasized several areas in which educators often differ markedly with regard to their professional perspectives—traditions, time, territory, taxonomies, talents, and trust. In these areas educators do not need to think alike—they just need to think together. The process of thinking together divergently is not an oxymoron. It is an intriguing process that can be very productive. Understanding the orientations of others toward the world and their work, and valuing preferences and perspectives of others, are key factors in having successful collegial relationships. Educators who make conscientious efforts to respect the individualism and independence of their students must also respect and value these rights for their colleagues and other co-educators, including students' parents as home educators.

One of the most overlooked but crucial elements in teacher preparation is cultivating the ability to relate constructively to school and home co-educators and address their differences with insight and sensitivity. Well-known educator Madeline Hunter (1985) urged teachers to move toward dialectical thinking. This would not mean abandoning one's own position, but taking the opposing view at least momentarily. As an example, Hunter urged all to "come out of armed camps . . . where we're not collaborating, so that 'I understand why you think it's necessary for your students to line up while I think it's better for them to come in casually'" (Hunter, 1985, p. 3). She stressed that when educators show respect for others' points of view, they model the cooperation and resilience that students need to learn for their lives and careers in the future. Differences in personality and temperament will be key factors in teacher effectiveness and learner success.

Personality is the sum total of physical, mental, and social characteristics of an individual—the embodiment of a collection of qualities (*Webster*, 1996). One's personality is a result of inner forces acting upon and being acted upon by outer forces (Hall & Lindzey, 1989). Personality traits distinguish individuals and characterize them in relationships with others. Any one of a person's individual instincts is not more important than any one of another person's instincts; what is important is the person's own preferences for personal functioning.

As discussed earlier, professional perspectives may be developed and refined in teacher preparation programs and professional development programs, but personalities tend to be brought to the profession by individuals. During the 1970s, 1980s, and 1990s numerous methodologies and instruments were developed to help people understand personality and human behavior and to improve human relationships. In fact, analyzing personality became quite faddish for a number of years. Several of the instruments were used in such diverse social service areas as education, counseling for marriage and family, personal awareness, career needs, religion, business and industry, and others. The brief introduction and attention to the topic here will be on self-study and a low-key look at various ways that personality shapes personal preferences in school environments.

Formal assessment of individual differences in personality can be done with one or more instruments selected from among a wide range of existing tools and techniques. Many of these tools have been decades in production and revision, with considerable research and theory to illuminate their usefulness across many fields of life, work, recreation, and for purposes here in particular, interpersonal relations. Numerous instruments for assessment and analysis are available online, often at no charge or minimal charge for trying out abbreviated versions and receiving simplified profiles and interpretations of results. Others provide cursory descriptions of the instrument and avenues through which they can be purchased for self-administration along with scoring and summary information. Some of the more widely used instruments are: Gregorc Learning Styles (1977), McCarthy 4MAT® Model (1990), Sixteen Personality Factor Questionnaire (16PF) (Cattell, Cattell, & Cattell, 1993), Keirsey Temperament Sorter (1984), and Myers Briggs Type Indicator (MBTI). The MBTI (Myers, 1962) is perhaps the best-known and most widely used instrument on the aforementioned list. Its popularity spans a wide range of countries and areas of life. It has been used for a wide range of counseling purposes, including career, marriage, educational, and business and industrial fields in the United States and beyond.

In addition to instruments that focus on individual preferences, contributions to team roles have also been studied using such instruments as the Team Roles Test (Belbin, 2010). Belbin suggests that, by understanding your role within a particular team, you can develop your strengths and manage your weaknesses as a team member, and so improve how you contribute to the team. Teams can become unbalanced if all team members have similar styles of behavior or team roles. The Belbin model can be used to help create more balanced teams.

Video Example from YouTube

▶

ENHANCEDetext
Video Example 2.1.

Teams perform best when each team member has clear responsibilities. A variety of roles are needed for best results. The value of each team role is explained here as an example. (https://www.youtube.com/watch?v=dXonkT2tekY)

Such assessments are used in a variety of contexts to increase awareness and understanding of human preferences that influence behavior. To balance the zeal of those who support each type of assessment for personality and personal styles, there are others who caution against generalizing and oversimplifying complex human attributes with dichotomous comparisons such as concrete/abstract, morning/evening, quiet/music-filled, extrovert/introvert, or impulsive/reflective comparisons. But Carl Jung, eminent Swiss psychologist on whose work the well-known Myers Briggs Type Indicator (MBTI) is based, was quite convincing over many years with his premise that people do differ in fundamental ways even as they all have the same instincts driving them from within (Jung, 1923).

The collective sum of individual preferences is a prime example of the "patchwork quilt" of human interaction that can be so constructive and facilitative in collaborative enterprises. For instance, the personal style of someone who looks for action and variety, shares experiences readily, likes to work with others, and tends to get impatient with slow, tedious jobs, is markedly different from another person who prefers to work alone, labors long and hard on one thing, and seeks abundant quiet time for reflection. As a second example, the personal style of an individual who is interested in facts, works steadily and patiently, and enjoys being realistic and practical, is a contrast during group work with the style of another who likes to generate multiple possibilities, attends to the whole aspect of a situation, and anticipates what will be said or done.

Yet another example is a person who needs logical reasons, holds firmly to convictions, and contributes intellectually while trying to be fair and impartial, contrasted with the style of one who relates freely to most people, likes to agree with others, and enjoys cultivating enthusiasm among members of the group. Finally, an individual who likes to have things decided and settled, prefers to move along purposefully, and strives to make conditions as they "should be," does not demonstrate the same preferences in a group as one who has a more live-and-let-live attitude, leaves things open and flexible, and functions with attitudes of adaptability and tolerance.

The beauty of Jungian theory, as characterized in the work of Isabel Briggs Myers (1962; 1974; 1980a), is the concept that every person is equipped with a broad spectrum of attributes and can use them as needed, but typically prefers to focus intensively upon one or the other at a time. Murphy (1987) explains this point by using the example of color. Just as red cannot be blue, one cannot prefer both polarities simultaneously. One might prefer having a red car, but could live with a blue one if circumstances necessitated it. If a person prefers to apply experiences to problems, that person cannot also prefer to apply imagination to those problems. But he or she can call forth imagination if need be, and may benefit from practicing the process of imagining or supposing in order to use that approach more productively.

Remarkably, one's less preferred functions often contribute to productivity and self-satisfaction because they provide balance and completeness. They are the well-springs of enthusiasm and energy. A person's least-preferred function is his or her most childlike (not childish—an important distinction) and most primitive function, and as such it can be quite helpful in that it creates a certain awkwardness and unrest that sparks innovation. But people will continue to call on their most preferred functions when they feel that ease, comfort, and efficiency are most important.

ACTIVITY 2.5
Comparing Preferences

Compare and contrast the following pairs of characteristics and think about which one of the pair suits you best in most instances:

__I offer my opinions to others readily.	or	I pause before responding.
__I am very interested in facts.	or	I am interested in many possibilities.
__I tend to hold firmly to my convictions.	or	I tend to compromise for agreement.
__I like to have things decided and settled.	or	I like things open and flexible.
__I like to work with others.	or	I like to work alone.
__I tend to work steadily.	or	I work in bursts, slack off, then return to work.

Now select another person who seems to differ from you in many ways, and talk about your preferences and theirs. Then reflect on how these characteristics might surface if you were co-teaching or partners on a team.

SELF STUDY OF YOUR PROFESSIONAL PERSPECTIVES AND PERSONAL PREFERENCES AS AN EDUCATOR

Unless individuals study their **personal preferences** and how those factors guide their own functioning, they are apt to view others through the biased and distorted lenses of their own unrecognized needs, fears, desires, anxieties, and sometimes unreceptive impulses (Jersild, 1955). Put more succinctly, educators will not make much progress toward understanding others or helping others understand themselves unless they first have self-understanding.

When co-educators are in collaborative and inclusive schools, to be successful they must develop and maintain superior working relationships. In an effort to develop collaborative norms for its school context, one district conducted enculturation activities that included getting-to-know-you activities using an instrument titled the *Keirsey Temperament Sorter* and a companion book *Please Understand Me* (Keirsey & Bates, 1984). Several years later, the participants reported that they still remembered the activity as their first glimpses of their co-educators' uniqueness and the group's diversity (Roy & O'Brien, 1991). Understanding and respect are crucial for nurturing a collaborative climate in which group productivity becomes more than the sum of its parts.

SITUATION 2.B

Comments by educators who have reflected on their own preferences and have now gathered to share them in a group discussion:

"I think I do have some good skills, but I don't seem to get them put together to do what I want."

"I get so fed up with the reports that have to be done on such short notice. If data are turned in hastily and carelessly, what is their value?"

"I worked really hard on a particular project and then when it came time to give out the recognition, everybody seemed to forget that the ideas were mine."

"I like to lead out and get things organized and finished, and I guess I'm not timid about saying what I think."

"I'm always wondering if I should say what I think or wait and see what everyone else thinks and then fall in line if I'm totally out in left field."

"It seems like what I do most in my department is put out fires."

"If I didn't show up tomorrow, I'm not sure any of my colleagues would notice or care, so long as there is a substitute teacher here to corral the kids."

"I really like the way my co-teacher supports me; I don't feel at all like the first-year teacher that I really am!"

Collaborating co-educators should reflect on their personal values and preferences before attempting to work intensively with other people who have their own packages of values and preferences. This can be done informally if the stakes are not too high and the process is just exploratory, not mandatory. Self-study analyses and follow-up discussions can be undertaken through a variety of methods and settings, including group work, role-playing, reading, conferences, and workshops. Tools for studying personality, temperament, and learning style such as those named earlier are useful when discussed in professional development sessions or department meetings that focus on small-group activities to bring out highlights of the rich variety inherent in human nature. Of course, no single journal article, book, conference, or training package will ever provide sufficient material to fully understand the sophistication and complexity of individual differences.

Self-study helps educators become more aware of their own attributes and weave their own best qualities into new combinations for helping students who have diverse interests and learning needs. Too few teacher preparation programs provide opportunities for this important self-exploration. Conoley (1987) and Dettmer (1981) were early advocates in promoting awareness of individual differences among collaborating adults as key to the theory and practice of school consultation. Safran (1991) criticized the shortsightedness of researchers who omit important factors in interaction such as personality, interpersonal affect, and "domineeringness," for example, from their research designs focusing on consultation and collaboration. Salzberg and Morgan (1995) report that while variability in personality is a key issue in human interaction, the topic was noticeably absent when they researched teacher preparation for working with paraeducators.

In the Special Education Consulting Project directed by Dyck, Dettmer, and Thurston (1985) at Kansas State University from 1985 through 1987 when the concept of collaborative consultation was emerging in the broad educational context and the first edition of this book was being launched, the researchers found on analyzing pre- and post-test data that the area of greatest gain among participants was in "awareness of self as a rudimentary variable in the collaborative consultation process." High rates of improvement also were noted for "ability to monitor and change my own behavior as needed to increase my effectiveness," and "skill when communicating for problem solving." In a survey of general education teachers (Tiegerman-Farber & Radziewicz, 1998) on development of their own competency skills for collaboration, special education teacher Shapiro emphasized that collaboration relies primarily on personality variables. It requires professional discipline and personal sensitivity, an understanding of the process, and a strong sense of self as a professional. She urged school personnel to develop a collaboration model and demonstrate it for the staff.

As stated earlier, oversimplification and generalization of complex constructs such as personality are to be avoided. Conclusions should not become labels. Rigid interpretations must give way to open mindedness and respect. With these cautions kept carefully in mind, teachers can begin to deal with their colleagues and students more effectively. As an additional incentive for the study of personality and preferences, it generally is lots of fun!

It is not necessary to use a formal personality assessment to explore the constructive use of individual differences. In fact, there is inherent value in keeping the process informal and somewhat fuzzy. The goals should be simple—to increase self-understanding in a nonthreatening manner, then broaden one's ability to respect and truly value differences in others, and finally, use that wide range of differences constructively for the benefit of students.

RESPECTING DIFFERENT VIEWPOINTS AND DIFFERENT INCLINATIONS AS COLLABORATORS

Teachers may differ dramatically from each other with regard to their perspectives and preferences so that a collaborative school consultation could involve one teacher who pays close attention to detail, examining every test score and asking questions about particular assignments, and another teacher who scarcely looks at the test scores, preferring instead to solicit verbal, generalized assessment of the student's capabilities from other professionals. A study by Lawrence and DeNovellis (1974) revealed that teachers with different preferences tend to behave differently in the classroom. Learning styles of teachers as well as students can contribute to these tendencies. Lawrence (1993) issues a broad analysis of such aspects:

- Cognitive style of preferred patterns of mental functions such as information processing and formulating ideas
- Attitudes and interests that influence what someone attends to

- Disposition to seek out learning environments to fit one's cognitive style and interests, and to avoid environments that do not fit
- Disposition to use certain learning tools and to avoid others As teachers learn more about their own preferences, they become even more adept at tuning in to student styles in ways that will help teachers work together to provide the differentiation students need. They also relate more efficiently to colleagues' personal preferences, not to do the same work in the same ways, but to understand the work of others (Clark et al., 1996).

■ ■ ■ ■ ■

ACTIVITY 2.6
Sharing a Professional Experience

In a group of four or five educators, describe an experience from your teaching or school days in which you put forth significant effort but in the end you felt unappreciated, unaffirmed, and perhaps a bit of a failure in that situation. After all in the group have shared a personal example (with the option of passing) discuss how members of the group felt about each disappointing professional experience. To practice feeling empathy for one whose preferences differ from yours, show an attitude of caring about a person's disappointment, especially if it was not something that would have bothered you all that much.

When a group of educators with different preferences collaborate, they have the opportunity to contribute a variety of strengths within the interaction. Those who like to bring up new possibilities and suggest ingenious ways of approaching problems will benefit from having other people supply pertinent facts and keep track of essential details. When some are being "devil's advocate" in finding flaws and holding out for existing policy, others can contribute by conciliating and arousing enthusiasm to sell the idea (Myers, 1980b).

Opposite types may or may not attract, but they definitely need to be available in order to achieve maximum team productivity. Managing differences elegantly is a tremendous challenge for a collaborative consultant or co-teacher. As stressed earlier, the primary goal in consulting, collaborating, and working as a team is not to think alike, but to think together. Each one's personal preferences and professional perspectives are important elements in effective interaction. Differences in schools and classrooms are not just role-related disagreements between adult and child, teacher and student, administrator and teacher, or paraeducator and supervising teacher. They reflect individual orientations to the world, unique learning styles, variability in personal values, and differentiated work styles. These differences, when understood and appreciated, can be quite useful in collaborations and consultations.

Some researchers and practitioners focus on the need for collaborators to view problems from mutual perspectives and shared frames of reference using a common language (Friend & Cook, 1990; Lopez, Dalal, & Yoshida, 1993). These mindsets are assuredly important for rapport-building and initiating exploration of a problem or need. However,

FIGURE 2.3   Viewing Matters Through Different Lenses

greatest team success will come from making sincere efforts to respect members' differences, value the contributions, and communicate in ways that respect and accommodate a variety of verbal and nonverbal styles.

Needing to view matters through a shared "lens," yet doing so with different "eyes," may be a conundrum but nevertheless a useful one. (See Figure 2.3.) As Lopez et al. (1993) note, consultants and consultees must understand how divergent points of view may predispose them to see problems in conflicting ways. Divergence is an asset in problem solving and not a liability when utilized by skilled collaborators. Educators can learn a great deal from talking with (and listening to!) colleagues with whom they differ both in theory and in practice. If a common vocabulary is used and a framework of respect for individuality is in place, teamwork will be much more productive. Furthermore, when individuality is looked on as pleasant and interesting, teamwork will be much more enjoyable.

Many communication problems among team members are due to professional differences and personality differences. A statement that seems clear and reasonable to one person may sound meaningless or preposterous to another (Myers, 1974). One person may want an explicit statement of the problem before considering possible solutions. Another might want at least the prospect of an interesting possibility before buckling down to facts. Yet another may demand a beginning, a logically arranged sequence of points, and an end (especially an end, Myers cautions). Still another will really listen only if the discussion starts with a concern for people and any direct effects of the issue on people. Myers stressed, "It is human nature not to listen attentively if one has the impression that what is being said is going to be irrelevant or unimportant" (Myers, 1974, p. 4). Communication is such a critical part of successful consultation and collaboration that it will be the focus of concern in a later chapter.

Individual differences can be useful in problem finding and problem solving. One person may focus more on the problem and the facts, while another focuses on the process and meanings behind the facts. If someone has to solve a problem alone, he or she will want to approach it from multiple perspectives in order to have all the benefits of each type. Problem-solving teamwork by a well-mixed team of collaborators enables most perspectives to be represented efficiently. Again, the adage "Many heads are better than one" applies here. No specific personality preferences are predictive of success in communication or problem solving within groups; however, research shows that teams with a complete representation of types outperform virtually any single-type or similar-type team (Blaylock, 1983). The likelihood of having such team versatility in one's collaborative situation is better than might be expected, for a group of several individuals typically contains many various perspectives.

As stated earlier, perhaps no area of teaching creates more tension and potential discord than testing and grading, whether it be among teachers, between teachers and students, between teachers and parents, between teachers and administrators, or even between teachers and coaches who need to keep athletes eligible to play. Consensus on evaluation methods will probably never be reached across all factions, but thoughtful and candid discussion sessions are a place to start. Having an opportunity to express one's viewpoints and to explain professional perspectives on assessment, grading, and reporting results may defuse potential flare-ups of disagreement and quell discord between teachers, within departments, throughout the school, and among parents of students. Using consultation services in this area can be particularly productive. For the services to be successful, good questions, open minds, and forthright sharing of opinions are musts. Collaboration and teamwork to develop viable policies on assessment and evaluation for the entire school context can help an individual teacher, and especially a preservice teacher, feel less isolated and more involved.

■ ■ ■ ■ ■

ACTIVITY 2.7
Reflecting on Plans for a Collaborative Activity

With a partner, choose a favorite lesson or subject area that you could team-teach. How would you go about setting this up? Although it is important to know something about your co-teacher's perspectives and preferences, what things should you study about yourself first before embarking on this collaborative endeavor? Then how can each of you share that information pleasantly and agreeably, in order to co-plan and co-teach more effectively?

It is important to keep in mind the phrase, "A little knowledge is a dangerous thing," when reflecting on individual differences. As indicated earlier, educators can work from knowledge of personality assessment or learning style concepts without having the formal profiles of individuals in that group; in fact, they probably should do so. It is not always possible, necessary, or even desirable to ascertain people's preferences with a standardized instrument. (This chapter's numerous application sections are provided as a very informal and hopefully an enjoyable means of finding out interesting and useful things about oneself and one's colleagues.) The most important purpose is instilling the attitude that human differences are not behaviors acted out with intentions of irritating and alienating each other. Rather, they are systematic, orderly, consistent, often unavoidable realities of the way people prefer to use their perception and judgment. Each set of preferences is valuable and at times indispensable in every field of endeavor.

Well-researched personality theory does not promulgate labeling of individuals. Learning styles theory and right–left brain function research have fallen victim on occasion to unwarranted use of labels; "He's so right-brained, that he can't . . ." or "She's a concrete sequential, so she won't . . ." The world probably does not need any more labels for individuals, and this is particularly cogent in the field of special education where labeling has been problematic and opposed vigorously for many years.

USING ADULT DIFFERENCES TO FACILITATE COLLABORATION

Individuals have far more potential than they use at any one time, and the power of this potential in team settings is exponential. Team building has been articulated helpfully in Johnson and Johnson's description (1987) of helpful elements within teams (Welch et al., 1992). Elements are: positive interdependence, individual accountability, face-to-face interaction, collaborative skills, and group processing. Such elements are particularly important in preparation programs of preservice teachers who need specific practice and modeling in interaction before they join experienced teachers in meetings and co-teaching activities.

ACTIVITY 2.8

Sharing Perspectives and Preferences in a Climate of Trust

Visit with co-educators or classmates about open-end topics such as:

- What do I think is good and not good about being a teacher?
- What changes do I hope will take place in education in the next ten years, and are there any ways that I will need to change if they do come about?
- What are my best attributes as a teacher?
- What do I need to work on most if I am to reach my potential as a teacher?
- What teaching strengths do I value in others?
- What teaching strengths within this group do I value most? (if group members know and trust each other well at this time)

**Video Example
from
YouTube**

▶

ENHANCEDetext
Video Example 2.2.

Listen to these collaborating
teachers describe how their
differences contributed to their
becoming a strong partnership.
(https://www.youtube.com/
watch?v=85HUMHBXJf4)

A team of educators should use the strengths of each person to draw out the problem or need, to generate ideas for serving that need, to organize and divide up what needs to be done, to prepare evaluation procedures, and to follow up with the evaluation and further planning if necessary. The variety of backgrounds and training can be rich sources of new ideas when conventional thoughts are not productive. However, it is not feasible and also not very helpful to contrive artificial arrangements that would provide a complete representation of types as featured in a personality assessment. As previously mentioned, variability among humans is rich enough that most groups of even a few will have a significant diversity of skills to contribute.

Some pertinent questions to consider when organizing teams or when discussing how each member can contribute best to the group are:

- Does our team have a mix of experiences, talents, and preferences? If we think we don't, is there something practical that can be done about it?
- Does the group appreciate the constructive potential of adult differences?
- Is everyone ready and willing to contribute in her or his own way?
- Is each person looking forward to having a good time together in finding ways to help our students learn, help teachers grow, and help school programs improve?

By valuing the contribution of each member on the team, the group can come to more fully-formed, student-centered decisions to serve special needs. Valuing individual differences will require more than merely tolerating them. It means accepting the fact that people are different and the world is the better for it. Teacher preparation programs must be enterprising in preparing graduates to have superlative aptitude for understanding individual differences among co-educators. Much more research is needed on the constructive use of individual differences for collaborative consultation and working in teams.

Teachers who devote considerable attention to accommodating student individuality may still find it difficult to recognize, much less respect and adapt to, adult differences. Educators should give consideration to divergent points of view and be ready, willing, and able to change their minds when the evidence warrants it. This is particularly important when they will be co-teaching.

Some cautions must temper the study and use of information about individual differences. Self-study and ensuing group discussions can be quite interesting, for just about everybody likes to share their own viewpoints and react to those of others. But occasionally participants may become so enthused that they share inappropriately, generalize unadvisedly, stereotype inadvertently, or draw others out indiscriminately. So it is always wise for not only the leader, but for each member of the group, to monitor events and do their part to keep discussions practical and helpful while appropriately personal and objectively impersonal.

The persuasive and personal aspects of consultative service require a close, careful monitoring of ethical concerns (Ross, 1986). Empathy for all, and an interactive manner of

onedownsmanship, which is defined as de-emphasis of prior knowledge in order to maintain relationships (Henning-Stout, 1994), along with communication in a climate of parity as equal partners and agreement of mutual ownership, are essential behaviors for ethical collaborators.

A collaborative school consultant must be open to new perspectives and ideas, giving colleagues every opportunity to share and letting them enjoy the benefit of contributing. Disagreements must not be taken personally. Co-educators must keep their channels of interaction open and friendly.

Groups can have profound influences on individual behavior; conversely, one principled person can exert considerable influence and good conscience on the group. Confident teachers demonstrate a willingness to learn from others. They draw others helpfully into productive sharing sessions. They promote strong respect for individual variability and work at deep understanding of human development and learning theory. They strive to nurture the cognitive, affective, sensorimotor, and social growth of co-educators as well as students.

 ENHANCEDetext **Application Exercise 2.1.** Click to apply your understanding of co-educator differences as you create an outline for staff development around the topic.

TIPS FOR USING CO-EDUCATOR DIFFERENCES CONSTRUCTIVELY

1. Respect the rights of others to hold different beliefs. Even if people do not agree, they should assume that others are acting in ways they believe are appropriate.
2. Reasons exist for things that people do or say, so try to discover them.
3. Try not to press for one's own favorite methods of serving school needs, educator needs, or student needs, but rather to encourage collaborative plans when problem finding and problem solving.
4. Have lunch, workroom breaks, and informal visits with other staff members often.
5. Ask others for their input when you are facing a problem, because it has a humanizing, rapport-building effect.
6. Listen to the other person's point of view and seek to understand that person's ideas and meaning.
7. Take time to assess preferences of others before deciding upon a collaborative interaction for a consultation method.
8. Appreciate perceptions and preferences that are different from one's own by engaging in a dialectical conversation. Do not feel that it is necessary to change your position or to convert the other person to your position.
9. Really care about other persons' feelings and ideas, and show it through actions.
10. Be available, available, available when others would like to share or just talk.

CHAPTER 3

STRUCTURING FOUNDATIONS FOR COLLABORATION, CONSULTATION, AND TEAMWORK

Collaboration, consultation, and teamwork probably began around cave fires and on hillsides ages ago, as our ancestors found that it was good to talk things over. It is likely that they formed connections as they learned to explore wider territories, produce useful things, and trade their surpluses. Through social interaction they acquired helpful information and enjoyed sharing their views with others. It was productive to communicate, whether in person, or by messenger, smoke signal, or drumbeat. They developed networks with those whom they trusted. As they planned hunting and gathering forays and eventually began to plant and harvest, they honed methods for teamwork that brought even more success. They learned, and taught, and progressed.

So it has been throughout the ages that people most likely improved their quality of life by interacting with others and working together. Now, in this increasingly complex and interconnected twenty-first century, individuals may have their own perspectives and preferences, and exercise them in relevant contexts, but those who interact with others and endeavor to work together will fare best. They will learn, and teach, and progress.

The role of educator has never been an easy one, and it is becoming more and more challenging in these times. Responsibilities have escalated for teaching, guiding, counseling, coaching and mentoring, preparing and managing learning environments, assessing student achievement, and networking with a wide array of professional colleagues and students' families and communities. Those who model collaboration and encourage teamwork are teaching learners how to succeed in the world they will inherit and manage someday.

CHAPTER OBJECTIVES

On completing this chapter, the reader should be able to:

1. List the four basic elements that are essential for effective collaboration in the school environment.
2. Identify the twelve essential components within the four elements of collaborative school consultation.
3. Describe briefly the six facets that should be employed to determine collaborative school consultation methods.
4. Compare and contrast at least three models that are used widely for collaborative school consultation.

5. Illustrate a collaborative school consultation method that delineates selected facets of system, perspective, approach, prototype, mode, and model.

6. Apply principles and practices of collaborative school consultation to selected situations.

KEY TERMS

formative evaluation

iatrogenic effect

interfering themes

mentor, mentee

novice teacher

onedownsmanship

parity

preservice teacher

professional learning

community (PLC)

summative evaluation

triadic model

SITUATION 3

The setting is a school administration office where the superintendent, the high school principal, and the special education director are having an early-morning conference.

Special Education Director: I've assigned five people on our special education staff to be collaborative consulting teachers in the schools we targeted at our last meeting.

Principal: I understand the high school is to be one of those schools.

Special Education Director: Yes, several classroom teachers will be involved. I've visited briefly with the English teacher who's getting a new student with learning disabilities, and I've also had a special ed staff meeting to discuss the concept of collaborative consultation.

Principal: I don't mind trying a new approach, but, to be honest, at this point I'm not sure the teachers understand very much about how this way of doing things is going to affect them or improve things for students.

Special Education Director: Indeed, several questions have come up about how that concept would be put into practice, and why.

Superintendent: Are you saying we need to spend a little more time at the drawing board to get the kinks out of the plan before handing it to the teachers?

Principal: Yes, and I think parents also will want to know what will be happening. They'll want us to tell them specifically how this will benefit students. Any time families of kids with special needs think direct services are in jeopardy of being reduced, they get anxious, which is understandable.

Special Education Director: I've been compiling a file of theory, background, research studies, program descriptions, teacher viewpoints, even some cartoons and funny sayings to add a little humor and wit if there are tense moments—you know the kind, like, "A consultant is the one who stops by to borrow your watch and tell you what time it is." I'll get copies of the best ones to you and our colleagues in the other designated schools. Maybe we should plan an inservice for teachers and some awareness sessions for parents, too, before we proceed, especially if we anticipate (dare I say this?) that there may be some co-teaching.

Superintendent: That sounds good. Draft an outline and it will be first thing on the agenda at next week's meeting. I'll get the word out to the other principals to be here. And by the way, I heard that consultant joke like this, "He drives over from the central office to borrow your watch and tell you the time!"

ELEMENTS FOR COLLABORATIVE SCHOOL CONSULTATION

Development of a collaborative school consultation program calls for structuring the intended program and specifying intended outcomes. When preparing teachers and students for a collaborative school consultation model, school educators and home educators (family members) should express their viewpoints and concerns early in the program-planning stages and work through any feelings of uncertainty and confusion about their roles and responsibilities. All educators should participate collaboratively to structure the proposed program's framework and specify the resources needed, as well as to determine methods of assessment for evaluating the outcomes.

One factor not to be overlooked in the installation of complex, sophisticated programs such as collaborative school consultation is the reality of educators' *prior experiences*. Some educators are parents and others have worked with children and youth in a variety of venues beyond schools. Some have fond memories of their school days; others—not so much. Some may be embarking on teaching as a second career, while others are just launching their careers. Still others plan to teach for only a few years and move on to other fields of endeavor. However, all have had prior experiences from which they have learned much. These life experiences mold their educational perspectives and personal preferences and enhance the value of wisdom they bring to services in the classroom. An instructive equation might be: "Knowledge + Experience = Wisdom."

Video Example from YouTube

ENHANCEDetext
Video Example 3.1.

Watch this video for ways collaboration can facilitate differentiated learning, teamwork, and communication among co-educators in a variety of roles. (https://www.youtube.com/watch?v=0ukO7YUOYTM)

COMPONENTS FOR COLLABORATIVE SCHOOL CONSULTATION

The clock-like figure (see Figure 3.1) names the four elements and twelve components within those elements that lay the foundation and provide a sequence for integrating collaboration, consultation, and teamwork into teaching and learning environments:

- Preparation—preservice, professional development, advanced programs
- Delineation of role—role clarification, role parity, role expectations
- Framework—structure, resources, management
- Commitment—assessment, evaluation, acceptance

Placement and sequence of each element and its components are very important. Note the starting point in Figure 3.1. It is essential for educators to begin "early in the day" with preparation for collaborative consultation, as shown at the 6:00 a.m. starting position. For example, commitment to collaborative consultation cannot be expected to happen until preparation, roles, and frameworks have been addressed.

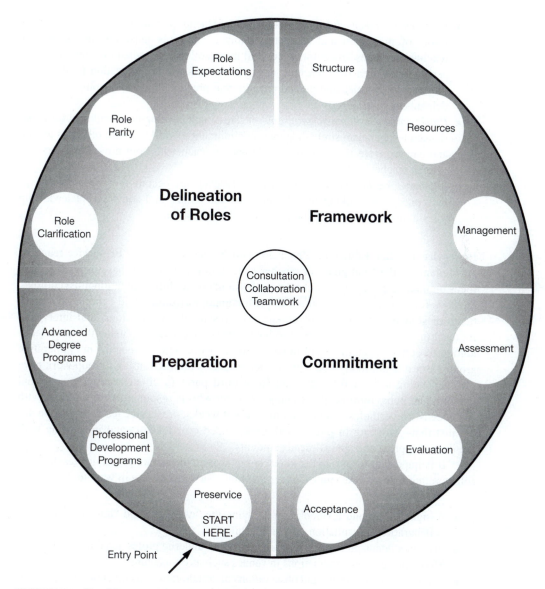

FIGURE 3.1 Key Elements for Collaborating Effectively

Preparation for Collaborative School Consultation

When collaborative school consultation is embraced as best practice for helping students with exceptional needs, all who are involved can benefit from preparation activities, including administrators, general education and special education teachers, counselors, school psychologists, related services and support staff, and family members and other caregivers. Preparation is fundamental for educators in four areas:

- *Preservice teacher education*—Instructors of teacher preparation courses and supervisors of practicum and student teaching experiences must prepare **preservice teachers** for roles less autonomous and more collaborative than they may have experienced in their own teaching days. Students in teacher education need to have orientation activities and guided practice that prepares them to become active participants as co-educators.
- *Professional development programs*—Professional development activities for experienced teachers can strengthen their commitment to working with others as a team and can motivate them to collaborate and co-teach with both novice teachers and veteran teacher colleagues.
- *Advanced teacher education programs*—Teachers are becoming more supportive of the concept of working in collaborations and teams, and some accept leadership roles in implementing collaborative school consultation.

Preservice Teacher Education Programs and Novice Teachers.   **Preservice teachers** are students in the final phase of teacher education programs. In these programs, they focus on many aspects of their chosen profession: curriculum, educational psychology, methods for teaching, development of professional portfolios, field experiences, practicum or student teaching, involvement in professional organizations, and interviews for teaching positions. Today's preservice teachers have grown up using the latest technology to connect, interact, and to some extent, work with colleagues in cooperative groups. But it is not likely that a preservice teacher's interactions and group work have involved being a bona fide advocate for a third party (a client) having exceptional learning and behavioral needs or being a teacher who is responsible for children with such needs. Nevertheless, in only months, if not weeks, preservice teachers will be doing just that—working in **parity** with experienced co-educators and interacting with families of typical and special needs students.

It is important for programs in teacher education to prepare preservice teachers for collaborating with co-educators. College and university educators will want to:

- Assign articles and textbooks for studying the "what for" and "how to" aspects of collaboration, consultation, and co-teaching.
- Instruct students in sociological principles that underlie professional interactions.
- Model professional interactions in venues such as co-teaching.
- Arrange demonstrations and observations of collaboration in authentic settings, such as teachers' interactions with family members of students, and simulated or actual IEP conferences, with signed permission of students' parents and teachers and coaching by the teachers on how to preserve confidentiality.
- Present situations and case studies where preservice teachers can respond to new situations that call for collaboration.

Videotaping or audiotaping sessions with follow-up self-critique or critique by others may not be the most fun experience for an educator but certainly can be valuable experience to help novice teachers get ready for their very first professional roles. Frankly, the more modeling of collaboration and consultation and teamwork that postsecondary personnel can provide for preservice teachers, the better.

One increasingly utilized structure for collaboration in schools is the **professional learning community (PLC)**, which is a group of educators who meet regularly and work in collaboration to share their knowledge and skills for serving students' needs. A PLC can provide structure, practice, encouragement, and positive feedback for the functions of collaborative school consultation. DuFour (2004) suggests that while educators in the professional learning community (PLC) may equate collaboration with congeniality and camaraderie, they must have the right structures to work in if they are to build a culture of collaboration. Thessin and Starr (2011, p. 51) assert that, "Simply putting well-meaning individuals together and expecting them to collaborate was not enough." They continue by stating that, "Teachers do not magically know how to work with colleagues, so districts must support and lead that work if PLCs are to live up to their potential" (Thessin & Starr, 2011, p. 49). In their analysis they found that when common planning periods were scheduled, the time tended to be spent in planning events and field trips. Then if the focus was turned toward supporting and improving student achievement, the immediate result was confusion and frustration. So educators determined that districts needed to provide guidance for administrators and teachers on how to work together in PLCs effectively.

An example of collaboration at an institutional level is the Professional Development School (PDS). PDS partnerships around the country are multi-institutional endeavors to review teacher education and K–12 schools simultaneously. One such partnership is the collaborative reconstruction process for PDS involvement at Kansas State University. Members of the College of Arts and Sciences faculty, the College of Education faculty, and K–12 public school educators work together in collaboration, inquiry, program assessment, and professional development experiences (Shroyer, Yahnke, Bennett, & Dunn, 2007). This collaboration on behalf of students has resulted in college course modifications that entail curriculum redesign and development of new teacher education programs. Other universities are working with K–12 schools in PDS activities to improve teaching and learning at all educational levels, and professional development personnel have opportunities for key parts in PDS collaborations.

Although PLC and PDS are two promising trends, some contend that even when university instructors emphasize the importance of collaborative teaching and learning in K–12 schools, not many of them *model* collaboration in their courses (Jones & Morin, 2000). Jones and Morin contend that preservice teachers need opportunities to observe collaborative teaching, not simply tag-team teaching, in college classrooms and have opportunities to develop a collaborative mindset. In some districts **mentors** and support groups have been established for new teachers to help ensure that they have a good first-year experience and do not fall into the ranks of teachers making early departures from the profession. With dedicated effort on the part of teacher education personnel and school district teachers working as partners, new teachers will be more prepared and comfortable with collaborative consultation and co-teaching formats from their very first moments in schools alongside experienced teachers.

Novice Teachers.   One beginning teacher (novice teacher) called that first year in the classroom "my first year of learning" (McCaffrey, 2000). Her school setting had class sizes of eight to twelve students, a teacher and three or four paraeducators and students with needs from physical disability to speech to occupational therapy, moving in and out of the classroom throughout the day. In preparation for each day she came in early and stayed late, but the result was frustration nevertheless on her part and confusion among her students.

New teachers will be apprehensive about their roles when they think that by discussing problems they may be having, they will be spotlighting professional weaknesses (Carver, 2004). Some put it this way: "I don't want to appear to be dumb." But it is not a sign of weakness to ask an experienced teacher, "Am I at about the right spot in the text for this time of year?" or "Is my instructional pace in this subject about right?" or "Have I set my expectations for students too high (or too low) or just about right?"

Although first-year teachers have been the focus of numerous studies, few of those studies have focused on first-year special education teachers. Whitaker (2000) speaks out on the difficulty of being a beginner in special education and reports on focus groups that were conducted to explore their concerns. Categories of need that were volunteered by the groups included:

- Mentoring accompanied by emotional support
- Information about special education paperwork
- IEP development and conferencing
- Awareness of school policies and procedures
- Means of locating and accessing materials
- Methods of discipline
- Curriculum building (a standard responsibility for serving special needs)
- Management of routines
- Interaction with co-educators in order to work with them more effectively

To this list it would be realistic and practical to add time management, and interaction with families of students.

Novice teachers can benefit greatly from observing more experienced colleagues and participating in consultations, working as part of teaching teams, and collaborating with a wide range of school personnel. They need knowledge about resources and strategies for sharing them, practice in interactive situations such as IEP conferences and parent conferences, and ways of showing accountability for their expenditures of time and energy in collaboration with co-educators. A particularly important area of preparation for novice teachers while they are still forming their teaching philosophies and strategies is that of partnering with families of students and valuing them as co-educators.

Some veteran educators may be reluctant to have novice teachers engage in collaboration and consultation practices before they have had teaching experiences in the "real world." Nonetheless, the seeds of awareness can and should be planted early to bear fruit later in important ways. After all, for most new teachers there is not much time to acquire experience between the last day of a teacher education program and the first day of stepping into a bustling school environment and their own multidimensional classroom.

Mentoring of preservice and novice teachers by experienced teachers in a collaborative atmosphere will benefit those who are mentored. Effective leaders and enthusiastic followers are positioned well for roles as mentors and their mentees. The mentorship concept originated and was recorded many centuries ago in Greek literature to describe the relationship of Odysseus, son of Telemachus, and Mentor, chosen by Telemachus to be Odysseus's model and guide. Mentor was directed to be part "parent" and part peer model as guide on the side, expert, diagnostician, appraiser, and advocate for Odysseus—all taking place in the full press of daily business and Mentor's own work.

In modern times, the relationship between mentor and **mentee** is based on shared talent and passion for the field of common interest; it is special, personal, and indeed collaborative. The mentor recognizes budding talent in the mentee but does not push for the mentee's commitment or achievement of greatness. The mentor does have a sense of timing—when to bear down, when to ease off, and when to take advantage of a teachable moment in which to lead. A mentor coaches toward the bent of the mentee, modeling indirectly through experience rather than dispensing information to be gathered in (or in some cases simply ignored). A mentor–mentee relationship is an ideal collaborative school consultation situation that allows novice teachers to interact with master practitioners.

Mentorships can encourage beginning teachers early in their careers so as to *keep them in the profession*, thus avoiding burnout and attrition from teaching. Special education teachers have been in short supply for many years. When studying effects of mentoring on special education teacher retention, Whitaker (2000) noted alarming statistics that approximately 15 percent of new special education teachers leave after their first year and 10 percent to 15 percent more do so after the second year, compared with an overall annual rate of 6 percent attrition for general education teachers nationally. Conversely, the national shortage of highly qualified special education teachers has been assessed at more than 10 percent and demand is expected to increase by 17 percent through 2018 (Bureau of Labor Statistics, U.S. Department of Labor, 2016).

Whitaker's research indicates that the effectiveness of mentoring correlates significantly with special education teachers' plans to remain in special education. A careful matching of a special education teacher mentor with one who teaches students having the same disabilities is particularly relevant. Unstructured, informal, and frequent contacts are very important in the mentor–mentee relationship.

Consultation, collaboration, and co-teaching are superb conduits through which modeling and mentoring can occur. Some interesting mentorship programs have been developed using the services of retired teachers who welcome the opportunity to become involved, just as grandparents welcome grandparenting—loving every minute spent with their young charges to share their years of experience and wisdom, then going home at the end of the day invigorated and satisfied. Some mentorships develop serendipitously and phase out casually. However, for a more planned and structured arrangement, it is helpful to match mentor and mentee by teaching styles,

---

Video Example from YouTube

▶

ENHANCEDetext
Video Example 3.2.

A mentor can guide and unlock the potential of passionate novice teachers. As you view this video, watch how the mentor observes and gathers evidence to then use for discussion with the teacher as they debrief about what went well and how the lesson might be improved. (https://www.youtube.com/watch?v=tVoyzliq7Ro)

FIGURE 3.2   Mentorship Means Caring and Sharing

curricular specialties, and extracurricular interests such as sports, music, or debate. (See Figure 3.2.) In a rich collaborative environment, both mentor and mentee will gain, as will their students.

Mentor relationships must be voluntary for both mentor and mentee. An unstructured and informal mentorship is often most effective. One caution pertaining to this professional relationship is that there must be advance preparation for the inevitable termination of the relationship. Mentorships do end eventually and when this is taken into account at the outset, most often in the format of a mutually agreed-on limit of weeks or months, the way is prepared for the time when and how it will be concluded. In this way neither participant feels "stood up" or let down. Formal mentorships that are terminated smoothly often develop into long-lasting professional friendships.

Professional Development Programs. Although teachers may enter the profession with competence in content areas and skills in methods, they are more likely to succeed if they are able or willing to work collaboratively with their colleagues and in partnerships with family members of their students. Consultation and collaboration programs can be implemented through professional development activities that are tailored to each school context. When carefully planned and well delivered, these activities strengthen interactive processes.

Special education personnel often are called on to lead or participate in planning and presenting staff development for their colleagues. There are disadvantages as well as advantages to this. It can be difficult to serve as "a prophet in one's own land" and conduct an inservice session. However, it is an advantage to understand the school context and to be aware of what participants probably already know but still need to know or want to learn more about. Their colleagues know them and know when and where they can be reached for more information or answers to questions. A staff development plan that features teachers collaborating on preparing curriculum and assessments, examining student work, observing each other's classrooms, and mentoring new teachers can have significant impact on student achievement.

The following steps are important in preparing useful staff development experiences and can be adapted to a variety of schools and personnel needs:

- Discuss attitudes and expectations toward staff development with various colleagues.
- Conduct a needs assessment and from it then select a topic to be featured.
- Determine the specific audience for whom the staff development will be provided.
- Select and arrange for presenters to conduct the activity.
- Decide on an engaging title, incentives, promotion of the activity, and publicity.
- Outline the activity, preparing the opening *and* the closing material carefully.
- Make arrangements for the facility, equipment, and materials needed.
- Plan and rehearse the content, then deliver it (*ending on time!*).
- Assess the outcomes with an evaluation of the activity.
- Follow up on further individual or group staff development as needed.

Advanced Programs. Graduate degree programs provide experiences that extend beyond a "mentioning" mode and short-term, superficial exposure to collaboration. Small-group activities, simulations and role-plays, interviews, videotaped and audiotaped consultation practice, reaction-and-reflection papers, resource gathering, practice with tools and strategies of technology, and assessments to determine outcomes will help even the most experienced educators to be more amenable to collaborations and establishing partnerships and more comfortable and proficient in interactive school roles.

It is *very* important for special education teachers who will be collaborating with general education colleagues to know the scope and sequence of grade-level curriculum content. They also must understand the functions involved in roles such as school psychologist and school counselor. By the same token, general education teachers and other school personnel should know the curriculum and teaching strategies of special education

ENHANCEDetext
Video Example 3.3.
School psychologists are
school-based mental health
professionals who support
students in a variety of ways.
Watch this short presentation
to learn more about what
school psychologists do.
(https://www.youtube.com/
watch?v=R_DQGJsV_hg)

teachers and be able to apply instructional and behavioral techniques needed by students with disabilities.

A source for standards pertaining to collaboration among special educators, families, other educators, related service providers, and community agency personnel is the updated 2015 *NCATE/CEC Initial and Advanced Preparation Standards for Special Educators*. Standard 7: Collaboration calls for special educators to collaborate with co-educators to ensure that the exceptional learning needs of students are addressed in schools. It refers to special educators as resources for their colleagues to create learning environments that meaningfully include individuals with exceptionalities and that facilitate positive social interaction and active engagement. One of the key elements in the collaboration standard is that special educators use collaboration to promote the well-being of individuals with exceptionalities across a wide range of settings and collaborators.

Some states require preparation in consultation skills for teacher certification. Inclusion of this training in standards for accreditation of teacher education programs is one way to put more emphasis on the presence of collaborative teachers and school environments. Astute school administrators will recruit people who welcome opportunities to work collaboratively with their colleagues. Every teacher preparation program and school administration program for collaborative consultation and co-teaching is unique.

When educators collaborate to achieve a common goal, the results are better than when they work in isolation. Recall the familiar phrase "Two heads are better than one," and add to that, "Several heads working together are better yet." The whole of efforts combined is greater than the sum of its parts. A collaborative effort channels each individual educator's strengths and talents into a combined pool of rich resources for serving students' needs.

Delineation of Roles

A school role such as counselor, general classroom teacher, learning disabilities specialist, speech pathologist, or facilitator for gifted education programs does not automatically determine a role for collaborative consultation. Rather, the consultative role emanates from the situational need. For example, the consultant might be a parent who provides information to the school administrator on the community's views about a school issue, or a learning disabilities teacher helping the sports coach assess a student athlete's difficulty in learning the play book, or a mentor giving the gifted program facilitator suggestions for materials to use with a student for enrichment and acceleration.

The consultee, on the other hand, collaborates with the consultant to be prepared for providing needed direct service to the client. The client is the one with the identified need or problem. Student *needs*, not student labels, determine services and delivery method, and an array of services is targeted and made available to address those needs. As indicated in an earlier chapter, these three roles—consultant, consultee, and client, are interchangeable based on the student's need and the educator's qualification to serve.

Role Clarification. In the process of collaborative school consultation, the initial phase of role delineation is clarifying how it will be consultative and collaborative. Until educators become comfortable with the collaborative concept, ambiguous feelings may persist. Even now teachers and school staff may be unsure of what consulting teachers are supposed to be doing. Classroom teachers may blame their own heavy responsibilities on the seemingly lighter caseloads of consulting teachers. One high school English teacher told a newly appointed consulting teacher, "If you were back in your classroom teaching five hours of English instead of 'facilitating' for a few high-ability students part of the time, my own student numbers wouldn't be so high." Some traveling teachers are envied for having their lunch periods on the road in between schools. Paradoxically, consulting teachers often have excessively demanding workloads due to travel time from school to school, conferences with teachers and students and perhaps parents. Their responsibilities include preparation of IEPs and gathering of appropriate curriculum and materials. During one meeting of a half-dozen or so itinerant special education teachers in a state known for its harsh winters, those in the group found that all of them had gone off the road during snow or ice storms at one time or another in their careers. If the workloads and hazards of the work are too great, effectiveness of services will be diminished. Time and energy needed for coordination and communication will be compromised.

Seamless, well-coordinated instructional plans for students with special needs require keen awareness of role responsibilities and service possibilities among all involved. A classroom teacher and a reading specialist may have information to share in addressing a struggling reader's strengths and deficits, yet know relatively little about each other's curriculum, instructional strategies, or teaching techniques. They must coordinate their efforts or those efforts might be counterproductive. Consider this unfortunate situation: A learning disabilities teacher was instructing a student with reading problems to slow down and read more deliberately, while the reading teacher was encouraging him to read much more rapidly and had referred him to the gifted program facilitator. Before the situation came to light in the course of that referral process the student, a pleasant and cooperative child, was trying valiantly to please both teachers simultaneously. Classroom teachers who have functioned autonomously for years may question how collaborating with special education personnel or other classroom teachers can be expected to help their students. It is a fair and thought-provoking question that deserves careful consideration.

Teachers may have doubts about the ability of a consulting teacher or co-teacher to fit into their classroom structure, especially if that other person is young and inexperienced. As one classroom teacher put it when asked about involving the special education consulting teacher, "I'd never ask *her* for help. What does she know about managing a full classroom of students whose needs are all over the chart? She's never dealt with more than five or six at a time, and she's not been responsible yet for a regular classroom an entire school year." A few educators are not prepared to trust novice-teacher colleagues, or abandon lingering school traditions, or respect the budding talent of less experienced co-educators. Collaborative school consultation calls for people to relinquish traditional roles in order to engage in partnerships and occasionally mentorships for sharing their knowledge and expertise and furthermore, to be ready to learn from the "new kid on the block." More than a few simply do not welcome changes in the usual school structure and routines. The reality of such viewpoints should be addressed forthrightly in staff development sessions or faculty meetings.

Role Parity.   Along with lack of clarification that leads to ambiguity and misunderstanding, special education teachers who travel back and forth among several schools, or who work somewhat apart in the building, may feel an absence of **role parity**, or equality that puts them on a par with general education teachers who stay put all day, because they do not belong exclusively to any one school or faculty group. They may feel minimally important to students and uninvolved in the educational mill of things, cut off from general classroom teachers, and even somewhat isolated from special education colleagues due to distance and schedules.

As one obvious example of non-parity, when consulting teachers are absent, substitutes often are not provided for them. In fact, on occasion they may even be taken away from their own assignments to substitute for absent classroom teachers or perform other functions that come up suddenly. Consulting teachers have been asked to guide visitors on a school tour, drive the school bus, and fill in for the secretary. These feelings of non-parity are accentuated by the misconception that they have little to no ownership in student welfare and development. Some who travel extensively, usually in their own cars or vans from school to school, have been dubbed "windshield" personnel. As collaborative consultation becomes more widespread, these conditions are improving but the problems still are far from being overcome. These policies could be discussed in staff development sessions in which building administrators are included and may require negotiation with the school administration.

Lack of parity could broadcast a message of diminished importance for roles of some educators. Teachers who feel like second-class colleagues, not accepted or appreciated as a vital part of the staff, develop defenses that erode their enthusiasm and effectiveness. Confusion about role parity fuels stress that can lead to burnout from the profession. Continuous, specific recognition and reinforcement of consultation and collaboration services for student development are important for credibility and professional morale.

General education teachers may feel that because they have not been trained as specialists they are less able than the special education teachers to consult and assist. They have their own complaints about lack of parity when overlooked as important resources for helping students with special needs. Some special education teachers pick up on this and wonder why no one acknowledges what *they* learn from their general education collaborators (Pugach & Johnson, 1989). Meanwhile, classroom teachers are not going to wait with open arms for the specialists to come and save them. School life will proceed even in the absence of a consulting teacher. School bells will ring, classroom doors will open, and the school day will go on.

Role Expectations.   Sometimes co-educators have unreasonable expectations for partnerships or team involvement. They may be anticipating instant success and miraculous student progress in a very short while. Then if positive results with students are slow to come about, attitudes may range from guarded skepticism to open disapproval of collaborative efforts. But they may simply be expecting too much too soon. A co-teacher or a special services consultant cannot be an instant panacea for every student's difficulties. Furthermore, teachers sometimes neglect to monitor and record results carefully, so day-to-day improvement in work does not stand out and the teacher may think, "I'm not being successful with this child." Some consultees have been known to pressure consultants unfairly by expecting them to "fix" the student, and then if this does not happen quickly, or alas, at all, they write off the concept of consultation and collaboration as a waste of precious time.

As noted earlier, some consulting teachers expect to work only with students, not adults, and they prefer it that way. "I was trained to work with kids, and that's what I enjoy," confessed one consulting teacher when assigned to an indirect service role. This situation presents a problem for both consultee and collaborator. A team approach or co-teaching format may be awkward for the staunchly autonomous teacher at first. Unrealistic and unreasonable expectations must be put aside in the early planning stages of school collaboration practices. Co-educators should set reasonable goals for themselves and not expect "the moon." Small, sure steps with a few enthusiastic collaborators will mark the smoothest path to success with their more reluctant colleagues.

Some collaborating consultants may wonder, "If I consult effectively, I may be working myself out of a job." However, that is not likely to happen. The more successful the consultants' services are, the more their fellow teachers and administrators are prone to value them for their contributions toward initiating long range, positive ripple effects. As one example, students who are missed in initial referrals often are noted and subsequently helped as a result of the interactions among classroom teachers and consulting teachers.

Two other points need to be considered. One is that sometimes the most difficult part of a collaborative consultation experience is stepping aside once the consultee experiences some success with students. Another is that in rare situations where collaborative consultation is not working and considerable efforts have been made without success to resolve difficulties and move on, the collaboration must end for the welfare of all, especially the student who may be caught in the middle. As noted earlier with mentorships, winding down or ending a collaborative relationship can be a sensitive process. It is a joint decision in which communication skills are of utmost importance and proper timing is crucial. There is no textbook approach to this (Dougherty, Tack, Fullam, & Hammer, 1996); therefore, it is essential for those involved to prepare themselves for mixed feelings that may include both relief and disappointment when professional and personal relationships must come to an end.

Involvement of as many co-educators as possible through needs assessments, interviews, professional development activities, and both formal and informal communications, will do much to alter inappropriate expectations for consulting and partnership roles. If collaborators can engage in successful teamwork with the more receptive and cooperative colleagues in their schools, it will generate confidence in the approach among others who are not so receptive initially.

Frameworks for Collaborative School Consultation

The third of three key elements in collaborative school consultation is the framework in which it is organized. Collaboration and co-teaching call for structures that provide adequate blocks of time, adequate resources, suitable facilities in which to meet, efficient management of schedules, and careful organization of details so that the interactive processes are carried out as smoothly as possible. These conditions are deceptively simple to describe but much more difficult to put into operation.

Structures for Consulting and Collaborating.   The most essential structure in the framework is allocation of time. Time is the ultimate nonrenewable resource and most would agree that one of the most overwhelming and frustrating obstacles to collaborative activity is the lack of time to do it. Interfacing with colleagues calls for blocks of time that fit into schedules of everyone involved. Sometimes willing teachers use their own planning time for consultation, but that is not an ideal way to instill positive attitudes toward a collaborative approach and it "robs Peter to pay Paul." The typical school day is simply not designed for incorporating collaboration time into the schedule without careful planning, some give and take, and occasionally, personal sacrifice by the collaborating teachers.

Even when a schedule for meeting and following up can be arranged, it may be next to impossible to find adequate blocks of time that are the same for all potential participants. Working out such a plan is often like working a complex puzzle; it is one of the most formidable tasks of those who want to collaborate, particularly those who have direct teaching responsibilities at set times in specific buildings, and especially for secondary-level teachers. Thus it is up to administrators to acknowledge the need for this quality time and to exert strong leadership in enabling it to happen. When administrators lend their authority *and* their approval to this endeavor, school personnel are more likely to find ways of getting together and to use that time productively.

Unfortunately, when consulting teachers *first* initiate consultation and collaboration, if it is without formal arrangement, it is very likely that it will come out of their own time, that is, before school, after school, during lunch hours, perhaps even on weekends. If this happens, it should be regarded as a *temporary* accommodation and replaced as soon as possible with a more formal allocation of time and designation of a suitable place during the school day. This is not only for their well being but to emphasize that consultation and collaboration are not simply add-on services to be carried out by a zealous, dedicated, almost superhuman few.

As time is made available for working together, facilities must be accessible in which to conduct the consultation. The area should be comfortable, quiet, convenient, and relatively private for free exchange of confidences. Such a place is often at a premium in a bustling school community.

Resources for Consulting and Collaborating.   It is no secret that districts struggle to find money for their ever-increasing expenses. So there is a risk of letting fiscal issues, rather than factors that focus specifically on student needs, dictate the service delivery method. One such factor is the teacher caseload issue, and it must be addressed carefully.

Large caseloads may seem to save money in the short run but not in the long run if student performance declines or if there is much attrition from the teaching profession because of heavy assignments. If a collaborating teacher's caseload is too great, direct services will be inadequate, indirect services will be diminished, acceptance of the collaborative approach falters, and the method of service risks rejection.

Recommended caseload numbers vary depending on school context, travel time required, grade levels, exceptionalities and special needs served, and structure(s) of the interaction method, but the numbers must be kept manageable to fulfill the intent and promise of consultation and collaboration. Part of the solution lies in documenting carefully *all* collaborative consultation and team activities to show the time and personnel required *and* making specific note of what should have been available but due to fiscal constraints was not. Consultants must negotiate with their administrators for reasonable caseload assignments and blocks of time to interact. It bears mentioning here that some collaborative school consultations to be described later in the chapter have more costly dimensions than others.

Although time is at a premium for busy educators, recent trends in computer technology and other electronic media are improving their situations. Teachers who work in partnerships with colleagues must be very organized and efficient. In recent years, tedious, time-consuming tasks such as developing IEPs, preparing reports, collecting academic and behavioral data, and communicating with families and support staff have become easier with technological advances. Online templates, email, shared electronic calendars, and a variety of other organizational tools help teachers maximize their time. Tools and vehicles such as these also have allowed teachers to be more connected in networks that enhance collegiality and teamwork.

Management of Collaboration and Consultation.   It is one thing to design a hypothetical method of consultation but quite another to plan multiple methods for application in different situations, and even more challenging to organize and put into motion the right method for each situation. It will be easier, of course, if preceded by thoughtful role clarification and genuine role parity, within a climate of appropriate role expectations.

Those who collaborate will want to generate a number of methods for consultation and collaboration in a variety of grade levels, subject areas, and special needs categories, and in suitable contexts for school, community, and families. The consultation structure should fit the context of the system. Some traditional models exist, and newer models for a variety of school contexts have been developed and put into practice. But school personnel should collaborate to design the methods that are custom fit to school and student needs. Taking a survey of teachers to ask how they would use collaborative activities would be a good way to begin. Studying and observing promising structures in other school systems also can be helpful.

Scientists note that astronomers from all parts of the world collaborate often because there is no one place from which every part of their "work area," the sky, can be observed. This analogy also applies to educators and parents as they address each child's total needs in the cognitive, affective, sensorimotor, and social domains to develop learning and behavior goals. The goals become building blocks for decision-making, and without them, the decision-making is like a hammer without nails. Educators have long-range and short-term goals. Students have IEPs with annual goals and learning objectives.

Schools have mission statements and program goals. Educators' aims, schools' missions, and students' goals should be bases on which to make decisions in educational environments. A goal catalyzes action and provides direction for that action. Reviewing goals will help educators stay focused to sort out and promote the things that are vital in addressing students' needs.

Commitment to Collaborative School Consultation

The fourth of the key components in collaborative school consultation is commitment. Commitment can be demonstrated in a number of different ways and at several different levels. Co-educators must document the effectiveness of consultation and collaboration, as noted earlier, to ensure continued support for collaborative consultation service and take note of small, consistent gains. School personnel are understandably skeptical of indirect services that do not prove their mettle. The old ways of doing things were isolation, "ownership" of students (yours, mine), and tendencies to sweep problems under the rug or hand them off to others for direct service "over there in another area of the school (or the district)."

Co-educators may be involved initially because they are told to be involved or because they have been talked into giving it a try or even because they are intrigued with the possibilities and just want to be collegial. But their interest will wane if the processes become a hassle and a burden, especially if positive results are not forthcoming and convincing.

Assessment of Consulting and Collaborating.   Assessment is essential for providing evaluative data to measure outcomes of collaborative school consultation and co-teaching. School personnel will be more accepting if success is demonstrated with carefully collected, reliable, and valid data. Unfortunately, assessment of collaboration and consultation processes has been minimal or murky. Too often results are clouded in what might be called "data dust."

A few procedures such as rating scales of judgments directed at a variety of skills and activities, and survey estimates of engaged time for the activities, have been tried. Administrators, advisory council members, and policymakers should study those carefully and use the most promising ones to develop assessment techniques that fit their school contexts. In keeping with the philosophy of collaboration, personnel from diverse roles should design the assessment tools and procedures cooperatively. A needs assessment instrument can be drawn up and field-tested, with the outcomes used to develop a structured and comprehensive evaluation plan.

Evaluation of Consulting and Collaborating.   With the assessment data from self-reports, interviews, and observations, formative and summative evaluation tools can be developed. **Formative evaluation** is ongoing and provides information to guide adjustments in the program. **Summative evaluation** is conducted at designated times and places to determine program value and make decisions about continuation of the program.

Not only should processes and content be evaluated, but the context of the school setting should be evaluated as well. For example, a consultant may have excellent communication skills and a wealth of content with which to consult and collaborate, but if the existing school context provides no time and space for interaction, positive results will be slim to none. Consultants will want to evaluate every stage of the collaborative processes to keep focusing on the right goals.

Assessment and evaluation should include a variety of methods for data collection to provide the kinds of information needed by target groups. Consultation and collaboration practices must not be judged inadequate for the wrong reasons. If time has not been allocated for collaboration, if school personnel have not had preparation and encouragement, and if administrator support is lacking, those components should be targeted for improvement before the collaborative process itself is faulted. Suggestions for planning, conducting, and using evaluation for collaborative school consultation will be addressed in a later chapter.

Acceptance of Consulting and Collaborating.   Participation in collaborative programs must be a willing decision among co-educators who volunteer to adopt this method of serving special needs. There must be parity for all involved, and encouragement by administrators will help to a great extent. By using techniques such as publicizing successes and promoting benefits of consultations and teamwork as they are realized, schools may get the collaboration bandwagon rolling with even the most reluctant persons on board. Most important is involving people right from the start in needs assessments, advisory committees, planning efforts, professional development activities, follow-up activities, and more and more personal contacts.

True collaboration requires time, energy, and practice. Genuine co-teaching necessitates trusting, sharing ownership and territory, and taking risks. These realities make involvement by school personnel more difficult and acceptance more challenging. In the minds of many educators, consultation has been associated with exclusionary special education programs and assistance in mainstreamed classes. So if teachers miss the opportunity for developing collaborative consultation service and then come to resent having more responsibility for teaching special education students, they may blame the collaborative approach and those willing to collaborate for the failure.

Special education teachers and support personnel need a well-designed plan and a spirited, collegial vision that will intrigue and excite them about joining in partnerships. They need to have families of students informed and on board with this approach to helping their children. Most of all, they need strong administrator support or it will be difficult for positive things to happen. Those who would consult, collaborate, team and co-teach, must recognize and build on every opportunity to have commitment by all.

FACETS OF METHODS FOR COLLABORATIVE SCHOOL CONSULTATION

A foundation for an educational philosophy of collaborative school consultation encompassing preparation, delineation of roles, frameworks, and commitments was shown in the Figure 3.1 clock-like graphic. Now it is time to focus on frameworks in which to develop methods of addressing the needs of learners, school educators, and home educators. The methods will be composites of purposes and parts, namely *systems* in which they will be

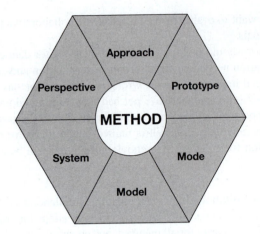

FIGURE 3.3   Structural Facets of Collaborative School Consultation

used, *perspectives* on which they are based, *approaches* emanating from specific needs, *prototypes* that have been designated for use, *modes* in which to develop a method, and *models* that have been developed and put to use.

Overlapping philosophies of collaborative consultation and working in teams evolved from a blending of theory, knowledge, and practices in several fields of human services. This overlap creates a tangle of philosophy and terminology that could be problematic. So a practical way of viewing collaborative school consultation and designing a *method* for the school context is to describe it as a blend of facets, like segments of a cut-and-polished gem. These segments (see Figure 3.3) highlight six parts of the collaborative consultation method, or "gem," that are organized and illustrated in Figures 3.4 through 3.9 as:

1. **System:** An entity of many parts that serve a common purpose.
2. **Perspective:** A particular viewpoint or outlook.
3. **Approach:** An initial step toward a purpose.
4. **Prototype:** A pattern.
5. **Mode:** A form or manner of doing.
6. **Model:** An example or a replica.

For brevity and clarity, written presentation of the facets begins with the uppercase form of their first letter. If two components begin with the same letter, another letter of the word is used. Thus, the six categories are *S* (system), *P* (perspective), *A* (approach), *R* (prototype), *E* (mode), and *M* (model). The letters form a little word that has no meaning itself but helps to keep in mind the order of the letters **SPAREM**. It is important to keep in mind that these six facets are constructed to reflect the experiences and the preparation, delineation of roles, frameworks, and commitments of educators in all walks of life and influences on learners. Note that many of them are well established, as evidenced by references to them that date back to the 1970s and 1980s. Most can be considered tried-and-true for their purposes well into the twenty-first century. (See Figure 3.3.)

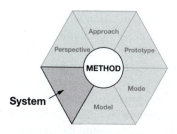

FIGURE 3.4   System for Collaborative School Consultation

Systems

A system is a unit composed of many diverse parts serving a common purpose. (See Figure 3.4.) *Systems* (*S*) in which educators function to serve special needs of students include school, home and family, community, medical and dental professions, mental health, social work, counseling, psychology, extracurricular functions, and advocacy and support groups. Other systems with which consultants and collaborators might be involved from time to time in addressing very specialized needs include, but are not limited to, therapy, industry, technology, mass communications, the arts, and other special interest areas for talent development. (See Figure 3.4.)

The most natural system within which to conduct school consultation and collaboration is, obviously, the school context. Educators are involved beyond the academic or cognitive aspects of student development to address physical, emotional, and social aspects. School educators include not just teachers both general and special but administrators and related services and support personnel. Home educators include parents or other caregivers and the community in general.

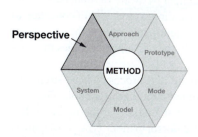

FIGURE 3.5   Perspective for Collaborative School Consultation

Perspectives For Consulting and Collaborating

A *perspective* (*P*) is an aspect or focus of thought from a particular viewpoint or outlook. Consultation perspectives that have evolved in education and related fields fit into three categories—purchase, doctor-patient, and process. (See Figure 3.5.)

A *purchase perspective* is one in which a consumer shops for a needed or wanted item. The consumer, in this case the consultee, "shops" for services to help the consultee address the client's need. For example, the teacher of students having intellectual disabilities might ask staff at the instructional media center for a list of low-vocabulary, high-interest reading material to help the student have immediate success in reading. This "purchase request" makes several assumptions (Neel, 1981) that 1) the consultee describes the need precisely; 2) the consultant selects the right "store" and "goods" in the store for that need; 3) the consultant has enough "inventory" (strategies and resources) to fill the request; and 4) the consultee can "afford" the time, energy, and modification of classroom strategies. The consultee is free to accept or reject the strategy or resource or decline it as a "bad buy." Even if the strategy is effective for that situation, the consultee may need to go again to the consultant for similar needs of other clients. Little change in consultee skills for future situations is likely to result from the consumer-type interaction. Thus, the overall costs are rather high and benefits are limited to specific situations. However, if the need is immediate and severe, then the purchase approach is useful.

A *doctor–patient perspective* casts the collaborating consultant in the role of diagnostician and prescriber. Consultees provide helpful information to the consultant. With this perspective there are several different assumptions: 1) The consultee describes the problem to the consultant accurately and completely; 2) after making a diagnosis, the consultant explains it clearly and convincingly to the consultee; and 3) the prescribed remedy is a promising one, not **iatrogenic**, a term used in the medical profession where a treatment is more debilitating than the illness it was designed to treat. An **iatrogenic effect** of educational service would result in more problems for students, educators, or the school context than the initial condition created. For example, taking high-ability students from their general classrooms to meet with gifted program facilitators may result in resentment by their peers and perhaps even their classroom teachers, so that students reject the opportunity for academic enrichment and perhaps even overcompensate with underachievement in order to have a desired status with their friends. Another example would be keeping a restless, misbehaving primary-level student inside during playtime as a corrective measure so the child is even more restless for the next lesson.

A classroom teacher might use a doctor-patient perspective by calling on a special education teacher and describing the student's learning or behavior problem. The collaborative consultant's role is to observe, review existing data, perhaps talk to other specialists, and then make diagnostic and prescriptive recommendations. As in the medical field, there is generally little follow-up activity on the consultant's part with the doctor-patient perspective, just as very few doctors call their patients the morning after a procedure to see how they are doing, and the consultee does not always follow through with the consultant's recommendations.

In a *process perspective*, the consultant helps the client be aware of, understand, and act on the problem. Consultative service does not replace direct service by a consultee to the client, and in contrast to the purchase and doctor-patient perspectives, the consultant neither diagnoses nor prescribes. As Neel (1981) stated it, the consultee becomes the consultant's client for that particular problem.

All of these perspectives—purchase, doctor-patient, and process—have strengths; therefore, any of the three might be employed at one time or another in schools. One factor influencing the adoption of a particular perspective is the nature of the problem. For example, in a crisis situation the consultee may need a doctor-patient type of diagnosis and prescription, even if temporary. But in a non-crisis situation the consultee may choose the process approach because many skills and resources developed for solving that particular problem could be used again and again in situations presenting similar problems. This makes process consultation both time-efficient and cost-effective for schools.

■ ■ ■ ■ ■ ▬▬▬▬▬

ACTIVITY 3.1
Determining an Appropriate Perspective for a Special Needs Situation

Have you had occasion to observe a situation where the purchase perspective was used in a way you consider appropriate to address a special need of a client (student or teacher or parent)? If you are a general education teacher, discuss this with special education teachers. If you are a special education teacher, discuss this with general education teachers. Aim for discussions at two or more student age or grade levels.

What about a situation where the doctor-patient perspective seemed appropriate? The process perspective? (When discussing your examples, use pseudonyms for names of people and schools.)

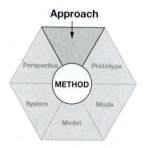

FIGURE 3.6   Approach for Collaborative School Consultation

Approaches for Consulting and Collaborating

An approach (*A*) is a *formal* or an *informal* preliminary step toward a purpose. (See Figure 3.6.) Formal collaborative consultations occur in preplanned gatherings such as staff meetings, conferences for developing IEPs, arranged interactions between school personnel and support personnel, and organized staff development activities. They also take place in scheduled conferences with families, related services personnel, and community resource personnel.

In contrast, informal consultations often occur "on the run." These interactions have been referred to as "vertical consultations" because people tend to engage in them while standing on playgrounds, in parking lots, at ball games, even in grocery stores. They are dubbed "one-legged consultations" when they happen in hallways "with one leg propped up against the wall" (Hall & Hord, 1987; McDonald, 1989). Conversations also take place frequently in the teachers' break room. It is very important to note and record informal interactions like these as consultations because they do cause expenditures of time and energy by both consultant(s) and consultee(s) and should be accounted for in the scheme of things. Highlighting them as consultations will promote the concept of collaborative school consultation. So take note of the general topic and document the time expended for purposes of accountability. The approach facet underscores efforts to construct a suitable framework for allocating high-quality interaction time. Informal consultations are to be encouraged because they can open the door for more structured collaborative consultation later. Sometimes they become catalysts for meaningful professional development activities as well. In other cases, they may activate team effort that would have been bypassed in the daily hustle and bustle of school life.

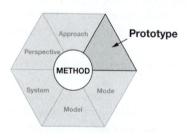

FIGURE 3.7   Prototype for Collaborative School Consultation

Prototypes for Consulting and Collaborating

A *prototype* (*R*) is a pattern. (See Figure 3.7.) Consultation prototypes include mental health consultation, behavioral consultation, process consultation, and advocacy consultation. Only the first two will be addressed here.

The *mental health prototype* has a long history (Conoley & Conoley, 1988). The concept originated in the 1960s with the work of psychiatrist Gerald Caplan, who conceived of consultation as a relationship between two professionals in which responsibility for the client rests on the consultee (Hansen, Himes, & Meier, 1990). Caplan (1970) proposed that consultee difficulties in dealing with a client's problems (think of "teacher" dealing with "student need") usually are caused by any one, or all of four **interfering themes** that can cause ineffectiveness:

1. Lack of *knowledge* about the problem and its conditions
2. Lack of *skill* to address the problem (or need) in appropriate ways
3. Lack of *self-confidence* in dealing with the problem (or need)
4. Lack of *professional objectivity* toward the situation

Reduction in theme interference helps a consultee break loose from constricting thoughts or feelings about the student or situation (Conoley & Conoley, 1988). The consultant not only addresses and helps resolve the problem at hand but also enhances the consultee's ability to handle similar situations in the future. When the mental health prototype is used for consultation and theme interference is accounted for, consultee change may very well produce client change. Therefore, assessment of success should focus on consultee attitudes and behaviors more than on client changes (Conoley & Conoley, 1988). School-based mental health consultation is characterized by the consultant's attention to the teacher's feelings and the meaning that the teacher attaches to the student's behavior (Slesser, Fine, & Tracy, 1990). This prototype supports Guskey's (1985) recommendation for staff development. It should be:

1. Designed to bring about changes in teacher classroom practices
2. Then focus on changes in student learning outcomes
3. Finally, only then expect changes in teacher beliefs and attitudes

The *behavioral consultation prototype* also purports to improve the performance of both consultee and client. It features clear, explicit problem-solving procedures (Slesser, Fine, & Tracy, 1990) and is based on social learning theory in which skills and knowledge contribute more to consultee success than less definitive themes like objectivity or self-confidence (Bergan, 1977). Behavioral consultation is probably the most familiar prototype to educators, therefore it is more easily introduced into the school context than mental health consultation. Indeed, it is the prototype on which the majority of collaborative consultation models are based. The consultant defines the problem, isolates environmental variables that support that problem, and plans interventions to reduce the problem. Bergan's four-stage model of a consultative problem-solving process was grounded on successful identification of the problem as the first stage (Bergan, 1995), with problem analysis, implementation, and evaluation following that stage.

According to Conoley and Conoley (1988), behavioral consultation is the easiest prototype to evaluate because problem delineation and specific goal setting occur within the process itself. Evaluation results can be used to modify plans and promote consultation services, among other potential consultees. But behavioral consultation can fail to bring results if it focuses on problematic social behavior such as aggression or being off task when that behavior really emanates from poor or inadequate academic skills (Cipani, 1985). This could be an example of lack of knowledge and lack of objectivity. If a plan for dealing with the aggression is recommended by the consultant but not put into place by the consultee, this could reflect lack of self confidence and skill development.

Modes for Consulting and Collaborating

A *mode (E)* is a particular style or manner of doing something. (See Figure 3.8.) Modes for school consultation are either direct or indirect, with the consultant in direct consultation

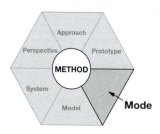

FIGURE 3.8   Mode for Collaborative School Consultation

delivering service to the client or in indirect consultation delivering service to consultees for the client.

In a *direct mode* the consultant works directly with a special-needs student. For example, a consulting teacher for learning disabilities or a speech pathologist specialist might use a particular technique with the student while a parent or classroom teacher consultee observes and assists with the technique. Direct service generally is provided to students subsequent to a referral (Bergan, 1977). The consultant may conduct observations and discuss the learning or behavior with the student (Bergan, 1977; Heron & Harris, 1987). The consultant becomes an advocate, and the student has an opportunity to participate in decisions made pertinent to that need. Another example of direct service is teaching coping skills or study techniques to students for use at home or at school (Graubard, Rosenberg, & Miller, 1971; Heron & Harris, 1987).

The *indirect service delivery mode* calls for "backstage" involvement among consultants and consultees to serve client needs. The consultant and consultee interact and problem-solve together. Then the consultee provides related direct service to the client. So school consultation is indirect service to students resulting from the direct service to teachers or parents. This mode is particularly useful when the consultee lacks situational self-confidence and objectivity.

MODELS FOR CONSULTING AND COLLABORATING

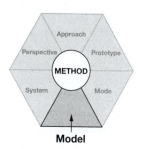

FIGURE 3.9   Model for Collaborative School Consultation

Models are the remaining facet of the SPAREM method for collaborative consultation and teamwork. A model is a representation in miniature, used for comparison, imitation, description, analogy, or display. It is not the real thing, just an approximation of it. (See Figure 3.9.) The *model* functions as an example with which to study, replicate, or manipulate intricate things. Models are presented here as examples for replication in learning environments where special needs of learners are of paramount concern.

Many models have been developed for serving special needs of learners in a variety of learning environments. A few well-known models adopted or adapted to guide collaboration and consultation processes are:

- The triadic model
- Resource/Consulting Teacher Program model (R/CT)
- Instructional Consultation model (IC)
- School Enrichment Model (SEM)
- Teacher Assistance Teams model (TAT)
- Conjoint Behavioral Consultation model (CBC)
- Biopsychoeducational model (designated by the acronym BPE for purposes here)

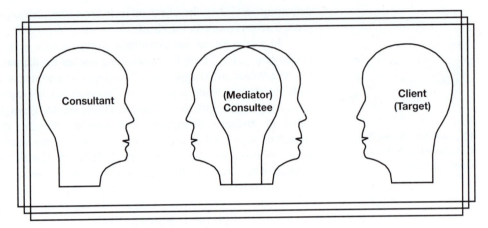

FIGURE 3.10   Example of a Basic Triadic Consultation

Models described herein are available on line and in educational, psychological, and medical periodicals for studying the procedures and analysis of relevant research, determining goodness of fit in designated school settings, and making decisions about them.

The **triadic model**, developed by Tharp and Wetzel (1969) nearly a half-century ago and embellished later by Tharp (1975), heads the list as the classic model from which many school consultation and collaboration models have evolved. It includes the three roles of consultant, consultee (or mediator), and client (or target). In this most basic of the existing models, services are not offered directly, but through an intermediary (Tharp, 1975). The service flows from the consultant through the consultee to the client. The consultant role is typically, although not always, performed by an educational or medical specialist such as a learning disabilities teacher, school psychologist, pediatrician, social worker, or school counselor. The consultee is usually, but not always, the classroom teacher. The client (or target as Tharp termed it in the early years of development) is most often but not always the student with special needs.

An educational need may be a disorder, a disability, or an advanced ability requiring special services for the student. With the triadic model, both consultant and consultee take ownership of the problem and share accountability for the success or failure of the service (Idol, Paolucci-Whitcomb, & Nevin, 1995). (See Figure 3.10.)

It is important here to review the previous material about roles. Roles are interchangeable among individuals, depending on the school context and the educational need. For example, on occasion a learning disabilities consulting teacher might be a consultee who seeks information and expertise from a general classroom teacher consultant. At another time a student might be the consultant for a resource room teacher who is the consultee, and for parents as clients for the interventions designed to help their child. Tharp (1975) gives the following example:

Ms. Jones the second-grade teacher may serve as mediator between Mr. Brown, psychologist, and John, the problem child. At the same time, she may be the target of her principal's training program and the consultant to her aide-mediator in the service of Susie's reading problem. The triadic model, then, describes relative position in the chain of social influence. (p. 128)

Over the years Tharp and others have identified several strengths of the triadic model, including the clarity it provides in determining social roles and responsibilities, and the availability of evaluation data from two sources—mediator (consultee) behavior and target (client) behavior. However, it may not always be the most effective model for every school context and content area, given the process skills and resources that are available.

Analysis and observation of program models for collaborative school consultation will suggest both strengths and potential drawbacks to be considered when planning, implementing, and assessing outcomes. Here is a brief summary highlighting the triadic model's strong points and potential drawbacks:

- Potential Strengths:

  Is appropriate for crisis situations

  Is a good way to get started with the consultee

  Tends to be quick and direct, while being informal and simple

  Keeps the concern in perspective

  Has objectivity on the consultant's part

  Provides for student anonymity if needed

  Is time-efficient

  Can lead into more intensive collaborative consultation

  May be all that is needed

- Potential Drawbacks:

  Is expected to have little or no carryover to other situations

  Probably will be needed again for same or similar situations

  Makes only one other point of view available

  Requires expert skills of communication by the consultant

  Could call for data that are unavailable

  May hold the consulting teacher accountable for lack of progress

The **Resource/Consulting Teacher Program model** (R/CT), based on the triadic model, is an integrative, collaborative model implemented at the University of Illinois and replicated in both rural and large urban areas (Idol, Paolucci-Whitcomb, & Nevin, 1986). It provides numerous opportunities for interaction among teachers, students, and parents. The resource/consulting teacher offers direct service to students through tutorials or small-group instruction and indirect service to students through consultation with classroom teachers for a portion of the school day. Students not in special education programs can be served as well, and parents sometimes are included in consultations. This model requires close collaboration between the R/CT and the classroom teacher so that teacher expectations and reinforcements are the same for resource room and general classrooms (Idol-Maestas, 1981).

- Potential Strengths:

    Can serve students not in special education programs

    Supports strong parent involvement

    Is an "in-house" approach to learning and behavioral needs

    Provides ownership in the problem-solving from many roles

    More closely approximates the classroom setting

    Provides opportunity to belong as a teacher/consultant

- Potential Drawbacks:

    Needs extensive teacher preparation

    Is energy draining

    Often demands more time than is available

    Produces high caseloads for the consulting teacher

    Requires support and involvement from school administrators

The **Instructional Consultation** (IC) **model** merges skill in collaborative consultation with expertise in specific areas. The model underscores several premises that have been offered by educational experts. First, teacher behavior does make a crucial difference to children's achievement (Rosenfield, 1995). Second, many tasks assigned to students are not well matched to their instructional levels. Children should be regarded as having learning disabilities only if they fail to learn *after having appropriate instruction* (Rosenfield, 1995). When students are referred for special services, their classroom teachers should have ongoing assistance in developing and managing their learning programs. Teams of participants include the principal and the team facilitator for that school, and resource specialists such as school psychologists and counselors who are designated for particular situations.

The IC process begins with entry-level discussion between consultant and teacher about roles, expectations, and commitment. Consultants relinquish the expert role and configure their professional relationships to be collaborative and egalitarian. Steps proceed through problem identification and analysis, classroom observation, procedures such as curriculum-based assessment, implementation of interventions, ongoing evaluation, and termination of the consultation relationship. At termination, a written record of agreed-on findings is submitted to involved parties.

- Potential Strengths:

   Follows the existing stage of consultation

   Calls into question attitudes that deficits within child or family have created the problems

   Helps transform schools into learning communities

   Focuses on academic concerns *within the ecological framework*

- Potential Drawbacks:

   Requires a .5 full-time equivalency facilitator in each building

   Does not absolve teachers of responsibility for student learning

   Must provide intensive training for the IC team

   Requires data-collection time and skills from teachers

   Is even more problematic at the secondary level due to the number of teachers involved

   Due to expenses of training and including the .5 facilitator factor, can be costly

The **Conjoint Behavioral Consultation model** (CBC) provides home and school collaboration with shared problem solving (Wilkinson, 2005). Behavioral problems in classrooms are distracting to learning, but many classroom teachers have had little training in behavior management techniques. This indirect, structured model of consultation service delivery is for parents, teachers, and school personnel to participate and share responsibility for addressing academic, social, or behavioral needs. The collaborators work to pinpoint the problem(s), develop a plan, and assess outcomes of the plan. The method of data collection for behaviors is developed conjointly. In recent years, the model has been expanded to asssess its application to children with medical conditions—attention-deficit/ hyperactivity disorders in particular (Grier & Bradley-Klug, 2011).

- Potential Strengths:

   Combines perspectives and information from school, home, and health-care providers

   Crosses the barriers that often occur between medical and school personnel (Shapiro & Manz, 2004)

   Conjoint involvement received well by families, teachers, and school psychologists

   Allows key persons in the student's life to feel more involved and responsible

- Potential Drawbacks:

   Needs more robust research designs to help draw better conclusions about the model (Wilkinson, 2005)

Needs more study having direct involvement by pediatricians in the CBC meetings with parents and teachers

Lack of time and availability of pediatricians who are involved

The **Teacher Assistance Teams model** (TAT) provides a teacher support system for clasasroom teachers. It was developed in the 1970s as a way for classroom teachers to self refer for assistance from a team of two or three skilled teachers in their attendance center who have been elected as a problem-solving team (Pugach & Johnson, 1995). The team typically meets in problem-solving sessions for about thirty minutes. It is intended as a means of reducing referrals to special education. In this non-directive, prereferral model, the teachers are regarded as capable of using the problem-solving process effectively. It has been used by special education pairs and others with similar roles. It also is helpful as an in-house assistance plan for novice teachers who might otherwise be reluctant to ask for help due to apprehension that they might be regarded as less than competent. A similar plan, the PAR Mentoring Program for teachers (Stedman & Stroot, 1998), helps novice teachers who may be struggling to benefit from experience of consultants or mentors who are experienced teachers remembering what their first teaching years were like. Yet another plan, known as the Teachers Helping Teachers (THT) plan has teachers taking turns in presenting favorite teaching techniques to their co-educators in different attendance centers throughout the school district.

■ Potential Strengths:

Creates a sense of appreciation and support for clasasroom teachers

Presents several teachers as experts

Treats the consultee as a capable professional even when requesting assistance

Can reduce the number of inappropriate referrals

Addresses the interfering themes problem in constructive, positive ways

■ Potential Drawbacks:

Even though nondirective, still needs structure in the collaborations and formal meetings

Requires teacher commitment to the agreed-on interventions and changes

The **Schoolwide Enrichment Model** (SEM) (Renzulli & Reis, 1985) is a long-standing model that addresses needs of gifted and talented students. It requires close collaboration among general education teachers, gifted program facilitators, and outside resources to provide three types of enriching and accelerative learning experiences for gifted and talented students. In the first layer of service, Type I enrichment activities such as centers and field trips are offered for all students in the regular classroom. Type II process-building activities such as problem-solving practice and simulations are offered in a resource room setting for students with above-average ability, creativity, and strong task commitment. Type III independent-study activities are research- or project-based for students identified as gifted and talented who need the services of a gifted program facilitator and resources beyond the school environment. The SEM model is built on intensive staff development for classroom teachers, school counselors, central office staff, and other school personnel such as media specialists to prepare them for their roles.

- Potential Strengths:

   Enrichment activities provided to very able students not identified as gifted

   Places gifted and talented students with other very able students to enjoy learning in areas of common interest

   Can reveal exceptional abilities and talents among all students

   Encourages opportunities to differentiated learning activities for all students

- Potential Drawbacks:

   Requires intensive staff development programs before implementation

   Necessitates involvement by all general education teachers, special education teachers, and other school personnel

   Requires time, energy, talents, and organizational skills of all co-educators to reap full benefits

The **Biopsychoeducational Consultation model** (with BPE used here as a defining acronym) is based on a problem-solving process for serving children affected by health issues in school settings (Grier & Bradley-Klug, 2011). It brings together all those working with the child, including family members, pediatricians, medical specialists, and school educators, with direction and guidance from the school psychologist. Communication and collaboration are strong features of the model, with interventions tailored to provide positive educational experiences for students with asthma, cancer, seizures, central nervous system disorders such as traumatic brain injury, and biopsychosocial disorders including attention disorder/hyperactivity and substance abuse. The health revolution of the past two decades has shifted what was sole responsibility for health needs of children from the medical personnel to shared responsibility with schools, families, and community agencies.

The BPE model has strong roots in collaborative problem solving and key personnel include school educators, home educators, and medical specialists including the student's primary care physician. Problem identification is one of the model's critical stages, and this topic is to be addressed in a later chapter.

- Potential Strengths:

   Emphasizes the importance of the student's ecological system (culture, parents, peers, teachers, welfare system, social services)

   Fosters improved health care and development

   Can be used to develop protocols for children with cancer who are returning to school

■ Potential Drawbacks:

Opportunities for school psychologists to use the model limited by their traditional training, lack of preservice experiences with clients' health issues, and role identification that does not encourage collaborative endeavors

Need for stronger communication between school personnel and the medical community than evidenced in the past

Lack of time and accessibility to school personnel identified by pediatricians as greatest obstacle to collaboration

The **Responsive Systems Consultation** (RSC) **model** appears briefly here to emphasize a position taken by educators in regard to learning disabilities. This position is that learning and behavioral labels delegated to students are too often *curriculum and instruction* problems that should be assigned to learning environments instead. As some school personnel and families would put it, the problem lies in a misfit of the learning environment for the student rather than a misfit of student who happens to be in that learning environment. To put it more succinctly, the student has been placed in a setting that could be described as *a school with curriculum disabilities*. The RSC model would design the learning environment for the student's needs rather than forcing the student into the existing school setting. This model takes a behavioral approach with collaborative consultation characteristics (Denton, Hasbrouck, & Sekaquaptewa, 2003). Parents and teachers work together in interview settings to achieve a goodness of fit for students with the curriculum and instruction.

Summary of Collaborative Models Contributions

In collaborative school consultation, the consultant and consultee are equal partners having diverse expertise in identifying problems and planning intervention strategies (Idol et al., 1986; Raymond, McIntosh, & Moore, 1986). The communication is not hierarchical or one-way. Rather, it broadcasts a sense of parity that blends skills and knowledge of both consultant and consultee, and disagreements are viewed as opportunities for constructive extraction of the most useful information (Idol et al., 1995).

In their research investigating teacher responses to consultative services, Schulte, Osborne, and Kauffman (1993) have found that most teachers who were surveyed viewed collaborative consultation as an acceptable alternative to resource rooms. However, coordinating schedules and finding congruent time slots for interaction, much less finding time at all, do impose limits on effectiveness.

Idol et al. (1995) recommend that for collaborative consultation to be perceived as a success, participants will need to develop appropriate interview skills, active listening skills, effective oral and written communication, positive nonverbal language, and well-developed structures for problem solving and conflict resolution. The collaborative school consultation process must be voluntary and nonsupervisory, and carried out in a climate of parity with a demeanor of **onedownsmanship**—in other words, a de-emphasis on one's knowledge and skills in the interest of maintaining positive relationships.

■ Potential Strengths of Collaborative Models:

Fits current school reform goals

Inspires professional growth for all through shared expertise

Provides many points of view

Focuses on situations encompassing the whole school context

Involves general <u>and</u> special education staff and often resource and support personnel as well

Generates many ideas

Maximizes opportunities for constructive use of adult differences

Allows administrators to assume a collaborative role

Facilitates liaisons with community agents

Pleases families because many school personnel are working to address their child's special needs.

■ Potential Drawbacks of Collaborative Models:

Little or no training of educators in collaborative consultation and teamwork

Shortage of time and compatibility of schedules for interacting

The reality that working with adults is not preferred by some educators

Requires solid, not just token, administrator support

Confidentiality is harder to ensure with many people involved

Could diffuse responsibility so much that no one feels ultimately accountable

Can take a long time to see results

DEVELOPMENT OF METHODS FOR COLLABORATIVE SCHOOL CONSULTATION

When planning for collaborative school consultation, it is helpful to use an informal, journalistic-style template that directs the study and discussion, such as:

- Why is this type of service best?
- What do we expect to occur?
- Who will be involved?
- When will it take place and for how long?
- Where will it be happening?
- How will we put the plan into operation?
- How will we evaluate the results?
- Who will be accountable for the outcomes?

Then, returning to the six components shown in Figure 3.3 for constructing a method, it will be helpful to decide which components and to what extent they will be structured to frame the plan:

1. *S*ystem (school systems, other social systems)
2. *P*erspective (purchase, doctor-patient, process)
3. *A*pproach (formal, informal)
4. *Pr*ototype (mental health, behavioral)
5. Mod*e* (direct, indirect)
6. *M*odel (triadic, Resource/Consulting Teacher Program, Instructional Consultation, Conjoint Behavioral Consultation, Teacher Assistance Teams, Schoolwide Enrichment Model, Biopsychoeducational Consultation, and other collaborative consultation variations

Looking again at Figure 3.3, the Method area in the center draws a component from each of the six facets in order to synthesize all six into a method having a goodness of fit for the particular school situation or student concern. Several situations that follow will provide opportunities to practice collaborative consultation as thought problems and then later in interaction with co-educators.

Thought problems provide opportunities for intently reflecting on real problems and possibilities before presenting them for discussion and critique by others. This abstract way of pondering problems rather than manipulating components is a practice that master thinker Albert Einstein employed quite successfully. Indeed, this kind of thinking often occurs informally when co-educators are contemplating multifaceted processes such as collaborative consultation or co-teaching. Several of the activities in this book can be regarded as thought problems.

To work through one or two of the situations, it will be helpful to consider the why, who, what, when, where, and how, and choose among options for system, perspective, approach, prototype, mode, and model. It is not necessary to dwell on interaction and coordination processes at this time; the goal is an appropriate structure for a school context. When thinking about a situation or concern, it is stimulating to address complex circumstances in the way Einstein did—that is, explore in the mind's eye and not in a laboratory or a classroom. The idea is to manipulate variables and concepts mentally, "seeing" them from all angles as facets of the gem structure described earlier and withholding judgment until all conceivable avenues have been explored in one's mind before putting them into practice or even discussing with colleagues.

■ ■ ■ ■ ■ ▬▬▬▬▬▬▬▬▬▬▬▬▬▬▬▬▬▬▬▬▬▬▬▬▬▬▬▬▬▬▬▬▬▬▬▬

ACTIVITY 3.2

Illustrating a Collaborative Consultation Model

How do you think an artist might depict educators working together to help a child learn at school? Would your thoughts form an abstract design with geometric shapes, and lines to show the interactions? Or would it be a sketch with stick figures to show teacher problem-solving for the child who might be in the middle of the sketch? Or would it be a sculpture made of clay or sand? Some interesting and instructive ideas that have been put forth by others to depict a collaborative school consultation enterprise include: crafting the plan into a mobile, illustrating it as points in the Big Dipper constellation, laying out the steps as if on a baseball diamond, or placing the problem-solving process into a spiral that moves inward from observation and data collection to focus on a plan.

If you like to draw or sculpt, you could turn your thinking into action and try your hand at making an illustration of the idea. If you don't care to do that but you have a graphically talented friend, you could explain the concept and collaborate with that person, asking if it suggests a picture. The most fun of all might be to ask a school child to make a drawing. It would be interesting to see how the young student perceives adults working together to help every child do well in school.

As a further challenge, think of an illustration for a co-teaching partnership. If you like your idea very much, find a way to make it into a chart or mural for display in your school to draw attention to the process of collaboration and what it offers learners and teachers who experience it.

SITUATIONS IN WHICH TO IMPLEMENT COLLABORATIVE SCHOOL CONSULTATION

Methods for collaborative consultation in schools are as varied as the situations calling for service and the school personnel who will address them. Ultimately the development process will be a collaborative endeavor. Co-educators must keep in mind that any method will be counterproductive if it shortens the service time and decreases the instruction that students need. Some parents use this possibility as a reason for opposing inclusive classrooms co-teaching practices. So the potential must be examined with objectivity and discussed frankly.

ACTIVITY 3.3

Situations for Constructing Methods of Collaborative Consultation

The following situations have occurred in educational contexts. Select one of them to address with another person or a small group, and propose how it could be managed or resolved. Is the best choice to use the *triadic* model and a *purchase* perspective, with *indirect* service from the consultant to the client, in an *informal, mental health* prototype of interaction within the *school system*? Would a variation of a *collaborative consultation* model and a *process* perspective be effective, using *direct* service to the client from both consultant and consultee in a *formal* way that approximates a *behavioral* prototype within a *community work setting* as the system? What other possibilities do you and your colleague or group of colleagues think could be promising methods?

Select a situation from the examples provided, or from others generated by you and your colleagues, and propose a method of addressing the need that is composed of an element from each of the six facets—System (context), Perspective (viewpoint), Approach (formal or informal), pRototype (pattern), modE (form), and Model choices. When thinking about the possibilities, it will be useful to consider potential drawbacks and strengths of the plan.

Situation 1: A third-grade child with intellectual disability hits other children for no apparent cause in the inclusive classroom where other students have been prepared for his presence in the class. The teacher has tried behavior management strategies and time-out periods. But the child impulsively strikes out whenever another child enters his physical space. Sometimes he waits in the restroom to jostle and punch other boys when they enter. The maternal grandmother, as the child's caregiver, is very involved with his IEP, his curriculum and instruction in the classroom, and his social interaction both in and out of school. How could the school and home personnel address the situation so that his classmates and teachers can continue to support and assist him appropriately?

Situation 2: Ten-year-old Clarisse is new to the school and is placed in a program for students with intellectual disabilities. Her teacher quickly learns that Clarisse prefers to observe rather than participate, and she will not join group activities. In her previous school, according to her parents, Clarisse had been allowed to lie on the floor most of the day so she would not have tantrums about participation. Her new teacher and paraeducator want Clarisse to demonstrate her capabilities but do not want her to get off to a bad start in the new school and do not want the parents to feel negative toward her new teachers. The teacher knows this is a crucial time for Clarisse's development and wonders what to do.

Situation 3: The speech pathologist has been asked by the gifted program facilitator to consult with her regarding a highly gifted child who has minor speech problems and some behaviors suggesting mild autism spectrum disorder, but is being pressured by his parents and kindergarten teacher to "stop the baby talk." The child is becoming very nervous and at times withdraws from conversation and play. How can the speech pathologist, general and special education teachers, and school psychologist engage in collaborative consultation to help?

Situation 4: A fifth-grade boy with learning disabilities, having a quiet and sensitive nature, and little interest in sports and team games is not accepted by other boys in his class, many of whom are quite sports-minded and team-oriented. He is being harassed and bullied by some boys and a few girls on the playground, sometimes in the restroom, and occasionally on the bus ride home. He has not opened up about this to any of his teachers (classroom, phys ed, music, art), but two classmates have described some incidents to a paraeducator who supervises recess. What should the para do about the boy, the alleged bullies, and the informers?

Situation 5: The school psychologist and school counselor are conferring with a teacher about a high school student who is often a behavior problem, and the psychologist is discussing methods for setting up behavior limits with appropriate contingencies and rewards. The teacher makes numerous references to the principal as a person who likes for teachers to be self-sufficient and not "make waves." How should the counselor and psychologist handle this?

Situation 6: Parents of a student with learning disabilities have asked the special education consulting teacher to approach the student's classroom teacher, who is in his first year of teaching, about what they think is excessive and too-difficult homework. The parents say it is disrupting their home life and frustrating the student. But they do not want to undermine the confidence of the novice teacher or add to their child's resentment toward him and increase the student's dislike of school. How can this situation be addressed?

Situation 7: A high school special education teacher who is assigned to plan and lead staff development, is meeting in the fall with the building principal at that principal's request. The meeting is supposed to be about planning the next staff development activity aimed at promoting collaborative consultation practices during the spring semester. But the principal uses their limited time to express concern about the quality and practices of instruction demonstrated by another faculty member. Knowing that the special education teacher is often in this teacher's classroom, the principal asks her for feedback concerning that classroom teacher's instruction and demeanor toward students. How should the special education teacher handle this situation?

Situation 8: A pediatrician contacts the director of special education and asks her to gather some of the special education staff and join a group of local doctors for the purpose of discussing characteristics and needs, including medications and restrictions, of children with disabilities. The paramount concern is finding congruent blocks of time and an appropriate place to meet. How should this opportunity be planned and structured in the almost-overwhelming schedules of these doctors and teachers that can be expected to provide maximum benefit for all?

Situation 9: A middle school student has been failing in several subjects during the semester and has become increasingly sullen and withdrawn over the past several weeks. Two of her teachers have arrived independently at the strong possibility that a male relative who is living with her family is abusing her. What actions need to be taken here and by whom?

Situation 10: A high school student went hunting over the weekend. He had lost his hunting knife with which he dressed out game, so he borrowed one from a friend. He drove to school on Monday with the knife in his backpack, intending to return it to his friend in the parking lot. But they did not connect and, distracted by an altercation in the parking lot, he forgets about the borrowed knife and makes his way into the building with the backpack. Another student finds out what is in the backpack and reports it. Soon the knife-borrowing student, who has learning disabilities with attention deficit disorder, is summoned to the office where his father, the principal, the football coach, and the school's security guard are gathered. The big game of the season is Friday night and the student with the knife is the team's star. How and by whom should this situation be handled?

Situation 11: A school district is experiencing discord for not allowing a middle-school transgender student to use the bathroom of that student's choice. The parents say that after several years of working through gender-related matters involving clothing, toys, activities, and at one point changing schools to make life more tolerable for the student, now it comes to this. School officials propose that the student use the faculty restroom and parents of other students are conflicted about the situation. Who should join the school counselor to study it from all sides and come to agreement on a course acceptable to all?

Situation 12: A primary-grade teacher and the school health nurse are distressed that a student who enrolled two weeks ago comes to school hungry, dirty, seemingly malnourished, and usually tardy. She walks alone several blocks to school. In the classroom she holds her head to one side, confuses words in simple readers, and needs markers to locate and keep her place in materials. The teacher suspects hearing and visual impairments and has requested she be tested as soon as possible. No caregiver for the child has been seen at school since her enrollment day and her records from the previous school have not caught up with her. How does she get immediate help?

Those who will be participating in collaborative consultation services must:

- Be knowledgeable and prepared
- Know their roles and express their concerns when situations call for it
- Participate actively to structure a suitable climate for co-educating
- Work through their thoughts and feelings about the dynamics of the challenge, especially if it is a new role for them.

Key elements and components for meeting the challenges are preparations (preservice, professional development, advanced programs), role delineation (clarifications, parity, and expectations), frameworks (structure, resources, management), and commitment (assessment, evaluation, acceptance).

Collaborative school consultation with reflective listening and assertive teamwork is not easy to accomplish; it takes significant amounts of effort and energy for relatively autonomous individuals to arrive at shared goals along different pathways. An issue is explored, options are analyzed, and often the best solution is not a favorite choice of each person, but everyone's acceptable choice that can be adopted with enthusiasm—a new and collaboratively formulated plan for the benefit of all.

 ENHANCEDetext Application Exercise 3.1. Click to apply your understanding of collaborative school consultation methods.

TIPS FOR STRUCTURING COLLABORATIVE SCHOOL CONSULTATION

1. Be knowledgeable about the various collaboration, consultation, and co-teaching methods.
2. Keep up to date on professional issues and concerns because education and the area of special education in particular undergo frequent changes in policies and practices.

3. Be on the alert for new methods or revisions of existing methods through which consultation and collaboration can occur in your school context.
4. Read current materials on school consultation and collaboration and highlight references to these processes in other professional material you read.
5. Visit programs where models different from those in your school(s) are being used.
6. Be realistic and understanding about the demands placed on classroom teachers, support personnel, administrators, and family members of students in their roles.
7. Seek out sessions at professional conferences that feature different models and methods and attend them to broaden your knowledge about educational systems.
8. Devise specific ways that co-educators can get your help and make those ways known to all.
9. Clarify what is expected of collaboration, consultation, and teamwork by having dialogue with people in all roles in the school context, for expectations will vary from person to person.
10. Be flexible and adaptable, because change takes time and must be preceded by awareness of the *need* to change.

CHAPTER 4

COMMUNICATING EFFECTIVELY FOR COLLABORATION AND TEAMING

When we are with others, we are always communicating—even if we aren't saying a word. Communication is not simply delivering a message. It involves body language, attitude and thoughts, facial expressions, listening, and yes, talking. Successful communication is much more complex than its individual components, or to borrow again a well-known quote from Aristotle, "The whole is greater than the sum of its parts."

Effective consultants are aware of many elements that make up communication. Key components of successful communication are understanding, trust, autonomy, and flexibility. Effective communicators withhold judgment and minimize efforts to control the path of communication. They manage interpersonal conflict and address concerns together. The finer points of communication are paramount for collaborating and consulting teachers who are constantly interacting with general education teachers, related service personnel, administrators, paraeducators, families, and members of the community. Your messages must be clear and delivered in a way that is both assertive and open to hearing what others have to say. Communication is the foundation of cooperation and collaboration among educators.

Collaborating educators in the twenty-first century have technology tools that educators in years past could not envision. Tech-savvy consultants must think about how technology-related tools can enhance their roles but also recognize the pitfalls these tools may pose and use them in ways that will communicate their intentions clearly.

Problems and conflicts are unavoidable elements of life and unavoidable elements in the context of collaboration in schools as well, but good communication skills will facilitate problem solving and resolution of conflicts. Ineffective communication creates a void that breeds misunderstanding and distrust. Elements of trust, commitment, and effective interaction are critical for conflict-free relationships. Effective communication becomes a foundation for cooperation and collaboration among school personnel, students, families, and others involved in education.

CHAPTER OBJECTIVES

Upon completing this chapter, the reader should be able to:

1. Give examples of how communication for effective school relationships has become both simpler and more complex.

2. Describe challenges in communicating effectively.

3. Demonstrate effective communication skills.

4. List major roadblocks to communication.

5. Illustrate techniques for conflict management, coping with resistance, and defusing anger, negativity, and resistance.

6. Determine ways of using electronic communication, social networking, and other Web 2.0 tools to communicate ethically in a collaborative climate.

KEY TERMS

assertive or active body language

assertiveness

body language (kinesics)

microaggressions

mindful communication

rapport building

responsive listening

roadblocks to communication

Web 2.0 tools for collaboration

SITUATION 4

The setting is the hallway of a junior high school in mid-afternoon, where the general math instructor, a first-year teacher, is venting to a colleague.

Math Teacher: What a day! On top of the fire drill this morning and those forms that we got in our boxes to be filled out by Friday, I had a disastrous encounter with a parent. Guess I flunked Parent Communication 101.

Colleague: Oh, one of those, huh?

Math Teacher: Jay's mother walked into my room right before fourth hour and accused me of not doing my job. It was awful!

Colleague: [nods head, showing empathy]

Math Teacher: Thank goodness there weren't any students around. But the music teacher was there telling me about next week's program. This parent really let me have it. I was stunned, not only by the accusation, but by the way she delivered it. My whole body went on "red alert." My heart was pounding and my stomach was in a knot. Then my palms got sweaty and I could feel my hands shaking. I could hardly squeak out a sound because my mouth was so dry. I wanted to yell back at her, but I couldn't!

Colleague: Probably just as well. Quick emotional reactions don't seem to work very well when communication breaks down. I found out the hard way that it doesn't help to respond at all during that first barrage of words. Sounds like you did the right thing.

Math Teacher: Well, it really was hard. So you've had things like this happen to you?

Colleague: Uh-huh. I see we don't have time for me to tell you about it because here come the thundering herds. But I'll tell you all about it later if you want. Come to my room after school and we'll compare notes—maybe put our heads together to plan some strategies for the future, just in case. And, by the way, welcome to the club!

COMMUNICATION FOR EFFECTIVE SCHOOL RELATIONSHIPS

Teachers manage many kinds of relationships in their work with students who have special needs. Some relationships grow throughout the year or over several years; others are established and stable; and still others are new, tentative, and tenuous. No matter what the type of relationship, and no matter whether it is with families, co-educators, paraeducators, or related-service providers, communication is the key to successful collaboration and productive relationships. Furthermore, communication in the twenty-first century has become, paradoxically, simpler and more complex due to the effects of modern technology.

In the chapter "Enter Technology, Exit Talking" of her book *How to Talk So People Listen: Connecting in Today's Workplace*, Sonya Hamlin (2006, p. 3) says that "even hello has changed" as a result of modern technology. Her discussion includes examples of how technology has changed the ways we communicate:

- We email the person in the office next door.
- We have a list of fifteen phone numbers to reach our family.
- We pull up in our driveway and use our cell phone to see if anyone is home to help carry in the groceries.
- We get up in the morning and go online before getting our coffee.

Computers, cell phones, the Internet, and even television have changed communication in the last decade. However, while all these media may be part of our repertoire when it comes to collaborating with school, home, and community partners, face-to-face interactions are still the standard and the most effective type of communication for most collaboration. People typically communicate in one form or another for about 70 percent of their waking moments. Unfortunately, lack of effective communication skills is a major reason for work-related failure.

A supportive, communicative relationship among special education teachers, general classroom teachers, students, and their families is critical to the success of children with exceptional learning needs in inclusive classrooms. Special educators must model exemplary communication and interaction skills.

Preceding chapters described the contexts of collaborative school consultation and identified potential areas of differences and disagreements among educators who are poised to work together in a number of ways. Now it is time to move ahead to the challenge of honing communication processes that are the nuts and bolts of collaboration and teamwork.

CHALLENGES IN COMMUNICATING EFFECTIVELY

Consulting is not a one-person exercise. A consultant will pay a high price for using a ramrod approach to push ideas onto others. But communication that minimizes conflict and enables teachers to maintain self-esteem may be the most important process in collaborative consulting. Unfortunately, development of communication skills is not typically included in teacher education programs. Because the development and use of "people skills" is the most difficult aspect of collaboration for many educators, more and more educators are stressing the need for specific training in collaboration and communication skills if they expect to help students with special needs be successful in inclusive settings. In your role as a collaborative teacher, you are likely to be working with others across different generations, personalities, genders, and cultures. Each brings its own nuances to the mix.

Verbal Aspects of Communication

Semantics play a fundamental role in both sending and receiving messages. As stressed earlier, a person who says, "Oh, it's no big deal—just an issue of semantics" is missing a major point. The semantics frequently *are* the issue and should never be taken for granted. The vital role of semantics in consultation, collaboration, and teamwork cannot be ignored.

Body language also plays a key role in communication. Studies of **kinesics**, or communication through body language, show that the impact of a message is about 7 percent verbal, 38 percent vocal, and 55 percent facial. We communicate *non*verbally much of the time and in many more ways than we tend to acknowledge. Being aware of your posture, position of your arms and feet, eye contact, and facial expressions really do matter. Giving attention to other things such as the clock, someone walking by the door or outside the window, checking messages on electronic devices, or even having the screen open on a laptop may communicate unintended messages.

Miscommunication breeds misunderstanding. A saying attributed to noted theologian John Powell stresses that, "I can't tell you what you *said*, but only what I *heard*." A person may send the message, "You look nice today," and have it understood by the receiver as, "Gee, then I usually don't look very good." A classroom teacher wanting to reinforce efforts of the special education teacher might say "Gerry seems to get much better grades on tests in the resource room," but the resource teacher may hear, "You're helping too much and Gerry can't cope outside your protection." Figure 4.1 graphically illustrates a potential range of distorted communication.

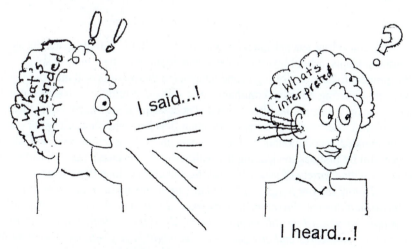

FIGURE 4.1   Miscommunication

Differing values, beliefs, ambiguous language, stereotypes, assumptions, and personal experiences, such as previous encounters with a person, all can serve as filters of language. Often these filters are unconscious and we don't realize how much they come into play (Treasure, 2011). Preconceived ideas constantly filter the messages we receive, thus preventing us from hearing what others are saying and providing only what people want to hear (Buscaglia, 1986). This can be demonstrated with the well-known game "Telephone." Players stand in a long line or a circle, while one of them silently reads a note or quietly receives a whispered message. Then that person whispers the message to the next one, and the message is delivered to each one in turn. After passing through the filters of many people and being stated aloud by the very last person, the message in most cases is drastically different from the original message. The game results are usually humorous. Real-life results are not always so funny.

■ ■ ■ ■ ■ ▬▬▬▬▬▬▬▬▬▬▬▬▬▬▬▬▬▬▬▬▬▬▬▬▬▬▬▬▬▬▬▬▬▬▬▬▬▬

ACTIVITY 4.1
Hearing Messages Through Our Filters

Join several others and designate one person to describe something that happened at school or another familiar context. Before the person recounts the event or situation, decide what *hat* each of the others in the group will wear. One might be designated as wearing the *administrator hat*, another might listen through the filtered ears of a parent, a student, general education teacher, a related service person, etc. If it is not a school-related issue, think of other appropriate *hats* that could be assigned. Listen to the person recount the situation while hearing it with the filter of your designated role. Jot down things you are feeling and hearing while you listen. Now take turns sharing what each person heard through their personal filters. Did the re-telling of the situation change depending on the filter? Think about times when you have been part of a conversation or meeting and each person walks away having heard a slightly different version of the same words.

A consulting teacher interacts with other teachers, parents, paraeducators, administrators, students, school board members, and countless others in their sphere of influence. It is prudent to be aware of filters and understand that what is said may or may not be what is heard. Utilizing effective communication skills can remove or lessen the impact of filters by acknowledging the filters exist and addressing issues surrounding them. For example, if you are working with a reluctant teacher who doesn't want to implement recommended accommodations for a student in the classroom, you will likely be more successful by first acknowledging the realities of the teacher's task of working with many students with a variety of needs. Try saying something along these lines:

"I know you are juggling a lot of balls in the air when trying to meet the needs of all students in a diverse classroom such as yours. I want to collaborate with you to make this workable for you, while still meeting the needs of the student. Tell me a little about how your classroom works and any concerns you might have about implementing this accommodation. This will help us figure out how to make it work within the context of your

specific classroom. Please know that I will assist you in any way that I can. I think you'll see benefits not only for this student, but possibly others as well. If our plan is not working or other issues arise, we can address them together."

The reluctant teacher who came in with filters of resentment and feelings that you "just don't understand" is likely to be more open to listening and carrying out an accommodation knowing you recognize it is not easy teaching twenty-five fourth-graders. You conveyed genuine interest about the classroom structure before pushing yet another expectation on the teacher. Finally, you worked together to develop an implementation plan rather than just expecting the teacher to "figure it out." Remember, once you leave and the teacher closes the door, a well-intentioned idea or suggestion will die on the vine unless the person feels it is worth the effort. Don't confuse head nods and smiles with agreement for carrying through with a plan. Successful consultants address underlying issues and are aware of how filters impact communication.

Nonverbal Aspects of Communication

Words are only one component of the message that is sent. The way we talk, walk, sit, and stand all say something about us, and whatever is happening on the inside can be reflected on the outside, sometimes without our awareness. Successful collaborating teachers are in-tune with their body language and other nonverbal elements of the message. These nonverbal components can result in very different messages, even when the same words are used. Nonverbal communication can be organized into six categories: eye contact, gestures, paralanguage (volume, rate, pitch, and tone), posture, overall facial expression, and yes, even clothing and the physical setting chosen for the interaction. Any of these could influence the message (White, 2000). A consulting teacher serving two different schools once admitted to changing her outfit at lunchtime to fit in better with her afternoon colleagues.

Our facial expressions convey our thoughts and feelings. Be aware of what pushes your buttons and how you react in difficult situations. It is wise to heed the advice of the saying "fake it till you make it," by controlling your reactions—including your voice volume, speed, tone, facial expressions, and body language—in stressful or uncomfortable situations. Practice maintaining your composure under pressure. Voice tone, pitch, volume, and speed can affect the receiver of a message in positive or negative ways. Sometimes the speaker is unaware of the way a message is being interpreted due to these subtle nonverbal communication messages. Simply slowing down the rate of speech can make a person appear more confident and calm, thus impacting the overall message. Stress or nervousness might be misinterpreted and interfere with the words or perceived interest in the topic being discussed. A slouching posture, folded arms, or turning away will imply lack of interest or rejection. As receivers of information, it is important to be in tune when seeing these body language signs in others. Arms crossed in front of the body, eyes downcast or little eye contact, minimal facial expressions are warning signs that your message is falling on deaf ears or not being received positively. People in some cultures—teachers or parents—may feel demeaned when consulting teachers dress too

Video Example from YouTube

▶

ENHANCEDetext
Video Example 4.1.

View this video on types of nonverbal communication. (https://www.youtube.com/watch?v=csaYYpXBCZg)

casually and communicate in an overly friendly way. Of course, the opposite can be true as well. A consulting teacher who arrives over-dressed to a "Casual Friday" event can send the message, "I'm more important or above you." Knowing your audience or the culture of the situation is important.

Cultural Differences in Communication

Language is the window through which the realities of experiences are revealed. A number of factors may cloud that window and lead to misjudgments in interpreting communication. Misunderstanding may not be due simply to miscommunication. Cultural background of the sender or the receiver may affect both sender and receiver.

Most consultants are aware that different languages or different dialects may have different words for the same object. Some languages have no words for terms the way educators use them in education. Verbal and nonverbal communication must be attuned to ethnic, racial, linguistic, and cultural differences. Because language and culture are so inextricably bound together, communicating with potential collaborative partners who are from different cultural and linguistic backgrounds is a very complex process. For example, eye contact in a classroom may signal disrespect and inattention in one culture but may mean respect in another culture. Typically, intermittent eye contact is considered a way to convey interest and attention, but it can be interpreted differently depending on the background, and sometimes gender, of the receiver. Cultural differences can extend to use of space, touch, appearance, voice tone, and body language. Educators will continue to be challenged by the cultural diversity of collaborators. Increases in diversity among colleagues, families, and community members require that educational consultants recognize and respect the impact of culture on communication in their work and the respect they will be accorded when they do. When interacting with others from cultures different from your own, be particularly observant and follow their lead. Consultants can show their interest in getting to know about the person by asking questions. Being curious about other people and their cultural backgrounds indicate you care and wish to know them better. It shows you are a good listener, one of the most important components for successful communication and collaborative interactions.

■ ■ ■ ■ ■ ■

ACTIVITY 4.2
Sending, Receiving, and Sharing Messages

In groups of three, with one person designated as interviewer, another as interviewee, and the third as responder, conduct three-minute interviews to learn more about one another. After each of these segments, the three change roles so that each person has a turn to serve in all three capacities. Each responder may make brief notes to use during a follow up, one-minute share time for introducing his or her interviewee to the whole group. Use questions of this nature or others given by the convener: Why did you decide to enter into the education profession or special education? What are your interests? Pet peeves? Long-range goals? Things you want to learn more about?

BUILDING SKILLS FOR COMMUNICATING

With well-developed communication skills, consultants and consultees will be able to engage more effectively in collaborative problem solving. In order to be effective communicators, senders and receivers of messages need competence in five major sets of skills:

1. Rapport building
2. Responsive listening
3. Assertion
4. Conflict management
5. Collaborative problem solving

Rapport building is essential in establishing a collaborative relationship. Responsive listening skills enable a person to understand what another is saying and to convey that the problems and feelings have been understood. When the consultant uses listening methods appropriately, the consultee can have an active role in problem solving without becoming dependent on the consultant. Assertion skills include verbal and nonverbal behaviors that enable collaborators to maintain respect, satisfy their professional needs, and defend their rights without dominating, manipulating, or controlling others. Conflict management skills help individuals deal with the emotional turbulence that typically accompanies conflict, and they have a multiplier effect of fostering closer relationships when a conflict is resolved. Collaborative problem-solving skills help resolve the conflicting needs so that all parties are satisfied. Problems then "stay solved," and relationships are developed and preserved. Problem solving is the focus of the next chapter.

Rapport-Building Skills

Collaboration with other professionals for best interests of students with special needs often means simply sitting down and making some joint decisions. At other times, however, it must be preceded by considerable rapport-building efforts. Involved parties should work to identify the problem(s) and to provide ideas toward solving the problem(s). Respect must be a two-way street for generating and accepting ideas and building an appropriate climate of collaboration. We encourage others to be part of the problem-solving team when we encourage them in positive ways. Perhaps legendary Alabama football Coach Paul "Bear" Bryant showed how to lift others up and make them work for the team when he said, "If anything goes bad, *I* did it. If anything goes semi-good, then *we* did it. If anything goes really good, then *you* did it. That's all it takes to get people to win football games for you." Educational consultants will be well served by adopting this philosophy from Coach Bryant's playbook of successful coaching.

When we take time to build positive relationships that are based on mutual respect and trust, others are more likely to:

- Want to work with us
- Care about our reactions to them
- Try to meet our expectations

- Accept our feedback and coaching
- Imitate our behavior

We are more likely to:

- Listen to and try to understand their unique situations
- Accept them as they are and not judge them for what they are not
- Respond appropriately to their concerns and criticisms
- Advocate for, support, and encourage them in their efforts to serve student needs

What behaviors are central to the process of building a trusting, supportive relationship? When asked this question, many teachers mention trust, respect, feeling that it is okay not to have all the answers, feeling free to ask questions, and feeling all right about disagreeing with the other person. Most of all, people want to feel that the other person is *really* listening. Trust is developed when one addresses the concerns of others and looks for opportunities to demonstrate responsiveness to others' needs (Combs, Harris, & Edmonson, 2015). A consultant can communicate care by becoming aware of something personal such as learning that a team member's child is considering college options and asking about how the process is progressing, or asking another how the preparation is going for an upcoming marathon. These small gestures of interest show you care and help build trust in relationships. Parents want to be treated with dignity and know that professionals respect their concerns and value their contributions and suggestions about their child's education. When parents feel heard and have been shown genuine concern, trusting relations will develop and parents will be more inclined to be active participants in their child's education (Park, Alber-Morgan, & Fleming, 2011).

Respecting differences in others is an important aspect of building and maintaining rapport (forging a partnership). Although teachers and other school personnel are generally adept at recognizing and respecting individual differences in children, they often find this more difficult to accomplish with adults or they simply do not think about it, much less treat it as an important consideration. Accepting differences in adults may be particularly difficult when the adults have different values, skills, expectations, and attitudes. Effective consultants accept people as they really are rather than wishing they were different. Suspend all unrelated thoughts, and start with a clean slate. Rapport building is not such a formidable process when the consultant respects individual differences and conveys high esteem for others.

ENHANCEDetext
Video Example 4.2.

In this video, observe how the school team members and parents are respectful and welcoming of each other's ideas. As a result, they are building a climate of trust and collaboration for the present and for the future.

Responsive-Listening Skills

Plutarch said, "Know how to listen, and you will profit even from those who talk badly." Shakespeare referred to the "disease" of *not* listening. Listening is the foundation of communication. Of course, first and foremost, one listens to hear the message but a person also listens to establish rapport. People listen when others are upset or angry, or when they do not know what to say or fear that speaking out will result in trouble. People listen so others will listen to them. Listening is a process of perpetual motion that focuses on the other person's ideas as speaker rather than concentrating on one's own thoughts and feelings as listener. Thus, effective listening is **responsive listening** because it is responding, both verbally and nonverbally, to the words and actions of the speaker. In his TED Talk, "5 Ways to Listen Better," Julian Treasure (2011) refers to this as "conscious listening." Conscious listening creates understanding. The practice of nonjudgmental awareness can help consultants communicate more effectively and meaningfully with others.

Successful consultants listen responsively and empathically in order to build trust and promote understanding. Responsive listening improves relationships and minimizes resistance and negativity. Although most people are convinced of the importance of listening in building collegial relationships and preventing and solving problems, few are as adept at this skill as they would like to be. There are several reasons for this. First, most people have not been taught to listen effectively. They have been taught to talk—especially if they are teachers, school administrators, or counselors. One study (Martin et al., 2006) found in observations of more than 100 Individual Education Plan (IEP) meetings that special education teachers talked 51 percent of the time, whereas family members talked only 15 percent of the time. This lopsided ratio may be attributed to teachers feeling pressure to report student progress to parents, but it doesn't leave much opportunity for parents to express their goals and interests during the meeting. This may result in parents feeling that their concerns are not valued, thus marginalizing the opportunities for successful collaboration. Educators are good at talking and regard it as an essential part of their roles. But effective talkers must be careful not to let the lines of communication get tangled up in a tendency to talk too much or too often. "The aim should be for teachers to be able to talk *with* parents instead of only talking *to* parents in order to cooperate and be in true dialogue" (Symeou, Roussounidou, & Michaelides, 2012, p. 82).

According to Thomas Gordon, one of the early promoters of effective communication, listening helps keep the "locus of responsibility" with the one who owns the problem (Gordon, 2000). Therefore, if one's role as a consultant is to promote problem solving without cultivating dependence on the part of the consultee, listening will keep the focus of the problem solving where it belongs. According to Gordon, listening also is important in showing empathy and acceptance, two vital ingredients in a relationship that fosters growth and psychological health. Chapman (2012) talks about *mindful presence*, an awake body, tender heart, and open mind and *mindful listening* that allows us to see the value in others and envision their potential. Without this mindset for communication, it is easy to enter into meetings with hidden agendas and preconceived ideas about the actions and motives, and therefore, not open to truly listening.

Responsive, effective listening makes it possible to gather information essential to one's role in the education of children with special needs. It helps others feel better, often by reducing tension and anxiety, increasing feelings of personal well-being, and encouraging greater hope and optimism. This kind of listening encourages others to express themselves freely and fully. It promotes self-understanding and problem-solving abilities.

Why is responsive listening so hard? First of all, listening is difficult because it is hard to keep an open mind about the speaker. Furthermore, people may be hesitant to listen because they think listening implies agreeing. There is a difference between agreeing versus simply acknowledging or showing respect for someone's idea (Becker & Wortmann, 2009). When listening to others, it is important for the person to feel comfortable and know you value their opinion, even if you disagree. Decide how you're going to validate: A head nod? Listening? Paraphrasing? By saying something like, "I'm glad you are bringing that idea or point of view into our discussion" not just, "That's a good idea," you validate the person's contribution and they know that you are listening. However, listening is much more than just hearing. Many people believe they are good listeners, but in reality, they are only *hearing* and not *listening*. The difference is that in listening, you're actually processing what you heard. Openness is important for effective communication. Co-educators must demonstrate tolerance toward differences and appreciation of richly diverse ideas and values while they are engaged in collaborative and consultative relationships. A consultant's own values about child rearing, education, or the treatment of children with special needs become personal filters that make it difficult to really listen to those whose values are very different.

Listening is indeed hard work. If the listener is tired or anxious or, conversely, bursting with excitement and energy, it is particularly hard to listen carefully. Feelings of the listener also act as filters to impede listening. Other roadblocks to responsive listening are making assumptions about the message (mind-reading), thinking about our own response (rehearsing), and reacting defensively. Think of it this way: listening attentively compliments the other person, and who doesn't like to be complimented?

Improving one's own listening skills can help establish collaborative relationships with colleagues, even those with whom it is a challenge to communicate. When collaborators improve their listening skills, they have a head start on solving problems, sidestepping resistance, and preventing conflicts. The three major components of responsive listening are:

1. *Nonverbal listening*—Discerning others' needs and observing their nonverbal gestures
2. *Encouraging the sending of messages*—Encouraging others to express themselves fully
3. *Showing understanding of the message*—Reviewing what they conveyed, or paraphrasing

Nonverbal Listening Skills.   Responsive listeners should use their faces and bodies to show they are listening and totally engaged in what is being said. Nonverbal listening may not be so effective for people who try to multitask while listening, such as peruse their email, text messages, talk to a colleague or grade papers during a meeting, or when a parent is busy preparing dinner while listening to a child's synopsis of the day. This is because nonverbal components of listening should demonstrate to the speaker that the receiver is respecting the speaker enough to concentrate on the message and is following the speaker's thoughts to find the *real* message. An exception to the examples above could involve taking notes during a meeting while someone is talking. This can actually show you value what the person is saying and respect their thoughts enough to write them down. Be mindful of switching between note-taking and eye contact so you look and feel totally engaged. A person who is attentive leans forward slightly, engages in a comfortable level of eye contact, nods, and gives low-key responses such as "oh," and "uh-huh," and "umm-humm."

The responsive listener's facial expression matches the message. If that message is serious, the expression reflects seriousness. If the message is delivered with a smile, the listener shows empathy by smiling.

The hardest part of nonverbal listening is keeping it nonverbal. It helps the listener to think about a tennis game and remember that during the listening part of the "game," the ball is in the speaker's court. The speaker has the privilege of saying anything, no matter how seemingly inconsequential or irrelevant. The listener just keeps sending the ball back by nodding, or saying "I see" or other basically nonverbal behaviors, until he or she "hears" the sender's message. This entails observing and listening to the nonverbal as well as the verbal messages of the sender. The listener recognizes and minimizes personal filters, perceives and interprets the filters of the sender, and encourages continued communication until able to understand the message from the sender's perspective. Responsive listeners avoid anticipating what the speaker will say and *never* complete a speaker's sentence.

After listeners have listened until they really hear the message, understand the speaker's position, and recognize the feelings behind the message, it is their turn to speak. But they must be judicious about what they do say. Several well-known humorous "recipes" apply to this requirement:

- Recipe for giving a good speech: add shortening.
- It takes six letters of the alphabet to spell the word *listen*. Rearrange the letters to spell another word that is a necessary part of responsive listening. (What is the word?)
- In the middle of listening, the *t* doesn't make a sound.

Verbal Listening Skills.   Although the first rule for a good listener is to keep one's mouth shut, there are several types of verbal responses that show the listener is following the thoughts and feelings expressed by the speaker. Verbal encouragers are added to nonverbal listening responses to communicate that the listener understands what the other is saying from the speaker's specific point of view. Certain verbal aspects of listening are intended to keep the speaker talking. There are several reasons for this which are specific to the consulting process:

- The consultant will be less inclined to assume ownership of the problem inappropriately.
- Speakers will clarify their own thoughts as they keep talking.
- More information will become available to help understand the speaker's point of view.
- Speakers begin to solve their own problems as they talk through them.
- The consultant continues to refine responsive listening skills.

Three verbal listening skills that promote talking by the speaker are inviting, encouraging, and questioning cautiously. "Inviting" means providing an opportunity for others to talk by signaling to them that you are interested in listening if they are interested in speaking. Examples are "You seem to have something on your mind," and "I'd like to hear about your problem," and "What's going on for you now?"

Video Example from YouTube

▶

ENHANCEDetext
Video Example 4.3.

View this video to learn more about key skills that will improve your listening skills. Which ones will be most helpful for you? (https://www.youtube.com/watch?v=D6-MleRr1e8)

Verbal encouragers are words added to nodding and mirroring of facial responses. "I see," "uh-huh," and "oh" are examples of verbal behaviors that encourage continued talking. These responses by the listener suggest, "Continue. I understand. I'm listening" (Gordon, 1977). You may decide to take verbal encouragers a step further and interject some validating phrases. Some examples of stock phrases you might consider using include:

"That's helpful to know."

"I appreciate your input."

"That is certainly one piece of the puzzle."

You should think about what phrases feel and sound natural to you and practice them so you sound like you really do mean them. Remember, voice tone can make the words sound sincere or phony. Add the word "because" at the end of each stock phrase, and fill in blank. If you appreciate the reason why the stock phrase is true, your voice will likely reflect it (Becker & Wortmann, 2009). In your next conversation with someone, listen for statements from the other person that you want to validate and try out the skill to see how it makes you more engaged in the conversation.

Cautious questioning completes the promoting of continued talking. Most educators are competent questioners, so the caution here is to use minimal questioning. During the listening part of communication, the speaker controls the message. It is always the speaker's "serve." Too intensive and too frequent questioning gives control of the communication to the listener. This is antithetical to the consulting process, which should be about collaboration rather than power and control. Questions should be used to clarify what the speaker has said, so that the listener can understand the message—for example, "Is this what you mean?" or "Please explain what you mean by 'attitude problem." Sometimes you might interject, "That's interesting. Tell me more."

Paraphrasing Skills.   Responsive listening means demonstrating that the listener understands the essence of the message. After listening and using nonverbal and minimal verbal responses, a collaborator who is really listening probably will begin to understand the message of the speaker. To show that the message was heard, or to assess whether what was "heard" was the same message the sender intended and was not altered by distortion, the listener should paraphrase the message. This requires the listener to think carefully about the message and reflect it back to the speaker without changing the content or intent of the message.

There is no simple formula for reflecting or paraphrasing, but two good strategies are to be as accurate as possible and as brief as possible. A paraphrase may begin in one of several ways: "It sounds as if . . ." or "Is what you mean . . . ?" or "So, it seems to me you want [think] [feel] . . ." or "Let me see if I understand. You're saying . . ." Whatever words you use, they should be your own and not "pat phrases" that might be interpreted as manipulative and not sincere. Paraphrasing allows listeners to check their understanding of the message. It is easy to mishear or misinterpret the message, especially if the words are ambiguous. Correct interpretation of the message will result in a nod from the speaker, who may feel that at last someone has really listened. Or the speaker may correct the message by saying, "No, that's not what I meant. It's this way . . ." The listener may paraphrase the emotional part of the message back to the speaker by saying, "You appear to be very frustrated about . . ." By paraphrasing appropriately, a listener demonstrates comprehension of the message or receipt of new information. Just by recognizing a consultee's anger, stress, or frustration, a consultant can begin to build a trusting relationship with a consultee. The listener doesn't necessarily have to agree with the content or emotion that is heard. Rather, the goal is to develop a supportive working relationship via effective communication, paving the way to successful cooperation and problem solving while avoiding conflict and resistance. Practicing reflecting and paraphrasing will make it more natural with time.

Parents often comment that they have approached a teacher with a problem, realizing that they didn't want a specific answer but just a sympathetic ear—a sounding board or a friendly shoulder. This is a very important consideration. Teachers can communicate clearly to parents their interest in the parents' perceptions and ideas by following three simple steps: listen, empathize, and communicate respect (McNaughton & Vostal, 2010). After listening to the parent's concern, teachers can make a statement of empathy (for example, "I can understand why you are concerned."). Consultants communicate respect by thanking the parent for contacting them and arranging their schedule to attend the meeting and by using all of the nonverbal listening skills described in the previous discussion. Responsive listening is important in establishing collaborative relationships and maintaining them. Listening helps build trust over time, the foundation for a good relationship that will be sustained and nurtured over time. It is also a necessary precursor to problem solving in which both parties strive to listen and get a mutual understanding of the problem before a problem is addressed.

So when is responsive listening to be used? The answer is *all* the time. Use it when establishing a relationship, when starting to problem-solve, when emotions are high, when one's conversation doesn't seem to be getting anywhere, and when the speaker seems confused, uncertain, or doesn't know what else to do.

This complex process may not be necessary if two people have already developed a good working relationship and only a word or two is needed for mutual understanding. It also may not be appropriate if one of the two is not willing to talk. Sometimes "communication postponement" is best when one is too tired or too emotionally upset to be a responsive listener. When a consultant cannot listen because of any of these reasons, it is not wise to pretend to be listening while actually thinking about something else or nothing at all. Instead, a reluctant listener should explain that he or she does not have the energy to talk about the problem now but wishes to at a later time (for example, "I need a chance to think about this. May I talk to you later?" or "Look, I'm too upset to work on this very productively right now. Let's talk about it first thing tomorrow."). Responsive listening skills that help avoid blocked communication are summarized in Figure 4.2. The checklist might be useful to review as a reminder of one's goal to be a responsive listener before entering a conversation or problem-solving meeting with a parent or colleague, and then again after the interaction to reflect on the listening skills for future refinement.

FIGURE 4.2 **Responsive Listening Checklist**

	Yes	No
A. *Appropriate Nonverbals*		
1. Good eye contact	_____	_____
2. Facial expression mirrored	_____	_____
3. Body orientation toward other person	_____	_____
B. *Appropriate Verbals*		
1. Door openers	_____	_____
2. Good level of encouraging phrases	_____	_____
3. Cautious questions	_____	_____
C. *Appropriate Responding Behaviors*		
1. Reflected content (paraphrasing)	_____	_____
2. Reflected feelings	_____	_____
3. Brief clarifying questions	_____	_____
4. Summarizations	_____	_____
D. *Avoidance of Roadblocks*		
1. No advice giving	_____	_____
2. No inappropriate questions	_____	_____
3. Minimal volunteered solutions	_____	_____
4. No judging	_____	_____

■ ■ ■ ■ ■ ■

ACTIVITY 4.3
Putting Responsive Listening into Practice

Using the responsive listening checklist in Figure 4.2, find a willing partner such as a classmate, colleague, family member, or friend and have them share a problem situation or something that is bothersome to them. Practice your responsive listening skills. After the interaction, review the checklist together to reflect on what you did well and what areas need improvement. What did you find most difficult to do in responsive listening?

Assertiveness

By the time a consultant has listened effectively and the collaborative relationship has been developed or enhanced, the consultant may be more than ready to start talking. Once the sender's message is understood and emotional levels are reduced, it is the listener's turn to be the sender. Now the consultant gets to talk. However, it is not always easy to communicate one's thoughts, feelings, and opinions without infringing on the rights, feelings, or opinions of others. This is the time for **assertiveness**.

Assertiveness skills allow consultants to achieve their goals without damaging the relationship or another's self-esteem. The basic aspects of assertive communication are:

- Use an "I" message instead of a "you" message.
- Say "and" or "so" instead of "but."
- State the behavior objectively.
- Name your own feelings.
- Say what you want to happen.
- Express concern for others (empathy).
- Use assertive or *active* body language.

Open and honest consultants say what they want to happen and what their feelings are. That does not mean they always get what they want. Saying what you want and how you feel will clarify the picture and ensure that the other(s) won't have to guess what you want or are thinking. Even if others disagree with the ideas and opinions, they can never disagree with the feelings and wishes. Those are very personal and are expressed in a personal manner by starting the interaction with "I," rather than presenting feelings and opinions as truth or expert answers.

In stating an idea or position assertively, consultants should describe the problem in terms of its impact on them, rather than in terms of what was done or said by the other person. "I feel let down" works better than "You didn't follow through on what we agreed to." If a consultant makes a "you" statement about the consultee that the consultee thinks is wrong, the consultant will only get an angry reaction and the concerns will be ignored.

When communicating, collaborating consultants should avoid the mannerism known as a rising inflection, where one's voice rises at the ends of sentences in a questioning way and is heard as being unsure and indecisive.

Video Example from YouTube

ENHANCEDetext
Video Example 4.4.

Watch American poet and teacher, Tayor Mali address this issue. (https://www.youtube .com/watch?v=SCNIBV87wV4)

Concern for Others During the Interaction. Expressing concern for others can take many forms. This skill demonstrates that although people have thoughts and feelings that differ from those of others, they can still respect the feelings and ideas of others. "I realize that this student's outbursts can present a tremendous challenge when you are trying to manage twenty-five other children in your classroom." This statement shows the consulting teacher understands the management problems of the classroom teacher. As the consultant goes on to state preferences in working with the teacher, the teacher is more likely to listen and work cooperatively. The consultee will see that the consultant is aware of the problems that must be dealt with daily. "It seems to me that . . .," "I understand . . .," "I realize . . .," and "It looks like . . ." are phrases consultants can use to express concern for the other person in the collaborative relationship. If the consultant cannot complete these sentences with the appropriate information, the next step is to go back to the listening part of the communication and encourage the person to tell you more.

Also important when considering the feelings of others and moving a relationship forward, is to think about the *way* questions are asked. Do your questions empower or disempower a colleague or parent? Contrast these disempowering questions, "Why hasn't this been implemented?" or "Whose idea was this?" with questions that empower the individual, "How do you feel about the way the plan is being implemented?" or "Describe the way you would like this project to turn out." By learning how to use questions in an empowering way, consultants encourage teamwork and build relationships (Marquardt, 2014).

How To Be Concerned and Assertive.   Assertive people own their personal feelings and opinions. Being aware of this helps them state their wants and feelings. "You" sentences sound accusing, even when that is not intended, which can lead to defensiveness in others. For example, saying to a parent, "You should provide a place and quiet time for Hannah to do her homework," is more accusatory than saying, "I am frustrated when Hannah isn't getting her homework done, and I would like to work with you to think of some ways to help her get it done." Using "and" rather than "but" is particularly important in expressing thoughts without diminishing a relationship. "But" is an erasure word. This is a particularly challenging assertion skill. To the listener the word "but" deletes the preceding phrase and prevents the intended message from coming through. Starting with validation builds trust, and when you use connective words like "and" or "so" instead of "but," it allows you to deliver your message in a way that will be heard and better received. It doesn't mean that you need to get rid of the word "but"; it means that when giving negative feedback, or conversing in emotionally charged situations, avoid using the word.

It is important to state behaviors specifically. By describing behaviors objectively, a consultant or consultee sounds less judgmental. It is easy to let blaming and judgmental words creep into language. Without meaning to, the speaker erects a barrier that blocks communication and the relationship. Be concise, rather than verbose, in your communication. Otherwise, your important message is likely to get lost because the other words distract the listener. Also, be careful not to disqualify your statements before, during or after you reply. Examples of disqualifying phrases are: "I think," "I don't know," or "I guess." Sometimes people wait until they get to the end of a statement and then say something like: "I'll implement this one, I guess." Be definitive and decisive in the words you use.

Conveying concern and assertiveness at the same time might not come naturally at first. If you are confronting a difficult situation, you might find it helpful to write down how you will phrase what you want to say and practice saying it aloud until it feels natural and you are comfortable with the words and phrasing. If you are writing a letter, email or text, you can often catch yourself when you reread a message and see how it sounds. If you are saying it verbally, on the spot, you can't go back and erase what you said. Think before you speak. Silence is a powerful tool. It allows you to stop the noise and collect your words, and it reels your audience back in.

Assertive communication includes showing supportive body language. A firm voice, straight posture, eye contact, and body orientation toward the receiver of the message will

■ ■ ■ ■ ■ ■

ACTIVITY 4.4
Communicating Positively

Compare the following two statements:

1. "I would like to have a schedule of rehearsals for the holiday music program. It is frustrating when I make a special trip to the school to work with Jillian and Emilio, only to find they are practicing for the musical program and can't come to the resource room."
2. "When you don't let me know ahead of time that the girls won't be allowed to come and work with me, I have to waste my time driving here and can't get anything accomplished anywhere."

Which of these two statements is less judgmental and accusatory? How might these two contrasting statements create differing listener attitudes toward the speaker? For many listeners, the judgmental words and phrases in the second sentence ("you don't let me know," "won't be allowed," "waste my time") sound blaming. They introduce an array of red flags. With a discussion partner or small group, discuss times you felt someone was being judgmental or accusatory toward you. Think of some difficult conversations you might encounter and work together to write down ways to say what you want to happen using the skills discussed here.

have a desirable effect. Assertive body language affirms that the sender owns his or her own feelings and opinions but also respects the other person's feelings and opinions. This is a difficult and delicate balance to achieve. Body language and verbal language must match or the messages will be confusing. Skills for being assertive are given in Figure 4.3.

FIGURE 4.3   Assertiveness Checklist

	Usually	Sometimes	Never
1. Conveys "I" instead of "you" message			
2. Says "and" or "so" rather than "but"			
3. States behavior objectively			
4. Says what he or she wants to have happen			
5. States feelings			
6. Expresses concern			
7. Speaks firmly, clearly			
8. Has assertive posture			
9. Avoids aggressive language			

What we say and how we say it have a tremendous impact on the reactions and acceptance of others. When consultants and consultees communicate in ways that accurately reflect their feelings and focus on objective descriptions of behavior and situations, and then think in a concrete manner about what they want to happen, assertive communication will succeed in building strong, respectful relationships. Assertive communication is the basis for solving problems and resolving conflicts.

How to Practice Mindful Communication. In her book, *The Five Keys to Mindful Communication*, Susan Chapman (2012) uses the metaphor of a changing traffic light in thinking about the communication interaction being open, closed, or somewhere in between. When the light is green, there is a two-way traffic flow to the conversation. The red light symbolizes that communication has shut down and at least one person is no longer listening. This red light phase can be brief or prolonged, but in the context of our discussion here, it is clearly something consultants want to avoid. If the communication light turns yellow, we should engage in what Chapman calls mindful communication. What do you do when you approach a traffic light and it turns yellow? People usually respond in one of two ways; they speed up or they slow down and proceed with caution. The latter reaction will likely result in the best outcome when applying this metaphor to communication and consultants working with others. Consider a situation where a parent or colleague becomes accusatory or makes a comment that causes you to feel defensive. The comment can trigger many responses. Your muscles might tighten, and your first thought is to defend yourself or even lash out with a comment that you will later regret. These reactions will only serve to halt the communication. If we apply **mindful communication** strategies, the symbolic yellow light reminds us to slow down and take a closer look at what is happening. It is a moment of choice, and the way we respond will take the communication interaction, and the relationship, back to green or to red. Often, this is when we need to listen more or say, "Tell me why you feel that way or why you asked the question." At times like this, you must muster all you have learned about responsive listening and withholding judgment. Be mindful of the filters both parties have in place when we communicate with each other. In your mind, imagine a fork in the road where you have the power to take the communication and relationship down one of two paths. Which will serve the student best and increase the likelihood of future effective collaborations?

The Art of Apologizing

Sometimes, despite good communication skills and careful relationship building and problem solving, consultants make errors and mistakes. Good consultants never blame someone else for communication breakdowns; they accept responsibility for their own communication. This is demonstrated when a consultant says, "Let me explain in a different way" instead of conveying, "Can't you understand?" Good collaborative consultants cultivate the art of apologizing.

One of the biggest misconceptions in the area of consultation and collaboration is that apologizing puts consulting teachers and classroom teachers at a disadvantage when working with colleagues and parents. It is simply not true that strong, knowledgeable people never say they're sorry. In fact, apologizing is a powerful strategy because it demonstrates understanding, honesty, confidence, and trust. Apologizing offers a chance to mend fences in professional relationships so that all can continue to trust in one another and in the relationship. When you make a mistake that has in some way hurt or offended others, start with an apology. An apology is a statement that sincerely conveys your regret for your role in causing—or failing to prevent—pain or difficulty to others (Patterson, Grenny, McMillan, & Switzler, 2012). "I'm sorry I didn't consult with you before I brought this up to the student's parents. I can understand why you felt blindsided when his mother called you and asked about the new schedule. I apologize." Remember, an apology isn't really an apology unless you truly regret what happened. To offer a sincere apology, your motives have to change. You may have to sacrifice a bit of your ego by admitting your mistake, but by doing so, you acknowledge it and can then put it aside and move forward with a healthy dialogue without unspoken resentment in the air. Some suggestions from psychologist Barry Lubetkin (1997) about how to apologize include allowing the person you've wronged to vent her or his feelings first, apologizing as soon as possible, and refraining from inserting "but" after "I'm sorry." State the apology once and let that be enough. Most importantly, apologies are empty if you keep repeating the behavior or the mistake.

Sometimes you need to fix a misunderstanding rather than apologize. Someone on the team may feel disrespected even though you feel you did nothing disrespectful. When others misinterpret your purpose or intent, step out of the argument and rebuild a healthy dialogue by using a skill Patterson et al. (2012) refers to as "Contrasting." Contrasting is a don't/do statement that:

- Addresses concerns of others that you don't respect them or have an ulterior motive (the *don't* part)
- Acknowledges your respect or clarifies your purpose (the *do* part)

For example:

[The *don't* part] "The last thing I wanted to do was to communicate that I don't value the time you spend at home working with Abby on her reading.

[The *do* part] I think your commitment to listening to Abby read every night is commendable."

Now you are able to move on and continue problem solving having addressed the hard feelings that were unintended consequences of something you or others said.

ROADBLOCKS TO COMMUNICATION

Roadblocks to communication are barriers to successful interaction, halting the development of effective collaborative relationships. They may be verbal behaviors or nonverbal behaviors that send out messages such as, "I'm not listening," or "Your ideas and feelings are not important." Responsible collaborating consultants most assuredly do not intend to send blocking messages. But by being busy, not concentrating, using poor listening skills, or allowing themselves to be directed by filters such as emotions and judgment, well-meaning collaborating consultants inadvertently send blocking messages.

Nonverbal Roadblocks

Nonverbal roadblocks include facing or looking away when the speaker talks; displaying inappropriate facial expressions such as smiling when the sender is saying something serious; distracting actions such as repetitively tapping a pencil, twirling hair around your finger, or checking messages on your cell phone or other device while "listening." Interrupting a speaker to attend to something or someone else—an alert message on a cell phone, someone walking by or a conversation in the hall, or a knock at the door—also halts communication and contributes in a subtle way toward undermining the spirit of collaboration.

Verbal Roadblocks

Gordon (1977) proposes twelve verbal barriers to communication. These have been called the "dirty dozen," and they can be grouped into three types of verbal roadblocks that prevent meaningful interaction (Bolton, 1986):

1. Judging
2. Sending solutions
3. Avoiding others' concerns

The first category, judging, includes criticizing, name-calling, and diagnosing or analyzing why a person is behaving a particular way. False or nonspecific praise and evaluative words or phrases send a message of judgment toward the speaker. "You're not thinking clearly," "You'll do a wonderful job implementing the RTI (Response to Intervention) curriculum-based assessment model in your classroom," or "You don't really believe that—you're just tired today" are examples of judging. (Notice that each of these statements begins with the word "you.") Avoiding judgment about parents or others helps teachers avoid deficit-based thinking which hurts everyone it touches. If the goal is to impact the lives of students in sustainable ways, collaborating teachers must play the role of partner with families and help them support their children's needs. Communicate by listening to co-workers' or families' concerns and work together (Edwards & Da Fonte, 2012). Nonjudgmental communication conveys equity in the relationship, which is a critical factor in teamwork.

Educators are particularly adept with the second category of verbal roadblocks—sending solutions. These include directing or ordering, warning, moralizing or preaching, advising, and using logical arguments or lecturing. A few of these can become a careless consultant's entire verbal repertoire. "Stop complaining," and "Don't talk like that," and "If you don't start monitoring Jim's oral reading fluency on a more consistent basis . . ." are examples of directing or warning. Moralizing sends a message of "I'm a better educator than you are." Such communication usually starts with "You should . . ." or "You ought to . . ."

When consultees have problems, the last thing they need is to be told what they *should* do. Avoid giving the impression that you are more concerned with rules or *shoulds* than with the relationship.

Advising, lecturing, and logical argument are all too often part of the educator's tools of the trade. Teachers tend to use these roadblock types of communication techniques frequently with students. The habits they develop cause them to overlook the reality that use of such tactics with adults can drive a wedge into an already precarious relationship. Consultants must avoid such tactics as assuming the posture of the "sage-on-the-stage," imparting wisdom, lecturing, moralizing, and advising. Unfortunately, these methods imply superiority, which is detrimental to the collaborative process.

Avoiding others' concerns is a third category of verbal roadblocks that is often entered into with good intentions but without thinking what message is being received. This category implies "no big deal" to the message-receiver. Avoidance messages include reassuring or sympathizing, such as "You'll feel better tomorrow" or "Everyone goes through this stage." Other avoidance messages include intensive questioning in the manner of "The Grand Inquisition," and humoring or distracting, "Let's get off this subject and talk about something more pleasant." Avoiding the concerns that others express sends the message that their concerns are not important.

When consultants use roadblocks, they are making themselves, their feelings, and their opinions the focus of the interaction, rather than allowing the focus to be the issues, concerns, or problems of the consultee. Because it is so easy to use a communication block inadvertently through speaking, it is wise to remember the adage, "We are blessed with two ears and one mouth, a constant reminder that we should listen twice as much as we talk." Indeed, the more one talks, the more likely a person is to make errors, and the less opportunity that person will have to learn something.

ACTIVITY 4.5

Roadblocks You Use or May Have Used Unknowingly

After viewing this video (https://www.youtube.com/watch?v=RBXOjvWbtJk&spfreload=1) about roadblocks to communication, did you find yourself thinking, "I've done that, but I didn't think about it being perceived that way. My intentions were good"? Which of the roadblocks have you used that you will now be more aware of and try to avoid in the future?

Terms, Labels, and Phrases as Roadblocks

Inappropriate use of terms and labels can erect roadblocks to communication. Educators should adhere to the following points when speaking or writing about people with disabilities:

- Do not focus on the disability label, but focus instead on educational needs or accommodations or issues affecting quality of life for them, such as housing, assistive technology needs, and employment opportunities.

- Do not portray successful people with disabilities as superhuman, for all persons with disabilities cannot achieve this level of success.
- Use people-first language, such as "a student on the autism spectrum" rather than "an autistic student."
- Emphasize abilities and not limitations, such as "uses a wheelchair" rather than "wheelchair-bound."
- Terms such as "physically challenged" are considered condescending, and saying "victim of " is regarded as sensationalizing.
- Do not imply disease by saying "patient" or "case" when discussing disabilities.

Acceptable, up-to-date terminology facilitates active listening and verbal communication.

Microaggressions

Microaggressions are best described as brief, everyday exchanges that send denigrating or disparaging message to a target group like multicultural and multiracial persons, religious and ethnic minorities, women, persons with disabilities, and LGBT individuals (Sue, 2010). Examples might include:

"You speak good English" sends the message, "You are not American."

"We're not going to worry about her taking upper-level math classes; the basics will be sufficient" sends the message, "Females are less capable in STEM-related areas."

Someone begins pushing a student's wheelchair without asking if assistance is needed sends the message, "You can't do anything by yourself because you have a disability."

Only recognizing holidays of the dominant culture in the school sends the message, "Your holidays need to be celebrated on your own time or with your own family; they aren't important."

Students using the term "gay" to describe a fellow student who is seen as different or not fitting in sends the message, "People who are weird and different are 'gay.'"

Staring or making under-the-table remarks when two same-sex partners come for a child's parent-teacher conference sends the message, "Your relationship is not acceptable in school."

Collaborative consultants must be aware of their own language and actions and the resultant messages. Modeling appropriate attitudes, language, and behavior and standing up for others when microaggressions occur, is both good professional practice and the ethical course of action. Often, a person doesn't realize the microaggression or was unaware of how words or actions were interpreted. Making the person aware in a private, tactful, and sensitive way, without lashing out or embarrassing them will send the right message. Educating students and co-workers about microaggression shows that insensitive and hurtful comments will not be ignored.

MANAGING RESISTANCE, NEGATIVITY, ANGER, AND CONFLICT

Communication is the key to collaboration and problem solving. Without back-and-forth discussions, there can be no agreement. Problem solving often breaks down because communications break down first, either because people aren't paying attention, or they misunderstand the other side, or emotions were not dealt with as a separate and primary issue.

In problem solving, it is critical to separate the person from the problem. Collaborative consultants will often find themselves needing to deal with emotions, along with any errors in perceptions or communication, as separate issues that must be resolved on their own. Masking emotions and avoiding difficult issues may seem like the most professional and appropriate way to handle emotional encounters, but studies suggest this often leads to deterioration in the relationship (Kramer & Tan, 2006). Expressing the emotions and addressing the issues can lead to positive outcomes if done in the proper time and place. Ignoring emotions during conflict is unrealistic. Conflict is rarely a dispassionate exercise between relative strangers weighing the pros and cons of an issue objectively. Rather than ignore emotions as being counterproductive, we should accept them as an integral factor in the conflict process. Emotions may take the forms of resistance, anger, negativity, or outright conflict. If emotions are not recognized and dealt with skillfully, they may become barriers to effective communication. Sometimes, regardless of how diplomatic people are in dealing with the emotions of others, they run into barriers of resistance in their attempts to communicate.

It is estimated that as much as 80 percent of problem solving with others is getting through the resistance. Resistance is a trait of human nature that surfaces when people are asked to change. Researchers have found that people resist change for a number of reasons. They may:

- Have a vested interest in the status quo
- Have low tolerance for change
- Feel strongly that the change would be undesirable
- Be unclear about what the change would entail or bring about
- Fear the unknown

Resistance often has nothing to do with an individual personally, or even with the new idea. The resistance is simply a reaction to change of any kind. Change often makes people defensive. However, it is good to remember the adage from a wise person, "Change is the only thing that is permanent."

Many people get defensive or resistant or just stop listening when others disagree with them. This may happen because they feel they are being attacked personally. Parents who are asked what time a sleepy student goes to bed at night may become defensive because they feel you are attacking or questioning their parenting, even though you may just want to rule out lack of sleep for some of the behaviors the child is exhibiting in the classroom.

Why Collaborative Partners Resist

It is human nature to be uncomfortable when another person disagrees. It is also human nature to get upset when someone resists efforts to make changes, implement plans, or modify programs for children with special needs. The need for change can generate powerful emotions. Most people are uncomfortable when experiencing the strong emotions of others. When someone shouts or argues, the first impulse is to become defensive, argue the other point of view, and defend one's own ideas. Although a school consultant may intend to remain cool, calm, and collected in the interactions that involve students with special needs, occasionally another individual says something that pushes a "hot button" and the consultant becomes upset, or angry, or defensive.

Special education consulting teachers who had been asked to describe examples of resistance they have experienced from classroom teachers toward their roles provided these examples:

- Some classroom teachers won't come right out and say it, but they feel they aren't responsible for students on IEPs.
- They act excited about an idea when it is proposed but never get around to doing it.
- They won't discuss it with you, but they do so with others behind your back.
- They may try initially but then give up too soon.
- They take out their frustrations on the students.
- They say that a proposed strategy won't work in their situation.
- They dredge up a past example where something similar didn't work.
- They keep asking for more and more details or information before trying an idea.
- They change the subject, or suddenly have to be somewhere else.
- They state that there is not enough time to implement the strategy.
- They are simply silent.
- They make it clear that they just prefer the status quo.

When resistance spawns counter-resistance and anger, an upward spiral of emotion is created that can make consulting unpleasant and painful. Bolton (1986) describes resistance as a push/push back phenomenon. When a person meets resistance with more resistance, defensiveness, logical argument, or any other potential roadblock, resistance increases and dialogue can develop into open warfare. Then the dialogue may become personal or hurtful. Nobody listens at that point, and a potentially healthy relationship is damaged and very difficult to salvage.

How to Deal with Resistance and Negativity

An important strategy for dealing with resistance and defensiveness is to handle one's own defensiveness, stop pushing so that the other person will not be able to push-back, delay reactions, keep quiet, and *listen*. This takes practice, patience, tolerance, and commitment. It is important to deal with emotions such as resistance, defensiveness, or anger before proceeding to problem solving. People are not inclined to listen until they have been listened to. They will not be convinced of another's sincerity and openness, or become capable of thinking logically, when the filter of emotions is clouding their thinking.

Negative people and negative emotions sap the energy of educational consultants. Reactions to negativity, conflict, and resistance can block communication and ruin potentially productive relationships. It is important to remember that negative people are not going to change. The person who has to change is the consultant. Negative people tend to harp on the bad things and ignore the positive. They also have a tendency to exaggerate issues, making the situation seem worse than it actually is.

The first point is not to engage in the negativity. When you converse with the negative person for the first time, provide a listening ear and empathy. If the person keeps harping on the same issues after the first few conversations, then it is time to disengage. Try changing topics, and if the person insists on continuing the negative banter, let it continue but don't engage in the negativity. Give a simple reply such as "I see" or "Okay." If you hear anything positive from the person, be sure to give affirmation and reply with enthusiasm.

Refrain from taking negativity personally. Negative people can be quite critical at times. If the negative comments are directed at you, it is natural to be bothered by the words and start questioning whether there is something wrong with you. If you observe their interactions with others, you may see similar negativity being directed at them as well, and realize the person's comments are not so much personal attacks but just the way the person deals with everyone. It is more about personality style than about you or something you did or didn't do. Such individuals just may be having a bad time at that point in their lives. A positive approach would be to deal with negativity as a challenge from which much can be learned about working with people. When there is a breakthrough in the communication and problem solving, such folks can become one's staunchest allies and supporters.

Accommodating negative or resistant school colleagues or family members of students at their best times and on their turf can be a first step toward this alliance. Communicate in writing in order to diffuse emotional reactions and convey the message one wishes to send. Following up later and remaining patient will model a spirit of acceptance that is spiced with invincibility and yet grounded in purpose.

One of the keys to working with difficult people is controlling one's own behavior (Ury, 1991). The natural reaction to resistance, challenges, and negativity is to strike back, give in, or break off the communication. But a negative reaction to resistance leads to a vicious cycle of action and reaction and eventual breakdowns of communication and relationships.

■ ■ ■ ■ ■ ▬▬▬▬▬▬▬▬▬▬▬▬▬▬▬▬▬▬▬▬▬▬

ACTIVITY 4.6
Managing Resistance

Construct a problem situation involving another person that could happen, or has happened, in your school context, and interact with a colleague to try these communication techniques:

Dismiss the negativity with "You may be right" and keep moving forward. Be assertive, as in, "I am bothered by discussing the negative side of things." Ask for complaints in writing (because some people don't realize how negative they sound). Ask for clarification, also, by suggesting that the person describe the problem and clarify the desired outcome. This leads people to think about positive actions. Don't defend attacks, and invite critique and advice instead. Ask what's wrong. Look for interests behind resistance, negativity, and anger by asking questions. Tentatively agree by saying "that's one opinion."

Switch roles and try another episode. Then have a debriefing session to critique the interactions.

Consultants must "hear their way to success" in managing resistance. This may take five minutes, or it may take months and months of careful relationship building. Colleagues cannot always avoid disagreements that are serious enough to create anger and resistance. A comment or question delivered in the wrong manner at the wrong time may be the "hot button" that triggers the antagonism. Consider remarks such as these:

"How can you expect the student to become independent if he always has a para at his side?"

"It doesn't appear that the behavior plan is being implemented in your classroom as it is written. Aren't you aware that you are legally responsible for implementing it?"

"Why don't you teach in a way to accommodate different learning styles?"

"You penalize students who are academically advanced when you keep the class in lockstep with basal readers."

"Shouldn't students be learning their own material rather than tutoring their peers (or younger students)?"

Such remarks can make harried, overworked classroom teachers defensive and resentful. If an occasion arises in which a teacher or parent becomes angry or resistant, responding in the right way will prevent major breakdowns in the communication that is needed.

Why People Get Angry

Anger is felt when a situation is perceived as unfair or threatening, and the person angered feels helpless to rectify that situation. Differences of opinions, values, and behaviors exacerbate these feelings. Coyle (2000) explains anger as a secondary feeling that follows frustration, unmet expectations, loss of self-respect, or fear. The anger is accompanied by anxiety and powerlessness, changing into feelings or actions of power and fight. Anger is directly proportional to a person's feeling of powerlessness. If you ask angry people to tell you what they want, you give them power, thereby reducing their feeling of powerlessness. A growing body of evidence indicates that even minor shifts in a person's mood can exert strong influences on ability to act and think clearly (Axelrod & Johnson, 2005). A person who is in a positive mood tends to see the world in a more positive way, stating that the glass is half full. In contrast, when people are in a negative mindset, they are more receptive to negative interpretations of events and a cynical outlook on life and those around them. For them the glass is half empty. Strong emotions create what has been identified as a cognitive deficit, a reduced ability to formulate rational plans of action, or to rationally evaluate potential outcomes of behaviors. This heightened emotional state can cause people to act in ways that are self-defeating and interfere with the rational pursuit of their actual interests. And sometimes "people vent their anger at those giving them the most help because they feel comfortable directing it there. In most instances, angered people feel unjustly victimized and blame others for their pain and anguish" (Coyle, 2000, p. 43).

How to Deal with the Anger.   Are you a person who avoids conflict at all costs? Do you prefer to avoid disagreements and arguments because you don't like conflict? Do you put your head in the sand and wait for the disagreement to blow over? "Conflict" is not a dirty word and it is not effective to simply ignore or avoid it. Avoiding a difficult conversation *is* a response. Unresolved conflict leads to anger, which undermines morale and thwarts productivity. Many avoid confronting conflict out of a fear of what might happen if they address it. They may fear hurting someone's feelings, worry they won't have control of their emotions, or they just don't want to "stir the pot." Just as the concept of emotional intelligence has been identified with successful people who have the ability to regulate and learn from their emotional experiences, Axelrod and Johnson (2005) have proposed that people would be well served by developing a form of conflict intelligence. It is important for the collaborative consultant to respond appropriately to angry people. Resist the temptation to react negatively toward the other person, even if you think it is deserved. A harsh response can escalate the conflict, undermine your position, and make it less likely that you will resolve the issue in a positive manner. Instead, use techniques to preserve your calm and de-escalate the other person's negative emotions. The first rule is to address the problem rather than the person, and then seek to find a shared goal with the angry person. Defer judgment and together explore options. When an angry person is loud and belligerent, speak more softly and calmly. Listen intently with responsiveness, not reaction.

When someone is difficult or challenging, try to see the situation from that person's point of view. Put aside any negative feelings about the situation or the other person and focus on the person's feelings about the situation. Give the person an opportunity to air their grievances or vent and be heard. Perhaps say something along the lines of, "Tell me what happened" or "Tell me what's upsetting you." Get to know them as people, not problems. Let the person know ways you appreciate them, such as how they greet all the students as they walk into the classroom or how that person always shows support of students by attending the extra-curricular activities. The idea is to find something where you can show your appreciation in a personal and individualized way and in a manner that is genuine and feels authentic to the receiver. Even saying, "I appreciate your being honest with me and sharing your concerns. I value our working relationship and I know this meeting was not easy," will set the course of future encounters in a positive direction. Transform an "I versus you" conversation into a "we versus the problem" dialogue.

Why Conflict Occurs in School Contexts

Conflict is an inevitable part of life. It occurs when there are unreconciled differences among people in terms of needs, values, goals, and personalities. If conflicting parties cannot give and take by integrating their views and using their differences constructively, interpersonal conflicts will escalate. It is important to develop tools for transforming vague and ambiguous sources of conflict into identified problems that can be solved collaboratively. Conflict is inevitable when working with others around difficult issues, and there are many positive aspects to be valued. Conflict can help clarify issues, increase involvement, and promote growth, as well as strengthen relationships and organizational systems when the issues are resolved. It is not advisable to avoid conflict when there is genuine disagreement because resentments build up, feelings get displaced, and unpleasant conditions such as backbiting, gossiping, and general discontent may result.

Teachers, administrators, and parents face many possible occasions for conflict when they are involved with educating children who have special needs. Some conflicts occur because there is too little information or because misunderstandings have been created from incorrect information. These instances are not difficult to resolve because they require only the communication of facts. Other areas of conflict arise from disagreement over teaching methods, learning and behavioral goals, assessment methods, and values.

Parent goals and teacher goals for the exceptional student may differ significantly, and support personnel may add even more dimensions to the conflict. At times a parent may criticize a general education teacher or lash out at administrators or school/district policies they feel are standing in the way of their child's success. When this occurs, consulting teachers who do not have a well-practiced communication strategy might fall into the trap of criticizing those who are not present. This might be done because they too feel some of the same frustrations as the parent or maybe they want to position themselves on the side of the parent in contrast to their absent colleague. Showing empathy is one thing, but if the consultant criticizes others, it may further erode the parents' confidence in their child's teacher or the school or district.

In addition to cautioning teachers not to criticize others to parents, McNaughton and Vostal (2010) also remind us not to react hastily and promise something we can't deliver. A wise building contractor once said, "It is better to under-promise and over-deliver than to over-promise and under-deliver." Consultants might find that helpful in their roles as well. Some conflict can even be beneficial if it clears the air of lingering disagreement and doubt so conflicting parties can move ahead. But if differences cannot be resolved through formal or informal conflict-resolution processes, then relationships will surely disintegrate.

Perhaps the most difficult area of conflict relates to values. When people have differing values about children, education, or educator roles within the learning context, effective communication is a challenging goal. As discussed earlier in this chapter, rapport building, listening, and paraphrasing are significant in building relationships among those whose values are in conflict. The most important step is to listen courteously until a clear message about the value comes through, demonstrating respect for the value even if it clashes with yours. Then it is time to assert one's own values and, along with the other person, try to reach a common goal or seek a practical issue on which to begin problem solving (Knackendoffel, Robinson, Deshler, & Schumkaer, 1992).

How to Resolve School-Related Conflicts

Some conflicts, particularly those involving values, are difficult to prevent and may seem at the time to be irresolvable. However, if all can agree to common goals or common ground for discussion, conflicts can be resolved.

Resolving conflicts within an "everybody wins" philosophy requires using the listening skills described earlier in the chapter to find common ground. In dealing with emotions of the speaker, the listener must concentrate with an open mind and attend to the speaker's feelings as well as facts or ideas that are part of the message. The listener must strive to hear the whole story without interrupting, even if there are strong feelings of disagreement. Conflict usually means that intense emotions are involved. Only by concentrating on the message with an open mind can all parties begin to deal with the conflict. Emotional filters often function as blinders. If the emotions cannot be overcome, the best tactic is to postpone the communication, using assertive responses to do so.

Consultants and consulting teachers must put aside preconceived notions about their own expertise and learn from those who often know the student best—family members and classroom teachers. Such consultees respond positively to open-ended questions that let them know they are respected and needed. When consultants open their own minds, they unlock the potential of others.

■ ■ ■ ■ ■ ■

ACTIVITY 4.7
Practice Makes Perfect, or Easier at Least!

With a partner, practice the following ten uncomfortable or embarrassing situations. Use the figures in this chapter to monitor verbal and nonverbal communication, for both sending and receiving.

1. Ask a person who drops by to come back later.
2. Say "no" to someone who is urging you to help with a project.
3. Answer the phone when you have at least three things going on. (Voice tone and rate are particularly pertinent here.)
4. Receive a compliment graciously.
5. Deliver a compliment so that it is not a distorted message or patronizing in tone.
6. Ask a colleague to please (for once!) be on time.
7. Ask an IEP team member to please refrain from checking text messages during a meeting.
8. Respond when someone has interrupted you.
9. Break into the conversation when someone has monopolized the discussion to everyone's frustration.
10. Apologize for an oversight or an ill-chosen remark you made.

As you feel more confident in these real-life "peak" and "pit" situations, think of similar difficult situations you have faced and practice your responses until they become second nature. Then use them!

After listening constructively, consultants need to help establish ground rules for resolving the conflict. The ground rules should express support, mutual respect, and a commitment to the process. Again, this requires talking and listening, dialoguing, and keeping an open mind. It is important not to dominate the dialogue at this time, and by the same token not to let the other person dominate the conversation. This part of the

FIGURE 4.4   Checklist for Managing Resistance and Conflict

A. *Responsive Listening*

1. Had assertive posture   _____

2. Used appropriate nonverbal listening   _____

3. Did not become defensive   _____

4. Used minimal verbals in listening   _____

5. Reflected content   _____

6. Reflected feelings   _____

7. Let others do most of the talking   _____

8. Used only brief, clarifying questions   _____

B. *Assertiveness*

9. Did not use roadblocks such as giving advice   _____

10. Used "I" messages   _____

11. Stated wants and feelings   _____

C. *Recycled the interaction*

12. Used positive postponement   _____

13. Did not problem-solve before emotions were controlled   _____

14. Summarized   _____

15. Set time to meet again, if applicable   _____

communication might be called "agreeing to disagree," with the intent of "agreeing to find a point of agreement." It is important to share the allotted interaction time equitably and in a way that facilitates understanding. Consultants must use precise language without exaggerating points, or, as discussed earlier, flaunting "educationese" or taking inappropriate shortcuts with jargon and alphabet soup acronyms.

Although there may be resistance after each assertion, it will gradually dissipate so that *real* communication and collaboration can begin to take place. Figure 4.4 summarizes useful steps for managing resistance and conflict.

WAYS TECHNOLOGY FACILITATES COMMUNICATION FOR COLLABORATION

A chapter about communication without a discussion about the role of technology in collaboration would be incomplete. The Pew Research Center's report, "American's Internet Access: 2000–2015 (Perrin & Duggan, 2015) reports that more than 84 percent of the U.S.

population had Internet access in 2015, and 94 percent of that group uses the Internet to send or read email. If the growing number of instant messages and text messages—not to mention tweets and numerous other forms of social media—are added, the volume of electronic messages sent daily for work and pleasure is staggering. Many do not stop to consider how these hurried messages are being received or interpreted. Even in school settings, educators are sending electronic messages instead of writing letters, calling, or meeting face-to-face—amazingly, sometimes to colleagues just down the hall. Lines have become blurred regarding what is acceptable practice concerning the use of electronic communication with students, families, colleagues, and others. Privacy issues must be considered as well.

Over the past forty years, we have seen unprecedented advances in electronic communication. Today, numerous devices such as smartphones and portable tablet devices provide constant and instant access to information via the Internet. The Internet facilitates access to information, allows for asynchronous communication (i.e., outside the constraints of time and place), and thus increases opportunities for collaboration. New and different ways of communicating and collaborating with each other are appearing almost daily. **Web 2.0 tools**, such as Twitter, YouTube, Google Search, Google Docs/Drive, Dropbox, Facebook, WordPress, Skype, Evernote, Pinterest, and Linkedin, to name just a few, have grown from relative obscurity a few short years ago into the emerging top ten tools for learning in 2015 (Center for Learning and Performing Technologies, 2015).

Email has largely taken over the letter's place as a ubiquitous form of communication. It has many advantages over more abbreviated types of instant messages when used for school-based collaboration with colleagues, community organizations, and families. Yet, it can facilitate *or* can hinder ongoing collaborative efforts. Because electronic communication lacks "tone of voice," body-language signals, and other nonverbal elements, it will be more difficult for educators to get a message across clearly; the unfortunate result could be serious miscommunication. An unread email, a misinterpreted message, or unclear communication related to an email, tweet, or text message requires extra time and work to repair the damage caused. Once the "send" button is pushed, you can't get it back. The adage "You can't un-ring a bell" comes to mind. Sometimes in our haste to send a message quickly, we forget to double-check our spelling as carefully as we might if we were sending a printed form of communication. Who hasn't experienced the embarrassment of "auto-correct" disasters? When we sent something to teachers, staff, administrators, or families, we want to represent ourselves in a professional way.

Figure 4.5 includes a list of "educators' spelling demons." Many are troublesome to spell, others are hard to select because another word is similar, and even with spell check, some can be missed.

Some might argue that even email is now outdated with the rise of rapid-fire messaging. The incoming generation does very little with email (Pogue, 2015). They may have an email account but they rarely check it and prefer the more direct, more efficient electronic memos, such as texting, Facebook, and Twitter messages. The reason? Time is often cited. It is much quicker to send a text and it often results in an instant response. However, those advantages may also come with a high cost to consulting teachers. The same cautions discussed throughout this chapter about responding too quickly, without reflection on how a message will be perceived, can have disastrous consequences in the context of school collaboration. As younger generations of teachers enter the profession, they would be wise to

FIGURE 4.5   Educators' Spelling Demons List

Educators' Spelling Demons List

Here is a list of spelling "demons" that haunt educators who are not good spellers. Written communication must be as clear and as accurate as possible; parents and students do notice. The focus is on words that teachers use often in their professional notes and letters.

abbreviate	complement, compliment	parallel
absence	consensus	penicillin
albeit	consistent	personal, personnel
all right	criticize, criticism	persuade
a lot	critique	pompon
accelerate	curiosity	principal, principle
accept, except	curriculum	precede, proceed
accessible	data are, datum is	professional
accommodate	definitely	pronunciation
accompany	dependence	pursue
achieve, achievement	desert, dessert	questionnaire
acquaintance	develop, development	receive
adolescence, adolescent	documentary	recognize
advice, advise	embarrass	recommend
affect, effect	exceed	referral
agenda	existent, existence	relevant
allotment	expertise	repetition
analyze, analysis	fulfill	resistant
apparent	grammar	scenario
assessment	harass	separate
athletic	implement	stationary, stationery
baccalaureate	individualize	strategy
behavioral	irrelevant, relevance	succeed
beneficial	its, it's	superintendent
benefitted	kindergarten	their, there
biannual, biennial	knowledgeable	therefore
calendar	liaison	they're
capabilities	license	thorough, through
capital, capitol	lightning, lightening	thought, through
changeable	maintenance	to too, two
choose, chose	marshmallow	truly
collaboration	misspelled	unmistakable
colleagues	niece	usable
concede	occurrence	weather, whether
commitment	okay	who's, whose

Each of these words has been spelled incorrectly in some papers submitted by both preservice teachers and experienced teachers during teacher education classes.

carefully consider the pros, cons, and appropriate use of new and emerging technologies for communicating with staff and families. Whichever communication tool is being considered, one should always ask, "Is this the best way to communicate for this situation?"

Online technology tools mentioned here and many others that are available can be used effectively as tools for collaboration. They offer a range of opportunities for interaction, information, and community participation among people of all ages, cultures, and socioeconomic classes. With appropriate technology, collaboration among those in a virtual community is not hindered by language, culture, or disability.

Just as with social etiquette rules that are designed to help people "think before they act," a network etiquette ("netiquette") is designed to make communication easier and safer. Netiquette-conscious users of technology are less likely to create problems for themselves and their recipients through stray or misguided comments or actions via the Internet. Strawbridge (2006) and other experts in Internet etiquette have offered more than 150 netiquette rules for email, mail lists, blogs, online services, and websites. Several of these suggestions are especially relevant to educators and others who engage in team-building and collaborative work. Technology supplies us with many devices to help us stay connected. That can be a double-edged sword. We may be more connected, but are we engaged in meaningful communication? Do we make good decisions about what forms of communication are appropriate for different audiences and purposes? For example, a text message to a co-teacher or other staff member in your building or on your team might be appropriate to confirm the time of the meeting or to ask what materials to bring for your joint planning session, but sending a text message to a parent to inform them of a student needing to stay after school because of poor behavior, or say to that the student is going to be moved to a different reading group, or have a different para next week would not be appropriate. When dealing with sensitive issues, talking to the other party face-to-face or over the phone is preferred. Consulting teachers need to use caution with email as well. Just because an email is sent, doesn't mean it is received or read.

Technology can serve as a barrier between people and difficult issues. It might be easier to send a text or email rather than talking face-to-face when we don't want to deal with a difficult issue, but the loss of the nonverbal aspects of the message (e.g., facial expressions, tone, body language, etc.) will likely make the outcome worse rather than better. Often, emails are composed quickly, without careful attention to our word choice, or recipients, and then sent in haste. The send button is pressed and it's gone. How often have we wished for an "undo" button after it was sent? This is especially true if there has been a heated interaction. We have all heard the expression, "when you are angry, count to ten before you say anything." A similar principle could be applied to responding with a quick email when you hear from a parent or colleague about something that pushes one of your hot buttons. If it makes you feel better to compose a response, do so, but resist the temptation to hit the send button. Wait a few hours, reread your email, and then ask yourself, "Would this be handled better with a phone call or face-to-face meeting?" Electronic communication can be a wonderful resource when used well. However, many organizations, businesses, and more and more schools are adopting and implementing etiquette rules for Internet activity by their employees so that they will be more efficient and have better protection from liability issues. Rules of politeness, consideration, and respect afforded by netiquette are important to follow for emails or other types of electronic communication.

Fisher and Sharp (1999) suggest that many collaboration setbacks can be traced to four problems: telling others what to think or do; not separating the person from the problem; blaming others; and having flawed assumptions about other teachers, families, community agencies, and even students.

When engineers stress collaboration, they often use the bumblebee analogy. According to the laws of aerodynamics, people have flawed assumptions that bumblebees cannot fly. But as everyone knows, they do fly. By the same token, some might say that groups cannot function productively because of the conflicts, personal agendas, and individual preferences that exist among the members. But they do function productively. Groups of people play symphonies, set up businesses, write laws, and develop IEPs for student needs.

An understanding of adult individual differences, styles, and preferences, as discussed in an earlier chapter, will encourage participants in consultation and collaboration to listen more respectfully and value differences among colleagues. Educational consultants maximize their effects on the lives and education of children with special needs by using good communication skills. They should always keep in mind the ancient rule we instill in children for crossing the street: "Stop, look, and listen." For the collaborative school consultant it means:

- *Stop* talking, judging, and giving advice.
- *Look* at the long-term outcome of good communication (keep your eyes on the prize).
- *Listen* to families, colleagues, and others who work in collaboration for children with special needs.

The stop, look, and listen rule sets up consultants for success—in establishing collaborative relationships, in developing rapport, in dealing with conflict and emotions, and in solving problems.

It is often helpful to write down what one plans to say to a teacher or a parent before an interaction and reflect on what the effects might be (Laud, 1998). Novice teachers and more experienced teachers who are still honing their communication skills could keep a log for recording selected interactions, analyzing them, and reflecting on alternative ways to communicate if those interactions were not productive.

Along similar lines, when sending written communication, and especially the irretrievable email, select words and expressions carefully. When in doubt, it is a good idea to have a colleague read the communication before sending it on its way. It is essential to put aside anger or frustration, begin the note on a positive tone, state the problem or concern carefully and objectively in the middle of the communication, and conclude with additional words that are positive and encouraging.

Listening instead of arguing, establishing ground rules that are considerate of the values and opinions of others, and working toward common goals and expectations for student success will help bring teams to the problem-finding and problem-solving stages with parity and respect. Consultants who remain calm and listen—always listen—will be "hearing their way to success" and helping to create an ethical and collaborative climate.

ENHANCEDetext **Application Exercise 4.1.** Click to apply your understanding of using assertive statements in your communication.

TIPS FOR COMMUNICATING EFFECTIVELY

1. Avoid communication roadblocks. Research shows that positively worded statements are one-third easier to understand than negative ones (Rinke, 1997).
2. Listen. Doing so helps dissipate negative emotional responses and often helps the other person articulate the problem, perhaps finding a solution then and there.
3. Be clear about your goals, needs, and preferences. Failing to let others know your needs and preferences can lead to disappointment and resentment.
4. Be aware of your hot buttons. Knowing your own responses to certain "trigger" behaviors and words will help you control natural tendencies to argue, get defensive, or simply turn red and sputter.
5. Attend to nonverbal language (kinesics, or body language) as well as to verbal language when communicating. Remember listening filters, yours and theirs.
6. Don't "dump your bucket" of frustrations onto the other person. Take a walk or a jog, shout, engage in your favorite forms of exercise or yoga, turn on your favorite playlist and sing along to avoid pouring out anger and frustration on others. Fill the buckets of others with "warm fuzzies" of empathy and caring.
7. Develop a protocol within the school context for dealing with difficult issues and for settling grievances.
8. Deal with the present. Keep to the issue of the current problem rather than past problems, failures, or personality conflicts.
9. Use understanding of individual differences among adults to bridge communication gaps and manage conflicts in educational settings.
10. Advocate for training that focuses on communication, problem solving, and conflict management.

CHAPTER 5

USING THE PROBLEM-SOLVING PROCESS IN COLLABORATIVE SCHOOL CONSULTATION AND TEAMWORK

Using a collaborative school consultation plan is like preparing food with a recipe. After the fundamentals of cooking have been mastered, the basic processes of food preparation can be adapted to other preferences and situations. Similarly, the fundamentals of a process for collaborative school consultation are applicable in many settings and adaptable to other grade levels, subject areas, and student needs. Just as recipes for food preparation should be flexible for adjustment to individual tastes and nutritional needs, so should individual education plans be flexible for adjustment to student interests and needs. Collaborative school consultants draw upon problem-solving strategies that call for ingenuity and various divergent thinking tools in designing appropriate educational plans for students.

The collaborative school consultation process is based on participant respect for and trust in one another. Participants include co-educators in schools, students' families, and students themselves. With appropriate problem-solving tools and techniques, co-educators can identify student needs and develop instructional plans for those needs. Schools will be contexts where teachers and learners can perform at their best. Working collaboratively as a team builds esprit de corps.

CHAPTER OBJECTIVES

Upon completing this chapter, the reader should be able to:

1. Describe the fundamental components of a problem-solving process.
2. List the ten basic steps in problem-finding and problem-solving processes.
3. Give examples of what collaborators should say and do when problem solving.
4. Illustrate useful tools, techniques, and interaction formats for problem solving.
5. Compare-and-contrast positive and not-so-positive interactions for problem solving
6. Propose what to consider if collaborative problem solving fails to resolve an issue.

KEY TERMS

brainstorming
concept mapping (webbing)
follow through and follow up

iatrogenic effect
Janusian thinking
metaphorical thinking

multiple intelligences
problem-solving process
synectics

SITUATION 5.A

The setting is the office area of an elementary school, where a special education teacher has just checked into the building and meets a fourth-grade classroom teacher.

Classroom Teacher: Hello [introducing self]. I understand you're going to be a consulting teacher in our building to work with us on students' learning and behavioral disorders.

Consulting Teacher: Hi [introducing self]. Yes, I hope to meet with all of the staff very soon to find out what you need and what would be helpful.

Classroom Teacher: Well, I for one am glad you're here. I have a student who is driving me and my other twenty-two students up the wall.

Consulting Teacher: How so?

Classroom Teacher: Since she moved here a few weeks ago, she's really upset the classroom management system I've been using for years—successfully, I might add.

Consulting Teacher: Is she having trouble with the material?

Classroom Teacher: No, she's a bright child who finishes everything in good time, and it's mostly correct. But she's extremely active—I'll use the word "frenetic"—as she busy bodies around the room.

Consulting Teacher: What specific behaviors concern you most?

Classroom Teacher: Well, for one thing, she tries to help everyone else when they should be doing their own work. I've worked a lot on developing the students' independent learning skills and they've made good progress. They don't need to have her tell them what to do.

Consulting Teacher: So her behavior keeps her classmates from being the self-directed learners that they can be.

Classroom Teacher: Right. I have to monitor her activities constantly, which means diverting my attention from all the other students. She bosses her classmates in the learning centers, and the media center, and even in the lunchroom and on the playground.

Consulting Teacher: How has she done with making friends so far?

Classroom Teacher: It's hard to say. So far I've been proud of the kids because they seem to be giving her some time and the benefit of their doubts while she settles in. But I think their tolerance is wearing thin. At this rate, she'll soon be having serious difficulties with maintaining peer relationships, let alone developing close friendships. This is probably the thing that will concern her socially prominent mother the most. I've only had one interaction with mom and it wasn't very promising. She seemed to not want to hear about any problems.

Consulting Teacher: Okay. For now shall we concentrate on the daughter? Which of the behaviors would you like to work on first?

Classroom Teacher: Well, I need to get her settled into some activities by herself so she's not bothering other students. Then she would learn more, too.

Consulting Teacher: What have you tried until now to keep her involved with her own work?

Classroom Teacher: I explain to her what I expect, and then I try to reinforce appropriate behaviors with things she likes to do. I've also used time-out, but she doesn't seem to understand what that is and why it's being imposed.

Consulting Teacher: We could make a list of specific changes in behavior you'd like to see and work out a program to accomplish them. In fact, the technique of webbing might help us explore the possibilities and focus on some options. It might help us identify some of her interests that we could channel into directed activities. How about doing one together on this chart paper? That way we'll have a record of our ideas, too. [Consultant and teacher work together to make a web of the student's behaviors and ascertain how one behavioral event seems to lead to another. (They begin to talk about a plan the teacher could initiate in the classroom.)] Uh, oh, there's the bell, and I know you have to go. Want to meet tomorrow to add any afterthoughts to our webbing chart and finalize the plan?

Classroom Teacher: Sounds good. I'd like to get this student on track so the class is more settled. We're getting into some new material that will require everybody's attention. If she can stay on track, I think the other children will like her better, and she'll enjoy learning new things, too. Besides, standardized tests are coming up soon, and then it will really be a challenge to keep her settled for her sake and also for the good of the others. I could meet with you here tomorrow, if that's okay. It might seem like a small problem to some, but to me it's a big problem that clouds the whole day. I must say, it helps a lot to have someone to talk with about it in a problem-solving manner.

PROBLEM-SOLVING PROCESS FOR ADDRESSING SPECIAL NEEDS

Collaborative school consultation calls for critical thinking and creative ideas, with all who are involved contributing in practical ways. The ultimate goal is to provide the best learning opportunities possible for students with special needs. Collaboration and consultation are not interchangeable because consultation is not always collaborative (Kampwirth, 1999). At this point, it may be helpful to review the descriptions of *consultation*, *collaboration*, and *teamwork* presented in earlier chapters and explore the viewpoints of co-educators toward these interactive processes.

Consultation provides direct service as advisement, counsel, or deliberation, either formal or informal, for a client's special needs. Recall that the client is typically a student, or a general education or special education teacher, family member, or resource personnel. *Collaboration* is the process where two or more work together to provide service toward achievement of a shared goal. When participants engage in *teamwork*, they subordinate personal prominence and contribute collaboratively to achieve a shared goal. Collaborative school consultation is an interactive process in which teachers, students, family members, and resource and support personnel combine their knowledge and skills to determine the student's educational needs, develop a plan with specific goals, implement the plan, assess the outcomes, and follow up as needed.

ACTIVITY 5.1

Queries and Responses about Collaborative Consultation

Interview three school professionals (one each at elementary, middle school, and high school levels if possible) to ascertain their perspectives and preferences regarding consultation services, collaborative activities, and co-teaching in schools. If they ask "What do you mean by collaboration, and consultation, and co-teaching?" you could address this in one of two ways—by sharing descriptions you have formed or by encouraging them to offer their own descriptions. Compare your interview results and draw inferences from your findings. Note any indication of budding interest in collaborative consultation and desire to learn more about the processes, and consider how these positive signs might be followed up productively.

Co-Educator Differences in Perceptions of Collaboration and Consultation

Most educators are attuned to the need for responding to individual differences of their students; however, much less attention has been given to individual differences of opinions and styles among school personnel and ways in which those differences affect school contexts and professional interactions. It is easy in the busy and public but paradoxically autonomous setting of school life to overlook the impact that differing personal preferences and professional perspectives of colleagues have on the complex process of working together. The study of adult differences and subsequent attention to constructive use of those differences is, for the most part, overlooked or neglected in teacher preparation programs and professional development experiences. Yet the school environment sparkles with variability among the adults who work there.

Important areas of variation among co-educators include: age, years of teaching experience; types of teacher education programs completed for certification; assigned grade level(s); curricular areas of teaching; general or special education focus; teaching experiences in rural or urban areas and small or large schools; personal preferences and professional perspectives regarding instruction for student learning and behavior; and much more. Co-educator differences in professional perspectives affect professional interactions when discussing students' needs and exploring ways of serving those needs.

Friction caused by disharmony among disparate types is reduced when the basis of disagreement is understood. When engaging in collaborative consultation and working together as co-teachers or team members, the more prickly areas of disagreement concerning professional perspectives and personal preferences can be discovered and discussed frankly in a spirit of camaraderie and collegiality. Co-educators do not need to teach in the same way; they just need to understand and respect the work of others. Then teachers and students alike will benefit from the rich array of individual differences.

As emphasized in an earlier chapter, adult differences can be used to significant advantage in teamwork and problem solving. When all aspects of team members' preferences are available to contribute diverse viewpoints and ideas, the multiple facets of problems can be analyzed and wide ranges of options generated. The most effective teams are those with the greatest variety of perspectives and the greatest tolerance for considering the views of others.

■ ■ ■ ■ ■   ■

ACTIVITY 5.2
Discovering Co-Educator Uniqueness and Commonality

This activity is interactive and constructive. The convener provides a few basic materials and brief instructions. Materials include, for each participant, from one to three "flower petals" pre-cut from colored construction paper (large enough on which to print a phrase or sentence); a brown "flower center" of generous size around which to attach the printed petals; a solid-color 8 ½ × 11-inch construction-paper background page for each group on which to "plant" the flower, and a bottle of school glue. (Figure 5.1 in this chapter could be used as a pattern for the blossom.) Groups composed of four to six participants are formed to discuss the following two items.

"First, discuss and discover one or two ways in which each of you is different from everyone else in the group and print each of your unique attributes on a single petal. Second, find several attributes of your group that are true for *all* participants, with the convener printing those on the flower's centerpiece. Glue the centerpiece and petals onto the background page to form a blossom. Then display pages of all groups to form a flower garden of diversity and commonality.

One group of six educators learned this about their differences: "I was born in a taxicab." "I paint watercolor landscapes." "I have two grandchildren." "I forgot to turn on the crockpot when I left for work this morning." "I cannot ride a bicycle." "My favorite recreation is riding horses." The six learned they are alike in that, "We are all women." "We all are wearing jeans this evening." "We all like to read a lot." "We all love chocolate." "None of us has ever gone skiing, but we all would like to someday."

Similarities among another group's participants were: "We all have pierced ears." "All of our children love sports." "We like to dance." "We are all over twenty years old." "We are not good pianists." "We are all special education teachers." These teachers differed in several ways such as "I hate shopping." "I haven't been on TV." "I *hate* to exercise!" "I'm working on my Ph.D." "I love to play tennis." "I teach fifth grade." "I live in a house with wheels."

Many seeds for starting conversations and building interrelationships can be planted with this simple activity. It most likely will be fun as well.

Co-educators exercise perception and judgment in order to determine students' needs and set learning and behavioral goals for them. This requires well-honed problem-solving skills because no two students or educators are alike. Most approaches have similar steps in the process. The problem-solving skills can be developed with practice and critique. Teachers who observe, collaborate with, and practice the techniques in simulated situations will be developing skills for practical use in a wide range of situations.

Pugach and Johnson (1995) suggest that co-educators configure two general categories for problem solving in the context of teacher collaboration: school-wide problems and specific student problems. Full inclusion is an example of school-wide problem solving undertaken in a collaborative way by all school personnel. Other school-wide examples are programs to eliminate bullying and programs to encourage good sportsmanship.

Problem solving for specific student needs is a more frequently occurring kind of situation that teachers must deal with in a problem-solving mode. For instance, should a developmentally delayed student be retained for another year in kindergarten or move on with inclusionary-classroom schoolmates? What problem-solving strategy will help a teenage student who has a serious obsessive-compulsive disorder but does not take the medications regularly that can help control this disorder? Both school-based and student-based categories are areas in which problem-solving skills can yield positive results in planning educational options for students. A problem-solving process that includes good communication skills and effective teamwork will enable educators to share their expertise.

It is helpful to begin with a study of the fundamental **problem-solving process**. Key components for addressing learning and behavioral needs of students are:

- Data gathering
- Problem identification (*very* important) and description
- Exploration of possibilities
- Development of a plan
- Implementation of the plan
- Follow through to assess progress on the plan
- Follow up on continuing the plan, adjusting it, or having closure

Collaborators will need to keep in mind that learning and behavior problems do not always emanate from student disabilities. It is possible that some students are "curriculum-disabled" (Conoley, 1987), meaning that the curriculum and school environment do not allow them to function successfully. They just need a modified or expanded approach to the existing curriculum in order to succeed (Pugach & Johnson, 1990). To make adaptations and accommodations for special needs, school co-educators and home co-educators must identify and modify aspects of the learning environment, both curricular and extracurricular, that are affecting student development.

Gathering Relevant Data

Data from multiple sources will contribute multifarious kinds of information pertaining to learning and behavior needs, along with information about the settings in which the needs are evidenced. These information points can be aggregated into a description of specific concerns and suggestions for constructing a plan. Figure 5.1 lists sixteen possible data sources. The more segments representing data sources for the client that are shaded, then the richer and more complete the identification from that overlay would be. Problem-solving tools such as brainstorming, concept mapping (webbing), and others presented in this chapter can activate thinking so collaborators select appropriate options and form suitable plans for student needs.

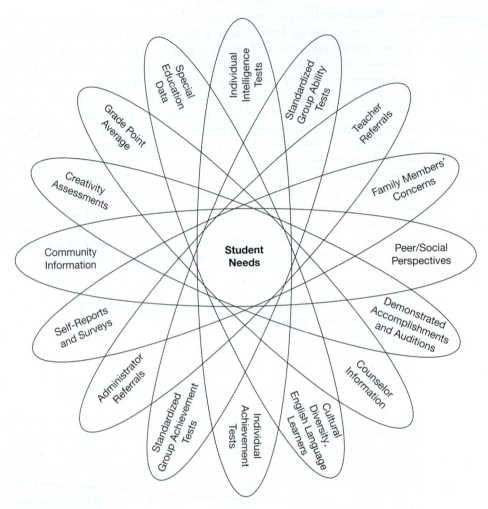

FIGURE 5.1   **Data Sources for Assessing Needs**

Identifying the Problem

The most important step in a problem solving process is *identifying* the problem, need, or concern. Sophisticated teaching methods and expensive instructional materials cannot be helpful if student needs are misidentified or overlooked. They might even produce an **iatrogenic effect**—or intended remedy that causes more harm than good. Identification of the problem requires concentrated, uninterrupted time and keen focus to zero in on all available data relevant to the need. If the problem is delineated appropriately, the problem-solving process is much more likely to be successful. (See Figure 5.2.)

FIGURE 5.2   First, Identify the Problem

Co-educators will want to analyze their own abilities and shortcomings in regard to problem solving. The four interfering themes introduced by Caplan (1970) are helpful to review here as a prompt for listening carefully and planning wisely on the client's behalf. Collaborating educators should ask:

- Do I need more knowledge and understanding about the student's needs?
- Do I lack skill in choosing options for courses of action that could be taken?
- Do I lack objectivity, letting my beliefs or former experiences have undue influence?
- Do I need more self-confidence in dealing with this situation?

It is important for collaborating teachers to focus on the problem, not on who "owns" the problem. When the problem area is identified, then and only then is it productive to focus on the planning that can lead to short-term progress and long-term solutions. One astute consulting teacher prepares for this by making a note of things she wants to say and ways she will try to say them when she interacts with co-teachers and family members. Then she rehearses, recording them in front of a mirror to check for voice tone, body language, and semantics.

Generating Possibilities

After the problem has been identified, the process of generating ideas can begin. Divergent thinking is important during this step in order not to get stuck in routine answers or come up with weak or unworkable plans. Some consultants find it helpful for the person who "owns" the problem to have the first opportunity for making suggestions.

Another important reason for prompting the owner of the problem to give initial suggestions is that consultants should avoid giving advice and being perceived as the experts. Several researchers in the past have shown that a non-expert approach to educational consulting is especially effective in special education (Idol-Maestas, Lloyd, & Lilly, 1981; Margolis & McGettigan, 1988). Initial suggestions and opinions of all participants should be listened to with respect before additional suggestions are offered. Communication skills that are such an important aspect of successful problem solving were the focus of an earlier chapter. When people participate actively in decision-making, they feel more ownership toward the results than when they feel coerced into approving a particular plan. People are more apt to support decisions they helped create than those imposed on them.

A problem will never be solved if all parties suspect that they are working on different issues. Problems are like artichokes: They have layers. Only after the outside layers are stripped away can problem solvers get to the heart of the matter. Expressing thoughts and feelings with clarity in order to generate best ideas requires reflective listening skill and appropriate assertiveness. Good listening skills will facilitate moving to the heart of issues.

Video Example from YouTube
▶

ENHANCEDetext
Video Example 5.1.
We see in this animated presentation on collaborative problem solving involving a business marketing example that the elements of effective problem solving are the same as what has been discussed here: working as a team, using effective communication skills, brainstorming solutions, and creating an implementation plan. (https://www.youtube.com/watch?v=0iaB72tHLYU)

Developing a Plan

Problems that come up in collaborative school consultation often signal the need for changes in classroom practices. This can cause resistance and negativity from co-educators. Advice giving and postures of role hierarchy could be communicated unintentionally. Furthermore, if one role is regarded as the expert role, there is pressure on that person and false expectations may be formed. It is hard to win in this kind of situation. The best practice for a collaborating consultant is to demonstrate parity, flexibility, and a caring, sharing attitude.

It is difficult when problem-solving to avoid the "quick fix." Furthermore, it can be demeaning to the co-educator who has been struggling with the problem for some time. Others need to feel that the collaborating consultant fully understands their unique situation and the source of their frustrations. If they don't, they may resist participating in problem solving and listening to the suggestions of their colleagues. Consulting teachers must listen before they can expect to be listened to and treated with parity or be approached voluntarily for help by consultees. Good collaborative consultants do not "solve" problems—they see that problems get solved. So they "nix the quick fix" and engage in a dedicated way to facilitate problem solving.

All learning situations and all students are unique. In response to a question about a hypothetical classroom-management scenario, an understanding high school teacher replied, "I don't know all the answers because I haven't seen all the kids." Although students and situations may appear similar in some ways, the combinations of students, teachers, parents, and contexts of school and home are unique for each problem. Furthermore, in many cases the people with problems already have arrived at their answers. They just need help to clarify issues or receive reassurance. When co-educators talk and listen and talk some more with their colleagues, they will begin to work through their own problems and find courses of action to solve them. Joint problem identification and idea generating should assure that professional relationships are preserved. Then communication is enhanced and all who are involved have stronger feelings of self-esteem and situational control.

Busy teachers do not need to take on the problems of others, but everyone who owns a part of a problem should participate in solving it. That may involve collaboration among a number of roles—teachers, administrators, vocational and technical arts counselors, social workers, justice system personnel, students, family caregivers, and others. Again, consultants and consultees must focus on the problem rather than on establishing ownership or assessing blame for the problem. The suggestions and actions of collaborative consultants have far-reaching ramifications and must be taken very seriously. Co-educators in inclusive settings with joint responsibility for students must share their concerns, pool their expertise, and collaboratively make decisions for the welfare of students and others who could be affected, including the students' families.

Implementing the Plan Agreed Upon

A problem-solving group should select a workable solution that all are willing to adopt, at least on a trial or experimental basis. There should be mutual participation in making the decision. Group members will accept new ideas and new work methods more readily when they have opportunity to participate in decision making. Many times, a complex problem can be solved when each person in the group discovers what the others really want, or conversely, dread what they will get. Then solutions can be proposed to meet the goals and protect the concerns of all involved.

Co-educators need to ask, "Did we have enough information to create options we may not have realized before this? Have we thought through the consequences of each option?" Taking time to ask all the necessary questions is a key to the decision-making process. Asking many questions and expecting clear answers will help to make options and choices obvious.

Co-educators should participate in the problem-solving process in such a way that all participants feel their needs are being satisfied and an equitable and professional relationship is maintained. Members of the problem-solving team will want to critique all the suggestions made, presenting both merits and disadvantages of the suggestions from their own perspectives. Honest and open communication, good listening skills, and an appropriate level of assertiveness are vital at this step.

Following Through and Following Up

After sorting through data, scheduling and arranging meetings, planning the agenda, and facilitating and participating in the meeting, it is tempting to breathe a sigh of relief when the agreed-on plan is ready, and then move on to other issues. But collaborators, busy as they are, must **follow through** on progress of the plan to be sure it is implemented as planned. Then later at a designated time they need to **follow up** on how the plan succeeded. If the follow-up process indicates that no progress was made or unexpected problems surfaced, then the problem-solving activity should be repeated.

■ ■ ■ ■ ■

ACTIVITY 5.3
Learning Disability or Curriculum Disability?

Review the term "curriculum-disabled" as it was presented earlier in the chapter and discuss it with colleagues whom you trust to be candid and nonjudgmental in expressing their viewpoints. What do you and they think and feel about this term? Should school curriculum and instruction be modified in order for students to fit in and be successful, or should students always be expected to adjust within existing school structures? This activity will require critical and creative thinking. It may generate some provocative comments and innovative ideas, and if so, what could you do with those ideas?

Problem-Solving Examples Emphasizing Consultation

Situation 1: A preschool teacher is concerned about a child in the group who is not fluent in speech. So the teacher asks the speech pathologist to help determine what to do about it. The speech pathologist consults with the teacher and the child's family to get more information about the observed behavior and makes additional observations. The consultant applies her expertise in speech pathology to address the questions and concerns of the teacher and the family members.

Situation 2: A physical therapist provides individualized therapy for a preschool child who has cerebral palsy. The therapist wants to know about the child's social development as well as performance in pre-academic skills such as letter recognition and sound discrimination. The therapist asks the teacher to serve as a consultant regarding this issue, and the preschool teacher provides the information requested.

Problem-Solving Situations Focusing on Collaboration

Situation 3: A kindergarten teacher and a music teacher are both concerned about a child's tendency to masturbate during group time while sitting on the classroom rug. The two teachers meet to discuss their mutual concern. Both parties discuss their observations and engage in problem-solving activities to identify the problem clearly and select possible actions. Both parties agree to make some changes in their respective settings to address the problem. If these collectively determined revisions do not work, they commit to trying other possibilities, including consultation with the child's parents, the school psychologist, and the health nurse.

Situation 4: A teacher of students with behavioral disorders, along with the school counselor, three classroom teachers, and a student's parents, meet to discuss inappropriate behavior of that student. The individuals involved in the meeting engage in collaborative problem solving to formulate a plan for addressing the problem. Each individual has a role in defining the problem, generating possible actions, and implementing the plan.

Problem-Solving Examples Featuring Teamwork

Situation 5: A special education teacher and a general classroom teacher wish to try co-teaching. The teachers meet weekly to co-plan. During the co-planning they decide when, where, and how to share which responsibilities for the instructional needs of all students in the classroom during a specified period of time each day. Each contributes information about personal areas of expertise and strength whenever feasible. The co-teachers come to consensus on what evaluation method to use and determine that they will assign grades for all students by mutual agreement. They do not refer to "my students" or "your students." Instead, they speak of, plan for, and teach *our students* as a team.

Situation 6: A team of professionals provides services for infants and toddlers with severe and profound disabilities. Each professional has an area of expertise and responsibility. The social worker has the leadership role because she is responsible for most family contacts and often goes into homes to provide additional assistance for families. The nurse takes responsibility for monitoring the physical well being of each child and keeps in close contact with other medical personnel and families. The speech pathologist works with the children to develop speech and language skills. The occupational therapist is responsible for teaching the children self-help skills. The physical therapist follows through with the medical doctor's prescribed physical therapy. Special education teachers provide language stimulation and modeling, coordinate schedules, and facilitate communication among the team that meets twice weekly to discuss individual cases.

Video Example from YouTube

▶

ENHANCEDetext
Video Example 5.2.

View this video to see a series of "what if" statements that challenge you to think differently when problem solving and interacting with colleagues. [https://www.youtube.com/watch?v=ue3hCVHtZZY]

A TEN-STEP COLLABORATIVE PROBLEM-SOLVING PROCESS

Fundamental principles of a typical problem-solving process for addressing special needs have been discussed, and distinctions have been made for problem solving that emphasizes direct consultation, that focuses on collaboration, and that features working as a team. It is now timely to outline a ten-step process for collaborative school consultation and teamwork.

The ten-step process presented in Figure 5.3 will help consultants and consultees communicate effectively and coordinate their efforts efficiently as they identify learning and behavioral problems of students and design programs for their needs. Co-educators will find it helpful to have a copy of this ten-step outline available for handy reference in problem-solving situations. When the outline is committed to memory or stapled into a plan book, it can be a good organizational tool and a reassuring resource for every co-educator.

FIGURE 5.3   The Ten-Step Problem-Solving Process

1. *Prepare for the consultation.*
   1.1 Focus on major topic or area of concern.
   1.2 Prepare and organize materials.
   1.3 Prepare several possible actions or strategies.
   1.4 Arrange for a comfortable, convenient meeting place.

2. *Initiate the consultation.*
   2.1 Establish rapport.
   2.2 Identify the agenda.
   2.3 Focus on the tentatively defined concern.
   2.4 Express interest in the needs of all.

3. *Collect and organize relevant information.*
   3.1 Make notes of data, soliciting from all.
   3.2 Combine and summarize the data.
   3.3 Assess data to focus on areas needing more information.
   3.4 Summarize the information.

4. *Isolate the problem.*
   4.1 Focus on need.
   4.2 State what the problem is.
   4.3 State what it is not.
   4.4 Propose desirable circumstances.

5. *Identify concerns and realities about the problem.*
   5.1 Encourage all to listen to each concern.
   5.2 Identify issues, avoiding jargon.
   5.3 Encourage ventilation of frustration and concerns.
   5.4 Keep focusing on the pertinent issues and needs.
   5.5 Check for agreement.

6. *Generate solutions.*
   6.1 Engage in collaborative problem solving.
   6.2 Generate several possible options and alternatives.
   6.3 Suggest examples of appropriate classroom modifications.
   6.4 Review options, discussing consequences of each.
   6.5 Select the most reasonable alternatives.

7. *Formulate a plan.*
   7.1 Designate those who will be involved, and how.
   7.2 Set goals.
   7.3 Establish responsibilities.
   7.4 Generate evaluation criteria and methods.
   7.5 Agree on a date for reviewing progress.
   7.6 Follow through on all commitments.

8. *Evaluate progress and process.*
   8.1 Conduct a review session at a specified time.
   8.2 Review data and analyze the results.
   8.3 Keep products as evidence of progress.
   8.4 Make positive, supportive comments.
   8.5 Assess contribution of the collaboration.

9. *Follow through and follow up on the consultation about the situation.*
   9.1 Reassess periodically to assure maintenance.
   9.2 Provide positive reinforcement.
   9.3 Plan further action or continue the plan.
   9.4 Adjust the plan if there are problems.
   9.5 Initiate further consultation if needed.
   9.6 Bring closure if goals have been met.
   9.7 Support effort and reinforce results.
   9.8 Share information where it is wanted.
   9.9 Enjoy the pleasure of having the communication.

10. *Repeat or continue consultation as appropriate.*

Step 1: Prepare for the Collaborative Consultation

Co-educators focus on the major areas of concern and reflect on the circumstances surrounding this concern. (Refer to Step 1 in Figure 5.3 here and in the other nine steps of the process.) They prepare helpful materials and organize them in order to use the collaborative time efficiently. It is helpful to distribute information beforehand so that valuable interaction time is not consumed reading new material. But they must take great care to present that material as tentative and still open to discussion. It is not always constructive to plan in detail prior to consultations. Furthermore, confidentiality is to be maintained by everyone at every juncture.

Occasionally consulting activities happen informally and without notice—between classes, during lunch periods, or on playgrounds. Educators usually will want to accommodate colleagues on these occasions when time and place permit. However, they should look beyond these events for opportunities to engage in more in-depth sessions.

Each collaborator needs to have enough advance notice and time to prepare. There should be provisions for convenient and comfortable settings for the interaction, seating that provides an adult, collegial atmosphere, no phone or drop-by interruptions, and assurance of privacy. Serving coffee and tea can help set a congenial tone for meetings.

Step 2: Initiate the Collaborative Consultation

Educators need to exert much effort in this phase. When resistance to collaborating is high, or the teaching staff has been particularly reluctant to participate, it is difficult to establish first contacts. This is the time to begin with the most receptive staff members in order to build in success. Rapport is established by addressing every consultee as special and expressing interest in what each one is doing and feeling. Teachers should be encouraged to talk about their successes but some are modest and reluctant to do so. The consultant needs to display sensitivity to teachers' needs and make each one feel important. The key is to listen, observe, and defer judgment.

The convener will want to identify the agenda and keep focusing on the concern. It is helpful to have participants write down their concerns before the meeting and bring them along. These can be checked quickly for congruence and major disagreements. (As stated in step 1, refer again to Figure 5.3 here and in each of the remaining steps.)

Step 3: Collect and Organize Relevant Information

The data should be relevant to the issue of focus. However, data that might seem irrelevant to one person may be the very information that is useful to another and essential for identifying the real problem. So participants must be astute in selecting appropriate data that include many possibilities but do not waste time or resources. This becomes easier with experience, but for new teachers, having too much information is probably better than having too little, while bearing in mind that time is limited and must be used judiciously.

Because problem identification is the key factor in planning for special needs, it is critical that sufficient data be obtained from multiple sources. Refer back to Figure 5.1 for identifying up to sixteen data sources of information for problem solving to address a student's needs. The more sources that are tapped, the more easily and clearly the need is understood. Think of sections in the figure as being shaded with colored pencils, paint, tissue-paper overlays, or computer-printed designs. The darker the center becomes, the more assured co-educators can be that needs are being assessed comprehensively.

Step 4: Isolate the Problem

It cannot be stressed too strongly that the most critical aspect of problem solving involves identifying and defining the problem at hand by focusing on needs, not handy solutions. Without problem identification, problem solving cannot occur (Bergan, 1995). The most common problem-solving error is to short circuit the problem definition step and hasten to traditional solutions rather than developing individually tailored solutions (Conoley, 1989). Henning-Stout (1994) notes that less experienced consultants in particular tend to spend insufficient time with the consultee on the nature of the problem and proceed too quickly to developing "the plan." A clear problem statement should be agreed upon by everyone before moving forward or solution finding will not be as focused, resulting in dissatisfaction with the outcome. Extra time spent for reaching agreement on the problem is time well spent (Knackendoffel, Robinson, Deshler, & Schumaker, 1992).

Step 5. Identify Concerns and Realities about the Problem

All concerns and viewpoints related to the problem should be aired and shared by each participant. A different viewpoint is not better or worse, just different. An effective consultant keeps participants focusing on the need by listening, observing, and encouraging everyone to respond. A certain amount of venting and frustration is to be expected and accepted. Teachers and parents will be less resistant when they know they are free to express their feelings without retaliation or judgment. Consulting teachers should remain nonjudgmental and assure supportive confidentiality, always talking and listening in consultees' language. As information is shared and discussed, the consulting teacher will want to make notes. It is good to have everyone look over the recorded information from time to time during the session as a demonstration of trust and parity, and a check on accuracy.

Step 6: Generate Options

Now is the time for creative planning. If ideas do not come freely, or if participants are blocking productive thinking, the consultant might lead the group in trying one or more of the techniques described later in the chapter. A creative problem-solving technique not only unleashes ideas, it sends a message about the kinds of behavior and attitudes needed to solve problems. "Straw votes" can be taken periodically if that helps the group keep moving toward solutions. "Thinking outside the box" and combining ideas are desirable processes at this stage. It is productive to separate the discussion into two topics, one focusing on benefits and the other on concerns. These two sharing periods would be initiated with the word stems "I like . . ." (in which the benefits are shared), and "I wish . . ." or "How could . . .?" (in which concerns are aired). At this stage, the group should modify, dismiss, or solve problems for each concern.

Step 7: Formulate a Plan

After options have been generated, wishes and concerns have been aired, and modifications have been recommended, it is time to make the plan. Participants must remain on task. They need to be reinforced positively for their contributions. Consulting teachers will want to be ready to make suggestions, but they should defer presenting them so long as others are suggesting and volunteering. They must avoid offering ideas prematurely or addressing too many issues at one time. Other unhelpful behaviors are assuming a supervisor/expert role, introducing one's own biases, and making suggestions that conflict with existing values in the school context.

As the plan develops, the group should be clear on just who will do what and when, where, and how. Evaluation criteria and methods that are congruent with the goals and plan should be developed at this time, and arrangements made for assessment and collection of data on student progress. A vital element to success in collaborative problem solving will be the commitment by all participants to follow through with the plan, as noted later in Step 9.

Step 8: Evaluate Progress and Process

Assessment of student progress toward the goals is a key component that should be discussed and planned for during the problem-solving process. Also, evaluation of the collaborative consultation process and the problem-solving process must not be overlooked or treated lightly.

The convener will want to make positive, supportive comments while drawing closure, and at that time evaluate the session informally with consultee help, taking care to record the information for later analysis, or to evaluate formally by asking participants to complete brief written responses. This also can be a good time to plan for future collaboration.

Step 9: Follow Through and Following Up on the Consultation about the Situation

Of all ten steps, Step 9 may be the most neglected. Unsuccessful consultation outcomes often can result from failure to follow through on commitments and to follow up on progress made and new issues that may have surfaced. For follow through, it is in the best interest of the client, consultee, consultant, and future opportunities for consultation to revisit the situation periodically. Participants will want to adjust the student's program if necessary and initiate further consultation if the situation seems to require it. Informal conversations with consultees at this point are very reinforcing. The sweetest words a consultee can hear are "What can I do to help you?" However, this question must be framed in the spirit of "What can I do to help you that you do not have the time and resources to do?" and not with an implication of "What can I do for you that you do not have the skill and expertise to accomplish?" Another useful question to ask may be, "What would you like to see happen in this situation (or with this student, or at this point in time)?" Consultants should respond immediately with materials, information, actions, or further consultations that have been promised, and take special care to reinforce things that are going well. Figure 5.4 is an example of a form that could be used for that purpose.

During follow up, consultants have opportunities to make consultees feel good about their participation. They can make a point of noting improved student behaviors and performances, as well as positive effects that have resulted so far from the collaboration. Also,

FIGURE 5.4   Memo to Follow Through

From: _____ to _____

              (consultant)   (consultee/s)

Date: _____   Re: _____

I am eager to follow through on the plan which we developed on the date above, and also to assist in other ways that may have occurred to you since then.

How do you feel things have progressed since that time? Please be forthright.

_____

_____

What else may I do to help?

_____

_____

                                     (List here any times, descriptions, etc., that would help me respond specifically to your needs.)

_____   Information   _____

_____   Resources   _____

_____   Meet again   _____

_____   Classroom visit   _____

_____   Conference with   _____

Thank you so much! I enjoy working with you to serve our students and schools.

they may volunteer to help if things are not going as smoothly as anticipated or if consultees have further needs.

Step 10: Repeat or Continue Consultation and Collaboration as Appropriate

Further consultation and collaboration may be needed if the plan is not working, or if one or more parties believe the problem was not identified appropriately. On the other hand, consultation also may be repeated and extended when things are going well. The obvious rationale in this case would be that if one modification helped, more will help further. This is very reinforcing for those who are consulting, collaborating, and working together as a team. It also encourages others to participate in consultation and collaboration processes.

SITUATION 5.B

Using the Ten-Step Problem-Solving Process

When implemented, a ten-step scenario for problem solving might go something like this:

A first-year special education consulting teacher asks to meet with the veteran classroom teacher about their student with hearing impairment. The student's response to instructional strategies and curricular adaptations that focus on the IEP goals has been good. However, the special education teacher believes more could be done in the school environment to help this student fit in socially, emotionally, and physically. In a brief exchange during shared hall supervision with the classroom teacher, she senses that he has some concerns as well, and she suggests a meeting before contacting the parents to see if adjustments to the IEP are warranted.

She prepares for their meeting with an agenda and some tentative ideas and examples for adaptations. She asks to meet in the classroom on the teacher's "turf." As a novice teacher, she wants to use her most polished collaborative consultation skills with this veteran teacher. She knows that as an intuitive thinker her preferred problem-solving style includes a tendency to gloss over facts and move too hastily (eagerly) perhaps to looking at ideas for solutions. This is something she has been working on, and it will serve her well today because she has observed that this classroom teacher has an opposite style of stating problem, issues, and factual data in succinct detail. She believes that these differences in style can work to their advantage and benefit the student.

During the interaction, she listens and waits appropriately. She uses verbal forms such as "we" and "How can I assist you in planning for this student's needs?" She asks the teacher about his concerns and listens reflectively until the teacher concludes his comments. She describes a few of what she considers the most powerful items on her idea-suggestion list. They review the student's IEP and then brainstorm, using their concerns and suggestions as a launch pad. This is where the novice teacher feels she can shine. Next, they generate a description of modifications focusing on the areas of student need and they outline what would be each teacher's responsibilities. Both contribute their personal expertise on how these modifications can be integrated into general curriculum and other parts of the student's school day. This includes more appropriate placement in the music room, in assemblies, at lunch, and in playground games.

The two teachers work out details of the plan, which surprisingly does not take all that much time to accomplish, and they include an early conference with parents for going over the plan. They want to be sure all facets are in compliance with their student's IEP and that they have family support. They make a note to solicit additional ideas from input by the parents. They also plan the means by which they will elicit support from other personnel including the music teacher, physical education teacher, bus driver, cafeteria personnel, and school nurse. As they wrap up, the novice teacher informs the classroom teacher that this has been one of her first consultations, and she is grateful to him for his part in making it a success. She will be even more comfortable now in the role and enthused about working with other teachers. Her collaborating teacher commends her for her innovative ideas and says he is sure that more good consultation and collaboration experiences are in her future.

This meeting carries the joint consultation through Steps 1–8 of the problem-solving process. Steps 9 and 10 for following up/following through and repeating the consultation process are yet to come. But both co-educators leave the meeting on this day feeling very good about their collaborative effort. As evidenced by the final exchange between the two, the event was a special boost to the first-year teacher's confidence.

ACTIVITY 5.4
Application of the Problem-Solving Process

Review Situation 5.B. Then, using the ten-step problem solving that was outlined earlier, ask these questions:

1. Who initiated the collaborative effort? (Step 2)
2. What additional information would be helpful? (Step 3)
3. What was the problem and how was it identified? (Step 4)
4. What other realities and concerns became evident? (Step 5)
5. What were options for possible actions? (Step 6)
6. What plan was formulated? (Step 7)
7. What went well? Why? Did anything not go well? If so, why? (Step 8)
8. What should happen in follow-through and follow-up processes? (Step 9)
9. At this point, are further interactions or actions called for? (Step 10)

WHAT TO SAY AND DO DURING THE PROBLEM-SOLVING PROCESS

This is a good time to consider sample phrases of communication that can be helpful in implementing each phase of the ten-step problem-solving process. Copies of these might also go into the consultant's plan book for quick reference during consultations. A consulting teacher does not want to parrot points from an outline or appear to be reading instructions as if assembling a piece of furniture. But practicing verbal responses for problem-solving steps will help the teacher be more natural and automatic when the need arises. Each number for the phrase sets that follow corresponds to a number of the ten-step consultation process outlined previously. Of course, it is unlikely that all of the comments suggested here would be needed or would fit any one conference.

1. *When planning the consultation* (Comments in this step are made to oneself.)

   (What styles of communication and interaction can I expect with these consultees?)

   (Have I had previous consultations with them and if so, how did they go?)

(Do I have any perceptions at this point about client needs? If so, can I keep them under wraps while soliciting responses from others?)
(What kinds of information could help with this situation?)

2. *When initiating the consultation* (In this step and the rest of the steps, say to the consultee and others who are involved:)

You're saying that . . .
The need seems to be . . .
May we work together along these lines?
So the situation is . . .
I am wondering if . . .
What can we do in regard to your request/situation?

3. *When collecting information*

Tell me about that . . .
Uh-huh . . .
What do you see as the effects of . . . ?
I'd like to rephrase my question.
Let's see now, your views/perceptions about this are . . .
Tell me more about the background of . . .
Would you give an example of that?
Sounds tough . . .
To summarize our basic information then, . . .

4. When isolating the problem

The major factors we have brought out seem to be . . .
I'm wondering if we are asking the right questions.
Could you be more specific?
What do you perceive is the greatest need for . . . ?
What circumstances have you noted that may apply?
Are there other parts to the need that we have not considered?
So to summarize our perceptions at this point . . .
Are we in agreement that the major part of this issue is . . . ?

5. When identifying the concerns and stating the realities

You say the major concern is . . .
How do you feel about this?
Let me see if I understood that.
But I also hear your concern about . . .
You'd like this situation changed so that . . .
How does this affect your day/load/responsibilities?
You are concerned about other students in your room . . .
What are some ways to get at . . . ?
You're feeling . . . because of . . .
This problem seems formidable. Perhaps we can isolate part of it . . .
Would you say that this situation . . . ?
Perhaps we can't be sure about that. . . .

The major factors we have brought out seem to be . . .

If you could change one thing, what would you change first?

6. *When generating possibilities*

How does this affect the students/the schedule/the family?

Do we have a good handle on the nature of this situation?

We need to define what we want to happen. . . .

How would you like things to be?

What has been tried so far?

What happened then?

Is this the best way to get it done? The only way?

How could we do this more easily?

Could we try something new such as . . . ?

Could you add to what has been said?

What limitations are there on the things we might suggest?

Let's try to develop some ideas to meet the need . . .

Your idea of . . . also makes me think of . . .

7. When formulating a plan

Let's list the goals and ideas we have come up with . . .

So, in trying . . . you'll be changing your approach of . . .

To implement these ideas, we would have to . . .

What I heard you say was . . . and is that what you meant?

I'm wondering if we have considered every possibility brought forth.

The actions in this situation would be different, because . . .

We've discussed all of the alternatives carefully, so now should we choose?

We need to break down the plan into steps. What should come first? Next?

When is the best time to start with the first step?

8. When evaluating progress

Have we got a solid plan?

One way to measure progress toward the goals would be . . .

Some positive things have been happening... .

How can we build upon these gains?

Now we can decide where to go from here. . . .

In what ways did our getting together help?

I can see [the student] progress every day. . . .

You're accomplishing so much with . . .

How could I help you and your students in more and better ways?

9. When following through and following up

How do you feel about the way things are going?

We had set a time to meet again. Is that time still okay, or should it be sooner?

I'm interested in the progress you have observed.

I'm following up on that material/action I promised.

I just stopped by to . . .

I wondered how things have been going for you . . .

How are things in your corner of the world these days?

I'm glad you've hung in there with this situation.

You've accomplished a lot that may not be apparent when you're with it every day.

You know, progress like this makes teachers look very good!

10. *If repeating the consultation*

Should we have another go at discussing this situation?

Perhaps we overlooked some information that would help. . . .

We got so much accomplished last time. How about getting together again to . . . ?

That's a great progress report. Would another plan session produce even more of these very positive results?

TOOLS, TECHNIQUES, AND FORMATS FOR COLLABORATIVE PROBLEM SOLVING

The collaborative format of working together and drawing upon collective expertise to solve problems is widely practiced in business and professional worlds. In the effort to use the best ideas of bright and innovative minds, astute leaders employ a number of group problem-solving techniques. One of the most frequent venues for problem finding and problem solving in schools is the conference for development of an Individual Education Plan (IEP). The collective thinking in which the interactive IEP team engages is a collaborative method of finding solutions to problems (Clark, 2000). With all participants knowledgeable about the problem-solving process and skilled in using key phrases, the conference should go well. However, many co-educators have expressed dissatisfaction with the IEP development process, citing blizzards of terms, forms, and paperwork as factors, and concern that input by the student and family was not encouraged strongly and valued highly. As noted by Menlove, Hudson, and Suter (2001), dissatisfaction was higher among secondary teachers than elementary teachers. Reasons given were team disconnect, time and preparation involved, training needed for pertinent knowledge and skills, and IEP relevance to their school context. General educators had the view that the IEP meeting is a special education teacher's meeting, not a team meeting, and when parents were present they did not like to push issues.

On the positive side, general education teachers have been signaling some improvements in time available, information received, communication skills in group settings, and preparation for problem delineation. This is a promising area in which IEP participation can be improved through programs that focus on development of skills for collaboration and teamwork. Another useful activity is rubric development as a group for a specific purpose, such as laying out expectations for learning and behavior on a class trip or designing procedures and assessments to structure a cooperative learning activity.

A large number of effective, easy-to-use techniques for group problem solving are available. These include brainstorming (Osborn, 1963), Six Thinking Hats and Plus-Minus-Interesting (de Bono, 1973, 1985, 1986), concept mapping, idea checklist, metaphorical thinking, role play, and TalkWalk (Caro & Robbins, 1991). Teachers often incorporate such kinds of group problem-solving activity into their curriculum planning for students, but may overlook their potential as tools for problem solving with adults. Some of the techniques will be described briefly here, while many more are available online and in books featuring creative and innovative production.

Brainstorming

Brainstorming is a mainstay of creative problem-solving methodology. It facilitates generating many unique ideas. When a group is brainstorming, participants should be relaxed and having fun. There are no right or wrong responses during the process because problems seldom have only one right approach. No one may critique an idea during the brainstorming process. All ideas are accepted as plausible and regarded as potentially valuable. Each idea that is expressed is recorded. In large group sessions, it is most efficient to have a leader for managing the oral responses and a recorder for getting them down on a board or chart visible to all.

The classic rules developed by Osborn (1963) and others for **brainstorming** and used in countless business, education, industrial, and community settings since then are:

1. Do not criticize any ideas at the time they are offered.
2. Remember that the more wild and zany the ideas are, the better.
3. Think up as many different ideas as possible.
4. Try to combine two or more ideas into new ones.
5. Hitch-hike (piggyback) on another's idea. A person with a hitchhike idea is to be called on before those who have unrelated ideas, so indicate a signal for doing that.

Note that when coaching others (children in particular) in brainstorming techniques, it is good to introduce them to the concept of "the humanitarian principle" before the very first session. This means that an idea will not be accepted if it is obviously a harmful or hurtful one. A response to "What are new ways to use old bricks?" that comes out as "To drown kittens" (typically followed with a pause and a quick glance at the teacher by its contributor to wait for classmates' chuckles or teacher's shocked expression) would be handled with a brief but firm, "Sorry, but as you know, we abide by the humanitarian principle here." Then the teacher would move quickly on without accepting the idea or scolding the contributor. This response would remain true to the spirit of brainstorming.

Brainstorming is useful when the group wishes to explore as many alternatives as possible and defer evaluation of the ideas until the options have been exhausted. People who cannot resist the urge to comment prematurely on ideas during brainstorming must be reminded on the spot that evaluation comes later. Leaders should call on volunteers quickly and politely ignore those who seem to want to bend the rules. When the flow of ideas slows, it is good to persevere a while longer. Often the second wave of thoughts will contain the most innovative suggestions. Each participant should be encouraged to contribute, but be allowed to pass if desired.

Video Example
from
YouTube

ENHANCEDetext
Video Example 5.3.

Brainstorming as a group process depends upon good group dynamics to succeed. Useful ideas can be gathered with the brainstorm techniques recommended in this video. (www.youtube.com/watch?v=9K8W4ooygUU)

Individual brainstorming can be a very productive activity and has become increasingly popular as an alternative to, or a precursor for, group brainstorm sessions. Recall that personal preferences often have effects on instruction in unexpected ways, and this is one example. Some people like to brainstorm privately, rather like an incubation process, before joining in a group effort. Others enjoy getting right to it. When brainstorming by the group will be used as a tool in a meeting, advance notice of the topic to be discussed will allow those who wish to reflect on it come better prepared to contribute enthusiastically.

Reverse brainstorming is an unusual technique that can be useful on rare occasions if the group is stuck and wishes to find another approach. With this technique, participants propose what would be considered the opposites of good ideas, such as, "If someone wanted to *increase* bullying and extortion on the school grounds, how could that be done?" Or, "If we *didn't* want students to read widely from many sections in the library, how would we discourage them from doing so?" On a cautionary note, participants need to know exactly what the purpose of this somewhat sophisticated technique is, and then should bring closure to the activity in a positive way by restating, "These are things we want *not* to do, so things we don't want to happen will not." It would be unfortunate if there were accidental eavesdroppers to a reverse brainstorm session who did not know the technique and were not informed as to the intent of the exercise!

Using the Brainstorm Technique.   A partner- or small-group brainstorming session would be appropriate for the following situation: A first-grade student has read just about every book in the small, rural school. The first-grade teacher and gifted program facilitator brainstorm possibilities for enhancing this student's reading options and augmenting the school's resources as well.

Another use for brainstorming would be thinking of ways to welcome and include new students into classroom and extracurricular activities. A third would be to brainstorm ways of getting children who are neglected socially chosen to be on teams.

Concept Mapping

Concept mapping (referred to by some as mind-mapping [Buzan, 1983], semantic mapping, webbing, or trees of knowledge or information) is a tool for identifying concepts, showing multiple relationships among them, and reflecting upon the degree of generality and inclusiveness that envelopes them (Wesley & Wesley, 1990). This visual technique allows users to display ideas, link them together, elaborate upon them, add new information as it surfaces, and review the formulation of the ideas. The process begins with one word or issue, written on paper, screen, or chalkboard, and enclosed in a geometric shape. Then other circles of subtopics, ideas, words, and concepts are linked to that central theme by lines or spokes, connecting and interconnecting where the concepts relate and interrelate. Colors and simple sketches can be used to enhance the graphics. More possibilities and new areas open up as the webbing is extended. Relationships and interrelationships that can help verbalize problems and interventions are recorded for all participants to see. If the concept map is displayed as a large mural about a topic of general interest, the process can go on and on as more ideas are generated and added.

**Video Example
from
YouTube**

▶

ENHANCEDetext
Video Example 5.4.

Watch this video to see a
demonstration of how groups
can use concept mapping
as a tool for collaborative
planning and problem
solving. (www.youtube.com/
watch?v=A625Yh6v6uQ)

Buzan (1983) offers strategies for mind mapping in which learning techniques such as note-taking can be structured to show interrelationships easily. Many students have been introduced to the concept of webbing to focus on a problem of interest and plan an independent study or develop a project. Sometimes college students are encouraged to try mind mapping by combining lecture notes and text reading to study for exams. Concept mapping is a powerful tool for generating ideas in groups as well as for enhancing individual learning. As the scope and sequence of topics become wider, concept maps can be used to structure meaningful and productive professional development activities (Bocchino, 1991).

Using Concept Mapping.   A classroom teacher has agreed to work with a new student diagnosed with Asperger syndrome. The student has acceptable social skills in some instances, and for the most part is friendly and cooperative. But he needs individual instruction, is functioning about two years below grade level, and occasionally makes threatening comments impulsively to other students. During previous visits, the teacher had indicated to the special education teacher that things were going well. But now, in the middle of November, she asks for consultation immediately. She is upset, saying things such as, "It just isn't working" and "I've tried so hard," but she has not really described the problem. How might concept mapping or webbing help in this situation? What word or phrase could go into the center to initiate the webbing process?

Synectics, Metaphors, and Janusian Thinking

Innovators in many walks of life work to develop their creative thinking skills by "seeing old things in new ways." This technique, known as **synectics** (Gordon & Poze, 1975; 1979) encourages participants to "make the familiar strange" or "make the strange familiar." Mental connections are made with facts and feelings and then broken up so that new connections can be made with new facts and feelings.

When co-educators interact to discuss their differing perspectives and preferences in the spirit of nonjudgmental curiosity and inquiry, they are helping to make what is strange become more familiar and anticipating that a gem of an idea will begin to form. This can be a welcome kick-start on the road to solving a problem.

Using Synectics.   A secondary-level teacher of students with developmental delays thought, "If I take something that was designed to challenge very bright students, and redesign it for my students, couldn't it challenge them also?" After much individual brainstorming, planning, trial and error, revision, brainstorming with selected others, and preparation of a procedural plan, he set up the catering system described in an earlier chapter in which his students provided snacks at first, then full-fledged meals after the plan was going well, for special events in the schools. The results for students' academic skills, social skills, practical skills in running the business, and feelings of self-confidence and self-esteem were immeasurable. The program became the talk of not only the school but also the entire community. After presentations at special education meetings, it received statewide attention and accolades. Creative problem-solving tools and activities *can* have real and positive outcomes.

Using Metaphorical Thinking. Metaphors are a kind of synectics, or mental maps, that permit the connection of different meanings through some shared similarity. They appear often in spoken and written communication. For example, poetic sentences such as "Life is a loom," and "The fog swallowed the ship," are metaphorical. Ordinary phrases used every day also are beautifully metaphorical, such as "Her flower garden is a paint box of intense colors, " and "It was a zoo at school today."

Metaphors connect in order to illustrate and explain. Many creative people in diverse fields have set aside conventional thinking on occasion to engage in **metaphorical thinking**. The metaphor uses one subject to strengthen and deepen understanding of another. Metaphors can guide groups to activate change processes, generate new ideas, and teach new concepts (Garmston, 1994). Some of the most important scientific, philosophical, and technical insights were conceived from an imaginative image (Pollio, 1987). Educators can use metaphors to connect two different viewpoints so one idea can be understood by means of another. They can build bridges of understanding with families and others in the community by using metaphorical language to discuss schools and student needs.

Metaphors can be tools for achieving new perspectives on unfamiliar and very familiar concepts; however, they also can be stereotypical, imprisoning our thinking if they are ill-chosen, narrow, and biased. Four types of metaphorical language that should be avoided as potential straitjackets in describing schools and students are:

- <u>Military</u>, suggested by words such as "target," "objectives," "training," "standardized," "discipline," "schedule," "information systems"
- <u>Industrial</u>, reflected in terms such as "product," "feedback," "efficiency," "quality control," "management," "cost effectiveness"
- <u>Disease</u>, implied in terms such as "diagnostic," "prescriptive," "treatment," "remediation," "monitoring," "labels," "referral"
- <u>Business</u>, where knowledge is perceived as a "commodity," intellect and talent are regarded as "capital," and research becomes a "marketable enterprise"

For example, military-metaphor language sounds like this: "After targeting areas of weakness cited by diagnostic testing, instructor(s) will schedule remedial drills for strengthening performance to meet designated objectives." Educators should choose positive terms and phrases that are free of military, disease, industrial, or business overtones. A metaphor that can set the scene for many positive approaches to learning and teaching is gardening. With this metaphorical backdrop, concepts and vocabulary can be assimilated that suggest budding potential and a harvest of productive outcomes. A gardening metaphor could include language such as the following for positive imagery and constructive planning:

- Seeds—the students
- Climate—the learning environment
- Rich soil—curriculum differentiation

- Sunlight—bright ideas
- Rain—refreshing materials and resources
- Fertilizer—curiosity, fun, stimulating activities
- Seasons—ample time, appropriate rhythms, cycles of development
- Harvest—achievement, satisfaction, accomplishment, fulfillment

Occasional "weeds" of unsuccessful methods and temporary setbacks along the way can be eliminated "organically," just as in good gardening, with techniques such as peer tutoring and cooperative learning. With continued focus on student achievement and unwavering expectations for their success, co-educators ("gardeners") will be motivated to plan wisely and students will be inspired to succeed.

■ ■ ■ ■ ■

ACTIVITY 5.5

Engaging in the Power of Metaphorical Thinking

With a group of colleagues, generate free-association responses to open-ended phrases such as:

- "Life is a _____ (party/pressure cooker/bank/car lot/battle)."
- "School is a _____ (zoo/prison/smorgasbord/twelve-act play/game)."

A second part of the activity is to continue from the image chosen, as in the following examples:

- "If school is a zoo, then teachers are ____ and students are _____."
- "If school is a twelve-act play, students are _____, teachers are _____, and principals are _____."

Open-ended phrases could move on, expanding on concepts like this:

- "Team teaching is a _____ (basketball game?) and the teachers are _____ (demonstrating a variety of skills?)."
- "Professional development activities are a _____ (battery charger?) and teachers are the (dead batteries now all charged up?)."

(Metaphors can be served as tart lessons sweetened with humor and a twist of wry!)

Using Janusian Thinking.   The process described as **Janusian thinking** was acknowledged by Rothenberg and Hausman (1976) when they studied the Eugene O'Neill play, *The Iceman Cometh*. The term was coined from the Roman god Janus, who looks backward into the old year and forward into the new (beginning in January). The process involves entertaining two or more contradictory or opposite ideas *simultaneously*—for example, sweet and salty. This simultaneous consideration of opposites creates tension that can spark original thought. As an example, Mozart told aspiring musicians that the rests in between the notes are as important, if not more so, than the notes themselves. Frank Lloyd Wright probably employed the concept of Janusian thinking because architects need to conceptualize the elements and shapes. The outer shapes must be reconciled with the inner shapes to plan a structure.

■ ■ ■ ■ ■ ■

ACTIVITY 5.6

Exploring Opportunities Provided by Janusian Thinking

With colleagues, use the technique of group brainstorming, permitting no judging of the ideas, and having a disposition where the strange become familiar—such as Sweet Tarts®, dry ice, jumbo shrimp, snow blanket—to generate more examples of Janusian thought. After thinking of several clever product-type examples, the power of the process becomes evident.

But that was the easy task. Now strive for new, Janusian-based concepts that can help students, such as creative homework, innovative drill, elementary/secondary student mentorships, and more. Teachers might be surprised at some profound combinations generated by students if they put them to the task of generating Janusian-structured school terms. Not so many years ago, some considered collaborative consultation to be a Janusian phrase, but no more.

More Techniques for Collaborative Problem Solving

A number of other collaborative activities for nurturing creative thinking are useful for exchanging information and generating ideas among co-educators to the ultimate benefit of their students. Many of them can be retrieved at websites under their descriptive names or under key words such as "creative problem solving," "creative thinking," and even "creative collaboration." A few are summarized briefly here:

Plus-Minus-Interesting.   The simple Plus-Minus-Interesting (PMI) process (deBono, 1986) can be completed in a half-hour or so, often stimulating rearrangement of perspectives and sometimes recasting values placed on those perspectives. As an example, in a school considering use of active senior citizens as reading aides, the collaborative team would generate a three-part list to show aspects that rate as pluses, then as minuses, and then as things that are interesting but the team would like to investigate further before making a decision. In making a decision, it is not necessary that the pluses exceed the minuses, and sometimes the "interesting" features may win out as the most contributive to decision making. The discussion and potential resolution that the PMI technique offers can be very helpful in problem solving.

Role Play.   A fundamental purpose of role play as a problem-solving practice is to produce new perspectives. For example, for new perspectives in a teacher-parent conflict, the teacher could take the role of the parent, and the parent that of the teacher. Other participants also have specific parts to play. At a critical part in the interaction, the leader stops the players and has the whole group explore options that would be possible from that point. Then new solutions may emerge (Torrance & Safter, 1999). In role play, the convener must be skilled and facilitative, so that the role players understand the purpose and participate intently without self-consciousness.

Talking Stick.   A very simple device for encouraging participation in discussions is the use of the talking stick, a practice ascribed to some American Indian tribes. Each person in turn takes the talking stick, restating the previous point made, even if contrary to his or hers, before adding a personal viewpoint to the discussion and then passing the stick on.

TalkWalk.   In this unique form of small-group interaction, participants engage in collegial dialogue focused on instructional and curricular issues while they walk together in an open environment (Caro & Robbins, 1991). The fresh air, physical and mental exercise, and exploration of ideas frees up thinking and expression. These domains of activity are reflective of the taxonomy domains discussed in an earlier chapter—cognitive, affective, sensorimotor, and social. The technique itself was the collaborative idea of Caro, a physician, and Robbins, an educational consultant. It calls for an element of trust among collaborators who sometimes are reluctant to seek advice from colleagues for fear of seeming incompetent. It can be used as part of a workshop or simply as an informal arrangement among colleagues.

Caro and Robbins suggest that groups of two or three work best. They propose that TalkWalk provides educators with four E-points for problem solving:

- Expertise from collective experience
- Enrichment to improve sense of self-worth and problem-solving capacity
- Expediency to obtain rapid solutions through assistance
- Exercise to bring a fresh attitude and perspective to the problem

One walk, for example, might focus on the group's vision for students who are in transition from school to work and independent living. Another might be to join preschool teachers and primary teachers in a TalkWalk to discuss that transition period for very young children. An outcome of such talks could be a plan that will help make it possible for the vision to become real.

Use of Multiple Intelligences.   A unique way to generate many perspectives and perhaps arrive at some clever solutions for problems is to frame the questions and approach them in terms of Gardner's (1993) **multiple intelligence** categories. For example, to build interest, rapport, and skills for team teaching among staff with no experience in team teaching, these questions could help with planning efforts:

- *Linguistic*—How can we use words and stories to describe team-teaching?
- *Logical-mathematical*—How might we measure the benefits and drawbacks of a team-teaching approach in our school?
- *Musical*—Should we create a team song, or motto, or cheer?
- *Spatial*—Should we make a physical map of where everything will be and what more, or less, should we include in the spaces we will share?
- *Interpersonal*—What kinds of differences in interests, preferences, values, and personal habits would be important to discuss before embarking on a team teaching mission?
- *Intrapersonal*—How would I describe my feelings about giving up some of my professional autonomy and sharing many of my ideas and techniques?
- *Bodily kinesthetic*—How can we move throughout the room, arrange materials, and get students' attention when we are teaching together in the same spaces?
- *Naturalistic*—Will our school environment accommodate the aspects of team teaching so that students are comfortable, parents are satisfied, and teachers are positive about the experience?

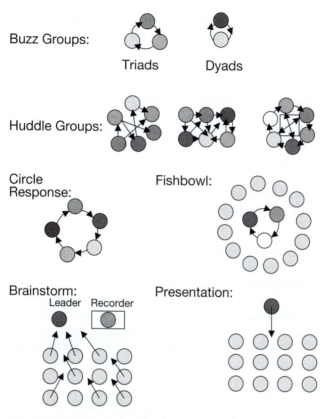

FIGURE 5.5   Interaction Structures

Interaction Formats

When assembling collaborators for group work, conveners will want to have several formats in mind for arranging physical settings and facilitating interactions that are stimulating and productive. Useful formats are: (See Figure 5.5.)

Buzz Groups.   Buzz groups work well in a group of fifty or fewer. This format ensures total participation and is easy to set up. The leader presents a topic or problem, provides minimal directions for subgrouping by twos or threes, and invites everyone to consider all aspects of the problem in the time allowed. The main disadvantage is a high noise level if the physical space is small.

Huddles.   Huddles work best with groups of five or six discussants. The leader arranges the groups, defines the topic, announces the time limit (with six minutes working well), and gives a two-minute warning that time is expiring. Each group designates its own reporter. The leader usually passes from group to group facilitating and encouraging if needed. In this structure, the participants tend to build on colleagues' contributions. The reporting process can vary, from a simple "most important points" to ranking of major points, to a written summary that is collected by the leader.

Circle Response.   Small groups of collaborators sit in a circle. The designated leader begins by stating or reiterating the topic. The response pattern moves to the left, with each taking a turn or saying, "I pass." At the end of a stipulated time, the leader summarizes the ideas and integrated thinking of the group. If discussion continues for a round or two, those who pass in the first round may choose to enter in on subsequent rounds.

Fishbowl, or Concentric Circle.   A few participants form a small circle within a larger circle of participants. The inner circle discusses an issue or a situation and the outside circle listens. Then the discussion process is reversed. Movable chairs are needed for making format changes quickly, and the issues for discussion should be chosen with needs of all participants in mind.

Presentation, Lecture Style.   Co-educators (consultees?) make a commitment to listen to the presenter (consultant?), by giving a focused hearing to the material both physically and mentally. They concentrate on the presenter as communicator, using their facilitative listening skills and focusing on the issues, not on self. The presenter states the purpose of the presentation and the expected outcomes. Sometimes a question-and-answer discussion closes the session, or a brief paper- or electronic-form survey is given to participants for ascertaining outcomes of the session. Surveys might include questions raised by the presentation that could be addressed in future presentations or in small-group collaborations with co-educators.

Other Formats.   An enterprising consultant also could consider other formats such as structured role-play, a structured or unstructured interview forum, panel discussion, reader's theater, research-and-report, and a film talk-back session as ways of encouraging interaction and information exchange among educators.

ELEMENTS THAT INTERFERE AND ELEMENTS THAT ENCOURAGE WHEN PROBLEM SOLVING

Co-educators must examine their own perspectives and preferences to identify any potential aspects that will impede their abilities to consult and collaborate on behalf of the student. Recall the four interfering themes (Caplan, 1970) that can decrease teachers' effectiveness—lack of knowledge and understanding, lack of skills for approaching problems in multiple ways, lack of objectivity, and lack of self-confidence.

Educators must be knowledgeable, skilled, objective, and self-confident, with a bit of risk-taking mixed in, to engage in divergent-thinking strategies with colleagues. When collaborating, they should:

- Use every opportunity to reinforce the efforts and successes of their colleagues.
- Take risks with curriculum and instruction for the right purposes so long as the risks are not regressive or harmful.
- Convey a desire for learning from colleagues and *their* experiences.

Too often classroom teachers, in occupying non-specialist roles among specialists, and parents, knowing their children best but entrusting them to schools for hours each day, are somewhat removed from the discussion and overlooked when ideas for addressing special learning and behavior needs are explored.

When communicating and cooperating with consultees to identify the learning or behavior need, it is important that collaborating consultants avoid sending messages intimating that classroom teachers and parents are deficient in skills that only special education teachers can provide (Friend & Cook, 1990; Huefner, 1988; Idol, Paolucci-Whitcomb, & Nevin, 1986). Good communication skills and cooperative attitudes will encourage feelings of parity and voluntariness among all school personnel and parents in the problem-solving process. Students assigned to go back and forth among resource settings in other schools for part of the week or school day may have teachers who fail to communicate about them and their work. This is a serious drawback of some cluster group arrangements where students travel from one school to another with no planned interaction among school personnel taking place. Coordination of collaborative effort is vital. This is easier said than done; sometimes it is hard even for bus drivers to coordinate the comings and goings of students among buildings.

Special education teachers who cannot identify basal reading curriculum used in various levels, and classroom teachers who cannot identify the nature of instruction taking place in the resource room, make problem identification more difficult (Idol, West, & Lloyd, 1988). Their lack of shared knowledge may even intensify the problems. Solutions should be based on sound instructional practice and take into account what we know about learning and behavior. If a solution is chosen because it is a quick fix but won't stand up over time, the person with specialized knowledge in the area needs to point out the flaws of a hastily conceptualized solution (Knackendoffel, et al., 1992). All parties must think about their own roles in a problem situation and endeavor to learn from each other by interacting, deferring judgment, and coordinating services. A team approach is a productive way to assess the context, conditions, interfering themes, and circumstances surrounding the student's needs and the school programs designed to meet those needs.

Positive Situations

Some collaborative consultations are more successful than others, while occasionally they are disappointing or downright discouraging. The following are examples of collaborative school consultants feeling positive and successful in their roles:

- Primary-level teachers and I sat down and discussed what materials they thought would be good to order and place in the resource room for their use as well as mine. Everyone had a chance to share needs, express opinions, and offer some recommendations.
- An undergraduate asked me about my student teaching and substituting days. She was feeling very down and unsure of her teaching abilities. I reassured her by telling of some things that had happened to me (and why). I encouraged her to find a dependable support system and gave her some ideas and things to think about.

- A teacher I have spent several weeks with stopped me in the hall yesterday to ask for an idea to use in her class that next hour. Before she finished putting her question into words, she had thought of an idea herself, but she still thanked me!
- I participated in a parent conference in which the parent wanted to kick the daughter out of the house and into a boarding school. It ended with the daughter agreeing to do more work at home and the mother agreeing to spend one special hour of togetherness a week with just her daughter.
- I talked with a physical education teacher about student responsibilities to learn health vocabulary. She had already shortened the assignment to five or ten words as individual needs dictated. I agreed to reinforce learning with some drill and memory of the words in my classroom, which I did. Students seemed very pleased that their teachers were working together.
- My son has several visual problems that may result in blindness. I talked with his first-grade teacher to discuss ways of helping him. She was feeling overwhelmed. I was in a position to suggest ways she could modify the classroom. She mentioned several times how much she appreciated having a parent, who is also a teacher, having helped her and especially having helped my son.

Not-So-Positive Situations

The following are examples of collaborative consultation attempts that did not turn out so well. These could be topics for discussion among co-educators as to what could have prevented the disappointing outcomes and importantly, whether these instances could be rectified after they occurred.

- A kindergarten child was staffed into my program, but the teacher wouldn't let me take her out of "her" class time. So I arranged to keep the child after school. The first night I was late coming to get the child, and the teacher blew up about it.
- Our music teacher asks students who cannot read to stand up in class and read, and then berates them when they stumble over words. I approached the teacher about the situation, but the teacher would have nothing to do with me, and after that made things even worse for the students.
- In visiting with the principal about alternatives in altering classroom assignments, it ended with his speaking harshly and suggesting that I was finding fault with the school staff, which I had not done.
- I give a sticker every day to a student who has learning disabilities if he attends and does his work in the resource room. His classroom teacher complained to the principal about it because "other students work hard and don't get stickers."
- A teacher of a student with a developmental disability wanted to obtain a computer for him. I made numerous calls, read a lot of material, and visited a computer store. The child, the child's father, and I went to another facility that cursorily assessed the child's potential for using a computer. But when I tried to communicate the assessment particulars to the teacher, I couldn't remember many of them.

I kicked myself for not writing things down, and I've ended up having little impact on this situation.

- At the present time I am working with a homebound sixth grade student with learning disabilities. One of his classroom teachers does not seem to be aware of the learning problems this student faces or the limited time he receives for instruction. I spoke up and tried to talk with her, but I was so emotional about the child that I felt I didn't communicate well.

WHAT TO DO IF COLLABORATIVE PROBLEM SOLVING FAILS TO ADDRESS AN ISSUE

There is no universal agreement on what makes group problem solving effective, and there is too little research to guide consultants as to what should be said and done in collaborative consultation. The ten steps outlined earlier have worked well for many consultants and consulting teachers. However, if this method of ten steps does not work, consultants can put forth questions such as:

- Was the problem defined accurately?
- Did all participants practice good listening skills?
- Were feelings addressed empathically?
- Were the nitty-gritty details worked out?
- Were pertinent hidden agendas brought to light and handled?
- Were all participants appropriately assertive?
- Was the consultation process evaluated and then discussed?
- Could any other problem-solving tools have facilitated the process?
- Did follow-through and follow-up activities take place after the conference?
- Should participants convene in groups to practice problem-solving techniques?

When practicing collaborative consultation techniques, which ones worked best? How did individual differences influence the activity? Were these individual differences used constructively, and if not, what could have been done to capitalize on the diversity? Did participants become better collaborators as they tried more scenarios?

When groups of co-educators gather (keeping in mind that for some IEP conferences the number of adults in attendance may be as many as a dozen), responsibility for handling confidential material is compounded. Also, co-educators need to be watchful for unwanted outcomes that can result from "groupthink," where negativity, bias, failure to examine risks of proposed choices, and failure to work out plans carefully can be detrimental to any and all involved (Murray, 1994). Ethical principles of collaboration and teamwork will guide co-educators in discussing sensitive matters efficiently, objectively, and respectfully. This is a "win-win" situation for all.

 ENHANCEDetext **Application Exercise 5.1.** Click to apply your understanding of the ten-step problem-solving process.

TIPS FOR PROBLEM SOLVING WITH COLLABORATIVE SCHOOL CONSULTATION

1. Have data, relevant materials, and thoughts organized before consultations, and develop a list of questions that will help ferret out the real problem.

2. Develop a checklist of information typically needed. Do not be reluctant to say that you do not have the answer(s). If it is something you should know, find out as soon as possible and get back to the person who asked.

3. Have strategies and materials in mind that may be helpful to the situation, but do not try to have all of the answers or offer solutions too readily because this discourages involvement by others who may have been struggling with the situation for some time.

4. Avoid jargon, and shun suggestions that conflict with school policies or favored practices of individual teachers; whenever possible use the terms "we" and "us," not "I" and "you."

5. Make it a habit to look for something positive about the teacher, the class(es), and the student, and comment encouragingly on those things by providing positive feedback, not just negative perspectives.

6. Don't try to "fix it" if it is not "broken," or wait for the consultee to make the first move, or expect that teachers will be enthused and flattered to field questions about their classrooms and teaching methods.

7. When school co-educators or home co-educators seek advice about a student, first ask what they already have observed. This gets them involved and encourages their ownership in the situation, along with providing more information that can be helpful.

8. Know how to interpret test results and how to discuss those results clearly with other participants in the conference setting; if insecure about it, have a practice session with a supportive colleague.

9. When possible, provide family members with samples of the student's schoolwork to discuss during the conference, remembering to refrain from talking while they are perusing the materials. Have a list of resources ready to share for helping with homework, suggesting incentives and reinforcements, and providing study tips.

10. Maintain contact with teachers during the year. The collaborating teacher or family may have detected an improvement that is directly related to your work, and it will be uplifting and energizing for you to know that!

CHAPTER 6

USING TOOLS FOR ORGANIZING, MANAGING, AND EVALUATING COLLABORATION

Schools are bustling arenas of activities, with much more activity for students than simply books and studies, and much more responsibility for teachers and support staff than just instructing and disciplining. Not only do school personnel teach students in academic settings, they also feed them, transport them, keep records, coach, counsel and advise, dispense materials and resources, address social and health problems, and much, much more. If the services of various school-related roles such as library and media specialist, speech pathologist, school psychologist, social worker, counselor, and nurse, were included, the list of responsibilities for educators would be even more daunting. With all of these working pieces in the school landscape, organization and management are key components of successful collaboration and consultation. Consultants run the risk of spinning their wheels if efforts aren't well coordinated with clear goals directing their activities. In addition, consultants cannot know if consultation activities are effective unless they evaluate their efforts and the results. We have all heard the familiar directives of the flight attendant who instructs passengers, in the case of an emergency, to take care of yourself first and then help your traveling companions. Similar advice should be heeded by collaborating teachers. Consultants must have all the working pieces under control or risk falling prey to stress and burnout. An over-extended consultant who feels out-of-control and frazzled is unlikely to have energy for thoughtful communication and problem-solving exchanges. Enthusiasm for coming to work each day and creativity for problem solving will likely be in short supply. Therefore, collaborating teachers need to periodically take their own inventory but also implement strategies to assist co-educators in dealing with issues of stress and burnout, meetings, schedules, recordkeeping, and confidentiality.

CHAPTER OBJECTIVES

Upon completing this chapter, the reader should be able to:

1. Describe aspects of education that make school personnel vulnerable to stress and burnout and suggest stress reduction strategies.

2. Propose ways of managing time and turf so as to find time for collaboration and teaming.

3. Indicate procedures for conducting meetings, interviews, and observations that can contribute to success in collaborations and teamwork.

4. Illustrate ways collaborating school consultants can manage records and resources more efficiently, using up-to-date technology.

5. Identify ways consultants can use self-assessments to improve their skills.

6. Explain why evaluation is important for collaborative school consultation in educational and community settings.

7. Describe the steps in designing and implementing an evaluation of collaborative school consultation programs and activities, including some important considerations when doing so.

KEY TERMS

attrition
burnout
consultation log or journal
eustress

evaluation
formative evaluation
impacts
logic model

self-efficacy
stakeholders
summative evaluation
time management

SITUATION 6

The setting is a coffee shop in a university's Student Union facility. Three faculty members from the College of Education—one who teaches educational psychology for education majors, another who teaches a methods class for education majors, and a third who teaches a class on exceptional children in the inclusive classroom, are sharing views about their new students for the semester.

Educational Psychology Instructor: I am impressed with the new group of students we have this semester in our teacher education program.

Instructor for Exceptional Child Class: I haven't been here as long as you have, but from what I have observed during my first two class sessions, I agree that they seem to be strong and very capable and dedicated as a whole.

Methods Class Instructor: They're so idealistic. They are sure that they will be able to inspire kids and excite them toward learning. They say they want to make a positive difference in their students' lives. I hope that in two years or so they'll be well prepared and strong enough to deal with all the challenges out there, especially if they accept positions in tough schools with many difficult students.

Instructor for Exceptional Child Class: Yes, or all too soon they'll be joining the ranks of teachers who burn out after just three or four years in the profession. I'm alarmed at the attrition rate for new teachers in this country.

Methods Class Instructor: We should all be alarmed about the data on teacher burnout and attrition. The statistics are an urgent message to us in teacher education programs to prepare them as best we can. Of course, we all think our own classes are vital toward that effort! But besides knowing their subject matter well, new teachers will need to be competent in many kinds of things. I believe a key area of competence that novice teachers need to develop is collaboration and consultation, with a lot of teamwork.

Educational Psychology Instructor: You raise a good point. Even though we offer that in a graduate-level course, the knowledge and practices it provides are needed by all teachers from day one, not just after they are out in the schools for several years and working toward a master's degree.

Instructor for Exceptional Child Class: And it shouldn't be only for special education majors. It's just as important for the general education teachers to develop those skills, for they are the other side of the equation.

Both Educational Psychology and Methods Instructors, in Unison: Well said!

TEACHER ATTRITION, SATISFACTION, AND EFFICACY

The dedication and enthusiasm of educators wishing to mold younger generations and make the world into a better place must be retained and maintained. However, in the complex hubbub of school life, demands on the professional educator can be overwhelming. When consulting teachers are asked to name the biggest obstacle for performing these responsibilities to the very best of their abilities, the overwhelming response is, "Time!" A study released by the Council for Exceptional Children in October, 2000 (*CEC Today*, Nov. 2000), cited overwhelming paperwork, pressure of high caseloads, lack of needed support by administrators, and shortage of qualified special education teachers as major concerns. Teachers stressed that they needed more time for collaborative planning, and 15 percent of the respondents reported having *no* time for individualized instruction. Only 26 percent reported having more than three hours a day with their intact classes of students. An aspect of their work was a lack of time for the planning and collaborating that are vital components of instructional accommodations and modifications for special needs.

Teacher retention has been a burning issue in education for decades, particularly in areas of science, math, the arts, and *special education*. Levine (2006) points out that due to population increases, immigration of students, and the inevitability of teachers reaching retirement age, numbers of school-age population are rising while numbers of teachers are decreasing. Recruiting and preparing strong, effective teachers must be a top priority, but several factors erode preparation of teachers and support for teachers after they enter the profession. These include ever-expanding costs of maintaining schools, public criticism as reflected in polls and the media, low morale among educators, and an avalanche of regulations and paperwork. Nearly one-fourth of new teachers leave after only two years, and one-third leave within five years (Ingersoll, 2002; Millinger, 2004).

Stress and fatigue take a toll, with burnout and **attrition** from the teaching profession as all too frequent results. The challenge of professional accountability for student achievement is a heavy burden. High-stakes testing to the neglect of the subject matter they love takes a heavy toll on teachers as well as on students. When teachers are not satisfied in their roles, they become candidates for burnout and attrition. But role-related stress can be minimized. The heavy responsibilities fueling that stress can be controlled by organizing and managing time and resources wisely.

More recent studies indicate that attrition in the first few years of teaching is an escalating situation, with an alarming one-third of new teachers leaving the profession within five years (Darling-Hammond, 2003). Shortages of special education teachers plague school districts; the attrition rate among special education teachers is 13 percent annually (Plash & Piotrowski, 2006). Newly hired special education teachers are 2.5 times as likely to leave teaching compared to other beginning teachers (Smith & Ingersoll, 2004). Sadly, teacher turnover is 50 percent higher in schools with high poverty levels than in other schools (Ingersoll, 2001). Special education teachers as advocates for children with special learning and behavior needs may be setting unreasonably high expectations for themselves and others. Lack of administrative support, along with heavy caseloads, confusion over role responsibilities, and not much decision-making authority are additional stressors, particularly for special education personnel (Vittek, 2015).

An unfortunate reality of the teacher shortage is the distressing exodus of experienced teachers in special education. Many leave their special education positions within a few years, with some of those quitting the profession altogether, but nearly half transfer to general education positions (Plash & Piotrowski, 2006). As needs for special education teachers mushroom, the numbers of educators who prepare for special education and subsequently enter the field have been dwindling. Demands imposed on classroom teachers by high-stakes testing and recent federal mandates have weighed heavily on teachers, making it hard for them to feel good about what they do. One fourth-grade teacher spoke for many of her colleagues when she put it this way: "I wanted to be a teacher, and I'm glad to be a teacher, but it's just not fun anymore."

Professional satisfaction is a key variable in the effort to increase retention and enhance the work settings of special education personnel. Some educators remain in the profession and juggle their daily routines within a burgeoning agenda of reform and mandates. Others burn out and leave the profession. Still others simply "fizzle out," "rust out," or "coast out." This last group tends to go through the motions of their profession in lackluster fashion, just getting by until retirement age arrives or a better opportunity comes along. These educators create situations that are particularly penalizing for students who have special needs and are most vulnerable to the effects of uninspired teaching.

One factor that can influence professional satisfaction is teacher **self-efficacy**. This is the belief that teachers have the ability to mold their own actions in ways that affect the learning and behavior of their students. Teacher efficacy correlates positively with higher student achievement, effective teacher practices, increased family involvement, decreased referral rates to special education, and higher job commitment by teachers (Hoy & Woolfolk, 1993). Importantly, teacher self-efficacy has an inverse correlation with burnout among general educators (Friedman, 2003.) More recently, Leko and Smith (2010) and others (Viel-Ruma, Houchins, Jolivette, & Benson, 2010) recommend professional development programs and strong induction programs to promote self-efficacy. They also advocate for school improvements in curriculum, discipline, and school status within the community as ways of enhancing collective efficacy.

Reducing Teacher Stress and Teacher Burnout

Teacher **burnout** can come about from physical and emotional exhaustion. Prolonged stress or the buildup of stressors causes fatigue and frustration. According to Maslach (1982), a researcher of burnout among service professionals for many years, there are three basic components of burnout:

1. Emotional exhaustion ("I'm tired and irritated all the time. I am impatient with my students and colleagues.")
2. Depersonalization ("I am becoming emotionally hardened; I start to blame the students or their families for all the problems.")
3. Reduced accomplishment ("I feel like I'm not making a difference for my students.")

The results of burnout can be attrition, alienation, cynicism, and physical problems such as heart disease, hypertension, ulcers, headaches, and psychosomatic illnesses. Stressors that cause stress reactions are many and varied. For the general education teacher as well as the special education teacher, a stressor could be a new special education regulation, being asked to provide services to students outside the scope of training or certification, too much paperwork, too many meetings that seem to go nowhere, an angry parent, a student who is behaving in a violent manner, or some or all of the above.

Most educators have a vast repertoire of coping skills, and we all know that stress in general is a normal life process. In fact, there is **eustress** (Schultz, 1980), a little-discussed phenomenon of proactive, positive response to a stimulus, such as that experienced by artists, entertainers, athletes, speakers, and yes, teachers, before going "on stage" that helps people perform at their best. It can even help us learn and grow. Those who have experienced some conditions such as eustress probably are more likely to have good coping skills and to be empathetic with others under stress than people who have not.

On the other hand, *dis*tress (anxiety, sorrow, pain, trouble) wears us down physically and emotionally. Busy, conscientious educators will never be able to reduce or eliminate all the stressors in their lives, but they can develop some positive coping skills that lessen the burden and strengthen resolve to overcome the difficulties.

Teacher education programs must be strong learning centers for preparing pre-service teachers to succeed as novice teachers so that they will want to remain in the profession. Management techniques for time and other resources, organizing structures for some of the more burdensome tasks, evaluation procedures that provide careful analysis of the outcomes, and the assistance of technology, are four areas that can minimize stress and reduce attrition from the profession.

Undergraduate students, when queried about their greatest concerns for their first years in the profession, have named areas that fit remarkably into Caplan's (1970) four "lack-of" themes noted in earlier chapters: knowledge, skill, objectivity, and self-confidence. Their questions, as major concerns driven by these themes, are: Will I know my subjects well enough? Will I be able to prepare good, motivating lessons? Can I manage the classroom and discipline the students appropriately? How will I be when it comes to working with parents? Will I know how to serve all students' special needs? Do I have the skills to provide appropriate feedback and grade students fairly?

Can I be confident that I can handle everything and not be a big failure? Teacher efficacy is needed here.

Novice teachers have many pressures that dampen their enthusiasm in the first years of teaching. This is the time when temptation to leave the profession is high. New teachers may be very stressed emotionally, physically, and socially. Understandably, new teachers fear being judged as incapable and failing if they ask for suggestions or outright assistance. Given the importance of perceived self-efficacy, it is important to build it up as a way of retaining new special education teachers.

Strategies for Reducing Stress

Developing adaptive strategies to reduce stress is crucial to maintaining emotional and physical health for all teachers, whether novice or veteran. Occasional, moderate stress can be positive and challenge us to be resourceful, but too much stress can be harmful. The techniques individuals use depend on their preferences and life styles. Collaborators must learn to "work smarter, not harder" to accomplish goals for students who are at risk of failure in school. They must take care of themselves so they do not lose their energy and enthusiasm, and students with special needs do not lose their good, caring teachers.

One group of special education teachers makes a commitment to meet each Friday at a centralized place for lunch and lively conversation. Ground rules stipulate there will be no talking about students, schools, or staff in that public place. The camaraderie and conviviality of the weekly event, looked on favorably by district administrators, is an effective support system for teachers whose roles invite stress.

Building mutually supportive networks of co-educators will minimize, if not totally eliminate, feelings of isolation and helplessness for those in demanding roles. It helps to talk things out with others and develop new outlooks when in the throes of the complex responsibilities inherent in working with special needs students.

In a cover article about managing stress in *ASCD Education Update* (January, 2012), Julie Proctor, a health and wellness coordinator at Oakland University in Rochester, Michigan, advises us to laugh every day and do something fun. When you feel yourself getting anxious, take three deep breaths and focus on your breathing. Outside activities can be a great stress reliever, so unplug the TV, computer, and cell phone. Develop a healthy social life. Support systems are crucial for handling stress; thus, a healthy social life is important.

What if burnout has occurred or is at least in the glowing embers stage and ready to flare up at most any time? What if an educator is experiencing low self-esteem, emotional distress, and physical exhaustion now? Strategies such as these can help:

1. Talk to someone, give a positive comment, let it be known you could use one in return, and share ideas.
2. Find a former teacher who was very important in your life and tell that person how much you learned with his or her guidance.
3. Schedule some time to be alone and reflect on your profession. Some find keeping a journal or blogging as a way to reflect. Reading the blogs of others such as CEC's *Reality 101* blog for new special education teachers can help a new teacher feel not quite so alone.

4. Laugh out loud. Each person should have his or her "laugh ration" every day for mental and physical health. So read, or watch a funny show, or subscribe to a daily comic in your inbox, or simply observe children or animals at play. A little diversion from the stresses of the job and life is good for the soul.

5. Move, stretch, jog. Mild exercise gets the blood flowing and transports more oxygen throughout the body, helping you feel alert and alive. Sunlight and fresh air help body and mind function well. A fifteen- to thirty-minute walk before work in the morning or in the evening can be good for the mind as well as the body. If alone, use the time to clear your mind, reflect on a situation, or just listen to your favorite music or audio book. Having a walking partner can provide a social break while getting exercise. One group of teachers meet in the school gym each day after school and walk several laps around the gym or building together feeling somewhat more invigorated before returning to their classrooms and tackling their end-of-day to-do list.

6. Play energetic, happy music. Classical music is best. Listening to sixty-cycle music such as that by Bach, Handel, and Mozart has been shown to increase alpha brain wave, the relaxation wavelength (Douglass & Douglass, 1993).

7. Break the routine. Take a different route when driving to work. Treat yourself to your favorite morning beverage on your drive to work. Rearrange your schedule or your furniture. Take a vacation if you can and when you do, leave worries and cares behind. Give yourself over to relaxation and rejuvenation.

8. Keep a jar of little treats on your desk, such as encouraging statements, or an envelope with a five-dollar bill to splurge on yourself now and again. Positive reinforcement is not just for kids.

9. Use reminders to help remember these and other prevention and intervention strategies. When placed in a planner or calendar, they can be self-motivating.

10. Remind yourself often that prevention and remediation of stress and burnout are the concern of the individual adult, not family or friends or colleagues. Every person needs to make deposits into a personal bank of techniques for keeping the flames of motivation and enthusiasm alive.

MANAGING TIME AND TURF

School improvement issues and legislative mandates may have convinced educators that the concept of collaborative school consultation is a promising method for helping students with special needs. However, for some teachers, the conversion to co-educator concepts and collaborative practices is not so simple and can be unsettling. As for novice teachers who did not have collaborative experiences in their teacher preparation program, collaborative principles can put them off balance just when they are starting out in their first teaching role. They may be thinking:

- Will participation in collaboration and consultation make me appear to be less competent?
- How much of my classroom time with students will be needed to provide this method of service to kids, and how do I go about allocating that time?

- Don't I need to work out a plan for my classroom and get experience with that before I collaborate with others and certainly before I co-teach?
- When in the world will I find time and space to interact like this with other teachers anyway?

Studies have shown that collaborating teachers chafe under time pressures of attending meetings, preparing and planning, teaching, conferencing with parents and students, administering tests, communicating with related services and support personnel, observing, evaluating, and problem solving. (See Figure 6.1.) Time, the precious, nonrenewable commodity everyone receives equally, requires decision-making about allocation and management. We should devote more time to organizing and managing time, and seek out tools that will help us put it to good use in the most powerful ways possible. Educator ingenuity can produce innovative ways of carving out time in an already-packed day if it becomes a top priority to do so.

A key factor in managing time and arranging schedules is the teacher's caseload. Those with both direct and indirect service roles should have their ratios classified for each category, and students receiving consultative services as well as direct services should be counted twice on the consulting teacher's caseload. Solutions to the time element lie in how educators choose to use the time available to them. Time may not be adaptable, but people are. An ancient Chinese proverb says, "You cannot change the wind, but you can adjust the sail." **Time management** skills can be learned and improved. Because time management is about choices, it is very personal. The best management plan for one is not the best one for another. A basic five-step plan is useful for making one's own time management plan:

FIGURE 6.1   "I Need a System Here!"

**Video Example
from
YouTube**

ENHANCEDetext
Video Example 6.1.

After watching this video, reflect on areas at school and home where you aren't as productive as you'd like to be. Identify your time-wasting habits and prioritize what you need to accomplish. (https://www.youtube.com/watch?v=VUk6LXRZMMk)

1. Analyze your current use of time.
2. Establish your goals and priorities.
3. Allocate your time and work.
4. Use positive time management techniques.
5. Review the results, rethink any problem areas, and reinforce successes.

Accountability for Collaborative Consultation Time

Many consultants, when asked specifically how they use their time, rely on memory or perceptions. However, to make significant improvements in time management, busy consultants must accurately observe and *record* their use of time. Time logs are a valuable way to observe personal use of time and they ultimately save time rather than waste it. Consultants may choose to use a diary time log, recording everything they do, when they do it, and how long it takes. Another option is to record time in fifteen-minute segments, or use a matrix that lists times of the day in segments and highlights elements of the consulting role. The matrix can be used to check off quickly those responsibilities that were handled in each segment. Then time spent on each activity can be totaled at the end of the day. When recording use of time, remember to begin early in the day, not waiting until the end of the day and then trying to remember it all, for the log record will come up short almost every time.

It is helpful to review long-term goals daily. They should be posted on the desk, the wall, or in a planner. This simple activity makes goals visual and helps one stay focused. Long-term goals should be subdivided into short-term goals, weekly goals, and daily goals. Keep a master "to do" list with priority codes matching items to your goals, assigning a due date to each project, because due dates keep tasks from being put off and they foster a sense of completion when accomplished. There are many existing systems that can help with this organizational task. Some find a technology-based app or system works best for them, while others prefer using a paper-based system such as a Bullet Journal or one of the many popular teacher planbook/calendar systems. Find the system that works best for you and then be diligent in recording your goals and to-do list every day so it becomes a habit.

Putnam (1993) offers a number of practical tips for making every minute count, including establishing goals and staying focused during work time; delegating routine tasks when possible to students, aides, and parent volunteers; minimizing procrastination; and learning to say "no" when warranted by practicing until it feels firm and guilt-free, and then really doing it.

Time management procedures encourage efficient use of abilities and strengths. The purpose of time management is not to get *everything* done, but to meet high-priority goals successfully. Being busy is not the same as being productive. Time management is a skill that can be learned and improved. See Figure 6.2 for one consulting teacher's weekly organizer form.

WEEKLY ORGANIZER

Dates: _____ to _____

Week at a Glance				
Monday /	Tuesday /	Wednesday /	Thursday /	Friday /

To Do (Priority)	To See	
	Person/Place	Time

To Do (Eventually)	To Phone/E-mail	
	Person	Phone number/E-mail address

☺ Notes & Reminders ☺

FIGURE 6.2   A Weekly Organizer Form

ACTIVITY 6.1
Using Time Wisely

Physicists define time as nature's way to keep everything from happening at once. By planning time and managing time-wasters, educators can be more productive and less stressed. Try one or more of these strategies and then reflect on how they helped:

1. *Make "to do" lists—monthly, weekly, and/or daily lists.* Make each list at the same time of day on the same kind of paper. Write down all that needs to be done and plan all activities, even those such as talking with friends or playing with the family. Then prioritize the list. Lakein (1973) suggests "ABC-ing" the list, with A as top priority for only those items that *must* be done. Designate B priorities as "nice if done" and

C jobs as "maybe later." You might even end up with a D—or "So what?"—list. Handle the C tasks sensibly. If they can't be delegated or ignored, try putting them on an extra-minutes list.

2. *Say "no" when you need to.* Avoid saying "Well …," or "I'll think about it." Certainly avoid, "I will if you can't find anyone else" because they *won't* find anyone else. Responding with "This is so important that it needs more attention than I can give it now" is often very effective.

3. *Delegate.* This is the perfect solution for C priorities, if a helper is available. Teachers are habituated into functioning autonomously, but others may be just waiting for a chance to contribute and develop their own skills or to receive recognition for being a good team player.

4. *Set deadlines and time limits.* Plan a personal treat for accomplishing a task by a deadline. Limiting time helps get things done efficiently and prevents simple tasks from becoming major projects. It prevents letting the intentions to clean out one drawer become major cleaning of the whole desk, file cabinet, and book shelves, for example.

5. *Organize desk and office area.* A work area can be so cluttered that it is difficult, if not impossible, to find things, concentrate, or work efficiently.

6. *Get a "do not disturb" sign and use it without guilt.* Some teachers have had great success making and using work-status cubes for their desk *and* even encouraging their students to do the same. Faces on one's cube can convey messages such as "Please do not disturb right now," "I need help," "This is not a good day for me, so be patient, please," or "I'm available if assistance is needed."

7. *Plan time for yourself.* Busy educators often devote so much time and energy to taking care of others that it comes at the expense of neglecting themselves. Take time to relax, visit with others in the building, talk to a child, read a book, go for a walk, or sketch a picture. If you absolutely cannot get away, take a few minutes to imagine where you would like to be and "go there" in your mind for a while, or simply close your eyes while listening to your favorite music for a short mind break.

Finding Time for Collaboration and Teaming

Managing time and schedules in order to collaborate effectively is indeed one of the biggest challenges for co-educators. Co-planning and working in teams is needed for meaningful inclusion and supporting students in the least restrictive environment, but teachers need to have the time available in order to do that. Many educators believe outcomes-based education and performance-based assessment are promising innovations for schools, but they acknowledge that each plan requires additional teacher plan time. How to accomplish that is as yet unresolved.

Time has emerged as the key issue inherent in every school-change analysis for many years. Raywid (1993) found that strategies for gaining time included freeing up existing time used for some lesson priority, restructuring or rescheduling time, using available time more efficiently, or buying time from other facets of the school context. Examples from this research include:

- Teachers sharing the same lunch period with their planning period after lunch, which results in 90 minutes of shared time per day

- Teachers interacting while students leave the building a few hours weekly to perform community service
- Substitutes hired with money saved by increasing class sizes by one or two students
- Daylong staff development for three to five days per year in some districts
- Compensatory time for teachers participating in two- to three-day planning sessions during breaks between terms
- Staff development days, with as many as five or more instructional days waived by state legislatures
- Lengthened instructional days
- Special talents and skills programs provided by specialists or community service days for students while teachers meet to collaborate and plan
- University personnel working in partnership to provide activities that free up teachers to interact

Note that most of the ideas above would require administrator approval and assistance. Building administrators must be the driving force to make such things happen. In some areas, teachers meet to develop rubrics, tests, teaching ideas, and the like. They are not required to make reports or write summaries as justification for time spent. They are just asked to show the products that resulted from the shared time. Other faculties brainstorm in an initial collaborative effort to come up with unique ideas for carving out more extensive collaborative time. Still others have grade-level or departmental plan time on a regular basis during some music, art, and physical education periods.

In one district, teachers were convinced that their high school students didn't get enough sleep. These teachers also were looking for ways and means of collaborating. So a policy was put into place to have late-start days every other Wednesday, moving school starting time from 8:00 a.m. to 8:30, to allow teachers an extra 30 minutes to meet and students an extra 30 minutes to sleep in, visit, or study. Administrators and para-educators supervised the students who showed up early. The Professional Learning Communities (PLC) model that was first implemented in Adlai Stevenson High School in Lincolnshire, Illinois, guided the time allocated for meeting together. Even experienced teachers reported learning many useful things during their time together. Guidelines for the teachers required that there be no cell phones used and no complaining. Instead, teachers shared ideas and discussed ways to improve student achievement (Silva, Thessin, & Starr, 2011).

In another district, three building administrators made it possible for teachers to form interdisciplinary teams that meet on their own time—Saturdays for breakfast or before or after school—to work on instruction that would use authentic achievement criteria (Stewart & Brendefur, 2005). The trade-off was that they were excused from regular professional development days. As they participated in the learning team, they adjusted to the reality that their work was available for scrutiny by others. A master teacher marveled at how much she learned, saying she could only imagine how much a *new* teacher might have learned. Her administrator became convinced that learning teams could improve instruction.

Other educational leaders have found new ways of creating time to collaborate. Some work with the parent–teacher organization to implement volunteer substitute-teacher programs that free up teachers. Others revise schedules to provide shared planning time, and still others release teachers from school duties such as lunch and bus supervision, and student activities and assemblies. Peer-tutoring programs across classes can free up time for team meetings, although start time and monitoring time must be factored in. Many innovative ideas are available, but generating and implementing the ideas requires time to plan and coordinate them.

In an *Education Update* (ASCD, 2000) from the Association for Supervision and Curriculum Development, finding time for collaborating is described as "not a question of know-how, but of want-to." Teachers want collaborative time to be part of staff development that occurs during the school day, not after school or on Saturdays. They value sharing materials and ideas, developing rubrics, asking big questions, doing joint planning, and making presentations to one another on tried-and-true techniques. When teachers have premium time arranged for working collaboratively on creating helpful strategies for curriculum and instruction, they refrain from using the shared time for routine activities such as grading papers.

Even more strategies for increasing collaboration time have been used successfully at elementary, middle, junior high, and senior high levels, including ideas such as these (ASCD, 2000; West, 1990):

- Bringing large groups of students together for speakers, films, or plays
- Using volunteers such as grandparents, parents, community leaders, and retired teachers
- Hiring a permanent "floating substitute"
- Having the principal set aside one day per grading period as "collaboration day" with no other activities on this day
- Having the principal or another staff supervisor teach a period a day regularly
- Having students working on independent or study activities while clustered in large groups under supervision
- Having faculty vote to extend the instructional day twenty minutes for two days a week

TECHNIQUES FOR MEETINGS AND OBSERVATIONS

Who has not winced at the thought of having another meeting to attend? Meetings, interviews, and classroom observations command precious time as well as physical and mental energy. Collective time and energy are wasted when people are trapped in unproductive meetings. Educators who want to work smarter, not harder, should set goals for having group interactions that are efficient and productive for all.

Conducting Efficient Meetings

Special educators are busy, but classroom teachers are among the most overextended of all. Many express their frustration that the total time is appallingly short for having all of their students together for a class period without someone or another coming and going. Consultation and collaboration will be accepted more readily when consultees know that consultants respect their time and their students' time. So meetings should be planned only if they can contribute significantly to serving students' needs.

The first rule in planning an efficient meeting is to ask, "Do we really need to have this meeting?" If the answer is not a resounding "Yes," then the business probably can be handled in a more efficient way, perhaps by memo, e-mail, phone, or brief face-to-face conversations with individuals. Good reasons for having a meeting are:

- Fulfilling legal obligations (such as an IEP conference)
- Brainstorming about a need in order to generate many ideas
- Problem-solving with several people in diverse roles to explore options
- Reconciling conflicting views among school, students, and home
- Providing a forum for all to be heard
- Building a team to make and implement educational decisions

Video Example from YouTube

ENHANCEDetext
Video Example 6.2.

After watching this video, which ideas did you find the most helpful as you think about running effective and efficient meetings? (https://www.youtube.com/watch?v=FQYUHpi0fhk)

Unnecessary meetings do waste much school time and teacher time. They also erode participants' confidence in the value of future meetings that may be called. Meetings should be called only when there is verifiable need and an overall purpose with definite objectives. Only people who can make a contribution need to be there. An agenda should be prepared and distributed in advance, and the meeting room and any needed equipment should be made ready ahead of time. Most important, the meeting must begin on time with no waiting for latecomers, and end on time, or early if possible.

Leaders or chairpersons of meetings will be more prepared and organized if they follow a planning checklist. (See Figure 6.3 for an example.) The planning sheet should include general planning points such as date, start and anticipated end time, participants, and goals. Checklists designed to set forth preparations for the room and to note participant needs also will be useful.

Meeting groups should be as small as possible, adhering to the principle concerning meetings that the more who are involved, the shorter it should be. If a problem-solving group includes more than six people, it is likely that not everyone will have an opportunity to contribute. Agendas are also important. Sometimes e-mail or memos can be used to solicit agenda items from those who will participate. An e-mail agenda should be sent in advance to allow participants to add additional items to the agenda, and it also encourages everyone to come prepared. As a variation to the typical agenda format, the agenda topics could be given in question format. For example, rather than "Scheduling for the Resource Room," the issue might be "How can we construct a fair, workable schedule for use of the resource room on M–W–F?" With an agenda distributed beforehand and a stop-time given, participants will be more productive and less apprehensive. Sometimes a short, high-interest activity, relating to the topic can be displayed on a whiteboard or projected on a screen in the front of the room. Participants focus on the activity as they arrive, becoming centered on the meeting topic(s) as they do so. Meetings are more effective when participants can anticipate the task.

It is important to allocate time for each item on the agenda. It is counterproductive to focus too long on early items and fail to get to the last ones. If more important items are placed far down the agenda and time becomes short, it might even appear that they have

FIGURE 6.3   Checklist to Prepare for Meetings

Date: _____   Place: _____

Time: _____   Topic: _____

Participants: _____

Goals for Meeting: _____

_____

_____

Preparation of Room: Preparation for Participants:

_____ Technology for visuals   _____ Name tags

_____ Screen, bulbs, cord   _____ Pads and pens

_____ Display board and markers   _____ Handouts

_____ Charts, pens, tape   _____ Agenda

_____ Audio capture technology   _____ Ice-breaker activity

_____ Podium, lectern   _____ Map of location

_____ Tables, chairs   _____ Refreshments

_____ Breakout arrangements   _____ Follow-up activity

_____ Other?   _____ Other?

Room Arrangement: _____

_____

_____   (Sketch of Room)

_____

_____

been put there by the convener to avoid action or decision-making on those topics. Seating arrangements that facilitate interaction are important factors in the success of a meeting. For best interaction, there should be an arrangement where all can face one another. A circle for six to ten people, a U-shape with peripheral seating if there is to be a visual presentation, or a semi-circle of one or more rows for large groups, works well.

During the meeting, the first order of business is to make sure that all participants are introduced by name and role. All participants should be made to feel that they have important contributions to make. Talking and whispering in subgroups can be particularly distracting. Ironically, some teachers who will not tolerate such behavior by their students in the classroom are the biggest offenders. Astute group leaders have various ways of handling this disagreeable occurrence. They might go over to the offenders and stand alongside or between them, direct a question to one of them, or request a response from them. Each participant in a meeting should be thinking at all times about what will move the group ahead.

Time should be checked frequently but discreetly without calling attention to timekeeper or clocks so that the meeting can end on time. If a meeting's agenda and group progress become sidetracked, leaders should redirect attention by making a point to refocus the discussion. When time is up, the leader should review any key decisions made and, if needed, set the time and place for the next meeting, perhaps offering a preliminary overview of that agenda. Minutes are useful for describing plans and decisions, and for listing projected dates to complete tasks. They are necessary to reflect the group's decisions about what is to be done, by whom, and by what date. They should be brief and concise, but they do not need to include each point of the discussion.

Finally, some time should be reserved at the end of the meeting to discuss progress made and to evaluate the effectiveness of the meeting. This does not need to be a lengthy process. A brief checklist like the one in Figure 6.4 could be distributed or sent by e-mail to be completed on line and returned in short order. Participants should be thanked for coming, for being prepared, and for participating actively. Finally, there should be early follow up on any tasks assigned.

Brief-Agenda Meeting.   When educators have a single topic that can be handled in a quick meeting before or after school, they can structure the meeting with a brief-agenda

FIGURE 6.4   Checklist to Evaluate Meetings

	Yes	No	Don't Know or Does Not Apply
1. All participants were prepared in advance with an agenda.	____	____	____
2. The meeting began on time.	____	____	____
3. Facilities were comfortable and pleasant.	____	____	____
4. Privacy was ensured.	____	____	____
5. Participation was evenly distributed with everyone contributing.	____	____	____
6. Time was used well and the agenda was completed.	____	____	____
7. A summary of decisions was made, listing those responsible.	____	____	____
8. Follow-up activities and any needed repeats were planned.	____	____	____
9. The meeting ended on time.	____	____	____
10. Participants evaluated the meeting's structure and outcome(s).	____	____	____

Additional Comments: _____

_____

_____

FIGURE 6.5   Brief-Agenda Conference

Date, Time, and Participants

Data reporting: _____

_____

_____

_____ 3 minutes

1. Problem finding   5 minutes

2. Idea generating   5 minutes

3. Solution finding   12 minutes

4. Follow-through planning   5 minutes

meeting process. (See Figure 6.5.) After becoming familiar with this process, team members will be able to have short-agenda meetings without much ado. However, they should not try to squeeze a large agenda or issue into this format, for that would be self-defeating to the brief-agenda purpose.

Making Prudent Observations

Consulting teachers often need to observe a student, groups of students, or an entire program in operation, and it is becoming more common for general education teachers to observe in other educational settings as well. This is not an easy professional activity to conduct. Consultants who go into classrooms to observe can expect some discomfort and anxiety on the part of the observed. There may be latent resentment because the consulting teacher is more or less free to visit in other classrooms, something many teachers would like to do but rarely get the opportunity.

Consulting teachers can facilitate the process of observation, and ease the minds of those being observed, in several ways. First, they should provide a positive comment upon entering the room, and then sit unobtrusively where the teacher has designated. They should avoid getting involved in classroom activities or helping students, even those who raise their hands hoping to be attended to. The most effective observers blend into the classroom setting so they are hardly noticed. Regular visits minimize the likelihood of having students know who is being observed and for what reason. It is concerning to hear a student say, "Oh, here's that special education teacher to check up on you-know-who again." (See Figure 6.6.)

Records of behaviors must be done in code so that the physical signs of the observer's writing, watching, and body language do not reveal the subject or purpose of the observation. Each consultant should develop a personal coding system for recording information. Observers can watch the targeted student for one minute, and then divert their attention to another student for one minute, continuing the process with other peers. In this way the observed student does not feel "targeted" and the behavior can be compared with that of classmates. The consulting teacher might even teach a lesson while the classroom teacher observes. This can be helpful for both consultant and consultee. See Figure 6.7 for a sample classroom observation form.

FIGURE 6.6   Here's That Teacher Video Recording Again.

Finally, it is important for an observer to exit the room with a smile and a supporting glance at the teacher. Then very soon after the observation, the observer will want to get back to the classroom teacher with positive, specific comments about the classroom first, then feedback on the observation, suggestions for collaborating, and concluding with another positive comment. Although consultants do not observe in classrooms for the purpose of assessing teacher behaviors and teaching styles, it would be myopic to assume that they do not notice teaching practices that inhibit or enhance students' ability to succeed in the classroom. When the practices appear to be interfering with student achievement, the consultant might ask the consultee in a nonthreatening, onedownsmanship way whether the student achieved the goals of the lesson. If not, is there something the teacher would like to change so this could occur? Then what might the consultant do to help? If the practices are showing positive results, the teacher should be reinforced with recognition of the student's achievement.

To avoid gathering inaccurate information, consultants will want to make repeat observations. In doing so, they can use the opportunity to obtain additional information on antecedents to the problem. They also can record benchmarks that indicate progress or backsliding.

Achieving rapport with a consultee while targeting a teaching strategy for possible modification requires utmost finesse by consulting teachers. To reiterate, the observer should make an appointment as soon as possible after the classroom observation or interview to provide feedback and continue with steps of the problem-solving process.

ACTIVITY 6.2
Important Happenings

Once a week, take ten minutes or so at the end of the day to reflect on all the important things that happened in the classroom and in your collaborative consultations that day. Notice how observant one becomes after engaging in this practice for a while.

FIGURE 6.7   Classroom Observation Form

Classroom Observation Form
for Social and/or Academic Assessment

Student's Name _____   Teacher's Name _____

School _____   Grade _____

Date _____   Time _____   To _____

Consulting Teacher/Observer _____

_____

Location of Student in Room _____

Percent of Time Student Is: In Seat _____ In Group Activity _____ On-Task _____

Attends to Instruction of Teacher or Aide_____

Responds/Follows Directions _____

Complies with Teacher/Aide Requests _____

Complies with Class Rules _____

Works Independently _____

Completes Work _____

Seeks Help Appropriately _____

Is Distracted _____

Seems Confused/Unfocused _____

Distracts Others _____

Participates in Discussions _____

Participates in Group Activities _____

Shows Respect for Teacher(s) _____

Shows Respect for Other Students _____

Helps Others Appropriately _____

Other Observations _____

_____

Summary/Comments _____

MANAGING CONSULTATION RECORDS AND RESOURCES

A prominent space scientist commented that physicists can lick anything, even gravity, but the paperwork is overwhelming! Special education teachers can relate to that. They cite the avalanche of computer workflow, paperwork, and record-keeping that just keeps piling up, and the lack of time in which to deal with it adequately, as major causes of stress and burn-out. Writing and monitoring IEPs, data recording and analysis, and completing records and forms, rank high as major usurpers of their professional and, too often, personal time.

When asked to estimate the amount of time they spend performing their responsibilities, resource teachers unknowingly will often overestimate the time spent on direct instruction and staffing, and underestimate their preparation for instruction and clerical duties such as data gathering and record-keeping. If teaching is to be perceived as an important service profession, careful records are essential. Records and data, both formal and informal, must be written into the consultant's role description as major responsibilities, with time in the workday allowed for accurate management. Who would want to be treated by a doctor who did not write down vital information after each visit, or served by a lawyer who failed to record and file important documents? The key for educators is to manage their student and teacher information data and paperwork so that it does not manage them. Finding an electronic organizational system that allows for creating files for storing documents, e-mails, and completed forms around topics, teachers, or students will help keep large amounts of paperwork and correspondence organized and retrievable. Systems such as OneNote or Evernote are popular choices for electronic organizing. Developing efficient systems and standardized forms for record-keeping will help educators, and especially those who collaborate often with colleagues, to work smarter and not harder.

Using a Consultation Journal or Log

One of the most important formats for consultants to develop is a **consultation log or journal** or electronic file. Consultants should record the date, participants, and topic of each consultation on separate pages, along with a brief account of the interaction, plans made, and consensus reached. Space could be provided for follow-up reports and assessment of the consultation. (See Figure 6.8 for a sample format.) If collaboration and consultation are to gain credibility as essential educational activities, records must be kept to account for the time spent and the outcomes. While teachers typically cannot control the type of records required, they can streamline some of the processes and procedures for collecting and using the information.

It may be productive also to check with one's administrator to find out what specific information would be best. Busy co-educators should not spend time collecting information that is not wanted or needed.

One caution that all educators are aware of but needs to be stressed often is confidentiality in regard to consultation records. Important points of the discussion about student needs and progress might be entered; however, diagnostic classifications and specific planning information—the type that needs family-member permission, should not be recorded there because of privacy issues. A misplaced log or a glance by a curious onlooker could allow access to very personal, privileged information about students and their families. All co-educators will want to have a coding system and secure storage facility for managing confidential data.

Developing Memos and Professional Cards

A consultation memo is a communication tool and also a record of that communication. It must be clear and precise in order to convey, not confound, the message.

FIGURE 6.8 Consultation Journal Format

Client (coded): _____ Consultee (initials): _____

Initiator of Consultation: _____

General Topic of Concern: _____

_____

Purpose of Consultation: _____

_____

_____

Brief Summary of Consultation: _____

_____

_____

_____

Steps Agreed On—by Whom, by When: _____

_____

_____

_____

Follow-Up: _____

_____

Most Successful Parts of Consultation: _____

_____

Consultation Areas Needing Improvement: _____

_____

Satisfaction with consultation process (1 = least, 5 = most)

1. Communication between consultant and consultee   _____

2. Use of collaborative problem solving   _____

3. Consultee responsiveness to consultation   _____

4. Effectiveness of consultation for problem   _____

5. Impact of consultation on client   _____

6. Positive ripple effects for system   _____

Information expressed in a simple, organized manner will receive more attention from the recipient. Jargon, excess verbiage, and cryptic sentences are to be avoided. The first appearance of an acronym should be preceded with the full name it represents. Even idioms can be problematic, especially to family members who do not speak English as the first language.

Contrary to some beliefs and practices, memos should be rough-drafted and then re-written in best form, rather than dashed off hastily and flung into a mailbox or an e-mail inbox. This is particularly relevant to the electronic memo where the words must convey the message with no vocal or facial expressions to help and no retrieval possible after the send key is pushed. Furthermore, it is always "out there," as some public figures have learned to their dismay. The memo writer should put the message simply, telling just enough and no more, with accurate information (times, dates, meeting rooms, descriptions, names) in sharp focus that sticks to the point, and as grammatically correct and aesthetically pleasing as possible without spending hours doing it. Recall Mark Twain's note concluding his letter to a friend: "Sorry about the length of this letter; if I'd had more time, it would have been shorter." That is a good maxim to remember for communication with students, families, and colleagues.

Consultants will find it helpful to include a personalized logo on the memo forms they use to communicate with consultees. This logo identifies the consultant at a glance. Thus, a busy recipient immediately recognizes its source and can make a quick note to self about the information needed to respond now or later. It personalizes professional interaction by providing a bit of information about the co-educator, a humorous touch, or the creative element that educators enjoy and appreciate. A carefully designed logo can promote consultation, collaboration, and team effort in a positive light. For example, a lover of dogs might sketch his dog in the corner along with his initial. One who likes to quilt might have quilt designs as a logo. A word cloud of terms related to collaboration could serve as a visual reminder of important elements of collaboration. A profile-type logo showing several people working together would convey the desire to collaborate.

Another item that improves consultant efficiency is the professional card. Even in this technology-based era, business cards have been a mainstay for communicating basic information in many professions and can be useful in education as well. Administrators could increase recognition of their staff and enhance morale by providing them with attractive, well-designed professional cards. Educators find these cards helpful when they interact with colleagues at other sites or when they attend conferences and conventions. The cards are also convenient for quickly jotting down requests for information or promises of material to be provided. They help build communication networks among colleagues with similar interests. If cards are not supplied by the district, consultants can create and obtain cards using web-based online ordering sites. Visually appealing customized cards are easily created and ordered in quantities of 100–500, often at a nominal cost.

Organizing a Consultation Notebook

Some consulting teachers use a loose-leaf notebook divided into sections with index tabs; others accomplish this with electronic files. They categorize the sections by buildings served, students served, teachers served, or a combination of those. One very organized consulting teacher had a section of "Best Times to Meet with Teachers," listing the days and times available for every teacher with whom she collaborated. Each consultant will want to develop the style that works best in his or her school context and role. Figure 6.9 is a list of suggestions for a special education consultant's organization of sections. Figure 6.10 shows a different format used by a consulting teacher for learning and behavioral disabilities. Collaborative consulting teachers may not want or need all of these sections, and may come up with others of their own that they would like to include. Here again, personalizing the role and school context adds to the usefulness.

It bears repeating that a primary responsibility of the collaborator is to ensure confidentiality of information for both student and staff. This can be accomplished in at least two

FIGURE 6.9   Consultation Notebook Sections

Appointments:	One for week, one for year.
"To-do" lists:	By day, week, month, or year as fits needs. List commitments.
Lesson plans:	If delivering direct service, outline of activities for week.
Consultation logs:	Chart to record consultation input and outcomes.
Phone call log:	Consultation time by phone.
Observation sheets:	Coded for confidentiality.
Contact list:	Phone numbers, school address, times available, e-mail addresses.
Faculty notes:	Interests, social and family events and dates, teaching preferences of staff.
Schedules:	For faculty, paras, support staff, regular school events.
Student list:	Coded for confidentiality, birth dates, IEP dates, other helpful data.
Student information:	Anecdotal records, sample products, events, awards, interests, birthdays, talents.
Medication records:	If part of responsibilities.
Materials available:	Title, brief description with grade levels, location.
Services available:	School and community services for resources.
State policies:	Guidelines, procedures, names and phone numbers of agencies/personnel.
School policies:	Brief description of school policies regulations, handbook.
Procedural materials:	Forms, procedures, for standard activities.
Evaluation data:	Space and forms to record data for formative and summative evaluation, and coded if confidential.
Idea file:	To note ideas for self and for sharing with staff and parents.
Joke and humor file:	To perk up the day, and for sharing with others.
Three-year calendar:	For continuity in preparing, checking, and updating IEPs.
Pockets:	For carrying personalized memos, letterhead, stamps, hall passes, paper, professional cards.

FIGURE 6.10   Consulting Teacher's Notebook

Table of Contents

1. Student Information
   1.1 Personal Information
   1.2 Student Profiles
   1.3 A Quick Look at IEPs
   1.4 Student Schedules
   1.5 Medication Records

2. School Information
   2.1 Faculty-Staff Roster(s)/Faculty Notes
   2.2 Master Schedule(s)
   2.3 School Calendar(s)
   2.4 School Policies/School Handbook(s)

3. Calendars
   3.1 Daily To-Do Lists
   3.2 Personal Calendars (Weekly, Yearly)
   3.3 IEP Review Dates
   3.4 Three-Year Evaluation Dates

4. Forms
   4.1 Personal Motif Memos
   4.2 Consultation/Collaboration Request

   4.3 Observation Sheets
   4.4 Weekly Teacher Progress Report
   4.5 Consultation Logs

5. Lesson Plans
   5.1 Weekly Lesson Plans
   5.2 Student Matrix Worksheet
   5.3 Class Co-Planning Sheet
   5.4 Unit Co-Planning Sheet
   5.5 Co-Teaching Planning Sheet
   5.6 Para Schedule and Responsibilities

6. Consultation/Collaboration
   6.1 Advantages of Consultation/
       Collaboration
   6.2 Tips for Consultation/Collaboration
   6.3 Completed Consultation Logs
   6.4 Consultation Evaluation Forms
   6.5 Personal Journal

7. Resource Listing

ways—coding the names with numbers or symbols while keeping the code list in a separate place, and marking person-specific files as confidential. A "Confidential" stamp prepared for this purpose can be used to alert readers that the information is not for public viewing. These practices, along with the usual protection of information and data, and the practice of seeing that the recorded information is as positive *and* as verifiable as possible, are common-sense rules that should be sufficient for handling all but the most unusual cases.

An itinerant special education teacher who serves several schools may want to prepare a simple form for each school stating the date, teacher's name, and child's code, along with the topic to be considered. The list can be perused quickly before entering the building so that no time is lost in providing the consultative or direct teaching service. Some teachers block off and color-code regular meeting times and responsibilities. An electronic calendar makes easy work of this by allowing the consultant to easily set up a color-coding system for different buildings, teachers, and types of tasks. The electronic calendar has added advantages when entering a series of meetings, searching for information about a meeting or student or teacher, storing contact information, adding pertinent information such as an emergency contact or IEP annual review date, listing phone numbers, and inserting detailed information such as class schedule and names of teachers.

An online calendar allows consulting teachers to have access to their calendars from anywhere, any time. It provides a clearer picture of available consultation times. Sensitive information within contact files can be locked and password protected, making it much more secure than a paper-based calendar or notebook. Another helpful strategy is development of a comprehensive manual or electronic file of pdf documents that organizes standard procedures and forms used for the school district and required by the state.

Managing Consultation Schedules

The collaborative school consultation schedule is a vital management tool. It not only allows the co-educator to organize that precious commodity of time productively but also demonstrates to administrators and other school personnel by its very existence and the records it contains that the collaborative consultant is goal-directed, productive, and facilitative. Schedules should be posted online and left in hard copy with office staff or administrative assistants and in teacher workrooms so that colleagues have easy access to the information. School secretaries and teachers should be asked to refer to these schedules. Saying, "Gee, I don't know where the special education teacher is; I can't keep up with those people" does *not* present collaborative consultation in a positive way.

Consultations and collaborative experiences can be keyed on the consultant's schedule with code letters for efficiency. Two collaborating teachers use this code in their notebooks:

- *ID*—informal discussion, spontaneous meeting
- *PM*—planned, formal meeting
- *PC*—phone conversation
- *EM*—e-mail message
- *MM*—major meeting of more than two people
- *FT*—follow-through activity
- *SO*—scheduled observation

The general classroom teacher may use the coded memos in his lesson plans on a daily or weekly basis. The special education teacher may use hers by buildings, teachers, or students in her management book.

Commercial resources are available that provide sample letters and forms adaptable to a variety of educational purposes, from writing a letter of congratulations to thanking a resource speaker for a presentation. Although educators probably will not want to use these patterns verbatim, they can get a "jump start" in preparing some of the more difficult types of communications. Coordination and organization of student files, consultation logs, school procedures, and schedules will necessitate spending a little more time at the outset, but once the procedures are set up, they will be time efficient and cost effective in the long run.

Organizing and Distributing Materials

Many school districts now have extensive instructional resource centers where school personnel can check out a variety of materials for classroom use. Even with the busiest resource center in full operation, consulting teachers usually have their own field-related materials and information about special areas that teachers want and need. With little or no clerical help, and oftentimes little storage space available beyond the seats, floor, and trunks of their own vehicles, traveling school consultants need to develop simple and orderly check-out/check-in systems for loaned materials, or soon they will have little left to use and share. One traveling teacher described her unfortunate experience of opening the door to her van and having a strong prairie wind whisk away forever the materials she had brought to share.

Those who travel from school to school, or even travel from room to room in one school, have helpful tips to offer that they have learned about organization and management:

- Color-code electronic files and folders for schools and use a file box with a card for each day that has reminders.
- Keep an idea file of filler activities.
- Use tubs for storage of bulky materials. Plan ahead and put materials in varied colors of tubs for one week, one month, a season, or a thematic unit. Colored tubs help with organization; clear tubs facilitate identification of the contents.
- Have a retrieval box in a certain place for receiving borrowed items that are returned. Keep a check-out catalog so you will know where your materials are. When materials are due, remove due cards for the buildings where you will be that week and collect the materials while there.
- Mark materials belonging to a school with the school's stamp and mark personal materials with a personal label.
- Keep an up-to-date inventory of available materials in both personal and school libraries that are available for borrowing and are organized somewhat by specific student needs. In some school situations, library pockets and check-out cards will facilitate check-out and return. But the inventory can be most efficiently managed, updated, and made available if it is an interactive electronic file arranged by subject of the material, grade levels for which it is appropriate, alphabetized name of the item, recommended loan period, and space for a requester to enter name, date, and item borrowed for what length of time, along with the all-important space for the entry of *date returned*.
- Before traveling to a school, scan the check-out file for due dates and send a friendly e-mail reminder that you will be at their school later that day or the next and could pick up any borrowed materials they no longer need. An alternative would be to put memos into message boxes asking for their return and leave request cards for them to tell you of any additional needs.
- Periodically assess the usefulness of the materials by querying teachers and students who used them. These kinds of interactions build positive attitudes toward collaboration and teamwork, promote the effectiveness of school consultation, and extend the ripple effect of special services.

Teacher Portfolios for Data Keeping and Accountability

A teacher portfolio focuses on a *teacher's* learning and accountability to self, co-educators, and administrators. It is a useful vehicle for recording progress in collaborative experiences and team interactions, as well as in co-teaching and partnerships with co-educators. It is authentic in purpose and task, multi-dimensional, contributive to an ongoing learning process, and invaluable at teacher evaluation time. The teacher can reflect on the material regularly, streamline it periodically, and add to it from year to year for visible evidence of growth and improvement. The portfolio can be presented as an example of productivity when it is time for the teacher to be formally observed and evaluated by supervisor or administrator. After retirement, when purged of any confidential material, it becomes a fond-memories folio.

Importantly, portfolios are useful tools for sharing ideas during team meetings and professional development activities. They spark discussions about reforms needed in education and excellent practices that deserve replication. They can be shared with students and parents as models for student-developed portfolios. Portfolios can be fun to design and maintain.

The value of teacher portfolios as a record and repository of professional activities and experiences has not been fully explored, but possibilities abound. A few products that bear consideration for inclusion in portfolios are:

- Lesson plans that worked well
- Videotapes of classroom activity highlights (with signed parent permission, if students are identifiable)
- Sample tests
- Worksheets or packets that worked well
- An innovative teaching or grading technique
- A sketch or photo of an unusual bulletin board so it won't be forgotten
- A list of professional books read and a mini-review
- Any articles published in newsletters, newspapers, or other professional outlets
- Photos of special class sessions (with signed parent permission)
- Original computer software that worked well
- A highly effective management technique
- Notes from parents or students that were reinforcing (again, with signed permission)
- Inclusions in the portfolio that are especially relevant to collaborative consultation and teamwork could be:
  - Documentation of consultation episodes (coded for confidentiality)
  - Descriptions of team-teaching activities
  - Stimulating discussions or collaborative activities with co-educators
  - Special achievements by students for the participating team of teachers
  - *Pinterest*, an online social network, used for educational purposes when teachers post (i.e., known as "pinning" on *Pinterest*) visual images on boards organized around topics or themes that can be shared with others. This visual social network can be considered as one element in a portfolio.
  - Interesting contributions made to teaching and learning by related services and support personnel. (For example, a teacher of students with learning and behavioral disorders learned that the school custodian was an expert on bees. Several of her students became keenly interested in a science project on apiaries and apiarists. The teacher consulted with the custodian and together they made plans for a classroom presentation by the custodian. Multiple positive outcomes resulted from this collaboration and she entered a summary into her portfolio.)

■ ■ ■ ■ ■

ACTIVITY 6.3
Developing a Teacher Portfolio

Develop a plan for your own teacher portfolio. Include a table of contents and design a rubric for showing growth and progress toward your professional goals. Be sure to include a number of collaborative experiences in your collection. Decorate the portfolio in your personal style. It could be fun as well as rewarding to do this project in collaboration with co-educators, discussing elements to put in portfolios, and in particular developing rubrics for the portfolio assessment and perhaps some specific parts of it such as co-teaching skills.

Brief entries that result from actions and reflections activities in this book may be helpful "down the road." Some advanced degree programs in universities require a portfolio presentation as a final examination. Sharing these in a small-group session for professional development could be idea generating and enjoyable for all participants. (Recall the attention to professional perspectives and personal preferences in an earlier chapter; positive examples of these most likely would surface in a portfolio presentation.)

Administrators are interested in more than how effectively collaborating teachers communicate or engage in problem solving. They want to know about practical issues such as how collaborators use the time, types of issues addressed, and whether or not collaborative consultation has been helpful to the participants.

All collaborators, regardless of their general or special education role, should keep records of their consulting and collaborating activities in order to justify the time involved and to validate their roles. The consulting log in Figure 6.10 is a useful form for documenting these data.

Technology for Working Smarter, Not Harder, as Co-Educators

Many of the tools, forms, and resources mentioned throughout this chapter can be created and exchanged electronically. Some consulting teachers function best with a paper system such as a spiral planner, whereas others prefer a paperless system such as an electronic calendar that can be accessed anywhere and anytime from a smartphone, tablet, or computer with automatic updates across devices.

Currently, interactive teams that reach across organizational boundaries can use technologies such as e-mail, teleconferencing, and video conferencing to communicate with one another frequently and quickly. Information can be gathered rapidly and exchanged through databases and electronic networks. Cell phones make team members accessible, regardless of their location. Think of those traveling teachers not so many years ago, needing assistance to get their vehicles out of those snowy ditches! Modern technology can help in many ways. For example:

- *Text Messages*—Can be sent at the convenience of one party and then others read and respond to them at their convenience.
- *Databases and information on student progress*—Stored in a file server or on a secure password-protected website and accessed by any team member at a convenient time.

- *Shared Documents with Notes*—Added on by team members to keep everyone on the team apprised of information or items of concern. Google Docs has been a popular choice of many teachers for collaborating on lesson plans, adapting student materials and tests, and creating meeting agendas and presentations. Team members can share materials, collaborate, edit, and store documents online for easy access by all.
- *Scheduling/appointment calendar*—Appointments and other commitments are entered into the electronic calendar. One special advantage is the way the program can handle recurring appointments. For example, if a team-planning meeting is scheduled for 2:00 on Friday afternoons, the consultant can enter that information; the program will automatically write in meeting reminders on the appropriate dates. Another advantage is the ability to view and print out daily, weekly, or monthly calendars, to be shared through the network if desired. Sharing privileges can be customized to allow one or several individuals the right to view or schedule appointments for all or part of a colleague's calendar. Smartphones have made the work of busy educators more efficient and less stressful.
- *Meeting Scheduling Tools*—Thanks to online scheduling tools such as *Doodle* and *MeetingWizard*, finding available dates and times and scheduling meetings between several parties and sending reminders, becomes automatic and less labor intensive for busy consultants, teachers, and families. Some of these free apps are quite specialized. *NeedToMeet* creates a meeting event page to share with invitees, and from there they can register for any of your open slots. Everyone can see everyone else's availability. If most of the invitees who have already RSVP'd are only free for a limited span of time, all guests following will see that and can potentially adjust their own schedules to suit the group. This limits the back and forth and removes you as schedule moderator.
- *Managing student records*—Databases for organizing large amounts of information in electronic "filing cabinets" allow great flexibility in sorting and retrieving data. For example, a consultant might set up a database file on a caseload of students with each individual record containing a separate entry for categories selected, such as name, address, phone, age, grade, type of exceptionality, parents' name(s), address, and phone number. Once the format is established, the consultant or an assistant enters the information for each record. Then it can be searched and sorted for different types of reports. This search-and-sort capability gives databases flexibility, a considerable improvement over traditional paper filing systems. Confidentiality of the data is, of course, essential.
- *Recording consultations and collaborations*—Information is kept in electronic files rather than paper-pencil format. It can be searched and sorted in various ways to provide valuable information for making decisions about students and collaboration processes. For example, if one wanted to know how many times a certain consultant or service provider worked with the student during the year, the data could be sorted to have all the entries for the service provider appearing together. Later, one who needed to know what services were provided by whom on a particular date could sort the information by data field. Having a record of these activities helps validate the need for times and places to consult and collaborate. Communication between teachers and paraeducators can be easily facilitated and captured through these electronic formats as well.

■ *Preparing reports and other written products*—Word processors and desktop publishing programs are a *must* for busy consultants and other team members. Once text has been entered in a word processor, it can be changed easily, edited, added to, modified, or reformatted. This capability is particularly useful for routine writing such as consultation logs, letters to parents, memos to other team members, assessment reports, newsletters, and classroom materials. Creating templates that can be modified or adapted for specific purposes and for the needs of students can be a great time saver.

Educators have many decisions to make about what, when, and how to invest in emerging technology. Thoughtful planning and investment decisions are needed to ensure that team members have the right technologies in their schools for management and instructional purposes.

SELF-ASSESSMENT AND SELF-EVALUATION OF COLLABORATIVE CONSULTATION SKILLS

Important reasons for conducting self-assessment and self-evaluation are to examine one's own collaborative work and the processes used, as well as to glean information for professional development. Self-evaluation, self-assessment, reflection, and self-direction are excellent methods of professional development for teachers. Without some type of self-evaluation, a consultant may perpetuate ineffective processes, resulting in a decline of collaborative consultation quality over time. Three areas need to be considered:

■ Conceptualizing a framework for self-evaluation
■ Examining methods for self-evaluation
■ Using self-evaluation for self-improvement

A Framework for Self-Evaluation

Self-evaluation is not synonymous with the accountability that administrators require. Its purpose is to engage in self-improvement and make personal change. Results are only to be shared if the self-evaluating person wishes to do so. Self-evaluation is related to ongoing professional development and involves self-assessment and reflection as well as planning strategies for self-improvement. The three steps in self-evaluation are:

1. Self-assessment
2. Self-improvement strategies
3. Post-strategy self-assessment or reflection

When thinking about designing and implementing strategies to improve collaboration or co-teaching skills, ground the strategies for your performance on baseline data from your first self-assessment. If this is your first self-assessment, you can use any other existing data that are relevant. Critiques or evaluations from past assessments would be a possibility.

Write down goals and objectives. Prioritize the behaviors needing change and write behavioral objectives for them. State desired criteria for evaluation—for example, saying "Okay" no more than two times in a twenty-minute consultation session. Include dates for achievement of each objective.

Then select strategies that can help you make the needed changes you have targeted. Formulate the strategies from material presented in other chapters of this book, in other professional books and journals, or in professional development meetings and workshops.

After you have worked on the targeted behavior, skill set, or knowledge, collect feedback with the self-assessment method you used for your baseline data collection point. Chart your progress in achieving your goals. Periodically check to determine your progress in the self-selected area for change. It is very easy to assume (often erroneously) that change has taken place if this step is bypassed. If goals focus on verbal skills, audio recordings will probably be sufficient for follow-up data, but if they include nonverbal skills, use of video recordings should continue.

The final step is to celebrate! It's not easy to change. When a criterion is met, a self-reward is due for a job well done. Objective data can be shared with a supervisor. Growth could be charted in the manner that student progress is documented. Self-assessment should be an ongoing process propelled by realistic expectations.

Methods of Self-Assessment for Self-Improvement

Consulting teachers and co-teachers can choose from a variety of methods for conducting self-evaluations. Audio- or videotaped materials, portfolios, checklists, and reflective journals are some of the possibilities.

Audio or Video Recorded Materials. This method uses audio or video recording of collaborative activities such as teachers' meetings or parent conferences. Although it is time consuming and somewhat cumbersome, there are great payoffs in actually watching and listening to oneself collaborate with others. In choosing this method of self-assessment, here are several important tips:

- Set the consultee at ease by explaining the purpose of the video recording.
- Do a few trial runs before involving a consultee in order to become comfortable with the video camera and accustomed to seeing yourself on video.
- Don't focus on traits that have nothing to do with the quality of consultation. Specific skills must be targeted for observation. Observe or listen to the video several times, each time focusing on just one or two behaviors for data collection. Checklists and rating forms such as those in Figures 6.11 and 6.12 may be useful. Consultants can make their own checklists that focus on communication skills they would like to improve.
- Tabulate behaviors using a systematic observation method so information can be interpreted meaningfully and progress followed objectively.
- Be sensitive to the rights of privacy for the consultee. Arrange the seating during a video recording session so that you face the camera and the consultee's back is to the camera.
- Do not show the video without signed permission from the consultee.

FIGURE 6.11   Collaborative Consultant Behaviors Checklist

Consultant _____   Observer _____   Date _____

	Yes	Needs Work	Does Not Apply
1. *Welcome*			
Sets comfortable climate	____	____	____
Uses commonly understood terms	____	____	____
Is nonjudgmental	____	____	____
Provides brief informal talk	____	____	____
Is pleasant	____	____	____
2. *Communication Exchange*			
Shares information	____	____	____
Is accepting	____	____	____
Is empathic	____	____	____
Identifies major issues	____	____	____
Keeps on task	____	____	____
Is perceptive, providing insight	____	____	____
Avoids jargon	____	____	____
Is encouraging	____	____	____
Gives positive reinforcement	____	____	____
Sets goals as agreed	____	____	____
Develops working strategy	____	____	____
Develops plan to implement strategy	____	____	____
Is friendly	____	____	____
3. *Interpretation of Communication*			
Seeks feedback	____	____	____
Demonstrates flexibility	____	____	____
Helps define problem	____	____	____
Helps consultee assume responsibility for plans	____	____	____
4. *Summarizing*			
Is concise	____	____	____
Is positive	____	____	____
Is clear	____	____	____
Sets another meeting if needed	____	____	____
Is affirming	____	____	____

Teacher Portfolios. The teacher portfolio, as presented earlier in this chapter, is an effective vehicle for collecting the authentic assessment information that educators can use to evaluate their own skills and continuing development. A teacher portfolio focuses on the educator's learning. It is useful for evaluating progress in collaborative experiences and team interactions, as well as co-teaching and partnerships with co-educators. It is multidimensional and authentic in purpose and task, and it contributes to an ongoing learning

FIGURE 6.12   Consultee Assessment of Consultation and Collaboration

Please evaluate your use of the consulting teacher service provided in the _____
program by providing the following information. Respond with:

1 = Not at all   2 = A little   3 = Somewhat   4 = Considerably   5 = Much

1. The consulting teacher provides useful information.   _____

2. The consulting teacher understands my school environment and teaching situation.   _____

3. The consulting teacher listens to my ideas.   _____

4. The consulting teacher helps me identify useful resources that help with my students' _____
   special needs.

5. The consulting teacher explains ideas clearly.   _____

6. The consulting teacher fits easily into the school setting.   _____

7. The consulting teacher increases my confidence in the special programs.   _____

8. I value consulting and collaborating with the consulting teacher.   _____

9. I have requested collaboration time with the consulting teacher.   _____

10. I plan to continue seeking opportunities to consult and collaborate with the   _____
    consulting teacher.

Other comments: _____

_____

process. The material can be evaluated, streamlined, and added to from year to year as visible evidence of growth and improvement. When educators develop professional portfolios to evaluate their own professional growth and development, they demonstrate the value and importance of authentic assessment.

The mainstay of assessment by portfolio is development of sound rubrics. This could be accomplished with several colleagues who want to prepare their own teaching portfolios. As suggested earlier, designing a rubric for a collaborative activity is a good way to engage in meaningful collaboration. It is also a useful tool for professional development.

Checklists. A variety of tools throughout this book can be used for self-assessment, including the checklist in Figure 6.11 and the rating scale in Figure 6.12. Journal articles about teacher assessment often contain helpful checklists. Consultants may want to design their own checklists based on their specific professional duties and responsibilities. It is always helpful to have others read over self-made checklists to assure that they are clear and comprehensive.

Video recording, having a colleague observe and report, and often just reflecting on one's habits objectively are all potentially helpful ways of growing professionally. Reflection leads to insights about oneself, prompting changes in self-concept, changes in perception of an event or person, or plans for changing some behavior.

The purpose of evaluation of collaborative practice is not to add stress by judging and pointing fingers at others or to make collaborators feel lest competent. Evaluation of programs and self-evaluation should help us determine if what we are doing is effective and making a difference. If it is not, how can we make it better? Collaboration can nurture and support teachers who are experiencing stress and perhaps are on the verge of burnout from the profession. It is often the accumulation of mountains of little things—being "nibbled to death by ducks"—and not the big crises that push professional educators into disillusionment. Caring, supportive colleagues can make all the difference for the overwhelmed novice teacher, the burdened administrator, or the discouraged veteran teacher.

THE ROLE OF EVALUATION IN COLLABORATIVE SCHOOL CONSULTATION

Evaluation is a complex endeavor. There is a field of professional evaluation whose association, The American Evaluation Association, includes thousands of members who focus on the evaluation of such widely varying activities as school and community programs, federal policies, health-related programs, environmental issues, and international development. It seems like everybody is interested in evaluation because everybody wants to know "what works?", or "am I getting my (or the taxpayer's) money's worth from this public program?", or "how do we strengthen this program so it really makes a difference in the academic success of students with disabilities?" These are questions that can be answered by evaluators, using rigorous and appropriate methods. Collaborative consultants in school settings are not expected to be professional evaluators or to have the skills of a professional evaluator. However, education consultants should have a basic knowledge of evaluation; they may be called upon to conduct basic evaluations of collaborative efforts, to work collaboratively with evaluators, or to be one of many partners in large evaluations that involve services to students with special needs and their families. The answers to these questions provide basic information for consultants when they consider the evaluation of collaborative school consultation processes.

1. What is evaluation?
2. Who cares about evaluation?
3. What are the purposes of evaluation?
4. Who are **collaborative school consultation** programs evaluating?

What Is Evaluation?

Educators want to know the value of programs, products, and portfolios. In general, *evaluation* means to fix a value or determine the worth of something. In most education settings, **evaluation** relates to determining the worth of an educational program, such as an IEP, a peer tutoring program, an after-school program, a co-teaching arrangement, or a family involvement program.

Program evaluation is defined here as an activity directed at collecting, analyzing, interpreting, and communicating information about the workings and effectiveness of designated educational programs (Mertens, 2015; Rossi, Lipsey, & Freeman, 2004; Shufflebeam & Coryn, 2015). Evaluation of collaborative activities and programs is important for three reasons:

1. If the program is to be continued as an item in the school district budget and funded and staffed adequately, school administrators need to know about the impact of the program.
2. School personnel will want to know whether their hard work is paying off. They will want to continue successful practices and discontinue or modify activities that do not have an impact. Thus, evaluation data will help to continuously improve the program.
3. Evaluation results are an excellent source for explaining, validating, and providing accountability for collaborative consultation programs and efforts. Evaluation results provide justification for the time used to invest in these kinds of efforts. This is especially important when some are skeptical about indirect services and are pushing for more direct services to students with exceptional learning needs.

A school or district may have an assigned evaluator whose job it is to assess programs and activities within the school. Whether schools are working with outside professional evaluators or in-district evaluators, the process is a collaborative activity. A good evaluation involves stakeholders in all aspects of program evaluation.

Consultants understand the differences between research and evaluation. Although evaluators and researchers utilize many of the same methods, research and evaluation are different in several ways. Research and evaluation have different purposes, different users, different questions, and the findings are used in different ways. Evaluators respond to the questions of stakeholders and focus their methodology on answering those questions, such as "What is the impact of our parent reading program on the literacy achievement of their children?" Research questions are typically stated as hypotheses that the researcher either rejects or fails to disprove; research findings build a knowledge base about specific areas, such as the relationship of socio-economic status to referral for special education services. Research results are published in research journals for other researchers or for practitioners to use to inform their practice. Evaluation findings may be presented in a variety of ways to various program stakeholders. The users of evaluation findings are the **stakeholders**—funders, educators, parents, students, community members, and others.

Who Cares about Evaluation?

Stakeholders are invested in the expected outcomes of the program. They care about the benefits of a program or activity because their children are involved, their time is involved, or their money is involved. Stakeholders have legitimate reasons for wanting to know if programs are producing the outcomes they expect to see. Many evaluators involve stakeholders at the evaluation design phase of a project and ask them to help design the evaluation questions. For example, if school personnel want parents to believe in the home-tutoring program, they should find out what questions parents have about the program. Then they can design the evaluation to elicit responses for the questions. In interviewing parents or asking teachers to fill out a survey, evaluators should always make sure people know why they are being asked to participate in an evaluation and how the resulting data will be used.

What Are the Purposes of Evaluation?

Basically, the purpose of evaluation is to answer the questions the stakeholders have about a specific activity or program. These are called the evaluation questions and they are the basis for all evaluations, from small classroom-based evaluations of activities to large multi-million dollar evaluations of government programs such as the Drug Abuse Resistance Education (D.A.R.E.) program. Usually these questions are related to the expectations of school districts, families, communities, or other stakeholders. Questions may focus on how the program is progressing and what improvements are needed to make it better. Questions may also address the impact the program is having on participants.

How Are Collaborative School Consultation Activities and Programs Evaluated?

Professional evaluators use many types of program evaluations and methods for their work. But most educational program evaluation features the accumulation of information for one of two primary purposes—formative evaluation or summative evaluation.

Formative evaluation provides ongoing information for making decisions to modify, change, or refine a program during its implementation. If a program is not producing expected outcomes, then program staff and administrators want to know that so they can make immediate changes. The process of formative evaluation often suggests the need for specific program changes; thus, formative evaluation provides important information to assist with ongoing program improvement. Formative evaluation means continually examining the impact of a program to fine-tune it until it reaches the outcomes that are expected. Without formative evaluation, practitioners could spend their time and efforts on programs that do not result in the changes in students they expect. Furthermore, without formative evaluation, educators could keep changing a program that does not need modification because it "works as it is."

Summative evaluation provides documentation for the attainment of program goals and is used most often by administrators in determining whether programs should be started, maintained, ended, or chosen from among several alternatives. Summative evaluation usually includes an assessment of the impact of a program or activity; that is, can you attribute the changes in students to the program, or might the outcomes be the result of some other factor? Summative evaluation may be conducted to determine the collective impact of a project on students, teachers, parents, schools, and communities. Summative evaluation is completed at the end of the program, but data utilized are collected before and during the program. This type of evaluation is expected to provide information about the viability of the program, to test the effectiveness of a completed new program, or to indicate if a product or process is ready for dissemination or replication. Summative evaluation indicates the short-term and long-term outcomes of the project and should relate program activities to these outcomes.

EVALUATING COLLABORATIVE SCHOOL CONSULTATION PROCESSES, ACTIVITIES, AND PROGRAMS

Evaluation should be planned carefully before a project or activity begins. A variety of evaluation designs is used by professional evaluators, and consultants may work frequently with professional evaluators and teams to design and implement evaluations for educational activities and programs. When consultants need to evaluate collaboration, consultation, and co-teaching, they typically use a practical action research design in which the practitioner is the researcher, or in this case, the evaluator. Action research is an approach to investigation that enables teachers to find effective solutions to problems they confront in their daily professional activities (Mills, 2010). This simple pre-post evaluation design conceptualizes action research as an iterative process that provides formative evaluation information for those designing the activity or intervention. A teacher starts with a problem and tries out various strategies to solve the problem. Collecting data before and after the application of the problem-solving strategies allows the practitioner to test the impact of the interventions. This aspect of the action research cycle can be used to evaluate Collaborative School Consultation processes and activities.

Whether the consultant utilizes an action research model for evaluating an activity or process or collaborates with a professional evaluator or evaluation team, the steps of the process are somewhat similar. The process involves making decisions about the why, what, and how of collaborative school consultation evaluation.

Steps in Designing Collaborative School Consultation Evaluations

Professional evaluators use various approaches to designing and implementing evaluations. However, these six common inquiries are the foundation of the process:

1. What is the purpose of the evaluation? (Why?)
2. Who are the stakeholders and what do they want to know? (Who and what?)
3. What activities will the program implement to reach its goals? (What?)
4. How will the expected outcomes of the activities be measured? (How?)
5. How and when will the data be collected and analyzed? (How and when?)
6. How will the findings be reported and used? (Then what?)

Here is a discussion of each of these steps:

1. Purpose of the evaluation. The purpose of an evaluation is usually established by the people who will use the evaluation. Here is an example: A school district receives funding from the state library to develop a parent-teacher center for families of children with disabilities. This funding will provide for the site, furnishings, materials, and personnel to develop the center and get it started. However, future funding for the center depends on evidence that the center is having a positive impact on children, parents, siblings, and neighborhoods. A special education teacher consultant is

leading a team to develop the center. The funder, the school district, and the consultant and her team want to know whether or not the center will be used by parents, and what impacts it has on parents and on their kids. This sets the purpose of the evaluation—to determine the impact of the center on families and students with special needs.

2. Evaluation questions of the stakeholders. Most educational programs are expected to produce one or more of three categories of changes, awareness, knowledge and skills. For example, "Did awareness, attitude and/or knowledge change as a result of participation in this activity?" "What is the impact of the intervention on participants' behavior?" and "In what ways did the school environment, policies, or climate change as a result of the collaborative activity?"

3. The activities of the program. In planning a collaborative activity, describing the program, or planning an evaluation, an important step is listing the activities of the program. What is the program going to do to produce the outcomes desired? What series of activities will be part of the project that will, collectively, improve educational outcomes for students with special needs, provide information or services to parents, or enable teachers or faculty to be better at working with diverse students? The answers to this second question are the activities introduced to facilitate expected changes.

4. Measures of expected outcomes for each activity. In matching expected outcomes with goals and activities of the program, each collaborative program will have its own particular goals and have specific activities to help meet those goals. Step four is to assign specific measurable objectives or outcomes to each program activity. Next, an evaluator selects or designs measures that do this. For example, stakeholders involved in a tutoring program might want to measure achievement gains for tutees and possibly look at subject-matter grades. Self-efficacy, attitude toward the subject matter, perceptions of the teacher or attitudes of the parents might also be outcomes to be measured. To measure these outcomes, an evaluator could interview students and parents about their thoughts on the impact of the program; survey community volunteer tutors; and collect data on achievement, attitudes, grades, and self-efficacy.

5. Data collection and analysis. When the measures have been determined, methods to gather the outputs or outcome data are selected. An evaluation team will decide collaboratively on ways of obtaining the data. Much of the data will exist within classrooms, student files, or school computer data banks. The challenge is to determine what is needed and then plan a strategy for collecting and summarizing the data in a meaningful, time-efficient way. Evaluators need to be assured that important aspects of the program get measured and that the evaluation instruments are sensitive enough to pick up all outcomes that result from the project. An evaluation is only as good as the data. Incomplete, flawed, out-of-date, or irrelevant data lead to results that are not valid and in some instances just might be harmful. "Garbage in, garbage out" is a phrase frequently used by evaluators.

Instrumentation and data collection should be put into place at the beginning of a project. A consultant, working with an evaluation team, should decide how to evaluate the program as early as possible, during the planning of the program, activity, or intervention. Baseline data will need to be collected before the program activities are put in place or the intervention is stated. This language probably sounds familiar, for that is exactly what is required when an IEP is developed for a student. The similarity is not coincidental. Principles guiding IEP development must guide all good program development.

Evaluation instruments and procedures must be as objective and unbiased as possible, and information from multiple sources should be collected. The data analysis method must fit the chosen methodology. Some complex programs may require extensive databases and statistical programs; however, stakeholders may be interested only in pre-post comparisons, tables with collected information, or charts that visually represent the results of the evaluation. Most common software packages have database programs that will convert databases to charts or tables. Involving stakeholders in making decisions about the representation of the data will help ensure that they remain interested and involved through the entire process so that the hard work of evaluation pays off with smart decisions.

6. Data reporting and using findings. The final element of evaluation involves communicating or reporting the results of the evaluation in a manner that is useful. Evaluation has value only if the results will be used to facilitate improvement of programs or to develop better programs, lower the costs of the program, or improve methods of operation. Evaluation findings provide information about what works and what doesn't work. The data should promote self-reflection and evidence-based thinking and point out actions that need to be taken—for example, curriculum revisions and adaptations, testing modifications and accommodations, reassignment of school personnel, reconfiguration of schedules, reallocation of funds, and so forth.

■ ■ ■ ■ ■ ▬▬▬▬▬▬▬▬▬▬▬▬▬▬▬▬▬▬▬▬▬▬▬▬▬▬▬▬▬▬

ACTIVITY 6.4

Who Are the Stakeholders and What Do They Want to Know?

ENGINEERING SUMMER CAMP FOR MIDDLE SCHOOL STUDENTS WITH DISABILITIES

Three middle schools in a large city collaborated with two engineering companies and the Department of Engineering at the local university. The goal of the project was to create a residential summer camp for middle school students with disabilities who had interests and capabilities in taking science and math courses in high school and possibly attending college with a major in engineering. The expected outcome for the camp was increased interest and excitement about engineering and technology and ways it can be used to help individuals, organizations, and society. This camp developed activities to address academic skills and self-confidence in the areas of math and science and to promote taking four full years of mathematics in high school. Program activities included hands-on experiential workshops and field trips and exposure to role models (high school students, college students, and scientists with disabilities). Follow-up activities during the school year and outreach to parents were part of the intervention program. School math and science teachers were part of the camp's administrative staff, learning about engineering and career opportunities along with the students. The project was funded by engineering companies, the university's department of engineering, the State Department of Education, and the National Science Foundation.

1. Who are the stakeholders in the Engineering Summer Camp program?
2. What do you think those stakeholders want to know?
3. What evaluation questions might they have?

Video Example from YouTube

▶

ENHANCEDetext
Video Example 6.3.

Watch this video and notice how the school personnel featured worked as a team to analyze student data and make program decisions to improve teaching and learning. Instructional time was maximized and the ongoing data they collected confirm their positive results. (https://www.youtube.com/watch?v=J8DQugVxHv0)

The report of evaluation findings should be constructed to answer the evaluation questions in specific ways. Providing graphs, tables, and a brief summary of the results of the evaluation will be sufficient to make the report useful. Again, reports of findings should be based on stakeholder needs. Funders may want detailed reports much like a journal article or a corporate report. Parents may want a summary with examples, succinct graphs, and pictures. A school administrator or collaborating teachers may want an executive summary with the findings and recommendations listed. Matching the report type to stakeholder needs helps assure that evaluation findings are used in making decision about programs and activities.

Planning Evaluations Using a Logic Model

Educational consultants often find it helpful to develop an evaluation using a plan such as the one in Figure 6.13 that has the elements of program evaluation just discussed.

Figure 6.13 is a planning template for developing an evaluation and may be used as a guide when working with a team to make decisions about a program evaluation.

This plan can be developed into a model of the logic of how the program is expected to work, that is, how activities and programs are related to expected changes in attitudes, behaviors, and knowledge. The planning template includes all of the elements discussed earlier.

Program developers and evaluators use a similar planning tool to tie all elements of a program together in a logical form. This plan is called a logic model because it demonstrates the logic of how the program or activities are organized to produce the expected outcomes. A **logic model** describes the elements of program evaluation just described, inputs, activities, outputs, and outcomes of an activity or program. Many evaluators use a logic model to design their evaluation methods and to communicate evaluation processes to stakeholders. There are various formats for displaying the conceptual logic of a program. A quick Web search for logic models will deliver many logic model designs and information. Some websites even have templates for use in developing logic models. Whatever format is used, a logic model is a systematic way to visually depict relationships among resources for operating the program, activities that have been planned, and outcomes the program is geared to achieve. Figure 6.14 shows an example of a hypothetical logic model prepared for a collaborative family-school program of information exchange activities described by Hughes and Greenhough (2006) in their research about a parent-school partnership program.

FIGURE 6.13   Collaborative School Consultation Evaluation Planning Template and Checklist

Name of program or activity: _____

Purpose(s) of the program or activity: _____

Evaluation team members: _____

    1. Agreed purpose of the evaluation: _____

    2. A) Stakeholders: _____

       B) Stakeholder evaluation questions: _____

       _____

3. Activities:	4. Expected outcomes:	5. Outcome measures:
_____	_____	_____
_____	_____	_____
_____	_____	_____

    6. Date collection (using outcome measures):

Instrument	Date	Who
_____	_____	_____
_____	_____	_____

    7. Analysis of data: _____

    _____

    8. Report(s) of findings: _____

    9. Use of findings: _____

In considering a logic model, these definitions are helpful:

Activities: The events, strategies, implementations, workshops, etc. that a project carries out to meet its goals and produce expected changes in participants.

Outputs: Numbers/products related to project activities, such as number of teachers attending a workshop about universal design for learning attendance at a workshop, number of parents checking out books from a resource center, number of students with disabilities taking Advanced Placement courses, hits on a school homework website, student test scores, etc.

Outcomes: Results of participation in project activities, such as changes in knowledge or attitude, increased use of a specific practice, improvement in grades.

Impact: Lasting outcomes attributable to the project, such as changes in environmental conditions, increases in evaluation capacity caused by the project.

FIGURE 6.14   Logic Model for Home-School Collaboration Project

RESOURCES	ACTIVITIES	OUTPUTS	SHORT- & LONG-TERM OUTCOMES	IMPACT
In order to accomplish our set of activities we will need the following:	*In order to address our problems or assets we will accomplish the following activities:*	*We expect that once accomplished these activities will produce the following evidence:*	*We expect that if accomplished these activities will lead to the following changes:*	*We expect that if accomplished these activities will lead to the following impact on home-school collaboration:*
■ Government policies (Every Child Matters: Change for Children) ■ Primary and secondary schools in Bristol and Cardiff ■ Teachers and administrators in target schools ■ Students and parents in target schools ■ Funding of the Home-school Knowledge Exchange (HSKE) Project	■ Video Activity—Video based on literacy teaching to inform parents of new literacy methods used at school and to encourage parents to do literacy activities at home (school-to-home communication). ■ Shoebox Activity—Students filled shoeboxes with items from home that were special to them; contents were used as part of the curriculum across all subjects (home-to-school communication).	■ Feedback from parents ■ Feedback from teachers ■ Demonstrated evidence of teachers' knowledge of out-of-school lives of their students ■ Demonstrated increased parent-child school-related interactions ■ Demonstrated increased parent-teacher interactions	■ Better communication between school and home ■ Increased parental appreciation and support of school learning activities ■ Parents learning about how reading and writing were taught ■ Teachers providing curriculum enrichment that is relevant to students' out-of-school lives ■ Improved trust and mutual understanding between teachers and parents	■ Increased trust between parents and teachers ■ Increased willingness to listen to parents and their priorities ■ Increased parental appreciation of educational methods ■ Increased parental support of school activities ■ Students see link of out-of-school lives with classroom and curriculum ■ Ongoing exchange of "funds of knowledge" between school and home

Source: Based on Hughes, M., & Greenbough, P. (2006). Boxes, bags, and videotape: Enhancing home-school communication through knowledge exchange activities. *Educational Review, 58*(4), 471–487. Illustration courtesy of the W. K. Kellogg Foundation, Battle Creek, Michigan.

TEN KEY CONSIDERATIONS IN EVALUATIONS FOR COLLABORATIVE SCHOOL CONSULTATION ACTIVITIES AND PROGRAMS

The following ten points are important other key considerations in planning and implementing effective evaluations for collaboration, consultation, and co-teaching activity:

1. The evaluation process should be ongoing.
2. Multiple sources of information should be used.
3. Valid and reliable methods of gathering information should be used.
4. It should be limited to gathering data that will answer pertinent questions and document attainment of consultation goals.
5. It should be realistic, diplomatic, and sensitive to diversity issues.
6. Legal and ethical procedures, including protection of privacy rights, must be followed.
7. Anonymity of respondents should be maintained whenever possible, and they should be informed whether the data are to be reported as grouped data.
8. It needs to be cost-effective in terms of time and money (for example, whenever possible, use existing data).
9. Data that are collected must be put to useful purpose; if not, data should not be collected.
10. Formative evaluation should result in program change; summative evaluation should result in decision making about the program.

 ENHANCEDetext Application Exercise 6.1. Click to apply your understanding of collaborative school consultation.

TIPS FOR ORGANIZING, MANAGING, AND ASSESSING COLLABORATION

1. Don't schedule yourself so tightly that you have no time for informal interactions and impromptu consultations, because these can open the door for more intensive and productive collaboration; be even more protective of colleagues' time than you are of your own and make good use of it.
2. Consult a technology specialist regularly to remain current in the ever-changing uses of technology, especially for data collection and data analysis.
3. Make concise checklists for procedural activities, such as general items to tell parents at conferences or items to tell new students and their parents.
4. Go to classroom teachers and ask *them* for help in their area of expertise. Discuss a strategy that you have seen them use and like very much, asking if they would like to share it with others or keep it as a special part of their teaching repertoire, and then respect their views about it.
5. Do not expect a uniformly high level of acceptance and involvement from all, but keep aiming for it.

6. Build into evaluation procedures some ways of improving less-than-successful collaborations.

7. Keep public remarks about colleagues on a positive, professional level. This is especially relevant when evaluating oneself or others. It is easy to find reasons to blame; it is much harder to find solutions from which all can benefit and then set about to implement them collegially and constructively.

8. Observe programs in other schools and share observations with key people in your school(s).

9. Constantly monitor and update your methods of protecting confidential information. Before sending confidential information through electronic networks, make sure steps have been taken to protect the information, and the transmission of electronic information is secure.

10. Don't try to do everything yourself, especially when it comes to planning large-scale evaluation programs; involve stakeholders in every phase of the process.

CHAPTER 7

COLLABORATING AS INSTRUCTIONAL PARTNERS AND TEAMS

Student abilities and needs lie along a continuum of learner differences; they do not fall into discrete, separate categories. It follows that there is no uniform instructional strategy for every student's needs. Alternatives must be available to provide accessible curriculum and appropriate instruction for individual learners. In the past, many educators aimed at teaching to the middle of the class, all the while knowing that did not meet the needs of all students but doing the best they could under the circumstances.

A one-size-fits-all approach to instruction can be particularly detrimental to students with disabilities and is stunting to students with high abilities. Teachers are challenged to develop and deliver lessons that provide multiple pathways to accessing information, learning content, and demonstrating their learning in a variety of ways. Educators differentiate learning goals for students' special needs and make adaptations for students to those goals when necessary. Adaptations can be in the forms of accommodations (aids and supports) or modifications (altered goals and expectations).

Co-planning and co-teaching are useful practices for providing differentiated curriculum in inclusive classrooms. Such curriculum may be remedial, review, student-interest based, accelerated, enriched, or a combination of differentiations. Regardless of the intervention or interventions to be used, it is important for special educators and general educators to work together so appropriate differentiated curriculum and alternatives for learning are developed and made available to fit all students' needs.

CHAPTER OBJECTIVES

Upon completing this chapter, the reader should be able to:

1. Describe how to prepare and plan for differentiated instruction.

2. Identify ways the Universal Design for Learning (UDL) framework can be applied within co-teaching structures.

3. Give examples of appropriate curricular adaptations for students with disabilities that can be developed collaboratively between general and special educators.

4. Discuss ways teachers in school-based teams work together to deliver a multi-tier system of supports (MTSS) for all learners.

5. Describe the characteristics and needs of exceptionally able students that have implications for their curriculum and learning resources.

6. Summarize ways school collaborative school consultation can address the learning needs of very able and talented students through curriculum differentiation, acceleration, and enrichment.

KEY TERMS

acceleration
co-teaching
curriculum accommodations
curriculum compacting
curriculum
    modifications

enrichment
flexible pacing
homeschooling
multi-tier system of supports
    (MTSS)
preassessment

Response-to-Intervention
    (RTI)
Schoolwide Enrichment
    Model (SEM)
Universal Design for
    Learning (UDL)

SITUATION 7.A

At lunchtime, two secondary-level teachers take their trays from the salad bar to a relatively quiet, cleared area where they can talk. Lori asks Mark about a professional development activity that she was not able to attend the previous week.

Lori (Secondary Classroom Teacher): Mark, you were going to fill me in on last week's session about Universal Design for Learning [UDL] that I missed. Is this a good time?

Mark (Secondary Classroom Teacher): Sure. And it will be good for me to wrap my thoughts around it again, because I think you and I might want to work together to give some of it a try with our classes. It was presented as a collection of best practices that are to be strategically placed at each phase of the teaching and learning process. These maximize learning and give all students access to the curriculum. In thinking about all of the needs in our inclusive classes, that has appeal, don't you think?

Lori: So, we wouldn't make adaptations for certain students after the fact, but plan lessons at the front end so that they're accessible to the broad spectrum of students we have?

Mark: That's the main idea I took away from the session. The overall concept is an outgrowth of the universal design movement in architecture. As you know, architecture is my true love, so I really related to that. As a result of the Americans with Disabilities Act, the universal design movement shelved the "one size fits all" mentality about architecture and the environment to accept one that's precisely the opposite—multiple ways of getting in, out of, and around buildings and functioning successfully in the environment. Regardless of whether someone can see, hear, walk, read, or speak, appropriate alternatives are provided so that anyone who can't do what others might be able to do can experience the environment in a fair and equitable way.

Lori: So this brick-and-mortar plan for using physical space became a concept that works for curriculum. That's interesting.

Mark: Yes, UDL provides supports for students in the classroom and reduces the barriers curriculum often throws up that shut them off from learning. It maintains high achievement standards for all learners, too. Here, I have an extra copy of the handout from the session that explains what the presenters called multiple pathways for using UDL.

PREPARING AND PLANNING FOR DIFFERENTIATED INSTRUCTION

The manner in which special education services are delivered today is practically unrecognizable when compared to services when PL 94-142 was passed and enacted in the mid-to-late 1970s. In years past, students who were unable to meet the standards in general education were referred and tested for special education. Qualifying for special education usually meant a ticket out of the general education classroom with its rigid curriculum and little to no differentiation of instruction. It was a widely held belief that these students needed specialized instruction that could only take place outside the general education environment. Ironically, this initial version of what is now known as the Individuals with Disabilities Education Act (IDEA) was often referred to as the "mainstreaming law," but more often than not, students with mild to moderate disabilities were pulled out of the general education classroom for specialized instruction. The way in which the least restrictive environment (LRE) has been interpreted over the years has evolved to what we more commonly see today—students with disabilities, even those with more severe disabilities and extensive needs, being educated alongside their age peers with supports being provided in general education settings. As a result of recent federal legislation and policy changes related to the education of students with disabilities, these students are being held to high expectations and must be assured access to the same general education curriculum as students without disabilities to the maximum extent possible. Accountability for all students means making not just social gains, as was typical of mainstreaming in years gone by, but ambitious academic gains as well (Dukes & Lamar-Dukes, 2009). Clearly, for this mandate to be fulfilled, general and special educators must work together in planning and delivering instruction to shared students. A multitude of options exist for this joining of special and general education. Some of the factors that will influence the service delivery option include the needs of the student, administrative support, joint planning time, paraeducator support, teachers' preparation and ability to work side-by-side in the same classroom, effective communication, and professional development activities to support the chosen model. Many schools are opting for co-teaching models where special and general educators teach shared students together.

Co-teaching is an instructional delivery model used to teach students with disabilities in the least restrictive integrated classroom settings where general and special educators collaboratively plan and deliver instruction for all students. Co-teaching has rapidly evolved and has been recognized as one way to ensure students with disabilities have access to the general education curriculum; they are taught by highly qualified teachers while still receiving the individualized, special education and other supports to which they are entitled (Friend, Cook, Hurley-Chamberlain, & Shamberger, 2010).

Co-teaching allows teachers the opportunity to share professional expertise with general educators who have knowledge of the curriculum content and special educators who know the instructional strategies most appropriate for students who learn differently. Put another way, general educators are considered *masters of content*, and special educators are viewed as *masters of access* (Villa, Thousand, & Nevin, 2008). Unfortunately, these potential benefits also create challenges. Attempts to merge the knowledge bases in co-teaching settings often creates confusion between teachers and causes issues to arise. When a group of educators were asked about their current challenges, the intricacies of co-teaching was reported as of the most common challenges teachers face (Scherer, 2016). Co-teaching, when done right, can look effortless and run like a well-oiled machine, but experienced co-teaching partners know there is a lot going on "under the hood." Successful co-teaching requires tough work, making thoughtful and difficult decisions, preparation, ongoing planning, serious reflection, and careful evaluation. It also requires a commitment to deal with difficult issues and fix problems as they arise rather than abandoning the co-teaching arrangement and leaving it on the side of the road like a car with a flat tire or stalled engine.

First Things First

Before co-teaching takes place, there is much to consider. First, does a co-teaching arrangement make sense? Who are the students, and what are their needs? How will a co-taught classroom benefit students? What co-teaching arrangement is best suited for identified needs? How will other support staff, such as related service personnel, and para-educators, be utilized? As for staffing—who, where, when? How will this arrangement be explained to parents of children with and without IEPs? What type of professional development will occur, and how will it be delivered? Will co-teaching arrangements be voluntary or mandated? When will planning time occur, and how often? The list could go on and on, but the point is that there are many decisions to be made and a great deal of planning to do.

Rather than jumping head first into co-teaching, some schools start with developing an inclusion mindset prior to introducing the concept of co-teaching with staff. It involves inclusion of all students and making sure that every teacher feels invested and responsible for the learning of all students. Once a school has an inclusion mindset, the next logical step is often co-teaching. Professional development is an effective way for teachers to learn about the nuts and bolts of co-teaching. This can be done through activities such as school-wide professional development workshops; online webinars; book study; visits to successful co-teaching programs; and attending state, regional, or national conferences/workshops on the topic. After gaining knowledge about co-teaching considerations through professional development, teachers should debrief about what was learned and determine which elements are a good fit for their particular school and student population.

Teaching partners come together in a number of ways. Sometimes two teachers already have established a professional relationship and are open to working together in a co-teaching model. They are early adopters and like to try innovative practices. They don't mind making a few mistakes along the way and they have a level of comfort and trust in each other. In other situations, the students on a special education teacher's caseload will drive the decision of the co-teaching partnership. The special education teacher may have several students in a particular grade or in one teacher's class. This could be intentional or just the way it works out. In this case, circumstance rather than choice determines the pairing of two teachers. Finally, sometimes an administrator believes two teachers would form an effective partnership and assigns them to work together. This last scenario begs the question, "Should educators only work together if they want to?" Some argue that *requiring* educators to work together somehow violates theirs right as a professional and can result in "contrived congeniality" rather than a true collaborative culture (Hargreaves, 1991). But time spent collaborating with colleagues is considered essential to success in most every profession, and this principle is no different in education (DuFour, 2011).

Opting out of collaboration should not be an option. School leadership organizations have advised principals that one of their key responsibilities and a core strategy for improving student learning is building the capacity for faculty to work together as members of a collaborative professional learning community. DuFour (2011), reminds us that when advocating for collaboration, professional associations have never added the caveat, "but only if each person wants to."

Preparation for Co-Teaching

Once teaching partners are identified, the next step is to get to know each other. This step is not so much about exploring a friendship as it is about discussing their teaching philosophies, curriculum, teaching routines and procedures, grading, and assessment practices. In other words, discuss the things that really matter in terms of teaching and student learning. These are best discussed in the beginning, with each teacher sharing what is really important to them, identifying shared beliefs, noting areas where each will compromise, and bringing forth issues where serious differences exist. Nitty-gritty details about shared classroom space, noise levels, and discipline need to be addressed (Sileo, 2011). The key to avoiding problems is being proactive and setting up routines and protocols at the beginning—saying, "Here's how I envision this. What thoughts do you have?" Parity should also be addressed. Parity in co-teaching implies equal status and shared responsibilities. This includes shared responsibility for instructional planning and delivery, discipline, and grading, among other tasks. In the process, it is also good to develop comfortable lines of communication and get to know each other on a more personal level. A teaching partner doesn't have to be one's best friend, but it never hurts to know a partner's favorite coffee drink (or that they detest coffee but like a particular soda at the end of the day), or whether the partner is one of the first to arrive at school in the morning, or prefers to stay late and work at the end of the day. Asking about hobbies outside of school, parents, and family members is helpful. Difficult conversations assuredly will be needed at times, so having established a personal relationship based on respect and trust will make those easier.

This is also a good time to discuss the what's and when's of face-to-face, joint planning time and frequency, and what can be done using technology such as file-sharing to collaborate on teaching ideas, lesson plans, accommodations, and adaptations. Designating a set time for joint planning and keeping it a priority on calendars will ensure that time is allocated for initial planning that can be continued independently and shared though electronic formats.

Teachers need to prepare the classroom before implementing co-teaching. As Keefe, Moore, and Duff (2004) note, "As a successful co-teacher, you need to a) know yourself, b) know your partner, c) know your students, and d) know your "stuff" (p. 37). Co-teaching partners will need to discuss their views on teaching and learning and resolve any major differences. (Refer to earlier chapters for discussions on teacher differences in perspectives and preferences.) In addition, they should agree on how grades will be assigned to students. Other matters to resolve are whether substitute teachers will be needed, roles of para-educators, how to inform parents of the co-teaching approach, and most importantly, a schedule for planning time together at least once weekly.

■ ■ ■ ■ ■

ACTIVITY 7.1
Variations in Teacher Perspectives

With colleagues or classmates, brainstorm and compile a list of teaching style differences that could be problematic when two teachers are paired for co-teaching. For starters, on that list put preference for direct versus indirect teaching approaches, hands-on learning compared to reading about a topic, and assessment of student learning through student-directed projects or by using paper-pencil, objective-style tests. What kinds of classroom behavior might be tolerated or even encouraged by one teacher but be upsetting to another? Start this list with behaviors such as: getting out of seat during the lesson; talking; making noises; being habitually late; and so forth. Discuss the importance of the behaviors on your lists through the lenses of an individual teacher's perspectives. What differences surface about their importance and possible responses or actions to take? Then discuss how these variations in teacher perspective might affect co-teaching relationships.

Co-Planning

Without co-planning, co-teaching often involves a special educator helping the classroom teacher, or the classroom teacher helping the special educator, or "turn-taking" at best. This arrangement brings little satisfaction to either teacher and is not likely to result in the high-quality student outcomes that educators and parents desire. When co-planning. special educators and general educators must blend differing approaches to planning lessons.

General classroom teachers typically plan for groups of students, whereas special education teachers tend to plan for individuals. Research conducted by the Joint Committee on Teacher Planning for Students with Disabilities (1995) indicated that general education teachers do not individualize instruction as a rule, although they might differentiate by planning for *all*, *most*, and *a few* students. They do not typically engage in a linear planning process of going from objectives to activities followed by determining evaluation methods. Even though general educators may know how to use that type of planning, they tend to start by selecting a theme or topic for a lesson and then planning content and activities for the entire class or large group.

Special educators, on the other hand, are trained, even required by federal law, to base lesson plans on individualized learner goals or what is specified in the learner's IEP. The planning steps are based on traditional lesson-planning models—goals, objectives, activities, and evaluation. This linear process may not be the best way for co-teachers to plan lessons, nor does it reflect the way teachers typically plan lessons. General classroom teachers obviously are concerned about student learning, but they tend to keep their groups of students engaged in activities throughout the school day for the sake of classroom order and whole-group learning. Advocates of students with disabilities often voice concerns that exceptional students' needs are not always being met in inclusive settings. These concerns have been largely focused on meeting students' needs through adaptations or modifications of the general education curriculum and instructional practices.

One possible reason for the struggle of students with disabilities in the general education curriculum and setting has to do with lesson plan development. Even if teachers believe accommodations are helpful for students, they often are unable to modify their instruction due to factors such as time limitations, classroom management issues, and the complexity of vastly different achievement levels of students in their classrooms. In short, many teachers feel ill equipped to plan for and teach students with disabilities.

The challenge for co-teachers is to reconcile the individualized and group planning processes and develop integrated lessons for the benefit of *all* students. This process must address the concerns of general educators mentioned earlier, such as sensitivity to time constraints, management issues, and engagement issues that address the needs of all learners. According to McTighe and Brown (2005), differentiated instruction has four guiding principles. It:

- Focuses on essential ideas and skills in each content area
- Is responsive to individual student differences
- Integrates assessment and instruction
- Adjusts content, process, and products to meet individual student needs

Universal Design for Learning (UDL) is a framework teachers can use when joint planning to meet the needs of all students within the general education classroom.

USING THE UNIVERSAL DESIGN FOR LEARNING FRAMEWORK TO DIFFERENTIATE INSTRUCTION

The paradigm for teaching, learning, assessment, and curriculum development that emerged in the 1990s when the Center for Applied Special Technology (CAST) coined the term "Universal Design for Learning" (UDL) is a refinement of **differentiated instruction** (Pisha & Coyne, 2001). "Universal" doesn't imply one optimal solution for everyone. Instead, it calls for multiple approaches to meet the needs of diverse learners. This involves:

- *Multiple means of engagement:* For purposeful, motivated learners, tap into their interests and offer practice opportunities that provide appropriate challenges and motivations for each student. Just as when a child is learning to ride a bike for the first time and the supervising adult needs to determine the right amount of support— when to remove the training wheels and how long to hold on while running alongside—teachers need to implement a scaffold that provides the right amount of support students need in acquiring new skills. This involves creating many pathways for students to learn the material presented. Some students may benefit from small-group learning opportunities, others may require more focused practice with precise feedback, and still others may benefit from working independently. Some students will need to write, some will need to talk through ideas before they understand, and others may need to represent their learning in physical ways. The goal is to have purposeful and motivated learners by providing options for self-regulation, sustaining effort, persistence, and creating interest in topics.

- *Multiple means of representation:* Content or information to be learned can be represented in different ways. For example, a teacher can present many books or websites at different reading levels that deliver the same information. Or a teacher can use a lecture to deliver information but also provide visuals, guided notes, and/or an audio file of main points for students to access at a later time. When content is presented in different ways, it gives learners the opportunity to become resourceful, knowledgeable learners.
- *Multiple means of action and expression:* For strategic, goal-directed learners, differentiate the ways that students can express what they know. Provide learners with alternatives for demonstrating what they have learned. The creation of many paths is key. Some students are good test-takers, whereas others are not. Some students write well and other students express themselves better orally. Most learning objectives can be manifested in multiple ways. Giving choices within a framework of options will likely provide increased motivation for students to participate meaningfully and demonstrate what they have learned. Options for execution functions, expression, and physical action will help strategic, goal-directed learners express what they know.

Another important element to UDL is understanding how the brain processes information for learning. Every brain processes information differently, and the way a person learns is as unique as an individual's DNA profile or fingerprints. In its research, CAST identified three primary brain networks and the roles they play in learning:

- *Recognition networks:* How we gather facts and categorize what we see, hear, and read. For example, think about how one recognizes a person's voice even without seeing the person, or automatically puts together a string of letters to form a word. These are recognition tasks—the "what" of learning.
- *Strategic networks:* How we plan and perform tasks, including organizing and expressing our ideas—the "how" of learning.
- *Affective networks:* How students get engaged and stay motivated. It is what piques their interest or excites them. These are affective dimensions or the "why" of learning.

Teachers can customize their teaching for individual differences in each of the three brain networks and thus reach and engage all students rather than just a few. The flexible UDL curriculum provides alternatives to address the broad range of learner differences. With this type of curriculum, it is imperative that special educators and general educators work together to ensure that appropriate alternatives are selected to address unique student needs. General education teachers are typically considered the content and grade-level experts, whereas special education teachers possess advanced training in matching specialized teaching methods and learning strategies to specific student learning needs, and provide the scaffolds to build a solid bridge between the content and the learners. In other words, general educators are in the best position to determine the big ideas that all students need to learn in their content area or grade level, and special educators can help determine if those goals are appropriate for individual students and suggest alternatives when necessary.

As noted earlier, if curriculum alternatives are insufficient for individual students, or if non-UDL curriculum is used, then the special education teacher has the additional challenge and responsibility of finding or creating accommodations, and in some cases, modifying the learning goals for students with disabilities.

Components of Universal Design for Learning

The purpose of UDL is to create expert learners who are: a) strategic, skillful, and goal-directed; b) knowledgeable; and c) purposeful and motivated to learn more. UDL provides teachers with the tools to design curricula-removing barriers that could prevent students from becoming expert learners. Four interrelated components comprise a UDL curriculum: goals, methods, materials, and assessments.

Goals are often described as learning expectations. They represent the knowledge, concepts, and skills all students should master, and they are generally aligned to standards. Within the UDL framework, goals are articulated in a way that acknowledges learner variability and offer more options and alternatives—varied pathways, tools, strategies, and scaffolds for reaching mastery.

Methods are typically defined as the instructional decisions, approaches, procedures, or routines that teachers use to enhance learning. Evidence-based methods are employed and methods are further differentiated based on learner needs. UDL methods are adjusted based on ongoing monitoring of learner progress.

Materials typically are media used to present content and demonstrate the learners' knowledge. Materials within the UDL framework are variable and flexible. For conveying conceptual knowledge, UDL materials offer multiple media and embedded supports such as hyperlinked glossaries, background information, and on-screen coaching. For strategic learning and expression of knowledge, UDL materials offer tools and supports needed to access, analyze, organize, synthesize, and demonstrate understanding in varied ways. UDL materials offer alternative pathways to success, including choice of content where appropriate, varied levels of support and challenge, and options for generating interest and sustaining motivation.

Assessment within the UDL framework is the process of gathering information about a learner's performance using a variety of methods and making informed educational decisions based on that information. The goal is to improve the accuracy and timeliness of assessments and to ensure that they are comprehensive and targeted. UDL assessments reduce or remove barriers so as to accurately measure learner knowledge, skills, and engagement.

UDL guides the design of instructional goals, assessment, methods, and materials that can be adjusted to accommodate and meet individual needs. UDL is a framework to improve and optimize teaching and learning based on what is known about how the brain functions and how learning occurs. There is no one optimal solution for everyone. The UDL framework has alternatives that make curriculum accessible and appropriate for individuals with different backgrounds, learning styles, abilities, and disabilities in widely varied learning contexts. CAST continues to evolve as it supports teachers in designing curriculum so that all students have access to rigorous curriculum. Special educators and general educators must work together to select appropriate alternatives that address the unique needs of students. When curriculum alternatives are insufficient for individual students, or when non-UDL curriculum is used, the special educator has an additional challenge of finding or creating adaptations to accommodate, and in some cases modify, the learning goals for students in accordance with their IEPs. The CAST website is a treasure trove of ideas and tools for implementing the UDL framework.

Incorporating UDL When Co-Planning Lessons

Spooner, Baker, Harris, Ahlgrim-Delzell, and Browder (2007) found that even a simple introduction to UDL can help teachers design lesson plans that are accessible for all students. These results were achieved by providing an introduction of UDL, including a description of the three principles of UDL and how to incorporate these principles into daily lesson planning (Spooner et al., 2007). In describing the individual components, visual cues were used, such as re**present**ation, **express**ion, and **engage**ment (that is, underlining and putting key words in bold print) to provide participants with a strategy to help remember the critical elements of UDL when planning their own lessons. It is important for teachers to remember the keyword "present" when thinking about the UDL concept of re**present**ation that includes creating innovative ways of presenting content material to students. Additionally, CAST provides some general recommendations on how teachers can use appropriate teaching methods to support the three primary brain networks.

To support diverse recognition networks:

- Provide multiple examples of critical content (including nonexamples).
- Highlight critical features or essential components.
- Provide content using varied media formats and tools.
- Support background knowledge through assessment and scaffolding when needed.

To support diverse strategic networks:

- Provide flexible models of skilled performance by demonstrating multiple times and at varying levels.
- Provide opportunities for supported and productive practice.
- Provide ongoing, relevant feedback, skillfully coaching and adjusting for students with a range of remediation needs (Ginsburg, 2010).
- Offer flexible opportunities for demonstrating the skill by varying the requirements and expectations for learning and expressing knowledge.

To support diverse affective networks:

- Offer choices of content and tools.
- Offer varying levels of challenge in materials and tasks, providing scaffolding as needed.
- Offer reward choices.
- Offer choices of learning context such as working independently or with a partner; resources to use such as book or web-based information; responding to questions through written (handwritten or word processed), scribed, or recorded formats.

FIGURE 7.1   UDL Lesson Analysis Form (Elements)

UDL Elements	Examples in Current Lesson	Ideas for Enhancing the Lesson
RePRESENTation (Content) Giving students various ways to acquire information and knowledge		
ENGAGEment (Process) Engaging students in activities that help them make sense of the content. Tapping into students' interests, offering appropriate levels of challenge and motivation.		
EXPRESSion (Products) Providing students alternatives for demonstrating what they know		

Using a simple planning format that incorporates the three primary UDL elements (see Figure 7.1), along with the related brain networks and the role they play in how students learn (see Figure 7.2), general and special educators are able to jointly analyze lessons already created and in use in the general education setting as their initial step in co-planning using existing lessons.

Teaching partners first look for examples of the UDL elements already in place within the lesson. Next, they brainstorm ideas for enhancing the lesson in each of the three primary UDL elements and the related brain networks, with each teacher bringing unique knowledge and expertise to the table. Additionally, the special education teacher might provide information regarding individual student characteristics and needs. For example, the special educator could note one student's difficulty in reading grade level material independently, or share how another student benefits from using a word processing program with word prediction capabilities and a talking spell checker for written assignments. This type of information could easily be shared using a form similar to the one shown in Figure 7.3. By using such a form, the general education teacher is better informed about the special learning needs of some students in the class and the potential barriers that printed textbooks or note-taking requirements might pose. Having this basic background knowledge, the teacher is in a better position to plan effective UDL lessons on the front end rather than having to retrofit lessons, which would be much like adding a ramp to the outside of a building that is inaccessible to some because of stairs. Such types of "add-ons" are never quite as elegant or work as smoothly as when these considerations are part of the initial plan. So by engaging in an initial "fix-up" of existing lessons, teachers begin to routinely incorporate these UDL principles into their initial planning stages.

Co-planning works best when teaching partners share a common planning period (Friend et al., 2010; Murawski & Bernhartd, 2016; Pratt, Imbody, Wolf, & Patterson, 2016)

FIGURE 7.2   UDL Lesson Analysis Form (Brain Networks)

Brain Networks	Examples in Current Lesson	Ideas for Enhancing the Lesson
Recognition • Provide multiple examples • Highlight critical features • Represent information in multiple media and formats • Provide supports for limited background knowledge and establish a context for learning		
Strategic • Provide flexible models of skilled performance • Provide opportunities to practice with supports • Provide ongoing, relevant feedback • Provide flexible opportunities for demonstrating skills • Provide novel problems to solve		
Affective • Offer choices of content and tools • Provide adjustable levels of challenge • Offer a choice or rewards • Offer a choice of learning content		

and, at least initially, can meet once a week for planning, with an aim to narrow this eventually to twice a month (Murray, 2004) as the teaching partners gain skills and knowledge from one another about content, teaching styles, UDL principles, and teaching options.

Lack of sufficient joint planning time is frequently high on the list of barriers to co-teaching. Therefore, using their limited co-planning time efficiently can help teachers maximize it to create universally designed and differentiated lessons for the inclusive classroom setting. Murawski (2012) offers several tips for using co-planning time more efficiently:

- Establish a regular planning time each week (20 minutes minimum) and hold the time sacrosanct.
- Meet somewhere without distractions.
- Save rapport building for another time.
- Have an agenda and snacks.
- Determine roles and responsibilities.
- Share equally in planning, teaching, and assessing.

FIGURE 7.3   Analyzing Student Needs with Potential Lesson Barriers

Students with Special Needs	Characteristics or Specific Needs	Potential Barriers to Learning
Student #1		
Student #2		
Student #3		
Student #4		
Student #5		

- Build in regular time for reflection, assessment, and feedback (at least monthly).
- Use a template for documenting and saving plans for future reference.

Teaching partners should think flexibly and creatively in terms of where and how co-planning can occur. While face-to-face joint planning may be the ideal, especially during the initial stages, teachers may find that sometimes they can utilize technology for collaborative planning. Charles and Dickens (2012) suggest that many Web 2.0 allow co-teaching partners to collapse time and space when it comes to many of the planning elements of effective co-teaching (i.e., managing the flow of content, developing accommodations for specific student needs, co-planning lessons and learning activities, and reflecting on assessment results). Web-conferencing tools allow users to share their computer screens, making it possible for teams of teachers to collaborate on upcoming lessons, accommodations, and modifications. Sessions can be recorded and used to document special educators providing consulting services to general education teachers. Using free web-sharing tools such as Google Docs, teachers can work collaboratively on a shared lesson, making recommendations and adjustments in their own time, with a final copy for each teacher that clarifies the responsibilities of each partner during delivery of instruction. A sample template for a co-planning form can be downloaded free at the 2 Teach LLC website. It divides the lesson into three parts (beginning, middle, and end) and includes columns to list responsibilities of the general education teacher and the special service provider, along with a column to list considerations such as student specific needs, accommodations, and adaptations. Cloud-based document management services such as Dropbox provide space in the cloud and access to the most current versions of their files, regardless of the device they have on hand to access a file. Users are able to see changes made to files on each device as soon as they are made. Multiple documents can be shared for collaboration with either editing rights or shared as a view-only document. It provides an anytime, anywhere work space.

Stewart and Brendefur (2005), in their study of collaboration among teacher teams, were told by participants that they found power in collaborative planning and value in observing colleagues teach. Collaboration helped organize teachers' thoughts about teaching a lesson and bringing instruction to a higher level with more student-centered lesson planning.

Delivering Differentiated Instruction

For students with disabilities, deficits in basic core content areas (e.g., reading and math) may limit access to the general curriculum and require teachers to plan interventions addressing these deficits. For multiple areas of focus and instruction, teachers need useful methods to collaboratively monitor the effectiveness of their instruction and to track student progress. Using familiar data collection methods, such as anecdotal, interval, duration, latency, and event recording techniques, the special educator and general educator can collaborate and contribute to specific roles (Lingo, Barton-Arwood, & Julivette, 2011). For example, the special educator can assist in providing examples of different recording formats, explaining the purpose of each and the pros and cons. The special educator has expertise in defining behavior and can provide information on differentiated instruction and formative evaluation. The general educator can be involved in collecting data, implementing both academic and behavior interventions, carrying out the formative assessments, and participating in refection and data analysis.

Three factors have been identified as critical to the success of a multi-tiered model of instruction: the curriculum used, fidelity of implementation, and behavior management (Barnes & Harlacher, 2008; Fuchs & Fuchs, 2007; Glover & DiPerna, 2007). Educators should ensure that the curriculum being used is supported by research to give students the best chance to be successful. Evidence-based practices (EBPs) are recommended when working with students with disabilities. Teachers should be aware of the underlying principles as to why an EBP works and then monitor the implementation of the program to determine if it is being implemented with fidelity (i.e., as it was intended). When implementing an EBP, it is of utmost importance to have a sound, data-driven reason for any adaptations that are made, and it is imperative to evaluate their effectiveness (Leko, 2015). If adaptations are made, they should be documented and considered when evaluating progress-monitoring data. Collaboratively, educators should create an effective learning environment by proactively and explicitly presenting positively stated expectations to students and providing frequent reinforcement (Harlacher, Walker, & Sanford, 2010). One of the hallmarks of effective interventions for students with disabilities is to intensify the instruction. This can be done by manipulating different variables that include:

- Amount of time allotted for instruction (in minutes per day)
- Duration (in weeks)
- Instructional group size

These are all variables that collaborating teachers should consider when differentiating instruction for shared students. General education teachers play an important role in identifying content to be mastered at their grade level or content area. Special educators can contribute to decisions on how to best intensify instruction for students who aren't meeting critical benchmarks jointly identified by the co-teachers.

A key element of co-teaching is the shared responsibility of teachers in both planning and delivering instruction. Co-teaching usually occurs for a set period of time, such as one class period each day, certain days of the week, or for one lesson topic. Some teachers have been misled to believe that co-teaching is necessary for every inclusionary situation and that students should never be taken out of the general classroom for special help. However, co-teaching should only be used when it is the best option for meeting the needs of a significant number of students. Pairing two teachers to deliver instruction to one group of students is a relatively expensive option and should only be utilized when the number of students with disabilities in the inclusion class justifies the presence of two teachers (Friend & Bursuck, 1996).

That being said, a number of studies report teachers benefiting professionally from co-teaching experiences. This includes general educators learning how to adapt lessons for all students and special educators gaining a better understanding of the critical content for students and teaching realities of the general education classroom (Scruggs et al., 2007). In a meta-synthesis of qualitative research on co-teaching in inclusive classrooms, Scruggs, Mastropieri, and McDuffie (2007) reported increased cooperation among students in co-taught classrooms and academic benefits as a result of extra teacher attention.

Selecting the Best Co-Teaching Approach

Co-teaching is not one teacher leading instruction while the other grades or prepares lesson materials. It's also not both teachers having the same role all of the time—a special education teacher moving students to the back of the room to work with them while the main teacher instructs the rest of the class, or one teacher in the role of the expert and the other always being the helper. Rather, co-teaching is a partnering of two teachers with different expertise, in this case, one being a special educator and the other a general education teacher, to provide more effective instruction to students in a general education classroom. Some co-teachers strive to be indistinguishable from one other so that to the observer it wouldn't be apparent which teacher is the special educator, but others disagree with this often held notion of co-teaching. Instead of making co-teacher clones of one another, Beninghof (2016) encourages just the opposite. Good co-teaching partnerships should celebrate and embrace the difference they bring to the classroom. With that in mind, how should co-teachers structure their co-teaching?

Benninghof (2016) believes the greatest positive effect on students in a co-taught classroom results when the specialist is doing something special. In contemporary co-teaching arrangements that Friend (2016) refers to as "Co-teaching 2.0," educators should focus on integrating special education strategies and teaching techniques that will enable students to meet the goals on their individual education program (IEP) and not just providing on-the-spot prompting and coaching to pull students through the general education curriculum. Co-teachers can use one of several approaches to present their lessons to heterogeneous groups, and they should vary the approaches often. Some examples of approaches are Teach and Monitor, Parallel Teaching, Station Teaching, and Team Teaching. Vaughn, Schumm, and Arguelles (1997), Bauwens and Hourcade (1997), and Friend and Bursuck (2009) provide descriptions of additional co-teaching arrangements.

Teach and Monitor.   One of the most common approaches is for both teachers to be in the classroom during instruction. One has primary responsibility for lecturing or presenting the lesson and the other helps monitor performance of students and provides additional assistance to students who need it. This approach does not require as much advanced planning as other approaches and is simple to implement. However, the teacher who circulates around the room could easily begin to feel like a "teacher's aide." One parent recently reported that her child came home from school saying they had a new "student teacher" in her room. In reality, the "student teacher" was the special education teacher who was co-teaching in the classroom. This observation is not provided to minimize the role of student teachers but to illustrate the point that both teachers might not be recognized as co-equals by students and as such may not be equally effective in providing direct instruction. To lift the status of the "support" teacher, the tasks assigned to each co-teacher should be of equivalent value in the eyes of both teachers and students (Kusuma-Powell & Powell, 2016). Establishing co-equal status doesn't happen by accident; it requires deliberate planning. To minimize potential limitations of the Teach and Monitor approach to co-teaching, the teachers should alternate roles regularly.

Variations of this approach are Speak and Chart, and Speak and Add. With Speak and Chart, one teacher lectures while the other writes the outline or notes on the chalkboard. With Speak and Add, one teacher lectures and the other occasionally jumps in to add or clarify points from time to time. Duet is a planned variation of Speak and Add in which each teacher takes turns presenting portions of the material in a coordinated fashion. This co-teaching structure also allows the monitoring teacher to gather formative assessment data, which can inform a teachers' next steps of instruction. Research suggests that monitoring students, adjusting instruction, and offering feedback can be powerful tools in teaching (Marzano, 2007). Collecting data and monitoring student progress is an essential part of making sound instructional decisions. Cornelius (2014) suggests using an enlarged seating chart diagram, with an open square shape to represent each student's desk. Using what she calls an "Anecdotal Seating Chart" placed on a clipboard, one teacher can make notes about student engagement while the other teacher is presenting a lesson. The monitoring teacher might stop next to a student who is not actively participating and pose a couple of questions to see if the student is understanding or if the student is confused. If the student answers the questions correctly, a brief note can be made on the chart, thus providing a quick record of progress monitoring data. If the student was not able to answer the questions, the teacher can quickly assess why the student was off task and possibly make some on-the-spot adjustments such as helping the student get started on the worksheet or adjusting the task and noting it on the chart for later review in teacher debriefing about the lesson and making adjustments for the next day. These co-teaching structures often become blended, as the example of Lori and Mark's co-teaching experience later in this chapter's activity will illustrate.

Parallel Teaching. A second form of co-teaching is Parallel Teaching. It involves placing students into two equal groups, with each teacher simultaneously teaching the same material to the small

---

Video Example from YouTube

▶ ENHANCEDetext
Video Example 7.1.

The Teach and Monitor co-teaching structure has many variations. Watch this video to see how one of these variations, might be implemented in practice. (https://www.youtube.com/watch?v=S3AK33YOZfE)

group. This co-teaching structure can be used in many different ways. It enables teachers to work with a smaller number of students, thus providing an opportunity for all students to have individualized and hands-on learning. Both teachers plan a lesson, but they split the class and each delivers the lesson to a smaller group at the same time. Parallel Teaching might also utilize a parallel curriculum where both teachers teach a similar topic but one teacher teaches it at a more advanced level than the other. For example, after having read a story to the entire class, one teacher takes the highest achievers to create a new ending for the story, while the other teacher works with the other students on vocabulary meaning and retelling the story sequence.

Station Teaching. A third method of co-teaching is Station Teaching. This approach occurs when teachers co-plan instructional activities that are presented in "stations" or learning centers. Typically, co-teachers arrange students into two or three equal groups and students rotate in groups through one of three stations. If there are three groups, teachers teach in two of the stations and students work somewhat independently in the third station with a para or peers. Each station presents a different aspect of the lesson and allows teachers to work with small groups of students. This way, each teacher works with all students in the class as they rotate through the stations.

Team Teaching. Team teaching is sometimes used as a synonym for co-teaching. Both teachers deliver instruction simultaneously to the whole class. This is often used when new material is being presented and the co-teachers question one another or when one teacher provides an example or clarifies with a visual as a difficult concept is presented, taking pressure off students who may have difficulty understanding the material. Teachers find that this approach helps them support each other as they present the material to ensure they included the necessary information and reinforced the concepts.

A variant of team teaching can involve special education teachers joining together to form a team. The team is responsible for all of the children in the classroom or ones at a particular level. Team teaching was observed in one school that involved ignoring disability labels for service of students. All students identified for special education services were assigned to special educators according to their age or grade-level placement. The special educators, regardless of categorical specialization, were assigned to grade-level teams and assumed primary responsibility for all students with special needs at the assigned grade level. The special educators met weekly to discuss matters of concern. Each special educator was a member of a grade-level team and met regularly with that team to discuss common issues. The special educators moved in and out of the classrooms at that grade level to co-teach as needed, to adapt materials, or sometimes to present a special lesson.

A high school math teacher described a pre-algebra class that she and the special education teacher co-teach. They have a shared planning time every other day because the school uses block scheduling. Within that time, they are usually able to set out a general plan for the week and then attend to specific problems or coordinate activities as needed. They share actual teaching responsibility more than they use a Teach and Monitor approach. This is purposeful so that students will perceive them ***both*** as math teachers, and not one as a math teacher with the other as special education teacher for certain students. What one of the co-teachers likes best about the approach is the camaraderie she shares with another adult. It lessens her feelings of isolation. However, she is quick to point out that co-teaching in situations when partners do not share a similar philosophy of classroom management, or do not appreciate and value temperament differences, would be challenging.

Co-teaching occasionally transpires almost spontaneously. Two third-grade teachers had adjoining classrooms, and early in the school year they could see that some students' math skills had slipped during summer vacation. So one teacher worked on basic skills with a blended group of students from both rooms while her colleague provided **enrichment** activities for students who were ready to move on. Then one day they had a "light-bulb moment." The curriculum and students were mismatched! So the co-teachers exchanged the curriculum plans. The enrichment group did modified bundling to grasp the concept of huge numbers after they complained about hearing adults on TV stammer over keeping words like "billion" and "trillion" straight because the amounts were almost beyond comprehension. The other group was more enthusiastic about math after constructing geo boards and building birdhouses and figuring out recipes, and they began to understand tens and ones through these construction activities. The teachers continued to monitor, co-plan, and move students back and forth among groups from time to time.

■ ■ ■ ■ ■ ▬▬▬▬▬▬▬▬▬▬▬▬▬▬▬▬▬▬▬▬▬▬▬▬▬▬▬▬▬▬▬▬

ACTIVITY 7.2

Co-Teaching with UDL—Plan in Action

Recall the conversation at the beginning of the chapter between Lori and Mark regarding the staff development session on UDL. As a result, they decide to co-teach an American history lesson about the Battle of Gettysburg during the Civil War:

■ First, Mark provides his lecture materials from past lessons. They review the lecture outlines, textbook materials, and assignments and discuss what could be eliminated or added to the original lecture and textbook material. They decide that all students can benefit from the lecture, including Randy, who is developmentally delayed. Most students can read the textbook assignment, which is ten pages, except Colin who needs it read aloud and Randy who cannot read it at all.

- They decide that most students, with the exception of Randy, will benefit from two of the assignments in the textbook.

- Mark is concerned about the ability of some students with learning difficulties to benefit from some of the content. Lori wonders if students with high ability will be challenged. They decide to use cooperative learning methods to deal with some of those concerns. Lori will prepare "challenge tasks" that will be required for the students with high ability, although anyone who wishes can try to do them. Mark has group-study worksheets they could use, but Lori recommends several changes. Mark thinks of some other items that could be eliminated or added to help the students in the class who have learning difficulties.

- Mark volunteers to make the revisions since he has the original worksheets on his computer.

- Although Lori is the teacher assigned for the course, they decide Mark should present the lecture because he has done it many times previously. However, Lori will be in the classroom to add information whenever it seems appropriate to help clarify a point.

- Lori will direct the cooperative learning activities. She has already established teams in the class and this content fits that structure well. Mark will have his para come into the classroom during that time, freeing him up to consult with another teacher.

- Lori thinks the students need a summative experience requiring them to demonstrate individual accountability. Mark and Lori discuss what the activity could be and Lori agrees to prepare it (a test this time). They will divide the tests, each grading half. When the tests are graded, Lori will record the scores in her grade book and Mark will give team rewards. Mark will give the test orally to the students with learning disabilities and prepare a modified test for the para to administer to Randy in the resource room.

Now, based on the information provided in this co-teaching example thus far, partner with a colleague or classmate and fill in a blank copy of the interactive lesson planning forms presented earlier (see Figures 7.1 and 7.2). Did the format and prompts built into the planning form spark ideas for other things that Mark and Lori might do or help you elaborate on some of their ideas?

No matter how well the teachers plan, some co-teaching actions must be spontaneous. This became obvious as Lori and Mark put their plan into action. Mark presented the lecture, while Lori monitored, as planned. But Lori spontaneously "jumped in" from time to time to clarify information. At one point, she went to the chalkboard and drew a diagram to more clearly illustrate a point that seemed confusing to students. The next day, as planned, Lori took over when the class began team study in the cooperative learning format. She instructed students to get into their teams, gave instructions for team activities, and told how they could earn bonus points. Now the para was monitoring and noticed that Randy needed more explanation, so he wrote out the steps for Randy. Once students were engaged in teamwork, Lori and the para "cruised" the classroom, stopping to help individuals or teams as needed and providing positive reinforcement for team effort. Later they met to reflect on results of the plan.

On Friday, both teachers were present while students took individual tests. The para took Randy to the resource room to help him take a modified test while Mark read the test to the students with learning disabilities. He read questions orally for them when needed. He noticed two students were having difficulty writing their answers and pulled them aside one-by-one to let them dictate answers to him. Then he asked them to do an additional task while the rest of the class finished their tests. Lori involved the very able students in other activities after they finished their tests, and Mark continued to monitor the test-takers. Lori and Mark divided the tests to grade as planned. Later they met to reflect on results of the UDL plan.

Collecting data and using the results to guide instruction is critical. Both formative and summative assessment should be part of the co-teaching. Wormeli (2007) describes formative assessment as monitoring student progress and adjusting instructional practice based on information gathered. Just as a good map or GPS can effectively guide a journey from start to finish, formative assessment can guide a plan for effective instruction. Gathering anecdotal notes during instruction can be a useful tool for this purpose.

Cornelius (2014) suggests a quick and simple way to track student progress on IEP objectives is to create a spreadsheet with students' names in the first column and an objective or two for each student in the second column. These are followed by columns titled "Opportunity" and "Occurrence," where the teacher can place a tally mark for each time the student has the opportunity to demonstrate a skill during a given day or lesson and then a tally mark for each time it occurred. The final column can be used to record the percentage achieved. For example, if one of the IEP objectives was to determine the main idea of a passage, the student might have four opportunities to do so and was able to do it successfully three times. So in the final column, 75 percent would be recorded. This formative assessment data can be combined with summative data on the same objective using end-of-unit tests, standardized test data, or some other summary assessment. The formative data will be the most powerful information for adjusting the "GPS teaching plan." When you get off course, it reminds you that you must "recalculate" the original route and make a detour to get back on track.

DESIGNING CURRICULAR ADAPTATIONS COLLABORATIVELY

Federal law requires that accommodations be made for individuals who qualify for certain types of carefully defined disabilities. Section 504 of the Rehabilitation Act of 1973 calls for public agencies to provide reasonable accommodations for individuals with disabilities, even those who do not qualify for IDEA, such as some students with attention deficit disorders or health impairments. The intent of both laws is to provide access to participation in school programs. Although Section 504 provisions and IEPs may specify accommodations needed by individual students, consulting teachers should help all parties who are involved in teaching these students to plan and prepare accommodations. Many authors use the terms "adaptations," "accommodations," and "modifications" interchangeably. For purposes here, curriculum "adaptations" are delineated as accommodations and/or modifications.

Curriculum accommodations are assistive aids and supports that help a student achieve the same outcomes as most other students in the class by adjusting the requirements. Therefore, an accommodation changes the path the student takes and the way he or she demonstrates learning, but it doesn't modify the initial learning goal or the final learning outcome. Accommodations change *how* a student learns the material. An accommodation can be made for *any* student, not just students with a 504 plan or an IEP. An accommodation does not alter what the student is expected to learn; it merely makes learning accessible to the student and allows students to demonstrate what they know. Accommodations do not alter the content of the assignments, give students an unfair advantage, or in the case of assessments, change *what* the test measures. They make it possible for students to show what they know without being impeded by their disability. Typical accommodations include extended time, frequent breaks, varying of activities, preferential seating, minimizing distractions, emphasizing varied teaching approaches (visual, auditory, multi-sensory), and use of manipulatives or graphic organizers. Teachers might highlight material, provide guided notes, allow use of a calculator or word processor or provide reading material in Braille or large print. Students with reading difficulties are often provided with text in digital formats so that a screen reader can be used. Tests may be read aloud, or the student might be allowed to give an oral rather than written response. Change in the test format (multiple choice vs. fill-in-the-blank) is yet another example of how accommodations are made for students.

Curriculum modifications involve changing the goals or the content and performance expectations for what the student should learn. Modifications are generally made for students with significant cognitive or physical disabilities. A modification does alter content knowledge and expectations as well as assessments. Modifications involve lowering the level of materials presented. An example of a modification is using a specialized curriculum which is written at a lower level of understanding. Materials or tests might be modified by simplifying vocabulary, concepts, or principles. Grading standards might also be modified based on the students' IEP goals.

Accommodations *level* the playing field while modifications *change* the playing field. Often the distinction is very black and white, but sometimes, it is not as clear. For example, reducing the number of spelling words on a weekly spelling test might be considered an accommodation if all the test words have a common spelling pattern that is being mastered. If, on the other hand, all of the words are considered key vocabulary terms that students are expected to write correctly and a student is only tested on half of the list, then it might be considered a modification. Sometimes the distinction comes down to what is being assessed. Consider the example of a student being allowed to make an outline of major points rather than writing an essay with complete sentences when responding to a short answer test question. Whether it is considered an accommodation or a modification will depend on whether the purpose was to test the student's ability to write a response in connected complete sentences or if the focus was merely on the content and not *how* it was written. In the UDL co-teaching activity, Randy took part in the American history class and then completed a modified test.

The key to effective accommodations and modifications is the word "appropriate." Today, because students with disabilities are included in high-stakes testing, accommodations must be appropriate without reducing the minimal objectives expected of all students. Accommodation strategies—for example, to "Read tests aloud and provide extended time"—should be individualized to meet the learner's needs and not generically applied to all special education students. Just as in the story about Goldilocks and the bear family, we don't want to choose an accommodation or modification that is too easy or too hard, but one that is just right. Once an accommodation is agreed upon, special educators and general education teachers should informally evaluate its usefulness for student learning by observing learning that occurs with use of the accommodation. Ask the question, "Do the accommodations cause the student to learn or show what he or she knows in an improved manner?" Formal measures should be in place as well when recommending an accommodation. The National Center on Educational Outcomes recommends six steps for teachers, IEP teams, and administrators in determining the best use of accommodations:

1. *Know the rules and regulations for accommodations.* Federal laws such as IDEA require states to monitor and show evidence of the effectiveness of accommodations chosen for instruction and assessment. Improved outcomes should be evident.
2. *Document decisions about accommodations.* IEP teams may need training regarding the correct way to choose accommodations and track their use.
3. *Document the use of accommodations*, noting accommodations that are listed on IEPs and the consistency with which the instructional and assessment accommodation are used.
4. *Review accommodations decisions and use*, documenting accommodations for state assessments to include listing the accommodations chosen and how they are used. Teachers should be aware of any accommodations that will invalidate assessments and know which are and are not allowed on high stakes testing. If a student is accustomed to having an accommodation and then is not allowed to use it for high stakes testing, it can be pointless to provide it at all unless the team determines that the accommodation provides other value beyond the test. At the very least, the student should have practice opportunities without the accommodation in place. If a student is to be granted permission to have an accommodation on a standardized test, educators must show that the accommodation has been provided on a regular and consistent basis, and not just for the standardized test.
5. *Evaluate and report on accommodations.* There may be times when an accommodation is recommended for a student in the IEP, but the student chooses not to use the accommodation. This should be noted. Likewise, if an accommodation is recommended but inadvertently is not provided, this must be noted as well.

Recommending blanket accommodations for students simply based on a disability label doesn't serve the student well and runs the risk of having general educators feel that the accommodations aren't fair because they give the student an unfair advantage. Special education teachers occasionally wonder why accommodations are not implemented by general education teachers. It could be that there is confusion about the intent or need of a particular IEP accommodation. Byrnes (2008) has proposed following five steps when selecting test accommodations:

1. State the disability or condition.
2. Describe the educational impact of the disability.
3. Consider upcoming educational tasks.
4. Identify barriers related to the disability.
5. Write unambiguous accommodations.

Byrnes recommends team members adopt four practices to increase the likelihood that accommodations will be implemented as intended. These require attention to:

- The number of accommodations selected
- Specifics about use of accommodations
- The process for reviewing accommodations
- Special considerations during transitions

Teams should guard against including accommodations in an IEP that just seem like they would be good rather than hone in on what is appropriate for a student's needs based on the disability. The decision regarding accommodations and modifications that are needed should not be taken lightly. It should be carefully considered by the IEP team and then communicated to all teachers who have the responsibility of providing that accommodation or modification. Teams should remember these points:

1. Keep lists of accommodations concise.
2. Specify when an accommodation is needed.
3. Review accommodations regularly.
4. Review accommodations during times of transition such as having a new teachers or being in a new school.

Consulting teachers might want to draw on the concept of scaffolding rather than accommodations. Scaffolding, as presented by Vygotsky (1978) is a structure for learning in which adults or more accomplished peers can help develop a student's independent problem-solving skills with collaboration and guidance to facilitate cognitive development. The scaffolding is used temporarily for helping a student benefit from classroom learning and then it is faded once the student no longer needs it. While that is the goal of general educators and is reasonable for some students with disabilities, many individuals with disabilities will need scaffolding or accommodations for a lifetime. For example, consider the special needs of students who are deaf or hard of hearing.

Making Text Accessible

In the upper elementary and secondary grades, the textbook has an increasingly prominent role; it is often the primary source of information about a subject. Unfortunately, printed textbooks and instructional materials used in the general education curriculum are not useful to many students with disabilities. The very materials that are there to support learning actually create barriers to learning for students who are not able to glean information from these materials. No reasonable person would question converting printed text for someone who is blind to another format such as Braille or audio format, yet some would expect students who are challenged by printed text because of a learning disability to read unaltered grade-level printed text.

Another way must be found for students with print disabilities to learn from materials that seem inaccessible to them. Hehir (2007) argues that school time devoted to activities focusing on changing the disability may take away from valuable time needed to learn academic material. Academic deficits may actually be exacerbated by ingrained prejudice against performing activities in more efficient, nontraditional ways, such as reading with Braille or text-to-speech software. For example, in inclusionary classrooms many older students with dyslexia and other specific learning disabilities have been expected to handle grade-level or higher text rather than having the book made available in a digital format. Disabilities such as dyslexia that affect ability to handle print can pose grave consequences for student success if accommodations aren't made.

National Instructional Materials Accessibility Standard (NIMAS).   Until recently, few students with disabilities had access to books they needed. Sometimes the problem was technical because schools did not have the technology they needed to provide accessible versions to students even if available. In other cases, the problem was lack of awareness: Many teachers and schools did not understand the issue of access or potential solutions. But for too many students the problem was the result of a frustrating distribution system where students couldn't get the materials in a timely fashion. The dissemination of accessible materials was inefficient and raised barriers rather than opportunities.

One of the most frustrating barriers to accessibility is created by multiple formats. The U.S. Department of Education has endorsed a common National Instructional Materials Accessibility Standard (NIMAS). NIMAS is a technical standard used by publishers to produce source files using Extensible Markup Language (XML) that may then be used to develop multiple specialized formats for students with print disabilities. Source files are prepared using XML tags to mark up the structure of the original content and thus provide a way to present content in any number of formats such as Braille, large print, talking books using human voice, and text-to-speech.

New to IDEA with the 2004 amendments, NIMAS is designed to maximize access to the general education curriculum for students who are blind or have print-related disabilities through timely provision of accessible instructional materials created from NIMAS source files. As a result of this standard, the printed instructional materials, including textbooks, are to be made available free of charge by publishers in the NIMAS-specified format to students who are blind and other persons with print-related disabilities in elementary and secondary schools. As a result of the adoption of NIMAS, print and digital materials can be converted more quickly and the quality and consistency of books converted into specialized formats has improved.

Zabala and Carl (2010/2011) outline four steps that IEP teams should follow in order to ensure that students who need accessible instructional materials (AIM) have them available and receive them in a timely manner: 1) Determine the need, 2) select the format(s) needed, 3) acquire formats, and 4) select supports needed for use. How does a specialized format of a print-based material differ from an alternative material? The specialized format includes exactly the same information as the print version of the material. It doesn't change the content, it merely changes the way in which the content is presented (Braille, audio, large print). An alternative material, on the other hand, may address the same general goals or content but the material is changed in some way, usually making it less complex, so that it can be understood by the student. This could be reducing the complexity of the vocabulary, reducing the length of text or sentence complexity, or a host of other options.

When general education teachers and special educators collaborate on decision making such as seeking out and arranging for appropriate materials, the match between the integrity of the content and the individual needs of the student with a disability can be realized.

Adapting Tests

Many students with learning and behavior problems have difficulty taking tests about subject matter they have learned. As a student progresses to higher grade levels, the ability to demonstrate knowledge through tests becomes more and more important. Consultants at upper grade levels will need to give careful attention to the test-taking skills of students with learning and behavior difficulties.

When students have difficulty taking teacher-made tests in content subjects, consulting teachers should give attention to a number of elements about the nature of the tests and ways to help students take the tests as written, or collaborate with the teacher to make test adaptations. Students can benefit from being taught effective study skills and test-taking strategies. Other suggestions to consider when consulting with classroom teachers about how to prepare students for tests, alternative test construction, and test administration include:

- Preparing study guides to lead students through reading material, emphasizing important information
- Giving practice tests
- Having students test one another and discussing answers
- Giving more frequent mini-tests rather than one test on large blocks of content
- Backing up the written tests with audio-formatted tests
- Providing extra spacing for essay questions and short-answer items
- Underlining key words in test directions as well as test items
- Providing additional time for students who have processing difficulties or write slowly
- Administering tests orally or converting to a digital format that will convert text to speech

Teachers are likely to be more resistant to test adaptations than to adaptations of classroom materials. Likewise, even when they believe it is a good thing to do, they are not very likely to make the adaptations themselves, either because they lack knowledge in this area or they feel they don't have sufficient time. Collaborative school consultants can teach classroom teachers elements of accessible test construction. For example:

- Sentence structure should be as simple as possible, including only words essential for responding to the item.
- Vocabulary and item stem should be grade appropriate when a readability analysis is applied.
- Test questions should be directly related to the objectives of the class.
- Item stem should be as direct as possible and use active voice.
- Item stem, answer stem, and any related visuals should be on the same page.
- Item stem should be worded positively (in other words, avoiding *not* questions).
- Bold font is needed on essential words or vocabulary terms.
- Answer choices should be about equal length.
- Have all text printed in standard typeface, using a minimum of twelve-point text.
- Allow for sufficient space between lines.
- Include ample white space to prevent the item from appearing cluttered.
- Keep the right margin unjustified (staggered).

An existing teacher-made or publisher-produced test can be adapted using some of these guidelines:

- Change the format so the items are easy to read, more space is allowed for discussion, or the order of items is rearranged to make them more predictable.
- Rewrite directions or provide cues such as highlighting, underlining, and enlarging.
- Provide prompts such as "Start here" or "Look at the sign on this row."
- Adjust the readability level of the questions.
- Provide outlines or advance organizers.
- Provide spelling of difficult words.
- Allow students to use outlines, webs, or other visual organizers.

Adapting the Curriculum

Students whose cognitive disabilities prevent them from benefiting from the general classroom curriculum, even with accommodations, need curriculum modifications. Students with mild or moderate cognitive disabilities may need adapted outcomes while students with severe cognitive disabilities will need different goals or outcomes. Whenever possible, a theme or topic studied by the rest of the students in the classroom should also be studied by these students.

Adapted Outcomes.   Students with moderate learning and behavior problems can succeed very well in most classrooms but may need modified outcomes such as a reduced number of practice problems or highlighted text. Other examples include the following: In math, the student works on the same concept but the number of required practice problems may be reduced; in social studies, the teacher might mark certain

FIGURE 7.4   Suggestions for Adaptations

Instructional Level
Let student work at success rate level of about 80%.
Break down task into sequential steps.
Sequence the work with easiest problems first.
Base instruction on cognitive need (concrete, abstract).

Curricular Content
Select content that addresses student's interest.
Adapt content to student's future goals (job, college. . .).

Instructional Materials
Fold or line paper to help student with a spatial problem.
Use graph paper or lined paper turned vertically.
Draw arrows on text or worksheet to show related ideas.
Highlight or color-code on worksheets, texts, tests.
Mark the material that must be mastered.
Reduce the amount of material on a page.
Use a word processor for writing and editing.
Provide a calculator or computer to check work.
Tape reference materials to student's work area.
Have student follow print text, listening to audio format.

Format of Directions and Assignments
Make instructions as brief as possible.
Introduce multiple long-term assignments in small steps.
Read written directions or assignments aloud.
Leave directions on chalkboard during study time.
Write cues at top of work page (for example, noun = . . .).
Ask student to restate/paraphrase directions.
Have student complete first example with teacher prompt.
Provide folders for unfinished work and finished work.

Instructional Strategies
Use concrete objects to demonstrate concepts.
Provide outlines, semantic organizers, or webbings.
Use voice changes to stress points.
Point out relationships between ideas or concepts.
Repeat important information often.
Use color-coded strips for key parts.

Teacher Input Mode
Use multisensory approach for presenting materials.
Provide a written copy of material on chalkboard.
Demonstrate skills before student does seat work.

Student Response Mode
Accept alternate forms of information sharing.
Allow audio-recorded or written report instead of oral.
Allow students to dictate information to another.
Allow oral report instead of written report.
Have student practice speaking to small group first.

Test Administration
Allow students to have sample tests to practice.
Teach test-taking skills.
Test orally.
Supply recognition items and not just total recall.
Allow take-home test.
Ask questions requiring short answers.

Grading Policies
Grade on pass/fail basis.
Grade on individual progress or effort.
Change the percentage required to pass.
Do not penalize for handwriting or spelling on tests.
Use scoring templates and rubrics.

Modifications of Classroom Environment
Seat students according to attention or sensory need.
Remove student from distractions.
Keep extra supplies on hand.

parts of the text material that must be read, with the remainder to be skimmed; and in science, the teacher might limit the number of concepts within a domain to be mastered. In short, these students are expected to master most but not all of the content. Most of the items listed in Figure 7.4 are adapted outcomes.

Functional Outcomes.   For students with severe cognitive challenges, curriculum goals may focus on areas such as social/behavioral development, language development, concept development, basic skills, or self-help skills. For example, if the class is studying plants, but a certain student's goals have to do with counting and language development, that student may count, sort, and talk about seeds. These students may also need accommodations to help them attain their goals. The primary reason for inclusion in the class is to participate in the social context and culture of the group.

Enhanced Outcomes.   Students with high ability also need modified curriculum. Cooperative learning is an effective instructional strategy for many students for a variety of reasons. However, it should not be justified for gifted students through inference that they require remediation in social skills. Nor should it be used to make gifted students available as handy tutors (Robinson, 1990). While occasional peer tutoring can be challenging and rewarding for the very able student, collaborative activities are not intended to set very able students up as surrogate teachers for other students.

When students with high ability are included in general classrooms, as the majority are for most of their school day, their learning needs also must be considered. Providing appropriate learning environments for them necessitates intensive collaboration and consultation among gifted program facilitators, classroom teachers, and resource personnel so that classroom modifications and resource adaptations will help these students develop their learning potential. This is discussed in more detail later in the chapter.

Classroom teachers may believe they do not know how to adapt instruction, but the most plausible explanation is that they do not have time to do it. Consultants and collaborators must consider whether their suggestions for classroom modifications are reasonable and feasible for the situation. (See an earlier chapter for ways of dealing with consultee resistance.)

Many of the resources available for helping teachers make classroom modifications represent the views of special educators rather than the collaborative views of classroom teachers and special education teachers. However, the list given in Figure 7.4 was prepared jointly by elementary classroom teachers and special education collaborating teachers, and as such it can be a helpful resource to share with classroom teachers during collaborative consultations.

Using IEP Information Collaboratively

When teachers and other instructional support personnel such as paras collaborate about shared students, it is important to use sensitive information from IEPs in a way that is useful but also maintains the confidentiality of the information. General education teachers having a classroom of many students should not be burdened with sifting through massive IEP documents to keep track of goals and objectives of students with special needs who are part of their classroom. Likewise, paras need the big picture of what goals the student is working toward and clear directions and guidance in terms of what they are to do while working with students on IEPs in the general classroom.

Consultants should devise a way to provide IEP highlights to teachers and paras in a format that will be useful to them without violating a student's rights. This might be a document called "IEP at a Glance" or "IEP Snapshot." To protect this information, it could be shared in a password-protected computer file or a paper copy placed in a locked file cabinet. Only individuals who know the password or who have been given access to the locked file could access the information. However, one limitation of putting information in locked files is that it is too easily forgotten—out of sight, out of mind. Perhaps a periodic e-mail message with the relevant information and a personal note about the student's progress or lack of it would be a way to keep everyone informed about progress toward meeting IEP goals and objectives. Of course, the e-mail material must be kept as secure as any printed, and perhaps even more so because of its potential for being sent far and wide erroneously.

TEAMING IN A MULTI-TIER SYSTEM OF SUPPORTS (MTSS)

The terms, **response to intervention (RTI)** and **multi-tier system of support (MTSS)** are often used interchangeably among many educators, but in fact, they are not quite the same.

Response to Intervention

Response to intervention is an instructional framework many schools use to help students who are struggling academically. It involves providing effective instruction and intervention across three tiers to all students. Assessment, progress monitoring, and data-driven decision-making are all components of the RTI process. Response to intervention has been gaining momentum and expanding across grade levels and content areas since it first came on the scene as a result of two major efforts by the federal government. The Reading First program that was ushered in with No Child Left Behind in 2002 encouraged schools to use the RTI framework for their literacy programs. Two years later, the 2004 reauthorization of IDEA also changed federal law concerning identification of children with specific learning disabilities. The concept of RTI was included in IDEA (2006) in order to allow local education agencies to "use a process that determines if the child responds to scientific, research-based interventions as part of the evaluation procedures"—specifically, for identification of specific learning disabilities (20 U.S.C. §1414[b][6]). As a result, schools were no longer required to consider whether there was a severe discrepancy between achievement and ability and could use RTI as one tool for determining if a child has a specific learning disability (SLD). While historically the focus of RTI was primarily on identification, it has become a mechanism of instructional delivery for all students, including students of high aptitude and talent. The broader conceptualization of RTI as an instructional delivery model allows for a more systematic delivery of services for all students, including those with a disability and those with high aptitude and talents (Johnsen, Parker, & Farah, 2015).

The long-standing discrepancy model of SLD identification has been criticized on many fronts, and it often is described as a wait-to-fail model where students had to wait to be so far behind before they became eligible for special education services. RTI was promoted as an alternative prevention model not only for students with potential learning disabilities but also as a built-in support and monitoring system for all students. This three-tiered prevention model works to support students with varying instructional and behavioral needs (Brown-Chidsey, 2007):

1. In Tier 1, research-based core group instruction is provided to all students. Universal screening of all students is done, typically three times a year. Students identified as at risk based on benchmarks established for the universal screen are then monitored on a more frequent basis while they continue in the core group interventions.

2. In Tier 2, students identified as at risk in Tier 1, who did not respond adequately to the core group instruction, are now targeted for additional small group interventions provided in the general classroom, and they continue to be assessed or to have their progress monitored more frequently. Those making too little progress are considered for Tier 3 interventions. States that include students with high aptitude and talents in the RTI framework use the screen process to identify those above grade-level standards, and they are provided with interventions to meet their needs at this level (Johnson, Parker, & Farah, 2015).

3. In Tier 3, students receive individualized, intensive interventions targeting their specific skill deficits. Those not responding at this level typically are considered for eligibility under IDEA. In the case of students who have a high aptitude or who are highly talented, they might be accelerated, or work with mentors to develop professional levels of expertise on research projects, or engage in leadership activities in community settings.

Response to Intervention has many beneficial features. It helps ensure that all students have equal opportunity to learn (Brown-Chidsey, 2007). It is a data-based, systematic method that lets co-educators know what is working and what is not working. The process has been growing exponentially and expanding far beyond its initial application to early literacy. A summary feature is that it reduces the number of children and youth who are referred for special education; the number of students identified for SLD has been steadily declining since 2005. Not surprisingly, it does require much collaboration between general education and special education teachers.

RTI comes with cautions. It should be implemented by educators who have training in the model. Identification of students for special education must focus on assessments that directly relate to instruction, and services must focus on intervention, not eligibility. Experts in the field of learning disabilities have spoken out against its sweeping application as a replacement model for SLD identification. However, as a preservice teacher noted while participating in a team, RTI was very helpful in improving a teacher's lessons and being able to learn from watching others teach. A number of websites, such as those of the National Center on Response to Intervention and Intervention Central, feature explanatory material, articles, and other materials teachers can use when implementing RTI. Initially, RTI was used almost exclusively for beginning reading skills but now is being

---

Video Example from YouTube

▶ ENHANCEDetext
Video Example 7.6.
This video illustrates how RTI is operationalized in a classroom. (https://www.youtube.com/watch?v=HWxsl2g5yp8)

implemented in early childhood settings through high school and has been moved into math, written language, spelling and even behavior benchmarking and monitoring.

Multi-Tier System of Supports

A multi-tier system of supports (MTSS) is more comprehensive. It may include the three levels of RTI, but MTSS goes beyond academics. Multi-tier system of supports encompasses RTI and then some. In addition to academic areas, it also covers social and emotional supports. That means it can include behavior intervention plans (BIPs). Multi-tier system of supports provides multiple levels of support for all learners (struggling through advanced). It aligns resources and support for students receiving instruction *and* for teachers and other support staff who are delivering the instruction. It requires greater focus on collaboration between general education and special education both within the school and between the school and the district office. Multi-tier system of supports requires that teachers, administrators, and student support specialists alter the ways they have traditionally worked together to include a more collaborative and cohesive culture. Response to Intervention and MTSS espouse common traits, but MTSS tends to reach beyond the typical response to intervention implementations. Both the MTSS and RTI frameworks provide student interventions designed to improve academic progress. Multi-tier system of supports uses the RTI model for intervention, and then provides support to make learning more effective. Behavioral and emotional interventions are provided where needed to support learning. Teachers and support staff receive additional resources and professional development. Partnerships are formed among educators, parents, and the community to provide integrated comprehensive services.

Proponents of MTSS see it as the evolution of the RTI model. Recently, many state educational agencies and school districts have adopted the MTSS approach over RTI because of the more comprehensive framework of MTSS. The chart in Figure 7.5 compares RTI and MTSS to demonstrate some of the similarities as well as differences between the two frameworks.

Positive Behavioral Interventions and Supports (PBIS)

Positive Behavioral Interventions and Supports (PBIS) is an approach for assisting school personnel in adopting and organizing evidence-based behavioral interventions. It is part of a comprehensive MTSS framework and includes the three-tiered framework (i.e., primary, secondary, tertiary) that provides a continuum of supports and services designed to promote appropriate behaviors and to prevent and address challenging behaviors. When applied at the schoolwide level, it is frequently referred to as Schoolwide Positive Behavior Support or SWPBS. When a school or district implements SWPBS, a team of representatives from the school, which typically includes administrators, classified, and general and special education teachers, receives training on the approach. The team works collaboratively with the school staff to develop three to five schoolwide behavioral expectations that are positively stated and easy to remember. An example might be, "Respect Yourself, Respect Others, and Respect Property." The team then creates a matrix of what each behavioral expectation looks like across settings (for example, classroom, playground, cafeteria,

FIGURE 7.5 Comparison between RTI and MTSS

	RTI	MTSS
Interventions	Academic	Academic, Behavioral, Social, and Emotional
Target Group	Students at risk of failing and those who might eventually qualify for special education	All students, including high achieving students
Collaboration	General and special educators work together on supports in Tiers 2 and 3	Even greater focus on collaboration between general and special education
Resources and Supports	Targeted for students	All students, teachers, and support staff
Focus	Intervention and remediation based on assessment results	Intervention, remediation, and a stronger emphasis on prevention
Scope of Interventions	Academic interventions centered within the school	Academic, behavioral, social, and emotional interventions centered in the school, community, and in the home

bus, restroom). For the behavior expectation of "Respect Property," examples of this for the restroom could include such things as: Flush the toilet after use, use two squirts of soap to wash hands, and throw used paper towels in wastebasket. School personnel make sure that all are consistent in carrying out the mutually agreed upon SWPBS system. Often schools will spend several days at the beginning of each year taking students around the school to stations, where the skills are taught and practiced in specific setting locations. Many schools choose to use the web-based School-Wide Information System (SWIS) that graphs office-discipline referral data. The program creates graphs of the data that can be displayed in a number of ways with many options. These data can then serve as information for discussion and decision-making by the school MTSS team.

PBIS is not a packaged curriculum or scripted intervention, and it does not come with a manual. It is a prevention-oriented way for school personnel to organize evidence-based practices, improve their implementation of those practices, and maximize academic and social behavior outcomes for students. Positive Behavioral Interventions and Support programs, like RTI, typically have three tiers. Tier 2 support is designed to provide intensive or targeted interventions to support students who are not responding to Tier 1 support efforts. Common Tier 2 support practices involve small groups of students or simple individualized intervention strategies. Individual PBIS plans at the Tier 2 level involve a simple assessment to identify the function a problem behavior serves (functional behavioral assessment or FBA) and a support plan comprised of individualized intervention strategies that includes a range of options such as teaching the student replacement behaviors for the problem behaviors, rearranging or changing the environment to prevent undesirable be-haviors, and monitoring the plan over time.

Monitoring Student Progress

Frequent monitoring of progress is a key component of MTSS and RTI. That has always been at the heart of what special education is all about. Special educators focus on daily and weekly student progress. Since it is rare in schools today for a special education teacher to provide all of the direct instruction to students with special needs, it is more important than ever to track progress and determine if the interventions being implemented in the general education classroom are working. In fact, it might be the most important function performed by the special educator in inclusive schools. Consider the example of a special education consulting teacher named Sara.

Sara was in her second year of teaching at an inclusive school. She had sixteen students in her caseload—mostly third- and fourth-graders. Sara spent at least one hour a day in each classroom where her students were placed. In addition, she taught math to several small groups in which her students were included. Although she believed her students were making satisfactory progress in basic skills, she wasn't sure. She began using curriculum-based measurement (CBM) procedures, taking reading and math probes once each week. After a few weeks of charting data, she realized that four of her students were not making progress in reading. She had not been working directly with these students in reading and did not realize the problems they were having. She immediately took steps to make changes in their reading instruction.

Monitoring Classroom Grades.   Both elementary and secondary-level teachers can monitor student progress by the number of completed assignments and grades in general classroom courses. This information must be interpreted cautiously, how-ever, because teachers' grading standards vary greatly. Special educators in inclusive schools should discuss grading philosophies and processes with each teacher and plan a system for grading students with adapted curriculum. This need for collaborative problem solving about grading processes was discussed in an earlier chapter.

Team Data-Based Decision Making

The mere mention of the word "data" puts some teachers on edge, largely because of fear of being judged on limited data (Swanson, Allen, & Mancabelli, 2015). Schools and dis-tricts that are successful at promoting data-based decision-making often have dedicated collaboration time for teachers. Without collaboration, data use is impossible, as noted by one principal (Datnow & Park, 2015). Teachers typically meet weekly or monthly in grade-level groups, groups that span across grade levels, or a combination of the two where weekly meetings occur for grade level teams and monthly meetings are used for school-wide data-focused team meetings. At the secondary level, the teams might be struc-tured around content areas. In effective team meetings, teachers examine a wide variety of data and support each other in improving instruction. This arrangement is often referred to as a professional learning community. In their decade of research on data use that included many observations of these types of team meetings, Datnow and Park (2015) distilled five essential components for quality conversations about data and how school leaders can support successful teams:

1. Students are the shared responsibility of everyone.
2. A healthy level of disagreement is essential for quality conversations about data.
3. Team members must respect each other and be less judgmental when examining the data. Data use is about determining how the school can improve rather than pointing fingers and playing the blame game (Swanson, Allen, & Mancabelli, 2015).
4. Data teams take a solution-oriented approach, with teachers engaging in reflective practice.
5. Everyone is clear about what they're to accomplish. However, expectations must be balanced. Too much structure might stifle teacher discussion, whereas too little could allow discussions to get off track and lose focus.

With RTI and MTSS being implemented in schools, special educators have a crucial role on these building-level teams. Their understanding of progress-monitoring data, intensive instructional strategies, and ways to observe and measure behavior to create positive behavior plans are all essential to the work of these teams. Collaborating special educators must advocate for being included on these teams if they are not part of the team structure.

Data-focused teams must be careful not to get too caught up in data and computer-generated reports. Teacher Karen Engles reminds us that some of the assumptions underlying schools' approaches to the RTI model can have unintended consequences in classrooms. Objective, standardized, and scientific measures of student achievement can have a great deal of appeal, but Engles (2015) suggests a common sense approach when examining RTI data. Formative assessment data are powerful and should not be dismissed over universal screening data. If students are tested too frequently, tests can become unreliable because students no longer put forth their best effort. They become test weary and results from two different measures may not match, leaving teachers to wonder which data are more accurate. Teaching is more like gardening than baking (Engles, 2015). When making a cake, measure and mix the ingredients precisely, bake it for the specified amount of time, and feel pretty much assured of success. Teachers, on the other hand are cultivating seeds, knowing the blooms may appear when they are no longer around to admire them. They must be sure at RTI meetings to discuss the students, not just the numbers. They need to consider all the data without over-reliance on standardized assessment. They should bring together authentic student work samples and consider social-emotional factors that are supporting or impeding academic performance. Data alone must not supplant professional judgment. Time will be required for collegial discussions of student needs.

A significant advantage of the RTI and MTSS models being implemented in schools is that they emphasize collaborative problem solving. When teachers come together in these team meetings, they get support from colleagues about successful approaches to Tier 1 and Tier 2 instruction. Collaborating special educators feel part of the larger school community rather than outsiders looking in. Participation in team meetings allows collaborating teachers to keep their fingers on the pulse of what takes place in general education classrooms and the expectations for students with disabilities who are an integral part of those classes.

CHARACTERISTICS AND LEARNING NEEDS OF STUDENTS WITH EXCEPTIONAL ABILITIES AND TALENTS

Many educators and policymakers believe that students with exceptional abilities and talents do not have special educational needs because they can "get it on their own" and they will be just fine. In their views, so many other students have major learning problems that teachers must address first and foremost. However, high-achieving students gain little if anything by "marking time in place." As some of these students put it, they feel as if they are "revving their motors with their brakes on." For them it is very frustrating and disillusioning. For the world at large, it is a waste of talents and abilities.

SITUATION 7.B

Alysia loves to high jump and she shows great promise in this activity as well as other track-and-field events. But the physical education teacher says that the high-jump bar will be set no higher than most of the students can jump. "Why not?" asks Alysia. "Well, for lots of reasons," the teacher responds. "The other kids can't go as high as you, and they need to work where everyone can be successful. So the bar should be kept in that range during the limited time we have to practice. We have only so much time to spend on high jump, you know, and it might discourage them to see you jump a lot higher than they can. Then, too, think about this. They might not even like you as much if you 'show them up.' So we need for you to just keep in step with everyone else and wait another year or two for raising the bar."

The irony of this situation is that if it *were* a competitive sports matter such as the high jump in a track-and-field event, it is likely that the bar *would* be raised for Alysia. Furthermore, she would be given time, equipment, space, instruction, and encouragement to develop her special talents. Similarly, a tall, very talented freshman basketball player would not be relegated to the bench for the next one or two years if a trophy for the school showcase could be won. It is unfortunate when schools and the public will forego age and grade-level constraints for performance areas in competitive events, yet "throttle down" bright minds that could contribute so much to the world.

Some might characterize high-jumper Alysia and the precocious basketball player as overachievers, but that is a misnomer because one cannot achieve more than one does. To say a student is "overachieving" is to be *under-expecting* for that student.

As pointed out in an earlier chapter, students differ in many ways, and the magnitudes of those differences can be great. Some educators overlook or ignore reality and strive to treat all students alike. They take very seriously the concept of equality without considering that "there is nothing so unequal as equal treatment of unequals." Noted educator Eisner (2003) questions the widely accepted assumption that the aim of schooling is to get all students to the same place at the same time. He presents a sharply critical analogy that compares schools to a railroad system and asserts that the *good* school:

does not expect all students to arrive at the same destination at the same time. Indeed, it provides conditions in which variability among students can be increased. What we ought to be doing in schools is increasing the variance in student performance while escalating the mean. In an ideal approach to curriculum and instruction—an approach in which every aspect of teaching is ideally suited to each student, and each aspect of curriculum is appropriate for the abilities students possess—variability among students will increase, not decrease. (p. 650)

Good teaching requires educators to make every effort to maximize the achievement of all students. In years past there have been efforts to have "No Child Left Behind," to "Race to the Top," to achieve "Common Core Standards," and to satisfy the "Every Student Succeeds Act" (LaPolice, 2016), but not much effort to set a goal of "No Child *Held* Behind." Programs for gifted and talented students have been implemented in most states but minimally funded and not often integrated into the school structure. Too much attention has been given to selection and placement processes for "pullout" programs of limited time and minimal interest or long-term value to students, with too little attention directed toward collaboration among school personnel and families of very able students to provide the enriched, accelerated curriculum they need.

How can school personnel determine which students have special needs for enriched and accelerated learning programs? Teachers have many opportunities to observe and evaluate student work in a variety of content areas. However, these opportunities have little value unless the curriculum (the body of coursework and planned school activities) is extended in ways that allow them to show their abilities and talents. Schools must provide responsive, nurturing school environments so that children's abilities will "bubble up" to be recognized (Clark, 2002). Such environments for learning also would encourage teachers to provide enrichment and **acceleration** opportunities for many more students than just the few who are formally identified for gifted program services.

Two useful tools for identifying high ability requiring differentiated learning experiences are preassessments and checklists. **Preassessment** determines what a student already has learned and should not have to repeat or "mark time in place" while it is being taught to others. It also provides evidence as to how far and fast the student can accomplish material that will be taught in the near future. Then differentiated learning programs can take the brakes off the learning process and allow students to progress farther and faster toward their potential. Without preassessment, it is unlikely that there will be differentiation (Rakow, 2012).

A simple preassessment technique to determine math achievement and predict potential would be to require less drill and assign fewer practice problems (perhaps just the last row of the hardest problems). Or allow the history student to stop off during a Civil War unit for more in-depth study on a topic of keen interest in that unit and catch up with the class later, having the content compacted by removing material already learned and testing satisfactorily on the unit after a period of four weeks or so. Or, a secondary student might be enrolled in two subjects simultaneously, attending each class half time and completing half of the assignments in each, then testing well on both subjects after a four-week or six-week period.

The collaborative consulting teacher can facilitate the preassessment process by administering tests, arranging materials and schedules, supervising where needed, evaluating the outcomes, consulting with family members about the student's progress, and convening a preassessment team to collaborate on analyzing the student's progress and planning next steps.

SITUATION 7.C

Anna, a second-grade student reading at the sixth-grade level, arrived home from school one afternoon and laid a second-grade basal reader on the kitchen table. She announced to her mother that the class's homework assignment was to read aloud to parents the word list in the back of the reader, practicing any words they did not know. Anna's mother sighed inwardly and strengthened her resolve to request a parent conference next week to talk about the snail's pace of reading in the class.

For now, to Anna she said, "Just put the book in your backpack and return it to school tomorrow. For your homework this evening, let's get your new dictionary and read as many pages in it as that word list takes up in the reader. We will see how many new, interesting words we find on those pages, and practice any that you don't know. OK?"

ACTIVITY 7.3
Anna's Homework Assignment

But what if Anna's teacher asks the children if they did the assignment? Should the mother send a note to inform the teacher of their substituted homework assignment? Should she coach Anna on how to respond to the teacher's question if it is asked? How would you have handled this situation as Anna's mother? As Anna? As the classroom teacher if she learns of the altered homework? With other teachers or classmates, role-play this situation to see what ideas emerge.

Roles of General Education Teachers

General education teachers are responsible for delivering instruction to all children in an inclusive classroom. They also should provide curriculum content in basic, differentiated, compacted, accelerated, and enriched forms as determined by student needs. But they should have assistance from special services personnel such as gifted program facilitators. It is important that co-educators understand and appreciate the characteristics and needs of students with high learning ability and draw on assistance from collaborative consultants.

Checklists for Identifying Exceptional Ability and Talent

In a very responsive learning environment, classroom teacher perceptions of student ability will be a good place to identify special needs. A collaborative consultant, typically the facilitator for the gifted education program, can introduce co-educators to purposes and procedures of the process in a one-on-one conference, or a brief inservice or staff development activity, or as part of a general faculty meeting. It will be important for the building administrator(s) to support this activity and highly desirable to participate in such meetings. One tool that can be introduced to teachers is the checklist of characteristics.

FIGURE 7.6 Teacher Referral Checklist

The following criteria are useful in assessing high potential of students. Please use one form per student to assign a value of *3* (to a considerable degree), *2* (to some degree), or *1* (to little if any degree) for each characteristic.

1. Learns rapidly and easily _____
2. Uses much common sense and practical knowledge _____
3. Retains easily what has been presented _____
4. Knows about many things of which other students are unaware _____
5. Uses a large number of words easily and accurately and appreciates word power _____
6. Recognizes relationships, comprehends meanings, and seems to "get more out of things" _____
7. Is alert with keen powers of observation and responds quickly _____
8. Likes difficult subjects and challenging tasks for the fun of learning _____
9. Asks penetrating questions and seeks out causes and reasons _____
10. Is a good guesser with an intuitive sense _____
11. Reads voraciously well beyond age level, and sets aside time for reading _____
12. Questions the accepted ways of doing things _____
13. Prefers to work independently with minimal direction _____
14. Has a longer attention span than age peers _____
15. Has little patience for routine drill and practice _____
16. Tends to be critical of self and others, with high standards and seeking perfection _____
17. Seldom needs more than one demonstration or instruction in order to carry out an activity _____
18. Perseveres on projects and ideas _____
19. Is withdrawn yet very capable when pressed _____
20. Demonstrates remarkable talent in one or more areas _____
21. Uses materials in innovative and unusual ways _____
22. Creates unusual stories, pictures, examples, models, or products _____
23. Has many interests and follows them with zeal _____
24. Makes extensive collections, with sustained focus _____
25. Invents contrivances, gadgets, and new ways of doing things _____
26. Prefers to be around older students or adults, communicating effectively with them _____
27. Has an advanced sense of humor and "gets it" when others may not _____
28. Influences other students to do things _____
29. Is serious-minded and intolerant of prolonged foolishness _____
30. Shows much sensitivity toward people, social issues, and right and wrong _____

Please check any of the following factors which apply. If present along with a number of the attributes above, they may provide additional validation of high ability.

A. A disability that affects learning and/or behavior _____
B. Living in a home where English is the second (or third) language _____
C. Transience (frequent moves) during the elementary school years _____
D. Social or educational isolation from resources and stimulation _____
E. Home responsibilities or employment that interferes with school _____
F. Irregular school attendance _____
G. Little or no interaction between school personnel and family _____

Additional comments:

ENHANCEDetext
Video Example 7.7.
There are many myths that surround students identified as gifted and talented. A few are presented in this short video clip. (https://www.youtube.com/watch?v=GoM0K5UfEdI)

An example of a teacher checklist for assessing high potential is shown in Figure 7.6. The form can be used as-is or modified to fit the school setting. A classroom teacher may want to use the checklist for only one student or several students, but better yet is to complete one for each student in the entire class.

After receiving checklist forms, a third-grade teacher focused on Chuck, a student whose uneven achievement across several subject areas concerned her. She pondered the butterfly net propped up beside his desk, the opossum skull he had secreted in the back of his desk, the array of reading materials he had bookmarked to study later, and various insightful comments he made during science lessons. When the gifted program facilitator collected the checklists, Chuck's teacher said: "I filled out twenty of these—one for each child in my classroom. Here is Chuck's page. He is a casual learner in some subjects, not always attentive to the lessons. Sometimes he just withdraws into his own world of thoughts. I am not going to recommend him for the gifted program just yet; however, I can tell you that *I'm thinking differently about him now*. I would like to meet with you and brainstorm for ways I might channel his attention toward *all* of the curriculum goals but also support him in his areas of keen interest and ability."

High scores on items 1–7 of the teacher referral checklist reflect the kinds of mental processes measured by standardized individual aptitude tests. Items 8–12 target learning styles, and items 13–19 signify performance styles. Items 20–25 predict creative thinking and doing. Items 26–30 are indicants of personal preferences that relate to learning. The seven lettered items at the end of the numbered list are factors that, if present, provide even more evidence of exceptional ability.

Secondary teachers often respond well to checklists in question format that describe specific (and to some adults, annoying) behaviors, such as:

Do you have a student (or more than one) who:

- Finishes what should have been a twenty-minute assignment in five minutes?
- Volunteers off-the-wall comments or suggestions during discussions?
- Is highly intolerant of stupidity, especially when perceived in an authority figure?
- Is impatient with sloppy or disorganized thinking to the point of rudeness?
- Recognizes sophisticated punch lines and gets more out of humor?
- Plans activities efficiently but can procrastinate to the point of desperation?
- Would rather argue than eat?
- Has probably read every book available on subjects of personal interest, but may tune out or lag behind when disinterested?

Educators who work with preschool children and kindergartners, and parents of preschool children who observe signs that lead them to think their child is precocious, will relate to checklists of characteristics such as these:

Do you have a child who:

- Asks many questions, often on topics that typically interest older children?
- Demonstrates early use of a large vocabulary and multiple meanings of words?
- Understands abstract concepts such as time, coins, larger numbers, calendars?
- Relates experiences in great detail and makes up vivid, dramatic stories?
- Has a long attention span and deep concentration level for such an early age?
- Learned to read at a very young age with little or no instruction?
- Expressed self in complete sentences at an early age?
- Shows precocious interest in values, purposes, and right-and-wrong issues?

Cultural differences such as deference to authority or reluctance to compete against friends can cover up talents and abilities. Illness or poor health and nutritional deficiencies may prevent students from showing their capabilities. The children of families who are poor, displaced, or disadvantaged, and have potential for exceptional achievement, must have teachers who recognize that potential and build upon it.

Collaborative consultants will want to discuss with teachers some validity issues that may influence completion of the assessments:

- Halo effect, where generously favorable attitudes can cause spuriously high ratings ("She's so sweet and always has her work done perfectly, so she deserves to be in a gifted program.")
- Logical error, in which two characteristics—for example, impatience with others and high ability, or giftedness while standing apart from others—are rated similarly due to raters' erroneous beliefs ("He must be gifted because he is disdainful of others, also introverted, and quite a loner.")
- Generosity error ("Everybody has gifts and deserves to be in a gifted program.")
- Severity error ("No one is gifted enough to necessitate providing a special program. Besides, it just isn't fair to those who don't qualify for a special program.")
- Central tendency (A more rare occurrence where everyone is believed to be average, sometimes dubbed the "Lake Wobegon" effect.)

Identifying Twice-Exceptional Students

Space should be left on checklists for including characteristics that suggest dual exceptionality. A student who is identified as gifted and also has a learning disability is twice exceptional. A visually impaired student who is a brilliant musician is twice exceptional. A child with cerebral palsy who is a deep thinker in science and math is twice exceptional. Twice-exceptional students benefit greatly when gifted program facilitators, special education teachers, resource and support personnel, family members, and classroom teachers all collaborate to provide classroom accommodations and extracurricular opportunities.

Collaborating consultants know that student potential too often is concealed by problems that do not allow their abilities and talents to "bubble up." Conversely, their abilities to compensate may mask problem areas or disabilities so that the needs are not identified. The student loses both ways: Ability is not served and disability is not addressed. To extend the point made just above, collaboration and consultation among family members, general education teachers, special education personnel, school counselors, school psychologists, mentors, and resource and support personnel, including those in the medical field, will factor positively into helping students reveal and develop their talents and skills.

Roles of Building Administrators

If building administrators do not support differentiated instruction, little is likely to happen that benefits students *or* their teachers. Administrators must provide the resources and support that very able students and their teachers need in order to maximize student achievement and productivity. They have responsibility for encouraging teachers to collaborate with their colleagues and with resource and support personnel to develop differentiated curriculum strategies and materials. Administrators also are integral in accommodating professional development for school personnel.

Figure 7.7 is a checklist for use by building administrators. They know all students even though they may not be familiar with as many facets of student performance

FIGURE 7.7   Building Administrator Referral Checklist

The following criteria are useful in assessing high potential of students. Please use one form per student to assign a value of *3* (to a considerable degree), *2* (to some degree), or *1* (to little if any degree) for each characteristic.

1. Is quite advanced in academic areas   _____
2. Shows superior leadership qualities   _____
3. Demonstrates a high degree of critical thinking and prefers intellectual challenge   _____
4. Is motivated by curiosity and seems to be self-directed   _____
5. Has many interests and is involved in many activities and projects   _____
6. Is full of ideas and demonstrates flexibility, originality, and resourcefulness   _____
7. Is keenly observant and questioning   _____
8. Is usually serious-minded and intolerant of foolishness   _____
9. Has a high energy level with unusual perseverance   _____
10. Has family members who are intensely concerned with enrichment and acceleration   _____
    in the curriculum and with the learning environment of the school

Please check any of the following factors which apply. If present along with a number of the attributes above, they may provide additional validation of high ability.

   A. Irregular school attendance   _____
   B. Limited contact between school personnel and family   _____

Additional Comments:

---

as classroom teachers are. They tend to see the bigger picture in which the student functions and often have interesting interactions with families regarding student capabilities and opportunities they need. Because they are inundated with information, they prefer brief, succinct fact sheets, information bulletins, and in this case, short and focused checklists. A formal note of explanation and request for input should accompany the distribution of several blank forms to them. If they have participated in meetings where teacher checklists were introduced and explained, they will be especially well informed and prepared for their part in the process.

As with the teacher checklist, administrator checklists should provide space for making additional comments. Confidentiality of the information during distribution and collection processes must be ensured.

Roles of Gifted Program Facilitators

Specialists in the education of highly able students have responsibilities for coordinating alternative learning activities, freeing up curricular options, gathering resources, and designing learning programs that can challenge students appropriately. Furthermore, they must familiarize themselves with classroom content of all grade levels they serve—a daunting assignment but important for building rapport with classroom teachers and contributing most helpfully in collaborative consultations and IEP conferences. They function as team members in classrooms, as consultants out of the classrooms, as communicators with administrators, and as co-educators with students and their families. They keep records on student talents and abilities, their needs, progress, and accomplishments, and they are in close contact with school counselors and school psychologists. They seek out resources and mentors in schools and beyond the school campus. Sometimes they provide professional development experiences for school personnel and awareness sessions for families, school boards, or community groups.

On occasion it is good for general education teachers and gifted program facilitators to exchange roles for a day. This lets the special education facilitator observe other students for manifestations of exceptional ability and allows the classroom teacher to direct accelerative, enriching activities with a single student or a small group of students.

■ ■ ■ ■ ■ ▬▬▬▬▬▬▬▬▬▬▬▬▬▬▬▬▬▬▬▬▬▬▬▬▬▬▬▬▬▬▬

ACTIVITY 7.4
A Middle-School Challenge

The consulting teacher for the district's gifted program headed toward the school office to announce her arrival in the building. The program was new and she had not assembled the students who would be in it or met with them individually. At a polite tap on her shoulder, she turned to see a seventh-grade student whom she didn't know but who obviously recognized her. He thrust a note into her hand and strode on down the hall. She stepped aside, unfolded it, and read:

I, as a concerned, bored student, am protesting against underestimating our abilities. I'm sorry to say that I'm writing this in math class. But what we do in here is really not worth working on. Review, review, that's all we do. This class is no challenge. If I've learned anything in this class, it is boredom. I want work! We want work! I have no intention of doing anything in this class except twiddle my thumbs. I've found no enjoyment in sitting here listening to the teacher repeat things I learned in 5th grade. I'm sure others feel the way I do. Please, we want a challenge.

Sincerely, Julio H_____

Attached to this note was a second paper with twenty-two signatures from other students, only twelve of whom she recognized as being on her gifted program student list!

Analyze this situation from several perspectives—the consulting teacher, the building administrator, the math department teacher in this large middle school, the petitioning student, and the interesting collection of twenty-two names. What should she do? Suggest next steps that could be taken from each of these perspectives.

Inventories of Interests and Learning Styles

As a part of an identification process, or a curriculum development process, useful information can be obtained from individual interviews in which collaborating educators gather information about student interests and goals. Sometimes the interest inventory is supplemented with a learning styles inventory to determine likes and dislikes in regard to structures for the learning process. Figure 7.8 is an informal instrument that includes both interests and learning styles to obtain rudimentary information about a student's learning wants and needs. Educators must bear in mind, however, that the best interest survey for any school's personnel is one that has been designed by the user(s) to fit that school setting. Other options include standardized instruments that are available online and from publishers.

More information can be obtained from a personal interview in which the collaborating consultant or classroom teacher serves as recording secretary, or at least shares the writing responsibility, than one in which a form is just given out for the student to fill out then or later. Occasionally, to save time, the teacher might solicit information from students in a group. But one drawback to this approach is that students, especially younger ones, may mimic preferences of others rather than concentrate on making their own wishes known.

DIFFERENTIATING CURRICULUM FOR EXCEPTIONALLY ABLE STUDENTS

The formula "Characteristics + Needs = Implications for Differentiated Curriculum" underscores Tomlinson's (1999) prompt that "one size cannot fit all." Differentiated curriculum for highly able learners, tailored to their capacity for learning and doing, has four criteria:

1. Release from repetition of material already learned (Why waste precious learning time redoing what one already has mastered?)
2. Removal of ceilings on prescribed curriculum (Why stop and wait until the rest of the class catches up?)

FIGURE 7.8 Inventory of Interests and Learning Styles

INTEREST INVENTORY

1. Name _____ Age _____ Grade _____
2. Gender _____ Brothers/Sisters _____
3. Community type (rural, urban, small town) _____
4. School(s) attended _____
5. My favorite subject(s) in school _____
6. What I like to read about _____
7. What I like to access on the Internet _____
8. My hobbies and collections _____
9. Lessons I take _____
10. What I like to watch on TV _____
11. My favorite recreation/sport _____
12. Where I have been on trips _____
13. Where in the world I would go if I could _____
14. What I would do in the world if I could _____
15. What I like best about school _____
16. When I have free time at school I like to _____
17. What I would like to learn more about _____
18. What careers I find most interesting _____
19. What I want to think about doing as a career _____
20. What I wish _____

Rate the next set of activities by putting:
1 = "Like very much," 2 = "It's OK," 3 = "Just so-so," or 4 = "Don't like."

_____ Doing things with a group
_____ Doing things on my own
_____ Reading assignments
_____ Writing reports
_____ Doing experiments
_____ Constructing things
_____ Drawing pictures
_____ Acting out things I'm learning
_____ Listening to teachers and speakers
_____ Watching films or television
_____ Working quickly in order to get done
_____ Working at a leisurely pace
_____ Being a leader most of the time
_____ Being a follower most of the time
_____ Planning my own learning activities
_____ Evaluating my own progress and development

3. Flexible pacing for progress through curriculum that provides for acceleration and enrichment (Why not go on to learn more about the subject?)
4. Engagement in self-directed learning and self-assessment (Why not continue learning in a self-selected topic of interest, designing assessment instruments and setting personal goals for achievement?)

These criteria may be easy to put into words but are not easily put into operation. Collaborators must exercise considerable skill in communicating with all parties, including families, to plan enriching and accelerating curriculum, coordinate the elements, and assess the outcomes carefully with attention to ever-expanding needs. Gifted program collaborators will want to acknowledge concerns of classroom teachers about possible gaps in learning content that students may experience. But with careful planning and directed assessment processes, as well as the assurances that research provides to the contrary, the concern about gaps in knowledge can be set aside. Collaborative consultation among general education teachers and special education teachers is the key to success with differentiated curriculum.

Acceleration or Enrichment?

Curricular content that accelerates student learning is enriching, and curriculum that enriches in appropriate ways will be accelerative. Classroom teachers are responsible for delivering content in differentiated formats, alternative options, accelerated pace, and enriching venues. Fundamentals should be presented at levels and paces (note the plurals) that can be accomplished by each student. No one should have to repeat again and again the content that has already been learned. **Flexible pacing** allows movement through the curriculum at differentiated speeds, breadths, and depths to stimulate and challenge exceptionally able learners.

In order for students to think and perform at complex and individually expressive levels beyond recall, recitation, explanation, and translation, teachers must convey that intent to students. Very able students tend to readily accept the challenge to analyze, synthesize, evaluate, imagine, and create. With encouragement, they can become active partners in their own curriculum development rather than just passive recipients of knowledge. They can be effective models for classmates who don't quite "get it" but could with modeling and a little help from their exceptionally able age peers (Vygotsky, 1978).

Discussion in an earlier chapter presented well-known educational taxonomies as powerful tools for focusing on higher-order levels of instruction that enable students to learn in increasingly complex, challenging ways. Figure 7.9 is a tool for introducing the concept to students from primary-level grades through secondary-level classes. The taxonomic "plant" illustration depicts growth in higher-order functions in a way that is readily grasped by most students. Learners progress beyond the familiar functions of rote recall and comprehension through application and analysis, creativity, and evaluation, to "bloom" into the most productive persons they can be in any area of learning and producing.

Classroom teachers are responsible for instructing a wide range of students, but with limitations on time, resources, and facilities they can overlook exceptional capabilities of their students and the need to challenge them appropriately. Teachers want all students to master basic skills but feel the brunt of pressures to provide differentiated opportunities. Furthermore it is easy to become defensive if their most able students complain that lessons are "boring." The "b word," when voiced with impatience, or delivered by a frustrated Julio as presented earlier in the chapter, can be overstated and overworked. Everyone benefits at one time or another from feeling bored; it causes "bored" individuals to fall back on their

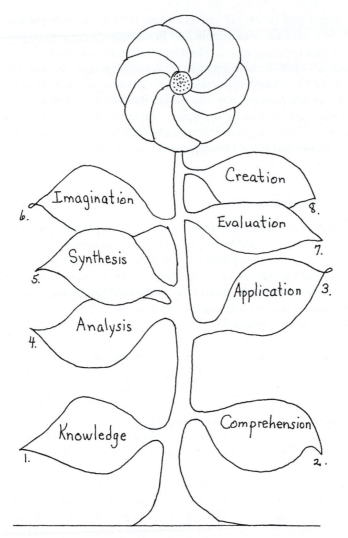

FIGURE 7.9 Blooms for Thinking and Doing

own resources and work to develop them. But sometimes teachers are not prepared to teach children who may be as knowledgeable or more so in subjects than they and need more. These situations call for a meeting of the minds among school co-educators and home co-educators for a collaborative approach to curricular issues that could impede student progress and dampen enthusiasm for learning. After preassessment is conducted to find which students have succeeded and need further challenge, it is time for curriculum compacting.

Curriculum Compacting

Just as teachers condense daily lessons and assignments for students returning to school after an illness, so can they compact curriculum for those who learn more quickly and easily than the majority of students (Renzulli & Reis, 1985). This "buys time" for learners to pursue individual interests and independent study in more challenging areas of regular or accelerated curriculum.

In order to structure a **curriculum compacting** plan for a highly able student, the teacher and student select a content area in which the student is very interested and has been very successful. Material can be compacted by unit, chapter, or topic. The teacher documents reasons for the modification and the proficiency level that will be expected. The collaborative consulting teacher for gifted education programs assists in creating opportunities and alternatives for enrichment and acceleration of content.

Reis, Burns, and Renzulli (1992) recommend starting the compacting process by designating a small group of students for whom it seems especially appropriate. Then:

1. Select one content area where the students seem most successful and for which the most resources are available.
2. Try different methods of finding out what students already know, including preassessment and interviews.
3. Compact the material by unit, chapter, or topic rather than by schedule.
4. Document a rationale for the compacted material and define proficiency as it reflects staff consensus and district policy.
5. Request help from collaborating teachers and resource personnel to create a wide range of opportunities and alternatives that justify replacing the eliminated content.

Very able students need not always accelerate at a *fast* pace through the curriculum. On occasion they may welcome the opportunity to slow down and study a subject in depth and detail, catching up with the class later by completing regular assignments on a curriculum-compacted basis. The Schoolwide Enrichment Model, based on an enrichment triad core curriculum structure, can provide the elements exceptionally able students need and also enrich the learning of all students in the general classroom.

The Schoolwide Enrichment Model

The **Schoolwide Enrichment Model (SEM)** is one of most long-standing and successful gifted education program models in the United States and in a host of other countries as well (Renzulli & Reis, 1985). As described in an earlier chapter, it is a differentiated and personalized curriculum model that promotes general education teacher and special education teacher collaboration and teamwork, and requires school-wide professional development for implementation. The curriculum structure of SEM is the Enrichment Triad, built on Type I, Type II, and Type III curriculum and a talent pool of students who are above average in ability, very creative, and task committed (highly motivated). The talent pool of students is not static; students may move in and out of the pool as their learning interests and needs dictate.

With the Enrichment Triad, *all* students in the general classroom participate in Type 1 exploratory activities on topics of interest through learning centers, field trips, resource speakers, learning packets, and more. *All* students in the classroom also participate in Type II process- and skill-building activities for problem solving, creative thinking, inquiry, vocabulary enhancement, extended reading, and more. For Type III's differentiated and personalized curriculum, the talent pool of students who are of above-average ability, highly motivated, and very creative are encouraged to participate in enrichment activities such as independent studies, research, and project development in a way and to an extent that would be done by professionals. These studies, processes, and products may need to be carried out beyond school campuses. Interest inventories and learning styles surveys guide the construction of Enrichment Triad activities.

The Type III experiences can take place in the classroom, in a resource room with other students in the talent pool, or beyond the classroom with mentors and content experts. The completed work is evaluated with authentic assessment methods using methods and rubrics such as performance critiques, product evaluations, observations, and interviews. Then it is shared with an authentic audience such as a community group or a news publication. The model is built on a solid foundation of intensive professional development for all staff and extensive collaboration among classroom teachers, special education personnel, and oftentimes mentors and other resource personnel in the community.

Roles of School Counselors and School Psychologists

These roles are integral in identifying student capabilities and needs, and addressing problems that can occur from failure of schools to meet those needs. In IEP conferences they often fill the required administrator role when the principal cannot attend. They can be helpful with practical suggestions for resources to optimize learning if encouraged to do so, and provide information in staff development activities if asked to do so. Secondary-level counselors can help by overseeing students' cognitive, emotional, and social needs in what are often explosive peer environments for them.

Assessment of progress by students of exceptional ability on goals and objectives can be problematic for a number of reasons. School psychologists can help in addressing issues such as:

- Difficulties in assessing high-order outcomes that cannot be measured as easily, precisely, or efficiently as basic skills and mastery outcomes
- Challenges of choosing standardized measures for goals and objectives that are highly individualized
- Statistical problems including testing error in measuring high-order processes and a slowing of gains at upper extremes of tests normed on general populations
- Low ceilings on many measures of achievement
- Regression effects that can cause high scorers to obtain more moderate scores on subsequent testing (which can be *very* hard for parents and teachers to understand and accept)
- Lack of norms for high-ability populations on some tests, which reduces their reliability
- Need for long-range goals that would require having outcomes studied for many years before valid inferences could be made

IEP Conferences for Exceptionally Able Students. A major area of contribution by school psychologists is participation in the individual education planning conference or, if IEPs for gifted students are not mandated in that state, any similar goal-setting conference for a student. IEP goals must be open-ended, aimed at complex learning, and focused on high-road transfer of learning that calls for application to new areas. Objectives should be developed with significant input from the student, and not remedial in tone but directed toward strengths for which the IEP is warranted. The student also should help plan the assessment process and evaluation of the learning.

Professional Development Leaders

As featured in an earlier chapter and noted throughout this book, professional development at pre-service, staff development, and graduate levels is a key element for classroom teachers in the context of collaborative school consultation. Novice teachers as well as veteran teachers must be ready, willing, and able to teach high-ability students who spend most of their school time in regular classrooms. Attention to special needs can have many positive ripple effects. Many teachers say their preparation for such students made them a better teacher for *all* of their students. Reis and Westberg (1994) indicated that the impact of the staff development philosophy presented by Guskey (1985) is significant in creating a positive response by teachers toward curriculum compacting, test-out, talent-pool participation, and other curriculum modifications for very able students.

Other Influential Role Groups for Special Needs

Policymakers, including legislators, school boards, and accrediting agencies, enact laws and regulations and allocate resources for schools. Advocates include parent groups, lobbyists for funding and lawmaking, business supporters, and other community factions interested in excellent education and the benefits good schools can provide for communities. Researchers contribute new insights into learning and teaching, and in working together within the sociocultural environments of schools. Some families who homeschool cite narrow school curriculum, paucity of enrichment opportunities and a generally slow pace of learning as compelling reasons for their decisions to make the efforts and sacrifices needed for homeschooling. This will be expanded on at a later point in the chapter.

University instructors of content-area classes and teacher preparation programs prepare students to know and teach content. Their coursework and assignments should include understanding of learning principles and motivation theory as they relate to the very able student. Curriculum developers and textbook authors have the means of including enriching, challenging content in basal materials if they can overcome pressures from interest groups whose agenda do not include focusing space and attention on "those who can get it on their own."

Media roles typically deal with good news about student achievements. Media slants on high performance by students can sway public opinions about needs of schools and the students who attend them, so those in such roles should be given information that enables them to provide their services ethically and supportively.

Mentors have opportunities for such profound influence on others that the relationship must not be left to chance happening. Mentorships allow students to apply and extend their learning beyond available school curriculum. Key steps in setting up and facilitating mentorships for students in gifted education programs are:

1. Designate student(s) who will participate in mentorships.
2. Ascertain student interests and learning styles. (Recall that they do not need to mirror those of a mentor.)

3. Locate mentors who may be a good fit for those interests and styles.
4. Discuss mentorship with the potential mentors to ascertain their feelings about it.
5. Temporarily match mentor with mentee and initiate casual interaction between them.
6. When a match is established, involve parents and develop a very general study plan, including a plan for eventual termination of the mentorship; this is important so that neither party is offended or let down when the mentoring relationship concludes.
7. Continue to monitor progress, from a distance if possible, handling any problems immediately; then bring closure as previously planned in Step 6.

For evaluation of their products and performances, and as a means of authentic assessment, students can be encouraged to solicit critique from outside experts, favorite former teachers, the principal, or even older students who are budding experts in that field. An example of a form for critique is provided in Figure 7.10.

Librarians, media specialists, and technology specialists are often the best resources for locating materials to lift students beyond mundane basal texts or to delve into an independent study or research project. They know where things are! They can help teachers build core skills practice into rich subject-matter investigations rather than rely on workbooks of mundane basal materials. They should be part of any team that is focusing on curriculum modification, independent study, research projects, individual study for testing out of courses, and other individual education plans. One way they could help is to collaborate with teachers on analyses of textbooks and accompanying instructor manuals to determine which ones provide the most useful enrichment instruction strategies and ideas for student projects and activities.

FIGURE 7.10 Request for Assessment

I, _____, would like for you, _____, to critique my _____
  (student name)   (evaluator's name)   (type of work)
It is included with this form. I have proofread, edited, revised, and improved it, and I now present it for critique and feedback from the evaluator I have chosen—You!
I am asking that you:

_____ provide comments on merits and strengths of this work.
_____ suggest any additions, deletions, revisions that could improve the work.
_____ comment on weaknesses, inaccuracies, errors, or misjudgments in the work.
_____ suggest resources I missed that would have added value to work.
_____ offer any ideas that come to mind for an extension of this work.

I will use your critique and feedback to:
_____ redo this work for the purpose of _____
_____ work more effectively on my next project which is _____
Thank you very much for your assistance! My teacher(s) and I value your help very much.

_____   _____
(student signature)   (facilitating teacher signature)

_____   _____
(date of request)   (date of returned assessment)

Homeschooling Very Able Learners

The research base for **homeschooling** students is limited, and the most common topic is a study of family reasons for the decision to homeschool (Jolly, Matthews, & Nester, 2013). Concerns of families in years past tended to center on religious and values-based issues, but more recently the concerns have focused on perceived lack of academic growth of their children and paucity of services to meet their advanced learning needs.

Homeschooling makes many demands on families to locate appropriate curriculum materials and assemble them into an enriching, sequenced program of study. Parents often seek out other families and build networks of relationships to share materials and ideas, locate tutors for specialized curriculum content and arts areas, and provide opportunities for participation in group-based activities such as sports, debate, drama and dance, and musical ensembles.

Jolly et al. (2013) make the case that when children leave school settings to be homeschooled, parental support for appropriate programming to meet special needs might dwindle and jeopardize the concept of free and appropriate public education for all children. Schools would be well-served to interact with families contemplating a homeschool process and build a connection with them if they do decide to homeschool that would include their input through occasional collaboration and consultation.

■ ■ ■ ■ ■

ACTIVITY 7.5
Textbook Analysis

Select a textbook for a grade level and curricular area that interests you. Analyze it and its instructor's guide for qualities that would make it suitable for enriched and accelerated learning. Compare and contrast best features and poorest features to personalize instruction for a very able student. Explain your reasons as if you were presenting it to your curriculum development staff, professional development staff, or an interested and concerned parent.

Then have a teaching colleague select and analyze a contrasting text, after which each one describes the merits and shortcomings for differentiating and personalizing instruction in an inclusive classroom. Do this with your colleague in roles as a member of a curriculum selection committee and as a marketing representative for the text's publisher. (Suggestion: This is more productive if the text has at least some desirable qualities, so be choosy and look until you find one that seems to fit that bill.)

Learning Options and Opportunities In and Beyond School

School personnel feel the brunt of parental pressure to provide advanced opportunities, and some become defensive on hearing that schools are not prepared to teach children who can pass tests over subject matter before opening their textbooks. These situations call for a meeting of the minds among all parties for collaborative resolution of curricular and extracurricular issues that can impede student progress and dampen enthusiasm for learning. A study by Purcell and Leppien (1998) highlights two facets of the collaborative process that can tap into its power for providing challenging instruction.

FIGURE 7.11   Learning Opportunities in the School Setting

- Differentiated curriculum in the classroom
- Curriculum compacting
- Use of books from the library as basal readers for both comprehension and skill building
- Telescoped curriculum where a time frame for course of study is collapsed or lengthened
- Continuous progress courses, moving ahead as content and skills are acquired
- Grade skipping
- Early entrance to school (however, not permitted in some states)
- Test out
- Cross-age tutoring, with very able students teaching younger students of high ability
- Programmed instruction packages for rapid progress in areas of keen interest
- Seminars within schools or in collaboration with other schools or universities
- Advanced Placement program
- Mini-replications of existing research studies
- Conversations with/observations of book authors, artists-in-residence, scientists
- Enrichment activity calendars for classroom teachers with a daily enriching activity
- Resource room time for independent study, research, or project development
- Honors classes
- Dual enrollment
- Discussion groups for moral dilemmas, great books, or current issues
- Special units of study that have a concentrated international perspective
- Biographies and autobiographies, to study great leaders of past and present
- Collection and analysis of the world's wisdom (proverbs, fables, maxims, or credos)
- Summer school enrichment courses
- International Baccalaureate program
- Extra classes for extra credit
- Cluster grouping to work with mental peers on advanced topics
- Extended library, lab, practice, or computer time, or more time to work on projects
- Small-group discussions and investigations with mental peers (and more)

1. Expectations for student learning must be discussed and made congruent.
2. Interactions among school personnel must facilitate differentiated curriculum.

Some arrangements that would benefit very capable students can take place in the general classroom. Others require a resource room or laboratory or library setting. (See Figure 7.11.) Still others are accessible only outside the school setting. When students leave their school campus for enrichment, or for accelerated coursework, group learning experiences, or individual arrangements, it is essential that special educators, classroom teachers,

FIGURE 7.12   Learning Opportunities Beyond the School Setting

- Early graduation from high school
- Early entrance to the university, with or without a high school diploma
- Career shadowing
- Academic competitions—regional, state, national, international
- Community service (sometimes for high school credit)
- Student exchange programs—urban to rural, west to east, north to south, United States to other countries
- Mentorships
- Tutorials with experts in a field of keen interest or exceptional talent
- Travel study programs
- Concurrent enrollment in high school courses and college courses
- Part-time enrollment in vocational-technical schools to learn a trade
- University credit by examination
- College correspondence courses
- Field trips
- College-level independent studies
- Internships and apprenticeships
- Periodic contributions of writing and reporting for newspaper and media
- Presentations and performances of advanced work to audiences outside the school (and more . . .)

counselors, and principals collaborate to ensure that the students accomplish school district and state academic requirements and continue to be involved in the life of the school. They also must deal with scheduling, student supervision, and liability issues. (See Figure 7.12.)

Ensuring Differentiated Curriculum in Inclusive Schools

An inclusive school increases responsibilities of classroom teachers to provide for learning needs of highly able students. VanTassel-Baska (1989) notes several mistaken beliefs that need to be altered regarding differentiation for highly able students. First, consultants and consultees should not assume that curriculum must *always* be different from what all learners have. Nor do all learning experiences need to be product oriented. Then, too, one curriculum package or a single learning strategy will *not* provide all that is needed.

It cannot be denied that many teachers feel negatively toward acceleration, or compacting of content for very able students. As noted earlier, some of their concerns must be addressed, such as the possibility that vital content and needed practice will be skipped; however, most such concerns are not justified. The research is clear that acceleration is *not* harmful as a general rule to the academic, emotional, or social well being of students who already may be tuned out, bored, or discouraged. Far worse is to languish for years craving more challenging work.

Research by Gerber and Popp (2000) indicates that collaborative programs should be explained thoroughly to those affected by them prior to the initiation of the programs. Students in particular need carefully presented, clear explanations about the purposes and potential benefits of consultation, collaboration, and co-teaching.

SITUATION 7.D

Oliver, a high school senior and aspiring playwright, while a lackluster student in most of his classes, had never participated in a gifted program. He did not care to be tested with the district's standardized measure of aptitude—and as for the program, he commented to the facilitator, "Activities like riding 100 miles in a school bus to tour an aircraft plant that doesn't interest me are not what I need." But when his drama teacher, after consultation with the gifted program facilitator and the building administrator, suggested that perhaps gifted program enrollment could make him eligible for curriculum adaptations in his senior year, he agreed to the testing. He tested very well, and after eleven years of "revving his motor with his brakes on" in many of his classes, he was given relatively free license to write the senior class play, cast, stage, and direct it, build stage sets, conduct rehearsals, and even advise the art department as to type of publicity material he wanted.

This was truly a co-teaching and collaborative consultation experience, involving school principal, gifted program facilitator, general classroom drama teacher, art teacher, vocational arts teacher, school psychologist, custodian, evening security guard, and family/consumer science teacher whose class made refreshments for the performance. Some teachers expressed doubts about the wisdom of giving such latitude to this student in their small-town, rural high school, but the principal endorsed the idea with only two stipulations—the consulting facilitator could edit any objectionable parts of the script, and there must be teacher supervision at all rehearsals. The play, though not well attended, was interesting and innovative, and Oliver graduated deeming his senior year a personal success.

ACTIVITY 7.6
Team Planning and Teaching

In collaboration with another teacher, co-plan a lesson at the elementary level that addresses curricular needs of highly able students in a typical classroom. Describe resources that will be needed and who will obtain them. Determine how you will assess the learning (entire class and smaller group) and how you will evaluate the success of the co-teaching process.

or

Describe a hypothetical situation at the secondary level in which you consult with a potential mentor about a student with high ability or talent. Draft ideas for addressing topics that might come up for discussion about planning, resource gathering, coordinating, supervising, and assessment. The ideas should be consistent with school policy, acceptable to the student's family, and above all, appealing to the student.

Not all teachers wish to team teach, or even to collaborate very much, and those wishes should be respected. Some classroom teachers are uncomfortable having other teachers in the classroom as they teach. Others do not like to make their best strategies and materials available for professional observation and scrutiny. As mentioned elsewhere in the book, teachers cannot be expected to hand off their personal best ideas to others even when engaging in collaborative activities. Building trust among collaborating teachers, families, and students as partners is a major determinant of success in co-teaching, and effective communication is a major tool in building that trust. Added to the element of trust is respect for a co-educator's territory, and that requires tact and finesse.

Classroom teachers and special education teachers may want to try co-teaching a lesson or perhaps even a unit at first. In this way, they can ease into a method of sharing space, direct-instruction time, preparation of materials, and assessment decisions. They might exchange roles for a time to gain new perspectives on the students and the material. They could opt to work together with a particular student in a partnership of three or more to plan, implement, and evaluate differentiated learning experiences. As they collaborate to design personalized programs and free up time for learning alternatives, they will be providing seamless attention to special needs. Schools will become more lively places for learning, staff members more enthusiastic, and families more supportive in a collaborative, ethical climate. When allowed and encouraged, students usually are delighted to have a "voice" in their learning. Teachers model interpersonal skills for their students and they find outlets for expression of their best and most creative ideas, which affirms and reinforces their decision to be an educator.

It cannot be said too often or too firmly that many positive benefits can be expected from consulting, collaborating, and co-teaching to tailor the curriculum and manage classroom procedures for students who learn differently, whether it is because of disabilities or exceptional abilities. As teachers work together, they have input from colleagues and with efficient management of processes they often gain precious time for getting to know students' interests, strengths, and areas of need. With this input and time they are able to plan accelerative, enriching, and personalized experiences for learning and doing by students who crave more work like Julio, or want more challenge like Alysia, or are hoping for interesting assignments like Anna, or seek a goodness of fit between ability and curriculum content like Oliver. When students can learn and progress in challenging and interesting ways, they leave the school environment with an ongoing love of learning and the preparation they need to fulfill their potential.

 ENHANCEDetext **Application Exercise 7.1.** Click to apply your understanding of determining exceptional needs and planning for collaboration and consultation with co-educators to address those needs.

TIPS FOR COLLABORATING AS INSTRUCTIONAL PARTNERS AND TEAMS

1. Co-teaching requires careful planning. Planning time must be built into the restructured school day.
2. Co-teachers will want to discuss their philosophies about teaching with their collaborator, especially in areas such as grading, accommodations and modifications, and interactions with families of students.

3. Seek out professional development opportunities to learn more about co-teaching such as webinars, professional journal articles, or resources on the Web. If you were already partnered with a co-teacher, engage in these activities together.

4. Offer to reformat a test for a teacher (to double-space, enlarge the print, or organize it differently) for use with any student who has a learning problem.

5. Have a favorite dozen or so successful strategies available for demonstration teaching or sharing.

6. Be understanding of classroom teachers' daily trials with some students having special needs. Celebrate even the smallest student progress and the general educator's role in making it happen.

7. Rather than just talking to classroom teachers about materials modification, *show* them how it can be accomplished. Give some examples or do an example for them. Better yet, do one together.

8. Learn about how MTSS is being implemented in your school or district and consider your role in that framework. Think about the expertise you have to offer in a decision-making team. If you're not invited to the "table," advocate for your inclusion with school leaders.

9. Talk with librarians and media specialists at school and in the community, asking them to order books and periodicals about needs of students that would appeal to families and community members. Give them the name, author, publisher, a brief description with rationale, and if possible the ISBN for efficient ordering.

10. Build networks of interaction among school personnel, parents, families who home-school, and community members who could serve as tutors, monitors, mentors, and independent study facilitators for special needs.

CHAPTER 8

BUILDING COLLABORATIVE RELATIONSHIPS WITH TEAM MEMBERS FROM DIVERSE POPULATIONS AND CONTEXTS

Creating just and equitable schooling for all students calls for renewed efforts in collaboration for educators, parents, family members, and, indeed, the whole community. This is a time of cultural transformation, and co-educators understand that school and community partnerships build solid foundations for positive outcomes for all students and stronger communities for all families.

CHAPTER OBJECTIVES

Upon completing this chapter, the reader should be able to:

1. Explain the impact of the multiple aspects of diversity on educational consultation and collaboration.

2. Develop diversity-related competencies for collaborating consultants.

3. Develop an awareness of and strategies for collaborating with team members from categorically diverse populations.

4. Develop an awareness of and strategies for collaborating with team members from diverse contexts.

5. Describe the social justice framework for consultation, collaboration, and teamwork.

6. Justify having social justice perspectives as collaborative school consultants.

KEY TERMS

contextual diversity	cultural competence	normativity
cultural and linguistic diversity	culture	privilege
	intersectionality	social justice

SITUATION 8

LeMay Jackson, a special education teacher who served Grandview elementary and middle schools as a consulting teacher, was absent-mindedly stirring sugar into his third cup of coffee before the bell rang at the middle school. He didn't notice the oak tree with its bright fall colors outside the teachers' break room. He didn't notice other teachers come and go to put their lunches in the big old refrigerator humming in the corner of the busy room. Mr. Jackson was thinking about his Program Action Team. The mission of this team, which included parents, teachers, and community members, was to work on improving services and resources for students in special education and their families. He had worked hard to invite individuals to the group who had been marginalized in the past, both in school efforts and community activities. So now the group included not only several teachers and volunteers who were usually part of school activities but also Janelle Smythe-Williamson who, with her partner, Matilda Smythe-Williamson were the parents of two students in Mr. Jackson's caseload at the elementary school; the Reverend Goody Mitchell of the New Church of the Liberal Agenda, whose daughter had just been diagnosed with ASD; Ahmed Asma, a newly arrived immigrant to Grandview; Rita Alhambra, a leader in the migrant workers' association; and retired General Charlie Sidmonds, whose grandchildren lived with him even though he had severe arthritis and used a wheelchair.

Yes, Mr. Jackson had a fine team. The problem was, they weren't very team-minded. They were clearly uncomfortable with the range of diversity among the group, and some were almost hostile to others. After two meetings and some surprisingly unanimous decisions regarding the renovation of a donated building as a family and community science center, they still weren't using each other's first names or engaging in dialogue before and after the meetings. The White members and the African American members sat on opposite sides of the table, and the seats beside Mr. Asma and his friend Janelle were the last to be filled. Would this exciting project get off the ground? Would half the group drop out before Thanksgiving?

When Dr. McDoogle (Dr. Mac), the school principal, came into the room to refresh his tea, he asked Mr. Jackson what was happening. Mr. Jackson was glad to explain the situation to his friend and colleague. "Why don't you try to organize the Program Action Team like a cooperative learning group?" Dr. Mac suggested. "Gloria Sapp uses it in her 6th grade, and those kids went from picking on each other, name calling, bullying, and refusing to work together to a high-achieving little family, despite the fact that there's a heck of a lot of diversity in that class and most of the old problems seemed to be based on identity like race, socioeconomic status, and perceived sexual orientation. Of course Gloria had the same group last year, so she's been working with them for quite a while. Maybe that would work with your group, although I'm sure they're not doing any name-calling."

Mr. Jackson thought about his group and recognized some of the bias he thought he saw might be based on unfamiliarity with diverse identities. He thought the group would probably get a lot more done if there was a welcoming, more democratic environment. He also remembered that when he recommended cooperative learning groups in classes where the students with disabilities in his caseload were ignored or taunted by other students, group goals and team success fostered interaction, comfort, and confidence, and new friendships were formed. He had read research that showed cooperative learning groups become less self-segregated and increased interaction leads to more compassion and understanding. Mr. Jackson decided to talk to Ms. Sapp, do a little more reading about the principles of cooperative learning, and use some of the strategies at the next team meeting. And he'd serve coffee, tea, and dessert and provide child-care by a qualified person. "Hmmmm, we just might have our science center after all! Let me get you some tea, Dr. Mac!"

DIVERSITY AND EDUCATIONAL COLLABORATION AND CONSULTATION

Understanding individual characteristics and group cultures is not an easy undertaking; nevertheless, it is a cornerstone for successful collaboration. Respecting individual, group, and **contextual** differences and similarities fosters collegial interactions and relationships. Consultants must acknowledge and understand the implications of the multiple aspects of diversity within society that affect all areas of the educational system.

Changes in U.S. demographics and predicted trends for continuing rapid change will have significance for the collaborative work done by educational consultants. Educators and others who work with students with special needs may move to a city or region where differences in values, culture, traditions, and customs seem to be overwhelming. Or the school district where a teacher works may change significantly because of industry leaving or coming to the area. Although demographics change, a co-educator's mission is the same: promoting the education of students with special needs. Therefore, educational consultants must respect and value the multiple diversities of their collaborators and consultants must demonstrate knowledge and competence in working with diverse populations and contexts in their schools and communities.

Multiple Diversities among Students, Families, and Educators

Educational consultants believe that all students, regardless of gender, disability, social class, ethnicity, race, or other cultural characteristics, should have an equal opportunity to learn in school and to become a successful part of our democratic society. Therefore, for educational consultants, it is appropriate to define "diversity" broadly. Current uses of the word "diversity" in educational settings relate to ethnicity, language, religion, disability, sexual orientation, and demographic factors and status variables of economic level, geographic location, age, gender, and other indicators of group uniqueness. Diversity includes historical and contextual bases, and it includes not just racial or ethnic groups but other groups or subgroups such as female, Deaf, rural, and military or ex-military. Educational systems will be called upon more and more during the next several decades to serve new pluralities with sensitivity and skill.

In addition, the teaching force does not reflect gender, racial, ethnic, and economic diversity, and it never has. Profiles of prospective teachers continue to be primarily white females from small towns or suburban communities who attended colleges or universities not far from home and plan to return to places similar to home for their teaching careers. These teachers reflect their own backgrounds and values, which are often unfamiliar to those of their students and their educational team members. Many teachers have limited experiences with diversity and feel unprepared to teach a diverse student population. Consultants from this population work hard to broaden their experiences and worldviews; they realize that they will be collaborating with a diverse array of educational partners.

It is essential for educators to become familiar with the complex diversities of their students, families, and other team members with whom they work. Deans and department chairs of teacher education programs are well aware that a critical element in gaining national accreditation for their programs is demonstration of diversity in student enrollment, instructional faculty, and sites for student teaching and field experiences. Once pre-service or newly credentialed teachers are placed in schools for that first year of teaching, experienced consulting teachers have an important role in mentoring and coaching them to work effectively with diverse families, colleagues, and community members.

Diversity-Related Terminology for Educational Consultants

Consulting educators may need to ask questions or research the meanings of terms related to diversity that are used in various local school programs. They may also need to provide explanations of educational terms to others with whom they collaborate, such as parents and community members.

Although the diversities discussed in this chapter go beyond culture, *cultural diversity* is a commonly used term in education. Banks and Banks (2010) describe **culture** as knowledge, concepts, and values shared by group members. Although different cultures tend to have different dress, language, food, housing, and other artifacts, it is the values, symbols, interpretations, and perspectives that most distinguish one culture from another. The American Psychological Association (2008) describes culture as the embodiment of a world view through learned and transmitted beliefs, values, and practices; and a way of living informed by historical, economic, ecological, and political forces acting on a group. Culture is a dynamic framework that provides guidelines and bounds for life practices. T. L. Cross, of the National Indian Child Welfare Association, described culture as an organized response to human needs. Food, safety and security, love and belonging, esteem and identity, and self-actualization are shaped by culture (Cross, 2003).

All members of a cultural group are not the same and individuals are not fixed in their attitudes, beliefs, or behaviors. Banks and Banks (2010) remind us that while membership in cultural groups can provide important clues about an individual's attitude or behavior, membership in a particular group does not determine behavior. Therefore, educators should avoid thinking about individuals in terms of their group or subgroup identity, such as Deaf, Latino, lesbian, or single parent. Individuals may or may not identify specifically with the group. These caveats should be called to mind frequently throughout this chapter. Strong group identification might provide vital cues for collaborative efforts; however, consultants should take care to avoid assumptions about individuals based on general characteristics of groups.

Other diversity-related terms relate to language, such as English language learner (ELL), English language development (ELD), English for speakers of other languages

(ESOL), cultural and linguistic diversity (CLD) and culturally and linguistically diverse students with exceptionalities (CLDE). The term "English language learner" (ELL) refers to students who are not proficient in English. "English language development" (ELD) refers to all types of instruction that promote the development of oral or written English language skills and abilities. This term often replaces terms such as "English as a second language" (ESL) and "English for speakers of other languages."

The phrase "minority group" is now used less frequently than in past decades unless it is in a numerical sense. Banks and Banks (2010) suggest the use of the term "ethnic group" to refer to a micro-cultural group that shares a common history and culture, values, behaviors, and other characteristics that cause members of the group to have a shared identity. Race and ethnicity are distinct, as defined by the National Center for Educational Statistics. Ethnicity is either Hispanic/Latino or Not Hispanic/Latino. Race is one or more of the following: American Indian or Alaska Native, Asian, Black or African American, Native Hawaiian or Other Pacific Islander, or White.

The National Science Foundation (NSF) and many other agencies of the federal government use the term "underrepresented minority" (URM) to refer to individuals from diverse groups who are underrepresented in specific areas such as postsecondary and graduate education in science, technology, engineering, and mathematics (STEM). For example, the NSF funds programs to promote and support STEM education for URMs. In the science field, that generally means women and girls, individuals with disabilities, and individuals from some racial and ethnic groups such as Native Alaskans, American Indians, Native Hawaiians, African Americans, Hispanics, and Pacific Islanders.

The term "tolerance" is used frequently by excellent resources found in the *Teaching Tolerance* magazine, a project of the Southern Poverty Law Center in Montgomery, Alabama. When those at the center were asked why they used the word "tolerance" rather than "acceptance," they responded that the term is the counter-position of intolerance. The center uses the definition established by the United Nations Educational, Scientific and Cultural Organization (UNESCO), which adopted a Declaration of Principles on Tolerance in 1995. UNESCO (1995) defined tolerance as "respect, acceptance, and appreciation of the rich diversity of our world's cultures, our forms of expression, and ways of being human." The organization understands that tolerance is fostered by knowledge, openness, communication, and freedom of thought, conscience, and belief; and that tolerance is harmony in difference. More information about this perspective can be found at the UNESCO website.

Privilege is a term used to denote a historical, traditional, or experiential status that reflects a dominant social position. Most people have heard the term "White privilege," which refers to the historical and traditional dominance and power of Western European culture in the current American society. Therefore, White privilege is implicitly granted to people of European descent because of history and tradition. It is not what they choose, it simply comes with the color of their skin; but this privilege is often taken for granted and it strongly shapes educational policies and practices. There are many kinds of privilege. Educators who work with students with disability understand the implicit privilege that comes with being able (and the implicit disadvantage, lack of power, that comes with being differently abled). Another example is the dominance and power granted to teachers because of their education, especially in parent-teacher relationship when parents may have little formal education. Students whose parents can afford to send them to computer camps and buy them computers, smartphones, and other equipment are privileged over students who have never had the opportunity to learn about and experience the digital world. Many consultants have White privilege, educational privilege, and economic privilege. These give consultants power to become change agents, but they also make collaboration and equal partnerships challenging. The most important concept for consultants is to understand their privilege and be careful not to take on characteristics of dominance and power in their consulting relationships.

There are many resources that can assist consultants who want to learn more about these areas, along with development of cultural identity, immigrant culture shock, culture-specific information, and important caveats for gathering this type of information. It is extremely important for educators who collaborate with adults from different cultural, racial, and economic backgrounds to study and reflect on the reality of diversity (see Figure 8.1).

Diversity and the Concept of Social Justice in Education

Diversity and appreciation of differences are inexorably tied to social justice and to the way power and privilege construct difference unequally in our society (Bell, 1997). **Social justice** is a complex term that relates to equity and multicultural education in that it has been defined as creating "an equitable and just learning environment for every student and family" (Gorski, Zenkov, Osei-Kofi, & Sapp, 2013, p. 1). Foundations for social justice in education are the works of John Dewey and Paulo Freire. Dewey (2012) writes about criticality of education to democracy. He grounds education on the principles of choice, discovery, and student-generated learning. Specifically related to social justice, he adds these purposes of education: students assuming agency, and effecting change in the time and place they inhabit. Freire (2000) contends that education is essential for societal transformation. He calls for personal, dialogic relationships to undergird education, because in such relationships, he argues, education acts to transform society (Shields, 2010). Social justice means addressing the axes of social difference—disability/ableism, gender/sexism, age/ageism, sexuality/heterosexism, race/racism, and the intersectionalities of oppression, power, and privilege that are central to lived experiences (Bell, 1997). Social justice education is an ongoing, contextual process that impacts inequitable social, economic, and political systems through critical examination and intentional advocacy for social justice.

FIGURE 8.1   Diversity Terms Word Cloud

DIVERSITY-RELATED COMPETENCIES FOR COLLABORATING CONSULTANTS

Consultants who work daily with students with disabilities are usually very aware of the harm to students when diversities of educational, physical, and cognitive abilities are ignored. Successful consultants understand that ignoring diversities in ability and all other aspects of diversity are harmful to developing relationships with adults with whom they collaborate. Saying "I don't see color in my classroom" or "I treat everybody the same" ignores the characteristics that make each person special and unique. Thus, efforts to become more inclusive in educational consulting relationships must include expanded knowledge about many aspects of diversity. Educators who collaborate with adults on behalf of children with special needs must foster positive attitudes toward multiple diversities and cultivate skills for developing and maintaining successful collaborative relationships with individuals who may be very different from themselves. Being sensitive toward differences in cultural traditions, values, language, age, ability, sexual orientation, country of origin, economic and educational status, and other diversities will enhance relationships and the process of collaboration.

Diversity-related competencies allow consultants to function comfortably in diverse settings and to interact harmoniously with people who differ from them. Diversity-related competencies are skills and attitudes that allow collaborators to move toward building trust and establishing relationships. Diversity-related competence is a reflective stance of continuously learning, unlearning, and re-learning. Striving for improved **cultural competence** is a journey that involves continual, reflective work.

There is no magic formula for success on this journey; however, many who write about cultural or diversity-related competence suggest that it involves these goals:

- Develop a social justice lens as a guiding framework for considering diversity.
- Study and become aware of one's own multiple diversities.
- Increase awareness of multiple aspects of diversity among collaborators.
- Increase knowledge and understanding of diverse populations and contexts.
- Develop skills to work effectively with a variety of collaborators on behalf of students with special needs.

Each of these areas of development of diversity-related competence is discussed in the sections below.

DEVELOPING A SOCIAL JUSTICE LENS AS A GUIDING FRAMEWORK FOR CONSIDERING DIVERSITY

Collaborative school consultants who are conscious of the shifting kaleidoscope of diversity in schools and their own roles in promoting educational opportunities and success for all students, understand the usefulness of a social justice lens in developing relationships and successful collaborations. A guiding framework, based on the social justice perspective, includes these dimensions:

1. Encourage families and communities to look at the bigger picture beyond a single characteristic. Individuals exist within multiple inequitable social, economic, and power relationships, institutions, and policies that limit their access to societal resources such as health care, jobs that pay a living wage, healthy living environments, and out-of-school resources. Consultants are challenged to relate to team members by looking at these institutionalized inequities in their lives. Considering structural inequities helps consultants avoid getting trapped into generalizing, falling back on common stereotypes (girls aren't good at math; people in wheelchairs can't play basketball; African American middle schoolers hanging around a street corner are up to no good; Alaska Native children don't care about education). It's so much easier to *problematize* an individual, a family, a group, or a community and to ignore the big picture—the built-in inequities of access to societal resources that most of us take for granted: proximity to a library or a discount grocery store, or public transportation to get to museums or to programs at a local university or a free health clinic. Social justice education means *not* interpreting problems of people of color, individuals with disabilities, and gay youth as *personal failures,* and looking at the bigger picture of unfair policies and systems that is part of a backstory restricting their access.

2. Reject deficit thinking that leads to negative assumptions about diverse populations. Deficit thinking is the perspective that team members from non-dominant groups or who are different from the perceived norm are inferior, needy, or at fault for their differences (Gorski, et al., 2013). The dominant culture, both overtly and covertly, promotes the idea that the elements of their culture are the "norm" and thus elements of other cultures or differences are "not normal." This is obvious with individuals with disabilities, where a disability is seen as "abnormal" and something that needs to be "fixed." (Note: Not all societies have this perception of differences in abilities.) If an able-bodied person is the norm, then someone who uses a wheelchair is seen as having a deficit. If heterosexism is perceived as normal, then other sexual orientations are seen as needing to be fixed. If English is the norm, then non-English speakers are problematic. Although it may sometimes be very difficult, consultants must try to avoid thinking differences are deficits and are abnormal. Deficit thinking leads to problematizing individuals because of their differences and therefore affording individuals who are different with less respect or credibility. Historically, difference has been used to marginalize, segregate, and disempower those marked as "different." Teachers with a special education background can recall the history of thinking about individuals with disabilities remember how they have been marginalized, segregated, and disempowered (Collins, 2013). Successful consultants consider structural inequities; reject deficit thinking; focus on strengths; and recognize the knowledge, resilience, culture, and experiences of their co-educators.

3. Recognize that the power of culture makes one relatively oblivious to the limitations of our own perspectives, behaviors, and values. This chapter has introduced some thoughts and concepts that may have made some readers uncomfortable or even resistant. For example, some may have never thought about how categories, group identities, or individual characteristics are sometimes used to justify discrimination

or unequal educational opportunities and practices. They may have never thought about how difference has been translated too often to mean "not normal," pathological, or problematic. This is not surprising; it shows the power of culture to form our thinking, beliefs, and values. Recognizing the power of our own culture, history, and background helps us become better collaborators. When we recognize our own limited perspectives, we are better able to develop diversity-related competencies that can help build teams and coalitions for excellence in the education of students with special needs.

■ ■ ■ ■ ■

ACTIVITY 8.1
"What's Normativity Got To Do with It?"

Normativity is the stance that what is deemed "normal" is right and what is "not normal" is wrong. "What is right?" and "What is the norm?" are age-old philosophical questions. A *norm* has been called an arbitrary line drawn in the sand. Consultants working with diverse educational colleagues need to consider: "Who decides what is normal?" This is important in education, as in all other areas of life and society, because we perceive that the flip side of "normal" is "abnormal" or "problematic" or "something that needs to be fixed" or "something that needs to be hidden or marginalized." Think about the history of educating (or not educating) individuals with cognitive or physical disabilities. How does that history tell the story of normativity? How have individuals with disabilities in most Western cultures suffered from or benefited from being perceived as abnormal, problematic, or needing to be fixed or hidden? One can see that defining what is "normal" or "the norm" serves as a lens through which to view a person. When we look through that "not normal" lens, our expectations of, and responses to, the "not normal" person shifts. When a student is diagnosed as having attention deficit with hyperactivity disorder (ADHD), how might that normativity lens shift expectations or and responses to the student? When two-parent (one male and one female) homes are considered normal, what happens when the normativity lens sees a single parent? (Think of the term "broken home.") Then recall other areas of diversity that have been discussed in this chapter. How has normativity impacted those who are perceived as representing the norm and those who are marginalized? Who decides what is normal? How might this impact your collaboration and your efforts to build relationships and equal partnerships?

Studying and Becoming Aware of One's Own Multiple Diversities

A primary part of developing diversity awareness is to understand one's *own* culture, identities, beliefs, and values. Recognizing characteristics of one's own culture is especially important for European Americans because of their tendency to view culture through an ethnocentric lens, often believing, somewhat naively, that theirs is the primary or prevailing culture (Ayers, Quinn, & Stovall, 2009; Spalding, Klecka, Lin, Odell, & Wang, 2010). Consultants should accept their own identities and the strengths and limitations of their own backgrounds and experiences. Educators need to constantly examine their own values and assumptions, so understanding how their culture, history, and identities influence their values and assumption is a first step in developing higher levels of diversity-related competencies.

■ ■ ■ ■ ■

ACTIVITY 8.2
Reflecting on One's Own Multiple Diversities

Think about your own culture, family history, and identity groups. How would you describe yourself? First think about your cultural background. What language did your great-grandparents, or more distant ancestors, speak? When did they come to the United States? Why did they come? What customs, such as holidays, foods, and traditions, in your family reflect the culture of your ancestors? How does your family value education? What other values are part of your family history and culture?

What other diversity characteristics describe you? With what groups or characteristics do you identify? Examples are: English-speaking, teacher, African American, Christian, middle-aged, male, middle-class, heterosexual, and others. Think about how these diversities and your culture and family history have shaped your education and your decision to become an educator. How do these characteristics make it harder or easier for you to establish collaborative relationships with those with similar characteristics? With very different characteristics?

Increasing Awareness of Multiple Aspects of Diversity among Collaborators

Just as Sonia Nieto (2000) suggests that educators become learners of their student's realities, consultants should become learners of the realities of their collaborators. These realities include many dimensions of diversity such as race, ethnicity, language, age, gender, religion, gender identity, sexual orientation, educational and socioeconomic status. Consultants need to understand and appreciate multiple diversities of the individuals with whom they collaborate. Educational consultants and their collaborative team members are self-identified as belonging to many diversity groups, such as Deaf, female, African-American, and immigrant. Although this chapter will focus on some generalized characteristics of diversity populations or cultural groups, it is important to keep in mind that diversity or cultural groups are not homogeneous. Within diverse groups there are those who share other factors, such as country of origin, religion, marital status, and education. Within considerations of diversity for consultants is the diversity of contexts from which or in which their collaborative partners live. These contexts have characteristics, as do cultural groups. Contexts of collaborative team members can be very influential in the consulting process, but they are also changeable. For example, partners who are connected to the military exist within a very specified context, but they are no longer a part of the military culture when they leave the military. Rural families may not always be rural; homeless families will not always be homeless.

Increasing Knowledge and Understanding of Diverse Populations and Contexts

After we have assessed our own attitudes and values toward diversity, we must examine our attitudes and practices about diversities and contexts different from our own. One way to start increasing knowledge and understanding of diverse populations and contexts is with a self-assessment.

Figure 8.2 shows some sample items for assessing one's diversity-related attitudes and practices. The items, or other items or checklists, can be used for personal reflection, self-study, or guided professional development. Discussion and expansion of the

FIGURE 8.2   Self-Assessment of Diversity-Related Competencies

A = Always; U = Usually; S = Sometimes; R = Rarely; N = Never

Personal Sensitivity

_____   1. I realize that any individual in a group may not have the same values as others in the group.

_____   2. I learn about and avoid words, statements, expressions, and actions that members of other culture groups and orientations could find offensive.

_____   3. I read books and articles to increase my understanding and sensitivity about the hopes, strengths, and concerns of people from other cultures, experiences, and backgrounds.

_____   4. I counteract prejudicial, stereotypical thinking and talking whenever and wherever I can.

School Context Efforts

_____   5. I include contributions of people from diverse populations as an integral part of the school curriculum.

_____   6. I strive to nurture skills and develop values in students and colleagues that will help members of minority groups thrive in the dominant culture.

_____   7. I know where to obtain bias-free, multicultural materials for use in my school.

_____   8. I have evaluated the school resource materials to determine whether or not they contain a fair and appropriate presentation of people in diverse populations.

Parent/Community Relations

_____   9. I invite parents and community members from various cultural backgrounds to be classroom resources, speakers, visiting experts, or assistants.

_____   10. I value having a school staff composed of people from different cultural backgrounds.

_____   11. I exhibit displays showing culturally diverse people working and socializing together.

_____   12. I advocate for schools in which all classes, including special education classes, reflect and respect diversity.

■ ■ ■ ■ ■

ACTIVITY 8.3
Planning for Learning about Diverse Colleagues and Collaborators

1. Complete the checklist in Figure 8.2, Self-Assessment of Diversity-Related Competencies. These are just examples of items related to competencies, so you may want to add others and talk with your class or a group about a more complete list, based on your understanding of diversity-related competencies.

2. When you have finished, discuss each of the categories of items and talk about your strengths, giving examples of your actions. For example, if you wrote in "Usually" for #3 (reading to increase your understand of people from other cultures, experiences, and backgrounds) you might say, "I got the children's book, *Saltypie: A Choctaw Journey from Darkness into Light* by Tim Tingle for my nephew for his birthday, and we are reading it together when he visits me." Or you might say, "The Girl Scout troop I lead is reading *Beyond Central, Toward Acceptance: A Collection of Oral Histories from Students of Little Rock Central High School* edited by Mackie O'Hara and Alex Richardson.

list can form guidelines for staff development or can be administered as part of a study module for a teacher preparation course on consultation and collaboration. Additional items might be added after discussions about diverse identities and characteristics in schools and communities.

Recognition and acceptance of individual and group diversity promotes effective interactions among individuals and groups. Clare (2002) suggests that a person's worldview and perspectives of diversity expand as a result of experiences with individuals from cultures, races, ethnicities, traditions, and characteristics different from that person's own. These experiences create avenues for personal reflection and shift the way consulting teachers envision a social justice framework for collaborative efforts and educational practices.

Appreciation and understanding evolve from direct interpersonal contact and from knowledge of the history and culture of diverse groups, including their stories, values, myths, inventions, music, and art. When considering methods for improving cross-cultural awareness and sensitivity, the best way for consultants to learn about other cultures is by learning from the people themselves, rather than learning about them secondhand. Awareness of differences and respect for customs within diverse cultures are major factors for interacting within school settings and engaging in collaborative efforts with school personnel.

Many consultants report that making the effort to become involved with families, colleagues, and communities not only improves their collaborations, it also enriches their own lives. When consultants

---

Video Example from YouTube

▶

ENHANCEDetext
Video Example 8.1.

How can you create a welcoming, inclusive environment where everyone feels they belong? View this video to learn about strategies that help us challenge our own biases in order to create more inclusive environments for all. (https://www.youtube.com/watch?v=2hZzPPcOg4U)

learn about and honor the culture, language, history, and customs of their students and the adults with whom they collaborate, they begin to mitigate the negative impact of prejudice and racism, and utilize customs and traditions as strengths. When consultants become familiar with the diversities of families and other school personnel on the education team, they are more able to:

- Consider the strengths that come with the diversity of experiences, backgrounds, histories, and cultures of various collaborators on their teams.
- Use technology in ways that are sensitive to cultural and individual differences. Technology is not culture-free; it reflects the cultural perspective of software developers.
- Develop a critical understanding of the social-cultural context of interactions and instruction in the setting, and allow this understanding to guide their work.
- Promote a positive cultural identity, because all cultures add value to schools and to society and are a powerful resource for group members.
- Develop multicultural connections in the school area.
- Prepare for and facilitate collaborative relationships among team members in a changing climate when mismatches among school personnel, students, and their families are likely.

The last part of this chapter contains information about some of the diverse contexts and characteristics consultants may encounter in their work.

FIGURE 8.3   Suggestions for Social Justice Thinking for Consultants and Collaborators

Do	Don't
Do . . . consider structural inequities.	*Don't* . . . think that "normal" means right or best.
Do . . . reject deficit thinking.	*Don't* . . . think the words you use don't matter.
Do . . . learn about other cultures and personify the identities.	*Don't* . . . blame individuals when they personify results of inequities.
Do . . . view collaboration from a social justice lens.	*Don't* . . . tolerate "isms" in your school. *Don't* . . . ignore the impacts of your own culture.
Do . . . consider impacts of intersectionality.	*Don't* . . . let disagreement with choices or viewpoints block building collaborative relationships.
Do . . . remember your own privileges.	*Don't* . . . make differences problematic.

Developing Skills to Work Effectively with a Variety of Collaborators on Behalf of Students with Special Needs

Many of the collaboration skills addressed in this book are essential for working effectively with diverse partners. Family and community members, as well as colleagues in the school setting, will have diverse backgrounds, histories, educational attainment, cultures, and individual characteristics such as race, ethnicity, gender, and ability status. Effective collaboration in diverse contexts and with individuals from diverse backgrounds and characteristics means coping with the stress in dealing with the unfamiliar, establishing rapport with others, sensing other people's feelings, and communicating effectively.

Communication skills and interpersonal skills are important for collaboration with educational partners. Collaborative consultants benefit from understanding interrelationships between language and cultural meaning. Not all individuals and groups share American middle class values or definitions of terms such as "disability." Some cultures throughout the world have very different perceptions of disability from those of Anglo Americans; those with "disabilities" are accepted as having a place in the community with no stigma or problem because they are viewed as having talent or uniqueness to contribute. This is an intriguing concept that poses a challenging topic for educators to address among themselves and with students.

Knowledge of cultural differences in nonverbal communication is important for educational collaborators. For example, knowing that avoiding eye contact is a sign of respect in some cultures will help consultant and consultee avoid interpreting this as disrespect and rudeness. Although it is the opposite of the cultural norms in most educational settings, looking away from the speaker in some cultures indicates paying attention. Variations of actions involving handshakes, head nods, eyebrow raising, and finger-pointing have widely different meanings in different cultural settings.

Consultants strive to avoid negative words and use language instead that indicates a desire to help students expand their abilities, in contrast to "helping them get better." They need to exercise caution in discussing poor work, bad behavior, or poor attitudes because what is perceived as mild criticism or simply a suggestion in one culture may lead to severe punishment of the child or disillusionment about the student's ability from a family of another culture. Idioms should not be used that might be misunderstood in another language— for example, "Let's put this on the back burner for now," "We need to get her to up to speed in that," "Students need to toe the line in his classroom," or "That's a Catch-22." Consultants need to be sensitive to the types of colloquialisms having negative connotations that they use in day-to-day conversations. Some common colloquialisms are based on cultural stereotypes and may be offensive to others. Examples are "circle the wagons," "that cotton-pickin' regulation," "low man on the totem pole," or "Even Ray Charles could see that."

Gendered language also affects interactions. Collaborators must monitor their own behavior for use of fair and balanced gender-specific language. For example:

- Use "persons" or "women and men," not "men" or "mankind."
- Avoid saying "female doctor" and "male nurse," saying simply "doctor" or "nurse."
- Instead of saying "He adds the balances," when the sex of the accountant is unknown, say, "The accountant adds the balances."

- Do not avoid recognizing same-sex partnerships. Same-sex partners are typically referred to as "partner" rather than "significant other."
- Refrain from terms like the "fair sex," "woman's work," and "man-size job."
- Identify someone as a "supervisor" rather than a "foreman."
- Say "students" or "class" instead of "boys and girls."

These recommendations for fair and balanced communication may seem like unimportant details. However, the most important part of establishing a successful collaborative relationship is demonstrating respect.

ACTIVITY 8.4
Planning for Improving Diversity-Related Competencies

Revisit your self-assessment in Figure 8.2. Select one or two items you would like to work on, and incorporate them into a plan of personal/professional development for the next month. Your plan might include volunteering at a soup kitchen and talking with individuals and families who participate in the meal. You might commit to subscribing to *Teaching Tolerance* (free) and reading it regularly. Share your plans with others in a small group. Work with a colleague to set target dates for accomplishing your plan and commit to getting back together in person or via electronic communication on those dates to evaluate the outcomes. As reinforcement for making significant progress, treat yourself to something special!

As we work at broadening the limitations of our thinking, will we be able to develop and strengthen our skills for working with collaborators from diverse populations and contexts? When we hone our competencies, we are better equipped to promote understanding and appreciation of diverse individuals and groups and develop collaborative relationships to provide better educational outcomes for students.

Video Example from YouTube

▶ ENHANCEDetext
Video Example 8.2.
View this video to learn about important tips to ensure you embrace cultural diversity and communicate with cultural awareness. (https://www.youtube.com/watch?v=ZDvLk7e2lrc)

COLLABORATING WITH DIVERSE TEAM MEMBERS

Consultants have an instrumental role in bringing together diverse groups of educators, including teachers, administrators, related services personnel, families, and community members. They use communication and collaboration skills to help the educational team address and resolve problems and to work for creative solutions.

Collaborative consultation within a true collaborative environment, rather than within an expert model of consultation, is the preferred mode of consulting with diverse team members. In this approach, the expertise of one partner in the team is not valued over that of another; all are recognized as vital to the collaborative process and the education of students.

This section of the chapter discusses several categorical diversities. These are non-changeable identities such as culture, language, disability and sexuality orientation/gender identity. The next section discusses diverse contexts, which relate more to place or circumstance that may change. Examples are rural, homeless, and military or military-connected.

Culturally and Linguistically Diverse Team Members

As consultants develop their knowledge, awareness and appreciation for cultural and linguistic differences, they need to keep in mind that generic cultural characteristics are not the be-all and end-all of cultural diversity. Any person or family may differ markedly from cultural or group generalities. Although many researchers provide lists of generic cultural characteristics of specific diverse groups, consultants must guard against the myopic perspective that culturally diverse educational partners are a homogeneous group. Educators should respond in individually relevant ways to those with whom they collaborate rather than make assumptions based on group cultural characteristics.

Descriptions of characteristics provide only broad brush strokes for initiating multicultural interrelationships. Furthermore, brief descriptions of characteristics of specific cultures may erroneously imply that cultural differences are simple and easy to understand. Cross (2003) gives us an example from his own Seneca teachings. For this Native American group from the U.S. Northwest, the theoretical model for their culture is a relational worldview; this worldview, Cross says, is different from that found in most educational institutions. For the Senecas, human existence is understood in the form of a four-quadrant circle encompassing mind, body, spirit, and context. Health and well-being depend on the balance among the quadrants. Balance is a constant human process, and the Senecas rely on their culture to provide the resources within each quadrant for staying in balance. Cross points to this relational worldview as being different from a culture that relies heavily on linear thought and the scientific process to understand and solve problems in terms of causal relationships. Developing a cultural perspective is far from simple.

Cultural groups have differing rules about human communications and relationships (Conroy, 2012). For example, it is not acceptable in some cultures to share beliefs and opinions with people outside the group. In some cultures and traditions, being quiet in the presence of authority figures is a sign of honor and respect. Both of these examples show behaviors that could be disconcerting to school personnel when trying to solicit needed input from parents who regard the teacher as an outsider and an authority.

In some cultures, the way to respond to a question with finesse is to skirt the subject and arrive at it indirectly, while in another culture being direct and forthright is admirable. Public congratulation in certain cultures is offensive because group accomplishment is valued more than individual achievement, whereas in other cultures public congratulation would be an incentive to continue excelling. When Billy Mills, an Oglala Sioux from South Dakota, became a track star at the University of Kansas, he won an important race, but not by much. In the movie about his life, *Running Brave*, after the race his coach questioned Billy about his less than stellar performance, to which Billy replied that he had won the race as Coach wanted, but he would not shame a fellow athlete by beating him badly.

Team Members Who Are LGBTQ-Identified

The increasing diversity of family structures means that educators interact with those whom students consider to be their family, whether it is a single parent, grandparents, foster parents, multigenerational living groups, or LGBTQ parents. LGBTQ is the abbreviation for individuals who are considered to be in sexuality and gender-identity minority groups, such as lesbian, gay, bisexual, transgendered, or queer. "Gender non-conforming" and "queer" are common contemporary terms that are used in lieu of categorization as gay, lesbian, or straight. Families headed by gay and lesbian parents are becoming more numerous and more visible (Mayo, 2010; Ray & Gregory, 2001). Therefore, educators in areas where school personnel and communities are committed to inclusive schools and active parent-educator collaboration are likely to be interacting with family members who are gay or lesbian. In addition, as with other diversities, team members such as educators, administrators, other school personnel and community members may identify as LGBTQ. Some of these educational partners will be open about their identification; others may choose to not do so. Experienced consultants understand that it is likely they will interacting with LGBTQ individuals on their collaborative teams.

Golombok and colleagues (2003) offer important findings that help educators understand the reality of families with gay or lesbian parents. Three of these are:

1. The only clear difference between heterosexual and homosexual parents' child-rearing patterns is that co-mothers in lesbian-mother families are more involved in parenting than are fathers in two-parent heterosexual homes.
2. A longitudinal study of adults who had been raised as children in lesbian-mother families found that as young men and women they continued to function well in adult life and maintained positive relationships with both their mothers and their mothers' partners.
3. Research has consistently failed to find differences between children of gay and lesbian families and children in heterosexual families with respect to gender development or psychological well being. Sexual orientation of parent is not a predictor of successful child development.

Research by Ray and Gregory (2001) shows that children in gay and lesbian families have psychological adjustments similar to those of children growing up in more traditional family structures. They identified common concerns of gay and lesbian parents. First, their type of family structure usually was not included in the curriculum about homes and families, and this made the children feel isolated. Also, their children were apt to be teased or bullied, and were asked difficult questions by other children, or even teachers, such as, "Why do you have two mommies?" Educators should take note of these very real concerns as they consult and collaborate with gay and lesbian parents.

Bias, harassment, and bullying are concerns of LGBTQ families and teachers. LGBTQ parents face barriers to their participation in schools and understandably are concerned when their children are inadequately protected from harassment (Casper & Schultz, 1999). LGBTQ educators, too, face harassment and safety concerns (Wright, 2010). Many educators have come from homogeneous community and family backgrounds, and they may bring biases from the past or limited knowledge about issues related to families with LGBTQ team members. To establish crucial collaborative relationships and to understand more about a child's out-of-school context, educators must:

1. Examine their personal beliefs and feelings about individuals who identify as LGBTQ.
2. Examine their personal beliefs and feelings about families and family diversity in all its many facets (Koemer & Hulsebosch, 1996).
3. Understand that a consultant's role is not to approve or disapprove of sexual and gender diversity but to team effectively with all to produce positive outcomes for children.

Examining one's own beliefs and feelings is not always a comfortable activity. Consultants need to ask themselves: "In what ways can conscious awareness of my feelings enable me to consult with adults in my students' lives and be more inclusive in my interactions with them?" No matter what our personal beliefs, values, and experiences are, as educators we understand that it is not possible to be *for* children and *against* their families. Inclusiveness is a moral imperative in schools, as well as in family and community relationships.

Educators need to recognize that LGBTQ team members represent a range of diverse social, ethnic, and economic class backgrounds, as do any other group of parents. Along with questioning stereotypes, school personnel who strive for inclusive and respectful home-school relationships should strive to learn more about the families with whom they work.

Although debates take place at both national and local levels about the definition of family and the parameters of a "legitimate" family, educators have an ethical responsibility to collaborate with *all* significant adults in the lives of their students. Co-educators must help school personnel set a comfortable tone within which all team members can feel welcome in classrooms and comfortable with taking an active role in home-school interactions.

Educators play a powerful role in demonstrating dignity and respect toward all. Lamme and Lamme (2001–2002) offer several concrete suggestions for making schools more inclusive and friendly to gay and lesbian parents. Their suggestions extend to all LGBTQ team members. Five of the most important to include here are:

1. Refer to families or parents rather than mothers and fathers.
2. Refuse to tolerate harassment and homophobic teasing, just as racist remarks and behavior are not tolerated. None of the children of gay and lesbian parents whom Lamme and Lamme (2001–2002) interviewed had heard an adult intervene when a homophobic remark was made in school.
3. Model and teach respect for all. Do not let homophobic harassment continue unchallenged. Educators should not tolerate popular youth sayings such as "That's so gay," just as they should not tolerate the use of the pejorative word "retard."
4. Reconsider special-event, parent-focused activities. Emphasizing a stereotypical father's day or mother-daughter breakfast may stigmatize children in homes with gay or lesbian parents.
5. Learn about community resources for LGBTQ individuals, including faculty and staff in your own school who might provide support to parents, students, and other educators.

Another aspect of sexual orientation affecting school personnel is the increasing number of young gay and lesbian students who are coming out about their sexual orientation, especially those in their early teens who live in urban areas. Some educators might deny that this could be a problem, but others recognize the need that students with sexual-orientation differences have for sensitivity by school personnel. A few states have mandated sensitivity training in their teacher certification programs and developing guidelines and materials for making schools more inclusive places of learning (Anderson, 1997). When caring teachers and administrators provide support to gay and lesbian parents and gay and lesbian students, the instances of abusive language, harassment, and homophobia are reduced (Edwards, 1997). In years past, little information on this subject was available, but now educators, parents, and students talk more openly and share information that can help students feel safe in their school environments and neighborhoods (see *National Geographic Special Issue, Gender Revolution,* January 2017).

In addition, educational collaborators can provide leadership in improving a school climate of accepting diversity. Part of diversity training or professional development regarding community-home-school relationships and programs should include the concerns expressed by families with LGBTQ parents. Remember that many of the issues faced by LGBTQ students are also issues consultants need to consider when working with collaborators. One example is the controversy in many schools about gender-neutral rest rooms. Many schools and other organizations have handled the issue of "what restroom to use" for transgender, gay, and lesbian students by having a "family" restroom. It is a gender-neutral restroom with no stalls or one stall that only one family or person uses at one time. Often there is a chair for parents or nursing mothers and a changing table. A father can take his very young daughter into the room and a mother, her young son. Families can go into the room together so no young children are left alone in the hallway. A family restroom is convenient and respectful of all configurations of families and individual identities. And for team members from the school and community, having a family restroom demonstrates that school's respect for all partners in the schooling of students with disabilities.

Team Members Who Have Disabilities

One diverse group that seldom is discussed in educational literature is educators who have disabilities. Considering that an estimated 15 percent of the population has a disability and that this percent increases with age, consultants should expect that at least 15 percent of adults with whom they interact will have a disability. The teaching ranks undoubtedly include individuals with disabilities—physical, learning, perhaps behavioral—but this is not a widely investigated or talked-about topic. Some adults with physical disabilities such as a missing limb, hearing or visual impairment, disfigurement, or impaired mobility do enter the teaching profession, and it is quite likely that some adults with ADHD are in the education profession.

Educators with disabilities have found creative ways to focus on their strengths and to use their disabilities in important impromptu lessons. Teachers who have learning problems of their own with memory, spelling, or comprehension have opportunities to model tenacity toward reaching their goals and to share the learning strategies that have helped them be successful. They can inspire children with anecdotes about how hard it was for them to succeed in college, but by having solid goals and good habits to nudge them forward, and by taking advantage of resources offered in schools and communities, they succeeded in completing an education for the profession of their choice. Many adults with ADHD tend to excel in crises and have learned adaptive strategies for dealing with paperwork and details that they can share with students. Adults who have overcome anxiety disorders, eating disorders, obsessive-compulsive disorders, or alcohol and other drug dependency also have much to offer children and youth by modeling attitudes of coping, resilience, a regimen of good habits, and a conquering spirit.

A group of seventh graders asked their teacher, a combat veteran with a prosthesis instead of a right arm, "Where'd you get that thing?" It made for a good history lesson by that teacher on the aspects of war and its outcomes. In spite of their initial fascination, the group was almost nonchalant from then on, when their papers were handed back by prosthesis, or when they shook "hands" with their right-"handed" teacher in greeting.

School co-educators can expect that many of the home co-educators with whom they work will have disabilities. As with teacher-partners, using the strength approach is critical for effective collaboration that involves parent-child relationships. The principles of Universal Design and Universal Design for Learning (UDL) (Burgstahler & Cory, 2008) provide successful strategies for developing materials and workspaces that are open and accessible to all. Spaces at tables for wheelchairs, microphones (your "teacher voice" is not enough for those with hearing impairments), using large and easily distinguished fonts for print materials are common UDL strategies. Appropriate readability levels and language of print materials are critical. All these and other strategies, when combined with respectful and inclusive language and a welcoming school environment with pictures and materials that represent all diversities, including individuals with various disabilities, will convey respect and willingness to collaborate with all adults in the students' learning environments.

COLLABORATING WITH TEAM MEMBERS FROM DIVERSE CONTEXTS

Constant self-examination of values, assumptions, and privilege are the first building blocks of diversity-related or cultural competence. Consultants also work to develop an understanding of the diverse contexts in which collaboration occurs and the impact of context in the collaboration process. The variety of contexts for educational consultation is vast. In this section of the chapter, there are brief discussions of these contexts: rural and remote regions, frequent moves or transience, military, migrants, poverty, homelessness, and homeschooling. These are considered contexts because they are not characteristics of an individual or group, but rather they are situations or social conditions from which and into which individuals and families may transition.

Team Members in Rural and Remote Areas

About 9 percent of the nation's students attend rural schools. Students of color are about 25 percent of rural students. Schools in rural and remote areas are characterized by geographic isolation, cultural isolation, and distance that necessitates significant amounts of teacher time spent in travel from school to school. Often there are too few students for some kinds of grouping, too few staff members covering too many curricular and special program areas, reluctance of students to be singled out, and limited resources. Poverty is the biggest threat to educational achievement in rural schools; in the 800 poorest rural districts, the poverty rate is similar to that in urban districts in Los Angeles, New York, and Chicago (Kreiss, 2010).

The most obvious barrier to collaboration in rural and remote areas is the geography. Other rural barriers include lower levels of participation rates in IEP, often due to transportation problems, and limited access to resources such as parent support centers, educational libraries, and disability advocates (Stanley, 2015). Too often the challenges of rural life have a negative influence on teachers' abilities to achieve positive educational outcomes for their students with disabilities.

Hoover and Erickson (2015) determined that challenges in rural schools even more complex as rural communities demonstrate more **cultural and linguistic diversity**. They found that often educators in rural areas were not prepared for the diversity and poverty found in rural America. Researchers have noted that the lack of compatibility between home values, teachings, traditions, and customs of the students and those held by the teacher influence home-school partnerships, and this incompatibility may be more striking in sparsely populated areas. The lack of experts in specific disabilities, lack of options for care and services for students with disabilities, and the absence of formal support groups were problems discussed by rural African American mothers in a study by Stanley (2015).

Despite these barriers, qualities of rural school life create advantages for consulting teacher approaches. Few rural schools are prepared and able to meet the needs of special needs students without consultation and other indirect services, so it is necessary for consulting teachers to become intensively involved in providing learning options and alternatives for students. Consulting teachers use their roles to coordinate efforts among teachers, administrators, parents, and other community members so that only a few resources will seem like more. Many consultants appreciate that they are left much to themselves to solve problems and determine their own professional development that fits their unique needs. In rural settings, teachers tend to be highly visible and therefore especially vulnerable to community pressure and criticism. However, teachers have a greater opportunity to influence the school and community in producing positive educational and social outcomes for students with disabilities. They often function as influential change agents. Because rural areas have limited access and resources, experienced educational consultants tend to be creative and innovative problem solvers (perhaps paralleling the farmer/rancher who can fix almost anything with improvisation and what is on hand). They maximize sparse resources and lack of specialized personnel by playing on the strengths of the rural community, including smaller class sizes, more frequent interaction among students and staff, greater involvement of many rural families in the school and its activities, and the commitment of most communities to their local schools.

Team Members Who Move Frequently

Up to 20 percent of the population in the United States are on the move each year and many more are searching for ways they could relocate to new jobs and new homes.

Students who experience high rates of mobility, defined as changing schools a minimum of six times between 1st and 12th grade, were 35 percent more likely to fail a grade than other students and scored an average of four months behind peers on standardized tests (Astor, Jacobson, & Benbenishty, 2012; Kerbow, Azcoitia, & Buell 2003; Wood, Halfon, Scarlata, Newacheck, & Nessim, 1993). The mobility issues can be a factor in transfer-of-credit policies, placement on extra-curricular/co-curricular teams and activities, access to special education services, and personal and social (friendship) adjustments in new schools. Research conducted by Bradshaw and colleagues (2010) reported findings that indicate adolescents experience considerable stress when changing schools due to anxiety over friendships, acceptance in peer groups, and the ability to participate on sports teams and other select co-curricular opportunities. Many families find that their community lives are disrupted, just as school-age children's educational programs are disrupted. Moving and the events leading up to and following it can be traumatic for everyone—even the family pet; for a student with disabilities, they may be particularly troublesome. Records must be forwarded, new teachers and texts and classmates assimilated, and adjustments made to home conditions of sleep, meals, and schedules for routines while the child is getting settled in. For parents and other potential team members, these stresses also could include a different predominant language, dramatically different customs involving celebrations and holidays, lack of supportive friends and family, and unfamiliarity with neighborhoods, shopping areas, and community activities.

Neighborhood ties are disrupted by moves, and parents are adjusting to new jobs in many cases. Families and individuals forced to move due to eviction, ethnic or racial tension, or economic deprivation, will be particularly stressed.

Mobility affects not only the students and families who move, but also the institutions they use. Transience is a big hurdle in developing and maintaining collaborative relationships. Consultants can build relationships with partners who move frequently by:

- Forming peer support groups, particularly helpful when newcomers need to learn about local resources and opportunities
- Setting up a buddy system that could involve matching the student with an older, confident, and popular student
- Finding mentors to serve as the newcomer's advocate and confidant
- Forming parent support groups
- Having periodic orientation programs at various times of the year
- Providing professional development programs for school personnel that focus on the needs of transient students and families, particularly those with disabilities, in their adjustment to the new school and neighborhood

Team Members in the Military and Military-Connected Families

Army Captain Joshua A. Mantz, who was shot by a sniper in Iraq, was pronounced dead for fifteen minutes but recovered, thanks to heroic efforts of Army medical personnel. Five months after he recovered, he returned to duty in Iraq. Speaking at a conference in Manhattan, Kansas, Captain Mantz described characteristics of military personnel returning

FIGURE 8.4   "This Isn't Like What I Had in My Other Three Schools."

from battle situations: "I'd like you to throw out the word 'wounded' as meaning a guy who got shot or burned. Rather, start thinking about it as—nobody who deploys to combat comes back not-wounded. Everybody who experiences combat comes back wounded in one way or another" (Mantz, 2010). Partnerships among consulting teachers, classroom teachers, and individuals such as Captain Mantz and other combat-wounded veterans are essential in serving the needs of their children.

Understanding the culture of the military family, and the unique dynamics and contextual factors that are a part of the military lifestyle, will give educators a better insight into facilitating collaborative relations with military-connected adults for the education of students with disabilities.

Children and youth who are military dependents tend to move frequently as their military parent moves to an assigned military installation, or they need to live in a new place because the military parent is assigned to an overseas post. Military-connected children average moving and changing school districts six to nine times prior to high school graduation, three times more often than civilian families (Astor, Jacobson, & Benbenishty,

2012; MCEC, 2012). When families move from site to site, they frequently become frustrated with the tangled web of records (or having *no* records for long periods until files do arrive), referrals, screenings, and conferences. When school records and student information are slow to catch up with the student or are misplaced, then students are at risk of being misplaced in school programs. Frequent school changes involve stressors, such as deployments, demands of assignments and homework, school attendance, and parental engagement (Richardson, et al., 2011). These frustrations and concerns are part of the life of military-connected students and families.

Values and behaviors that are inherent for success in the military are not those that automatically lead to success in the nonmilitary environment (obeying orders, depending on a team, and protecting team members at great personal cost). When families are separated by deployment of fathers, mothers, or sometimes *both* parents to trouble spots and active war zones around the world, consulting teachers become sources of assurance for anxious families who have students with special needs. These caring professionals can provide continuity in learning programs and support for the social and emotional needs of students who may feel afraid, lonely, and confused.

Consultants in schools must also recognize that returning military personnel and veterans face many challenges in reintegrating with their families and communities. Trauma experienced by military personnel in the line of duty may have affected the way in which new information is processed, how relationships are managed, and response modes to situations and surroundings.

For many military-connected individuals, the mental health concerns and issues grow to be hidden disabilities. Recent surveys rated concerns of anxiety, depression, hyper-vigilance, stress, post-traumatic stress disorder (PTSD), and sleeping problems as moderate or high concerns (Hamrick, Rumann, & Associates, 2013). Rudd, Goulding, and Bryan (2011) reported the increasingly high rate of suicide and suicidal ideations among veterans. Living with family members who are suicidal or experiencing deep depression often leads to family challenges. Working in a team with families, school administrators, teachers, health and social service personnel, and military staff who oversee family and school concerns will help ensure a stable learning environment for military-dependent students.

Teacher strategies that provide students with transitional success both entering and exiting a school, as well as resilience-building opportunities in the classroom, are tools that every educator can leverage to have a more successful academic environment. Providing understanding, support, and opportunities for student success also provides support for parents and other family members as they weather transitions and concerns attached to moving and deployment. Resources are available to help consultants understand military-connected students and educational partners. The American Association of Colleges for Teacher Education (AACTE) and the Military Child Education Coalition, commonly referred to as MCEC, developed a set of guiding principles for working with military-connected students. These principles were the framework for an initiative called Operation Educate the Educators, a program that helps better prepare pre-service and in-service school personnel to meet the needs of military-connected children. The MCEC is focused on ensuring quality educational opportunities for all military children affected by mobility, family separation, and transition and provides a variety of resources for educators. A helpful iBook, *Military Connected Students in the Classroom*, was developed at Kansas State University and is a widely-used resource for pre-service and inservice educators. It is available on iTunes or via the university's college of education website.

Much can be done toward making military-connected students, family members, and school personnel feel welcome in new school environments. Local partnerships among home, community, and military establishment are a first step that benefits all groups. Institutional partnerships among schools, military installations, and colleges and universities have initiated research and programs that help students succeed academically and socially (Keller & Decoteau, 2000; Mercer, Thurston, & Hughey, 2014). In all of these efforts, consulting teachers are the foremost facilitators of successful partnerships for students having special needs.

Migrant Families as Team Members

Migrant families are those who make frequent moves in search of temporary or seasonal agricultural or fishing employment. As students in schools across the country, children and youth in migrant families work with education consultants. Educational needs facing migrant students include low attachment to schools and community, lack of pre-school services, education gaps, transfer of records and credits (high school), and health issues. They face many of the same issues as rural and poor families. The impact of this lifestyle is that only one out of two migrant students graduates from high school. Some migrant students require special education services. Title I, Part C of the Elementary and Secondary Education Act was designed to meet the educational needs of migratory students who are qualified under the Migrant Education legislation (Devine, 2013).

Migrant families face many barriers that consultants should consider. Besides language barriers, common to most but not all migrant families, migrant families often live in poor and isolated locations and have less formal education. Consultants should remember that families often experience discrimination because of race, mobility, migrant status, and language. These family characteristics too often preclude parents from fulfilling the expected parental role in education (e.g., attending school events or responding to teacher requests); this leads educators to assume that parents do not value education or care about the education of their children. However, most migrant families place a high value on education and parents are very involved in developing non-academic education, such as developing responsibility and respect for self and others (Devine, 2013; Gonzales, Borders, Hines, Villalba, & Henderson, 2013). Consultants should acknowledge and respect the contributions migrant parents make to their children's education.

Successful efforts in collaborating with migrant families are based on recognizing strengths they bring to the situation as well as the challenges of the lifestyle. California has a state-wide Migrant Education Family Biliteracy Program that draws migrant families into the school community by valuing the cultural and linguistic assets the family possesses. The program integrates the family unit into the educational experience by utilizing the family's first language to teach and model literacy strategies that families may replicate at home in the absence of the teacher. Other examples are Kentucky's provision of continuous access to online links to college and ESL classes, and Head Start's specific programs for migrants that involve family and community collaboration.

Team Members Who Are Poor

In the last census (2011), 46.2 million people (about 15 percent) living in the United States were living in poverty (U.S. Department of Commerce, 2012). Poverty is defined by governmental guidelines that vary with family size and geographic location. Generally, poverty guidelines set the poverty line as below an annual income of less than $12,000 for one person to less than $40,000 for a household of eight family members. Smiley (2012) estimated that nearly 2 million U.S. families with children live on less than two dollars a day.

An obvious effect of poverty is hunger. Hunger deprives children of sufficient calories and the vital nutrients that significantly impact children's ability to learn. Initial consequences of hunger are seen in many classrooms. Signs include fatigue, irritability, dizziness, and difficulty concentrating. Other signs might be behavioral problems, apathy and passivity, frequent headaches and stomachaches. Researchers have also found that depression, anxiety, withdrawal, and social skills deficits may be the signs of persistent hunger. Often these signs are interpreted as laziness, hyperactivity, attention deficit, or lack of cognitive abilities. These consequences of hunger also can be seen in adults who are poor and who are, nevertheless, expected to be equal partners in the education of their children.

Although educational personnel cannot end hunger in their communities, they can play a role in supporting children and families who face food insecurity. Spies, Morgan, and Matsuura (2014) suggest educators develop relationships with children and families, identify signs of hunger, and carefully lead families to resources in the community that support the nutritional needs of the family such as food pantries and free family meals. School personnel should identify signs of persistent hunger, including any of the symptoms listed earlier. Teachers could note, for example, behavioral signs of hunger such as the speed of eating lunch, the amount of food eaten, and possibly attempts to take food home. Care should be taken not to single out children who may have nutritional or other needs related to poverty. Schools can consider providing breakfasts for all students, snacks in the classroom or at breaks, and a school food pantry. There are many example programs, such as Breakfast in the Classroom, sponsored by the Walmart Foundation, and Kids Café (Feeding America, 2013). Educators can work with other community organizations that address local poverty issues and provide services for families who may need food, clothing, medical services, and shelter.

Consultants using the social justice approach to collaborating with team members in poverty strive to understand the relationships between poverty, class, and education. They know that all too often, the educational approach to individuals in poverty is framed by studying behaviors and cultures of poor students and their families rather than studying the structural inequities and inequitable conditions (Gorski, 2007). The so-called "culture of poverty" mindset suggests we need to "fix" poor students and their families. The social justice approach means we need to take action about social conditions such as access to health care, affordable housing, reasonably safe living conditions, safe school with quality educational practices, and living wages. Gorski (2007) has these suggestions for engaging individuals who live in poverty:

- Do not use communication that requires Internet access or other costly resources.
- Make sure that engagement with partners is affordable and convenient by providing transportation, on-site childcare, and time flexibility.
- Hold meetings in a public place where everyone feels comfortable and safe, such as a church or library that is on a bus line.
- Keep supplies on hand for meetings, such as paper, pencils, and notebooks. Provide these for everyone, not just those who are poor.
- Be persistent and courteous in reaching out to parents; keep trying.
- Challenge colleagues when they marginalize poor students, parents, and team members by reminding them of the inequitable conditions in our schools and communities.

ACTIVITY 8.5
Exploring Beliefs and Realities about Poverty

This was designed as a group activity. If you are working in a large group, a very small group, or by yourself, you may need to modify some of the directions. For this activity you will need two pieces of paper for signs; several classified (rentals) sections and some grocery ads from the local paper; and copies of the Cost-of-Living Calculations worksheet for each group. (See Figure 8.5.)

1. Post a sign in one corner of the room that says "Strongly agree" and one in the opposite corner that says "Strongly disagree." Make a line connecting the two corners with tape, chalk, or string.
2. Read aloud the following statement: "Individuals are responsible for living in poverty. They have no one to blame but themselves." Think about this statement for a few moments, then go stand anywhere along the line that shows how strongly you agree or disagree with it. When everyone is standing on the line, talk with the people nearest you about why you chose that place to stand. Explain to each other your beliefs about who is responsible for poverty.
3. Form a group with three or four of the people who are standing nearest you on the line. With your group, look at the Federal Poverty Level (FPL) for 2011. The FPL is meant to identify what it would cost a family of a specific size to meet its basic needs, such as food, clothing, transportation, and shelter. It is developed annually by the department of Health and Human Services.

Family Size	Pre-Tax Income
2 people	$14,710
3 people	$28,530
4 people	$22,350

Does it seem high or low to you? What is your reaction to this amount of money being defined as poverty?

1. Think of your group as a household. Make a list of what your basic needs are and use the Cost of Living Calculations sheet (see Figure 8.5) to record your work. Start with housing and food. What else is essential for your household? For example, is a car essential? A cell phone? Health insurance? This may not be as clear-cut as you think, and your group may disagree at first. The members of your group will have to come to agreement about what you need and what you can live without.

2. Find out how much these essentials cost in your community. To find the cost of housing, for example, look at rental notices, keeping in mind that you need to decide how many rooms your household needs. To find the cost of food, make a shopping list of what your family would need for a week, then go to a supermarket and price the items or use the grocery ads. You might assign different items to different people to price. When each person has gathered his or her data, reconvene.

3. Calculate the monthly costs of basic needs for your family group. Write them on the sheet on which you have listed the items. Add up the monthly costs, and then multiply by 12 to find out the amount of money a family of your size would need in order to survive in your community.

4. Compare your group's cost of basic needs in your community with the FPL's poverty level for 2011. What do you notice?

5. Using federal minimum wage, calculate the annual income of someone who works full time (40 hours a week) at a minimum-wage job. How does this annual income compare with the federal poverty rate? How does it compare with the cost of basic needs in your community?

6. Look back at your household's expenses. If your expenses are more than you would make working full time at minimum wage, try making ends meet in two ways. First, what can you cut from your list? For example, could you live in a smaller apartment? Could you do without health insurance? Could you buy less expensive food? As you make the cuts, think about how your life would be without the items that you had considered basic needs. List some of the effects these cuts would have on your quality of life. Then try another approach: Figure out what hourly wage someone would need to earn in order to meet his or her basic needs in your community.

7. Now return to the original activity. Listen again to the opening statement: "Individuals are responsible for living in poverty. They have no one to blame but themselves." Think about it for a few moments, then go stand on the place on the line that shows how strongly you agree or disagree with the statement.

8. Discuss the following questions with the people near you on the line: Has your position changed? If so, what has caused it to change? If not, why not? Then return to your seat and write a response to someone who says that anyone who works hard can rise from poverty.

9. Reflect on how this activity influences your thoughts about collaboration, consultation, and teamwork for students with special needs.

Adapted from http://www.tolerance.org/lesson/what-poverty

FIGURE 8.5 **Cost-of-Living Calculations Worksheet**

Think of your group as a family that lives together in a household. (The size of your group will be the size of your household.) Make a list of what your basic needs are. Calculate the monthly costs of basic needs for your group's family. Write them on the sheet where you have listed the items. Add up the monthly costs, and then multiply by 12 to find out the amount of money a family would need in order to survive in your community.

BASIC NEEDS PER MONTH	COST IN YOUR AREA

Size of family: _____

Total cost of basic needs per month in your area: _____

Total cost of basic needs per year in your area: _____

Federal poverty level: _____

Federal minimum wage: _____

　　　　Per hour: _____

　　　　Annual income: _____

Minimum wage required for worker in your area to meet basic needs: _____

Team Members Who Are Homeless or Who Serve Homeless Students

There are many reasons that families don't have a home; it is estimated that about a third of the workforce is one bad accident, one large medical bill, or one missed paycheck away from losing their homes. When families are homeless, they live in motels or shelters, in cars, on the couches or floors of friends or relatives, in abandoned buildings, or on the streets. Sometimes when a family becomes homeless, the family must separate, with children going to live with relatives, friends, or on their own. As many as one third of homeless adults are employed, but low-wage jobs do not provide enough income to meet the needs of the family.

Consultants need to be aware of the students who are homeless because they are not with their families. Each year, between 1.5 and 1.6 million youth run away from home or are forced out of their homes by their parents (Toro, Dworsky, & Fowler, 2007). Unaccompanied homeless youth are young people experiencing homelessness and not in the physical custody of a parent or legal guardian. Many are runaways. These youth have fled their homes for various reasons such as drug abuse or physical abuse (Greene, 1995). Studies have found that 20–40 percent of unaccompanied youth were sexually abused in their homes, while 40–60 percent were physically abused (Hammer, Finkelhor, & Sedlak, 2002). Others, called throwaways, have been ejected from their homes by parents because of pregnancy (Toro, Dworsky, & Fowler, 2007), sexual orientation (20–40 percent of unaccompanied youth identify as gay, lesbian, bisexual, or transgender) (The National Gay and Lesbian Task Force and the National Coalition for the Homeless, 2007). Educating homeless children and youth involves challenges related to homelessness and to education system requirements, such as residency, guardianship, and transportation.

The McKenny Homeless Assistance Act of 1987 guarantees a free, appropriate education to all homeless children (National Center for Homeless Education, 2012). Educational consultants will partner with a variety of community service and advocacy organizations in educational efforts for unaccompanied homeless youth. Programs for homeless youth include comprehensive referral and placement services, transitional schools (separate schools), and shelters that include schools. An example of a school for homeless children that includes services for families promoting future financial independence (e.g., job training) is Positive Tomorrows, a program in Oklahoma City. Transitional schools shelter students from the stigma of poverty and homelessness. The mainstream approach educates homeless students in regular education programs, with the philosophy that homeless children are just like other children, except that they don't have a permanent home. Modifications to regular programs include additional or adapted academic support services, special transportation, homework assistance, and after school recreational programs that serve meals.

Consultation, collaboration, and teamwork are keys to the success of educational programs. Understanding homelessness is critical to overcoming the barriers of educating homeless students; educational consultants may have the role of providing staff development about the special needs of these students. Educators may work with McKinney-Vento liaisons. Federal law requires every school district in the country to designate a McKinney-Vento homeless liaison that identifies and provides data on homeless children and youth in the district as well as ensures these youth enroll in and attend school and receive support to succeed. A consultant with expertise in special education is an invaluable collaborator for McKinney-Vento liaisons.

Consultants may want to learn about innovative programs such as the Conscious Caring Curriculum, a series of customizable lessons that use art, poetry, and stories to nurture empathy and teach children about homelessness and its effects on children and their families. Information about this curriculum is found at the Homeless Children's Education Fund's website (http://homelessfund.org). First Book is an enterprise that provides new books and educational materials to families that have few resources.

Information about First Book can be found on their website. An excellent source for resources about homelessness is the website for the National Association for the Education of Homeless Children and Youth (NAEHCY).

Team Members Involved with Homeschooling

Reports on numbers of students homeschooled in the U.S. vary widely, and not all children who are homeschooled are reported. However, the National Center for Education Statistics (NCES) in the U.S Department of Education states that approximately 3 percent of the school-age population was homeschooled in the 2011–2012 school year. Consultants may work with parents who homeschool their children, and they may also work with community partners who homeschool their children. Therefore, it is important that consultants understand family motivations for schooling at home as well as laws involving school responsibilities for providing services for students who are homeschooled.

Families' reasons for homeschooling have been categorized as academic, value-driven, or religious; parents are concerned about moral issues, lack of differentiated instruction, negative peer pressure and bullying, more help for special needs including disabilities and giftedness, and problems that include student suspension or pregnancy. NCES reports that 91 percent of homeschooled students had parents who said that a concern about the environment of many schools was an important reason for homeschooling their child. As homeschooling becomes more accepted and prevalent, educators are seeing the need to develop collaborative partnerships with families who homeschool. These partnerships facilitate responding to family requests for the use of school services, including but not limited to speech therapy, foreign language classes, extracurricular activities/sports, enrichment programs, and libraries and other materials. As taxpayers they are entitled to these resources and by law they are entitled to special education services for their children with exceptional needs.

Evidence that homeschooling is successful for most of the students has been documented through such means as success rates in university classes and scores on standardized tests. However, there are not many safety nets for the student if homeschooling does not work. Good homeschooling experiences require tremendous commitments of time, effort, focus of both student and homeschool teachers, and often a loss of a second-income source by families. This is a huge sacrifice, especially if there are disabilities in the family that require special attention.

The homeschooling process has benefited greatly from distance learning curricula and from resources available on the Internet. Many homeschooling families also take advantage of nearby community colleges and universities. Some parents do not want to commit to schooling their children at home as a full-time activity, preferring instead to send their children to school while supplementing their education with downloaded curricula or community-based experiences to give them additional opportunities for learning.

Many homeschooling families *do* want to remain a part of the public school community with the understanding that all privately schooled and homeschooled students are eligible to receive services (Council for Exceptional Children, 2000). A growing trend is one in which personnel from public schools and homes work together to educate children.

By collaborating with school personnel for a child's special needs, families can be assured that they have taken advantage of everything both home and school have to offer in order to maximize their child's opportunity for success. Collaborative partnerships will allow home and school educators to provide the utmost benefits available for students in whom they have a shared interest. Consultants should keep this in mind when working with partners who homeschool: Just as with other dimensions of diversity in team members, you may not agree with their choices or their ideas, but you must allow for differences and continue your work to build trusting and collaborative relationships.

SOCIAL JUSTICE FRAMEWORK FOR COLLABORATION, CONSULTATION, AND TEAMWORK

Educational consultants who approach their work from a social justice framework develop partnerships that have a transformative influence on students, colleagues, families, schools, and communities. This framework guides the way consultants think about and relate to their educational partners. It guides a critical shift in the way one views the world, one's place in it, and one's relationship to others. This shift starts with realizing the limitations of their own understandings and the influences of their own culture on their perceptions of differences and diversities. They recognize the social and political structures that offer support or deny access to education, power, and opportunity for their students and collaborators.

Just as examining your own biases, privilege, and cultural limitations in recognizing and understanding the social justice perspectives related to collaboration and consultation may be stressful and difficult, you may find that other educational partners will struggle with ideas such as normativity, privilege, and structural inequities. Just invoking the name of John Dewey will probably not be enough to appease the resistance you may experience. It may help to go back and study the chapter about communication and dealing with resistance. Remember: You don't have to agree with a team member or approve of their values, life style, customs, or religious faith—you just have to treat them with honor and respect. As difficult as this may be at times, the winners will be the students.

A critical understanding within the social justice framework is the idea of intersectionality. **Intersectionality** describes the recognition of multiple identities and the interaction of those identities. No one is defined by a single characteristic or factor. Using one factor, such as Latino, female, poor, Jewish, heterosexual, single father, or homeless puts individuals in a box from which escape is difficult. This keeps collaborators from seeing a whole person, with strengths and positive experiences.

Although it is easier to interact with team members if we think of them as having only one diversity characteristic, single identities can lead to stereotyping, marginalizing, and silencing many voices. In reality, identities and affiliations are multiple, fluid, and shifting. And all aspects of one's social identity simultaneously interact (Goodman, 2011). One's constellation of identities may mean one is part of a privileged group that intersects with an identity that is part of a marginalized group. Consultants strive to value group membership and individual identities without reducing the complexity of multiple diversities.

ACTIVITY 8.6
Develop Your Character

This intersectionality activity is designed to be conducted in groups of about six. The purpose is to explore and discuss beliefs, stereotypes, assumptions, and intersectionality. You will need 24 index cards, six cards for each of four colors. Prepare four sets of index cards with the words or phrases below. Each set is a different color to represent one of four different categories: Role, Characteristic, Group Identity, and Description. You will have six blue Role cards, and each blue card will have a different role written on it (mom, teacher, PTA president, grandfather, school counselor, and foster parent). You may choose to make your own list of roles, characteristics, group identities, and descriptions for this activity.

Role (blue)	Characteristic (red)	Group-Identity (yellow)	Description (green)
Mom	tall	Mexican	in a wheelchair
Teacher	white-haired	White	in a burka
PTA president	blind	migrant worker	in a Land Rover
Grandfather	Spanish-speaking	African American	in a doctor's coat
School counselor	single	Jewish	in a large family
Foster parent	lesbian/gay	Muslim	in a beat-up truck

Each person draws a card from each category. For example, one person's cards may depict: An African American lesbian foster parent who is in a wheelchair. Each of these characters is a participant in your school's New Student Orientation.

1. What were your first thoughts when you learned the description of your character? What emotions did you have? What questions did you have? How do you think others in school settings respond to this person and her or his intersection of identities?

2. Think about your character. What is your name? What is your history? Who is your family? How do you deal with intolerance you may face? What do you do for fun? How do you think your multiple diversities intersect to influence your identity? Your interactions with school personnel? Your interactions with a student with a disability?

   How might both privilege and marginalization impact your life? What is your motivation for working with others in the best interests of students with special needs?

3. You are all members of a team working in the community to develop a summer recreational program for students with disabilities. Introduce yourself to others in the group. Have a group discussion, taking the part of your character, about a community summer recreational program for students with special needs.

4. Debrief as yourself with the group. What did you learn about yourself? About the process of collaboration?

As an extension of this activity, decide on four different sets of categories and make different characteristics cards for each set; then play the game again.

Educators who build their work on the social justice framework build learning communities; engage in collaborative problem-solving; listen and take advice from families, parents and community members; attend to the immediate needs and requests of their educational partners with respect; and share power with partners from diverse identities, backgrounds, and contexts.

 ENHANCEDetext Application Exercise 8.1. Click to apply your understanding of diversity-related terminology for educational consultants.

TIPS FOR WORKING WITH DIVERSE COLLABORATORS, FAMILIES, AND STUDENTS

1. Learn about the values, beliefs, and traditions of other cultures or identity groups in your school by attending community activities sponsored by those groups.
2. Talk to your parents, grandparents, or older relatives about your family history and about the intersections of their experiences and their cultural and historical identities.
3. Carefully consider the traditional "helping" activities such as gathering food for food banks or collecting winter coats for poor children. Research has shown that conducting such activities, without addressing some of the reasons for hunger and poverty, increases rather than decreases stereotypes.
4. Get to know the families of culturally and linguistically diverse students by making special efforts to reach out to them. Let them know you want to learn more about them because you care about their children.
5. Sit in on classes in bilingual education programs. Better yet, learn a new language.
6. Develop collaborative relationships with teachers of English language learners or culturally and linguistically diverse students with exceptionalities, even if you are not working with any of the students at the present time.
7. Support leadership among people from marginalized groups.
8. Speak up when you see or hear something that perpetuates inequality.
9. Ask families from diverse groups what their family goals are and discuss with them a variety of ways those goals could be addressed in the school curriculum.
10. Be realistic about what collaborative consultation can do, and celebrate even the smallest successes.

CHAPTER 9

ENGAGING FAMILIES IN HOME-SCHOOL COLLABORATIONS AND PARTNERSHIPS

A well-known consultant about child behavior and parenting issues once told one of the authors something like this: "I can offer parents a few generalizations that fit most parent-child relationship issues; but I don't know all the answers because I haven't met all the kids." We offer this same caveat about the information in this chapter. We will provide information about developing and sustaining collaborative relationships with members of students' families; and this information can be generalized to many parents. However, all families are unique and all parents and caregivers have a unique history and perspective. So be aware that we will provide the best information we can about collaborating and teaming with families, but "we don't provide the answers for such work with all families."

Education of students with special needs is a shared responsibility. Education of the whole child rests on solid, well-functioning partnerships among school, family, and community. Family members are a child's first and most influential teachers. The nature of education puts families and schools into shared roles for educating children and especially those with special needs. Too often the conventional patterns of relationships between schools and parents is limited to having parents as donors of craft materials; as "room parents" and classroom volunteers; or as passive recipients of information via newsletters, texts, and websites. Cultivating home-school collaborations that engage school personnel and family members together in maximizing each child's potential is as challenging as it is important. Beneficiaries of home-school partnerships are students, families, school personnel, and communities.

CHAPTER OBJECTIVES

Upon completing this chapter, the reader should be able to:

1. Explain the rationale for family partnerships and benefits to students, their families, teachers, schools, and communities from the partnerships.

2. Describe ways collaborative teachers are moving toward equal partnerships with families.

3. Outline key elements, components, and steps in developing empowerment-based home-school partnerships using the Equal Partnership Model.

4. Provide examples of potential challenges to home and school collaborative partnerships.

5. Identify ways to work collaboratively and respectfully in formal, mandated family, educational, and transition meetings.

6. Identify important considerations when instituting a home visit program.

KEY TERMS

Equal Partnership Model   family empowerment

SITUATION 9

The setting is early on a school morning at a middle school. The consulting special education teacher has just arrived at the building, hoping to make much-needed contacts with two teachers before they start their classes, when the principal walks out of her office briskly, with a harried look.

Principal: Oh, I'm glad you're here. I believe Ronnie is part of your caseload this year, right? His mother is in my office. She's upset. She says that everybody's picking on her son and he refused to come to school.

SPED teacher: That's serious. It's really early; she must be upset.

Principal: Well, she's on her way to work; she has two jobs and her day job starts pretty early.

SPED teacher: Do you know what happened?

Principal: It seems that yesterday he broke a beaker in the science lab and then he got into a shouting argument with his lab partners about whose fault it was. The science teacher needed to remove him from the classroom, so she sent him to me. After he cooled down and we had a talk, it was time for classes to change, so I sent him on to his next class. But he skipped out. The office administrative assistant texted his mother to inform her about his absence. Ronnie must have really unloaded on her last night, because she's here now, quite upset, and saying that the teachers do not care about her son and his problems. Could you join us for a talk?

SPED teacher: Okay, sure. [Enters the principal's office and greets Ronnie's mother.]

Mother: What is going on at this school? Ronnie and I have been working every night on homework the teachers send; and I'm making an effort to keep track of the work to be sure it's done. I thought things were going better for Ronnie. Now this problem with his science teacher has him refusing to come to school! Ronnie has his issues, but he's never refused to go to school before.

SPED teacher: You're right, that's serious. We all want Ronnie to be in school. I know you've been working with Ronnie on getting his homework completed; his teachers tell me he's doing better. I'd like to visit with you about this, and it would probably be good if Ronnie could join us. I realize you're on your way to work; do you have time to get our calendars together or do you want me to call or e-mail you?

Mother: [Gives a big sigh.] Yes, I'd like to talk. And the sooner, the better. I don't want him missing school. Let's catch this before it gets worse. I get off work at 4 today and don't go to my other job until 7; so maybe I can pick up Ronnie from my mom's and meet you at 4:30.

SPED Teacher: Hmm . . . that sounds fine. Do you want to meet here at the school or is someplace else more convenient?

There is a colorful children's book by Robie H. Harris with illustrations by Nadine Bernard Westcott called *Who's in My Family?* The book depicts a universe of families that is very different from the typical family of several decades ago. The reality reflected in the picture book requires educators to consider new ideas, new paradigms, and new models for home-school collaboration. In the history of parent-teacher relationships, "parent" has almost always meant biological parent, and "family" has meant two biological parents and their children. Other configurations were considered un-normal, problematic, and "broken" (consider the phrase "broken home"). The traditional thinking about "parent," "family," and "home" is no longer appropriate for school personnel.

Educational consultants and their colleagues must be aware of the realities and new legislation facing today's families. Special education legislation no longer uses the term "parent." Part H and Section 619 of the Individuals with Disabilities Education Act (IDEA) refer to "families" rather than "parents." The U.S. Census defines a family as a group of two people or more (one of whom is the householder) related by birth, marriage, or adoption and residing together; all such people (including related subfamily members) are regarded as members of one family. This reflects the reality that many children do not live with one or more biological parents. Others offer alternative definitions of family. For example, family could be defined as a group of people who are important to each other and offer each other love and support, especially in times of crisis. Other definitions relate to legal or blood relationship of the family members. Many consultants consider the parent to be the person with whom the school communicates. This might be a grandparent or other relative, a foster parent, or a caseworker in a group home. Other realities relate to the *home*; a child's home may be in an apartment with other families, a trailer, Grandma's residence, a homeless shelter, or a group home. Consultants who are collaborating with other adults for the development and well-being of children with special needs should use broad, inclusive definitions of "family," "parent," and "home."

Increases are evident in poverty levels, births to adolescent parents, and the rise of nonbiological parents as primary caretakers (foster care, grandmothers, extended family, adoptive parents, and so on). There are increasing numbers of families with cultural minority backgrounds, single-parent families, parents with disabilities, gay or lesbian parents, immigrant families, and blended and extended families. Consultants need to help other school personnel recognize and respect differences in family configurations. Educators should respond in individually relevant ways rather than make assumptions about families based on the nature of the home, family, and parent. In this book, we use the terms "parent," "family," and "home" in the most inclusive and broadest sense.

RATIONALE FOR COLLABORATIVE FAMILY-SCHOOL PARTNERSHIPS

When school personnel and family members work together in a collaborative, respectful, and trustful manner, the results are dramatic. Such partnerships enhance the educational attainment of students. Benefits, including increased satisfaction for parents as well as school-based educators, are evident in a number of research studies. Family-school partnerships are mandated by legislation pertaining to the education of students with special needs. So collaborating with parents and caregivers is not just the "right thing to do"; it is required by law.

The importance of parent and family engagement in educational efforts on behalf of their children is becoming a priority for many school and districts (Reid, 2015). In 2014, the U.S. Department of Education released a family- and community-engagement model to encourage districts and states to adopt parent-engagement efforts linked directly to student learning. Also in 2014, the National Association for Family, School, and Community Engagement was formed. The group is helping lead the momentum of prioritizing home-school partnerships. Cities such as Boston, MA; Albuquerque, NM; and New Haven, CT, are implementing city-wide family engagement programs, and states such as Oregon are developing state-wide systems. Massachusetts is one of the states that are including family-engagement in their teacher-evaluation systems. The field of education is recognizing that parents and families are natural partners in producing positive student outcomes.

Benefits of Family and School Partnership

School, family, and community provide overlapping spheres of influence on children's behavior and achievement. All spheres should be included for involvement by the collaborative team in partnerships with students at the center. Student development and learning at all levels of education are supported by strong home-school relationships.

Extensive research shows that family involvement can enhance a student's chances for success in school and significantly improve achievement. Students have higher attendance rates, more pro-social behavior, better test scores, and higher homework completion rates when their families are engaged in home partnerships with schools. Level of family involvement predicts children's academic and social development as they progress from early childhood education programs through K–12 schools and into higher education (Caspe, Lopez, & Wolos, 2007; Goodall & Montgomery, 2014; O'Donnell & Kirkner, 2014; Wilder, 2014).

For preschool children, family involvement means improved cognitive and social development. In an experimental research study on parent involvement at the early childhood level, the Harvard Family Research Project found that family participation in school activities is associated with child language; self-help; and social, motor, adaptive, and basic school skills (Weiss, Caspe, & Lopez, 2006). Their research showed that frequency of parent-teacher contact and involvement at early-childhood sites is associated with preschool performance.

Relationships between homes and schools have positive short-term and long-term benefits for elementary school students as well. Barnard (2004) showed that when low-income African American families maintained continuously high rates of parent participation in elementary school, children were more likely to complete high school. Dearing, Kreider, Simpkins, and Weiss (2006) conducted a longitudinal study that showed consistent family involvement was predictive of gains in children's literacy performance. Dyson (2010) found family involvement had a significantly positive effect on students with disabilities. In a meta-analysis of studies examining the relationship of parent involvement with student academic achievement in urban elementary schools, Jeynes (2007) discovered that continuous and consistent parent involvement shields and protects children from the negative influences of poverty. This study suggests home-school collaboration may be one approach to reducing achievement gaps between white student groups and students-of-color groups.

At the middle and high school levels, family involvement is a powerful predictor of various positive academic and social outcomes (e.g., Froiland & Davidson, 2014; Jeynes, 2014). Because of the adolescent's increasing desire for autonomy and changes in school structure, family engagement in education tends to decrease in middle and high school. Nevertheless, family involvement in learning remains important in the adolescent years. Parents can monitor their adolescents' academic and social progress and acquire information they need to make decisions about their children's future. When parents partner with educators, they have the opportunity to learn skills that help with their student's needs as the child moves into adulthood, such as social skills, independent living, and preparation for further education and careers.

School personnel also benefit from working collaboratively with parents. Families and caregivers can provide information about children's histories and experiences and include their own wisdom about their children's interests and needs. Teachers learn more about students' backgrounds and receive support from family members who can provide encouragement to their children as they study and learn.

School systems benefit from home and school collaborations through improved attitudes toward schools and advocacy for school programs. A positive home-school relationship helps others in the schools and the community. Family involvement increases positive communication among all who are involved on the education team.

ACTIVITY 9.1
Communicating the Benefits of Home-School Collaboration

Write a letter to the editor of your local paper, describing the importance of home and school relationships. Or, prepare a short talk about that topic for the local school board or parent group. Show your letter to a community leader who is concerned about student success in the schools or practice your talk to others in your group. What are the strongest points of your ideas? How could your presentation of ideas be improved? Consider actually sending your letter or giving your talk in a public forum.

Legal Mandates for Family Engagement

Families of children and youth with special needs are among the strongest advocates for programs that function in our country. Legislators have been known to tell persons who lobby for special interests that they should model their zeal and intensity of preparation on what the parents of children with disabilities bring to legislative offices and meeting chambers. So a brief overview here of legislative action concerning families and schools will be enlightening. School personnel need to be aware of several mandates intended to ensure and strengthen educational partnerships between home and school. The Education for All Handicapped

Children Act of 1975 (EAHCA) prescribes several rights for families of children with disabilities. Succeeding amendments have extended those rights and responsibilities.

Legislation mandating family involvement is part of EAHCA, the Handicapped Children's Protection Act, Early Intervention for Infants and Toddlers (Part H of P.L. 99-457), and the Individuals with Disabilities Education Act (IDEA, P.L. 101-476). Passage of P.L. 94-142 in 1975 guaranteed families the right to due process, prior notice and consent, access to records, and participation in decision-making. To these basic rights the 1986 Handicapped Children's Protection Act added collections of attorney's fees for parents who prevail in due process hearings or court suits. The Early Intervention Amendment was part of the reauthorized and amended P.L. 94-142. Passed in 1986, it provides important provisions for children from birth through five years and their families. Part H addresses infants and toddlers with disabilities or who are at-risk for developmental delays. Procedural safeguards for families were continued and participation in the Individualized Family Service Plan (IFSP) was added.

The IFSP is developed by a multidisciplinary team with family members as active participants. Part B, Section 691, mandates service to all children with disabilities from ages three to five and permits noncategorical services. Children may be served according to the needs of their families, allowing a wide range of services with parent training. This amendment fosters collaboration based on family-focused methods. The legislation speaks of families in a broad sense, not just a mother-father pair as the family unit, and families' choices are considered in all decisions.

The 1990 amendments under P.L. 101-476 increased participation by children and adults with disabilities and their families. An example is the formation of community transition councils with active participation of parents in the groups. Subsequent court decisions and statutory amendments have clarified and strengthened parent rights (Martin, 1991). The spirit of the law is met when educators develop positive, collaborative relationships with families.

The IDEA Amendments of 1997 were signed into law in June 1997, after two years of analysis, hearings, and discussion. This reauthorization of IDEA, as Public Law 105-17, brought many changes to P.L. 94-142. Parent participation in eligibility and placement decisions, and mediation as a means of resolving parent-school controversies are two critically important areas of change. P.L. 105-17 strengthened the involvement of parents in all decision-making involving their children (National Information Center for Children and Youth with Disabilities, 1997). The 1997 amendments were reauthorized in 2004 as P.L. 108-446, the No Child Left Behind (NCLB) legislation. NCLB mandated that schools give parents the tools they need to support their children's learning in the home and also that they communicate regularly with families about children's academic progress, provide opportunities for family workshops, and offer parents chances to engage in parent leadership activities at the school site.

MOVING TO EQUAL PARTNERSHIPS WITH FAMILIES

Successful educational consultants realize that involvement is not synonymous with collaboration. Goodall and Montgomery (2014) describe a continuum between parental involvement with schools to parental engagement in children's learning. Their model is not a simple progression with steady movement toward an equal partnership. Families may be at different places along the continuum, depending on the age of the children, family history and characteristics, and experiences with schools. Goodall and Montgomery call this a "messy web of interactions." Consultants should not expect parents to be on similar spots on the continuum or make a steady, unswerving journey to full partnership. Consultants have found that sometimes just the initial stages of establishing trust and mutual respect will take a year or two to develop.

Most educational consultants recognize the importance of family engagement, but moving beyond the "What can parents do for the school?" question poses a challenge for some educators. Christie (2005) believes it is easier to talk about what parents can do for the school than it is to listen to parents about what they know their children need. Sometimes when parents appear not to care, Christie says, it is because they know that what they have to say probably will not be heard. In her study that involved fifty-seven parents, Wanat (1997) found that parents had specific ideas about what constituted meaningful involvement. One parent summarized legitimate parent involvement as "everything you do with the child, because education involves a lot more than just sitting at school." It would be good for education consultants to remember this statement when they work collaboratively with parents.

True partnership features mutual collaboration and respect for the expertise of all parties. Authentic partnerships between schools and families are represented by the **Equal Partnership Model**. Too often parent involvement is perceived as teachers and school personnel *giving* parents "things to do, things to read, things to change." True equal partnership calls for consultants to promote mutual trust, respect, and parity. Not only should families be involved with schools, but educators also must be involved with families. In these cases, the teacher is the person who "calls the shots," who has the control in the situation. Developing a parent workshop on discipline or a volunteer program without considering strengths, needs, and goals of parents is a failure to respect the parents. This may communicate that educators know more about what parents need that do the parents themselves. This is not an equal partnership.

Success of the Equal Partnership Model for home-school collaboration is based on these principles:

- Families are a constant in children's lives and must be equal partners in all decisions affecting the child's educational program.
- Family involvement includes a wide range of family structures.
- All families have strengths and coping skills that can be identified and enhanced.
- Families are sources of wisdom and knowledge about their children.
- Diversity and individual differences among people are to be valued and respected.

Video Example from YouTube

▶ ENHANCEDetext
Video Example 9.1.

As you watch this video, listen to how school personnel and parents discuss the partnership between home and school. (https://www.youtube.com/watch?v=ZYbhnsmF--U)

The Equal Partnership Model

The Equal Partnership Model includes specific skills, attitudes, and behaviors on the part of educational consultants. The model defines home-school collaboration as the development and maintenance of positive, respectful, egalitarian relationships between home and school.

It includes mutual problem solving with shared decision-making and goal setting for students' needs. The five steps of the Equal Partnership Model are described in the next section, and tools for developing the model are provided.

Central to the model are respect for family concerns and priorities, awareness of family skills and assets, and use of family and community resources and supports. Family-centered programs are flexible and individualized; they focus on communication and developing and maintaining relationships. Building home-school collaboration takes time and expertise. This is a tall order for educational consultants, but empowering relationships and better outcomes for students depend on this shared sense of respect and care.

DEVELOPING HOME-SCHOOL PARTNERSHIPS: THE EQUAL PARTNERSHIP MODEL

Home-school collaboration practices have many variations. Effective collaboration efforts depend on school policies; attitudes of teachers; their beliefs about family roles and the efficacy of family involvement; school and community resources for families; and the experience, trust, and communication skills of school personnel and family members. When school personnel collaborate with family members, they nurture and maintain partnerships that facilitate shared efforts to promote student achievement. As families and teachers plan together and implement plans of action, they find that working as a team is more effective than working alone. Each can be assured that the other is doing the best for the child and each can support the other, thus producing positive educational outcomes for children with special needs.

Five basic steps of the Equal Partnership Model will assist school personnel in developing successful home-school partnerships:

Step 1: Examining personal values, attitudes, and perceptions
Step 2: Building collaborative relationships
Step 3: Initiating home and school interactions
Step 4: Individualizing for families
Step 5: Evaluating home and school collaborations

Step 1: Examining Personal Values, Attitudes, and Perceptions

Value systems are individualistic and complex. Our values influence our viewpoints toward cultural backgrounds, gender, age, education, family structures, sexual orientation, and many other issues that are part of working collaboratively with families. Therefore, an initial step in collaborating with families is to examine one's own values and beliefs about parents and their interactions with their children and teachers. Figure 9.1 is a checklist for examining one's own values and attitudes toward parents and other family members. Inventorying and adjusting one's attitudes about families are the hardest parts of consulting with them. Attitudes and perceptions about families and their roles in partnerships greatly influence implementation of the collaborative consulting process.

FIGURE 9.1   Examining Own Values

Instructions: Rate belief or comfort level, from 1 (very comfortable or very strong) to 5 (very uncomfortable or not strong at all).

How comfortable do you feel with each?

_____ Parents and others whom you think are overly protective

_____ Homeless families

_____ Families who send their children to school without breakfast

_____ Parents who have lost control of their children

_____ Volunteers in the classroom

_____ Being invited to students' homes

_____ Teachers who do not follow through

_____ Families that include gay or lesbian parents

_____ Students attending conferences

_____ Parents who do not allow their children to be tested

_____ Families of a different racial or ethnic group from yours

_____ Family members who do not speak English

_____ Others who think special needs children should be kept in self-contained classrooms

_____ Teachers who think modifying curriculum materials or tests is watering down the lessons

_____ Family members who drink excessively or use drugs

How strongly do you believe the following?

_____ Family members should be able to call you or e-mail you at home.

_____ Newsletters and listservs are important communication tools.

_____ Family members should volunteer in the classroom.

_____ General classroom teachers can teach students with special needs.

_____ All children can learn.

_____ Family members should come to conferences.

_____ Resistance is normal and to be expected in educational settings.

_____ Children in divorced families have special problems.

_____ Family influence is more important than school influence.

_____ Sometimes consultants should just tell others the best thing to do.

_____ Consultants are advocates for children.

_____ Teachers should modify their classrooms for children with special needs.

_____ It is a teacher's fault when children fail.

_____ Consultants are experts in educating special needs children.

_____ Some people do not want children with special needs to succeed.

Do you think all teachers, administrators, counselors, psychologists, parents, grandparents, social workers, and students would have responded as you did? What happens when members of the same educator team have different views?

In addition to examining values and beliefs related to specific parent and teacher roles, consultants should think about their personal values and skills that relate to home-school collaboration. Figure 9.2 provides a self-assessment rating scale for reflecting on personal attitudes and perceptions concerning the collaboration of parents and educators.

School personnel also must keep in mind that family members are not a homogeneous group; therefore, experiences with one family member cannot be generalized to other family members. A grandfather and a teenaged mother do not have the same life

FIGURE 9.2   Self-Assessment of Attitudes and Perceptions

Rate yourself on the following, from 1 (very little) to 5 (always).

1. I understand the importance of home-school collaboration.	1	2	3	4	5
2. I recognize the concerns parents may have about working with me.	1	2	3	4	5
3. I recognize that parents of students with special needs may have emotional and social needs I may not understand.	1	2	3	4	5
4. I recognize and respect the expertise of families.	1	2	3	4	5
5. I feel comfortable working with families whose values and attitudes differ from mine.	1	2	3	4	5
6. I am persistent and patient as I develop relationships with families.	1	2	3	4	5
7. I am comfortable with my skills for communicating with families.	1	2	3	4	5
8. I am realistic about the barriers for me in working with families.	1	2	3	4	5
9. I find it difficult to understand why some families have the attitudes they have.	1	2	3	4	5
10. I recognize that some family members will have problems interacting with me because of their experience with other teachers.	1	2	3	4	5

experiences or ideas about education, although they may have many cultural, religious, or linguistic commonalities. Additional resources for examining values and for increasing cultural sensitivity are found in an earlier chapter.

ACTIVITY 9.2
Examining Your Personal Values and Attitudes

Work in small groups, choosing as a group to use either Figure 9.1 or 9.2 to examine and discuss your personal values, attitudes, and perceptions about parents and families or about family-school partnerships. Individually complete the chosen assessment. Then compare your responses. Discuss the similarities and differences. Why are some of the responses different within the group? Why are others similar? What experiences have you had as students, parents, educators, and community members that are reflected in your responses? Show respect for differences in your group as you discuss what you have learned.

Step 2: Building Collaborative Relationships

The second step in the Equal Partnership Model of collaboration with families is building positive, lasting collaborative relationships. This critical step involves:

1. Using appropriate communication
2. Focusing on family strengths and needs
3. Honoring parental expertise
4. Providing social support

Using Appropriate Communication. Friendly, positive relationships and honest, respectful communication can help bridge barriers that prevent effective home-school collaboration. As emphasized in an earlier chapter, basic communication and rapport-building skills are essential for establishing healthy, successful relationships with family members. Astute teachers avoid any words and phrases that may be perceived as thinking that having a student with one or more disabilities is undesirable. They listen for the messages given by parents and respond to their verbal and nonverbal cues. In addition, when communicating with families, school personnel must avoid jargon that can be misunderstood or misinterpreted. Parents often feel alienated by professional educators, and one common cause is words (e.g., pedagogy, rubrics, dual-immersion classrooms, response to intervention) and acronyms (e.g., IFSP, ITBS, FBA, 504 Plan) that pepper the conversation without explanation of their meaning. Word choice can either ease or inhibit communication with parents, and professional educators must respect language variations created by differences in culture, education, occupation, age, and place of origin.

Consulting teachers often find that one of the most important, but difficult, aspects of developing relationships with parents is listening to them. The challenge lies in listening to parents' messages even though the teachers might disagree strongly with family members because their attitudes and values might differ significantly. Although the quality of the interaction should be a primary focus in parent relationships, the numbers and variety of initiated communications are important as well. To initiate partnerships, educators have effectively used such communication tools as phone calls, introductory and welcoming letters, newsletters, teacher-to-parent calendars, and notepads with identifying logos. Each note, phone call, e-mail, conversation, or conference, whether taking place in a formal setting or on the spur of the moment at the grocery store, should reflect the willingness and commitment of school personnel to work with parents as they face immense responsibilities in providing for the special needs of their child.

It is important for teachers to arrange and encourage more regular, informal contacts with parents. Family members often report being put off by the formality inherent in some scheduled conferences, particularly as often happens at middle school and high school levels when limited to fifteen minutes, in a large, noisy gym with no privacy, after waiting in line for their turn, during scheduled district parent-teacher conferences or in a classroom with other families shifting from one foot to the other just outside the door. Teachers should ask parents to share their preferred modes of communication. Phone calls and e-mails or text messages are appropriate for positive reports, but should not be used to discuss weighty concerns. Families are usually happy to get Instagrams or texted photos of their child at school, but consultants should always be mindful of the underlying tone that each communication conveys. Many parents appreciate receiving individualized tips such as suggestions for discussion topics related to school work, developmentally appropriate education-related birthday gifts such as books or software, or simple do-it-yourself projects families can do together. Some consultants have found that group e-mails and school websites are an effective way to communicate with families. However, educators must keep in mind that some families do not have access to this technology and that providing information does not usually prompt interaction. Educators should never assume they have *communicated* something with a parent just because they sent it or posted it. When in doubt, it is best to call or set up a face-to-face meeting.

The effective collaborative partner provides support and reinforcement for family members in their family roles. In addition to listening to family members and acknowledging their expertise, it is crucial to empower families by giving them positive feedback about their efforts to support their child's education. Families often get very little reinforcement for parenting, particularly for the extra efforts they expend in caring for children with special needs. They should be encouraged and commended for providing time and space for homework and discussing school with their children. Too few families hear positive comments about their children. Some teachers send home "up slips," putting them in a different format from the "down slips" that families too often receive, and have conferences with families because the student is performing *well* in the classroom. Families appreciate having their special efforts recognized, just as teachers do.

Focusing on Family Strengths.   The Equal Partnership Model emphasizes an empowerment approach. Rather than focusing on what is going wrong, educational collaborators focus on family members and the strength of their experiences. The Equal Partnership Model stresses not only respect for the curriculum of the child's home and community, but also the importance of providing opportunities for family members to use their strengths and skills to contribute to the formal education of their children. This relationship is not based on a deficit model of blame and inequality, although it is often difficult for consultants to overcome the negativity trap when society is obsessed with finding fault.

Educational consultants should never assume that parents lack motivation, skills, and knowledge. Parents of students with special needs have played a significant part in policy, legislation, and programs for students. Parents have started national organizations; provided community leadership in developing new services; and written books, plays, and television shows about individuals with disabilities and their families.

Tools for assessing parent strengths include interviews and checklists that are useful in determining what types of contributions families can bring to the partnership. One example of a strength assessment is provided in Figure 9.3. Family assets can be conceptualized along four levels of involvement (Kroth, 1985), from strengths that all family members have to skills that only a few family members are willing and able to contribute. For example, all parents have information about their children that schools need. At more intensive levels of collaboration, some family members are willing and able to tutor their children at home, come to meetings, help make bulletin boards, and volunteer to help at school. At the highest level of collaboration, only a few parents can be expected to lobby for special education, provide community leadership and advocacy, or conduct parent-to-parent programs.

Educators can also use checklists, conversations, home visits, and community involvements to learn about the strengths, interests, and needs of parents and the communities in which the families live. If school personnel offer workshops and materials that are not based on family interests and needs, a message is communicated to parents that educators know more about family needs than the family themselves; then the family involvement is not a true partnership. Figure 9.4 provides an example of a needs assessment/interest inventory.

School educators who use strengths and interests of family and community members to engage them in education of infants and toddlers, preschool and kindergarten

FIGURE 9.3 Identifying Family Strengths

Families! We need your help. Many of you have asked how you can help provide a high-quality educational program for your children. You have many talents, interests, and skills you can contribute to help children learn better and enjoy school more. Please let us know what you are interested in doing.

_____ 1. I would like to volunteer in school.
_____ 2. I would like to help with special events or projects.
_____ 3. I have a hobby or talent I could share with the class.
_____ 4. I would be glad to talk about travel or jobs, or interesting experiences that I have had.
_____ 5. I could teach the class how to _____.
_____ 6. I could help with bulletin boards and art projects.
_____ 7. I could read to children.
_____ 8. I would like to help my child at home.
_____ 9. I would like to tutor a child.
_____ 10. I would like to work on a buddy or parent-to-parent system with other parents whose children have problems.
_____ 11. I would like to teach a workshop.
_____ 12. I can do typing, word processing, phoning, making materials, or preparing resources at home.
_____ 13. I would like to assist with student clubs.
_____ 14. I would like to help organize a parent group.
_____ 15. I want to help organize and plan parent partnership programs.
_____ 16. I would like to help with these kinds of activities:

At school _____

At home _____

In the community _____

Your comments, concerns, and questions are welcome. THANKS!

Name: _____

Child's Name: _____

How to Reach You: _____

students, as well as primary, middle, and secondary students, can approach this in many creative ways. Many schools are using an interactive web-based process for encouraging homework that counts on families to help students complete homework proficiently and earn better grades.

At the early childhood level, Mayer, Ferede, and Hou (2006) use storybooks to successfully promote family engagement. The online Family Involvement Storybook Corner that is found on the Harvard Family Research Program website promotes awareness and practice of family involvement through storybooks. Another example is the Raising a Reader Program, based on the work of Judith K. Bernhard. More information can be found on the

FIGURE 9.4   Identifying Family Interests

Families! We want to learn more about you so that we can work together helping your child learn. Please take a few minutes to respond to these questions so your voice can be heard. It will help the Home-Schools Advisory Team develop programs for families, teachers, and children.

Check those items you are most interested in.

_____ 1. Family resource libraries or information centers
_____ 2. Helping my child learn language and social skills
_____ 3. Support programs for my child's siblings
_____ 4. Talking with my child about sex
_____ 5. Helping with language and social skills
_____ 6. Mental health services
_____ 7. Talking with another parent about common problems
_____ 8. Respite care or babysitters
_____ 9. My role as a parent
_____ 10. Classes about managing behavior problems
_____ 11. Making my child happy
_____ 12. Managing my time and resources
_____ 13. Making toys and educational materials
_____ 14. Reducing screen time
_____ 15. What happens when my child grows up
_____ 16. Recreation and camps for my child
_____ 17. State-wide meetings for families
_____ 18. Vocational opportunities for my child
_____ 19. Talking to my child's teacher
_____ 20. Talking with other families
_____ 21. Learning about child development
_____ 22. Things families can do to support teachers
_____ 23. Home activities that support school learning
_____ 24. Information about the school and my child's classes
_____ 25. Helping my child become more independent
_____ 26. Others?

_____

_____

_____

Thanks for your help!

Name of family member responding to this form, and relationship to child:

_____

Child's name: _____

Raising A Reader website. She and her colleagues built their Early Programs on parent strengths that benefit children by giving parents a prominent role as their children's literacy teachers. Raising a Reader is a nonprofit organization in California whose purpose is engaging parents in a routine of daily "book cuddling" with their children birth through age five.

Siblings of children with disabilities often need information about disabilities, opportunities to talk about their feelings and concerns, and time to hear about the experiences of other siblings of children with disabilities. Some common feelings include guilt over a sibling having a disability while they do not, anger and resentment about getting less attention, and frustration or embarrassment over having to deal with a sibling who is different. Families need to know it is not uncommon for siblings to have these feelings and it is helpful for them to be able to discuss their feelings honestly with the parents and appropriate school personnel. Similarly, parents may feel guilty that they spend too much time focusing on the needs of the child with the disability and not giving other children in the family equal time and attention. A consulting teacher can facilitate these discussions and provide resources such as children's books that address sibling issues around disabilities. Families need others with whom to share their feelings of pride and joy, and to discuss ways of planning for the future (Cramer et al., 1997; Fiedler, Simpson, & Clark, 2007).

Including the Expertise of Family Members. Family members fulfill a range of roles from purveyors of knowledge about the child to advocates for political action. Indeed, they are experts about their children, their families, and often about their communities. What school educators learn from parents, siblings, caregivers, and community members makes them better able to be successful with students. Family expertise should be honored by remembering that families are:

- A group of individuals with initiative, strengths, and important experiences
- The best advocates and case managers for the child with special needs
- The best information resource about the child, the family, and their culture
- Partners in setting goals and finding solutions

Not all parents are ready or able to provide this expertise, as described in Kroth's four-levels model discussed earlier. The consultant must respect and support the courage and commitment of family members who struggle with the challenges of daily living faced by all families and those with exceptional needs in particular. Recognizing, supporting, and reinforcing interventions on behalf of the child with special needs will promote an increased sense of competency and help create a safe, nurturing environment for children, while maintaining the unique cultural and contextual characteristics of their family unit.

School personnel must guard against valuing or privileging teacher knowledge and experience over family knowledge and experience. As stated earlier, it is vital to recognize that parents are the experts when it comes to knowing about their children, no matter how many tests educators have administered to students or how many hours they have observed them in the classroom. If professional educators are perceived as *the* experts, and the *only* experts, false expectations may create unrealistic pressure on them. Some family members find it difficult to relate to experts. So a beautiful "boulevard of progress" becomes that one-way street where there are only narrow, one-sided elements of judging, advising, and sending solutions.

Communicating messages of equality, flexibility, and a sharing attitude will facilitate effective home-school collaboration. The message that should be given to parents of students with special needs is, "I know a lot about this, and *you* know a lot about that. Let's put our information and ideas together to help your child." Just as school personnel have much expertise to share with families about the education of students with special needs, parents have much to communicate to school personnel about their children. This parental expertise can be regarded as "curriculum of the home" and "curriculum of the community" (Barbour, Barbour, & Scully, 2008). Such information includes parent-child conversation topics, how leisure reading is encouraged, deferral of immediate gratifications, long-term goals, how homework is assisted and assessed, amount of screen time and how it is monitored, with whom the child plays, how affections and interests in the child's accomplishments are demonstrated, and what community activities are important in the family's life. If school personnel do not understand (or attempt to understand) the curriculum of the home and the community, equal partnerships are difficult to establish. When parents and teachers work together as equals, they have more opportunities to express their own knowledge and can come to respect each other's wisdom and expertise.

Providing Social Support. For many families with exceptional children, support networks are a vital part of their lives. Families rely on informal and formal social support networks for the information and guidance they need to carry out responsibilities for child rearing, children's learning, and child development.

For families of children with disabilities, supports are a crucial aspect of family-focused collaboration. Schools can provide a rich array of formal support for the child, parent, and family in the forms of information and environmental experiences to strengthen family and child competence and influence student outcomes. Families often need additional skills and knowledge to become strong advocates for their children and partners with their children's teachers. This knowledge includes information, communication skills, problem-solving skills, and life management strategies. Providing this support for parents, families, and siblings of children with exceptionalities also means fostering community support and advocacy (Fiedler, Simpson, & Clark, 2007). For example, resources for studying the interests and needs of siblings of people with special health and developmental needs are available online. An example is the Siblings Support organization's website.

According to extensive research by Dunst (2000) and his colleagues, informal support has a stronger relationship to many child, parent, and family outcomes than formal support. Parents often report feelings of isolation and of being alone in their commitment to their children's well-being. Informal social support means parents have a network they can call on for help, friendship, and advice. Families may have the capacity to garner support; however, many families, especially those with young children who have just been referred to special services or diagnosed with a learning or behavior problem, need help from schools in developing social support networks. Consultants should encourage activities that help families develop informal support networks such as parent-to-parent groups and informal multiple-family gatherings. Schools can also provide opportunities to access informal social support by arranging discussion groups, hosting potluck meals at school or in the community, having regular family coffee hours, and many other activities. Many parents of students with disabilities find that sharing experiences and learning from other parents is a critical source of support and encouragement. Some parents find advice from other parents to be more credible than advice from school personnel.

Step 3: Initiating Home-School Interactions

Parents want their children to be successful in school. Even parents who are considered "hard to reach" usually want to be more involved. Most, however, wait to be invited before becoming engaged with school personnel. Unfortunately, many have to wait for years before someone opens the door and provides them the *opportunity* to become a team member with others who care about the educational and social successes of their children. Parent satisfaction with their involvement is directly related to perceived opportunities for involvement (Goodall & Montgomery, 2014). They are more motivated to carry on when they are aware that the results of their time and energy are helping their child learn.

Successful educators establish rapport with families early in the school year. They contact parents right away, before problems develop, so that the first family contact is a positive one. Research has shown that when family members are welcome in schools and classrooms, and their child's work and experiences are meaningful to them, parents often experience new aspirations for themselves and for their children. This provides another important reason to work collaboratively and respectfully with parents. Many practitioners have found that the best practice is to ask parents to reflect on what has made schools and educators feel welcoming and inviting.

Step 4: Individualizing for Families

Special education professionals are trained to be competent at individualizing educational programs for students' needs. Nevertheless, they may assume that all family members have similar strengths and needs, thereby overlooking the need to individualize family involvement programs. Individualizing communications with parents is not the norm. A report of parent and family involvement in education (Noel, Stark, & Redford, 2015) showed that 87 percent of students (K–12) had parents who reported receiving school newsletters, memos, e-mail, or notices addressed to all parents from the school but only 57 percent of students had parents who reported receiving notes or email specifically about their child.

Individualizing for families means knowing the strengths and needs of family members. Using checklists and forms like those provided in this chapter help teachers learn about the needs parents have for information, translation, social support, advocacy, or referral. By using the assessments discussed earlier, and taking care to avoid stereotypes and judgments, educational personnel will be more successful in involving parents as partners in their child's learning program. Individualizing for families based on their strengths and needs promotes **family empowerment**, that is, the attitudes and skills for families to determine their own futures. When educators partner with parents and other family members on behalf of children with special needs, parents become more confident that they have the information and problem-solving skills they need in order to deal with current and future situations regarding their children and families.

Several program attributes can help assure consultants that school-home-community programming will result in family empowerment. Dunst (2002) lists and describes the principles of Family Support America that promote family empowerment. Examples of those principles are:

- Relationships should be based on equality and respect.
- Educators should enhance families' abilities to support growth and development in all family members.
- Schools should affirm and strengthen families' cultural, racial, and linguistic identities and enhance the abilities of families to function in a multicultural society.
- Services and systems for families should be fair, responsible, and accountable to the families served.

Successful work with parents calls for establishing respectful and trusting relationships, as well as responding to the needs of all partners. The degree to which parents are placed in an egalitarian role, with a sense of choice, empowerment, and ownership in the education process, is a crucial variable in successful collaboration.

Individualizing for families means considering the multiple diversities of the family, such as family structure, cultural heritage, language, country of origin, race, and other aspects of diversity discussed in a previous chapter. Traditional approaches to reaching out to families are not always appropriate for families from some cultural and some non-dominant groups. Educators must develop cultural competence that demonstrates acceptance and respect for diversity and differences. This allows for individualization of educational programs for students and individualization of parent interactions to be done in a manner that respects the family. Some consultants have been successful at learning about cultures they serve by observing influential members of different groups. Other recommendations include spending time with people of that culture, identifying a cultural guide, reading the literature (professional as well as fiction) by and for persons of the culture, attending relevant cultural events, and asking questions in respectful ways. Other recommendations for consults were discussed in an earlier chapter.

Educators collaborating with families who are culturally, linguistically, and in other ways different from that family must keep in mind that one approach does not fit all ranges of diversity (Iruka, Cureton, & Eke, 2014; Parette & Petch-Hogan, 2000). Schools can investigate programs that have been successful with parents and families coming from different cultural and socio-economic backgrounds such as the 'Ohana math program in Hawaii (Muccio, Kuwahara-Fujita, & Otsuji, 2014). One program, the Parent Institute for Quality Education (PIQE), started with Hispanic families and has been replicated in many communities across the country. It was started in California to connect families, schools, and community members as partners in advancing the education of every child through parent engagement. This organization includes parent engagement education classes, workshops for parents and educators, and activities to promote school success.

Step 5: Evaluating Home-School Collaboration

Evaluation of home-school collaborative activities and programs can indicate whether families' needs are being met and their strengths are being utilized. If you are starting a literacy program or a family engagement initiative, you will want to know if it's working. Evaluation will help consultants understand the impacts of their initiatives on students, parents, and schools and will point to ways to improve a program. Assessment tools used after a workshop, conference, or at the conclusion of the school year allow school personnel to ask parents, "How did we do in facilitating your learning of the new information or accessing the new services?" or "How do you see the new twenty-four-hour parent center benefiting your family?" If data show that the activity gave families the information they needed, provided them with the resources they wanted, and offered them the opportunities they requested, educators will know whether or not to continue with the program or modify it.

Educators also should evaluate their own involvement with families. This means assessing their inclusion of family strengths and skills to facilitate educational programs with children who have special needs. Did teachers get the information they needed from families? How many volunteer hours did parents contribute? What were the results of home tutoring on student achievement? What changes in family attitudes about the school district were measured?

POTENTIAL CHALLENGES TO COLLABORATING WITH FAMILIES

The success of family collaboration activities is based on partnerships developed and maintained by using interaction and communication skills such as those described in a previous chapter. However, other barriers may overshadow the need for effective communication. These surface as formidable challenges to educators even before lines of communication are established. Examples of such barriers are time limitations, anticipation of negative and stressful or punishing interactions, denial of problems, blaming, or a personal sense of failure in parenting and teaching. Collaborative consultants who recognize potential barriers to home-school partnerships will be better prepared to use successful and appropriate strategies in bridging the gap between home and school. Four potential challenges for educational consultants are discussed here: working with families with diverse characteristics and structures; the history and attitudes of parents and other family members; the ubiquitous Blame Game; and cultural and linguistic diversity.

Diverse Characteristics of Families

Major changes in immigration patterns and in the diversity of the U.S. population will add to the complexity of collaboration with families. Diverse and changing family characteristics and structures often make facilitating home-school collaboration challenging for consultants who are not familiar with specific family compositions or characteristics. For example, a consultant who has worked with families who are homeless may not be as challenged in engaging them as a consultant who has no experience or knowledge about families who are homeless. A consultant who has gay, lesbian, or transsexual friends will be less challenged collaborating with families with two mothers or two fathers. A consultant who grew up in a large city may be challenged by the context of rural families. And a consultant who has a family member with a disability may be less challenged working with parents or caregivers with a disability. Educational personnel should be cognizant that their own attitudes, perceptions, and parent engagement competencies are greatly impacted by their experiences with and familiarity of individual and family characteristics.

Parents of children with special needs face many economic and personal hardships such as work schedules and health concerns. Many types of disability are very expensive for families, and the impact on the family budget created by the special needs of a child may produce formidable hardships. Sometimes families arrive at the point where they feel their other children are being neglected by all the attention to the child with exceptional learning needs. This adds to their frustration and stress. In addition, children with special needs and their families are vulnerable to stereotypes of society about disabilities. The ways in which families cope with the frustrations and stress influence their interactions with school personnel.

Low-income families may have difficulty with transportation and childcare, making it hard to attend meetings or volunteer in school even when they would like to do so. A solo parent, already burdened with great responsibilities, may be particularly stressed in parenting a child with special needs. This role can be overwhelming at times. For collaborative efforts to produce results, the interaction must fit the single parent's time and energy level. (See Figure 9.5.) School personnel may need to tailor their requests for conferences and home interventions to the availability of the single parent. Sometimes a single parent may need additional emotional support or just someone to chat with about concerns.

A two-parent (or four-parent), two-home student may face struggles in dealing with repercussions from family strife leading to the divorce, breakup of the family, and passage back and forth between parents, oftentimes with stepparents and new brothers and sisters, and possibly a change of schools, in the mix. Educators at school and at home must organize a cooperative and collaborative team for managing the academic and emotional needs of the students. As just one example, homework assignments can be problematic for a child who will be with one parent for only a short time, then will move on for a turn with the other parent, and return to the first parent to repeat the procedure time after time. Teachers will need to develop strategies to keep both family units involved and informed.

Many families are overwhelmed by family crises and normal life events. Others face multiple stressors such as long work hours, illness and disability, and overwhelming responsibilities. Many are discouraged and burned out. Such situations make collaboration a challenge for collaborative consultants and many families. Despite these potential challenges, an Equal Partnership Model is the goal for home-school collaboration.

Attitudes and Perceptions of Parents and Caregivers

Historical, attitudinal, or perceptual factors in regard to work and to education can influence family participation. Parents of children with learning and behavior problems can be effective advocates and change agents for *their* children; however, they may be inhibited by their own attitudes or circumstances. For example, many parents, while very concerned about their child's education, are fearful and suspicious of schools, teachers, and education in general because of their own educational history or past negative interactions with school

FIGURE 9.5   "Keep Parents Informed"

personnel. Such attitudes provide a challenge; however, consultants use many strategies to demonstrate their respect for parents and their own non-judgmental attitudes. A key to success with wary parents is persistence and patience. Meeting outside of the school, conducting home visits, demonstrating support of efforts to help their children with schoolwork, and acknowledging small steps of trust and communication are common teacher strategies.

The Blame Game

Family members may avoid school interactions because they fear being blamed as the cause of their children's problems. Sometimes teachers do blame parents for exacerbating learning and behavior problems ("I can't do anything here at school because it gets undone when they go home!"). But blaming hampers development of mutually supportive relationships. Family members are very sensitive to blaming words and attitudes from school personnel. A teacher who is part of a therapeutic foster family reported that he felt "blame and shame" after a school conference about the child with emotional and behavior problems who had been his foster child for two months. It is fair to assume that this was not a productive conference.

Consultants need to be wary of unintended messaged that might be interpreted as blaming. Examples to a parent: "I can see that traveling so much with your job would prevent you from attending the therapy sessions at the clinic." "If you would just follow the math tutoring suggestions I sent home the first of the year, your daughter might be able to complete the course and move to basic algebra." And whenever consultants hear a colleague say, "If only that parent would come to the behavior workshop (or help with homework, or come to parent conferences), Matty would be doing so much better in school!" Perceptive consultants recognize this as the Blame Game.

Judging attitudes, stereotypes, false expectations, and basic differences in values also act as barriers and diminish the collaborative efforts among teachers and families. It is challenging to feel comfortable with people who have very different attitudes and values. Teachers should make every effort not to reproach family members and to work hard as non-judging partners on the child's team. Educators, including teachers and parents, must abandon postures of blaming or criticism, and move on to collaboration and problem solving. It is important to remember that it does not matter where a "fault" lies. What matters is: Who steps up to address the problems and needs?

ACTIVITY 9.3
Assumptions–Ours and Those of Others

You have already thought about the problematic nature of assumptions and biases in a previous chapter. This activity is an opportunity to reflect on how assumptions and biases inhibit the development of positive home-school-community relationships. **Assumptions** are usually generalizations we make when we assume that what we know about one person or family is true of other people or families, or when we assume that what has happened in the past will always happen. Think about what assumptions may be operating in this scene: *A father rushes in for a conference with you; he is late. The man is dressed in soiled and wrinkled khaki shirt and trousers and when he shakes your hand, his is rough and callused. "Lo siento," he says and apologizes for being late. "How can I help out today?"* What assumptions might the teacher make in this circumstance? In what ways might that assumption be wrong? Think about how the scenario would play out under various possible teacher assumptions (e.g., this is a migrant worker; the man owns a big construction firm; the man speaks very little English). Reflect about assumptions you have made about parents or families based on their names, dress, language, choice of words, demeanor, etc. What assumptions might people make about you when they first meet you? How can we overcome our natural tendency to make assumptions? How can we help others avoid making assumptions that would impede the development of strong, trusting relationships? What other examples can you think of?

Cultural and Linguistic Diversity among Families

Active parent and community engagement in educational programs for culturally and linguistically diverse (CLD) students is essential (Rodriguez, Blatz, & Elbaum, 2014). Yet the differences among cultural and linguistic backgrounds of school personnel and their students make home-school collaboration a challenge. The unfortunate portrayal of CLD families as deficient in skills necessary for school readiness is a huge barrier to active parent participation. Misconceptions about parental concern for their children's schooling are all too prevalent among school personnel (de Valenzuela, Torres, & Chavez, 1998).

Effective collaborative consultants recognize that sometimes there are differing views between home and school about the involvement of families in the education of their children and varying levels of visibility for that involvement. Consultants should realize that parental activities to support child learning may not be visible, but may be very powerful. Recent research has demonstrated positive impacts of family engagement with immigrant, Latino, and other diverse families (Sibley & Dearing, 2014; Sime & Sheridan, 2014; Wessels & Trainin, 2014).

Educators should take careful note that the concept of *disability* is culturally and socially constructed. Each culture defines the parameters of what is considered normal, with some cultures having a broader or different definition of disability from that in U.S. schools

(Linan-Thompson & Jean, 1997). This may be one reason ethnically diverse parents seem to be less involved and less informed about their child's school life than parents in cultures where there are very specific definitions of what is normal in terms of ability and disability. It is important to learn from family members how their beliefs and practices will affect programs for children with special needs. Educational consultants who work with families must be aware of the family's perceptions of disability and use other terms such as "educational needs and strengths." Linan-Thompson and Jean (1997) suggest taking time to learn about family perceptions of special needs before carefully and thoroughly explaining the whole special education process. Teachers should use informal assessments in addition to formal assessment tools to help explain the disability on less formal terms, and use parents' preferred forms of communication (written note, informal meetings, or video- or audio files). Teachers can have documents translated so that families who do not read English in the home can be kept informed. Google Translate is a free app that allows users to type text or upload documents to be translated and to select from a wide array of languages.

The following ten strategies are helpful when collaborating with families from diverse cultural groups:

1. Acknowledge cultural differences and become aware of how they affect parent-teacher interactions.
2. Recognize the dynamics of group interactions such as etiquette and patterns of communication.
3. Go out into the community and meet the families on their own turf.
4. Adjust collaboration to legitimize and include culture-specific activities.
5. Learn about the families. Where are they from and when did they arrive? What cultural beliefs and practices influence their child-rearing practices, health and healing processes, and disability-causation attitudes?
6. Recognize that some families may be surprised by the extent of home-school collaboration expected in the United States.
7. Learn and use words and forms of greetings in the families' languages.
8. Work with cultural mediators or guides from the families' cultures to learn more about the culture in ways that will facilitate communication between school and home. Examples are: relatives, church members, neighbors, or older siblings.
9. Ask for help in structuring the child's school program to match home life, such as learning key words and phrases used at home.
10. Most of all, understand your own values, and educational and cultural history, then root out and discard any lingering stereotypes or misconceptions.

Having well-publicized policies at the district level that encourage home and school collaboration is an integral part of providing opportunities for minority family members to become full partners with teachers. Traditional methods of parent involvement, such as PTA meetings, open houses, or newsletters, seldom permit true collaboration; they construct instead a "territory" of education that many parents are hesitant to invade.

Concern, awareness, and commitment on the part of individuals in the educational system are beginning steps in challenging limitations that inhibit collaboration between teachers and families who have language, cultural, or other basic differences. Supporting and reinforcing families in their life roles is not always easy. Members of families with multiple problems often are viewed as having defective or faulty notions of parenting, minimal problem-solving skills, and mental health problems. For families with different values and expectations who must deal with high-risk factors such as poverty, mental illness, or drug and alcohol involvement, focusing on strengths and providing positive supports are best approaches for collaborators.

ACTIVITY 9.4

Creating a Family Engagement Case Study

The Harvard Family Research Project uses family engagement cases to contribute to teachers' abilities to work with families. The project recommends both using cases found on their website, as well as developing one's own case. The project has a "Create Your Own Case Toolkit," which can be accessed on their website. The toolkit has six steps to build a case (a story about family engagement that invites critical thinking and problem solving). Go to the toolkit website and create a family engagement case; the case can be from your own experience, an experience of someone else, or your imagination. Share your case with your group and the group's cases as an opportunity for discussion, reflection, and collaboration.

COLLABORATING IN MANDATED AND REGULAR MEETINGS

Working collaboratively and respectfully with parents in formalized planning such as IEP meetings and regular classroom-progress conferences is a vital yet sometimes challenging aspect of home-school collaboration. If parents only hear from teachers when formal meetings are scheduled, they are less likely to see themselves as equal partners. As one parent said to a teacher, "I take care of her at home; you are in charge of the school part." Planning and progress meetings and conferences should be only one of the many points of contact between school personnel and family members.

ENHANCEDetext
Video Example 9.3.

Watch this video, and notice the spirit of family-focused collaboration and how negative interactions are avoided.

Family Partners in IEP, IFSP, and ITP Planning

The Individualized Education Plan (IEP), Individualized Family Service Plan (IFSP), and Individualized Transition Plan (ITP) conferences can be a productive time or a frustrating experience. Parents may be emotional about their child's problems, and teachers can be apprehensive about meeting with the parents in emotion-laden situations with sensitive issues to discuss. A number of researchers have found that too little parent involvement in team decision-making, particularly relating to IEP, IFSP, and ITP development, is a major problem in special education programs (Boone, 1989).

School consultants will improve school-home collaboration in these areas if they provide family members with information before the meeting. For example, teacher consultants could provide student assessment data two weeks before the scheduled formal meeting in order to work collaboratively with families to develop goals and objectives (Diliberto & Brewer, 2012). Contrast this approach with the often typical formal meeting where a predetermined draft of goals is presented by school personnel, leaving parents feeling the IEP, IFSP, or ITP document is a *fait accompli* and the primary purpose in attending the meeting is to obtain their signature on the document. When teachers collaborate with parents in advance of formal meetings, they show respect for the knowledge families bring to the table while demonstrating that educators care about the student and value family input. Even a form or note sharing information and/or thoughts about possible goals and asking for input from the family can go a long way in demonstrating a desire for true collaboration. Discuss or ask for information about the student beyond academic areas (i.e., social, behavior, health, etc.). Ask families if there is anything they would like you to know about themselves or their family that will help you better serve their child or if there is any disability-specific information about their child that they would like to share with you or the team (Edwards & Da Fonte, 2012). Consultants can communicate with family members by phone, letter, or informal interview to inform them about names and roles of staff members who will attend; typical procedure for meetings; ways they can prepare for the meeting; contributions they will be encouraged to make; and ways in which follow-up to the meeting will be provided.

Diliberto and Brewer (2012) propose six key elements for successful IEP meetings: 1) pre-meeting planning; 2) meeting facilitator; 3) meeting agenda; 4) ground rules; 5) essential knowledge; 6) limited jargon. IEP team members should plan the IEP meeting together to assure that all are familiar with the student. At the planning meeting, an agenda is developed and a facilitator is designated. [The facilitator guides the meeting while another member of the team completes the IEP forms.] Diliberto and Brewer suggest ground rules that include: communicate clearly and listen carefully; ask and welcome questions for clarification; respect others' views; share views willingly; be open to different ideas and views; and look to the future, not the past. Part of the agenda will include sharing essential knowledge from various members of the team (i.e., student background, laws and regulations, interpretations of assessment data, and general education curriculum). However, it is essential for the agenda to include soliciting parental expertise. No one knows the student better than the family, so it is important that they be asked to share background information on the student such as strengths and challenges and what they believe has or has not been successful in the past. At some time during the meeting, the LEA representative or school administrator should go over laws and regulations, making sure to use language that is easily understood and free of jargon or unexplained acronyms. Some teachers provide parents with a dictionary of terms frequently used in IEP meetings and go over the terms before the meeting.

Then the educator should wrap up the conference and ask for questions or feedback. Educators should keep in mind that family members may be anxious or nervous about the conference and may not have questions at the time of the conference. In addition, their emotions may prevent them from "hearing" everything said during the conference. Finally, parents may be on very strict time schedules for returning to work, picking up small children, or keeping a medical appointment. Their time must be valued and their schedules honored, so careful planning is essential. Before family members leave a meeting, ask if they would like to set up a follow-up communication or a regular communication schedule (e.g., a five-minute phone call during the noon hour, a weekly e-mail summing up the week's accomplishments). This is especially welcomed when meetings seemed to be consumed with checking off items on the agenda with little time to converse informally about the student.

Specific ways parents can be involved in IEP, ITP, or IFSP development and implementation before, during, and after the conference are provided in Figure 9.6. This list could be printed in the school handbook.

Student-Led Conferences

A student has the greatest investment and most important involvement in constructing an individual education plan for learning. Indeed, it is counterproductive to formulate goals and objectives without involving students in their conferences as members of the planning team. Having students help plan a student-led conference with family members will give them a sense of ownership in their own learning process. Students and their teachers should talk beforehand about the purpose of their conference and then set some goals for the meeting. If the teacher does not feel the student is ready or has not collected the appropriate materials, the conference should be postponed until those conditions are met.

A student will want to decide which samples of work to show and what learning activities to describe. Developing a sample rubric beforehand to evaluate the conference after it takes place will add to the learning process. The classroom teacher or special education teacher, or both, may want to have a brief practice session so the process feels familiar and the student is comfortable when the conference takes place. It will be helpful to for the teacher to coach the student in avoiding jargon and "educationese" and prefacing any acronym with an explanation of that term. Teachers should prepare family members ahead of time for the student-led conference with a phone call or a brief letter, focusing on the contributions it can make to their child's confidence and pride in achievement.

Parent partnerships can be particularly difficult to cultivate at the secondary level. Much of the difficulty stems from attitudes of adolescent students who would just "die" of humiliation if their parents were seen at school by their peers (McGrew-Zoubi, 1998). Other teens might head off a teacher's efforts to involve family members with "Go ahead, but they won't care/come/participate," or "They have to work," or "They don't think it's necessary," or even a harsh appraisal of parent interest such as "They don't have anything to contribute to any meeting about me." Parents probably are not immune from these perceptions and attitudes, and some acquiesce to them out of frustration or years-long weariness, while teachers are hard-pressed to find ways of countermanding them.

In some middle school settings where traditional parent-teacher interactions and conferences have been perceived as more problematic than helpful, an innovative student-centered model for conferencing has been developed and field tested. In this model, a structure is created in which students are helped to prepare for their own conferences. The new format is communicated to parents and colleagues and procedural operations are developed (Countryman & Schroeder, 1996). In the planning, development, and evaluation phases of this new approach, teachers found that students should have more participation

FIGURE 9.6   Checklist for Families in Developing IEPs

Throughout the year:

Read about educational issues and concerns.

Learn about the structure of the local school system.

Observe your child, noting work habits, play patterns, and social interactions.

Record information regarding special interests, talents, and accomplishments, as well as areas of concern.

Before the conference:

Visit the child's school.

Discuss school life with the child.

Talk with other families who have participated in conferences to find out what goes on during the conference.

Write down questions and points you would like to address.

Review notes from any previous conferences with school staff.

Prepare a summary file of information, observations, and products that would further explain the child's needs.

Arrange to take along any other persons that you feel would be helpful in planning the child's educational program.

During the conference:

Be an active participant.

Ask questions about anything that is unclear.

Insist that educational jargon and "alphabet soup" acronyms be avoided.

Contribute information, ideas, and recommendations.

Let the school personnel know about the positive things school has provided.

Ask for a copy of the IEP if it is not offered.

Ask to have a follow-up contact time to compare notes about progress.

After the conference:

Discuss the conference proceedings with the child.

Continue to monitor the child's progress and follow up as agreed on.

Reinforce school staff for positive effects of the planned program.

Keep adding to the notebook of information.

Be active in efforts to improve schools.

Say supportive things about the schools whenever possible.

in preparing conference scripts. They need a log to help them organize their products, and they must not overlook bringing to the discussion their classes, such as art, music, driver education, family and consumer science, and modern languages, or those subjects will not get discussed. Students reasonably express the need to see how teachers have evaluated them before it is revealed at the conference.

Teachers will want to plan carefully for a student-led conference in collaboration with parents or other family members. After planning, they should review the steps and prepare by rehearsing them, focusing especially on the opening few minutes and the

FIGURE 9.7   Rating Form, Student-Led Conference

Name: _____

Criterion	Needs Improvement	Fair	Good	Outstanding
1. Was prepared for the conference	0 1	2	3	4
2. Participated enthusiastically	0 1	2	3	4
3. Presented material in organized way	0 1	2	3	4
4. Explained learning process effectively	0 1	2	3	4
5. Assessed achievement realistically	0 1	2	3	4
6. Submitted ideas for next work/studies	0 1	2	3	4
7. Credited resources accurately	0 1	2	3	4
8. Involved all participants in discussion	0 1	2	3	4

Total: _____ of 32

Areas of strengths:

Areas that need more work:

closing of the conference. These steps will help guide student and collaborator through the process in advance of the event:

1. Decide what the goal(s) of the conference should be and why having a student-led meeting is a good idea.
2. Together, make a simple, uncluttered agenda, with time limits built in and a definite ending time imposed (preceded by a three-minute wrap-up). If you plan to use the checklist provided in Figure 9.7, go over those with the student to convey what is expected and how the event will be assessed.
3. Determine how families will be informed and invited, making sure to convey that the student will be in charge. This would be a good time to use an online format for the invitation if that is something the student can do well or would like to learn.
4. Have the student choose a preferred location and plan a seating arrangement.
5. Together, choose work samples and other information showing progress made, goals accomplished, and goals yet to be met. Think about what other information family members would like to have and what questions they might want to ask or answer.
6. Rehearse! Fix any problem areas. If needed, rehearse again.
7. After the conference, have a debriefing and talk about what went especially well, what needed improvement, and what would be good to do next time. Expect the student-led conference to be a very good learning experience for student, family members, and teachers.

A student-guided conference must not be hurried. A thirty-minute segment of time might be reasonable. Busy teachers, particularly those at the secondary level with dozens of students, will need strong administrator support and innovative scheduling ideas to make student-guided conferences successful. But for a courageous, energetic school staff, student-guided parent conferences can promote meaningful ownership by students in their own learning. Furthermore, they can impress upon families the importance of their partnerships with school personnel. Students and other participants also can benefit from an assessment of conference outcomes by using a rubric designed for the purpose. (See Figure 9.7.)

Benefits from having students participate in conferences for their individualized programs include:

■ Receiving information about their progress
■ Feeling involved in their own educational planning
■ Being more strongly motivated to improve and more enthusiastic about school-based learning
■ Being aware that home and school(s) are working collaboratively on their behalf

HOME VISITS

Ample evidence demonstrates that after-school, home, and community activities can enrich and support children's education and development. To learn about home and community supports for education, many educators find that home visits are an excellent way to better understand about the family and community context of students (Stetson, Stetson, Sinclair, & Nix, 2012). Home visits are becoming more prevalent as educators strive to develop collaborative relationships with families. Communication with families outside the school setting helps balance equity and builds trust and respect in home-school relationships (Byrd, 2012). Home visitors take the role as guests and learners; this reversal of roles is usually welcomed by families. Visiting students in their homes helps educators understand students' life experiences and may help educators identify needs for which they can provide resources.

A home visit program should be planned carefully and endorsed by school and district administrators. Protocols, purposes, and professional development should be in place before home visits are made. Visits should have a specific purpose, such as to welcome a student to a school, provide information about successful home tutoring practices, or simply to establish and build an equal partnership with parents. Plans and protocols for visits should also be based on family work schedules, teacher comfort levels with home visits, and community context (such as safety or language) (Spies, Morgan, & Matsuura, 2014; Middleton, 2008).

When visiting the home of a student, it is imperative that home visitors reserve judgment and avoid making assumptions. A large home in a suburban neighborhood may be empty of furniture. A tiny urban apartment in an ethnic neighborhood may be full of books and toys. A home visitor may be greeted with a lavish spread of traditional food items from the family's country of origin and at another home may be introduced to the three other

FIGURE 9.8 **"Teacher Says Thanks"**

families who live in the apartment. Most families welcome home visitors from their children's schools. They are glad to show how they support educational development in their own way and to discuss their beliefs, heritage, and customs. Remember, the educator is the guest, and the primary purpose of home visits is always to develop home-school relationships.

Maintaining Home and School Collaboration and Partnerships

Home-school collaboration is mandated, it is challenging, and it is rewarding. Educators have two choices in collaborating with families: to see school as a battleground with an emphasis on conflict between families and school personnel or to see school as a "homeland" environment that invites power sharing and mutual respect, with collaboration on activities that foster student learning and development (Epstein, 2011). The goal for educators and their partners is to integrate family engagement as part of the school instructional strategy, that is, as part of the curriculum rather than added on to school activities. Successful home-school-community partnerships (see Figure 9.8) are those that:

- Respect the family as the child's first teacher
- Empower families and communities to support and advocate for all students
- Understand learning as a lifelong endeavor involving families and communities
- Recognize that all families want the best for their children and can have a positive, significant impact on their children's education

Resources for School Educators and Home Educators

The Internet and local libraries and media centers are excellent sources of information about successful home-school-community collaborative efforts. Many state and national organizations are dedicated to providing helpful information about disabilities, special education, legal issues, and successful parent-as-partner strategies. For example, every state has at least one parent center that is funded by the U.S. Department of Education. Information about these centers can be located on the Parent Center Network website.

Most states have a Parent Training and Information Center and a Community Parent Resource Center that provides training and information for addressing learning or behavioral disabilities to families of children and young adults from birth to age twenty-two who have physical, cognitive, emotional, or social needs. They help families obtain appropriate education and services for children with disabilities and improve educational programs for all children. They train and inform parents and professionals on a variety of topics, help to resolve problems between families and schools or other agencies, and connect children with disabilities to community resources that address their needs. Other resources include, but are by no means limited to, the National Association for the Education of Young Children, the PACER Center, and the National Network of Partnership Schools and the Center on School, Family and Community Partnerships. Most of these sites have both Spanish and English versions and are excellent resources for both parents and educators.

Closing Thoughts

In their career-long efforts to establish and sustain healthy and powerful partnerships with families, educators demonstrate keen awareness of the realities, sometimes bright but oftentimes grim, in which today's families live and function. Many families are overwhelmed by family crises as well as everyday life events. Some face multiple and prolonged stressors such as poverty, addiction, long work hours or multiple jobs, health issues while having no insurance, bilingual or multilingual communication difficulties between home-school, and more. Families might include a single parent, a blended family, gay or lesbian parents, unwed adolescent parents, nonbiological parents serving as primary caregivers, foster caregivers, grandparents, extended families, and adoptive parents.

Collaborative consultants avoid judging attitudes, overtones of blaming, stereotyping, holding false expectations, and dwelling on basic differences in values. They are tolerant if parents wish to obtain second or even third opinions. They have empathy with families, with the awareness that parents may be having considerable difficulty in coming to terms with their child's disability or disabilities. Confidentiality of information and privacy pertaining to family matters is honored and preserved.

For an ideal partnership to be developed, families and school personnel must make every effort not to reproach each other, but to work together as partners on the child's team. They should strive to be honest with each other and willing to listen and empathize, acknowledging any anger or disappointment with patience and calmness. Teachers need to remain calm and open-minded in explosive situations and employ responsive listening to learn exactly what the family members' views and concerns are. Teachers who find out that they are wrong should acknowledge that before stating their views. They understand that all parties have the welfare of the child in mind.

Teachers and administrators, and any other school personnel included, will need to keep in mind that most families are doing the best they can; parents of students do not start out the morning saying, "I think today I will be a poor parent." Consultants understand that collaboration does not require total agreement in values or educational philosophy, but school personnel and families must focus on needs and interests of children and their families.

Students, schools, and families are strengthened by appropriate outreach efforts and partnership activities based on values and practices of a family-focused approach such as the Equal Partnership Model. Educators who empower and support families of their students recognize that they are part of powerful partnerships and the work they do with parents is part of the educational legacy they leave with students and their families.

 ENHANCEDetext **Application Exercise 9.1.** Click to apply your understanding of parent conferences and the core principles of IDEA.

TIPS FOR HOME-SCHOOL COLLABORATION

1. When working with families, be positive, proactive, and solution-oriented. But mostly, listen.
2. When developing transition plans, work with parents and students to assure that you understand their post-school aspirations and plans clearly link high school goals to these post-school goals.
3. Regularize your communication with parents. For example, use the same format for all homework messages, and a different format for all information. Use colorful folders or paper to give a signal "Please read" or "This needs to be signed." Or use Friday afternoon emails to maintain communication with families.
4. Ask parents about strategies or accommodations they use at home that have been successful. You may learn some new suggestions to pass on to other parents. Better yet, create opportunities for parents to share their successes with other parents.
5. When using an interpreter, look at the parent when speaking and listening, rather than at the interpreter.
6. Talk about the student rather than the disability. A disability is just part of the total child.
7. Facilitate family involvement in the whole school community, not just special education activities.
8. Parents of children who have disabilities report feeling isolated. Always be alert for opportunities to engage parents in school and community activities.
9. Consider providing developmentally appropriate child care for school events. Urge community groups to also provide child care by individuals who have experience with children with disabilities.
10. Engaging families should be systematic, not random. Careful plans should be developed and followed.
11. Get past "attitudinal hang-ups" about certain types of families (homeless, extended families, families with linguistic differences). Engage ALL families in some manner that is appropriate to their child.
12. No matter what happens, remember that families want the best for their children.
13. Provide name plates or table tents for IEP meetings, so that everyone can clearly read the names of those involved. Some consultants provide a folder for parents so they will have papers to use just as the school team does.

CHAPTER 10

WORKING IN COLLABORATIVE TEAMS WITH PARAEDUCATORS

The success of students with disabilities often depends on the support provided by **paraeducators** *(sometimes referred to as "paraprofessionals" or shortened to "paras"). Paraeducators are the primary support for students with disabilities in K–12 settings and often have the responsibility of implementing student programs in the general education setting. Without these often underpaid and overworked partners, including students with disabilities in general education settings would be difficult, if not impossible. The use of paraprofessionals in public schools has become one of the primary mechanisms by which students with disabilities are being supported in general education classes.*

Through the years, paraeducators have become increasing visible and important in schools. The No Child Left Behind (NCLB) Act specifically defined the title paraprofessional (paraeducator) and specified the roles and limitations of instructional paras. A designated amount of the 2004 Individuals with Disabilities Education Improvement Act (IDEIA) federal money is used to provide the services of paraprofessionals to assist students with disabilities. Para qualification requirements were maintained in the most recent Every Student Succeeds Act (ESSA) that replaced NCLB in 2015. Further, ESSA has given paraeducators a voice in key decision-making and professional developmental opportunities at the federal, state, and local levels. In doing so, ESSA promotes respect for paraeducators and the critical roles they play in educating students.

When paras were first introduced into schools, their primary role was to support the teacher in clerical tasks such as checking papers, preparing materials, and creating bulletin boards. Over time, the role of paras has changed rather dramatically. Paraeducators are now engaged in many other important tasks more directly linked with teaching and learning. Additionally, as more students with IEPs are being served in general education classrooms, paras have moved from working primarily under the direct supervision of the special educator in a special education classroom setting to the more typical role today, working directly with students in inclusion settings. Paraeducators are often supervised from a distance by the special educator who is assigned to the supervisory role. This service delivery option has had a tremendous impact on the special educators who supervise paras. It is not uncommon for special educators to be responsible for directing a half dozen or more paras. Special education teachers who entered the profession to work with children with special needs often feel more like an air traffic controller than a teacher. Scheduling and communication logistics dominate a large part of their role. These teachers frequently report that it is a role they felt unprepared for as a novice special education teacher.

Paraeducators and teachers have an important interactive relationship. On one hand, they are partners in accomplishing the tasks inherent in the teacher's role; however, the teacher has responsibility for supervising the para's work and assessing outcomes of the para's performance. Some have compared the role of the para to that of a sous-chef but in an educational setting. In short, teachers supervise and direct the work of paraeducators, but it is the qualified general or special education teacher who is responsible for planning, adjusting, and delivering the primary instruction.

CHAPTER OBJECTIVES

Upon completing this chapter, you will be able to:

1. Explain ways a paraeducator is a partner.
2. Discuss how the paraeducator's responsibilities should be determined and communicated with the para and general education teacher.
3. Review how paraeducators are selected and prepared for their roles.
4. Identify strategies for ongoing communication with paras.
5. Propose useful ways teachers can supervise and direct para activities.
6. Describe several important points to consider when utilizing para services.

KEY TERMS

paraeducator (para,   supervising teacher
   paraprofessional)

SITUATION 10

Jackie recently completed her teacher preparation program and was hired as a special education teacher in a community not far from where she attended school. She was excited when offered a job in a highly sought-after district with little turnover in the teaching staff. She couldn't have dreamed of a more perfect job, or so she thought. However, after being in the job for four short months, things weren't going as she had envisioned.

Jackie's biggest problem was with her paraeducators. This blindsided her because during her student internship semester and subsequent practica in special education classrooms, she found she really enjoyed working with the paraeducators in those programs and had considered them both friends and colleagues. After all, they were close in age to herself, and her cooperating teachers seemed to have a good working relationship with them. She even commented in her portfolio that they all functioned together as an effective team.

When Jackie walked into her new job, she looked forward to having the same type of working relationship with her paras. She felt fortunate when interviewing for the position that there would be four paras working with her to help support students in the various classrooms. All the paras had been there five or more years, and two had been there more than ten years, so she was encouraged by their dedication to their jobs. She felt fortunate that she would not have to do para orientation and training that was talked about in one of her university courses on collaboration in special education. She had enough on her plate just getting oriented herself.

Jackie welcomed the paras' knowledge of students on her caseload and how returning students had been served during the previous year. She felt like she was able to hit the ground running, due to the collective experience of her para team. It took about six weeks for things to settle in and as new students were placed on her caseload and she had a chance to visit classrooms and observe, Jackie felt she was ready to try some new things. Later in the chapter, the attention will focus on an activity in Jackie's context to see how her plan for trying new things has worked.

PARAEDUCATORS AS PARTNERS

Paraeducators are essential partners in providing special education services; therefore, teachers and consultants to whom these partners are assigned must give special consideration to their needs. Many of the concepts and skills presented in other parts of this book apply to working with paraeducators. This section emphasizes special skills that relate specifically to supervising, directing, and communicating with paras.

Since the early 1990s, significant changes in special education have fueled an increase in the reliance on paraprofessionals to support students with disabilities. In recent years, schools have turned increasingly to paras due to a number of factors, including large caseloads for special education teachers. Additionally, recent special education-related legislation mandates students be educated alongside their peers with access to the general education curriculum and instruction provided by highly qualified teachers. Providing para support in general education classrooms where students with disabilities are included has been the most commonly used type of support for these students.

As more students with low-incidence and high-need disabilities such as autism, intellectual and multiple disabilities, and emotional and behavior disorders are being served in inclusion settings, an increasing number of paras are being used to support the needs of these students in general education settings (Suter & Giangreco, 2009). In their review of a decade of literature on paraprofessional support of students with disabilities, Giangreco, Edelman, Broer, and Doyle (2001) noted that when the Education of All Handicapped Children Act (P.L. 94-142) was first passed in 1975, there were discussions concerning training a whole new cadre of personnel, essentially paraprofessionals, to meet the needs of the new population of students with more severe disabilities entering public schools. At the time, some believed these students did not need highly trained teachers with teacher education degrees. Others felt differently and assumed that given proper support and instruction, students with more severe disabilities were in fact educable, and needed specialized and individualized instruction from highly trained special educators. In the end, federal officials agreed with the latter group and advocated for professional teachers to serve students with severe disabilities. In looking at the landscape of services for students with moderate to severe disabilities in today's schools, we should note the increasing reliance on paraprofessionals to support students with more severe disabilities in the general education classroom. Some might ask whether we have come full circle.

Paraeducator Requirements

One outcome of the No Child Left Behind (NCLB) Act was that all paraprofessionals were to hold an associate degree, have completed two or more years of college, or passed a district- or state-approved paraprofessional assessment. Additionally, NCLB more clearly set the boundaries for roles instructional paras could fulfill by requiring that they act under the direct supervision of highly qualified teachers. With the passage of Every Student Succeeds Act (ESSA) in December of 2015, NCLB was replaced but some provisions remain. Any state receiving funding from ESSA must have a plan with assurances for professional standards for paraeducators. While each state will be responsible for its own standards for paras, it is likely that most will maintain the paraeducator requirements laid out in NCLB and paras will have a voice with regard to professional development.

While guidelines and standards for the use of paraeducators seems to be in flux, there is no denying that the use of paraeducators is a well-established and growing trend. Since 1992, the number of paraeducators has increased 131 percent, whereas for the same period the number of special education teachers has decreased (Data Accountability Center [DAC], 2010). Twenty-six states reported employing more special education paras than special education teachers (U.S. Department of Education, 2008). It has become common for special educators to be responsible for directing the work of more than four paras on average—and in some cases as many as fourteen (Giangreco & Broer, 2005). In 2012, the number of special education paraprofessionals in the United States (Bitterman, Gray, & Goldring, 2013) was over 450,000, and this number continues to rise. The 2016–2017 edition of the Bureau of Labor Statistics *Occupational Outlook Handbook* reports over 1.2 million jobs for teacher assistants in 2014 with projected growth predictions of 6 percent from 2014–2024 as a result of increases in student enrollment, class size, and continued demand for special education services.

Over the years, the manner in which paraprofessionals are used has also changed. Paras increasingly are being called on to support students with disabilities in general education classrooms with little direct supervision from special education teachers. In one statewide study, Fisher and Pleasants (2012) reported that 44 percent of the paraeducators indicated they had regular meeting time at least once a week with a special educator but the length of those meetings was generally short, ranging from 10–27 minutes. Another 44 percent of the paras indicated that they had no meeting time. Twenty-two percent indicated they were part of general education teams and met at least once each week with a general and special educator. The average length of these meetings was 14 minutes. But this lack of supervision was not always the case. Initially, paras employed in special education typically worked under the close supervision and direction of a special educator who was present with them in a resource or self-contained classroom all or most of the time. However, today, paras are more likely to be assisting students with disabilities within general education classrooms, often having limited contact with the special education teacher listed on the student's IEP as the one who supervises them (Giangreco, Suter, & Doyle, 2010). Even when paras spend all of their day in a special education setting, they perceive their role to be a one-to-one assignment (Fisher & Pleasants, 2012), thus begging the question, who designs instruction for students with IEPs? Are the roles and duties paras are asked to perform clearly delineated and appropriate? Do they have adequate training to carry out their duties? Are they being adequately supervised? The extensive literature review by Giangreco and colleagues (2010) indicates that often, through no fault of their own, too many paras remain inadequately trained and supervised to do the jobs they are asked to undertake. Overreliance on paras or inappropriate use of their services can result in a host of unintended negative consequences.

With the advent of the NCLB legislation, the intent was that teachers be held more accountable for supervising their paraeducators, and administrators be expected to give paras more support, avoid misassignments of their responsibilities, and provide professional development to help them perform their roles effectively. *Neither paras nor teachers typically have had formal preparation for collaborating with one another in productive ways.* Frequently, the relationship is hampered by inadequate communication, lack of time for planning together, and lack of clear job descriptions.

A fine line often exists between paras' assistance to teachers in implementing their plans and functioning as instructor and decision maker. With more pressures evolving from inclusionary practices, paras are sometimes being asked to extend their roles inappropriately to include assessment, curricular adaptations, instruction, and communicating with families. It is alarming that in one study, 27 percent of paras identified developing lesson plans as one of either their primary or secondary roles, and 31 percent believed this was an appropriate role for paraeduators (Fisher & Pleasants, 2012). Supervising teachers are responsible for collaborating with paras when delegating tasks to them within the inclusion setting. Capizzi and Da Fonte (2012) remind supervising teachers that:

> Delegation of a task does not release responsibility for the completion of this task. But, at the same time, the responsibility when delegating shifts to ensure that support is provided at a level to allow the paraeducator to complete the task. Collaboration and delegations are more effective when the teacher has taken an active role to build a team that is based on trust, respect, and hard work. (p. 3)

With these issues, along with heavy caseloads and lack of time, paraeducators have many pressures. They may feel a lack of respect, as is evident in a study of paras where 40 percent reported lack of appreciation as a major concern and 38 percent as a minor concern (Fisher & Pleasants, 2012). Their salaries tend to be appallingly low. Some resent the absence of opportunity for advancement. Many articulate a need for more intensive clarification and preparation for the para role. Research by Giangreco, Edelman, and Broer (2001) identified several themes suggesting how school personnel can respect, appreciate, and acknowledge paraprofessionals. They can receive:

- Non-monetary signs and symbols of appreciation
- Adequate compensation
- Trust for carrying out important responsibilities
- Non-instructional responsibilities
- The respect of being listened to
- Orientation experiences and support for their roles

Special education supervising teachers have little control over how much their paras are paid, but they could have substantial influence over most of the other identified areas.

Building on research that occupational stress can have a negative effect on employees' mental and physical health as well as longevity in a job, Shyman (2011) identified contributors to occupational stress in special education paraeducators. Based on those findings, he recommends developing better training of staff and organizing supervisor hierarchies. The importance of both role conflict and supervisory support were evident as factors related to occupational stress. There should be both clearer avenues of support and sufficient support provided to paras. Successful matches of role delineation, skill development, expectations, and support can help instill respect and appreciation for the role. Para-educators often serve as "connectors" between parties such as students, parents, teacher, and community service providers (Chopra, et al., 2004). Being a respected and valued member of the team is paramount for them to work effectively.

Determining When a Student Requires Para Support

One of the first important questions to be answered is, "Is a para needed?" Schools want to prevent overreliance on paraeducators but also need to assure levels of support are being provided to meet IEP goals, particularly when students are in inclusive settings with less direct contact with special education teachers. All stakeholders need to be on the same page during the decision process with the focus on student goals and the role of the para-educator with respect to these questions;

- What are the specific support needs of the student?
- How can independence be increasingly achieved?
- What natural supports can be utilized?
- How will social acceptance of the student be enhanced?

Mueller and Murphy (2001) developed a three-part instrument to be used by the IEP team and the paraeducator, where applicable, to aid in this process. The first part is an Intensive Needs Checklist. It is designed to develop an overview of the student's needs in direct relation to the classroom environment. Issues are addressed regarding safety concerns, level of prompting needed to complete work, assistance needed with basic functional skills such as toileting, mobility, feeding, dressing, and if the student requires specialized small or individualized instruction in specific academic areas. Completion of the checklist by the IEP team helps focus the discussion and determination of need for a paraeducator and, if so, in what ways para support would be provided. The second part of the instrument is the Student's Abilities and Assistance Needs Matrix. The matrix focuses on what the student can or cannot do and the extent of assistance needed. A matrix listing each period of the day in the first column is followed by five columns with these headings:

- What student can do *without assistance*
- What student cannot do and *needs accommodation* to complete
- What student cannot do and *needs assistance*
- What student needs to promote *social acceptance* and how peers will be utilized
- What areas will be targeted for *independence* (should be identified in the IEP)

Finally, the Plan for Paraeducator Assistance identifies where, when, and how the paraeducator will provide support. It should include the specific class activity, the need for the para, how natural supports and peers will be used to increase socialization, how independence will be encouraged, and how much time will be needed for para support. By completing all of these parts, the IEP team will have undertaken a thorough review of student needs and the environment where para support is needed, thus assuring that para support is provided according to real versus perceived need.

DELINEATING THE PARAEDUCATOR ROLE

Paraeducators may be found in virtually any educational setting, ranging from a preschool class for children with special needs, to a first-grade classroom having students with disabilities, to a grocery store for coaching adolescent students with developmental disabilities in learning a new job, to a resource room for gifted adolescents with needs for advanced and expanded curriculum. Paraeducator responsibilities vary widely, from teaching a lesson, to grading homework and tests, to participating in classroom activities, to sometimes just "being there" for the students and teacher.

An extensive literature review by Giangreco, Edelman, Broer, and Doyle (2001) noted the greatly expanding roles and duties for paraprofessionals during the 1990s, especially those where students with disabilities are served in general education settings. They found that paras continue to work with students who have the most challenging behavioral and learning characteristics, engaging in a broad range of roles without preparation for many of them. The researchers listed eight major role categories of such duties:

1. Providing instruction in academic subjects
2. Teaching functional life skills
3. Teaching vocational skills at community-based work sites
4. Collecting and managing data
5. Supporting students with challenging behaviors
6. Facilitating interactions with peers who don't have disabilities
7. Providing personal care
8. Engaging in clerical activities

In their updated review of previous findings, Giangreco and colleagues (2010) found that current literature supports the earlier findings that para roles have become increasing instructional. With the understanding that highly qualified educators, both general and special education teachers, are responsible for making the plans that the para then implements, evidence continues to appear that paraprofessionals work autonomously with very little direction. Paraeducators report making instructional decisions, providing the majority of instruction to some students, and doing so without adequate professional direction from the teachers who are their direct supervisors. This certainly begs the ethical question as to whether our least qualified personnel are being assigned to provide the bulk of instruction and support to our students with the most challenging behaviors and learning needs, often with little oversight or direction, overstepping the boundaries identified in IDEIA. With the current emphasis on Response to Intervention (RTI) and teacher and student accountability regarding instruction, it is more imperative than ever before that paras, as key players in academic programs for students with disabilities, be closely supervised in their performance of those duties. This is particularly important in situations where most students on a special education teacher's caseload are served in a full inclusion model. A special education teacher functions more as a case manager, overseeing and directing the activities of many paraprofessionals who work with students on IEPs in the general education classroom. These paras must not only be supervised in the performance of their duties, but they must also be guided and coached on the nuances of instruction for students with disabilities. Since paras often are trained on the job rather than being prepared in advance, several (Brock & Carter, 2015; Causton-Theoharis, Giangreco, Doyle, & Vadasy, 2007; Koegel, Kim, & Koegel 2014; Stockall, 2014) have proposed direct instruction and side-by-side coaching training models for teaching everything from literacy instruction to socialization skills for students with ASD and even training paras to implement peer support arrangements. Just as importantly, teachers who are planning the instruction for students must receive ongoing feedback from the paraeducator. Ongoing reporting systems should be in place that allow paraeducators to keep educators informed about both formal progress monitoring data as well as more informal feedback about a host of other variables that impact student performance and motivation. When such ongoing reporting systems are not in place, paras often are left to make instructional decisions beyond the scope of their role and supervising teachers no longer have working knowledge of a student's day-to-day performance.

The relationship between the special education teacher and paraeducator differs somewhat from the other collaborative roles. Unlike the consulting teacher and the consultee teacher, classroom teachers and paraeducators do not have parity in the school program because they are not equally responsible for decisions about student needs and instructional interventions. The teacher is expected to supervise and direct the paraeducator, who is employed to assist the teacher and, therefore, to follow the teacher's direction. Even so, the paraeducator is necessary as a partner to the teacher's success and to the success of the teacher's students. Indeed, the prefix "para" means "to come alongside," or "to help another." Paraeducators are employed in schools to work alongside teachers and help them with the demands of their jobs.

Some use the term "instructional paraprofessional" to designate a person who helps with instruction of students. Nevertheless, paraeducators do not plan instruction nor are they responsible for evaluating student performance. In some situations, it may be appropriate for the para to administer brief assessments and probes that are typically used in ongoing progress monitoring as part of RTI, as long as they have been trained and follow the administration and scoring guidelines, but evaluating the results of those assessments clearly falls in the role of the teacher. There is much paras can do to help students learn and gain confidence with their schoolwork and assist teachers and special educators in implementing the students' IEPs.

Prior to supervising or working with a paraeducator, it is helpful to identify key tasks as part of a teacher's role, specify what the teacher does when carrying out that role, and then stipulate what role the paraeducator might have in comparison to what the teacher does. This is a useful exercise for the teacher to clarify, distinguish between the two, and then articulate it to the para so both are clear about how their roles are intertwined but different. Figure 10.1 provides an example of what this might look like for a few key teacher and para tasks.

FIGURE 10.1   Interrelated Roles of Teacher and Para on Key Tasks

EXAMPLE TASKS	Teacher Role	Para Role
INSTRUCTION	Delivers whole class, small group, and one-on-one individualized instruction.	Reinforces lessons and skills introduced by the teacher or carries out individual and small-group instruction directed by the teacher and when para has been explicitly trained to deliver a specific instructional format.
PLANNING	Plans the lessons and determines which instructional procedures will be used.	Carries out the teacher's plans and reports to the teacher about student progress.
BEHAVIOR MANAGEMENT	Observes and analyzes student behavior (Functional Behavioral Assessment) and then, often in consultation with others, develops a behavioral intervention plan.	Observes and records student behavior and carries out any behavior plan that is in place for a student or other classroom management system.
WORKING WITH FAMILIES	Initiates written and verbal contact, conferences, and shares student progress.	Participates in conferences or other meetings with parents as appropriate and when invited by the teacher or supervisor.
ASSESSMENT	Administers, scores, and interprets both formal and informal tests and reports results to necessary persons.	Administers informal tests and routine progress-monitoring probes and CBMs with prior training and records results for the teacher to review and share.

Paraeducator Responsibilities

Every paraeducator position has its unique characteristics and responsibilities, but some are more commonly utilized than others. Paras report delivering instruction planned by professionals as one of the most common roles along with behavior support (Fisher & Pleasants, 2012; Giangreco & Broer, 2005). Less frequent, but still reported by paras and teachers as being part of a para's role, are supervision of students, assisting students with personal care, adapting lessons designed by general educators, and clerical tasks. These tasks might be in the forms of one of the following:

1. *Supporting and monitoring students*—Reading to students and listening to them read, providing guided practice for students needing scaffolding on a math lesson that was presented by the teacher, administering routine curriculum-based measurement (CBM) probes as part of ongoing student progress monitoring, helping students with health care or other personal needs, assisting with small-group activities, observing and recording student behavior, supervising playground activities.

2. *Preparing instructional materials*—Making materials for specific lessons, duplicating materials, taking notes in a secondary content class to help students fill in their own notes and prepare for tests, making instructional games and learning centers or self-correcting materials to provide additional practice on a skill or topic area, making arrangements for community-based instruction and field trips, collecting and compiling upcoming assignments from general education teachers to share with the special education supervisor for planning purposes, learning about a student's specialized equipment or assistive technology and helping with integrating it into the classroom.

3. *Communication support*—Participating in team meetings and parent conferences as appropriate, preparing student performance charts, providing feedback about student progress to supervising teachers.

4. *Support of routine business*—Recording attendance, checking papers, filing materials, entering data for progress monitoring.

As noted earlier, more students with disabilities are receiving their education in the general education classroom where paraeducators often are assigned to work with individual students or small groups of students to support them in the inclusion setting. This can present a challenge for a special educator who is responsible for supervising the work of the paras and monitoring student progress, but who may not be present to oversee day-to-day instructional activities and behavior support strategies being implemented. The special education para supervisor must have a system to ensure ongoing two-way communication between them. Often paras have the most direct avenue for contact and support of students with disabilities whose primary placement is in the general education classroom. In order for the special education teacher to develop appropriate interventions and ensure that instruction and behavior plans are being implemented appropriately, the special education teacher should build weekly meeting time with the para into their schedules. This meeting should have a consistent format and structure to promote most efficient use of time. This weekly meeting can fulfill the dual purpose of monitoring and planning for students as well as establishing and building a positive working relationship between the supervisor and paraprofessional. Depending on the situation, possible topics for discussion at such a meeting are outlined in Figure 10.2. In addition to the weekly meeting, it is helpful to have a daily communication procedure that provides a definite, reliable way to touch base with one another. This could be in the form of a student folder where the para records brief notes on a log sheet to keep the teacher informed about student day-to-day performance. It might be a list of words the student missed in the oral reading time, math concepts covered in the lesson on which the student needs additional guided practice, a sentence or two about behavior incidents, or notes about student successes. This can also be a place for the para to jot down questions or topics to be discussed at the next weekly conference. Rather than physically dropping off a student folder or clipboard with these notes to the special education classroom or teacher's office, some prefer using a more efficient tool such as e-mail or some type of electronic log sheet. As always, keeping such

| Video Example from YouTube |

ENHANCEDetext
Video Example 10.1.
Watch this video and identify the responsibilities of these paraeducators. (https://www.youtube.com/watch?v=0lNGlh8b_CE)

FIGURE 10.2   Topics for Para/Supervisor Weekly Conferences

Possible Discussion Topics for Weekly Conference Between Para and Special Education Supervisor include:

1. Schedule the para's time and delegate tasks for the upcoming week.
2. Discuss general role of the para in the classroom.
   - This is a good time to discuss how the para interacts with the student(s) and classroom teacher.
   - Share any feedback you have been given by the classroom teacher regarding the para or the students being served.
   - Ask the para for feedback about the effectiveness of interventions being implemented, student behavior, academic performance, progress toward goals and overall motivation and attitude.
   - Solicit input from the para in terms of how the students being supported in the classroom are fitting in and interacting with other students and the teacher. (Do they seem to be an integrated member of the class or more of a "visitor" on the side?)
3. Review any data being collected by the para regarding student performance and discuss what the next step should be. This might include progress-monitoring graphs or charts of basic academic skills, student work samples, behavior observation logs, anecdotal daily log notes, and the like.
4. Talk through your analysis of the information and seek input from the para.
5. Finalize plans for the upcoming week, including any changes that will be made, and ensure that the para has the necessary training and information to carry out the plan. Sometimes the special education teacher might need to provide a brief demonstration or model the teaching behavior on how to provide feedback to the student.
6. Finally, ask the para if there are any additional topics to cover or issues that need to be brought to your attention. Make sure to convey that you value their contributions and input.

communications private from other students, and even from adults who do not have permission for access, is mandatory. Electronic tablets and other such devices are becoming more common in the classroom for recording data and communication purposes, and this simply extends the application of that technology and puts it in the hands of paraprofessionals. Technology can be a bridge to the communication gap that often exists when paras and their supervising teachers have limited opportunity for face-to-face meetings. Paras can share student work samples, their notes and questions, and even collect student behavior data (e.g., video record some examples of baseline behavior and then use periodic video captures to document progress for monitoring the effectiveness of an intervention or behavior plan). These samples can be shared with supervising teachers in real time and have the added bonus of being captured for later discussion and used in a student portfolio to be shared during team problem-solving meetings and during parent-teacher meetings. While these are all benefits of using technology to streamline and enhance communication for the benefit of students, preparing the para for such responsibility also highlights the importance of providing paras with proper training and guidelines for the ethical use of technology and the importance of maintaining confidentiality.

As noted earlier, paraeducators may assume a range of job responsibilities while supporting students in the classroom. Depending on the skills and training of the paraeducator, this could include carrying out academic and social skill interventions designed by the teacher, making on-the-spot curricular modifications, and managing student behavior, all while developing working relationships with others on the team. Paraprofessionals and their supervisors and teachers should discuss what tasks are appropriate for the para to carry out, which should be done only by a qualified teacher, and which might be done by either the para or the teacher. Figure 10.3 provides an example of how this might look. It is designed so both the para and teacher fill it out separately and then compare their selections and discuss any items where there was not agreement. The items on this form can be easily adapted to more closely fit a particular situation.

FIGURE 10.3   Teacher and Para Role Clarification

Both the para and teacher should complete this separately and then compare and discuss any answers that vary.

ACTIVITY	PARA	TEACHER	EITHER
Listen to student read orally and record words read correctly and errors			
Monitor student progress by administering daily math probes			
Assist students with assignment			
Deliver rewards and consequences as indicated on the student's behavior plan			
Provide corrective feedback			
Help with arrangements for field trips or community-based instruction			
Prepare materials for lessons following teacher directions			
Observe and record student behavior			
Share academic or behavior information with a parent			
Supervise students (lunch, playground, loading bus)			
Complete routine paperwork			
Attend to student's physical needs in the bathroom or the lunchroom			
Program communication phrases into a student's augmentative communication device			
Gather instructional resources for a lesson on teaching fractions			
Read a test to a student			
Score an objective style test			

There is often a fine line between what is an appropriate responsibility for the para and is being clearly directed by a qualified teacher, and what crosses the line and borders on educational malpractice by essentially leaving paras on their own to teach students with special needs. In fact, many paraeducators appear to assume primary responsibility for students on IEPs in the general education classroom. Breton (2010) indicated that almost 40 percent of paras he surveyed interacted directly with the special education teacher on less than a weekly basis. Another 16 percent said they never received consultation on providing direct instruction to students from their supervising special education teacher. In one study of paras, more than half expressed concerns regarding being put in the role as the primary instructor for students on IEPs in the general education setting, resulting in general education teachers being less likely to interact with these students (Fisher & Pleasants, 2012).

Paras are often aware that it is the classroom teacher's responsibility to provide the primary instruction in academic and social skills, to make modifications, and to respond to student misbehavior. Nevertheless, some paras take on these responsibilities that go beyond their role and job description (Marks, Schrader, & Levine, 1999). Explanations for this behavior include:

- Paras don't want students to be a "bother" to the teacher.
- Paraeducators feel an urgency to meet a student's immediate academic needs.
- Paras may believe their own performance will be based on positive relations with the teacher.
- Paras are often faced with the need to make on-the-spot modifications when teachers are not readily available.

In many situations, paraeducators have become the primary vehicle for accommodation for students with severe or multiple disabilities in inclusive schools. Lohrmann and Bambara (2006) contend that providing in-class supports such as paraeducators is a critical factor in the acceptance by general education teachers of the inclusion of students with developmental disabilities and challenging behaviors in their classrooms. In most instances, paraeducators stay in close proximity to the student with a disability in these classrooms, attending to their students' physical needs such as toileting, and to instructional needs such as reading aloud to students or recording their answers. Paraeducators may even adopt an advocacy role, making it their responsibility to work toward acceptance of the included student, or to "represent" the student in ways that would support acceptance (Broer, Doyle, & Giangreco, 2005; Giangreco & Boer, 2005). While on the face of it, this may seem a laudable character trait of paraprofessionals to become so invested in the students they serve that they do whatever it takes for the student to be successful in the inclusive classroom. But, when paras take on roles that have been described in the literature as mother, friend, protector, and primary teacher (Broer et al., 2005) that can be cause for concern. Giangreco, Suter, and Hurley (2011) found that students with disabilities felt stigmatized and rejected by their peers and that paraprofessionals provided inadequate instruction due to lack of preparation.

Often, especially when paraprofessionals are assigned to individual students, a primary and sometimes-exclusive relationship develops between the students with a disability and the person who is literally at their side for a significant part of the school day. Giangreco and Broer (2005) found in their study that paras assigned to individual students reported spending 86 percent of their time within three feet of their assigned student. To an outside party looking at the situation, this might raise some warning flags as to whether this is a healthy situation if the goal is to help these students gain independence and develop friendships with their peers in natural settings. Possibly the bigger issue is that fewer than 15 percent of the paras in the study indicated a concern that this unusual proximity to students for so much of their time at school might be unnecessary and interfere with teacher and peer interactions.

Since the paras seem to be unaware of the harm they may be causing, it is important for teachers and supervisors of paraprofessionals to sensitize their own paras and teachers in those classrooms to reactions reported by some former students who had paras. It is not likely that many students would want to attend school all day with their mother always at their side, yet this is how many students have reported feeling about a para who is almost constantly within three feet of them. Mothering supports, no matter how well intentioned, perpetuate the thinking that what students with intellectual disabilities need in school is mothering rather than appropriate supports and effective instruction delivered by a highly qualified teacher (Broer et al., 2005).

It has also been suggested that in addition to making paras and teachers more sensitive to this issue, changes in program structure might be needed. This could include such remedies as rotating paraeducators, carefully analyzing the need for and assignment of one-to-one paras, exploring alternatives to the current use of paras, and developing more socially valid ways of providing needed supports in general education classrooms by means of peer tutors and similar peer-based models. When an exclusive para is deemed necessary, the goal should be to gradually but deliberately begin to fade out such intensive para support. Students with disabilities should also be given age-appropriate input about the types of support they will receive and be instructed in self-advocacy skills so they can share in the decision-making process. Given the long history of paras taking primary responsibility for students with more significant needs in the general education classroom, it may require a shift in mind-set of all members of the team. Rather than the general education teacher and the paraeducator thinking of the para's role as being one of primarily supporting the student in a one-on-one arrangement, it might be more helpful for all involved to think of the para's role as one of assisting the teacher in adapting instruction and materials in a way that will allow the student meaningful participation in the curriculum. The para knows the student's needs and can work with the teacher to develop adaptations, modifications, and solutions rather than engaging in these decisions unilaterally. This places responsibility for instruction on the teacher rather than the para. Collaborating teachers who serve as supervisors to paras in general education settings should lead this discussion so this is the mind-set of the team.

Supervision of paraeducators can be complex and challenging. Unfortunately, many teacher education programs give little or no attention to the topic in their programs. When it is addressed in preservice programs, it is most likely discussed with future special education teachers and rarely included in courses for general education teachers. This neglect is similar to that of neglecting collaboration and consultation skill development in preparation programs for general education teachers, thereby excluding one-half of the interaction process by this oversight. One could argue that a special education teacher is the person most likely to be responsible for supervising paraprofessionals (or collaborating with a co-teacher) and, therefore, the one most in need of the training. Yet it seems reasonable for the general education teacher to also have some knowledge about the para role and skill in interacting with special education colleagues. In reference to the paraeducator, awareness should include:

- What a paraprofessional can and cannot do
- How to best utilize para support in an inclusive classroom
- Ways to provide feedback and communicate effectively
- How to handle issues with paras
- Who to contact if the problem is not resolved expeditiously

Although most special educators today expect to direct the work of paraprofessionals, the majority report receiving little or no training in how to carry out this important function and most say they rely primarily on their on-the-job experiences. This might explain why many special educators responsible for overseeing paras fail to use effective supervision practices. French (2001) reported that in her research, the majority of teachers she studied did not plan for paraprofessionals, and most of those who did delivered plans orally rather than providing written directions the para could refer to when carrying out an instructional or behavioral plan.

So, while new special educators realize that paraprofessionals are very much a part of their role in the delivery of special education, few feel adequately prepared in exactly *how* to supervise paras and even fewer have had practice in doing so prior to their on-the-job experience. When novice special education teachers engage in para supervision without adequate training, they may make mistakes that could have long-term ramifications and need to be repaired. The situation could be compared to starting a building project without a blueprint. But people and relationships are harder to rebuild than bricks-and-mortar building, not to mention the lost opportunities for students that cannot be regained.

One area of particular importance in regard to para and teacher relationships and success of the supervisory relationship is that of personality variables. Discussions of individual differences among adults in the work setting were provided in an earlier chapter. Individual differences also can be problematic when there are large discrepancies in age, culture, educational level, or ethnic background. Young novice teachers may feel inadequate or awkward when having to supervise a para old enough to be the teacher's parent. In another supervisory relationship, a new teacher may be faced with supervising a para who has been in the position for several years and seems to be a lot more knowledgeable about the students, teachers, parents, and school culture than the supervising teacher, thus making it seem like the tables are turned.

In spite of challenges in addressing the roles and responsibilities of paras, there are positive effects of having paras as part of the special education team. As suggested earlier, many paras can be supportive links to the community. Those same characteristics mentioned earlier that might intimidate a novice teacher (i.e., older paras who have been in the role much longer than the teacher supervising them) can be an asset if used in a positive way. They likely have connections in the community and school that a novice teacher is just beginning to form. Their positions cost the schools relatively little. Laudably, most paras are pleased to work patiently and caringly with students who can be difficult at times. They often tend to view these students in different and positive ways. They are able to contribute information that helps classroom teachers and consulting teachers provide appropriate learning experiences. Much more effort should be made to prepare educators to collaborate with and supervise paraeducators, and schools should put strong emphasis on recruiting exemplary candidates for paraeducator roles and preparing them well.

Persons who are attracted to paraprofessional positions report some of the same reasons for choosing to become a para. Many like the schedule compatibility with family circumstances, and being involved in work within their communities that fulfills their love of working with children (Giangreco et al., 2010). These factors may attract a person to the job, but given the relatively low pay that most paraprofessionals earn, it is unlikely a skilled and motivated person will stay in the position very long if there aren't other factors that make the job enjoyable. A great deal of time and training is invested in a para during the first year or two of employment, so it only makes sense that retention of qualified and effective paras should be a priority of both the district and the supervisor. There are many intangible ways to foster retention of good paras. Simple gestures by administrators such as providing a mailbox for each para in the teacher's workroom and having the names of paraeducators listed as part the school staff on school websites and in printed staff directories recognizes that paras as part of the school team. A few kind words or small tokens of appreciation such as a thank-you card letting paras know you value their contribution to the team can go a long way in making their job worthwhile.

One special education teacher who has successfully retained many in her core group of paras for several years describes her team as being like a family. She meets with her paras as a group a few days before school starts to go over important information about the upcoming school year and students they will be supporting. When there are new hires, she uses the skills and experiences of her returning paras to help with the orientation and training of the new paras, thus communicating her confidence in their abilities and leadership skills. They all work together to prepare for the start of the school year, each contributing their own particular skills and interests. They organize and arrange the room, put together student folders and materials, discuss how they will communicate on a daily basis about each student, and determine topics of interest for professional development. The supervising teacher loves to cook, so she prepares a special lunch to serve when they meet on the first day. The group also shares a pizza lunch twice a month to bring everyone together. This not only helps them bond as a team socially but it is an avenue for group brainstorming and problem solving.

The paraeducator and teacher relationship can be likened to a couple on the ballroom dance floor. The two gracefully perform together to the rhythm of the music, one partner leading and the other following. Both partners use the same basic dance steps, but the unique timing of special moves, as guided by the leading partner, keeps them from impeding others or digressing from their areas. Some have described the role of the para like that of a sous-chef who supports the executive chef's goals in assigned ways and works under the direction of the executive chef (Causton-Theoharis, Giangreco, Doyle, & Vadasy, 2007). See Figure 10.4 for some examples of how a supervisory professional teacher might direct a paraeducator in much the same way as a sous-chef.

The para–supervisor relationship becomes less obvious when a para is employed to work with a team. In that case, it can be likened to having an orchestra: The para plays an important role in a group performance directed by a conductor. Co-teachers, in contrast, can be thought of as engaging in a musical duet. Each follows the same score but with different,

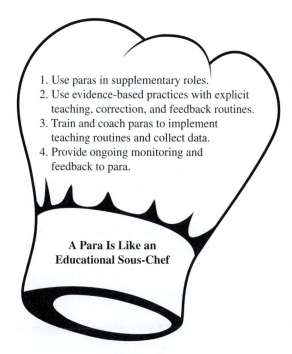

1. Use paras in supplementary roles.
2. Use evidence-based practices with explicit teaching, correction, and feedback routines.
3. Train and coach paras to implement teaching routines and collect data.
4. Provide ongoing monitoring and feedback to para.

A Para Is Like an Educational Sous-Chef

FIGURE 10.4   A Para Is Like an Educational Sous-Chef

preplanned parts. All must maintain the rhythm and harmony to produce a pleasant experience.

The co-teaching team will need to determine who is to assume the primary supervisory responsibilities for paraeducators. The best selection will likely be a person who:

- Holds ultimate responsibility for the outcomes
- Is in the best position to direct the para
- Can provide training for the assigned duties
- Can observe and document para performance

Supervision requires specific, sophisticated skills and behaviors. A supervisor must plan, schedule, coordinate, and evaluate another person's actions. As noted earlier, it is not unusual in these current times of fiscal austerity for special education teachers to be assigned as many as five or six paras whom they direct and supervise. The supervisor is responsible for the para's actions, and the para is accountable to the supervisor. Regardless of how much or how little education or preparation a person has before taking a para position, a supervisor should provide on-the-job training. For example, co-teachers may develop a teaching plan that includes the para for part of the implementation. For the plan to be successful, the supervisor or co-teacher must get the para ready for implementing the pertinent parts of the plan.

A number of functions associated with para supervision have been introduced thus far (French, 2000; Wallace, Shin, Bartholomay, & Stahl, 2001). They include:

1. Communicating and planning with the paraprofessional
2. Managing schedules (prioritizing tasks, preparing schedules)
3. Delegating responsibilities (assigning tasks, directing instructional supports, monitoring performance)
4. Orienting (introducing people, policies, procedures, job descriptions)
5. Providing on-the-job training (modeling teaching, coaching new skills, giving feedback)
6. Evaluating (tracking performance, providing a summative evaluation of job performance)
7. Strengthening public relations in the communities and managing the work environment (maintaining lines of communication, managing conflicts, solving problems)

The more individuals with whom the para works, the more complex the supervision processes. When paras are in the general classroom most of the school day, it is essential for the classroom teacher to be involved in the supervision. In some instances, the classroom teacher may take major responsibility for the supervision. If communication processes among all parties are open, this arrangement can work well. This is best discussed at a meeting with all three parties involved—para, classroom teacher, and special education supervising teacher. The general education teacher may not fully understand the para's role in the classroom and may not be well versed in what the para is permitted by law to do or not do as a paraprofessional. Having a meeting with all parties prior to placement avoids problems and misunderstandings down the road. The teacher and para are made aware of the proper channels of communication if a conflict develops between the two. Follow-up and periodic check-ins can be done with a brief form to survey the teacher and para about how things are going and whether there are any concerns that need to be addressed. Even if there are no concerns identified, arranging a face-to-face meeting with all three individuals at the end of each nine weeks or semester can provide an opportunity to discuss whether the para is being utilized in the most effective manner and how students are progressing.

The first section of the para orientation plan checklist (refer to Figure 10.5) identifies some topics that could be discussed at such a meeting.

SELECTION AND PREPARATION OF PARAEDUCATORS

Most paraeducators bring many useful skills to the job. Some have teaching experience. A few may even have teacher certification but may have been unable to find a teaching job available in the area where they must live. When selecting a paraeducator, administrators should look for a person with:

- A high school diploma, at least, so as to meet national entry standards for paraprofessionals such as those set forth by NCLB
- Evidence of good attendance at work
- Adherence to ethics and confidentiality in their work
- Ability to follow teachers' directions and written plans
- Ability to communicate effectively with students and adults
- Good relationships with young people
- Willingness to learn new skills
- Flexibility
- A sense of humor (It always helps!)

Many of the common difficulties between paraeducators and their supervising teachers can be minimized or avoided completely if the relationship begins with a well thought-out orientation session. A sample checklist of items to include during a para's orientation is included in Figure 10.5. As you will notice, orientation and training are not one-shot events. There are things a paraprofessional needs to know immediately and other things that are important but can wait until after a week or two on the job. Other information and training needs will be ongoing and almost indefinite as the paraeducator grows professionally. The foundation for the relationship is often built during the initial orientation. With development of a job description, trust can emerge along with high expectations and mutual support.

Many districts provide paras with a paraeducator handbook that outlines some important information about the district, their role as a paraeducator, and questions they may have.

FIGURE 10.5   Para Orientation Plan Checklist

Get to Know the People and the School
- Provide a tour of the school
- Introduce key people para needs to know
- Provide a school and student handbook and a school calendar
  - Highlight emergency procedures and other important information

- If the para is working with you in a special education classroom, go over classroom routines including:
  - general student behavior expectations
  - a schedule of when students arrive and leave
  - where materials and supplies are located
  - how to contact the office
  - any clerical or record-keeping duties the para might need to do

- If the para will be working in an inclusive classrooms supporting students, arrange a formal meeting with the teacher, yourself, and the para. Be sure to cover the basics including:
  - the role of the para in the class,
  - how the para will be introduced to the class and parents
  - having teacher share expectations for the para (such as where the para will be located in the classroom, classroom management policies, work style, and interaction preferences)
  - clarifying whether the para is to assist only a particular student, a group of students, or any student in the classroom even if they do not have an IEP, 504, or behavior plan
  - what records or log the para will keep to report on student progress (reporting to both the general and special education teachers)
  - discussing proper communication channels if there is an issue or concern (Will the teacher have a role in the para's evaluation?)
  - discussing how feedback will be given to the para and the special education supervisor

- Discuss confidentiality–VERY IMPORTANT

After a Week on the Job
- Introduce para to other teachers and staff
- Discover para's interests, skills and relevant background related to students or education (and consider using both an inventory or a checklist as well as an interview/discussion format)
- Discuss additional details about job-related tasks (answer para questions)
- Provide additional background on specific student characteristics and needs
- Provide ongoing mini "need to know" training sessions (how to provide positive corrective feedback, how to administer a word identification probe, and so forth)

After a Month on the Job (and continuing on an ongoing basis)
- Develop a plan for acquisition of new skills needed in carrying out the para's role (para, teacher, and supervisor all having input)
- Ask for input from para about program improvement and convey that you work as a team for the benefit of students you serve

Supervising teachers may find it helpful to provide an additional notebook that is specific to your school or the para's role as part of your team. In addition to the orientation checklist, it would be helpful to include frequently used forms such as ongoing communication and feedback forms and checklists, instructional lesson directions, building schedule, staff directory, school map, etc. In the front of the notebook, you should include basic contact information, the supervisory information, regular meetings times, and a reminder of professionalism and confidentiality. Confidentiality can never be overemphasized. (See Figure 10.6.)

Sometimes paras are asked directly for information that is confidential. Some rehearsed responses for confidential information such as those found in Figure 10.7 will help paras know how they can respond to these requests.

FIGURE 10.6   Important Information Regarding Para Communication and Professionalism

Contact Information Outside of School:

Supervising Teacher: Paraeducator:

Phone _____   Phone _____

Email _____   Email _____

If you have questions about your roles and responsibilities or any concerns about students, your duties, or those you work with, your primary contact regarding your position is _____ and is the person to whom you should go to with questions.

If you are ill or need to be absent, please call _____ and then _____ with as much advance notice as possible.

Paras on my team will meet weekly on _____ (day of the week) at _____ (time) in _____ (room or location). The purpose of the meeting is to plan and share information about students, responsibilities, and schedule changes. Please be prepared to share information and to bring up any concerns or questions.

We will meet monthly on _____ (day of the month) at _____ (time) in _____ (room or location) with the general education teacher. The purpose of the meeting is to coordinate planning, roles, and discuss any concerns or questions. Upcoming lessons or activities will be discussed as they relate to students on IEPs.

We will meet once each semester to evaluate job performance, discuss training needs/staff development, and your role as a para. Other teachers/related service personnel with whom you work, such as the classroom teacher, will be asked for input on your evaluation. You will also be asked to reflect on your performance and needs.

Professionalism:
- We work very hard to respect the privacy of our students and their families. Please remember not to discuss students in areas where you might be overheard. This includes the teacher workroom, lunchroom, hallways, playground, or any other public area at school or outside of school (e.g., grocery store, coffee shop, athletic events, etc.)

- If someone asks you about a student or the student's family, home, or disability beyond the scope of what is needed to work with the child in the classroom, please do not discuss the student; instead refer the person to your supervising teacher.

- If a parent, teacher, or friend asks you about a student, please tell them you are not allowed to discuss students and ask them to contact the supervising teacher.

- If you are asked about co-workers or any programming-related issues in the school, tell the person it would not be appropriate for you to discuss such matters.

FIGURE 10.7   Example Responses to Requests for Confidential Information

Request	Para Response
Parent of another child in Cassie's class: *"How much time does Cassie spend in the general education classroom?"*	*"Student placement is confidential. I'm not allowed to speak about placements outside of school."*
Friend and parent of a child on an IEP you work with in the science class: *"What's the deal with the new 6th-grade science teacher? Is she as disorganized as she seems?"*	*"I'm sorry. I'm an employee of the school/district and we aren't allowed to talk about other employees outside of school."*
Co-worker: *"Does Simone leave the classroom for reading?"*	*"Student information is confidential. I'm not allowed to share information about placements with anyone other than the teachers on a student's team. Sorry."*
Parent: *"Don't you think it is distracting and unfair to the other students in the class when _____ shouts out in the middle of a lesson and constantly has to be redirected during instruction?"*	*"I'm sorry. I'm not allowed to talk about students outside of school."* **or** *"Student information is confidential to everyone but the student's parents and teachers who work with the students."*
Friend: *"I heard Sara's son was arrested over the weekend. She must be so upset. What has she told you?"* (Sara is the supervising teacher)	*"Sara is a friend, but it would not be appropriate for me to talk about her private life since she is also a fellow employee."*
Teacher in the building: *"What's wrong with Paul? He seems bright enough but there's something a little odd about him, and I've seen him going into the special education classroom."*	*"Student information is protected by law. I'm not allowed to share information about any student other than staff who work directly with the student."*
Friend: *"I've heard the principal has all these crazy ideas about keeping all the special education students in general classes. What do the teachers think about that? I heard several are going to ask to transfer to other schools at the end of this year."*	*"I can't talk about what goes on in school since I'm an employee of the district and it wouldn't be appropriate."*

Supervisors are ultimately responsible for the actions of paraeducators in the classroom; however, a certain amount of leeway should be granted if the paraeducator has experience or insight into the behavioral or academic interventions that might be most beneficial. The para sometimes has the advantage of more frequent one-on-one contact with the student and may also see the student across different settings and with different teachers. With this additional insight, their ideas might improve effectiveness of the intervention. Ongoing communication, in which the teacher invites the paraeducator to provide input, will validate the para's ideas and knowledge gained from working with particular students in different classroom environments. Paraeducators should have differing assignments and responsibilities based on their experience, training, and confidence level.

The National Resource Center for Paraeducators (NRCP) has established three levels of responsibilities for paraeducators:

- *Level I* responsibilities include supervising and monitoring students, preparing learning materials, providing personal assistance to students, reinforcing learning experiences that are planned and introduced by teachers, and conducting themselves in a professional and ethical manner.
- *Level II* responsibilities include all Level I responsibilities as well as having more autonomy in delivering lessons developed by the teacher, assisting students in completing projects assigned by the teacher, collecting ongoing assessment data as directed by the teacher, implementing teacher-developed behavior management plans, and participating in regularly scheduled teacher and paraeducator meetings that may include other team members to plan for students in the general education setting.
- *Level III*, the highest level, responsibilities include additional tasks of collaboration and information sharing with teachers for planning purposes, modifying curriculum and instructional activities for individual students under the direction of teachers, and assisting teachers in maintaining student records.

ACTIVITY 10.1

Progress Monitoring and Para Communication — Who's in Charge?

Jackie, a second-year special education teacher, just completed a summer course on collaboration where she gained additional skills in directing and supervising paraeducators. One of her goals is to implement a communication system that would provide her with daily reports from the paras, including what happened in the classrooms each day and data that will assist her in monitoring student progress. She asked each para to keep a daily log as they worked with students and return it to her at the end of the day. She also wanted to begin weekly debriefings and training meetings with all her paras to start coaching them in the skills they would need to implement the new teaching routines.

Much to Jackie's disappointment, the logs were often incomplete and poorly written. When Jackie asked one of the paras to improve the quality of her logs, the para said it seemed pointless to have to write everything out that she already knew in her head. It didn't stop there. The paras found excuses to miss the weekly meetings or seemed disinterested in what Jackie was sharing. One even went so far as texting on her cell phone while attending one of the meetings. Jackie felt intimidated by a couple of the paras who were older than she was and had worked in the school much longer. They felt they knew better than she what the students needed.

Put yourself in Jackie's shoes. Discuss the situation with others in a small group to problem solve how Jackie might have approached this situation with her paras that would lead to a better outcome.

When training paraeducators, Pickett and Gerlach (2003) recommend that a teacher provide a rationale for a given skill or strategy, explain why it is important, and give a clear, step-by-step description. Next, the teacher should demonstrate or model the skill. Ideally, this would be done in the setting where the para is to implement it. Some supervising teachers have found it time efficient to video record the demonstration or model rather than finding time in an already busy schedule to meet one-on-one with the para. A video recording can be utilized by multiple paras, viewed at a time that is convenient for the para, and watched multiple times for clarification. The teacher should observe the para implementing the procedure and provide feedback. If it is not feasible to observe the para, the para can make a video recording to share with the teacher for feedback. Finally, the teacher should provide ongoing coaching unobtrusively while the para is working with students. Steinbacher-Reed and Powers (2012) found paraprofessional development models that include individual coaching to be more successful than large-group professional development sessions. A side-by-side coaching professional development technique is described by Stockall (2014) where the teacher identifies the goals and objectives and provides instruction while the paraeducator listens and asks questions. The teacher then demonstrates the instruction through modeling with explicit skill identification. These two phases are labeled "I Do It" phases. Next, "We Do It" involves guided practice where the para performs the skill or instruction with the teacher asking questions, encouraging, and providing feedback. Finally, the last phase, "You Do It," is independent practice with the para being self-directed and self-evaluating performance. The teacher and para debrief and feedback is provided. This side-by-side coaching technique assures paras receive the level of professional development needed to be effective in carrying out their role in inclusive settings where the special education teacher is not always present for more ongoing supervision.

Matching Paras with Teachers

When initially pairing paras with teachers, it is helpful to openly discuss work style preferences, both of the para and teacher. A number of such informal inventories exist but a **supervising teacher** can easily develop one like the example in Figure 10.8. This example has questions appropriate for the paraeducator, but the statements could be modified easily to develop a complementary version for the teacher or supervisor to complete. For example, item 2 could be changed from "I like to receive regular corrective feedback" to "I prefer to *give* regular corrective feedback rather than waiting until end-of-semester formal evaluations." Some items, such as item 6, "I am a detail person," could appear on both para and supervising teacher's form. Having both the para and teacher complete complementary forms such as this serves as a good discussion starter about work style preferences.

It is unlikely that two people will be a perfect match, and that isn't necessarily the purpose, nor may it even be desirable, but it starts the conversation about how the two can best work together. When responses on items are in conflict with one another, differences in styles and preferences can be discussed and followed up by discussion of ways to accommodate or work around them. Sometimes opposites work well together when strengths and preferences for different types of tasks can be identified. Recall the discussion earlier in the text about the value of differing styles in team situations. A teacher may enjoy the creative aspect of planning and teaching new and interesting lessons but detest the record-keeping part of the job. If the para who works with them enjoys tasks of recording student progress on charts and graphs and analyzing the data, then it may seem like a perfect

FIGURE 10.8   Work Style Inventory

	1 – Strongly Disagree to 5 – Strongly Agree				
1. I like to be supervised closely.	1	2	3	4	5
2. I like to receive regular corrective feedback.	1	2	3	4	5
3. I like to have clear guidelines and expectations.	1	2	3	4	5
4. I like to have written instructions when implementing instruction or a behavior plan.	1	2	3	4	5
5. I like to know exactly what I will be doing in advance.	1	2	3	4	5
6. I am a detail person.	1	2	3	4	5
7. I like to provide input regarding students.	1	2	3	4	5
8. I consider myself a very punctual person.	1	2	3	4	5
9. I need a quiet place to work without distractions.	1	2	3	4	5
10. I thrive on having a routine that is followed daily.	1	2	3	4	5
11. I like working with other adults.	1	2	3	4	5
12. I like to have choices in how I work or how I complete a task.	1	2	3	4	5
13. I prefer to be told exactly how to do each task.	1	2	3	4	5
14. I like tasks that require me to be creative.	1	2	3	4	5
15. I think of myself as being spontaneous.	1	2	3	4	5

marriage of opposite work styles. On the other hand, if one person is of a type who is neat and tidy and the other is much less so, then sharing a desk could present problems. Knowing these differences from the start can allow each to be a bit more sensitive to the other's style. If sharing a desk is the only option, maybe a compromise of each having a separate drawer and agreeing that shared space will be maintained at a certain level of organization will resolve the difference at a workable level.

With the rapidly increasing cultural and linguistic diversity of students in special education, having diversity among paraeducators who support them is important. Efforts should be made to create a staff of paraeducators who reflect the cultural and linguistic backgrounds of the students. This is especially important in communities where teachers may not be familiar with the culture and versed in the first language of students. As suggested earlier, paras often have fulfilled a role very effectively as a community partner and liaison in home–school relationships. They can serve as translators of the culture and language for both educators and families. Hispanic and Native American families especially rely on the interconnectedness of the extended family and informal community-based networks for emotional and social support (Geenen, Powers, & Lopez-Vasquez, 2001). Thus, paras from the community may be able to facilitate meaningful collaboration with culturally and linguistically diverse (CLD) families. Paras who are not familiar with cultural and linguistic diversity should participate in the same relevant staff development and self-assessment as other educators.

District-Level Staff Development for Paras

Although states are required to provide appropriate training, preparation, and supervision for paraeducators, the type and amount of training provided will vary from state to state. Lasater, Johnson, and Fitzgerald (2000), using more than twenty-five years of experience as staff developers and data from a nationwide survey validating guidelines on standards and skills required by paraeducators and teachers, recommend conducting needs assessments targeted specifically to para roles and issues. This should be followed by professional development sessions in settings similar to those for training other professionals, with professional credits and stipends provided for attendance. As stated earlier, the new ESSA legislation gives paraeducators a stronger voice than ever before in the areas of needs assessment and professional development. This renewed and extended commitment communicates that paraeducators are valued and important to the instructional process. Para should be actively involved in the needs assessment process to determine what skills are needed for their role, which skills they currently possess, and which skills will require more training. Just as important as identifying the areas of training needed, the supervising teacher and para should discuss and plan the best mode of delivery. For example, materials may be available in online modules that the para can complete independently or it may be decided that the para will observe the teacher performing the skills or lesson and then, through guided practice, will perform the skill or lesson and receive feedback. Another option is to have paras with more experience or levels of training teach other paras. During these professional development options, whether done online or with a teacher or other para, time should be allocated for questions, feedback, and discussion of issues. An effective way to start the discussion about needed training for paras is to use a form similar to the one in Figure 10.9 where the para can reflect on skills already possessed, areas where further training is needed, and areas where the para doesn't feel comfortable in carrying out a duty or skill. The supervising teacher should create lists of tasks/roles paras might be expected to perform based on the job description and student caseload. Those tasks can be listed on the form for the para to complete and then discussed to determine training needs and how those will be delivered or which tasks might be better carried out by another para or a qualified teacher.

The ultimate goal of paraeducator staff development is to build a solid knowledge base that reflects students' needs and goals. Paras, like teachers, value information they can take back to the classroom and implement immediately. So the training should be practical and provide alternatives for responding to implementation challenges.

On some occasions, it may be beneficial to have some joint professional development sessions with teacher and para partners. Topics for joint sessions could include exploration of roles and responsibilities, team-building activities, and communication skills. This dual training model not only provides needed information and skills to both teacher and the paraprofessional, but it also has the added benefit of enabling the partners to discuss the information and its application to their unique situation. Finally, no matter how much advance preparation the paraeducator has received, teachers to whom a para is assigned must provide orientation and on-the-job training. The job of the supervising teacher is to provide training that will help the paraeducator function in the specific situation of the assignment.

FIGURE 10.9   **Para Job Skills Inventory**

Task/Skill	I feel confident in carrying out this task.	I need more training.	I don't feel comfortable doing this task.
Examples:			
1. Provide corrective feedback to students.			
2. Carry out a lesson plan using _____ program.			
3. Supervise playground or lunchroom activities.			
4. Carry out a behavior plan with a student.			
5. Chart student performance.			
6. Administer reading probes.			
7. Conduct an individual lesson.			
8. Grade papers.			
9. Help a student implement _____ assistive technology in the classroom.			
10. Assist a student with toileting.			
11. Prepare learning materials.			
12. Record and chart behavior.			

Yet another option for providing training is to supply written as well as online materials that paras can study independently at a time convenient to them or access on a need-to-know basis. The supervising teacher can create or obtain a guide that can be given to the paraeducator for self-study. One example of such a resource is *Paraprofessionals in the Classroom: A Survival Guide* (Ashbaker & Morgan, 2013). This guide includes such topics as how para duties are assigned and defined, laws and regulations affecting para roles, learner characteristics, critical components of effective instruction, monitoring instructional effectiveness, student behavior and classroom management, recognition, praise and sanctions, professional and ethical behavior, and reflection and self-evaluation. Online training modules can serve a similar purpose. For example, paraprofessionals in Nebraska can access the Project PARA: Paraeducator Self-Study Program and receive feedback about their performance as they complete each module. A companion site for supervisors of paraeducators, Project PARA: Supervising Paraeducators, also includes modules that can be completed by teachers to aid in their supervision of paras.

Supervisors should discuss roles, skills, and needed training on an ongoing basis. Federal and state preparation and training requirements for paraeducators have created a need for documenting training and skill-development activities. At the very least, every paraeducator should maintain a file folder or online file documenting the training by means of certificates, transcripts, meeting/training agendas, products, or other evidence of completed activities. If some type of skill inventory has been completed, and training modules are selected and completed based on that inventory, this should be included in the documentation as well. The Project PARA: Paraeducator Self-Study Program mentioned above is set up to include eight units of instructional resources for paras, including pretests for self-assessment of skills prior to beginning each unit. After completion of the unit, a post-test is taken. The ParaEducator Learning Network is a commercial program used by many districts across the country to provide online training and documentation for paraeducators in a variety of skill areas.

Training Paras to Deliver Instruction

One of the primary instructional roles of paraeducators is carrying out plans developed by the supervising teacher. This instructional role often takes place away from the supervising teacher where direct observation and monitoring is not possible. In light of this, supervising teachers have an obligation to train and prepare their paraeducators adequately for delivering instruction and then provide the necessary supervision to assure it is being delivered as directed. A detailed lesson plan is the first step in clarifying what the teacher wants the para to do during the instructional session. The plan should include the objective(s) of the lesson; materials needed; a step-by-step outline of the activities; description of instructional procedures; reinforcements needed; and data collection, record keeping, and evaluation that will be required. The teacher's lesson plans should be explicit and provide a means for the paraeducator to communicate ongoing student progress and other daily and weekly anecdotal information from which lesson adjustments can be made. In the end, the supervising teacher needs to be informed and connected to each student who is working with a para in order to make knowledgeable and informed decisions about lesson and behavioral intervention plans.

During initial training with paras regarding teaching a lesson written by the teacher, the supervisor should use a sample lesson to explain clearly and demonstrate carefully each step by means of explicit modeling. In addition to the teaching procedures, the supervisor should also point out ways to keep students engaged and how to provide corrective feedback and effectively reinforce positive behavior and student learning. Record-keeping procedures and how to monitor and document student progress should also be discussed.

Figure 10.10 provides an example of a detailed instructional plan for a para. When this level of specification is provided, the paraeducator is not left wondering how to implement the lesson and instructional fidelity is ensured.

Short video clips can also be used for training purposes. The advantage of creating a library of video examples is that they can be viewed and reviewed anytime, anywhere. A video can be especially useful when new paras join the team at different times

FIGURE 10.10   Example Instructional Plan: Sight Word Recognition

Objective: When presented ten sight word flash cards one at a time, the student will name each Dolch Sight Word within three seconds with 90 percent accuracy.

Materials: 3×5 flash cards printed with sight words from the Dolch List.

Print a blank copy of the data table below and fill in the sight words across the top (see example "have")

Activity:

1. Have the student sit opposite you at a desk or table.

2. Show the student one flash card at a time.

3. Progress through the following steps while showing each flash card.

a) Say: "What word is this?" Record on chart "+" if student responds correctly, "−" if student doesn't respond correctly. Place the words said correctly in a separate pile.

b) If the student does not respond correctly, say: "This word is 'WORD.' What Word?" Be sure the student names the word correctly. "Yes, WORD."

c) Place the missed card in the back of the deck so it will be repeated.

4. After going through the deck successfully, mix up the cards and repeat the procedure marking the corrects and incorrects in the row labeled "Trial 2." Repeat again for Trial 3.

5. Work for ten minutes or until the student has successfully read the words three times each.

Reinforcement: After each correct response say: "Good job!" or "You're correct."

Recording Student Performance:

Student responses:

Have

Word	1	2	3	4	5	6	7	8	9	10
Trial 1										
Trial 2										
Trial 3										
Percent Correct										

Overall Percent Correct: # correct_____/ # attempted_____

Is the student consistent in saying the flashed sight word within three seconds?

Does the student name each word correctly 90 percent of the time?

Note:

Share the results with the supervising teacher to determine next steps.

of the year. Some paras on the team may already know some things that others need For example, many paras will not be trained in how to make corrections and provide feedback to students. Short video clips can be found online or made by the teacher to share with the para.

After describing and modeling the lesson, the teacher should have the para role-play the lesson while the supervisor takes notes and provides feedback. Teachers who are responsible for supervising several paraprofessionals and/or who routinely have their paras implement specialized-teaching routines might find it helpful to create some short instructional videos modeling how to teach a lesson (or find a similar, suitable example on the Internet that could be viewed by the para). These video mini-training lessons could then be archived on a webpage for paras to access when they need to learn a new skill or learn how to implement something directed by the teacher. An advantage of the video option is that a para can watch a video anytime, and the teacher and para don't have to wait until they have mutually shared planning time; another example of the asynchronous benefit of modern technology. Keep in mind that if the video training option is used for the demonstration and model phase, it is still important for the supervising teacher to directly observe the paraeducator practice-teach the lesson and provide feedback before assigning the para to teach a lesson independently. Paras could also capture their teaching of a lesson to show they are carrying out routines as instructed.

STRATEGIES FOR ONGOING COMMUNICATION WITH PARAEDUCATORS

A variety of ways are available for paras and supervising teachers to communicate; the method chosen will depend on the preferences of those involved. Logistics, access, level of comfort with technology, number of parties involved, caseload, and supervision load are factors and preferences to be considered. As mentioned earlier, some choose to use an ongoing paper-and-pencil log in a student folder in which the paraeducator and teacher can share information such as data on student progress, anecdotal notes, questions about adaptations or adjustments to lessons, and so on. In other situations, a supervisor may have opportunity to touch base with paraeducators and debrief at the beginning or end of the day. Still others may find technology applications helpful for sharing lesson notes, changes in schedules, and other necessary communication. Portable technologies such as tablets can be used to capture a picture of a student's work sample along with on-the-spot notes, which can be downloaded later by the supervising teacher or printed out and placed in a file for the teacher's review. If e-mail is used for communication between the para and teacher, it is important that paraeducators are informed about issues of confidentiality and how e-mail should and should not be used. Some teachers and paras have found that text messaging with cell phones is an unobtrusive way to send a quick message about an unexpected change in the schedule, or to alert the teacher to a problem that needs immediate attention, or to ask a quick question of the para or teacher. The use of cell phones in schools, whether for sending a text message, making or receiving phone calls, or reading e-mails, can be convenient for a variety of purposes that would otherwise be much more difficult or time-consuming. But, when cell phones are used, there is a risk that they will be used

ENHANCEDetext
Video Example 10.2.

In this video, special educator Shawn Heimlich describes how he utilizes six paraeducators in both the resource room and when they work with students in general education classes. How does he supervise and communicate with his paras?

inappropriately. If overused, cell phones could become a distraction and be counterproductive. Teachers should talk to paras upfront about whether cell phones are an appropriate way to communicate with each other and, if so, set clear guidelines for their use. If cell phones and other technologies such as tablets are being used for communication between the para and supervising special educator, that information should be shared with the general education teacher to avoid misunderstanding about uses in the classroom. This also will provide an opportunity to air any concerns on the part of the general educator.

Need for Confidentiality by the Paraeducator

The Council for Exceptional Children (CEC) has published standards for paraprofessionals working in special education, and the National Resource Center for Paraprofessionals (NRCP) also provides standards for knowledge that paraeducators are expected to possess if they work in special education programs. One of the CEC standards for paraprofessionals specifically addresses professional and ethical practice. It includes knowledge about ethical practices for confidential communication and kinds of biases and differences that affect one's ability to work with others. Because there is no single professional association for paraeducators, standards such as those proposed by CEC or NRCP are voluntary. No outside agency monitors unprofessional behavior, although school administrators can bring disciplinary action if a paraprofessional acts in a way considered inappropriate by school district standards.

Ashbaker and Morgan (2013) target criteria of professionalism for paraeducators such as dress and appearance, regard for health and safety of students and staff, communication and conflict resolution skills, collaboration with teachers and parents, and confidentiality in the use of information. It is of utmost importance that paraeducators understand the necessity for confidentiality when working with students. Teachers need to impress on paraeducators the importance of keeping confidential and secure any information such as academic achievement, test scores, descriptions of student behavior, attendance, family problems, and other information of a personal nature. Additionally, job descriptions for paraprofessionals should include ethical guidelines in dealing with students, families, and others (Trautman, 2004). A statement such as "Keep information that pertains to school, school personnel, student, and parents or guardians confidential" could be printed and placed on the covers of notebooks with student information, at the top or bottom of a memo pad used to communicate with staff, or as part of one's signature line on outgoing emails. This serves as a polite yet constant reminder about the confidentiality and ethical behavior related to their role and sensitive information. Paras should be directed to take any concerns they have directly to the supervising teacher rather than sharing those concerns with others. Figure 10.11 offers a dozen tips for carrying out paraprofessional duties in an ethical manner. This list should be shared on the first day with a new para, provided

FIGURE 10.11   A Dozen Tips for Carrying Out Paraprofessional Duties in an Ethical Manner

As a member of the educational team, you are expected to carry out your paraprofessional role with high ethical standards. You will be handling confidential information and need to act in an ethical manner in difficult situations. Use this information to guide your actions.

1. Read the district's paraprofessional handbook and school policy manual and follow the guidelines.
2. Only perform instructional and noninstructional activities for which you are qualified or have been trained. (If you do not feel you have the skills to perform a duty that has been assigned to you, you should tell your supervising teacher and seek needed training.)
3. Do not share confidential student information.
4. Do not engage in inappropriate conversations about students or staff.
5. Always follow the directions of your supervisor who bears the ultimate responsibility for managing instruction and behavior of students.
6. Any information about a student should only be shared with a parent when the supervising teacher is present. It is not the role of the paraprofessional to share student progress information, test results, behavior concerns, or any other similar type of information.
7. Respect the dignity and privacy of all students, families, and staff members.
8. Do not engage in discriminatory practices based on the student's race, disability, gender, cultural background, sexual orientation, or religion.
9. School matters and problems should only be discussed while on duty during the school day and with the appropriate personnel. Coffee shops, gyms, restaurants, sporting events, the family dinner table, and other social functions are not appropriate venues to share information that must be kept confidential.
10. Always present yourself as a positive adult role model to students and represent the school, its staff and programs in a positive light.
11. Respect the teacher as your supervisor. Follow the lessons and programs designed by the teacher. Discuss concerns involving teaching methods or other classroom issues directly with the teacher. If the issue is not resolved, then discuss your concerns only with your supervisor. Don't talk about it to other paras, parents, or teachers.
12. If issues arise regarding students, family members, or staff such as other paraeducators, only discuss them with your supervisor. If the issue is not resolved, follow the proper grievance procedures outlined by your district.

on a handout for the para's notebook, and revisited often at conference time or when needed.

When a teacher is absent and a substitute teacher is called in, confidentiality can be a concern if teachers have failed to plan ahead for ensuring para confidentiality (Fleury, 2000). Teachers will want to discuss with paras at the beginning of the year the possibility of teacher absence and of having a substitute teacher for a period of time. A teacher should provide guidelines on maintaining confidentiality in the presence of the substitute teacher and knowing the parameters for sharing information with the substitute only when it is absolutely needed. The para's role in the presence of a substitute teacher should be discussed. Many teachers have substitute-teacher notes or a special folder with basic information for the substitute that includes the schedules of the paras and the duties and assignments they perform throughout the day. Finally, teachers should convey in their notes to the substitute teacher how the paras can assist in maintaining the daily routine of the classroom, a concern that is so important for the students *and* their teacher.

Sometimes it is the paraeducator who will be absent and, again, advance planning for an unexpected or even a planned absence can go a long way in making for a smooth transition when a substitute assistant is called in (Fleury, 2000). Ideally, it is less complicated when the substitute is familiar with the program and students, and has filled in before for an absent teacher or para. These subs may be at the top of the "substitute call list." But it is not wise to assume that the person substituting understands issues of confidentiality. Those should be discussed at the beginning of the day. Much like a plan prepared for a substitute teacher, it is helpful to have a similar plan on file should the para be absent. This would include the para's schedule, a brief overview of specific methods or reinforcers used with students, and classroom management routines. It is important to be class specific, not child specific, at this time. If the absent para has been assigned to a student with unpredictable behavior, consider reassigning that student temporarily to someone who knows the student. Encourage the substitute to ask questions about your teaching methods or behavior management tools, but be aware that sometimes you will not be able to fully answer the question because of the need to preserve confidentiality.

FRAMEWORK FOR WORKING WITH PARAEDUCATORS

Para supervision requires skills beyond consulting, collaborating, or teaching. The supervisor is responsible for the para's actions and the para is accountable to the supervisor. Whereas collaborating teachers mutually develop a teaching plan, the supervisor will tell the para what parts of the developed plan to implement. Most paraeducators are assigned to one supervising teacher who is responsible for planning what paraeducators should do from day to day, and for scheduling where and when the paras will do it, as well as communicating this information to others. Because paras are frequently working alongside general education teachers rather than with their primary supervising special education teacher, it is critical that all members of the team have an initial meeting to discuss roles and communication. The general educator and the para need to be clear about the role of each when the para is working in inclusive settings. The consulting supervising teacher will meet periodically with the general educator about students on IEPs and will need to decide when a para should be part of those meetings. General education teachers serve as secondary day-to-day supervisors and should be consulted to provide input when the paras are being evaluated.

Video Example from YouTube

▶ **ENHANCED**etext
Video Example 10.3.

Watch this video for a top ten list of important strategies for working with paraeducators. (https://www.youtube.com/watch?v=0VJNdg-AiFM)

French (2000) suggests a number of practical ways a supervising teacher can select classroom tasks for delegating to a paraeducator. She describes delegation as getting things done through another who has been trained to handle them, by giving that person authority to do it but not giving up teacher responsibility. Selection of the task is determined by considering it in the light of time sensitivity and the consequences of *not* doing it. A task that needs to be done soon and that has major consequences should *not* be delegated. Such tasks include student behavior crises, meetings regarding the crises, student health crises, and monitoring of students in non-classroom settings. Tasks that are not time sensitive but have major consequences also should not be delegated. This might include such things as designing individual behavior plans, assessing student progress, developing curriculum, and planning instruction.

The following steps can be helpful in deciding what can be delegated to paras and how to set up the delegated tasks for successful completion:

1. Analyze the task and if it can be delegated, identify the steps it contains.
2. Decide what to delegate, keeping in mind the skills and preferences of those involved.
3. Create a plan that specifies the purpose of the task, how to do it, and criteria for successful completion.
4. If more than one para is available, match para skill sets to the task at hand and choose the best person for the job.
5. Make yourself available to answer questions and provide clarification.
6. Monitor performance without hovering over the para. When the task is complete, acknowledge the para's efforts and reinforce the good work. Be tolerant of the reality that the para may not do some things exactly as you would have done them.

Special educators responsible for supervising paras need to define clearly and monitor carefully the paras' responsibilities. Breton (2010) points out that the least professionally qualified individuals, the paraprofessionals, often have primary responsibilities for teaching students who present the greatest academic and behavioral challenges. Unfortunately, all too often students on IEPs are placed in general education classrooms without clear expectations established regarding the role each team member will play regarding planning, implementing, monitoring, evaluating, and adjusting instruction. These researchers suggest assigning paras as classroom assistants rather than as assistants for single students. They note that if co-teachers fail to plan instruction, the responsibility often falls on the para, which is clearly beyond reasonable expectation for them. Others recommend ongoing collaborative meetings for sharing expertise areas and for discussing and clarifying areas of responsibility, including strategies and a plan for "fading" the level of support provided by the paraeducator (Marks et al., 1999).

Sometimes paras unnecessarily separate and isolate students with IEPs from the general classroom group in an effort to help them understand or complete the lesson. Paras must be instructed that students are to be physically, programmatically, and interactionally included in classroom activities planned by qualified teachers. To help instill this awareness, teachers need to make sure they consider the para's role when co-planning lessons, and whenever possible include the para in the planning process.

ACTIVITY 10.2
Clarifying the Para Assistant Role

Jane is one of three paras assigned to Martin, a teacher of students with behavior disorders. Jane is an experienced para and has clear notions of what she should do in the inclusive classroom where Martin has assigned her. Martin told Jane simply to be in the classroom to intervene whenever a particular student, Bart, gets off task or refuses to do work. She is not to help him with his work, but only to take steps to keep him "under control." Jane doesn't think that is a good use of her time. She wants to help this student and others who might be having difficulty with the assignment. She thinks she should help clarify confusing information and outline class lectures on the chalkboard as she did in the previous school where she was assigned. Discuss the following questions with one or more in a small group. Is it appropriate for Martin to have these somewhat limited expectations for Jane even when she isn't pleased about it? Does the classroom teacher have a voice in this? How could this conflict be addressed?

Managing Schedules and Time

Challenges of arranging consultant and co-teaching schedules are magnified when several paraeducators are part of the scheduling demands. Because schedules are likely to change from week to week, it is helpful for everyone to have a schedule each week that indicates who does what, when, and where. The schedule should be available to all special service staff and the building office personnel. You never want your front office personal to tell a parent or administrator who comes to the office and asks to see you, "I can't keep track of where he or she might be. S/he doesn't really have a schedule." Likewise, a teacher might need to find a para who works in several classrooms. A whiteboard or some type of posted schedule listing all the members of the team (special educator and paras) and where they are from hour to hour can be used to keep track of all the moving parts. Sometimes it begins to look like one of these whiteboards you see on medical shows in an ER or surgery wing where names of doctors and patients are constantly being erased and new schedules posted. Keep in mind, if student names are needed on a white board visible to the public near the door of a special education classroom or office, be sure to protect the confidentiality by using student initials, and, even then, only if absolutely necessary.

The challenge of finding time to plan and discuss student needs with a para mirrors the issues of time discussed elsewhere for collaborating teachers. Teachers and paras in self-contained special classes may have break periods at the same time, but that is not likely when the para is working in a different classroom, as is often the case in inclusive schools. In an ideal situation, at least twenty minutes a day is set aside for para–supervisor planning.

The more individuals with whom a para works, the more complex the supervision process is. When paras are in the general classroom most of the school day, classroom teachers must also be in a supervisory role for them. If communication processes among all parties are open and ongoing, this arrangement can work well. Sometimes, however, much confusion can occur.

It is one thing to plan for oneself and quite another to organize and plan for another person such as a paraeducator. Capizzi and Da Fonte (2012) provide several examples of forms teachers can use to plan for paras. Another type of plan would be a daily schedule that would list all time periods through the day, where the para is to be during each time period (for example, "room 25" or "the work room"), and what activity or responsibility the para will have, such as co-teach the group with Martin or adapt the textbook for student Willy. Plans of this nature can be printed on paper or shared in a Web-based format using free and accessible Web-sharing tools such as Google Docs, where the paraeducator and professional can easily add comments and provide feedback to one another.

Another challenging part of supervising paras will be to determine *when* the supervisory responsibilities will be performed. Teachers who oversee paras must carve time out of their day to plan, schedule, and develop teaching activities for the paraeducator to implement with students. Additional time will be needed to train the para in how to deliver the plans effectively. This can be best described as on-the-job training, coaching, and feedback. According to French (1997), "Teachers who fail to spend outside time for planning, training, coaching, and feedback with paraeducators report that they are dissatisfied with the performance of the paraeducators with whom they work" (p. 73).

Examples of other information to provide the paraeducator are:

- A copy of school handbook(s) providing school policies and regulations
- Information about the students included in one's caseload
- Teachers' guides for instructional materials that will be used
- First aid information
- Emergency information, such as locations of storm shelters and safety procedures
- Classroom rules and other expectations for classroom management
- Behavior management guidelines for specific students
- Procedures for accessing media and checking out materials

Although supervising teachers are responsible for planning carefully and communicating responsibilities to paraeducators, it will not always happen. As part of the orientation and training of paras, it is good to remind them that not every situation they will encounter can be anticipated or clearly spelled out as to what they should do. There will not always be time to read the handbook (such as when a major storm is imminent). There will be times when they are uncertain about their responsibilities and the best advice you can give is to use common sense. Of course, they should be reminded to always request details about their designated tasks and to practice good communication skills; but when uncertainties arise, they may have to rely on their best judgment of what their cooperating teacher or supervisor would want them to do under the circumstances.

Some populations of students such as those diagnosed with Autism Spectrum Disorder (ASD) can pose special challenges for paras because the characteristics, behaviors, and skill levels of these students vary widely. The supervising teacher may have plans for the para to follow but the student may react in an unexpected way and the para must adjust lessons "on the fly" without specific directions. In this case, knowing some general guidelines for working with students with ASD can help guide the para's decision-making.

Evaluating the Paraeducator-Teacher Relationship

Extensive use of paraeducators has altered the role of teachers. Supervising and directing the work of paraeducators is an addition to the teacher's role. According to French (1999), "Even though teachers are no longer solely responsible for providing instruction, they remain wholly accountable for the outcomes of the instructional process" (p. 70).

Teachers may find evaluating paras neither easy nor particularly pleasant, especially when performance is substandard. However, the task may be made less discomforting by following three suggestions:

1. *Be clear and concise in telling paras exactly what you expect.* Preparing job descriptions will get you off to a good start. Say "When you help co-teach in science, please refrain from responding to questions, and show the student instead how to find answers in the textbook or other resource materials" rather than "Would you please help students in the science class during study time?"

2. *Tell paras what you like about the way they do their jobs.* Everyone likes to have good performance acknowledged.

3. *Tell paras if there are things that they are not doing well.* Talking about what you don't like as well as what you do like is not only a teacher's responsibility, it also shows you care about the personal relationship. Many teachers do not feel comfortable talking about problems, so they dodge around troublesome issues far too long. But constructive feedback gives you and the para a chance to work out differences and misunderstandings. (A previous chapter provided material to help with communication in sensitive areas.) If your paras see you engage in self-evaluation of your own teaching through video recording and analysis or even informal debriefing immediately after teaching a lesson, then they will view the self-analysis as an expected part of teaching and not punitive when they are asked to do it as they teach a lesson. You can also model this behavior by sitting down with paras and looking over student progress data, analyzing how, for example, you could change the level of corrective feedback during your lesson to see if it will have a positive impact on student performance.

Feedback should relate to the task or action, not the person. The tone should be objective and not blaming. Keep the focus on what you can do to improve student outcomes. Also, give feedback sooner than later. If too much time passes, it won't be as meaningful or as likely to be incorporated because the opportunity will have passed. If the feedback is at all personal or could be perceived as negative, be sure to choose an appropriate place and time and make sure it is done privately. Some examples of how the feedback might be given include:

- Start by describing the context: "I'd like to talk with you about what happened when you were in Ms. Winkler's room helping Davis and other students during the math lesson earlier today."

- Describe your reactions and reasons: "I noticed that some of the students who sit near Davis seemed distracted by your conversation with him and sometimes seem to struggle to see the teacher working the problems on the board because of where you were standing next to Davis when helping him."
- Ask for the change you'd like to see: "It might work better for you to let Ms. Winkler finish the lesson before you start assisting Davis with the assigned problems. Maybe you could discuss moving Davis's seat to a place where it would be less distracting to other students when you are helping him."
- Allow time for the other person to respond.

It is never easy to discuss problems. If a problem is of a more personal or difficult nature than the example here, consider planning out what you will say and rehearse it before you meet with the para. Remember, you can only control what *you* say and what *you* do. You cannot control the other person.

A supervising teacher should listen to the para's input and suggestions that result from his or her observations and knowledge of the students. It is important to learn what is happening to and for the students assigned to the para's responsibility. Sometimes the paraeducator is the only adult who observes what a student does during a particular activity. The para's observations and the way these are communicated to the supervising teacher are important factors in the decisions that will be made about that student. The supervising teacher should direct the para to report outcomes related to specific goals and objectives on students' IEPs, such as learning outcomes, specific behaviors, and relationships with others. Ask the para to provide information to answer the following questions:

- What was the event?
- Who was there?
- When did it take place?
- Where did it take place?
- What was going on before the event?
- How did the event take place? (What was said or done by all those mentioned in "Who" above?)
- What was the outcome (the natural consequence) of your intervention?

Caution the paraeducator to avoid interpreting, judging, labeling, speculating about the student's motives, dwelling on covert behaviors, or making judgments about feelings. Ask for only the facts and get them written out if at all possible. Once again, it is important to remember that paraprofessionals don't walk into the job having been trained in how to describe behavior objectively. Share some examples of poor interpretations of behavior (for example, "He was daydreaming.") as compared to more objective behavioral descriptions that would be more suitable for documenting student behaviors (such as, "He stared at the bulletin board with a blank look on his face for three minutes."). Figure 10.12 provides a checklist that may be useful in guiding evaluation before or after instructional activities.

FIGURE 10.12   Paraeducator Teaching Checklist

Ask yourself the following questions before and after teaching students. Identify those areas in need of improvement. Reward yourself for areas well done.

Getting Ready to Teach

> Do I know the special instructional needs of all the students I will be teaching?
> Is the teaching environment comfortable with no distractions?
> Do I have all the necessary materials for this lesson?
> Have I asked the teacher to clarify any parts of the lesson I do not understand?
> Have I adapted material if needed?
> Do I know the content I am preparing to teach?
> Am I prepared to use at least three different activities related to the lesson goal?

While You Are Teaching

> Do I take a few moments to establish rapport with students each time?
> Have I verbally cued students to attend before starting the lesson (for example, "Eyes up here")?
> Are my instructions concise and clear?
> Have I reviewed relevant past learning?
> Is the lesson goal clear to me and my students?
> Have I modeled a skill when appropriate?
> Do I keep the student(s) engaged in the task at least 70 percent of the time?
> Do I ask questions of selected students by name instead of calling on volunteers?
> Do I provide praise for effort?
> Do I give brief, immediate, corrective feedback to the student who errs?
> Does every student have an opportunity to respond many times during the lesson?
> Do I provide questions and cues to help students use what they already know to discover new information?
> Do students respond correctly 80–90 percent of the time?
> Do I check for skill mastery before closing the lesson?
> Do I change activities when it is clear a student is experiencing frustration?
> Do I keep the lesson interesting by changing activities?
> Am I using rewards for individual students correctly as instructed by my supervising teacher?

CONSIDERATIONS WHEN UTILIZING PARAEDUCATORS

Paraeducators can play key roles in supporting students in all service delivery models, including helping maintain their success in the general curriculum with inclusive settings. However, to maximize the effectiveness of paraeducators, consultants and teacher teams should be keenly aware of the need for well-designed preparation programs, role clarification, appropriate supervision, recognition, and adequate compensation for their work.

With the increasing utilization of paraeducators, we must ask ourselves what we want from special educators in inclusion-oriented schools. Do we want our special education teachers to be managers of paraeducators who provide the bulk of specialized instruction to students with disabilities? Or do we want special education teachers spending more time directly teaching students with IEPs and co-teaching with general education teachers? Giangreco and Broer (2005) report that special education teachers spend a significantly smaller percentage of time on instruction than do the paras they supervise. It raises a question about the quality of instruction these students are receiving, especially in the age of mandates for having highly qualified teachers work directly with students. If the tables were turned and we were doing this in general education, would it be accepted as good practice? What is a reasonable number of paraprofessionals for a single special educator to direct and supervise without tipping the scale of reasonableness? The Bright Futures Report (Kozleski, Mainzer, & Deshler, 2000) listed the relatively small percentage of time special educators spent in instruction as being one of the key contributing factors to explain why many special education teachers say they are leaving the field. Like other teachers, they went into special education to teach and work with students with special needs directly, not to be paper pushers and supervisors for other adults who teach for them.

Another ethical concern that warrants further scrutiny is the alarming number, over half, of all special education paraprofessionals, who are assigned to students on a one-to-one basis (Suter & Giangreco, 2009). Broer and colleagues (2005) reported the potential detrimental effects (for example, stigmatization, isolation, lack of friendships, over-dependency on the para, disenfranchisement) of having individual paras assigned one-to-one with students. Often, these one-on-one paras are described by their former students as being unnecessarily motherly or parental. At the very least, we need to consider alternatives to our current utilization of paraprofessionals and explore other options for providing students with the supports they need to be successful in inclusion-oriented schools.

 ENHANCEDetext **Application Exercise 10.1.** Click to apply your understanding of communicating expectations to paras and the teachers in the classrooms where they support students.

TIPS FOR COLLABORATION WITH PARAPROFESSIONALS

1. Develop a system for determining when a para is needed and how to best utilize the para based on student needs.
2. With paraeducators assigned to you, discuss your school district's mission statement(s) and attendance-center philosophies, and also your own teaching philosophy and values, before they begin working with you and the students.
3. Visit other schools where there are clear procedures for scheduling, directing, supervising, and evaluating the work of paraeducators. Implement practices that are promising for your school setting.
4. Encourage paras to share their ideas on student behavior and learning, and incorporate those ideas into the instructional plan when appropriate. (See Figure 10.13.)
5. Give constructive feedback frequently. Simple statements like "You did a great job modeling how you find the main idea" and "Maybe he would perform better if you changed the order and put his favorite task after a less favored task" are important communication examples to express to the paraprofessional.

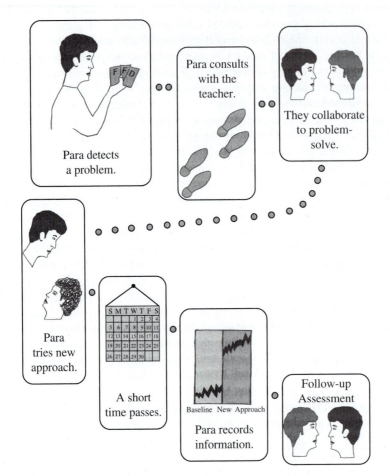

FIGURE 10.13 Step-by-Step Problem-Solving with Collaboration

6. Be aware of how you communicate. Different approaches work better with different people. Refrain from reproaches or put-downs, and strive to convey critique and information in your para's preferred communication style.

7. Introduce family members to the paraeducators who will work with their child.

8. When a para asks for advice, first ask what the para has observed. This gets the para involved and encourages active participation in observing students, deciding on a plan, and implementing that plan.

9. Advocate for well-designed, well-conducted, and carefully evaluated staff development activities for paraeducators based on their needs, and determine how these can best be accomplished.

10. Discuss ethical standards with your paras on a frequent basis by first providing staff development on confidentiality and ethical behavior for paraprofessionals. Provide examples of applications that are as close as possible to what the para might experience on the job.

CHAPTER 11

COLLABORATING THROUGH LEADERSHIP, ADVOCACY, AND COMMUNITY PARTNERSHIPS

Collaborations and networks among general and special education teachers, related services and support personnel, families, and the communities they live in can expand the multiple opportunities that students have to succeed in school and in local activities outside of school. Those involved in the formal and informal education of children and youth work in many arenas of school, work, play, and community life. As Helen Keller wisely said, "Alone we can do little, together we can do so much."

Envisioning collaborative educational and community environments is a relatively easy process; developing such environments and implementing them require much more effort. The leadership of experienced school administrators and well-prepared teachers can be catalyzing in a collaborative environment. Leadership in schools comes in many forms. It isn't so much a title or a position, as it is a way of thinking and doing. Effective leadership involves trust between stakeholders, close communication with parents, strong ties with community service providers, and ongoing team-oriented focus on improving teaching practice to impact student learning (Anrig, 2015). Leaders serve as mentors to new faculty and model collaboration at all levels. As leaders, administrators can forge alliances with other social service agencies, business partners and foundations, judicial systems, library and media centers, colleges and universities, families, civic groups, and members of the community. As leaders, mentors, student advocates, and professional developers, teachers can steer their colleagues toward determining what students can do and what more they could do with the assistance of special services. When schools collaborate with community partners it creates bridges between families, schools, and the community. Transitions are made easier for students when they walk out the school doors at the end of the day or at the end of their K–12 education.

CHAPTER OBJECTIVES

Upon completing this chapter, the reader should be able to:

1. Describe the rationale for a special education teacher's advocacy and collaboration beyond the school setting.
2. Outline how collaborative consultants can be regarded as practicing transformative and distributed leadership.

3. Describe specific actions consultants can do to advocate for students with disabilities and their families and to support students' efforts in self-advocacy.

4. Describe how collaborative consultants can facilitate communication and coordination among a variety of educational and community agencies for the diverse needs of students with learning and behavioral problems.

5. Discuss why collaboration with personnel from various community service agencies can benefit students who require services beyond the school environment.

6. Explain how can consultants work with educational and community organizations to assist children and youth as they make transitions at critical educational junctures.

KEY TERMS

civic engagement
critical junctures
curriculum of the
   community

distributed leadership
instructional leadership
mentoring

self-advocacy
self-determination
transformative leadership

SITUATION 11

Another school week is over. The events of the past week are history. What will happen beyond this moment is the future. As teachers finish their bus duties and other supervisory tasks and head for their rooms to pick up work they will take home for the weekend, one teacher, Mary Clements, stops by the break room to be sure the coffee pot is turned off. The teacher glances through an old issue of **Scientific American** *lying on a table among the other magazines teachers have brought to recycle:* **The New Yorker, Mother Jones, Science News, Self, Discover,** *and* **The Atlantic.** *She is intrigued by an article titled "The Limits of Intelligence" by Douglas Fox (2011). In it, she reads*

So have humans reached the physical limits of how complex our brain can be, given the building blocks that are available to us? . . . The human mind, however, may have better ways of expanding. . . . After all, honeybees and other social insects do it: acting in concert with their hive sisters, they form a collective entity that is smarter than the sum of its parts. Through social interaction we, too, have learned to pool our intelligence with others. (p. 43)

Mary's mind goes down the list for next week: city council meeting about universal design for the new city park and playground; committee on a community-inclusive theater project with the Fine Arts Center; meeting with advisors of the local community college about access for students with disabilities. The teacher puts the magazine and an old Halloween issue of *Simple Living* into her canvas tote. This is good material to ponder over a mocha latte this weekend.

SPECIAL NEEDS ADVOCACY AND EDUCATION ACROSS EDUCATIONAL, COMMUNITY, AND GOVERNMENTAL SPECTRUMS

Never in recorded history has so much of our world changed so rapidly and dramatically as it is changing today. We do not know for certain how these changes will affect schools and educators, but one thing is clear: Students now at risk with exceptional learning needs will be placed in greater jeopardy than ever by the accelerating demands on them to keep pace and measure up in competitive, high-pressure environments. Schools are not alone in their responsibility for removing barriers that keep students from succeeding in the adult world. Personnel in mental health; employment and training; child development; recreation, health, and welfare services; as well as education, have a vital interest in promoting school success for all children. Educational consultants must consider the community an integral part of the preparation of all students for a successful adult life. Building educational and community partnerships requires adaptation of the consultant role to become both an advocate and an educational resource working within other organizations. Figure 11.1 lists some examples of groups with which special education collaborators can partner to advocate for students with special needs.

Collaborative school consultation and teamwork among all educators in school, home, and community partnerships will provide support that is vital in preparing and enabling all students to be successful learners, self-assured individuals, and productive members of society.

Video Example from YouTube

ENHANCEDetext
Video Example 11.1.
Watch this video on the leadership and strengthening diverse teams. How can teacher leaders overcome challenges and lead and motivate individuals to build collaborative teams? (https://www.youtube.com/watch?v=Uv08ObnMOzl)

FIGURE 11.1 Educational and Community Partners for Collaboration and Advocacy

Educational Partners	Community Partners
Administrative and Office Assistants	After School Clubs
Assistive Technology Personnel	Attorneys and Hearing Officers
Building and District Administrators	Boys and Girls Club
Custodial and Maintenance Services	Big Brothers/Big Sisters
Food Services	Business Partners
Media/Library/Technology Specialists	Community Mental Health Providers
Mentors and Career-Shadowing Supervisors	Disability Support Groups
Paraeducators	Legislators
School Volunteers	Parks and Recreation
Reading Specialists	Physicians
Related Service Personnel	Public Library
Security Services	School Board Members
Special Education Administrators	University Disability Support Services
Student Teachers/Interns	University Special Education Faculty

LEADERSHIP FOR ADVOCACY AND ACTION

The leadership of experienced school administrators and well-prepared teachers can be catalyzing in a collaborative environment. Leadership in schools is not a position, but a *way of thinking and doing* in the educational setting. Because of their experience, education, and expertise, special education consultants are in a prime position to provide leadership in the community for efforts and initiatives that involve students with special needs and their families. They are committed to the continuing development of schools and communities that are inclusive and meet the educational needs of all students, including those with disabilities. Good leaders help others to progress in such a way that they think they did it all themselves. Eminent leader and former United States president Harry Truman said it in words something like this: "Great leaders have the ability to get others to do what they really don't want to do—and to like doing it!" The leadership style consultants often adopt is not the traditional "hero," "boss," or hierarchical type of leadership, but rather a collaborative type of leadership that combines what theorists call transformative leadership and distributed leadership.

Researchers and theorists studying social justice and leadership discuss both transformative and distributed leadership in educational settings. Leaders for social justice make issues of race, class, gender, disability, sexual orientation, or other historically and currently marginalizing conditions central to their advocacy, practice, and vision (Theoharis, 2007). He and others affirm that social-justice educational leadership centers on addressing and eliminating marginalization and promoting inclusive educational practices. Thus, consultants who practice school and community leadership by actively advocating for students with disabilities and their families practice social justice leadership in their schools and communities. Shields (2010) writes about leadership that has a goal of transformation to a just and equitable society (in which students with disabilities would have access, opportunities, and quality education as their peers do). Therefore, she uses the term **transformative leadership** to name educational leadership that practices and advocates equity for students with disabilities and others who are marginalized. Transformative leaders believe that every individual is entitled to be treated with dignity, respect, and absolute regard (Shields, 2010).

The concept of leadership as distributed has also been the subject of research and theorizing in the field of education (e.g. Bolden, 2011; Spillane, 2006). **Distributed leadership** is also an action-based leadership. It focuses on social interactions, social systems and how resources are shared to achieve something that an individual agent could not achieve alone (Bolden, 2011; Leithwood, Harris, & Strauss, 2010). Consultants recognize distributed leadership as somewhat akin to collaborative consultation in that it does not focus on the dichotomy of leaders-followers or experts and non-experts, but rather considers how all partners mutually constitute practice (of leadership or of consultation). Distributed leadership considers collaborative action and shared interests. It is synergetic and implies interdependency, with leadership seen as a collective responsibility. Factors related to distributed leadership include trust, support, recognition, common vision, willingness to share, good relations, and willingness to change.

These definitions and practices of transformative and distributed leadership are familiar to educational consultants. Consultation, collaboration, and teamwork for students with special needs has a goal of transforming schools and communities for optimal outcomes for students with disabilities. Collaborative practices that lead to such transformations are synergistic, supportive, and interdependent. Actions are based on shared interests and goals, and leadership is a collective responsibility. Special education consultants, by the nature of their work, practice transformative and distributed leadership. They make others feel more empowered. They thrive on the successes of those who follow their lead. They take pleasure in seeing a collaborative team spirit coalesce, and they constantly strive to help others improve and grow. Strong educators are not threatened when they note signs of leadership in others. They call on the combined strengths and efforts of others to address the concerns together to achieve success (Miller, Devin, & Shoop, 2007).

Instructional leadership is yet another type of leadership. Instructional leaders focus on student learning and the impact of teachers and other school and community factors that influence student learning. Hattie (2015) describes major mind frames that inform high-impact instructional leadership. One such mind frame is the belief that student success and failure is about what they, as teachers or leaders, did or didn't do. They view themselves as change agents. They understand the importance of dialogue and see assessment results as feedback on their impact.

In the everyday work world, leaders use phrases and expressions that make others want to succeed. They avoid phrases such as "It'll never work in our district," "That's been tried before with no success," or "We're too new/old/big/small/inexperienced/set in our ways to do that in our school." Expressions that leaders avoid because they dampen enthusiasm are, "It could never work here in our area," "We've done it before," "With more experience you would not even have suggested it," or "The time is not right for that." How much more effective communication would be if the mind frame was shifted to useful comments such as those suggested by Annunzio (2001)—for example, "It seems unworkable to me, so help me understand how it *could* work," "I'll explain what we tried before, and you can explain how your idea is different," or "That sounds innovative, but there may be some obstacles, and if there are, how could we overcome them?"

Transitioning into Leadership Roles

Increasingly, teachers are being appointed to such roles as instructional coach, lead teacher, mentor coordinator, and data analyst, thus becoming teacher leaders. In recent years there has been a shrinking pool of veteran teachers due to the aging of the teaching force that has resulted in large-scale retirements. This opens up leadership opportunities for teachers in the second stage of their teaching career, with four to ten years of experience, to take on these leadership roles (Johnson & Donaldson, 2007). In the case of special educators, leadership roles may present themselves even earlier in their careers due to the shorter longevity of special education teachers in the field. Factoring in some of the reasons that as many as 40 percent of new special education teachers leave their careers in the first three years of teaching (Billingsley, 2004), there is a compelling case for moving strong special education teachers into leadership roles where they can feel empowered, supported, and valued. Putting these teachers into leadership roles will increase the motivation for these teachers to stay in districts and support incoming special education teachers and general education teachers having increased diversity of student needs in their classrooms.

Video Example from YouTube

▶

ENHANCEDetext
Video Example 11.2.

Watch this video on the value of teacher leadership. What are the benefits of teacher leadership for teachers who are placed in leadership roles, their school, and the students? (https://www.youtube.com/watch?v=tMLIZHe0IEk)

These leadership roles are a natural progression for collaborative consultants who may find leadership roles attractive on a number of levels. First, many find they have unique and specialized knowledge and skills that they want to share with others. For example, most special educators have advanced preparation in assessments for progress monitoring, data analysis, behavioral observations, and specialized academic and behavioral interventions. Additionally, they often are able to assist general education teachers with making accommodations for students based on learning profiles, and they are skilled in knowing how to modify and differentiate the curriculum for diverse learners. Becoming a teacher leader reduces isolation and results in frequent collegial interaction and working on teams. It gives the teacher leader an opportunity to see many different classrooms and teaching styles. Finally, becoming a teacher leader offers an opportunity to change up responsibilities and to expand one's sphere of influence. Teacher leaders often have a voice at the decision-making table and are able to influence direction and change within the school and even the larger district.

While there are potential positive outcomes for teachers who enter into leadership roles, these roles can be met with resistance by others. Teachers are often protective of their instructional space and may be suspicious and even intimidated by a peer observing them teach. Resentment also can arise if the teacher leader is seen as "too young" or "too inexperienced" as a novice for having a leadership role Recognizing these potential obstacles that can undermine a teacher leader's effectiveness allows one to approach the role in a manner that lowers resistance and resentment that might otherwise occur.

Johnson and Donaldson (2007) have identified some proactive strategies that teacher leaders find helpful in avoiding the aforementioned barriers. The first involves "waiting to be drafted" rather than being the first to volunteer for a leadership position. Wait to see if more veteran teachers volunteer first. After being offered a position as an instructional coach by his principal, one teacher said, "he waited until his more experienced colleagues expressed no interest in the role and encouraged him to take it." By doing so, he avoided being seen as a hotshot who thought he knew more than others. He felt he could better enlist the support of others since they had turned down the role. Another strategy is to work with the willing. This is a strategy often recommended when first seeking out a co-teaching partner. Start with your most willing colleagues who welcome the opportunity to receive feedback, collaborate on ideas, and engage in coaching to improve teaching and learning. Starting with the willing also builds confidence and skills in the teacher leader. In time, others might be willing to invite the teacher leader into their classrooms. Finally, some teacher leaders have found that the best approach is to work side-by-side with colleagues. They cast themselves as sources of support; resources rather than supervisors. Their colleagues choose *if* and *how* to incorporate changes into their classrooms, and reinforce the notion that teacher leaders are no more expert than their peers. The leader is someone offering ideas that could be adopted or rejected, implemented in a way that fits the teacher's teaching style, and entered into as a problem-solving venture with no preconceived blueprint.

Mentoring—A Double-Sided Coin

Novice special education teachers often arrive on the job a little anxious but still full of anticipation, excitement, and confidence. This enthusiasm may begin to wane during the first months on the job and they may begin to doubt their abilities. Before long, they are at risk for burnout if they don't receive the supports they need. When questioned about leaving, novice special educators most often cite lack of support. This is especially true when teachers are hired at the eleventh hour or even after the start of the school year. They receive little mentoring and are often placed in a sink-or-swim situation. These special educators often feel unsupported, unprepared, and overwhelmed by student needs and job responsibilities. Many of the reasons cited here for burnout can be balanced with well-designed coaching and mentoring.

Effective leaders and novice special educators are positioned well for roles as mentors and mentees (those who are mentored). **Mentoring** means helping less experienced teachers observe, experiment, and evaluate different ways to instruct and carry out their roles; finding which strategies work best for them. Typically, the mentor is sharing ideas and providing direction for the mentee, but that is not to say that it is always a one-way street. The learning process often goes both ways. What novice teachers lack in experience is often countered with their fresh ideas and innovative teaching strategies based on current research they have acquired in their teacher education programs. The relationship between mentor and mentee is based on shared talent and passion for the field of common interest and is personal. The mentor recognizes budding skills in the mentee and helps guide and strengthen those skills. Timing is critical—the mentor must know when to bear down, when to ease off, and when to take advantage of a teachable, leadable moment. A mentor coaches toward the bent of the mentee, realizing the goal is not to mold each teacher to be an image of the mentor but to guide and play on the individual strengths of each mentee. Mentors model indirectly through experience rather than just dispensing information to be ingested (or, with some, simply ignored).

Special education teachers are especially vulnerable to early career burnout but having a fellow special educator mentor who has been carefully matched based on similar roles can increase teacher retention. A mentor–mentee relationship is an ideal situation for novice teachers to gain experiential learning from master practitioners. Such relationships can encourage beginning teachers early in their careers so as to *keep them there*, thus avoiding burnout and attrition. A strong mentoring program can also have a ripple effect in creating future mentors from those who were once the novice teachers. A teacher with just a year or two of experience can easily relate to new teachers in the school and can serve as an informal mentor and partner to new teachers. The novice teacher may be less intimidated by a relatively new teacher and the relationship can also inspire confidence and a sense of purpose for the teacher with a year or two of experience.

Not all districts or schools have formal mentoring programs and even when in place, there can be tremendous variation. Ideally, a

---

Video Example from YouTube

▶

ENHANCEDetext
Video Example 11.3.

Watch this video on mentoring and supporting new teachers. Notice how the different mentors help guide the novice teachers to discover ways to strengthen their own teaching rather than telling them what to do. (https://www.youtube.com/watch?v=ykxkt3Eq7ao)

mentor is someone who has experience in a role similar to that of the person being mentored. In the case of a novice special educator, a mentor may be assigned who does not have a special education background or someone who is not in the same building, yet comes to observe and meet on a regular, but infrequent basis. In situations such as these, novice teachers may want to seek out their own mentor or multiple mentors. There may be a teacher with lots of experience in the building who can help with many issues that arise, but another teacher in the district working in a similar role at a different school may provide a different kind of support. When finding a mentor, or being a mentor, whichever situation you find yourself in, establishing the right relationship is critical. To find the right match in a mentor, look for someone whom you respect and who has skills you want to emulate. Most people have more than one mentor. Different mentors serve a host of assorted roles and bring varied skills and knowledge to the table. Being open-minded to working with others who are different from ourselves will challenge mentees and help them grow in different and positive ways.

In addition to mentoring programs, many schools have found that developing learning communities helps promote relevant and lasting professional development and support. Faculty can choose from a list of recommended books that address a current educational trend or topic of interest to the teachers in the school. Discussing a book within a learning community serves as an avenue to engage all staff to work together and it provides opportunity for teachers to take a leadership role in guiding the discussion and implementation plan for any resulting actions. Engaging in a common read with several others can serve as a means to provide new teachers with a series of supports as they navigate their way through the early stages of their career. Reading also serves to inspire and reinvigorate. Kaufman and Ring (2011) provide a list of recommended readings compiled by veteran teachers, administrators, and instructors in special education across state and national levels to inspire novice educators. Topical areas are: inspiration, advocacy, and leadership; biographies, autobiographies, and parables to inspire; fiction and nonfiction to motivate and inspire; and instruction to guide, inspire, and motivate. A book study group using materials such as these can be a forum to explore current educational issues, share perspectives from different vantage points, and stimulate professional growth. When used for professional development, book clubs provide systematic, contextualized dialogue (Burbank, Kauchak, & Bates, 2010).

ADVOCATING FOR STUDENTS WITH SPECIAL NEEDS

Teachers who specialize in the education of students with special needs understand that part of their professional responsibility to their students is to advocate within the educational system and the community for individuals with disabilities and their families (see Figure 11.1.) They collaborate with parents, who are experts about their own children, and with public officials, who are experts in community-based programs or legal issues related to individuals with disabilities. However, special education professionals have extensive background and training in working with individuals with special needs. This experience and expertise may be called upon as communities strive to make their towns and businesses "disability-friendly." For example, in March 2011, the revised regulations

FIGURE 11.2   Advocacy: Carrying the Ball for Special Needs

implementing the Americans with Disabilities Act (ADA) took effect. These revised rules were the first major revision by the Department of Justice for its guidance on accessibility in twenty years and can be found on the ADA website. The new rules adopt the 2010 ADA Standards for Accessible Design, which have been retooled to be more user-friendly. As communities work to implement these standards that promote independent living for individuals with disabilities, the education consultant with expertise in disabilities can play an important advocacy role in these collaborative endeavors.

Advocating for students with special needs is an important role of a special educator, and advocacy guidelines are part of the Council for Exceptional Children (CEC) professional standards. These include working toward improving how government services are provided to individuals with exceptionalities, working in collaboration with various professionals to ensure appropriate services are provided, documenting evidence of inadequate services or resources, ensuring appropriate placements are provided, and adhering to federal and local legislative mandates to ensure a free and appropriate public education. Few would argue that advocating for students is the right thing to do, and yet, teachers are sometimes reluctant to do so. Special education teachers report administrative pressures to remain quiet or close their eyes to certain practices and even to act inappropriately in some situations (Whitby, Marx, McIntire, & Wienke, 2013). Examples include recommending less expensive or existing services for students instead of more appropriate services that aren't as readily available or that may require additional funds. This is common with assistive technology (AT) when teachers are told not to include any out of the ordinary AT devices or services on the IEP. Likewise, there may be pressure to conduct fewer assessments than the special educator believes are necessary for the student to receive a comprehensive evaluation due to shortages in personnel to conduct the evaluation or simply because it is not the standard of practice for the district.

When advocating for student services, special educators can sometimes feel at odds with an administrator or other colleagues who are in attendance at the IEP meeting. Some may believe there will be repercussions for speaking out and even fear nonrenewal of their contract. It is imperative that special educators understand the importance of advocating for students and learn how to advocate effectively. This is a subject that receives inadequate attention in most teacher education programs. Unless a novice teacher has a seasoned mentor who validates the importance of advocacy and models how to do it effectively, the next generation of special educators may lack the courage to recommend something that goes against the norm in a school or district and the skills to do so effectively. Whitby and colleagues (2013) recommend these advocacy strategies:

- Know special education law and its implementation at the district level.
- Place the child's needs first.
- Develop respectful relationships with the IEP team members.
- Use diplomacy and create win-win situations when negotiating for services.
- Control your emotions and always act in a professional manner.

Practicing effective communication skills discussed earlier in the book will be helpful when advocating for students. Remember to stay calm, listen to others, and take time to organize your response. Remind the team or administrator that it is your job to advocate for the student and reiterate IDEA guidelines while remaining respectful of those with whom you disagree. In the end, respect the final decision of the team, even if it differs from your professional opinion. Your role is to offer your professional expertise and make the team aware of what you think is in the best interest of the student. If team members are reluctant to implement something unfamiliar or new to them, offer support in setting up an intervention or modeling in the early stages. Collaborative problem solving with follow-up is critical for long-term success and receptiveness to your ideas in the future.

Decisions are made at many levels that impact students and their families, today and in the future. At a recent legislative forum, a state senator described her work on the education committee. The senator was a former teacher and she gave many examples of her legislative colleagues voting on issues related to education about which they knew very little. "We need the voices of those who know about such topics as child mental health, group homes, juvenile offenders, and educational policy that affects students with disabilities!" she told the group. She asked pointedly from her place on the podium, "Can you name the representatives and senators who serve you in our state legislature? Do you know their positions on issues involving children and families? Do you know how to communicate your expertise and to advocate for your students with your elected officials?" She then charged each one there to let not one more day go by without knowing such important answers to those questions.

Getting to know policymakers and elected officials, communicating with them about the needs of students, and building bridges of communication are responsibilities of collaborative school consultants and necessary steps of advocacy. When communicating with public officials, personal letters are more effective than form letters. Sending *many* letters will get more attention than sending copies of one letter signed by many. Letters that are short, concise, friendly in tone, and free of stereotyped phrases, derogatory comments, and unreasonable requests will have a positive impact. Thanking elected officials for their interest in the past and support they have given, along with descriptions of specific ways that their support already has helped communities, will be particularly powerful. Think of a letter as a vehicle of appreciation, information, and documentation, and also a vehicle to carry ideas for actions that would help, along with suggestions for ways in which they might be carried out. Because they often hear or read only negative news about students or hear of what is not working, let them know about successes. Examples of student work and achievement, and newsletters and clippings that commend students and schools, can provide convincing evidence when included with the letters (with parent and administrator permission, of course).

ACTIVITY 11.1
Creative Community Advocacy

There are many avenues for advocacy in your community. One example is keeping track of legislation involving education by engaging in educational or advocacy organizations and writing letters, visiting legislators, and organizing informational meetings. Here are some not-so-obvious ways to advocate for all students with disabilities. In each scenario, how might you be an advocate? What are other examples?

- The mayor has asked you to serve on the city housing board.
- You are a member of the youth development committee at your church.
- Your family is active in 4-H.
- The Boys and Girls Club is sponsoring a breakfast with a well-known sports figure.
- The local home improvement store is having a birdhouse-building class.
- Your best friend is a docent at the zoo.
- The city is going build a new playground.
- The local library is sponsoring a "Read to Dogs" program every Saturday.
- Others?

Supporting Student Self-Advocacy

A recent guest in a university classroom of preservice teachers talked about his identity as a person with learning disabilities. The guest, an award-winning high school history teacher, told the group that learning to name and describe his disability was one of the most important lessons in his life—a skill he used in school, in college, and in his adult life as a teacher, parent, and community activist for students with disabilities. Understanding your disability, your strengths and your needs, and asking for help in getting what you need to succeed is a form of **self-advocacy** that serves students throughout their lives. Self-advocacy skills should be taught as early as possible to empower students to have positive current and future outcomes. Teaching self-advocacy skills in earlier grades is especially important for students in inclusive settings because special, individually designed

educational goals, needed accommodations, and more. Students then use steps of the strategy to share the information during conferences, listen and respond to others, ask questions, and communicate their goals.

All of the ideas presented here can be modified up or down for students with lower or higher abilities as well as grade level. Using the last example of the student-led IEP meeting, for a student with lower ability, the PowerPoint slides or script could have prompts with basic language such as, "How I am doing," "My goal to improve," "My level of effort," "Help that I need from my teacher or parents." When playing the Self-Determination Game, some students may use a communication device or picture exchange to communicate roles and responsibilities, whereas a higher ability-level modification of this same activity could involve students serving as leaders in a cooperative learning group where the Self-Determination Game is being played. An important piece of gaining self-determination skills is observing and learning from persons with disabilities who are successfully working in careers. Employees from businesses who have disabilities can visit classrooms to talk about their jobs. Students can participate in career fairs or field trips to community businesses that employ individuals with disabilities. It is important for children to learn about the diversity of jobs that people with disabilities can perform and level of education or training that is necessary to obtain different types of jobs. Engaging families early in the process of developing self-determination skills and preparing for transition to post-school life is important. Parent expectations for postsecondary education and employment have been found to be a predictor of post-school outcomes (Mazzotti, Rowe, Sinclair, Woods, & Shearer, 2015).

Educators can help students become effective advocates for themselves by teaching them self-advocacy skills and supporting their use of self-advocacy skills in school and community settings. Students must be aware of their disabilities, be able to state the facts, describe their strengths and limitations, assess their problems, explore possible solutions, and ask for help if they need it.

Successful self-advocates know their rights, their needs, and their best supports. It is important also that they know the best times to approach others with requests that serve their needs. Students who learn to do this can gain a sense of control and influence over their employment conditions and living situations. A federal longitudinal study (Wagner, Newman, Carmeto, Garza, & Levine, 2005) found that while nearly seven in ten students with disabilities said they understood what services they would need to deal with their disability, less than a third said they often gave their opinions on services to professionals with whom they interacted. The support for self-advocacy is critically important for educational consultants and their partners. Consultants can work with team members and co-educators to help them understand the importance of student self-advocacy and to help other educational and community partners support students as they learn and practice this critical skill set. When educators see students trying to be self-advocates but being overly aggressive or passive in their efforts, it is important that educators give students feedback. Sometimes educators can model self-advocacy and provide opportunities for practice and reinforcement for using self-advocacy skills.

Consultants can also promote student self-advocacy by engaging students in community events, IEP meetings, and other occasions where students can speak up for themselves rather than have others speak for them. Involvement in extracurricular programs is

---

**Video Example
from
YouTube**

▶

ENHANCEDetext
Video Example 11.4.
Watch this video about self-advocacy featuring individuals who have become self-advocates. Think about the benefits to these lives because they have learned self-advocacy rather than waiting for someone else to advocate for them. (http://www.youtube.com/watch?v=78d8_BKojl0)

---

yet another way that has been suggested to help students with disabilities gain leadership skills and build self-determination and confidence (Vinoski, Graybill, & Roach, 2016). Partnerships for Success (PFS) is a school-based program funded by a grant from the Georgia Council of Developmental Disabilities. It was founded on principles of self-determination and inclusion and has been implemented in a number of different ways. Clubs are student-led and club co-officers are students with and without disabilities. Students develop a variety of social, athletic, community service, civic, educational, and fundraising activities. Club sponsors facilitate implementation of the activities and provide guidance and support for student leadership teams. As one example of a PFS project, clubs have partnered with businesses and corporations to raise money to build an accessible playground. A toolkit is available with information on how to form a Partnerships for Success Club and ideas for developing self-determination skills at the PFS website. Elementary, middle, and secondary schools across the country have similar programs where students with and without disabilities are joined together to work side-by-side in a variety of ways (Meadan, Shelden, Appel, & DeGrazia, 2010). Extracurricular programs involving students with disabilities are nonacademic learning opportunities that enhance life skills, and shape recreational pursuits, career paths, and social connections. If students aren't involved in extracurricular programs, they are not in a position to take advantage of the educational and social benefits these programs have to offer. As students gain in skills and enter middle or high school, some teachers have nominated them to be on committees or community boards to advocate for themselves and others with disabilities. These students become proficient at advocacy and experienced in **civic engagement**, that builds leadership skills for students as they enter adulthood.

INTERAGENCY COLLABORATION

All children have individual needs, and all are entitled to a free appropriate public education (FAPE) that addresses their special needs. In order to serve students in ways that are right for every child and are productive for society, educators should partner with many individuals, organizations, and agencies including:

- Related services and support personnel in public organizations
- Public, private, or community organizations and programs
- Government or community agencies that provide funding for services or enrichment programs that can be developed collaboratively for students and families

Figure 11.3 lists some examples of groups with which special education collaborators will want to partner in advocacy and education for students with special needs.

As a process, collaboration is a means to an end rather than an end in itself. The goal is success in school for students with special needs. But schools are not alone in the

FIGURE 11.3   Integrating Efforts through Collaboration

Collaborative consultants can integrate and collaborate with other educators in these ways:

With general education teachers:
1. Establish joint ownership of the student and the learning situation.
2. Respect the views of all.
3. Keep problems "in house."
4. Request regular interaction and feedback from them.

With other special education colleagues:
1. Openly deal with the discomfort of having others give critique and feedback.
2. Arrange and coordinate planned interactions.
3. Together develop support systems.

With support and related services personnel:
1. Become more knowledgeable about their roles and responsibilities.
2. Make sure to integrate major ideas they produce.
3. Plan and implement student programs that reflect coordinated involvement and not fragmentation.

With building administrators:
1. Inform them in as brief and practical a manner as possible.
2. Don't carry tales from a school/district to others.
3. Don't be a spy, or judge, even if asked.
4. Request regular feedback as to your own effectiveness.

With attorneys/hearing officers:
1. State your credentials, certifications, training, and experiences relative to the case.
2. State the nature and extent of knowledge about the student.
3. Discuss assessments, curricula, and modifications used, and their reliability, validity, and appropriateness.
4. Explain all terms, using no acronyms or jargon.
5. Remain calm, honest, and cooperative.

With legislators:
1. Be brief, accurate, and substantiating with all material delivered.
2. Thank legislators for their past interest and help.
3. State situations realistically without unreasonable demands.
4. Consider the whole picture, as the legislator must, and not just one's own primary interest.

With the public:
1. Be perceptive about issues of culture, diversity, and conflicting interests.
2. Demonstrate reasonable expectations while upholding standards and delivering challenges.
3. Express your dedication to students and commitment to excellent schools.

---

responsibility to help students succeed; they cannot do it all. Students are in school for much less time than it would seem. They typically attend six hours a day, 180 days a year for 12.5 years. Some educators describe the school time as "the thirteen percent factor"; others calculate sleep, school time, and inevitable absences a bit differently and come up with a "9/91 percent factor." Either way, it is an amazingly low figure. Furthermore, it is only allocated time, not actual time engaged in learning. And this is only the time *allocated* for learning; a measure of actual time students are *engaged* in academic learning would be much less. (This is also one of the shortest school years, if not *the* shortest, in the developed world.) For the remaining 91 or so percent of the time, the child is at home with friends, relatives, caregivers, or others elsewhere in a community, or alone.

Much of what students learn comes from experiences, associations, and interactions they have outside the scheduled school activities. This secondary curriculum may be a dominant part of any student's life (Barbour & Barbour, 2001), especially when traditional and formal school curriculums are not compatible with the special needs of many students. Community settings offer many alternative therapies or learning environments that promote socialization, language, and cognitive and physical development. Non-school facilities in the community provide the added component of parental engagement and links to the community and other institutions in the community.

This **curriculum of the community** (Barbour & Barbour, 2001) has great potential for enhancing the social networks of students and families; inculcating natural resources into the education of students; and providing services such as entertainment, recreation, and informal education. In addition, the informal curriculum enables the involvement and collaboration of several organizations within a community (Barbour & Barbour, 2001). Schools and communities can address their considerable responsibilities in helping students learn by employing a wide spectrum of resources and collaborating with many agencies to help them stay in school as active, successful learners.

Collaborating on Grant Proposals for Funding Special Projects

As school and community partners work collaboratively to improve the educational and social outcomes of children with disabilities, school consultants are often called upon to be part of a proposal-writing team to secure funding for new projects or programs. Grant money is available from a wide variety of sources, including the federal government, state governments, private donations, foundations, local businesses, local clubs and organizations, donations to fund-raising activities, and corporations. These sources have programs and projects in mind that fit their philosophies and goals. They set their own procedures, which must be followed explicitly by proposal writers if they wish to be in the running to receive the grant funding.

Several benefits can result from submitting a collaborative grant proposal. The first is the collaboration experience gained by the team regardless of whether the grant proposal is funded. Few significant proposals are developed in these times that do not include a number of colleagues interacting to conceptualize and develop the plan and then carry out the project after it is funded. Some people have major roles and others serve in minor ways, but all can participate and ultimately profit in tangible and intangible ways. Another benefit is the collection of resources and support needed to meet the goals of the grant. When multiple resources are targeted and letters of support are generated, more people become involved as supporters of innovative school programs. Even if a proposal is not funded, partnerships have been formed and more people are made aware of needs and the assistance that could have been provided for those needs. Another funding or support opportunity might present itself that will catch the attention of one of these earlier partners.

When a grant proposal is funded, the benefits soar. Money and resources become available for carrying out projects that were only dreams or wishes before funding. This has an energizing, morale-boosting effect that reverberates throughout a school system and community. Farmington, Illinois Superintendent John Asplund, during an interview as part of Education Week's Leaders to Learn From conference, spoke about a project idea brought to him by a history teacher in his district (*Education Week*, 2016). The proposal was to transform the traditional school library into a research center that would become a hub of activity as compared to the traditional library where students sit quietly reading a book. Asplund, as he does with everyone who comes forward with ideas needing funding, asked the teacher how the project fit into the district's core values, the estimated cost and his ideas for funding it, and how it would benefit students. Together they identified barriers and then Asplund stepped back to let the teacher work through the problems. By empowering the person with the original idea and others interested in the project, creative and workable solutions were created. Although some money was needed for adding some furniture, many elements required little or no money. They came up with features like displaying student artwork to make the space inviting and to transform it from formal library space, thus creating a win-win solution by showcasing student work with little cost. The research center at the high school was so well received that it sparked the initiative to go forward with transforming all the school libraries in the district to research centers. These hubs of activity are filled with student artwork on the walls and feature furniture arrangements that are conducive to student collaboration and research. Teachers in Asplund's district report being inspired by others when they see dreams and visions become reality. The Farmington district is finding ways to go forward with innovative projects despite serious budget constraints in their state. Asplund believes that when teachers hear the word "no" over and over again, they forget about the word "yes" and see an idea as unattainable. This superintendent has changed the culture and has found ways to say yes by asking teachers to answer these key questions: How does it fit into the district or school's core values? How will it be funded? How will it benefit students? When new programs are proposed, he also asks, what will it replace? Asplund points out that educators are really good at adding things in education but never subtracting, a point well taken for collaborating consulting teachers to note.

These same processes have relevance to developing proposals for outside funding. Starting with a vision that serves a need and that will benefit and involve many is often the first step. Next, identifying barriers and systematically figuring out solutions creates ownership and investment in the project. Whether preparing a modest proposal to be funded internally by the school board or a local community agency, or seeking larger grant monies from an outside source, there is value in having direct involvement from teachers in each step of the process. The amounts of money do not need to be sizable for these positive outcomes to be realized. Some of the most invigorating projects have resulted from relatively small grants, such as those from community groups or local businesses, but they always start with identifying a need, creating a vision, and developing a clear plan by thinking through all the steps and working through the barriers.

School consultants and collaborators are in ideal positions to work with others to secure grant funds. When projects impact students with special needs, school consultants provide an important voice in the development of such projects. Some larger districts employ proposal writers, but those individuals need to collaborate with other school and community personnel to develop successful proposals.

DEVELOPING COMMUNITY PARTNERSHIPS

It is a challenge for educators to form new paradigms that decompartmentalize services for students with special needs. But stepping outside the in-school educator role is necessary for providing the collaboration needed for student success. Service providers and agency personnel must step outside the boundaries of their job descriptions on occasion to do what needs to be done for individuals with special needs and their families. Educators need to remember that this may be challenging for those with whom they collaborate.

Many families of children with special needs face a multitude of problems and require services beyond the school environment. The reality is that no one agency can provide all of the necessary services for children with disabilities and their families. Educators can partner with others in the community to advocate for these services and educate others about programmatic issues. Collaborative strategies help provide better services to families using several human service systems and keep children and families from falling through the cracks by ensuring that they receive needed services.

When personnel within various systems collaborate, they avoid service duplication and reduce the total cost of services. Collaborative consultation ensures having fewer gaps in services, it minimizes conflict, and it clarifies responsibilities. And most importantly, it maximizes possibilities of positive educational and social outcomes for students with special needs.

The ultimate goal is ensuring the future success of students with special needs by eliminating or reducing difficulties that place them at risk—infant mortality, delinquency, violence such as school shootings and bomb threats, youth unemployment, child abuse and neglect, drug involvement, suicide, mental illness, and poverty. Interagency collaboration is not a quick fix. It is time-consuming and process-intensive. It takes commitment and flexibility to discover new roles and relationships. These new roles and responsibilities call for collaborative skills that require wide knowledge and much practice.

Consultants should plan carefully how to work with different services agencies, professional cultures, and norms and standards (Shaver, Golan, & Wagner, 1996). None of these entities likes to waste limited time engaging in meaningless meetings any more than busy teachers and consultants do. Many of the strategies addressed in previous chapters will guide educators in developing good working relationships with those who are not professional educators and help in resolving major obstacles to understanding.

A group of teachers in a special project to include students with severe disabilities in their general education classrooms reported that the most helpful aspects of the specialist support they received were these: a shared framework and goals, physical presence of the collaborator, validation of the classroom teacher's contribution, and teamwork (Giangreco, Dennis, Cloninger, Edelman, & Schattman, 1993). If problems did appear, they tended to be caused by separate goals of the related services specialist, disruption of classroom routine, or overuse of special education practices. In this project, both teacher and consultant needed to consider more fully the context of the regular classroom and show respect for values and needs of that classroom, its students, and its teacher(s). In this study, conducted to analyze the benefits of inclusion for students with severe disabilities, seventeen of the nineteen teachers reported that they were transformed by their experiences. Not only were their attitudes toward the students changed; in some cases the teachers said that they changed their attitudes about themselves as well (Giangreco et al., 1993).

Collaborative teams with support services and community personnel are not always easy to coordinate, even when the group has a common goal (for example, assuring the post-secondary success of students with learning disabilities). Sileo (2011) suggests that newly formed relationships must be nurtured and strengthened because the teamwork required is hard work and it is important that teams be successful and long lasting. In order to facilitate appropriate support services for students, collaborative co-educators can do several things, such as:

- Become knowledgeable about the roles, capabilities, and responsibilities of community agencies and support personnel.
- Within the bounds of necessary confidentiality and ethical school practices, ask support personnel for their viewpoints and opinions about helping students with special needs.
- Inform agency personnel about the collaborative consultation role, schedules, and responsibilities.
- Volunteer to provide professional staff development activities that focus on inclusion and collaboration and encourage involvement of community entities.
- Have professional development sessions that provide information about exceptional learning needs and the value of working as teams for these students

Here are several examples of interagency partnerships that combine the resources of schools, universities, families, volunteers, and community-based organizations to serve students beyond the school day:

1. The Parent Institute for Quality Education (PIQE) is a nationally recognized program that was started in 1987 by the Rev. Vahac Mardirosian and Dr. Alberto Ochoa of San Diego State University as a result of conversations with parents in a predominantly Latino elementary school in the San Diego area. Their first program, Parent Engagement Educational Program, evolved into a nine-week curriculum delivered to parents in their primary language to help parents become educational advocates for their children K–12. PIQE has operated offices in several states to offer classes in sixteen languages. Their website offers many resources and ways for parents, teachers, students, and volunteers to get involved with PIQE programs. Ongoing evaluation on the impacts of their programs has demonstrated the success of this collaborative effort.

2. Communities in Schools is a program that unites community resources such as health care and mental health professionals with teachers, parents, principals, and volunteers on behalf of children (Barbour & Barbour, 2001). Many highly successful outcomes have been realized for students and families. Business-school partnerships have also shown promise for impacting schools, communities, and students.

Critical features of these partnerships include strong leadership and support from local power brokers; open communication; respect for differences in skills, ideas, cultures, and values of other partners; decision making based on common ground; long-range goals; careful planning; continuous assessment; and keeping the community informed (Barbour & Barbour, 2001).

3. El Valor is a nonprofit community-based organization founded in 1973 by the late Guadalupe S. Reyes who dreamed of a community in which all members, including her son with special needs, could live, learn, and work. The collaboration started in the basement of a church in the Pilsen area of Chicago, where they started the first bilingual, bicultural rehabilitation center in Illinois. El Valor, meaning "courage," has grown into a multicultural, multipurpose organization that reaches thousands of families in the Chicago area and millions throughout the nation. El Valor has distributed evidence-based practices and curricula such as Mis Padres, Mis Maestros (My Parents, My Teachers), a program for parents with children ages birth to five years. Information about these programs can be found on their website. El Valor has worked with more than 1,000 individuals with disabilities and their families from diverse communities.

The participation of educators in these collaborations has had great benefits for students, families, and communities. After studying the development of interagency collaborative educational projects, the Southwest Educational Development Lab in Austin, Texas, offered these steps for organizing and managing collaborative interagency projects (SEDL, 2000):

1. Convene a group, including all stakeholders.
2. Assess student and community needs.
3. Establish purposes and priorities.
4. Study effective ways of working together.
5. Plan the project.
6. Implement the plan.
7. Evaluate the results.
8. Sustain the achievement.

Collaborations can be productive in terms of providing successful outcomes for students with special needs and in building exciting new partnerships among communities. Interactions with school personnel are essential for building successful interagency partnerships that focus on the success of students. However, working successfully to plan and implement high-impact programs for students with special needs requires a commitment of time and effort. How can groups work together despite differences in missions, expertise, philosophies, and resources? Suggestions involve efforts to:

- Work to assure that communication is clear, on-topic, and assertive. Use the skills for communication addressed in an earlier chapter.
- Take time to learn from each other. Listen respectfully and remember that all stakeholders have their own ideas and areas of expertise. Build a sense of community.

- Obtain and maintain high levels of support at all organizational levels.
- Keep in mind that the more democratic the process is, the better. However, build toward consensus rather than "majority rules." The idea is to construct a sustainable, successful project together.
- Work to develop high levels of trust. Keep "eyes on the prize" of having successful outcomes for students, families, and communities.
- Think long term; think firm foundations. As with the examples above, a few dedicated individuals from educational and community organizations worked collaboratively to build partnerships that sustained over time and produced positive outcomes for students.
- Most important of all, celebrate small successes and share the credit for successes with all partners.

ACTIVITY 11.2

A Ten-Year Dream

Reflect on the three examples of interagency collaborations above. Think of your current or future role with students having special needs—whether that role be parent, teacher, administrator, volunteer, community agency worker, advocate, or other. Put yourself ten years into the future. What would you like to see in a headline in your local paper related to students with special needs? Write down the headline. Now, think about how this accomplishment involved interagency collaboration. Who were the stakeholders? What were the headlining student outcomes? Finally, think about what you can do today, this month, and this year to get started on this dream to make the headline real. What will be the challenges? What new skills and understandings will you need to be a part of this future happening?

ORGANIZING INTERAGENCY COLLABORATION FOR CRITICAL EDUCATIONAL TRANSITIONS

"Transition" is an umbrella term for activities and opportunities that prepare students for significant changes in their lives. It can be described as the process of moving from one service delivery system to another (Fowler et al., 2000). Transition points can be called **critical junctures** between systems. These include such points in time as birth to preschool, preschool to kindergarten, elementary to middle school, and high school to work or postsecondary education. Transition calls for intensive collaborative efforts among educational institutions, families, and agencies such as those who provide rehabilitation or school-to-work services.

Collaborations in Early Childhood Education

Because education for students with special needs is most effective during the early childhood years, P.L. 99-457 requires family-centered and community-based direct services for all children from infant to five years old with special needs that call for direct services. Early childhood education (ECE) and early childhood special education (ECSE) reduce special education costs and improve teaching environments. Early childhood education programs can save school systems several thousands of dollars per child over the course of the child's K–12 school experience. Early intervention is cost-effective and educationally sound. Benefits to the child, the family, and the public are quite significant in reducing later academic failure and social problems such as teenage pregnancy, crime, and school dropout. There should be preparation and accreditation for early childhood teachers and a smooth transition plan in place for preschoolers from early childhood education to K–12 school. Part H created a new program for preschoolers from birth to three years of age and stipulated the development of an Individualized Family Service Plan (IFSP) for each child and family served. This amendment called for collaboration based on family-focused methods, and it continued procedural safeguards for families. The legislation expanded beyond academic concerns to include family members, social workers, speech and language pathologists, medical personnel, and other professionals. It authorized funding for state grants and multidisciplinary experimental, demonstration, and outreach programs.

Increased services such as these for preschool children with disabilities require dedicated cooperation among professionals, parents, and other caregivers, with collaboration at the heart of the programs. Making the services available and conducting them effectively is a challenging order for communities. But doing so is extremely important because these services are usually the first experience with schools for parents of young children.

Early childhood special education (ECSE) has moved toward full inclusion, with consultation services provided by ECSE consultants who have expertise across all disabilities including multiple disabilities. As they consult in settings such family daycare, child-care centers, child education centers, Head Start programs, and prekindergarten classes, successful delivery of inclusion support is dependent on teamwork.

Teams for ECSE can differ from K–12 teams in that the child may receive services across a variety of settings such as placement in a special education preschool class *and* after-school care in an inclusive setting. Multiple resources may be needed to address medical, financial, family counseling, rehabilitation, and other needs. Team leadership often falls on the ECSE consultant as case manager for orchestrating services as varied as occupational therapist, audiologist, and after-preschool caregivers. All team members must be knowledgeable about other members' roles and backgrounds, and they must communicate with their perspectives in mind and "on the table" for consideration without unwarranted delay. Early childhood special education personnel have many responsibilities as collaborative consultants and members of teams where the stakes are high for very young children and their families.

Transition from Early Childhood to Kindergarten

Early intervention programs for infants and toddlers with disabilities proliferated following the early childhood legislation. Parents and other caregivers outside the school now play a more integral part in the education and well-being of these children. Disabilities of children in the early intervention programs tend to be severe; therefore, the interventions require integration of multiple services from specialists in several disciplines. Recall the observation in an earlier chapter that an IEP conference might have a dozen participants.

Families are an integral part of the therapy in home-based programs. Therapists go into homes to provide stimulation for the children, and guidance and instruction for the parents. Staff and parents are in consultation and collaboration with all available resources, including health and medical personnel, social services personnel, public school personnel, and community resources such as preschool and day care centers. These programs typically are year-round, not nine-month programs. In addition, these programs can also be structured very differently from the elementary programs to which the children will transition. Parents may have concerns regarding how services will change and often aren't prepared for the transition. One parent expressed concern about her child moving from an early childhood program with multiple teachers and paraeducators working in tandem within a single classroom setting to an inclusive kindergarten classroom with one para and support services that were less integrated.

Federal legislation (P.L. 102-119) requires that states develop interagency agreements to address roles and responsibilities for transition from early intervention services to preschool services and to provide guidance for local communities through specification of state level responsibilities (Fowler, Donegan, Lueke, Hadden, & Phillips, 2000). Preparation of such agreements is a daunting task, requiring skillful collaboration by team members. Issues to be dealt with include ways of (Fowler et al., 2000):

- Transmitting information from one agency to another
- Preparing the child and family for services
- Providing services in least restrictive environments
- Delivering service for children who turn three late in the school year or in summer
- Using Individualized Family Service Plans
- Selecting methods to determine eligibility for services (The interagency agreement and its implementation should be monitored and evaluated on a regular basis.)

Transition from preschool settings to kindergarten school programs also calls for strong, continuous efforts in collaborative school consultation. Although there are many models and programs for early childhood education, P.L. 99-457 reaches far beyond classroom interventions. Preschool teachers should prepare children for the local settings into which they will make the transition. Children need special skills to be ready for kindergarten and sometimes they need preparation for the local setting. Contributions of early childhood educator personnel to elementary school programs are invaluable for getting new kindergarten students off to a successful start. Collaborative efforts between preschools and kindergarten and elementary school educators are essential for the success of students with special needs as they make this critical transition.

Transition from Middle School to High School

The most pressing need for a preteen is to make a comfortable move from elementary school to the very different middle school climate and then to high school. If support systems are not in place for students with disabilities at these important junctures, students may drop out, withdraw from participation, or experience failure in school. Services related to postsecondary education for students should begin much earlier than at the high school level. Students in intermediate and middle school grades can begin to set their life goals through career awareness, social skills, money management skills, involvement in extra-curricular activities, self-advocacy skills, and development of portfolios, to mention just a few examples.

A collaborative project by the National Association of Secondary School Principals, Phi Delta Kappa International, and the Lumina Foundation for Education, designed to collect opinions of middle school students about their current school activities and their preparation for success in high school and college, showed that the students were optimistic and positive but not necessarily attuned to the reality of American high schools (Bushaw, 2007). The researchers concluded that schools may be operating on a "sort and select" mission that reaches only some students. They urged that this mission be replaced with a goal of preparing *all* students for postsecondary opportunities linked to their interests. The responses of polled students, when asked how much information they had received about how to choose high school courses that prepare them to attend college, showed that 68 percent had "some or none." Only 11 percent had "a great deal." It does not take a giant leap of imagination to conclude where students with disabilities fit into this scene. Several suggestions by researchers can be summarized here as:

- Eliminating the sink-or-swim transition from middle school to high school, with ninth grade in particular being the key link in the school chain where students begin to disengage
- Partnering with parents and caregivers, beginning in middle school, to make more information available about postsecondary options
- Helping students better understand their interests and relate them to a program of study
- Enlarging perceptions of college to include community college, part-time study, work combined with study in the career environment, and study programs offered through distance learning

Each of these suggestions is relevant to success for students with special needs; each is also doable when they are the focus of a strong collaborative effort.

Transition from Secondary School to Postsecondary Opportunities

At the opposite end of the continuum from early childhood needs and continuing beyond those of the middle school child are the needs of students leaving school to enter the world of work and adult living. Heightened awareness of this important transition period for young people with disabilities grew in the 1980s, when program goals for serving students with disabilities were built on education services that could help them lead meaningful and productive lives. One of the realities was that no one parent, teacher, or school counselor could provide all the necessary assistance. All school professionals and agencies with services for the welfare of students need to be involved in partnerships and team efforts to assist the student and the family.

As in transition from middle school to high school, comprehensive assessment of student abilities, interests, and needs is vital. Curriculum selection and instructional strategies should include a variety of job-related and postsecondary education explorations. When college education is not a feasible option for young people because of their abilities, job training is essential, along with skills needed to succeed in that work and to experience pleasure and feelings of accomplishment by doing the work. In model programs, students spend part of their day on academic subjects and the rest of the day at work sites. Some programs even allow students to earn academic credits at the work site. Many postsecondary service organizations, such as rehabilitation agencies, are essential partners in the transition from school to work for students with special needs.

More students with disabilities are entering college or postsecondary training. Successful transition and adjustment require collaboration on the part of all those involved with educational and support services for students with special needs.

Students with disabilities who plan to attend a college or university also need preparation to use the transition services that will be available at that institution. Partnership with college student services offices is an important collaborative relationship to build for educators responsible for high school transition services. Students with disabilities are often reluctant to disclose their disability when they enter postsecondary settings. A myriad of reasons exist for this, including fear of stigma, lack of self-advocacy skills, believing they can get by without services, and lack of knowledge about what services are available or how to access them. Newman, Madaus, and Javitz (2016) found that the more transition orientation students receive in high school, the more likely they are to disclose a disability earlier in their college career. Transition planning in high school also increases the likelihood of students seeking out and receiving support services in post-secondary institutions. Given the low rates of disability disclosure and accessing of the services, both disability-related and generally available supports, efforts should be made to help students seek out supports at the postsecondary level

University educators and administrators must acknowledge the needs students have for developing skills to facilitate successful adjustment to college life and then assist them with those needs. Unfortunately, the dropout rate for students with disabilities is extremely high. The rate for students with disabilities attaining a college degree was reported as 14 percent in 2000 (Harris & Associates, 2004). In her extensive review of research about college retention of students with disabilities, Holley Belch (2004–2005) found that the key elements for success were a sense of belonging and inclusion, involvement in both in- and out-of-class activities, a sense of purpose and intentionality, self-determination, and integration of successful universal design strategies in the curriculum and co-curriculum. These four attributes are not typically developed or nurtured as part of the work of a transition team for students; however, these skills, along with self-advocacy, are essential for post-secondary success of students with disabilities.

Accommodations and services for students with disabilities after high school are no longer provided through the IEPs mandated in IDEA. Student rights and accommodations are provided through the legal framework of two other federal laws, the Americans with Disabilities Act and Section 504 of the Rehabilitation Act, which do not require the same level of supports.

An important community of practice for students transitioning to or attending post-secondary school is the DO-IT (Disabilities, Opportunities, Internetworking, and Technology) program at the University of Washington. This program focuses on promoting the success of individuals with disabilities and the use of computer and networking technologies to increase their independence, productivity, and participation in education and careers. DO-IT provides resources, publications, and videos that include information about evidence-based practices and universal design. Individuals can sign up as a member of the DO-IT community of practice and receive e-mail alerts about new research and other useful information. Educators have many partners in the transition to postsecondary education endeavor.

ACTIVITY 11.3
Searching for Resources

Knowing what resources are available in your community helps facilitate collaboration. A school-related group such as the parent/teacher organization (PTO), a committee of teachers, or a student group seeking a service project, could develop a community resources booklet for parents, teachers, and community agencies. To learn about resources in your community, have a personal scavenger hunt or go with a small group of your colleagues to discover new resources for students and families. Find people, places, and things that can enhance special abilities and serve special needs. As you do this, if someone asks what you are doing, explain and then engage them in conversation about education. Invite them to be advocates and collaborators in enterprises that will help students succeed in school.

Closing Thoughts

"If you think in-school collaboration and co-teacher consultation are challenging, wait until you try interagency collaboration!" says one experienced educational consultant. Turf issues, lack of clarity on fiscal responsibilities, and requirements for shared personnel, facilities, and equipment agreements are among the barriers to successful interagency collaboration. On the other hand, many educators have had experience with interagency collaboration while working with the Interagency Coordinating Council, established under Part H of P.L. 99-457 (the Handicapped Infant and Toddler Program), and with the Community Transition Council, as established under P.L. 101-476.

School–community collaboration requires patience, effort, and new perspectives about what is important in teaching and learning. A quote attributed to Mark Twain helps educators remember that collaboration is sometimes a slow process: "A habit cannot be tossed out the window. . . . It must be coaxed down the stairs one step at a time." Cross-agency collaboration creates multiple opportunities for learning and enhances the diversity of experiences for students with disabilities. It uses the informal curriculum of the community. The results will be longer-term, consistent, community-developed educational supports for student success. The challenges may be great, but there are resources in educators' own backyards to benefit students in a variety of ways.

 ENHANCEDetext **Application Exercise 11.1.** Click to apply your understanding of how consultants collaborate through leadership, advocacy, and community partnerships.

TIPS FOR COLLABORATING THROUGH ADVOCACY AND COMMUNITY PARTNERSHIPS

1. Don't try to do everything yourself.
2. Develop rapport with media specialists. Give them advance notice of upcoming topics and try not to make too many spur-of-the-moment requests.
3. Keep a log of positive activities and interactions with collaborating community organizations. Recognize their work and talk about it with others to establish communities of interest in serving students with disabilities and their families.
4. Keep public remarks about colleagues on a positive, professional level. If you must vent, try using a journal at home. Reviewing it now and then may show you the way to improve the situation.
5. Make a directory of community resources that serve students with disabilities; include those who serve all children and work with them to assure that they are inclusive. Share the directory with community and school partners and families.
6. Do not expect the same levels of involvement and commitment from everyone.
7. Have open houses, extending invitations to school board members and community organizations, with follow-up thank-you notes to those who visited.
8. Drop off samples of periodicals such as *Educational Leadership*, *TEACHING Exceptional Children*, *Phi Delta Kappan*, *Early Childhood Today*, *Journal of Emotional and Behavioral Disorders*, *Journal of Learning Disabilities*, and *Gifted Child Today* at offices of pediatricians, obstetricians, and dentists for their waiting rooms. If possible, have a brief visit with the medical staff about potential value of these materials to families and community members.
9. Build networks of interaction among school personnel, parents, and community members who could serve as tutors, monitors, mentors, and independent study facilitators for special needs.
10. Provide opportunities for volunteering and service by your students. This will help them develop social competencies and leadership skills. Too often students with disabilities are just recipients of services rather than providers.

CHAPTER 12

CHARTING YOUR COURSE FOR COLLABORATIVE SCHOOL CONSULTATION

Teaching was once a rather lonely endeavor in public, yet closed, environments. But that is no longer the case and most assuredly will not be so in the future. In these complex times, it truly will take "the whole village" to raise a child or youth. All school personnel, parents, students, and community members must work together to ensure that schools provide stimulating and safe environments in which to learn and grow. Collaboration will become an increasingly common process for working with students and co-educators in the future. Those who accepted the challenge early in this book to watch and listen each day for the word "collaborate" most likely found it many times in newspaper and news magazines, TV shows, science journals, sportscasts, music and movie reviews, economic reports, diplomacy efforts, political activities, homemaking and family material, and on and on. Working together has become essential for just about every component of life in this century. As educators collaborate and consult within their school contexts, they instill in students the skills for collaboration, teamwork, and networking that will be needed for their roles in an increasingly global world.

CHAPTER OBJECTIVES

Upon completing this chapter, the reader should be able to:

1. Predict challenges in education of the future that will need collaborative consultation.

2. Illustrate ways school administrators, policymakers for education, school psychologists, counselors, and various resource and support personnel can be involved in school-based collaboration.

3. Describe positive ripple effects of teaching and learning that can result from collaborative consultation and teamwork.

4. Differentiate levels of service that can be provided by collaborative consultation.

5. Point out benefits that successful collaborative school consultation can bring to schools and communities.

6. Summarize competencies (acquired skills or innate abilities) and ethics (principles based on what is good and what is not good) that are needed to ensure the success of collaborative school consultation and team efforts.

KEY TERMS

iatrogenic	onedownsmanship	synergy
multiplier effects	positive ripple effects	

SITUATION 12.A

An informal conversation is taking place before the monthly meeting of the local Board of Education. Several community members and educators who are there to observe the meeting are talking about recent problems within the community, including vandalism, outbreaks of violence, a teenager's death that is a suspected suicide, and several pick-ups and arrests by law enforcement officials.

Mr. Alvarez, Middle School Teacher: You know, I've been teaching for many years, and I remember when our main discipline problems in schools were running in the halls, chewing gum, and talking without permission. Today our problems are everything from drug abuse, sexual harassment, verbal abuse, bathroom-gender issues, sports-related concussions, and gun-carry laws, to destruction of property and assaults on people.

Ms. Cohen, Mother of an Elementary School Student: Yes, I hear you loud and clear. The violence and fear in our schools and communities undermine children's physical and mental health and their eagerness to learn. Events that frighten and injure our school-children, and can cause mental and emotional trauma, are happening all across this nation. This is unnerving. I find the incidence of young suicides across our nation to be especially troubling.

Mr. Adamson, School Board Member: Yes, the pressure for safe and orderly schools is strong. The latest national poll on public perceptions of schools shows that parents and community members name school safety as one of their top concerns.

Ms. Dinkens, High School Assistant Principal: I can tell you this; teachers have grave concerns about the welfare of their students and their own safety right in their classrooms.

Ms. Cohen: We need to promote more community awareness of the issues and promote policies that will help school officials set strong guidelines against violence and destruction. Schools must have programs and personnel for preparing young people to deal with apprehension and threats of violence before such conditions erupt into unfortunate incidents.

Mr. Adamson: Yes, absolutely. Then we all must work together as a community to figure out how we can make our schools and communities as safe and healthy and productive an environment as we can.

Mr. Alvarez: We hope our children and youth will become good citizens and lifelong learners here in this community or wherever they are. Schools are our country's lifeblood and the showcases for communities.

Ms. Dinkens: Indeed. We want our schools to succeed. Students should be able to work and play, have businesses and jobs, raise their families, contribute to their communities, and fulfill their dreams.

CHALLENGES IN WORKING TOGETHER FOR THE FUTURE

Co-educators are hardy pioneers and courageous trailblazers in their searches for better ways of helping children grow and develop into all they can be. Collaborative school consultants are often looked to for leadership. This calls for ongoing dialogue among teachers, school psychologists and counselors, district and school administrators, related services personnel, community leaders, social workers, medical personnel, local justice officials, families, and certainly students.

Eisner (2003), noted educator and administrator at Stanford University, underscores the collaborative perspective by emphasizing that instruction must teach students to exercise judgment, think critically, acquire meaningful literacy, serve others, and work with others in all walks of life. With school consultation and collaboration as a contributing process to teaching and learning, there is hope for creating both the social flexibility and the satisfying individuality that students will need. Collaborating educators can work together to enhance their repertoire of instructional and advisory practices so students succeed in spite of, perhaps even because of, their special needs.

The challenge of thinking in new ways about school-based education is not a desire to make it easier or to avoid accountability or abandon the values that historically have provided meaning and given direction to educators. Rather, it is a challenge to participate in creating a new vision of helping students achieve their potential in a connected world. The time to think and act in new, exciting ways is now. As that well-known adage reminds us, "The journey of a thousand miles begins with a single step."

ADMINISTRATOR AND SUPPORT PERSONNEL ROLES

The building principal's role and concomitant responsibilities are just short of overwhelming. So many school issues compete for a principal's time and energy that teachers must make a keen effort to accommodate their principals' heavily committed schedules when asking them to think about, much less become involved in, collaborative and team-based efforts. But building administrators *must* be involved; they have key roles in not only allowing but encouraging and endorsing collaboration and teamwork. They make the allocations of time, space, and other resources that are so necessary for effective consultation and collaboration. Much of their time and energy is spent in interactive processes of many sorts with numerous people. They meet formally and sometimes informally with family members who are not always supportive of schools and teachers. They assign paraeducators and coordinate teamwork that takes place among building personnel. They also promote staff development for educational reform and new programs.

SITUATION 12.B

Margo is the principal of an elementary school where a collaborative school reform approach is being implemented. The approach is a bold attempt to turn around a low-achieving school in which many students have failed to make adequate yearly progress. Margo knows that strong, successful teamwork will be central to success of the program's four distinctive features:

- Family and community partnerships in education
- Academic excellence focusing on reading, writing, math, science, social science, and technology instruction
- Citizenship efforts where students are taught to develop responsible behaviors with emphasis on treating others with respect
- Educator support that helps teachers make important decisions based on frequent reports of each student's progress throughout the year toward curriculum goals

In Margo's building, the teachers have been resistant toward making any changes. She has the challenge of leading them to a more positive and supportive attitude and to successful implementation of the approach. She makes it clear to the teachers that the approach *will* be implemented in the building and she is 100 percent behind it. She asks teachers who feel they cannot be supportive to consider transferring to another building in the district by the next school year. She invites teachers to discuss their concerns individually with her. She remains positive and supportive, yet firm in her goals for the school. She is careful to follow through to see that each implementation activity is completed and nothing slips through the cracks.

Margo confers with central office and program administrators, including the director of special education, to provide additional personnel and material support to the teachers during the transition time. With the help of the school counselor and music teacher, she organizes school-wide assemblies for Friday afternoons so teachers can have released time for planning collaboratively.

Margo also organizes a parent/community night for interacting with each other and showcasing the school's aims. She seeks written evidence of support from students, teachers, parents, and resource personnel. She continues to keep parents informed of changes taking place in the school and requests their input for important decisions that need to be made.

How Administrators Can Encourage Collaboration and Teamwork

Administrators can assist staff immeasurably by freeing up teacher time and arranging for substitutes and activities so consultation and collaboration among school personnel can take place. Building administrators should work with consultants to clarify collaborative consultation roles and ensure that such roles have parity among the school staff. They also should encourage interaction and staff development for all school personnel. When staff development sessions are promoted and attended by building principals, the positive ripple effects can be profound.

In a review of educational research on the principal's role in creating inclusive schools for diverse learners, Riehl (2000) notes that school leadership has moved well beyond application of knowledge and skills as a science of administration would suggest, and beyond finesse with processes as an art of administrative performance, to regarding school administration as a form of practice. This "creates a 'horizon' that envisions what schools create and where they might lead" (Riehl, 2000, p. 69). A study by Foley and Lewis (1999) indicated that the secondary administrator role of manager and primary decision-maker for operation and function of the school, with responsibility for centralized control of school activities and resources, does not mesh with principles of collegiality, parity, and shared decision-making that underpin collaborative structures. Foley and Lewis propose a shift in authority to regard the principal as a team member and supporter.

Principals are often referred to as instructional leaders. Indeed, schools today must be led by instructional leaders who value teamwork as a way to maximize student learning. Hattie (2015) describes what he calls high-impact instructional leadership and focuses on mind frames that inform leadership style. High-impact instructional leaders:

- Focus on learning and the impact of teaching
- Evaluate the effect everyone in the school has on student learning
- Believe student learning success or failure is about what teachers or leaders did or didn't do
- See themselves as change agents
- View assessment as feedback on their impact
- Value dialogue and listen to both teacher and student voices
- Set challenging targets for themselves and teachers
- Welcome mistakes, sharing what they've learned from their own mistakes, and creating a safe environment in which teachers and students can learn from their errors without losing face

In their handbook *A Principal's Guide to Special Education*, Bateman and Bateman (2001) point out the principal's role in special education and discuss what principals need to know in order to implement best practices for special education in their schools. Topics covered include eligibility and placement, the principal's role as an instructional leader, special education laws, policy issues concerning discipline and due process, accountability, staffing, working with school counselors, and more. It is vital for all school administrators to study and reflect on such issues. Administrators must be included as *participants* in professional development experiences so they are aware of special needs and the programs and personnel that can help serve those needs effectively.

To summarize the specific ways in which administrators can encourage collaboration, they should:

- Provide resources for collaborating and co-teaching
- Listen to, and gather feedback, from co-educators
- Serve as instructional resources themselves
- Function as liaisons between school and community
- Provide released time for professional development
- Participate actively in professional development programs

ACTIVITY 12.1
Questions to Ask the Building Administrator

With a colleague, simulate a conference between a building principal and a novice classroom teacher. Use these questions posed by a beginning teacher in dialogue with the administrator about consulting and teaming with her co-educators.

1. Do I *have* to have a student with disabilities in my classroom? If so, who is responsible for developing curriculum and lessons for them?

2. If I don't agree with what the special education teachers or support staff have asked me to do, and I've discussed the issues with them but still there is no resolution, what do I do next?

3. Why does the special ed teacher have a smaller caseload than I do?

4. Whose responsibility is it to supervise and evaluate special ed staff?

5. How may I request student services that are not available now?

6. Where will I find time to collaborate and consult with co-educators?

7. How would I go about setting up co-teaching experiences with a colleague?

8. If co-educating doesn't work out after a fair trial, what then?

9. To what extent will I be accountable for standardized test scores of *all* students in my room, including those with disabilities?

Getting Off to the Right Start with Administrators

The novice teacher who conferred with the building principal in Activity 12.1 was addressing concerns outlined very early in this book: how to prepare for collaboration; what the collaborative role will be; how to carry out responsibilities of the role; and how to evaluate one's success in the role. Sometimes just getting started is the hardest part of what has great potential for being a pleasant and fulfilling professional experience.

ACTIVITY 12.2
Ten-Plus-One Steps for Building a Path to Success

Develop a chart of a ten-plus-one-step process for participating in collaboration and teamwork as a general education teacher, or a special education teacher, or as one of a two-partner team. Keep this guide ready in your portfolio or desk for occasional review and quick referral when needed.

1. As the first step, read, study, think, interview others, and if possible complete coursework or professional development sessions to gain information and skills about collaborating and consulting as a team of co-educators.

2. Formulate your own personal philosophy of collaboration as a collaborator, co-teacher, and team member.

3. Meet with the administrator(s) in your assigned school(s) to learn their views on the collaborative consultant role or co-teacher role for the district, using exemplary responsive listening skills. *This is a very important step.*

4. If an advisory council is part of the district's administrative structure, request your administrators' permission to engage some of the members in informal discussion about consultation and collaboration roles. (An advisory council generally includes general and special education teachers, support personnel, administrators, parents, other community leaders, and perhaps a student or two.)

5. Meet with department heads of grade levels and curriculum levels with whom you will be interacting to find out their perceptions of collaboration and expectations for the role and what they think could work best.

6. At this point, rethink and reorganize your thoughts and ideas, and gather more information if necessary.

7. Develop a tentative role description and goals based on views expressed by central and building administrators, advisory council members, and department leaders, as well as your own viewpoints.

8. Return to the central-office administrator and/or building administrators, as appropriate for that district, conveying the description and goals to them and revising if necessary.

9. After honing your plan to a concise format, put it up for discussion, explaining it to department heads if that applies, to teaching staff and to non-teaching staff, refining it even further if needed as per their comments.

10. Convey the essence of the plan to co-educators during a professional development or staff meeting and to parents during a parent-teacher meeting or individually to family members whose children will be involved.

11. Last, but certainly not least, go over the plan with students who will be the focus of your efforts, encouraging their comments and and taking those comments very seriously.

School Board Members as Leaders and Partners in Education

School districts in the United States are governed by Boards of Education (BOE). The school board is arguably the most influential group in a community because it oversees education for children and youth of the community; therefore, BOEs are framing the future. Being a school board member in a community is one of the most significant responsibilities that a citizen of a community can accept. The school board sets policies for operation of the district's schools, including the hiring of staff, approving curriculum, and taking care of school buildings and other property. Personnel hiring includes the all-important task of selecting a superintendent of schools, who is the agent of the school board. The board is an agent of the state, directed by a State Board of Education. The aggregate of individuals making up a BOE speak as one body to formulate policy for the community's schools, enforce the policies, and evaluate the outcomes of policies.

Effective BOE membership calls for members to focus on policy and not become mired down in regulations or procedural matters. Although the details of "buses, ball-games, buildings, and budgets" are very important, it is vital that school boards also discuss and make decisions about matters such as curriculum, student achievement, teacher contracts, and the structure and mission statements of schools. Teacher leaders who aim to introduce concepts such as curriculum revision, changes in basal textbooks, block scheduling, *and collaboration among co-educators, or co-teaching arrangements* should bring their plans to the school board's attention and provide appropriate information.

Board meetings are held monthly, and sometimes more often; they tend to be long, often arduous, and sometimes contentious because of the high stakes involved—the community's children. Nevertheless, teachers should attend meetings now and then, even when their own topics of immediate concern are not on the agenda. This demonstrates to the board that teachers want to be informed and involved. A group of co-educators, representing all grade levels and curricular areas, could collaborate on occasion to present a report to the school board about a current topic such as efforts they are making to plan and teach together. Sometimes boards have additional meetings—typically a workshop or a public forum where parents and taxpayers can become more knowledgeable about their schools. Faculty and other school personnel should read and discuss school board meeting reports, which generally are available in local newspapers.

When school personnel want the news to flow the other way—from school to board—they must remember that board members are typically some of the community's busiest people. So they will react most favorably to comprehensive, concise written reports or "fact sheets." Examples of what teachers have done, what students have accomplished, and how the schools can be showcased can provide support and rationale for additional resources, policy changes, and innovations.

Too few educators and lay public know very much about school boards—how they are selected, qualifications for running (which are surprisingly minimal), term of office, whether reimbursed or not, and perhaps most intriguing, reasons a candidate puts herself or himself up to run for the school board. Teacher education programs should provide preservice teachers with more knowledge about school boards and practicing teachers should become familiar with who is on the board, why they are members, and what transpires at board meetings. Teachers can learn a great deal by attending their local school board meetings periodically, especially when they aren't there to advocate or ask something of the board. Too often, members of the school board and the community only see teachers in the audience when there is a controversial agenda item such as a proposed school closing or when it is time to negotiate teaching contracts. By attending more regularly, teachers send a message that they want to be informed and they are interested in all topics and board actions. Informal conversations often occur before or after the meeting with board members and other community members who have attended. This is a great opportunity to learn what is going on and have potential influence with those who make important decisions that impact teachers and students. A school board member who sees a teacher regularly attending meetings and conversing with others is more likely to seek that teacher's opinion about an issue or policy down the road. Connections are made and trust is established, thus contributing to the goal of collaboration.

School board members must be active listeners and skilled decision-makers. They also need to keep in mind the adage that no one can please all of the people all of the time. Nevertheless, they must give their best efforts in collaborating with fellow board members. Board members articulate policies to their constituents as a body, not as individuals. So collaboration, consultation, and team efforts are important tools for school boards as well as for school personnel.

School Psychologists and Counselors as Partners in Collaboration and Consultation

School psychologists and counselors have integral roles in assessing student abilities and needs and identifying problems if the needs are not served. They provide preassessment, assessment, and post-assessment data to teachers and parents. They contribute practical suggestions for resources to remediate in problem areas and optimize in strength areas, and they make recommendations for topics to feature in staff development activities.

Secondary level counselors oversee students' cognitive, emotional, and social needs in what are often explosive peer environments for them. As far back as the mid 1960s, school counselors began to promote the concept of proactive service in these cases, so that by the early 1970s consultation was being recommended as an integral part of contemporary counseling service.

A major area of contribution by school psychologists to the collaborative effort is in the individual education planning (IEP) conference. In IEP conferences school psychologists often fill the required administrator role when the principal cannot attend. Maureen Shapiro, regular education teacher (Tiegerman-Farber & Radziewicz, 1998, p. 207), describes her school's multidisciplinary team as including "the speech pathologist, classroom teacher, assistant teacher, psychologist, occupational therapist, music therapist, creative art therapist, and adaptive physical education or dance movement therapist, and administrators" to develop IEPs using a team approach.

School psychologists were part of the discussion and dialogue in a School for Language and Communications Development project aimed at formulation of collaboration (Tiegerman-Farber & Radziewicz, 1998). The project outcomes described competencies of the collaborative process as abilities to establish and maintain rapport, learn from others, be flexible and receptive, respect others' input, communicate clearly, support views of others, manage conflict, develop strategies and objectives, and make decisions. Success of inclusion was reported as depending on development of the collaborative process in the school, with the most important variables being the flexibility and time allocated for the teaming process.

Several points made by the researchers are pertinent to collaborative school consultation in inclusive schools. Collaboration can be

> **Video Example from YouTube**
>
> ENHANCEDetext
> **Video Example 12.1.**
>
> Watch this video and reflect on areas where the special educators and school counselors might collaborate based on common roles. (https://www.youtube.com/watch?v=aN0Q-R6Ruw8)

formal or informal, but at a formal level the process is more clearly defined and directed. Amount employed and success of the collaboration will "depend on the personalities of the individuals involved" (Tiegerman-Farber & Radziewicz, 1998, p. 203).

School psychologists perform many roles in schools that are vital to special educators and the students they serve. These include counseling, assessment, consultation and collaboration, crisis intervention, and academic and behavior intervention. They often have an active role in the Multi-Tier Systems of Support (MTSS) teams discussed in an earlier chapter. As part of those teams, school psychologists can provide assistance in data analysis and problem solving to develop behavioral and academic interventions for the various tiers in MTSS. They need to solicit input from parents and work with them so they are participants in the process. Equal status and confidentiality among school co-educators and home co-educators are critical to success of the process. Ability to communicate is a key factor in successful interaction. This includes not only spoken and written communication but facial expressions, gestures, posture, tone of voice, and timing. With these tools, the educator communicates facts, feelings, perceptions, and innuendoes.

Collaboration among special education and general education teachers, school counselors, and school psychologists can enrich the problem-solving process by focusing on all needs of the whole child. That said, preparation and internships in collaboration types are important experiences for the preparation of school psychologists and counselors.

Determining Professional Development Needs

The collaborative consultant role is ideal for coordinating useful inservice and staff development activities about special needs. Special education personnel often inherit these responsibilities either as a part of a plan or by default. Having school psychologists and counselors involved provides added benefits. Of course there are some disadvantages to being a "prophet in one's own land" for conducting inservice activities, but there are a number of advantages. One of the biggest is knowing the school context and being aware of what participants probably already know and still need or want to know.

This is a good point at which to distinguish between "training" and "professional development." When discussing training and professional development for teachers learning about technology, Patnoudes (2015) believes it is crucial to differentiate between the two. He describes training as the *how*—it is the user manual on devices, software, apps, or website. To broaden the scope beyond technology, this could include learning how to teach a lesson from a particular curriculum, demonstrate a strategy, or carry out the steps of a behavior intervention. Training is needed because teachers must understand the tool or strategy in order to use it. On the other hand, teachers need professional development to understand the *why*. Professional development focuses on why and when to use the tool or strategy. It focuses on building the teacher's capacity for understanding when the tool or strategy is needed and how to optimize the results. Understandably, teachers want training but they must have professional development as well in order to understand why to use the tool or intervention. It is easy to get drawn into a glitzy technology device or application, a well-packaged curriculum, or a novel behavior intervention and forget about the need to understand why it is or is not the needed intervention. Professional development can help teachers in the decision-making process.

"Becoming an expert special educator is not easy task! Even if you have mastered the basic expectations for your job, those expectations are continually evolving, becoming increasingly complex and rigorous," according to Benedict, Brownell, Park, Bettini, and Lauterbach (2014). Benedict and colleagues (2014) encourage special educators to take charge of their own professional development by:

- Analyzing their teaching
- Video capture themselves teaching
- Analyzing the videos
- Identifying an area to target for professional growth

To become an expert special education teacher, one must become a scholar of teaching, be relentless in developing deeper content knowledge, and acquire new pedagogical methods for helping students learn and master content. This can be accomplished in a number of ways, but one that is particularly relevant to the content of this text is to plan instruction collaboratively with peers and then observe their implementation of the plans. This practice helps teachers integrate new ideas and resources into their instructional repertoire. Another way to take charge of one's own professional learning is to peruse professional literature, especially articles from practitioner-type journals such as *Teaching Exceptional Children*, *Intervention in School and Clinic*, and other teacher-friendly journals having useful strategies or ideas. Getting involved with a teacher study group or professional book study is yet another way to increase one's knowledge and expertise. Whichever method one selects, it will take time to feel comfortable implementing the new skills effectively. First attempts to implement are likely to have a few bumps. The key is to stick with it and practice, practice, practice! Seek feedback and problem-solving support. Following this plan will help develop the skills needed by an exemplary teacher.

SITUATION 12.C

Several middle-school teachers are conversing in the break room on Friday afternoon.

Social Studies Teacher: What a week! I feel like I've attended to everything this week but students and curriculum. Maybe things will slow down a bit next week.

Math Teacher: Guess you didn't look at your office memo yet, hmmm? There's a reminder about the staff development sessions next Tuesday and Thursday mornings before school. Something about collaborative consultation with special education teachers, I think.

Social Studies Teacher: (with a hint of sarcasm) Consultation? You mean visits by those people who drive over from the central office to borrow your clock and tell you what time it is? Or do you mean the imported experts breezing in from more than fifty miles away with their briefcases and stacks of transparencies?

Math Teacher: I believe this group involves the school psychologist, counselors, and special education staff. We're supposed to find out about what we can do together and how we can manage it, now that so many students with learning and behavioral problems are in our classrooms most of the time.

Art Teacher: Oh, great. How does that involve me? I had my required course in special ed. What I *really* need is a bigger room and more supplies.

Social Studies Teacher: And if we're supposed to collaborate with these people, where will we find the time?

Physical Education Teacher: Uh–huh. It will be hard enough just carving out the time to go to the *meeting* about it.

Math Teacher: Now you know you'll just *love* congregating en masse to try and concentrate on some new-fangled proposal when you'd rather be in your classroom getting set for the day.

Social Studies Teacher: Well, let me put it this way. If they're not through by 8:20 sharp, I'm out of there!

Presenters of staff development must attend to different needs of participants, along with some occasional indifference or resistance. They will want to address the agenda of co-educators and note those who are:

- Looking for facts, data, and references
- Wishing to study the topic through interactions with colleagues
- Wanting to reason and explore
- Liking to adapt, modify, or create new ideas and processes (Garmston & Wellman, 1992)

Keeping adult learner characteristics and individual style variations in mind, professional developers should arrange for participant comfort, give them options and choices, manage the designated time well, deliver practical and focused help, and follow up on the effectiveness of the experience.

Busy educators value activities in which they work toward realistic, job-related, useful goals. They need to see results for their efforts as demonstrated by success when they use the material within their school context. Too often professional development is designed to focus on "attitude adjustment" before there are validations of successful strategies. So it begins at the wrong place—that is, telling teachers why they should something and then expecting them to want to do it.

In Guskey's (1985) well-received model aiming for teacher change, staff development is presented to *generate change in classroom teaching practices*. This brings about changes in student learning outcomes, causing changes in teacher beliefs and attitudes. Guskey stresses that staff development must illustrate clearly ways in which new practices can improve student performance, and how these practices can be implemented without too much disruption or extra work. This is particularly important when focusing on consultation and collaboration, because implementing this kind of professional activity often involves more time and effort at the outset.

Kelleher (2003) describes professional development as a form of adult learning that must be concerned primarily with student learning. A speaker or an activity might be interesting to participants, but the test of success is what teachers *do* with the new information they receive. Kelleher recommends allocating professional development budgets so as to encourage teachers to focus heavily on activities related to peer collaboration. A peer collaboration strand that features teachers collaborating in writing curriculum and assessments, examining student work, observing one another's classrooms, and mentoring new teachers can have significant impact on student achievement. What do co-educators already know about a topic such as collaborative school consultation at this point? What do they want to learn? How can they be involved in planning, conducting, and evaluating experiences for their individual needs? This information should be solicited through needs assessment instruments. Most school personnel have had experience with completing needs assessments. Formats for needs assessments include:

- Checklists
- Questionnaires and surveys
- Open-ended surveys of areas of concern
- Interviews
- Brainstorming sessions
- Informal methods such as observations and team-meeting buzz groups

Needs assessments might ask school personnel to check topics of need or to describe their concerns that can be developed into a staff development activity.

Garmston (1988) compares presenting staff development with giving presents. He suggests the "present" should be something participants (presentees) want or can utilize, personalized to individual taste as much as possible, attractively wrapped, and a bit suspenseful. The presenter will want to plan the following elements carefully and will find it useful to rehearse key parts of the session before the event, especially the opening and closing sections.

- Assess audience needs and interests.
- Have something on the agenda that appeals to everyone.
- Conduct the activity in an interesting, efficient, multi-modal format.
- Package the ISD material attractively.
- Pace the session to cover all major points and end on time.
- Ensure that no one's input is overlooked.
- Provide an element of surprise and intrigue.
- Assess and evaluate the outcomes of the staff development activity.
- Provide follow-up help, support, and additional information as requested.

Formal and Informal Approaches to Professional Development

Professional development can be formal or informal. Formal activities are conducted through scheduled sessions, conferences, presentations, webinars, modules, training videos found on the Internet, courses, brochures, retreats, and other planned activities. Informal activities occur in conversations, observations, reports about one topic that include another aspect of education, memos, references to media productions, online discussion board

FIGURE 12.1 Formal and Informal Professional Development

	Formal	Informal
Plan	Typically structured Example: Workshop	Usually casual Example: Newsletter column
Method	Designed with care Example: Speaker/discussion	Somewhat spontaneous Example: Hall chat
Evaluation	Data collection Example: Checklist	Reflection Example: Journal note

postings, chat rooms, mini-presentations by co-educators at faculty meetings, newsletters, and purposeful reading material or professional book study groups. (See Figure 12.1.)

Time is the enemy when planning and presenting whole-faculty or small-group faculty sessions where teachers will concentrate and reflect. Before-school and after-school hours might seem workable because participants are coming to school anyway or are required to stay after school for a specific length of time. But teachers dislike this, finding it hard to focus on their own learning at an early hour when their thoughts are centered on beginning the school day efficiently, and feeling that by day's end their energy and emotions may be lagging and other responsibilities beckoning. Saturday sessions are no more popular, as they encroach upon the family and community life so necessary for sustaining teacher vitality and support.

The arrangement preferred by most teachers for staff development is released time during the school day. This means that their responsibilities with students will need to be assumed by others. Numerous suggestions have been offered by professional development experts for carving teachers' time from their schedules and responsibilities, such as occasionally hiring substitute teachers, having a permanent substitute cadre that conducts planned enrichment activities for students, having a staff of roving substitute teachers, or making arrangements where one teacher teaches two classes to free up the second teacher. The substitute cadre eliminates the necessity for detailed lesson planning by the teacher, because the enrichment activities are planned and provided by the cadre. Roving substitutes allow released teachers to have short periods of time for observing, coaching, gathering research data, or assisting in another classroom. Loucks-Horsley and colleagues (1987) contend that the time issue surrounding staff development is a "red herring" because the problem often lies in *the constructive use of time*, not its availability.

> **Video Example from YouTube**
>
> ENHANCEDetext
> **Video Example 12.2.**
>
> This satirical video poking fun at traditional, district-wide inservice sessions, reminds us of the importance of making staff development activities relevant and engaging for both the novice teacher and those who feel they have attended way too many of these sessions and look for ways to check out mentally before the session begins. (https://www.youtube.com/watch?v=Mvu3HBQmPNk)

Attending Conferences and Conventions for Professional Development

Conventions, conferences, and workshops provide opportunities for personal and professional growth. At well-structured events, the atmosphere is charged with energy and enthusiasm and a smorgasbord of choices is offered to whet adult learners' appetites. Participants gain information and ideas from other educators. They renew acquaintances and make new connections. In-district partnerships can bloom if colleagues or parents are asked to go along. One concept that is effective for some convention themes is a team model of participants in which a classroom teacher or two, a special education teacher, and a building administrator attend the event together. Fruitful discussions can take place within the group who are often energized to bring back the ideas to their school. Initial implementation plans often begin while attending or traveling home from a professional conference. Networks of collaboration can be established among educators with common curriculum and special needs interests. Some gather to plan writing projects for professional journals or to prepare proposals for funding cross-country research projects or future co-presentations. The process of submitting proposals for making presentations is an intellectual exercise that contributes to professional development.

Professional events are meant to be invigorating and informative. Convention-goers can gain the most from the experience by planning their time carefully, getting to sessions early, making sure to visit exhibit areas for new ideas and materials (and sometimes publisher giveaways), taking advantage of sessions that showcase instructional strategies and student products, and allowing some time and energy to venture beyond the convention site for a little fun and relaxation. In order to achieve such positive outcomes, professional development experiences must be planned, conducted, evaluated, and followed up efficiently.

While there is much to be gained from attending conferences in person, budget cuts, time constraints, and staffing difficulties have resulted in more teachers and administrators turning to online professional development in the form of webinars. Webinars can be found on almost any topic, and many are free or at a nominal cost when compared to the cost of travel to an out-of-state conference. Some professional conferences have even created a virtual conference attendance strand, allowing teachers to attend sessions virtually from their offices or classrooms or from the comfort of their sofas at home. Presenters of webinars are typically experts in their area and have extensive knowledge and experiences. Webinars can be viewed during the live broadcast or an archived version can be watched after the session. If participating in the live webinar, questions can be posed through a moderator and answered during or at the conclusion of the session. If viewed by a group together, discussion can take place during and after the webinar to discuss the topic and how it could be implemented in their setting. Webinars offer affordable and accessible training and professional development to meet the learning needs of busy professionals at any time.

The Staff Break Room (Workroom, "Lounge")

Very little has been written about the staff break room that is sometimes referred to as "the lounge" even though as a general rule not much lounging goes on there. The lack of attention to this place where co-educators can interact with other adults is surprising because most teachers do drop in at some time or other. Some go there quite frequently, although others seldom do.

Visits usually fall within one of three purposes—physical, social, or personal. There may be the physical benefit of refreshment, a quick "nap," or a restroom break. Having a few minutes of socialization squeezed between intensive periods with children and adolescents is important to some. Professional benefits include catching up on tasks such as grading papers or reading materials, or getting one's thoughts and plans together for the next activity or class. But sometimes teachers want an opportunity to interact with colleagues and share reflections about teaching practices and student needs. Good ideas for collaboration and co-teaching can come from these brief moments, to be revisited in one's mind at a later time with more focused attention.

Break room conversations can be problematic if the discourse is quite negative and cynical. When this kind of talk affects one's morale negatively, going there for "down time" becomes **iatrogenic**, where the intended remedy is worse than the initial condition. But the break room/workroom/lounge typically provides a useful hub of interactivity for special education teachers to develop rapport with general education colleagues and learn more about their classrooms and students.

It is important that collaborative consulting teachers spend enough time in the teachers' workroom ("Don't the special ed people want to be a part of our faculty?"), but not too much ("Don't those special ed people have anything to do?"). Of course, care must be taken to keep professional conversation general in nature. Confidentiality and ethical treatment of information are necessary behaviors for all teachers, and special education teachers in particular. But in this room that is provided for relaxation, reflection, and refreshment, a collaborative spirit can be nurtured and then carried away to classrooms, offices, and meetings.

ACTIVITY 12.3
Designing a Staff Break Room

In your thoughts or on sketch paper, have fun creating a "dream break room" that could serve school personnel for physical, social, and personal needs. What would it look like? What would it sound like? Where would it be located? How might co-educators nurture the collaborative spirit there? What would it take to construct and outfit such a room? Could some of your suggestions be carried out right away with little cost and disruption to the school? Who would do this, and how would it be done?

POSITIVE RIPPLE EFFECTS OF COLLABORATIVE SCHOOL CONSULTATION

Collaborative consultation is not an oxymoron as some have suggested. It is **synergy**—"a behavior of whole systems unpredicted by the behavior of their parts taken separately" (Fuller, 1975, p. 3). Collaboration in conjunction with consultation requires harmonious, efficient teamwork. When interactive teamwork is effective, there is synergy. A synergistic combination of systems, programs, personnel, and support is a recipe for success in the school setting.

Positive ripple effects, sometimes referred to as **multiplier effects**, make compelling arguments for consultation, collaboration, and co-teaching. They provide benefits that can reach far beyond an immediate situation involving one student and that student's teachers. When collaboration occurs among co-educators, many skills and talents "bubble up" to be shared and expanded. Then all will learn and improve their skills. Here, it is important to revisit a point made earlier. Consulting teachers who are concerned that their positions could be eliminated when collaboration is successful in addressing the needs of students should not be anxious. As teachers become more proficient in helping students with special needs, they value collaborative consultation services even more and tend to include the process in their plans for instruction more frequently.

Using specialized intervention techniques for many more students than the ones formally identified for special education programs is a positive outcome to expect from collaborative school consultation. Multiple benefits can extend well beyond the immediate classroom because consulting teachers are in a unique position to facilitate interaction among many groups. The effects that ripple out from mutual planning and problem solving across grade levels, subject areas, and attendance centers in a school district are powerful instruments for initiating positive changes in the educational system. These ripples create multiplier effects that make convincing arguments for consultation, collaboration, and teaming processes. They augment benefits beyond the immediate situation involving one student and that student's teachers. Furthermore, co-educators in collaboration with their colleagues are modeling a powerful tool for their students who soon will be collaborating and teaming with others in their own workplaces. (See Figure 12.2.)

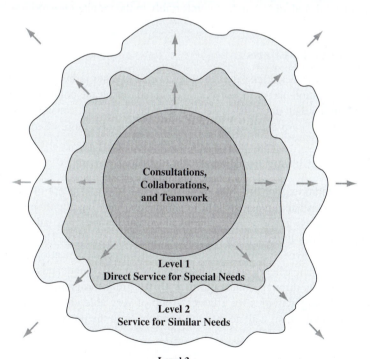

FIGURE 12.2   Three Levels of Service

LEVELS OF COLLABORATIVE AND CONSULTATIVE SERVICE

A positive outcome of collaborative school consultation is enhanced skills among teachers for providing interventions and remediation techniques to many more students than those identified for services. The services can be classified into one of three levels.

Examples of Level 1 Effects

Direct services for consultees mark the first level of effects. At this level, the consultation and collaboration are most likely to have been initiated for one client's need. (Recall that a client can be an entity such as a student group, school, family, or community, as well as a single student.) As examples, level 1 effects can result from the following types of school situations:

- The special education teacher for learning disabilities engages in problem solving with a high school teacher to determine ways of helping a student with severe learning disabilities master the minimum competencies required for graduation.
- The audiologist helps a teacher arrange the classroom environment to enable a hearing-impaired student to function comfortably in the regular classroom setting.

Examples of Level 2 Effects

Needs for special services often extend beyond level 1 to other individuals. At level 2, consultees use information and points of view generated during the collaboration to be more effective in similar but unrelated cases. Both consultant and consultee repertoires of knowledge and skills are enhanced so that they can function more effectively in similar situations.

Level 2 effects include these examples:

- The classroom teacher becomes more familiar with the concept of hyperactivity in children, subsequently regarding fewer children as having attention deficit disorder with hyperactivity, and adjusting the classroom curriculum to address very active children's needs more appropriately in that classroom setting. This reduces labeling of children as hyperactive and lessens referrals to special education programs.
- The classroom teacher becomes comfortable with enrichment activities provided for gifted students through collaboration with the gifted program facilitator, and provides enriching activities for a larger group of very able children in the classroom who can handle them with no difficulty and thrive in the process.

Examples of Level 3 Effects

When collaborative consultation outcomes extend beyond situations such as ones described in levels 1 and 2, the entire school system can be affected positively by level 3 outcomes. Organizational change and increased family involvement are potential results of level 3 outcomes.

Level 3 effects enable these kinds of outcomes:

■ The efforts toward collaboration and teamwork could result in a professional development plan called "Teachers Helping Teachers," during which teachers in a school system provide training for interested colleagues, and sometimes parents as home educators, in their areas of expertise.

■ The school district's emphasis on consultation, collaboration, and co-teaching pleases families who find that their children are receiving more integrated and personalized instruction for their learning needs. Families become more active and interested in the school's programs, and more positive and encouraging of their children's efforts at home.

All in all, the multiplier effect of these interactive processes is a powerful tool for serving *all* students in more personalized ways, with positive effects reaching far beyond school contexts as graduates enter their chosen fields of work and areas of community life. Just as ripple effects happen on the water, they can happen on land in the hearts and minds of students and their teachers.

REVIEW OF BENEFITS FROM COLLABORATIVE SCHOOL CONSULTATION

School environments that promote collaborative consultation tend to involve all school personnel in the teaching and learning processes. (See Figure 12.3.) Information is shared and knowledge levels about student characteristics and needs, with strategies for meeting those needs, are broadened. Importantly, many of the strategies are helpful with other students who have similar but less severe needs.

A number of specific benefits such as these can be expected from well-conducted collaborative school consultation and teamwork for special needs:

1. Augmented support and assistance for students are available in the inclusive classroom.
2. Collaborating special education co-educators help general education co-educators develop repertoires of materials and instructional strategies. Many resource teachers find this more efficient than racing from one student to another in a resource room while they all work on individual assignments. A special education teacher succinctly put it this way, "In my resource room, by the time I get to the last student, I find that the first student is stuck and has made no progress. So I frantically run through the whole cycle again. Tennis shoes are a must for my job!"
3. Consulting teachers find ways to help classroom teachers become confident and successful with special needs students. At times they assume an instructional role in the classroom, which frees the classroom teacher to study student progress, or set up arrangements for special projects, or work intensively with a small group of students.

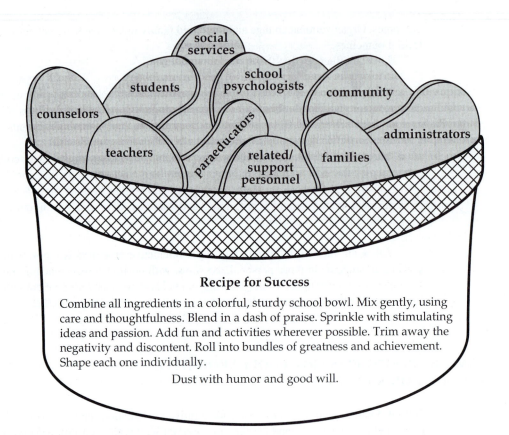

FIGURE 12.3   Ingredients for Success

4. When general classroom and special education teachers collaborate, each has ownership and involvement in serving special needs. In stressful situations, collaborators strengthen each other's resolve and effort by providing both material and emotional support (Conoley & Conoley, 2010). Such support is invaluable across all domains— mental, emotional, physical, and social.

5. Collaborative efforts to serve students in heterogeneous settings can help minimize stigmatizing effects of labels such as "delayed," "having disabilities," "exceptional," or even "gifted."

6. Collaborative efforts can reduce referrals to remedial programs. In a study of special education in an inclusionary middle school, Knowles (1997) found that collaboration and teamwork decreased special education referrals and grade-level retention of students.

7. Fewer referrals for special education services mean reduced expenditures for costly and time-consuming psychological assessments and special education interventions.

8. Educators can focus more of their limited time and energy on teaching and facilitating, and less time on repetitive processes of testing and measuring.

9. A ripple effect extends services to other students by encouraging use of modifications and alternatives for *their* special needs.

10. A successful consultation process becomes a supportive tool that teachers increasingly value and use.

11. Collaborative consultation services help to bridge gaps between parallel systems of special education and general education and are an effective way to alleviate confusion about goals and objectives of general education and special education.

12. When classroom teachers are efficient in working with a wide range of student needs, school administrators benefit from eased pressure of parent and student disgruntlements. Building principals find it stimulating to visit and observe in classrooms as part of the team, taking note of ways to ensure that every student succeeds in the school and reinforcing teacher successes with all students. This is for many administrators a welcome change from the more formal classroom visits they make for purposes of teacher evaluation.

13. Important but frequently overlooked is maintenance of continuity in learning programs as students progress through their K–12 school experiences. This is a savings in time, energy, and resources of the educational staff and often the parents as well.

14. A collaborative consultation approach is a natural system for nurturing harmonious staff interactions. Teachers who have become isolated or autonomous in their teaching styles and instructional outlook often discover that working with other adults for common goals is quite stimulating. Sharing ideas can add to creativity, open-endedness, and flexibility in developing educational programs for students with special needs. In addition, more emphasis and coordination can be given to cross-school and long-range planning, with broader accumulation of resources for student needs.

15. Collaborative consultants are integral in planning professional development experiences; they can identify areas in which teachers need awareness and information sessions, and they can coordinate workshops to help related services and support personnel become more knowledgeable about exceptional learning needs.

16. Parents or caregivers who have become extremely frustrated with the labeling, fragmented curriculum, and isolation from peers endured by their children with special needs, respond enthusiastically when they learn that several educators are functioning as a team for their child. Parental attitudes toward school become more positive. They are more likely to get involved in their child's learning program, more eager to provide input with their ideas, and more helpful in monitoring their child's work. They are particularly supportive when consulting services allow students in special education programs to attend inclusive neighborhood schools and receive more assistance from interagency sources for their child's special needs.

COMPETENCIES AND ETHICS FOR COLLABORATIVE CO-EDUCATORS

Throughout this book, competencies for collaborating, consulting, co-teaching, and working in teams as co-educators have been woven into descriptions of processes and content for various school contexts. Emphasis has been put directly or indirectly on these key points:

- Being knowledgeable about both special education and general education curriculum and methods

- Being interested in current trends and topics, and innovative in generating new ideas
- Recognizing and valuing diversity of preferences and perspectives among teachers and students
- Understanding how schools function and having a panoramic view of the educational scene
- Being practical and realistic, innovative, assertive, risk-taking as appropriate, and always fair and diplomatic
- Relating well to teaching colleagues, related services and support personnel, school administrators, families, and students
- Using good communication skills with patience and understanding
- Demonstrating objective viewpoints toward all aspects of education
- Keeping a professional perspective on the entire school context
- Linking people with resources, referring people to other sources as appropriate, and teaching when that is the most useful way to serve students' needs
- Being willing and not hesitant in seeking out help if needed
- Being comfortable and confident as an agent for change and progress

Again, as an experienced, long-time collaborative consulting teacher put it, "You have to be abrasive enough to create change, but pleasant enough to be asked back so you will do it some more" (Bradley, personal communication, 1987). The checklist (see Figure 12.4) that was introduced informally earlier in this book now summarizes the main competencies and can be used for self-assessment, evaluation by a supervisor, or assessment by a professional colleague whose views are valued highly.

The need to adhere to ethical principles within an ethical climate has been noted throughout this book. The sensitive and persuasive aspects of consultation require a close, careful look at ethical practices (Ross, 1986). Consultation, collaboration, and teamwork in school contexts will require particular emphasis on ethical interactivity for several reasons:

- Collaborative consultants have complex roles with many demands placed on them, but too often those in the roles have received little or no training for them.
- School consultation implies power and expertise until (and *only* until) a collaborative spirit has been cultivated in the school environment.
- Confidential data must be shared carefully among a number of individuals.
- Collaborative consultants are out and about much more than classroom teachers, interfacing with many people in homes and schools and across the community.
- Parent permission is not always required, but many issues will require the sensitivity and confidentiality needed in situations involving special learning and behavioral needs.
- Collaborative consultants may be asked on occasion to act inappropriately as a middle person or to form alliances or carry information, and ethically they must decline.
- There is some risk of diminishing return for collaborative efforts that may reduce the amount of time available for direct service to a student (Friend & Cook, 1992).
- Adults often have difficulty adapting to individual differences in teaching styles and preferences of colleagues, and some may erect barriers of resistance to working together.

FIGURE 12.4   Competencies Needed for Collaborative School Consultation

Criterion Area and Competencies	Needs Work	Improving	OK	Good	Excellent
Knowledge and Awareness of Collaboration/Consultation					
Understands concepts of collaborative consultation	1	2	3	4	5
Analyzes own perspectives/preferences	1	2	3	4	5
Shows respect for others' perspectives/preferences	1	2	3	4	5
Utilizes collaborative consultation theory and research	1	2	3	4	5
Understands collaborative models and programs	1	2	3	4	5
Application of Collaborative/Co-Educator Relationships					
Values diversity and individuality	1	2	3	4	5
Practices effective listening skills	1	2	3	4	5
Practices effective nonverbal skills	1	2	3	4	5
Practices effective verbal skills	1	2	3	4	5
Establishes co-equal relationships	1	2	3	4	5
Problem-Solving Techniques					
Demonstrates skill in problem finding	1	2	3	4	5
Collects and processes pertinent data	1	2	3	4	5
Uses effective problem-solving strategies	1	2	3	4	5
Selects appropriate methods for special needs	1	2	3	4	5
Follows through with decisions, follows up on plan	1	2	3	4	5
Organization and Management					
Manages time and resources efficiently	1	2	3	4	5
Coordinates collaborative consultation effectively	1	2	3	4	5
Conducts successful observation and interviewing	1	2	3	4	5
Provides resources and personnel for special needs	1	2	3	4	5
Conducts assessment of collaborations/co-teaching	1	2	3	4	5
Partnerships with Co-Educators					
Co-plans effectively with co-educators	1	2	3	4	5
Co-teaches successfully with co-educators	1	2	3	4	5
Directs paraeducators capably	1	2	3	4	5
Works well with related services/support personnel	1	2	3	4	5
Engages in respectful, productive family interactions	1	2	3	4	5
Change Agents for Positive Ripple Effects					
Provides leadership in collaborative settings	1	2	3	4	5
Interacts effectively with school administrators	1	2	3	4	5
Makes appropriate decisions for student well-being	1	2	3	4	5
Uses technology effectively and innovatively	1	2	3	4	5
Demonstrates skills of mentoring/modeling	1	2	3	4	5

■ Just as with mentorships, it is important to recognize those rare times when it is in the best interest of all concerned, but the student most of all, to withdraw from a consulting situation. Disengagement is recognized in psychological consultation as the termination of a consultative relationship. This is reality, so having a transition plan for moving into other relationships and experiences can ease feelings of inadequacy and help dispel feelings of failure.

Ethical collaborative consultation requires confidentiality in acquiring and using information about students, families, and individual school settings. It demonstrates a high regard for individual differences among colleagues and constructive use of those differences to serve students' needs. It gives evidence of concern and empathy for all, **one-downsmanship** (downplaying status differences and communicating as partners) in the consultative role, advocacy for those with special needs, and mutual ownership of problems and successes in the school environment.

Gullatt and Tollett (1997) note that society is becoming more complex and many legal issues now arise in school contexts. Yet few states require an educational law course as part of teacher education coursework for licensure, either at the graduate level or the undergraduate level. Broad issues needing to be addressed in the scope of school law include special education, student discipline including suspensions, liability, definition of negligence, student/teacher rights, confidentiality and privacy, photographing of students, conducting research in schools, freedom of student press, ever-changing laws and regulations, and much more. Occasionally school personnel are called to be expert witnesses and provide testimony and depositions involving student or family rights and due processes. So Gullat and Tollett (1997) recommend that universities and legal authorities collaborate with local educational authorities to design professional development workshops for informing teachers of current educational law and new legislation as enacted by state and national legislative bodies. They propose that each school designate a resource teacher to be responsible for collecting and distributing information about school law. Ethical issues could be included in this assignment and kept on the front burner of co-educators' group-focused agenda.

One dilemma for school personnel is that privacy or confidentiality may not be an absolute right, especially when minors are involved and there is risk of serious harm (Taylor & Adelman, 1998). Sometimes professionals cannot maintain confidences legally or ethically. Such conflicted intentions can interfere with trust between consultant and client or consultee, but the concern may be outweighed by a responsibility to prevent serious harm. Taylor and Adelman (1998) point out that most ethical guidelines recognize such extenuating circumstances. They suggest that the problem might be reframed and focused on ways of sharing the information appropriately.

Hansen, Himes, and Meier (1990) offer educators four general suggestions for exercising ethical behavior in their roles:

1. Promote professional attitudes and behaviors among staff about confidentiality and informed consent.
2. Take care with the type and tone of information that is entered in written records.
3. Be cautious and prudent in discussing problems of children and their families.
4. Focus on strengths of clients and share information only with those who need it to serve the student's needs.

Video Example from YouTube

ENHANCEDetext
Video Example 12.3.

Starting a new school year brings anticipation and excitement for both students and teachers. The ideas you've learned about in this book have no doubt stirred some excitement about collaboration as well. As you watch this video of a teacher's parody on Taylor Swift's song, "Blank Space," think about starting fresh with new ideas and enthusiasm for collaboration. (https://www.youtube.com/watch?v=uKZyUCLACIo)

Most issues involving special needs of children and adolescents are not so complex or fraught with legal entanglement. In these less complex and dramatic instances, several well-known maxims can be applied to defuse ill will and create a caring, facilitative, commonsense infusion of collegial and ethical practices into education for special needs:

- Keep your words sweet, for you may have to eat them.
- It's better to bend than to break.
- Only a fool would peel a grape with an ax.
- Eagles do not hunt flies.
- It is very hard to put the toothpaste back into the tube.
- And one cannot "un-ring" a bell.
- Lastly, what breaks in a moment may take years to mend.

Time to Chart Your Course

Educators, including preservice teachers in teacher education programs, novice teachers in their first position, experienced teachers, and veteran teachers as well, may look at the competencies checklist (Figure 12.5) and wonder, "Am I prepared for this kind of professional activity? How do I ensure that I am?" They can be confident of success if they are prepared to respond positively to the top-twelve collection of practical recommendations that are listed in Figure 12.5.

> ENHANCEDetext **Application Exercise 12.1.** Click to apply and synthesize your views on collaborative school consultation.

In Conclusion

The challenge of thinking in new ways about school-based education is not a call to make it easier or avoid accountability or abandon the values that historically have given meaning and direction to educators. Rather, it is a challenge to have a new vision of best opportunities for helping students achieve their potential in a wide-open, connected world. The time to envision new, exciting ways is now, repeating the well-known adage that "The journey of a thousand miles begins with a single step." Teachers are guides for today's children and youth along the course of that journey into their future. All students will need knowledge and skills they have developed in their homes, their communities, and most certainly their schools, that will prepare them for the challenges in their lives.

"An apple for the teacher" has been a traditional gift from student to teacher for decades, perhaps centuries. It represents the bright, caring relationship between teacher and student. But long gone are the days of the little red schoolhouse where an adoring student places an apple quietly with gratitude and respect on the desk of a single teacher. Much different conditions exist for teachers today in their crowded classrooms and huge, bustling school buildings teeming with a diversity of students—some of whom are outspoken and angry, others withdrawn and seemingly unreachable, a few wishing their

FIGURE 12.5   Readying Preservice and Novice Teachers for Collaborative School Consultation

A top-twelve list of practical recommendations for preservice and first-year teachers complements the general competencies checklist for all collaborative school consultants in general education and special education roles. Some have been sprinkled into various chapters, where featured, but they are collected here as a helpful dozen.

1. While in the teacher education program, including your field experiences and student teaching experiences, keep an idea journal.
2. If a teaching portfolio is required for graduation, plan the contents so they will be useful idea generators in your brand-new position.
3. Save your class textbooks and course packets for major subjects such as educational psychology, methods and content-areas, introductory special education, and assessment. Also, taking an assessment course is highly recommended. If taken as a graduate course, it can be a good launch pad for working toward a graduate degree.
4. When enrolled in courses such as educational psychology, look for ways of applying the material to future teaching situations; for example, when studying negative and positive reinforcement, or developing class rules, create sample plans that could be modified a bit and drawn upon later for a real, specific classroom. Talking through these activities collaboratively with classmates will result in even better products to stow away for use in the near future.
5. Video yourself teaching, lecturing, conferencing, and interacting with students, then study them just as a football team studies game films to improve their playing. Older teachers may dislike doing videos, but the younger generation tends to be more comfortable in front of video cameras. Of course, confidentiality and privacy of participants must be assured, so here again, written permission from all participants is a wise policy.
6. Join a new-teacher support group; if none is available, start one. Novices need high-quality feedback on their teaching performance. If none is forthcoming, ask for it (Grossman & Loeb, 2010); it is likely that your supervising administrator will be impressed with your request.
7. Find key "magnet-type" teachers in your first assigned building(s) and ask for some collegial time to draw upon their expertise. In exchange for the time, offer to take their bus or lunchroom duty for double the length of time the person contributed to you. This generous offer should ensure that you use the interaction time judiciously!
8. Return to your own early school days and visit with your favorite teachers, telling them how much you valued their guidance and asking them to talk with you about their teaching philosophy and practices. Most will be flattered and touched by your desire to do this. Perhaps you will receive such a visit from some of your own former students someday.
9. Take every opportunity to observe collaborative and co-teaching activities in schools during your field experiences or practicum. As noted earlier, it would be good experience to attend an IEP conference, but only with the administrator's written permission, written permission by the student's family, and your assurance of preserving complete confidentiality.
10. Take notes (without recording names—using code if necessary) when observing or working in schools. Sketch classroom layouts, catalog ideas for materials, and observe teaching procedures.
11. Make broad-stroke plans for your first day, month, week, and year. For example, a dedicated first-grade teacher would want to plan out that first day in 10-minute increments, with flexibility to tweak the plan in progress, of course.
12. Do not be concerned about appearing to be inexperienced. Every teacher has a first-year experience. Neither should you regard your veteran colleagues as "old school" and inflexible. All can learn from each other and enjoy doing it. The school environment has become much more collaborative and supportive in the past decade or two.

FIGURE 12.6

school days would never end, and too many thinking they just might opt out of it all tomorrow. (See Figure 12.6.)

The apple now signifies important work that is still to be done. As teachers step out of their classrooms, they know they are no longer addressing the challenges alone. They have opportunities to collaborate in diverse ways with many co-educators. When a person takes a symbolic apple and slices it, a bounty of seeds is revealed. If they slice it horizontally, the image of a star will appear—a beautiful, positive image. Then, if they envision the star, gather up the seeds, and plant them far and wide, who can count all of the apples that will grow from that vision and a few small seeds?

TIPS FOR SYNTHESIZING ELEMENTS AND CHARTING YOUR COURSE

1. Develop a personal philosophy of collaborative school consultation and be ready to explain it if asked.
2. Promote an exchange-of-roles day in which consultants teach classes and teachers observe, plan modifications, and consult with others.
3. Make a personal pledge to read at least an article a week from a professional journal.
4. Join a dynamic professional organization and become actively involved in it.
5. Observe programs in other schools and share observations with key people in your own school context.
6. Engage in research efforts for new knowledge about collaboration, consultation, teamwork, and networking with co-educators.
7. Remember that knowing how to collaborate does not guarantee one the opportunity to do it, so *create* the opportunity.
8. Advocate for students at every opportunity and in every way you can.
9. Reach out to preservice and novice teachers, new school staff, families of students, and new resource and support personnel to build their confidence, increase interactivity with them, and expand their skills.
10. Be available—and available—and never give up!

GLOSSARY

■ ■ ■ ■ ■

acceleration   Movement through the curriculum faster and farther than the typical pace.

assertive or *active* body language   Sitting or standing in an upright but relaxed, non-threatening posture with no barriers across the body such as arms folded or fisted hands.

assertiveness   The quality of being self-assured and confident without being aggressive. It requires being forthright about your wants and needs while still considering the rights, needs, and wants of others.

attrition   In the strictest application, it refers to teachers who leave the teaching field, but it could also apply to teachers who leave special education positions for general education teaching positions. It could also refer to when teachers leave one district for another.

brainstorming   Activity by a group or an individual to produce many diverse ideas, the more unusual the better, without passing judgment on any idea at that time.

burnout   Can be the result of physical and emotional exhaustion, often due to prolonged stress, depersonalization, and feeling a lack of accomplishment. This can result in attrition, alienation, cynicism, and physical problems.

civic engagement   Involvement in community activities and organizations, especially ones related to governance and policy.

client   An individual, a group, an agency, or other entity receiving consulting services in order to learn (know the material) and do (apply that learning) in school and beyond, who is often but not always the student.

co-educator   An educator who collaborates, consults, teams with, co-teaches, networks with other educator(s) to address students' needs for learning and doing. May be a school educator, home educator (parent or other caregiver), or community resource person.

co-teaching   A partnering of two teachers with different expertise to provide more comprehensive and effective instruction for students with disabilities or exceptional abilities within the general education classroom. In the context of this book, general and special educators collaboratively plan and deliver instruction for all students in the least restrictive environment.

collaboration   To labor together, or to work jointly in cooperative interaction to achieve a shared goal.

collaborative ethic   A philosophy promoting principles of shared purpose and interdependent practices among co-educators in working together for best interests of students and schools.

collaborative school consultation   An interactive process in which school co-educators, home co-educators, students, and resource and support personnel combine their knowledge and expertise to determine the student's educational needs, plan learning and behavioral goals, implement the plan, assess outcomes, and follow up as needed.

competencies for collaborative school consultation   Innate abilities or acquired skills for collaborating in schools.

concept mapping (webbing)   Linking of concepts to a central theme in order to illustrate relationships and make connections that generate more ideas and further connections.

consult   To advise or seek advice; to confer, consider, examine, refer to, communicate in order to decide or plan something, seek an opinion as a guide to one's own judgment, request information or facts, or talk over a situation with someone.

consultant   One who provides professional input or renders services in a field of special knowledge and training, or more simply, one who consults with another for a common purpose.

consultation log or journal   Used to record information about consultations. Typically includes the date, participants, topic, brief summary, outcomes. and any necessary follow-up.

consultation   Advisement, counsel, a conference; formal or informal deliberation to provide direct services to students or to work with co-educators in addressing special needs.

consultee   One who confers with a consultant to gather and exchange information and advice and apply it for the client's needs.

contextual diversity   Varied settings and circumstances of individuals, which may present challenges if a consultant is not familiar with the setting or circumstances. Examples include homelessness, those living in rural and isolated areas, and military families.

critical junctures   Important transition points between two disjointed progressions in education, such as high school to college or preschool to school.

cultural and linguistic diversity   Differences found among groups who have common values, beliefs, practices, language, and histories.

cultural competence   Skills, values, and attitudes that educational consultants need in order to work successfully in diverse settings with individuals having diverse identities, affiliations, characteristics, and experiences.

culture The embodiment of a worldview through learned and transmitted beliefs, values, and practices; and a way of living informed by historical, economic, ecological, and political forces acting on a group.

curriculum accommodations Assistive aids and supports that help a student achieve the same outcomes as most other students in the class by adjusting the requirements.

curriculum compacting After preassessment, to determine what parts of the curriculum have already been mastered, teachers replace content that students know or can learn rapidly and easily with new content, enrichment options, or other activities.

curriculum modifications Involves changing the goals or the content and performance expectations for what the student should learn. It generally lowers the level of the material or performance expectations.

curriculum of the community Associations, activities, and interactions outside the formal or informal school setting.

distributed leadership Educational leadership that focuses on shared interests and collaborative action; it does not focus on the dichotomy of leaders–followers or experts and non-experts, but rather considers how all partners mutually constitute practice.

enrichment Learning experiences and arrangements beyond the typical breadth and depth.

Equal Partnership Model The concept that parents and educators have equal status (parity) in the partnership focused on producing the best outcomes for student. The partnership is built on mutual trust, respect, and reciprocity.

ethical collaborative consultation Principles based on ideas about what is good and bad as it relates to school-based collaboration.

eustress Beneficial stress—a phenomenon experienced by entertainers, athletes, speakers, and yes, teachers, before going "on stage" that helps them perform at their best. "Eustress" is a term for positive stress versus distress, which refers to negative stress.

evaluation Program evaluation is a systematic process that involves collecting data regarding questions about a program. The data are used to judge the merit, worth, or value of the program that is being evaluated.

family empowerment Families develop or are recognized as having the skills and attitudes for making their own decisions about their children and determining their futures.

flexible pacing Provides for movement through the curriculum at differentiated speeds, breadths, and depths to motivate and challenge exceptionally able learners.

follow through and follow up Check up on progress made toward a plan that was developed, and then check up on whether that plan was successful.

formative evaluation Formative evaluation is ongoing and conducted for the primary purpose of improving a program.

hidden curriculum Curriculum that is taught and learned covertly in venues such as hallways, restrooms, athletic fields, meeting rooms, school handbooks, and wall charts, primarily in the social and affective domains.

home co-educator Family members and other caregivers for students who collaborate with school co-educators for student needs.

homeschooling A nonpublic school where children are provided an academic curriculum and learning experiences at home, primarily by parents but with occasional assistance from resource personnel.

iatrogenic effect Treatment is more debilitating than the condition it was designed to treat.

iatrogenic An intended remedy that makes the condition or situation worse rather than better.

impacts Evaluations are conducted to study the impacts of activities or program on the participants of a program. Data are collected about participant outcomes and impacts are usually demonstrated by showing a causal relationship between the outcomes and the activities.

instructional leadership Instructional leaders focus on student learning and the impact of teachers and other school and community factors that influence student learning.

interfering themes Impediments to the ability to listen and problem-solve.

intersectionality People's multiple identities and affiliations and the interaction of those identities and affiliations.

Janusian thinking Holding two or more contradictory or opposite ideas simultaneously in thought.

kinesics The interpretation of body motion communication such as facial expressions and gestures or nonverbal behavior related to movement of any part of the body or the body as a whole.

logic model A logic model is a visual representation of a program's or activity's theory of change. It shows the relationship of the program resources and activities to the expected outcomes or changes in participant behavior, attitudes, or knowledge.

mentor; mentee Guide, teacher, adviser, supporter; one who is guided, taught, and supported.

mentoring Helping novice teachers observe, experiment, and evaluate different ways to instruct and carry out their roles.

metaphorical thinking Mental mapping that provides different meanings through some shared similarity.

microaggression Small, everyday slights (intended or otherwise) that harbor an underlying attitude of racism, sexism, homophobia, or even ageism. They often happen below the level of awareness of well-intentioned members of the dominant culture.

mindful communication To be mindful of speech means to notice your intention before you speak and to listen with full attention and without judgment.

multi-tier system of supports (MTSS) Often includes three levels of support common in RTI, but it is more comprehensive, going beyond academics to cover social and emotional supports for all learners (struggling through advanced). It aligns resources and support for students receiving instruction and for teachers and other support staff who are delivering the instruction.

multiple intelligences A multi-intelligence profile developed by Howard Gardner to facilitate carrying out a diversity of tasks and solving various problems.

multiplier effects Another way of describing positive ripple effects.

network A system of connections among individuals or groups having similar purposes who interact and collaborate to accomplish shared goals.

normativity Assumption that some characteristics, contexts, experiences, affiliations, and other diversities are "normal" and therefore anything different is "not normal."

novice teacher Beginning teacher.

onedownsmanship Down-playing status differences and communicating as partners.

paraeducator (para, paraprofessional) A person who works alongside a teacher to support students with special needs.

parity Equality that puts one on a par with others in the group.

persona The public role a person assumes or is perceived to assume.

personal preference A selection or choice to which one gives personal priority.

personality Disposition or temperament.

positive ripple effects Effects that reach out beyond an initial happening in ever-widening circles.

preassessment A test, teacher observation, or other informal assessment to determine what a student already has learned or can learn rapidly and easily with minimal teacher assistance.

preservice teacher Students in the final phase of their teacher education program.

privilege An historical, traditional, or experiential status that reflects a dominant social position, often referring to skin color or gender.

problem-solving process A set of skills formulated to solve problems, progressing from data-gathering to problem identification, to development of a plan, to evaluation of progress, to the follow up of results.

professional learning community (PLC) A group of educators who meet regularly and work in collaboration to share their knowledge and skills.

professional perspective A mental view of facts and ideas, seeing relevant data through meaningful professional relationships.

rapport building Building relationships by gaining trust and respect or confidence in your skills, motives, and intentions.

response to intervention (RTI) Originally used as a process to determine if a child responds to scientific, research-based interventions as part of the evaluation procedure for identification of specific learning disabilities, but now has expanded to an instructional framework many schools use to help all students who are struggling academically. It is a prevention model that typically involves three tiers of increasing support for students who are struggling within general education settings.

responsive listening A method of communication that facilitates problem-solving by using opening acknowledgements, confirmation responses, and feedback to help build understanding between the speaker and listener.

roadblocks to communication Common responses that impact communication negatively. Roadblocks get in the way of good listening and create barriers to successful interaction.

school co-educator School personnel for students who collaborate with home co-educators and others for students' needs.

Schoolwide Enrichment Model (SEM) One of the most long-standing and successful gifted education program models in the United States, in which the curriculum structure is the Enrichment Triad, built on Type I, Type II, and Type III curriculum and drawing from a talent pool of students who are above average in ability, very creative, and possess high task commitment (highly motivated).

self-advocacy Understanding and speaking out about your strengths and needs and asking for what you need.

self-determination A characteristic of a person that leads to them making choices and decisions based on their own preferences and interests, to monitor and regulate their own actions, and to be goal-oriented.

self-efficacy The belief that people have the ability to mold their own actions in ways that affect the learning and behavior of their students.

social justice (in education) Creating a fair and equitable learning environment for all students and families.

stakeholders Stakeholders are intended users of evaluation findings. They are individuals and groups who have a stake or interest in the program or activity being evaluated.

summative evaluation Summative evaluation is planned and implemented to determine the merits of a program, usually the impact of the program on those in the program. It is usually completed after the program is designed and implemented.

supervising teacher The special education teacher serves as the supervisor to the para. The supervising teacher is responsible for planning what paraeducators do day to day, and for scheduling where and when the paras will do it, as well evaluating their job performance.

synectics Making the strange familiar and making the familiar strange; breaking up conventional mental connections and forming new connections.

synergy Behavior of whole systems unpredicted by the behavior of their parts taken separately.

taxonomic domains Organizational tools categorized in designated spheres to guide educators in developing instructional objectives and planning strategies for the instruction.

teamwork Joint action in which each person participates cooperatively and collaboratively to contribute to the goal and subordinates personal prominence to enhance the effectiveness of the group.

time management The analysis of how working hours are spent and the prioritization of tasks in order to maximize personal efficiency.

transformative leadership Educational leadership that practices and advocates for equity for students with disabilities and others who are marginalized.

triadic model A classic collaborative consultation model that includes three roles—consultant, consultee, and client.

Universal Design for Learning (UDL) A refinement of differentiated instruction that calls for multiple approaches to meet the needs of diverse learners. It involves multiple means of engagement, representation, action, and expression. Teachers customize their teaching for individual differences in each of the three brain networks (recognition, strategic, and affective).

Web 2.0 tools Technologies that focus on collaboration, sharing of user-generated content, and social networking. Users interact on a site and with each other by updating or adding content.

REFERENCES

American Psychological Association. (2008). *Report of the task force on the implementation of the multicultural guidelines.* Washington, DC: Author.

Anderson, J. D. (1997). Supporting the invisible minority. *Educational Leadership, 54*(7), 65–68.

Annunzio, S. (2001). *eLeadership.* New York, NY: Free Press.

Anrig, G. (2015). How we know collaboration works. *Educational Leadership, 72*(5), 31–35.

ASCD. (2000). Finding time to collaborate. *Education Update, 42*(2), 1, 3, 8.

ASCD. (2012). How to manage your stress. *Education Update, 54*(1), 1, 6, 7.

Ashbaker, B. Y., & Morgan, J. (2013). *Paraprofessionals in the classroom: A survival guide* (2nd ed.). Boston, MA: Pearson.

Astor, R. A., Jacobson, L., Benbenishty. R. (2012). *The teacher's guide for supporting students from military families.* New York, NY: Teachers College Press.

Axelrod, L., & Johnson, R. (2005). *Turning conflict into profit: A roadmap for resolving personal and organizational disputes.* Edmonton, Alberta, Canada: The University of Alberta Press.

Ayers, W., Quinn, T., & Stovall, D. (Eds.). (2009). *Handbook of social justice in education.* New York: Routledge.

Banks, J. A. & Banks, C. A. M. (Eds.) (2010). *Multicultural education: Issues and perspectives* (7th ed.). Hoboken, NJ: Wiley & Sons.

Barbour, C., & Barbour, N. H. (2001). *Families, schools, and communities: Building partnerships for educating children.* Upper Saddle River, NJ: Merrill Prentice Hall.

Barbour, C., Barbour, N. H., & Scully, P. A. (2008). *Families, schools, and communities* (4th ed.). Upper Saddle River, NJ: Prentice Hall.

Barnard, W. M. (2004). Parent involvement in elementary school and educational attainment. *Children & Youth Services Review, 26*(1), 39–62.

Barnes, A. C., & Harlacher, J. E. (2008). Clearing the confusion: Response-to-intervention as a set of principles. *Education and Treatment of Children of Children, 31,* 417–431.

Bateman, D., & Bateman, C. F. (2001). *A principal's guide to special education.* Reston, VA: Council for Exceptional Children.

Bauwens, J., & Hourcade, J. J. (1997). Cooperative teaching: Pictures of possibilities. *Intervention in School and Clinic, 33*(2), 81–89.

Becker, E. F. & Wortmann, J. (2009). *Mastering communication at work: How to lead, manage, and influence.* New York, NY: McGraw Hill.

Belbin, R. N. (2010). *Team roles at work.* New York: Routledge: Taylor & Francis,

Belch, H. (2004–2005). Retention and students with disabilities. *Journal of College Student Retention, 6*(1), 3–22.

Bell, L. A. (1997). Theoretical foundations for social justice education. In P. Griffin (Ed.), *Teaching for diversity and social justice: A sourcebook.* New York, NY: Routledge.

Benedict, A. E., Brownell, M. T., Park, Y., Bettini, E. A., & Lauterbach, A. A. (2014). Taking charge of your professional learning: Tips for cultivating special educator expertise. *Teaching Exceptional Children, 46*(6), 147–157.

Beninghof, A. M. (2016). To clone or not to clone? *Educational Leadership, 735*(2), 10–15.

Bergan, J. R. (1977). *Behavioral consultation.* Columbus, OH: Merrill.

Bergan, J. R. (1995). Evolution of a problem-solving model of consultation. *Journal of Educational and Psychological Consultation, 6*(2), 111–123.

Billingsley, B. (2004). Special education teacher retention and attrition: A critical analysis of the research literature. *The Journal of Special Education, 38,* 39–55.

Bitterman, A., Gary, L., & Goldering, R. (2013). *Characteristics of public and private elementary and secondary schools in the United States: Results from the 2011–12 Schools and Staffing Survey* (NCES Publication No. 2013–312). Washington, D.C.: National Center for Education Statistics.

Blaylock, B. K. (1983). Teamwork in a simulated production environment. *Research in Psychological Type, 6,* 58–67.

Bloom, B. S., Engelhart, M. D., Furst, E. J., Hill, W. H., & Krathwohl, D. R. (1956). *Taxonomy of educational objectives; Handbook I: Cognitive domain.* New York, NY: McKay.

Bocchino, R. (1991, March). Using mind mapping as a note-taking tool. *The Developer, 1,* 4.

Bolden, R. (2011). Distributed leadership in organizations: A review of theory and research. *International Journal of Management Reviews, 13,* 251–269.

Bolton, R. (1986). *People skills: How to assert yourself, listen to others, and resolve conflicts.* New York, NY: Simon & Schuster.

Boone, H. A. (1989). Preparing family specialists in early childhood special education. *Teacher Education and Special Education, 12*(3), 96–102.

Bradshaw, C. P., Sudinaraset, M., Mmari K. & Blum, R. W. (2010). School transitions among military adolescents: A qualitative study of stress and coping. *Psychology Review, 39*(1), 84–105.

Breton, W. (2010). Special education paraprofessionals: Perceptions of preservice preparation, supervision, and ongoing developmental training. *International Journal of Special Education, 25*(1), 34–45.

Brock, M. E., & Carter, E. W. (2015). Efficacy of teachers training paraprofessionals to implement peer support arrangements. *Exceptional Children, 82*(3), 354–371.

445

Broer, S. M., Doyle, M. B., & Giangreco, M. F. (2005). Perspectives of students with intellectual disabilities about their experiences with paraprofessional support. *Exceptional Children, 71*, 415–430.

Brown-Chidsey, R. (2007). No more "waiting to fail." *Educational Leadership, 65*(4), 40–46.

Brown, D., Wyne, M. D., Blackburn, J. E., & Powell, W. C. (1979). *Consultation: Strategy for improving education.* Boston, MA: Allyn & Bacon.

Brownell, M. T., Yeager, E., Rennells, M. S., & Riley, T. (1997). Teachers working together: What teacher educators and researchers should know. *Teacher Education and Special Education, 20*(4), 340–359.

Brownell, M., Adams, A., Sindelar, P., Waldron, N., & Vanhover, S. (2006). Learning from collaboration: The role of teacher qualities. *Exceptional Children, 72*(2), 169–185.

Burbank, M. D., Kauchak, D., & Bates, A. J. (2010). Book clubs as professional development opportunities for preservice teacher candidates and practicing teachers: An exploratory study. *The New Educator, 6*, 56–73.

Bureau of Labor Statistics. (2016). *Occupational Outlook Handbook, 2016–17.* U.S. Department of Labor: Washington, DC.

Bureau of Labor Statistics, U.S. Department of Labor. (2016–2017). *Occupational Outlook Handbook,* 2016–17 Edition, Teacher Assistants, Retrieved from http://www.bls.gov/ooh/education-training-and-library/teacher-assistants.htm

Burgstahler, S., & Cory, R. (Eds.), *Universal design in higher education: From principles to practice.* Cambridge, MA: Harvard Education Press.

Buscaglia, L. (1986). *Loving each other: The challenges of human relationships.* Westminster, MD: Fawcett.

Bushaw, W. J. (2007). From the mouths of middle-schoolers: Important changes for high school and college. *Phi Delta Kappan, 89*(3), 189–193.

Buzan, T. (1983). *Use both sides of your brain.* New York, NY: Dutton.

Byrd, D. R. (2012). Conducting successful home visits in multi-culture communities. *Journal of Curriculum and Instruction, 6*(1), 43–54.

Byrnes, M. (2008). Educators' interpretations of ambiguous accommodations. *Remedial and Special Education, 29*(5), 306–315.

Capizzi, A. M., & Da Fonte, M. A. (2012). Supporting paraeducators through a collaborative classroom support plan. *Focus on Exceptional Children, 44*(6), 1–16.

Caplan, G. (1970). *The theory and practice of mental health consultation.* New York, NY: Basic Books.

Caplan, G., Caplan, R. B., & Erchul, W. P. (1995). A contemporary view of mental health consultation: Comments on "Types of Mental Health Consultation." *Journal of Educational and Psychological Consultation, 6*(1), 23–30.

Caro, D. J., & Robbins, P. (1991, November). Talkwalking—thinking on your feet. *Developer, 3*–4.

Carpenter, T. (2016, January 20). Committee explores merit pay. *Topeka Capital-Journal,* pp. 1, 6A.

Carver, C. L. (2004, May). A lifeline for new teachers. *Educational Leadership, 58*–61.

Caspe, M., Lopez, M. E., & Wolos, C. (2007). *Family involvement in elementary school children's education.* Cambridge, MA: Harvard Family Research Project. Retrieved from http://www.hfrp.org

Casper, V., & Schultz, S. B. (1999). *Gay parents/straight schools: Building communication and trust.* New York, NY: Teachers College Press.

Cattell, R. B., Cattell, A. K., & Cattell, H. E. P. (1993). *16PF Fifth Edition Questionnaire.* Champaign, IL: Institute for Personality and Ability Testing.

Causton-Theoharis, J., Giangreco, M., Doyle, M., & Vadasy, P. (2007). Paraprofessionals: The "sous chefs" of literacy instruction. *Teaching Exceptional Children, 40*(1) 56–62.

CEC Today. (2011, March 29). *Common Core Standards: What special educators need to know.* Arlington, VA: Council for Exceptional Children.

CEC Today. (2000, November). Council for Exceptional Children. Arlington, VA.

Center for Learning and Performing Technologies. (2015). Top 100 tools for learning 2015. *Center for Learning and Performing Technologies Data.* Retrieved from http://c4lpt.co.uk/top100tools/

Chapman, S. G. (2012). *The five keys to mindful communication.* Boston, MA: Shambhala.

Charles, K. J., & Dickens, V. (2012). Closing the communication gap: Web 2.0 tools for enhanced planning and collaboration. *Teaching Exceptional Children, 45*(2), 24–32

Chopra, R. V., Sandoval-Lucero, E., Aragon, L., Bernal, C., De Balderas, H. B., & Carroll, D. (2004). The paraeducator role of connector. *Remedial and Special Education, 25*, 219–231.

Christie, K. (2005). Changing the nature of parent involvement. *Phi Delta Kappan, 86*(9), 645+.

Cipani, E. (1985). The three phrases of behavioral consultation: Objectives, intervention, and quality assurance. *Teacher Education and Special Education, 8*, 144–152.

Clare, M. M. (2002). Diversity as a dependent variable: Considerations for research and practice in consultation. *Journal of Educational and Psychological Consultation, 13*(30), 251–263.

Clark, B. (2002). *Growing up gifted* (6th ed.). Upper Saddle River, NJ: Merrill.

Clark, C., Moss, P. A., Goering, S., Herter, R. J., Lamar, B., Leonard, D, Robbins, S., Russell, M., Templin, M. and Wascha, K. (1996). Collaboration as dialogue: Teachers and researchers engaged in conversation and professional development. *American Educational Research Journal, 33*(1), 193–231.

Clark, S. G. (2000). The IEP process as a tool for collaboration. *Teaching Exceptional Children, 33*(2), 56–66.

Collins, K. M. (2013). A disability studies response to JTE's themed issue on diversity and disability in teacher education. *Journal of Teacher Education, 64*(3), 283–287.

Combs, J. P., Harris, S., & Edmonson, S. (2015). Four essential practices for building trust: Are you communicating in a way that inspires trust? *Educational Leadership, 72*(7), 18–22.

Conley, D. T. (2011). Building on the common core. *Educational Leadership, 68*(6), 17–20.

Conley, D. T. (March, 2011). Building on the common core standards. *Educational Leadership, 66*(6), 17–20.

Conoley, J. C. (1987). *National Symposium on School Consultation.* Austin, TX: University of Texas.

Conoley, J. C. (1989). Professional communication and collaboration among educators. In M. C. Reynolds (Ed.), *Knowledge base for the beginning teacher* (pp. 245–254). Oxford, England: Pergamon.

Conoley, J. C. (1994). You say potato, I say . . . : Part I. *Journal of Educational and Psychological Consultation, 5*(1), 45–49.

Conoley, J. C., & Conoley, C. W. (1982). *School consultation: A guide to practice and training.* New York, NY: Pergamon Press.

Conoley, J. C., & Conoley, C. W. (1988). Useful theories in school-based consultation. *Remedial and Special Education, 9*(6), 14–20.

Conoley, J. C., & Conoley, C. W. (2010). Why does collaboration work? Linking positive psychology and collaboration. *Journal of Educational and Psychological Consultation, 20,* 75–82.

Conroy, P. W. (2012). Collaborating with cultural and linguistically diverse families of students in rural schools who receive special education services. *Rural Special Education Quarterly, 31*(3), 20–24.

Cornelius, K. E. (2014). Formative assessment made easy: Templates for collecting daily data in inclusive classrooms. *Teaching Exceptional Children, 47*(2), 112–118.

Council for Exceptional Children. (2000). Home schooling—A viable alternative for students with special needs? *CEC Today, 7*(1), 1, 5, 10, 15.

Countryman, L. L., & Schroeder, M. (1996). When students lead parent-teacher conferences. *Educational Leadership, 53*(7), 64–68.

Coyle, N. C. (2000). Conflict resolution: It's part of the job. *Delta Kappa Gamma Bulletin, 66*(4), 41–46.

Cramer, S., Erzkus, A., Mayweather, K., Pope, K., Roeder, J., & Tone, T. (1997). Connecting with siblings. *Teaching Exceptional Children, 30*(1), 46–49.

Cross, T. L. (2003). Culture as a resource for mental health. *Cultural Diversity and Ethnic Minority Psychology, 9*(4), 354–359.

Darling-Hammond, L. (2003). Keeping good teachers: Why it matters, what leaders can do. *Educational Leadership, 60*(8), 6–13.

Data Accountability Center. (2010). Health Science Center/Human Development Center, Louisiana State University. New Orleans, LA: Author. Retrieved from https://www.ideadata.org

Datnow, A., & Park, V. (2015). Five (good) ways to talk about data. *Educational Leadership, 73*(3), 10–15.

de Valenzuela, J. S., Torres, R. L., & Chavez, R. L. (1998). Family involvement in bilingual special education: Challenging the norm. In L. M. Baca & H. T. Cervantes (Eds.), *The bilingual special education interface* (3rd ed.) Upper Saddle River, NJ: Merrill.

Dearing, E., Kreider, H., Simpkins, S., & Weiss, H. B. (2006). Family involvement in school and low-income children's literacy performance: Longitudinal associations between and within families. *Journal of Educational Psychology, 98,* 653–664.

deBono, E. (1973). *Lateral thinking: Creativity step by step.* Boston, MA: Little, Brown.

deBono, E. (1985). *Six thinking hats.* New York, NY: Harper & Row.

deBono, E. (1986). *CORT thinking: Teacher's notes* (Vols. 1–6, 2nd ed.). New York, NY: Pergamon.

Denton, C. A, Hasbrouck, J. E., & Sekaquaptewa, S. (2003). The consulting teacher: A descriptive case study in responsive systems consultation. *Journal of Educational and Psychological Consultation, 14*(1), 41–73.

Dettmer, P. (1981). The effects of teacher personality type on classroom values and perceptions of gifted students. *Research in Psychological Type, 3,* 48–54.

Dettmer, P. (2006). New domains in established fields: Four domains of learning and doing. *Roeper Review, 28*(2), 70–78.

Devine, D. (2013). Value/ing children differently? Migrant children in education. *Children and Society, 27*(4) 282–294.

Dewey, J. (2012). *Democracy and education.* New York, NY: The Free Press. (Original work published 1916.)

Diliberto, J. A., & Brewer, D. (2012). Six tips for successful IEP meetings. *Teaching Exceptional Children, 47*(2), 128–135.

Dougherty, A. M., Tack, F. E., Fullam, C. B., & Hammer, L. A. (1996). Disengagement: A neglected aspect of the consultation process. *Journal of Educational and Psychological Consultation, 7*(3), 259–274.

Douglass, M. E., & Douglass, D. N. (1993). *Manage your time, manage your work, manage yourself.* New York, NY: AMACOM.

DuFour, R. (2004). What is a professional learning community? *Educational Leadership, 61*(8), 6–11.

DuFour, R. (2011). Work together: But only if you want to. *Kappan Magazine, 92*(5), 57–61.

Dukes, C., & Lamar-Dukes, P. (2009). Inclusion by design: Engineering inclusive practices in secondary schools. *Teaching Exceptional Children, 41*(3), 16–23.

Dunst, C. J. (2002). How can we strengthen family support research and evaluation? *The Evaluation Exchange, 8*(1), 5.

Dunst, C. J. (2000). Revisiting "Rethinking early intervention." *Topics in Early Childhood Education, 20*(2), 95–104.

Dyck, N., Dettmer, P., & Thurston, L. P. (1985). *Special education consultation skills project.* Manhattan, KS: Kansas State University, College of Education, unpublished manuscript.

Dymond, S. K., & Russell, D. L. (2004). Impact of grade and disability on the instructional context of inclusive classrooms. *Education and Training in Developmental Disabilities, 39,* 127–140.

Dyson, L. (2010). Unanticipated effects of children with learning disabilities on their families. *Learning Disabilities Quarterly, 33,* 43–55.

Education Week. (2016, March 16). *Farmington, Ill., Superintendent John Asplund on his innovative school-leadership approach.* [Video File.] Retrieved from https://www.youtube.com/watch?v=QM807llK7S0&feature=youtu.be

Edwards, A. T. (1997). Let's stop ignoring our gay and lesbian youth. *Educational Leadership, 54*(7), 68–70.

Edwards, C. C., & Da Fonte, A. (2012). The 5-point plan: Fostering successful partnerships with families of students with disabilities. *Teaching Exceptional Children, 44*(3), 6–13.

Eisner, E. W. (2003). Questionable assumptions about schooling. *Phi Delta Kappan, 84*(9), 348–357.

Engels, K. (2015). RTI: What teachers know that computers don't. *Educational Leadership, 73*(3), 72–76.

Epstein, J. L. (2011). *School, family, and community partnerships: Preparing educators and improving schools* (2nd ed.). Boulder, CO: Westview Press.

Federico, M. A., Herrold, Jr., W. G., & Venn, J. (1999). Helpful tips for successful inclusion: A checklist for educators. *Teaching Exceptional Children, 32*(1), 76–82.

Feeding America. (2013). *Map the meal gap.* Retrieved from http://www.feedingamerica.org/hunger-in-america/our-research/map-the-meal-gap/overall-executive-summary.html?_ga=1.260216141.1315697720

Fiedler, C. R., Simpson, R. L., & Clark, D. M. (2007). *Parents and families of children with disabilities: Effective school-based support services.* Upper Saddle River, NJ: Prentice Hall.

Fisher, M., & Pleasants, S. L. (2012). Roles, responsibilities, and concerns of paraeducators: Findings from a statewide survey. *Remedial and Special Education, 33*(5), 287.

Fisher, R., & Sharp, A. (1999). *Getting it DONE: How to lead when you're not in charge.* New York, NY: HarperCollins.

Fleury, M. L. (2000). Confidentiality issues with substitutes and paraeducators. *Teaching Exceptional Children, 33*(1), 44–45.

Foley, R. M., & Lewis, J. A. (1999). Self-perceived competence of secondary school principals to serve as school leaders in collaborative-based educational delivery systems. *Remedial and Special Education, 20*(4), 233–243.

Fowler, S. A., Donegan, M., Lueke, B., Hadden, D. S., & Phillips, B. (2000). Evaluating community collaboration in writing interagency agreements on the age 3 transition. *Exceptional Children, 67* (1), 35–50.

Fox, D. (July, 2011). The limits of intelligence. *Scientific American, 305*(1), 36–43.

Freire, P. (2000). *Pedagogy of the oppressed, 30th anniversary edition.* New York, NY: Continuum.

French, N. K. (1997). Management of paraeducators. In A. L. Pickett & Gerlach (Eds.), *Supervising paraeducators in school settings.* Austin, TX: PRO-ED.

French, N. K. (1999). Paraeducators and teachers: Shifting roles. *Teaching Exceptional Children, 32*(2), 69–73.

French, N. K. (2000). Taking time to save time: Delegating to paraeducators. *Teaching Exceptional Children, 32*(3), 79–83.

French, N. K. (2001). Supervising paraprofessionals: A survey of teacher practices. *Journal of Special Education, 35,* 41–53.

Friedman, I. (2003). Self-efficacy and burnout in teaching: The importance of interpersonal-relations efficacy. *Social Psychology of Education, 6,* 191–215.

Friend, M. (1988). Putting consultation into context: Historical and contemporary perspectives. *Remedial and Special Education, 9*(6), 7–13.

Friend, M. (2016). Welcome to co-teaching 2.0. *Educational Leadership, 73*(4), 16–22.

Friend, M., & Bursuck, W. D. (1996). *Including students with special needs: A practical guide for classroom teachers.* Boston, MA: Allyn & Bacon.

Friend, M., & Bursuck, W. D. (2009). *Including students with special needs: A practical guide for classroom teachers* (5th ed.). Columbus, OH: Merrill.

Friend, M., & Cook, L. (1990). Collaboration as a predictor for success in school reform. *Journal of Educational and Psychological Consultation, I*(1), 69–86.

Friend, M., & Cook, L. (1992). The ethics of collaboration. *Journal of Educational and Psychological Consultation, 3*(2), 181–184.

Friend, M., Cook, L., Hurley-Chamberlain, D., & Shamberger, C. (2010). Co-teaching: An illustration of the complexity of collaboration in special education. *Journal of Educational and Psychological Consultation, 20,* 9–27.

Froiland, J. M., & Davison, M. L. (2014). Parental expectations and school relationships as contributors to adolescents' positive outcomes. *Social Psychology of Education, 17*(1), 1–17.

Fuchs, L. S., & Fuchs, D. (2007). A model for implementing responsiveness to intervention. *Teaching Exceptional Children, 39*(5), 14–20.

Fuller, R. B. (1975). *Explorations in the geometry of thinking synergetics.* New York, NY: Macmillan.

Gallessich, J. (1974). Training the school psychologist for consultation. *Journal of School Psychology, 12,* 138–149.

Gardner, H. (1993). *Multiple intelligences: The theory in practice.* New York, NY: HarperCollins.

Garmston, R. (1988, October). Giving gifts. *The Developer, 3,* 6.

Garmston, R. J. (1994). The persuasive art of presenting: What's a MetaPhor? *Journal of Staff Development, 15*(2), 60–61.

Garmston, R. J., & Wellman, B. M. (1992). *How to make presentations that teach and transform.* Alexandria, VA: Association for Supervision and Curriculum Development.

Geenen, S., Powers, L. E., & Lopez-Vasquez, A. (2001). Multicultural aspects of parent involvement in transition planning. *Exceptional Children, 67*(2), 265–282.

Gerber, P. J., & Popp, P. A. (2000). Making collaborative teaching more effective for academically able students. *Learning Disability Quarterly, 23,* 229–236.

Giangreco, M. F., & Broer, S. M. (2005). Questionable utilization of paraprofessionals in inclusive schools: Are we addressing symptoms or causes? *Focus on Autism and Other Developmental Disabilities, 20*(1), 10–26.

Giangreco, M. F., Dennis, R., Cloninger, C., Edelman, S., & Schattman, R. (1993). "I've counted Jon": Transformational experiences of teacher education students with disabilities. *Exceptional Children, 59* (4), 359–372.

Giangreco, M. F., Edelman, S. W., & Broer, S. M. (2001). Respect, appreciation, and acknowledgment of paraprofessionals who support students with disabilities. *Exceptional Children, 67*(4), 485–498.

Giangreco, M. F., Edelman, S. W., Broer, S. M., & Doyle, M. B. (2001). Paraprofessional support of students with disabilities: Literature from the past decade. *Exceptional Children, 68*(1), 45–63.

Giangreco, M. F., Suter, J. C., & Doyle, M. B. (2010). Paraprofessionals in inclusive schools: A review of recent research. *Journal of Educational and Psychological Consultation, 20,* 41–57.

Giangreco, M. F., Suter, J. C., & Hurley, S. M. (2011). Revisiting personnel utilization in inclusion-oriented schools. *Journal of Special Education, 47,* 121–132.

Ginsburg, D. (2010, October 5). Differentiated instruction: A practical approach. [Web log blog "Coach G's Teaching Tips"]. Retrieved from http://blogs.edweek.org/teachers/coach_gs_teaching_tips/2010/10/differentiated_instruction_a_practical_approach.html

Glover, T. A., & DiPerna, J. C. (2007). Service delivery for response to intervention: Core components and directions for future research. *School Psychology Review, 36,* 526–540.

Golombok, S., Perry, B., Burston, A., Murray, C., Mooney-Sommers, J., Stevens, M., & Golding J. (2003). Children with lesbian parents: A community study. *Developmental Psychology, 39*(1), 20–33.

Gonzalez, L. M., Borders, L. D., Hines, E. M., Villalba, J. A., & Henderson, A. (2013). Parental involvement in children's education: Considerations for school counselors working with Latino immigrant families. *Professional School Counseling, 16,* 185–193.

Goodall, J., & Montgomery, C. (2014). Parental involvement to parental engagement: A continuum, *Educational Review, 66*(4), 399–410.

Goodman, D. J. (2011*). Promoting diversity and social justice: Educating people from privileged groups* (2nd ed.). New York, NY: Routledge.

Gordon, T. (1977). *Leader effectiveness training, L.E.T.: The no-lose way to release the productive potential in people.* Toronto, Canada: Bantam.

Gordon, T. (2000). *P.E.T.: Parent effectiveness training: The proven programs for raising responsible children.* New York, NY: Three Rivers Press.

Gordon, W. J. J., & Poze, T. (1975). *Strange and familiar.* Cambridge, MA: SES Associates.

Gorski, P. C. (2007, Spring). The question of class. *Teaching Tolerance.* Montgomery, AL: Southern Poverty Law Center.

Gorski, P. C., Zenkov, K., Osei-Kofi, N, & Sapp, J. (Eds.). (2013). *Cultivating social justice teachers: How teacher educators have helped students overcome cognitive bottlenecks and learn critical social justice concepts.* Sterling, VA: Stylus Publishing.

Graubard, P. S., Rosenberg, H., & Miller, M. B. (1971). Student applications of behavior modification to teachers and environments or ecological approaches to deviancy. In E. A. Ramp & B. L. Hopkins (Eds.), *A new direction for education: Behavior analysis* (pp. 80–101). Lawrence, KS: University of Kansas.

Greene, J. (1995). Youth with runaway, throwaway, and homeless experiences: Prevalence, drug use, and other at-risk behaviors. *Research Triangle Institute.* Washington D.C.: U.S. Dept. of Health and Human Services.

Gregorc, A. F., & Ward, H. B. (1977). A new definition for individual: Implications for learning and teaching. *NASSP Bulletin, 61,* 20–26.

Grier, B. C., & Bradley-Klug, K. L. (2011). Collaborative consultation to support children with pediatric health issues: A review of the biopsychoeducational model. *Journal of Educational and Psychological Consultation, 21*(2), 88–105.

Grossman, P., & Loeb, S. (2010). Learning from multiple routes. *Educational Leadership, 67*(8), 22–27.

Gullat, D. E., & Tollett, J. R. (1997). Educational law: A requisite course for preservice and inservice teacher education programs. *Journal of Teacher Education, 48*(2), 120–135.

Guskey, T. R. (1985). Staff development and teacher change. *Educational Leadership, 42*(7), 57–60.

Hall, C. S., & Lindzey, G. (1989). *Theories of personality* (3rd ed.). New York, NY: Wiley.

Hall, G. E., & Hord, S. M. (1987). *Change in schools: Facilitating the process.* Albany, NY: State University of New York Press.

Hamlin, S. (2006). *How to talk so people listen: Connecting in today's workplace.* New York, NY: Harper Collins.

Hammer, H., Finkelhor, D., & Sedlak, A. (2002). Runaway/throwaway children: National estimates and characteristics. *National Incidence Studies of Missing, Abducted, Runaway, and Thrownaway Children.* Washington, DC: Office of Juvenile Justice and Delinquency Prevention.

Hamrick, F. A., Rumann, C. B., & Associates. *Called to serve*. (2013). New York, NY: Jossey-Bass.

Hanna, G. S., & Dettmer, P. A. (2004). *Assessment for effective teaching: Using context-adaptive planning*. Boston, MA: Allyn & Bacon.

Hansen, J. C., Himes, B. S., & Meier, S. (1990). *Consultation: Concepts and practices*. Englewood Cliffs, NJ: Prentice Hall.

Hargreaves, A. (1991). Contrived congeniality: The micropolitics of teacher collaboration. In J. Blace (Ed.), *The Politics of life in schools: Power, conflict, and cooperation* (46–72). Thousand Oaks, CA: Sage.

Harlacher, J. E., Walker, N. J. N., & Sanford, A. K. (2010). The "I" in RTI: Research-based factors for intensifying instruction. *Teaching Exceptional Children, 42*(6), 30–38.

Harris, L., & Associates, Inc. (2004). *National Organization on Disability (N.O.D.)/Harris survey of Americans with disabilities*. New York, NY: Author.

Harrow, A. J. (1972). *A taxonomy of the psychomotor domain: A guide for developing behavioral objectives*. New York, NY: McKay.

Hart, J. E., & Brehm, J. (2013). Promoting self-determination: A model for training elementary students to self-advocate for IEP accommodations. *Teaching Exceptional Children, 45*(5), 40–48.

Hattie, J. (2015). High impact leadership. *Educational Leadership, 72*(5), 36–40.

Hehir, T. (2007). Confronting ableism. *Educational Leadership, 64*(5), 8–14.

Henning-Stout, M. (1994). Consultation and connected knowing: What we know is determined by the questions we ask. *Journal of Educational and Psychological Consultation, 5*(1), 5–21.

Heron, T. E., & Harris, K. C. (1987). *The educational consultant: Helping professionals, parents, and mainstreamed students*. Austin, TX: PRO-ED.

Heron, T. E., & Kimball, W. H. (1988). Gaining perspective with the educational consultation research base: Ecological considerations and further recommendations. *Remedial and Special Education, 9*(6), 21–28, 47.

Hoover, J. J., & Erickson J. (2015). Culturally responsive special education referrals of English learners in one rural county school district: Pilot project. *Rural Special Education Quarterly, 34*(4), 18–28.

Hoy, W., & Woolfolk, A. (1993). Teachers' sense of efficacy and the organizational health of schools. *Elementary School Journal, 93*, 356–372.

Huefner, D. S. (1988). The consulting teacher model: Risks and opportunities. *Exceptional Children, 54*(5), 403–414.

Hughes, M., & Greenhough, P. (2006). Boxes, bags, and videotape: Enhancing home-school communication through knowledge exchange activities. *Educational Review, 58*(4), 471–487.

Hunter, M. (1985, May). Promising theories die young. *ASCD Update, 1*, 3.

Idol-Maestas, L. (1981). A teacher training model: The resource/consulting teacher. *Behavioral Disorders, 6*(2), 108–121.

Idol-Maestes, L., Lloyd, S., & Lilly, J. S. (1981). Non-categorical approach to direct service and teachers education. *Exceptional Children, 48*, 213–220.

Idol, L. (1988). A rationale and guidelines for establishing special education consultation programs. *Remedial and Special Education, 9*(6), 48–58.

Idol, L., Paolucci-Whitcomb, P., & Nevin, A. (1986). *Collaborative Consultation*. Austin, TX: PRO-ED.

Idol, L., Paolucci-Whitcomb, P., & Nevin, A. (1995). The collaborative consultation model. *Journal of Educational and Psychological Consultation, 6*(4), 329–346.

Idol, L., West, J. F., & Lloyd, S. R. (1988). Organizing and implementing specialized reading programs: A collaborative approach involving classroom, remedial, and special education teachers. *Remedial and Special Education, 9*(2), 54–61.

Inger, M. (1993, December). Teacher collaboration in secondary schools. *CenterFocus 2*. Available online at http://ncrve.berkeley.edu/CenterFocus/CF2.html

Ingersoll, R. M. (2001). Teacher turnover and teacher shortages: An organizational analysis. *American Educational Research Journal, 38*(3), 499–534.

Ingersoll, R. M. (2002). The teacher shortage: A case of wrong diagnosis and wrong prescription. *NASSP Bulletin, 86*(631), 16–31

Iruka, I. U., Curenton, S. M., & Eke W. A. I. (2014). *The CRAF-E4 family engagement model: Building practitioners' competence to work with diverse families*. San Diego, CA: Elsevier.

Jersild, A. T. (1955). *When teachers face themselves*. New York, NY: Teachers College Press.

Jeynes, W. H. (2007). The relationship between parental involvement an urban secondary school student academic achievement. *Urban Education, 42*(1), 82–110.

Jeynes, W. H. (2014). Parental involvement that works . . . because it's age-appropriate. *Kappa Delta Pi Record, 50*(2), 85–88.

John-Steiner, V., Weber, R. J., & Minnis, M. (1998). The challenge of studying collaboration. *American Educational Research Journal, 35*(4), 773–783.

Johnsen, S. K., Parker, S. L., & Farah, Y. N. (2015). Providing services for students with gifts and talents within a response-to-intervention framework. *Teaching Exceptional Children, 47*(4), 226–233.

Johnson, D. W., & Johnson, R. T. (1987). *Learning together and alone: Cooperative, competitive, & individualistic learning* (2nd ed.). Englewood Cliffs, NJ: Prentice Hall.

Johnson, L. J., & Pugach, M. C. (1996). Role of collaborative dialogue in teaching conceptions of appropriate practice for students at risk. *Journal of Educational and Psychological Consultation, 7*(1), 9–24.

Johnson, S. M., & Donaldson, M. L. (2007). Overcoming the obstacles to leadership. *Educational Leadership, 65*(1), 8–13.

Joint Committee on Teacher Planning for Students with Disabilities. (1995). *Windows on diversity*. Lawrence, KS: University of Kansas.

Jolly, J. L., Matthews, M. S., & Nester, J. (2013). Home-schooling the gifted: A parent's perspective. *Gifted Child Quarterly, 57(2),* 121–134.

Jones, S. L., & Morin, V. A. (2000). Training teachers to work as partners: Modeling the way in teacher preparation programs. *The Delta Kappa Bulletin, 67*(1), 51–55.

Jung, C. G. (1923). *Psychological types.* New York, NY: Harcourt Brace.

Kampwirth, T. J., (1999). *Collaborative consultation in the schools: Effective practices for students with learning and behavior problems.* Upper Saddle River, NJ: Prentice Hall.

Kaufman, R. C., & Ring, M. (2011). Pathways to leadership and professional development: Inspiring novice special educators. *Teaching Exceptional Children, 43*(5), 52–60.

Keefe, E. G., Moore, V., & Duff, F. (2004). The four "knows" of collaborative teaching. *Teaching Exceptional Children, 36*(5), 36–42.

Keirsey, D., & Bates, M. (1984). *Please understand me: Character and temperament types.* Del Mar, CA: Prometheus Nemesis.

Kelleher, J. (2003). A model for assessment-driven professional development. *Phi Delta Kappan, 84*(10), 751–756.

Kellems, R. O., & Morningstar, M. E. (2010). Tips for transition. *Teaching Exceptional Children, 43*(2), 60–68.

Keller, M. M., & Decoteau, G. T. (2000). *The military child: Mobility and education,* Fastback #63. Bloomington, IN: Phi Delta Kappa Educational Foundation.

Kerbow, D., Azcoitia, C. & Buell, B. (2003). Student mobility and local school improvement in Chicago. *The Journal of Negro Education, 72*(1), 158–164.

Kleinert, J., Harrison, E., Fisher, T., & Kleinert, H. (2010). "I Can" and "I Did"—Self-advocacy for young students with developmental disabilities. *Teaching Exceptional Children, 43*(2), 16–26.

Kluth, P., & Straut, D. (2001). Standards for diverse learners. *Educational Leadership, 59*(1), 43–46.

Knackendoffel, E. A., Robinson, S. M., Deshler, D. D., & Schumaker, J. B. (1992). *Collaborative problem solving.* Lawrence, KS: Edge Enterprises, Inc.

Knowles, W. C. (1997). *An investigation of teachers' perceptions of special education placement and inclusion: A qualitative case study of two middle schools.* Unpublished doctoral dissertation, Kansas State University, Manhattan, KS.

Koegel, R. L., Kim, S., & Koegel, L. K. (2014). Training paraprofessionals to improve socialization in students with ASD. *Journal of Autism and Developmental Disorders, 44*(9), 2197–2208. doi:http://dx.doi.org.er.lib.k-state.edu/10.1007/s10803-014-2094-x

Koemer, M. E., & Hulsebosch, P. (1996). Preparing teachers to work with children of gay and lesbian parents. *Journal of Teacher Education, 47*(5), 347–354.

Kozleskie, E., Mainzer, R., & Deshler, D. (2000). Bright futures for exceptional learners: An action agenda to achieve quality conditions for teaching and learning. *Teaching Exceptional Children, 32*(6), 56–69.

Kramer, M. W., & Tan, C. L. (2006). Emotion management in dealing with difficult people. In J. M. H. Fritz & B. L. Omdahl (Eds.), *Problematic relationships in the workplace* (pp. 153–178). New York, NY: Peter Lang.

Krathwohl, D. R., Bloom, B. S., & Masia, B. B. (1964). *Taxonomy of educational objectives; Handbook II: Affective domain.* New York, NY: McKay.

Kratochwill, T. R., & Pittman, P. H. (2002). Expanding problem-solving consultation training: Prospects and frameworks. *Journal of Educational and Psychological Consultation, 13*(1 & 2), 69–95.

Kreiss, C. (2011). What is rural America? *Teaching Tolerance 39,* 28–31.

Kroth, R. L. (1985). *Communication with parents of exceptional children: Improving parent-teacher relationships.* Denver, CO: Love.

Kusuma-Powell, O., & Powell, W. (2016). Lifting the status of learning support teachers. *Educational Leadership, 73*(4), 63–67.

Lakein, A. (1973). *How to get control of your time and your life.* New York, NY: McKay.

Lamme, L. L., & Lamme, L. A. (2001–2002). Welcoming children from gay families into our schools. *Educational Leadership, 59*(4), 65–69.

LaPolice, C. (2016). A critical moment. *Educational Leadership, 82*(4), 8–11.

Lasater, M. W., Johnson, M. M., & Fitzgerald, M. (2000). Completing the education mosaic: Paraeducator professional development options. *Teaching Exceptional Children, 33*(1), 46–51.

Laud, L. E. (1998). Changing the way we communicate. *Educational Leadership, 61*(4), 23–28.

Lawrence, G. (1993). *People types and tiger stripes: A practical guide to learning styles* (3rd ed.). Gainesville, FL: Center for Applications of Psychological Type.

Lawrence, G., & DeNovellis, R. (1974). *Correlation of teacher personality variables (Myers-Briggs) and classroom observation data.* Paper presented at American Educational Research Association Conference. Chicago, IL.

Leithwood, K., Harris, A., & Strauss, T. (2010). *Leading school turnaround.* San Francisco: Jossey-Bass.

Leko, M. M. (2015). To adapt or not to adapt: Navigating an implantation conundrum. *Teaching Exceptional Children, 48*(2), 80–85.

Leko, M. M. & Smith, S. W. (2010). Retaining beginning special educators: What should administrators know and do? *Intervention in School and Clinic, 45,* 321–325.

Levine, A. (2006, September). *Educating school teachers.* The Education Schools Project. Retrieved from www.edschools.org/teacher_report.htm

Lilly, M. S., & Givens-Ogle, L. B. (1981). Teacher consultation: Present, past, and future. *Behavioral Disorders, 6*(2), 73–77.

Linan-Thompson, S., & Jean, R. (1997). Completing the parent participation puzzle: Accepting diversity. *Teaching Exceptional Children, 30*(2), 46–50.

Lingo, A. S., Barton-Arwood, S. M., & Julivette, K. (2011). Teachers working together: Improving learning outcomes in the inclusive classroom—Practical strategies and examples. *Teaching Exceptional Children, 43*(3), 6–13.

Lopez, E. C., Dalal, S. M., & Yoshida, R. K. (1993). An examination of professional cultures: Implications of the collaborative consultation model. *Journal of Educational and Psychological Consultation, 4*(3), 197–213.

Loucks-Horsley, S., Harding, C. K., Arbuckle, M. A., Murray, L. B., Dubea, C., & Williams, M. K. (1987). *Continuing to learn: A guidebook for teacher development.* Andover, MA: Regional Laboratory for Educational Improvement of the Northeast and Islands.

Lubetkin, B. (1997, January). Master the art of apologizing. *The Manager's Intelligence Report.*

Maeroff, G. I. (1993). Building teams to rebuild schools. *Phi Delta Kappan, 74*(7), 512–519.

Mantz, J. (2010, October). *Combat Stress: Redefining the wounded warrior and family* [video file]. Retrieved from http://vimeo.com/16928841

Margolis, H., & McGettigan, J. (1988). Managing resistance to instructional modifications in mainstream settings. *Remedial and Special Education, 9*, 15–21.

Marks, S. U., Schrader, C., & Levine, M. (1999). Paraeducator experiences in inclusive settings: Helping, hovering, or holding their own? *Exceptional Children, 65*, 315–328.

Marquardt, M. J. (2014). *Leading with questions: How leaders find right solutions by knowing what to ask* (2nd ed.). San Francisco, CA: John Wiley & Sons, Inc.

Martin, J. E., Van Dycke, J. L., Greene, B. A., Gardner, J. E., Christensen, W. R., & Woods, L. L. (2006). Direct observation of teacher-directed IEP meetings: Establishing the need for student IEP meeting instruction. *Exceptional Children, 72*, 187–200.

Martin, R. (1991). *Extraordinary children—ordinary lives.* Champaign, IL: Research Press.

Marzano, R. J. (2007). *The art and science of teaching.* Alexandria, VA: ASCD.

Maslach, C. (1982). *Burnout: The cost of caring.* Englewood Cliffs, NJ: Prentice Hall.

Mason, C. Y., McGahee-Kovac, M., & Johnson, L. (2004). How to help students lead their IEP meetings. *Teaching Exceptional Children, 36*(3), 18–25.

Mayer, E., Ferede, M. K., & Hou, E. D. (2006). The family involvement storybook: A new way to build connections with families. *Young Children, 61*(6), 94–97.

Mayo, C. (2010). Queer lessons: Sexual and gender minorities in multicultural education. In J. A. Banks & C. A. M. Banks (Eds.), *Multicultural education: Issues and perspectives* (7th ed.) Hoboken, NJ: Wiley & Sons.

Mazzotti, V. L., Rowe, D. A., Sinclair J., Poppen, M., Woods, W. E., & Shearer, M. L. (2015). Predictors of postschool success: A systematic review of the NLTS2 secondary analyses. *Career Development and Transition for Exceptional Individuals,* doi: 2165143415588047

McCaffrey, M. E. (2000). My first year of learning: Advice from a new educator. *Teaching Exceptional Children, 33*(1), 4–8.

McCarthy, B. (1990). Using the 4MAT system to bring learning styles to schools. *Educational Leadership, 48*(2), 31–37.

McDonald, J. P. (1989). When outsiders try to change schools from the inside. *Phi Delta Kappan, 71*(3), 206–212.

McDonnell, L. M., McLaughlin, M. J., & Morrison, P. (1997). *Educating one and all: Students with disabilities and standards-based reform.* Washington, DC: National Academy Press.

McGrew-Zoubi, R. R. (1998). I can take care of it myself. *The Delta Kappa Gamma Bulletin, 65*(1), 15–20.

McKenzie, H. S., Egner, A. N., Knight, M. F., Perelman, P. F., Schneider, B. M., & Garvin, J. S. (1970). Training consulting teachers to assist elementary teachers in the management and education of handicapped children. *Exceptional Children, 37*, 137–143.

McLeskey, J., & Henry, D. (1998). Inclusion: What progress is being made across states? *Teaching Exceptional Children, 31*(5), 56–62.

McLeskey, J., Henry, D., & Hodges, D. (1998). Inclusion: Where is it happening? *Teaching Exceptional Children, 31*(1), 4–10.

McNaughton, D., & Vostal, B. R. (2010). Using active listening to improve collaboration with parents: The LAFF don't CRY strategy. *Intervention in School and Clinic, 45*(4), 251–256.

McTighe, J., & Brown, J. (2005). Differentiated instruction and educational standards: Is détente possible? *Theory Into Practice, 44*, 234–244.

Meadan, H., Shelden, D. L., Appel, K. & DeGrazia, R. L. (2010). Developing a long-term vision: A road map for students' futures. *Teaching Exceptional Children, 43*(2), 8–14.

Menlove, R. R., Hudson, P. J., & Suter, D. (2001). A field of IEP dreams: Increasing general education teacher participation in the IEP development process. *Teaching Exceptional Children, 35*(5), 28–33.

Mercer, D., Thurston, L. P., & Hughey, J. (2014). The college-wide military-connected learner initiative in K-State' College of Education. *ATE-K The Advocate, 22*(2), 24–30.

Mertens, D. M. (2015). *Research and evaluation in education and psychology: Integrating diversity with quantitative, qualitative and mixed, methods* (4th ed.). Thousand Oaks, CA: Sage.

Middleton, K. E. (2008). Sending teachers on visits to all homes. *School Administrator, 65*(2), 58.

Military Child Education Coalition [MCEC]. (2012). *Living in the new normal. Public engagement workbook.* Harker Heights, TX: Military Child Education Coalition.

Miller, T. N., Devin, M., & Shoop, R. J. (2007). *Closing the leadership gap: How district and university partnerships shape effective school leaders.* Thousand Oaks, CA: Corwin.

Millinger, C. S. (2004). Helping new teachers cope. *Educational Leadership, 61*(8), 66–69.

Mills v. Board of Education of the District of Columbia 348 F. Supp. 866 (D.D.C. 1972).

Mills, G. E. (2010). *Action research: A guide for the teacher researcher* (4th ed.). Upper Saddle River, NJ: Pearson.

Morel, N. J. (2014). Setting the stage for collaboration: An essential skill for professional growth. *The Delta Kappa Gamma Bulletin, 81*(1), 36–39.

Morsink, C. V., Thomas, C. C., & Correa, V. I. (1991). *Interactive teaming: Consultation and collaboration in special programs.* Columbus, OH: Merrill.

Muccio, L. S., Kuwahara-Fujita, R., & Otsuji, J. J. Y. (2014).'Ohana math: Family engagement to promote mathematical learning for Hawaii's young children. *Young Children, 69*(4), 24–30.

Mueller, P. H., & Murphy, F. V. (2001). Determining when a student requires paraeducator support. *Teaching Exceptional Children, 33*(6), 22–27.

Murawski, W. W. (2012). 10 tips for using co-planning time more efficiently. *Teaching Exceptional Children, 44*(4), 8–15.

Murawski, W. W., & Bernhardt, P. (2016). An administrator's guide to co-teaching. *Educational Leadership, 73*(4), 31–34.

Murphy, E. (1987). *I am a good teacher.* Gainesville, FL: Center for Applications of Psychological Type.

Murray, C. (2004). Clarifying collaborative roles in urban high schools: General educators' perspectives. *Teaching Exceptional Children, 36*(5), 44–51.

Murray, J. L. (1994). *Training for student leaders.* Dubuque, IA: Kendall/Hunt.

Myers, I. B. (1974). *Type and teamwork.* Gainesville, FL: Center for Applications of Psychological Type.

Myers, I. B. (1980a). *Gifts differing.* Palo Alto, CA: Consulting Psychologists Press.

Myers, I. B. (1980b). *Introduction to type.* Palo Alto, CA: Consulting Psychologists Press.

Myers, I.B. (1962). *Manual: The Myers-Briggs Type Indicator.* Palo Alto, CA: Consulting Psychologists Press.

Nagel, D. (2013). K–12 teachers out of pocket $1.6 billion on classroom tools. *THE Journal.* Retrieved from https://thejournal.com/articles/2013/07/01/k12-teachers-out-of-pocket-1-point-6-billion-on-classroom-tools.aspx?=THE21

National Center for Homeless Education. (2012). *Education for homeless children and youths program: Data collection summary.* Washington DC: U.S. Department of Education.

National Gay and Lesbian Task Force and the National Coalition for the Homeless. (2007). *Lesbian, gay, bisexual and transgender youth: An epidemic of homelessness.* Washington DC: Authors.

National Information Center for Children and Youth with Disabilities. The IDEA amendments of 1997. *NICHCY News Digest, 26,* 1–38.

Nazzaro, J. N. (1977). *Exceptional timetables: Historic events affecting the handicapped and gifted.* Reston, VA: Council for Exceptional Children.

Neel, R. S. (1981). How to put the consultant to work in consulting teaching. *Behavioral Disorders, 6*(2), 78–81.

Newman, L. A., & Madaus, J. W., & Javitz, H. (2016). Effect of transition planning on postsecondary support receipt by students with disabilities. *Exceptional Children, 82*(4), 497–514.

Nieto, S. (2000). Placing equity front and center: Some thoughts on transforming teacher education for a new century. *Journal of Teacher Education, 5*(3), 180–187.

Noel, A., Stark, P., and Redford, J. (2015). *Parent and family involvement in education, from the National Household Education Surveys Program of 2012* (NCES 2013-028.REV), National Center for Education Statistics, Institute of Education Sciences, U.S. Department of Education. Washington, DC.

O'Donnell, J., & Kirkner, S. L. (2014). The impact of a collaborative family involvement program on Latino families and children's educational performance. *School Community Journal, 24*(1), 211–234.

Osborn, A. F. (1963). *Applied imagination: Principles and procedures of creative problem-solving.* New York, NY: Scribner.

Page, S. E. (2007). *The difference: How the power of diversity creates better groups, firms, schools, and societies.* Princeton, NJ: Princeton University Press.

Papay, C., Unger, D. D., Williams-Diehm, K. & Mitchell, V. (2015). Begin with the end in mind: Infusing transition planning and instruction into elementary classrooms. *Teaching Exceptional Children, 47*(6), 310–318.

Parette, H. P., & Petch-Hogan, B. (2000). Approaching families: Facilitating culturally, linguistically diverse family involvement. *Teaching Exceptional Children, 33*(2), 4–12.

Park, J. H., Alber-Morgan S. R., & Fleming, C. (2011). Collaborating with parents to implement behavioral interventions for children with challenging behaviors. *Teaching Exceptional Children, 43*(3), 22–30.

Patnoudes, E. (March 27, 2015). What should come first, training or professional development? *EdTech* Focus on K-12. Retrieved from http://www.edtechmagazine.com/k12/article/2015/03/why-training-and-professional-development-go-hand-hand

Patterson, K., Grenny, J., McMillan, R., & Switzler, A. (2012). *Crucial conversations. Tools for talking when stakes are high* (2nd ed.). New York, NY: McGraw-Hill.

Pennsylvania Association for Retarded Citizens (PARC) v. Commonwealth of Pennsylvania, 343 F. Supp. 279 (E.D. Pa. 1972).

Perrin, A., & Duggan, M. (2015, June 26) *Americans' Internet Access: 2000–2015.* Pew Research Center. Retrieved from http://www.pewinternet.org/2015/06/26/americans-internet-access-2000-2015/

Phillips, V., & McCullough, L. (1990). Consultation-based programming: Instituting the collaborative ethic in schools. *Exceptional Children, 56,* 291–304.

Pickett, A. L., & Gerlach, K. (2003). *Supervising paraeducators in schools settings: A team approach.* Austin, TX: PRO-ED.

Pisha, B., & Coyne, P. (2001). Smart from the start: The promise of universal design for learning. *Remedial and Special Education, 22*(4), 197–203.

Plash, S., & Piotrowski, C. (2006). Retention issues: A study of Alabama special education teachers. *Education, 127*(1), 125–128.

Pogue, D. (2015). Is e-mail dead? *Scientific American, 312*(3), 27.

Pollio, H. (1987, Fall). Practical poetry: Metaphoric thinking in science, art, literature, and nearly everywhere else. *Teaching-Learning Issues, 3*–17.

Pratt, S. M., Imbody, S. M., Wolf, L. D., & Patterson, A. L. (2016). Co-planning in co-teaching: A practical solution. *Intervention in School and Clinic.* doi:1053451216659474

Pryzwansky, W. B. (1974). A reconsideration of the consultation model for delivery of school-based psychological services. *American Journal of Orthopsychiatry, 44,* 79–583.

Pugach, M. C., & Johnson, L. J. (1989). The challenge of implementing collaboration between general and special education. *Exceptional Children, 56*(3), 232–235.

Pugach, M. C., & Johnson, L. J. (1990). Fostering the continued democratization of consultation through action research. *Teacher Education and Special Education, 13*(3–4), 240–245.

Pugach, M. C., & Johnson, L. J. (1995). *Collaborative practitioners, collaborative schools.* Denver, CO: Love.

Pugach, M. C., & Johnson, L. J. (2002). *Collaborative practitioners, collaborative schools* (2nd ed.). Denver, CO: Love.

Purcell, J. H., & Leppien, J. H. (1998). Building bridges between general practitioners and educators of the gifted: A study of collaboration. *Gifted Child Quarterly, 42*(3), 172–181.

Putnam, J. (1993). Make every minute count. *Instructor, 103*(1), 39–40.

Rakow, S. (2012). Helping gifted learners soar. *Educational Leadership, 69*(5), 34–40.

Ray, V., & Gregory, R. (2001, Winter). School experiences of the children of lesbian and gay parents. *Family Matters, 28*–32.

Raymond, G. I., McIntosh, D. K., & Moore, Y. R. (1986). *Teacher consultation skills* (Report No. EC 182–912). Washington, DC: U.S. Department of Education. (ERIC Document Reproduction Service No. ED 170–915).

Raywid, M. A. (1993). Finding time for collaboration. *Educational Leadership, 51*(1), 30–34.

Reid, K. S. (2015, June 3). Parent engagement on rise as priority for schools, districts. *Education Week, 34*(32), 9.

Reis, S. M., & Westberg, K. L. (1994). The impact of staff development on teachers' ability to modify curriculum for gifted and talented students. *Gifted Child Quarterly, 38*(3), 127–135.

Reis, S. M., Burns, D. E., & Renzulli, J. S. (1992). *Facilitator's guide to help teachers compact curriculum.* Mansfield Center, CT: Creative Learning Press.

Renzulli, J. S., & Reis, S. M. (1985). *The schoolwide enrichment model: A comprehensive plan for educational excellence.* Mansfield Center, CT: Creative Learning Press.

Reynolds, M. C., & Birch, J. W. (1988). *Adaptive mainstreaming: A primer for teachers and principals.* White Plains, NY: Longman.

Richardson, A., Chandra, A., Martin, L. T., Setodji, C. M., Hallmark, B. W., Campbell, N. F., Hawkins, S., & Patrick, G. (2011). *Effects of soldiers' deployment on children's academic performance and behavioral health.* Retrieved from http://www.rand.org/pubs/monographs/MG1095.html

Riehl, C. J. (2000). The principal's role in creating inclusive schools for diverse students: A review of normative, empirical, and critical literature on the practice of educational administration. *Review of Educational Research, 70*(1), 55–81.

Rinke, W. J. (1997). *Winning Management: 6 fail-safe strategies for building high-performance organizations.* Clarksville, MD: Achievement.

Robinson, A. (1990). Cooperation of exploitation? The argument against cooperative learning for talented students. *Journal for the Education of the Gifted, 14*(1), 9–27.

Rodriguez, R. J., Blatz, E. T., & Elbaum, B. (2014). Strategies to involve families of Latino students with disabilities: When parent initiative is not enough. *Intervention in School and Clinic, 49*(5), 263–270.

Rosenfield, S. (1995). The practice of instructional consultation. *Journal of Educational and Psychological Consultation, 6*(4), 317–327.

Ross, R. G. (1986). *Communication consulting as persuasion: Issues and implications.* (Report No. CS506–027). Washington, DC: U.S. Department of Education. ERIC Document Reproduction Service No. ED 291–115.

Rossi, P. H., Lipsey, M. W., & Freeman, H. E. (2004). *Evaluation: A systematic approach* (7th ed.). Beverly Hills, CA: Sage.

Rothenberg, A., & Hausman, C. R. (1976). *The creativity question.* Durham, NC: Duke University Press.

Roy, P. A., & O'Brien, P. (1991). Together we can make it better in collaborative schools. *Journal of Staff Development, 12*(3), 47–51.

Rudd, M. D., Goulding, J., & Bryan, C. J. (2011). Student veterans: A national survey exploring psychological symptoms and suicide risk. *Professional Psychology: Research and Practice, 42,* 354–360.

Safran, S. P. (1991). The communication process and school-based consultation: What does the research say? *Journal of Educational and Psychological Consultation, 1*(4), 343–370.

Salzberg, C. L., & Morgan, J. (1995). Preparing teachers to work with paraeducators. *Teacher Education and Special Education, 18*(1), 49–55.

Scherer, M. (2016). What we didn't know when we co-taught. *Educational Leadership, 73*(4), 7.

Schulte, A. C., Osborne, S. S., & Kauffman, J. M. (1993). Teacher responses to two types of consultative special education services. *Journal of Educational and Psychological Consultation, 4*(1), 1–27.

Schultz, E. W. (1980). Teaching coping skills for stress and anxiety. *Teaching Exceptional Children, 13*(1), 12–15.

Scruggs, T. E., Mastropieri, M. A., & McDuffie, K. A. (2007). Co-teaching in inclusive classrooms: A meta-synthesis of qualitative research. *Exceptional Children, 73*, 392–416.

SEDL. (2000). Collaborative strategies for revitalizing rural schools and communities. Benefits 5. Austin, TX: Southwest Educational Development Lab, Retrieved from ERIC database. (ED444808)

Shapiro, E. S., & Manz, P. H. (2004). Collaborating with schools in the provision of pediatric psychological services. In R. T. Brown (Ed.). *Handbook of pediatric psychology in school settings* (pp. 49–64). Mahwah, NJ: Erlbaum.

Shaver, D., Golan, S., & Wagner, M. (1996) Connecting schools and communities through interagency collaboration for school-linked services. In J. G. Cibulka & W. J. Kritek (Eds.), *Coordination among schools, families, and communities: Prospects for educational reform.* Albany, NY: State University of New York Press.

Shields, C. M. (2010). Transformative leadership: Working for equity in diverse contexts. *Educational Administration Quarterly, 46*(4), 558–589.

Shroyer, G., Yahnke, S., Bennett, A., & Dunn, C., (2007). Simultaneous renewal through professional development school partnerships. *Journal of Educational Research, 100*(4), 211–224.

Shufflebeam, D. L., & Coryn, D.L. (2015). *Evaluation theory, models, and applications* (2nd ed.). San Francisco, CA: Jossey Bass.

Shyman, E. (2011). Examining mutual elements of the job strain model and the effort-reward imbalance model among special education staff in the USA. *Educational Management Administration & Leadership, 39*(3), 349.

Sibley, E., & Dearing, E. (2014). Family educational involvement and child achievement in early elementary school for American-born and immigrant families. *Psychology in the Schools, 51*(8), 814–831.

Sileo, J. M. (2011). Co-teaching: Getting to know your partner. *Teaching Exceptional Children, 43*(5), 32–38.

Silva, E., Thessin, R. A., & Starr, J. P. (2011). Supporting the growth of professional learning communities. *Phi Delta Kappan, 92*(6), 48–54.

Sime, D., & Sheridan, M. (2014). "You want the best for your kids": Improving educational outcomes for children living in poverty through parental engagement. *Educational Research, 56*(3), 327–342.

Simpson, E. J. (1972). *The psychomotor domain* (Vol. 3). Washington, DC: Gryphon House.

Simpson, R. L. (2004). Inclusion of students with behavior disorders in general education settings: Research and measurement issues. *Behavior Disorders, 30*(1), 19–31.

Slesser, R. A., Fine, M. J., & Tracy, D. B. (1990). Teacher reactions to two approaches to school-based psychological consultation. *Journal of Educational and Psychological Consultation, 1*(3), 243–258.

Smiley, T. (2012). Standing together against poverty. *Public Administration Review, 73*(3), 511–536.

Smith, S. J., & Ingersoll, R. M. (2004). What are the effects of induction and mentoring on beginning teacher turnover? *American Educational Research Journal, 41*, 681–714.

Smith, J. D. (1998). *Inclusion: Schools for all students.* Belmont, CA: Wadsworth.

Sondel, B. (1958). *The humanity of words.* Cleveland, OH: World Publishing.

Spalding, E., Klecka, C. L., Lin, E., Odell, S. J., & Wang, J. (2010). Social justice and teacher education: A hammer, a bell, and a song. *Journal of Teacher Education, 61*, 191–196.

Spies, T. G., Morgan, J. J., & Matsuura, M. (2014). The faces of hunger: The educational impact of hunger on students with disabilities. *Intervention in School and Clinic, 50*(1), 5–14.

Spillane, J. (2006). *Distributed leadership.* San Francisco, CA: Jossey-Bass.

Spooner, F., Baker, J. N., Harris, A. A., Ahlgrim-Delzell, L., & Browder, D. M. (2007). Effects of training in universal design for learning on lesson plan development. *Remedial and Special Education, 28,* 108–116.

Stainback, S., & Stainback, W. (1985). The merger of special and regular education: Can it be done? A response to Lieberman and Mesinger. *Exceptional Children, 51*(6), 517–521.

Stanley S. L. G. (2015). The advocacy efforts of African American mothers of children with disabilities in rural special education: Considerations for school professionals. *Rural Special Education Quarterly 34*(4), 3–16.

Stedman, P. & Stroot, S. A. (1998). Teachers helping teachers. *Educational Leadership, 55*(5), 37–38.

Steinbacher-Reed, C., & Powers, E. A. (2012). Coaching without a coach. *Educational Leadership, 69*(4), 68–72.

Stetson, R., Stetson, E. Sinclair B., & Nix, B. (2012). Home visits: Teacher reflections about relationships student behavior, and achievement. *Issues in Teacher Education, 21*(1), 21–37.

Stewart, R. A., & Brendefur, J. L. (2005). Fusing lesson study and authentic achievement: A model for teacher collaboration. *Phi Delta Kappan, 86*(9), 681–687.

Stockall, N. S. (2014). When an aide really becomes an aid: Providing professional development for special education paraprofessionals. *Teaching Exceptional Children, 46*(6), 197–205.

Strawbridge, M. (2006). *Netiquette: Internet etiquette in the age of the blog.* London, U.K.: Software Reference Ltd.

Sue, D. W. (Ed.). (2010). *Microaggressions and marginality; Manifestation, dynamics and impacts.* Hoboken, NJ: John Wiley & Sons, Inc.

Suter, J. C., & Giangreco, M. F. (2009). Numbers that count: Exploring special education and paraprofessional service delivery in inclusion-oriented schools. *Journal of Special Education, 43*, 81–93.

Swanson, K., Allen, G., & Mancabelli, R. (2015). Eliminating the blame game. *Educational Leadership, 73*(3), 68–71.

Symeou, L., Roussounidou, E., & Michaelides, M. (2012). "I feel much more confident now to talk with parents": An evaluation of in-service training on teacher–parent communication. *School Community Journal, 22*(1), 65–87.

Talley, R. C., & Schrag, J. A. (1999). Legal and public foundations supporting service integration for students with disabilities. *Journal of Educational and Psychological Consultation, 10*(3), 229–249.

Taylor, N., & Adelman, H. S. (1998). Confidentiality: Competing principles, inevitable dilemmas. *Journal of Educational and Psychological Consultation, 9,* 267–275.

Tharp, R. (1975). The triadic model of consultation. In C. Parker (Ed.), *Psychological consultation in the schools: Helping teachers meet special needs.* Reston, VA: Council for Exceptional Children.

Tharp, R. G., & Wetzel, R. J. (1969). *Behavior modification in the natural environment.* New York, NY: Academic Press.

Theoharis, G. (2007). Social justice educational leaders and resistance: Toward a theory of social justice leadership. *Educational Administration Quarterly, 43*(2), 221–258.

Thessin, R. A., & Starr, J. P. (2011). Supporting the growth of professional learning communities. *Phi Delta Kappan, 92*(6), 48–54.

Tiegerman-Farber, E., & Radziewicz, C. (1998). *Collaborative decision making: The pathway to inclusion.* Upper Saddle River, NJ: Merrill.

Tomlinson, C. (1999). *The differentiated classroom: Responding to the needs of all learners.* Alexandria, VA: Association for Supervision and Curriculum Development.

Toro, P., Dworsky, A., & Fowler, P. (2007). Homeless youth in the United States: Recent research findings and Intervention approaches. *Toward understanding homelessness: The 2007 National Symposium on Homelessness Research.* Washington DC: U.S. Departments of Health and Human Services and Housing and Urban Development.

Torrance, E. P., & Safter, H. T. (1999). *Making the creative leap beyond.* Buffalo, NY: Creative Education Foundation Press.

Trautman, M. (2004). Preparing and managing paraprofessionals. *Intervention in School and Clinic, 39*(3), 131–138.

Treasure, J. (2011, July). Julian Treasure: 5 ways to listen better. [Video file]. Retrieved from http://www.ted.com/talks/julian_treasure_5_ways_to_listen_better

U.S. Department of Commerce. (2012). *Income, poverty, and health insurance in the United States. Table number in poverty and poverty rate: 1959–2011.* Retrieved from http://www.census.gov/hhes/www/poverty/data/incpovhlth/2011/tables.html

U.S. Department of Education. (2008). Table 3-4. *Paraprofessionals employed (FTE) to provide special education and related services to students age 6 through 21 under IDEA, Part B, by qualification status and state*: Fall 2008 [Data file]. Available from Individuals with Disabilities Education Act (IDEA) Data Web site: https://www.ideadata.org

UNESCO. (1995). *Declaration of principles on tolerance.* Retrieved from http://portal.unesco.org/en/ev.php-URL_ID=13175&URL_DO=DO_TOPIC&URL_SECTION=201.html

Ury, W. (1991). *Getting past no: Negotiating with difficult people.* New York, NY: Bantam Books.

Van Reusen, A. K., Bos, C. S., Schumaker, J. B, & Deshler, D. D. (2007). *The self-advocacy strategy* (Revised). Lawrence, KS: Edge Enterprises.

Van-Belle, J., Marks, S., Martin, R., & Chun, M. (2004). Voicing one's dreams: High school students with developmental disabilities learn about self-advocacy. *Teaching Exceptional Children, 38*(4), 40–46.

VanTassel-Baska, J. (1989). Appropriate curriculum for gifted learners. *Educational Leadership, 46*(6), 13–15.

Vaughn, S., Schumm, J. S., & Arguelles, M. E. (1997). The ABCDEs of co-teaching. *Teaching Exceptional Children, 30*(2), 42–45.

Viel-Ruma, K., Houchins, D., Jolivette, K., & Benson, G. (2010). Efficacy beliefs of special educators: The relationships among collective efficacy, teacher self-efficacy, and job satisfaction. *Teacher Education and Special Education, 33*(3), 225–233.

Villa, R. A., & Thousand, J. S. (2003). Making inclusive education work. *Educational Leadership, 61*(2), 19–23.

Villa, R. A., Thousand, J. S., & Nevin, A. I. (2008). *A guide to co-teaching: Practical tips for facilitating student learning* (2nd ed.). Thousand Oaks CA: Corwin Press.

Vinoskie, E., Graybill, E., & Roach, A. (2016). Building self-determination through inclusive extracurricular programs. *Teaching Exceptional Children, 48*(5), 258–265.

Vittek, J. E. (2015). Promoting special educator teacher retention: A critical review of the literature. *SAGE Open.* doi: 10.1177/2158244015589994

Vygotsky, L. S. (1978). *Mind in society: The development of higher mental processes.* Cambridge, MA: Harvard University Press.

Wagner, M., Newman, L., Cameto, R., Garza, N., & Levine, P. (2005). After high school: A first look at the post-school experiences of youth with disabilities. A report from the National Longitudinal Transition Study-2 (NLTS2). Menlo Park, CA: SRI International.

Wallace, T., Shin, J., Bartholomay, T., & Stahl, B. J. (2001). Knowledge and skills for teachers supervising the work of paraprofessionals. *Exceptional Children, 67,* 520–533.

Walsh, J. M. (2001). Getting the "big picture" of IEP goals and state standards. *Teaching Exceptional Children, 33*(5), 18–26.

Wanat, C. L. (1997). Conceptualizing parental involvement from parents' perspectives: A case study. *Journal for a Just and Caring Education, 3*(4), 433–458.

Webster's new collegiate dictionary (8th ed.). (1996). Springfield, MA: Merriam-Webster.

Webster's Third New International Dictionary, unabridged: The great library of the English language. (1976). Springfield, MA: Merriam-Webster.

Weiss, H., Caspe, M., & Lopez, M. E. (2006). *Family involvement in early childhood education.* Cambridge, MA: Harvard Family Research Project. Retrieved from www.hfrp.html

Welch, M. (1998). The IDEA of collaboration in special education: An introspective examination of paradigms and promise. *Journal of Educational and Psychological Consultation, 9*(2),119–142.

Welch, M., & Sheridan, S. M. (1995). *Educational partnerships: Serving students at risk.* Fort Worth, TX: Harcourt Brace.

Welch, M., Sheridan, S. M., Fuhriman, A., Hart, A. W., Connell, M. L., & Stoddart, T. (1992). Preparing professionals for educational partnerships: An interdisciplinary approach. *Journal of Educational and Psychological Consultation, 3*(1), 1–23.

Wesley, P. W., & Buysse, V. (2006). Ethics and evidence in consultation. *Topics in Early Childhood Special Education, 26*(3), 131–142.

Wesley, W. G., & Wesley, B. A. (1990). Concept-mapping: A brief introduction. *Teaching Professor, 4*(8), 3–4.

Wessels, S., & Trainin, G. (2014). Bringing literacy home: Latino families supporting children's literacy learning. *Young Children, 69*(3), 40–46.

West, J. F. (1990). Educational collaboration in the restructuring of schools. *Journal of Educational and Psychological Consultation, 1,* 23–41.

West, J. F., & Idol, L. (1987). School consultation (Part I): An interdisciplinary perspective on theory, models, and research. *Journal of Learning Disabilities, 20*(7), 385–408.

Whitaker, S. D. (2000). Mentoring beginning special education teachers and the relationship to attrition. *Exceptional Children, 66*(4), 546–566.

Whitby, P. J. S., Marx, T., McIntire, J., & Wienke, W. (2013). Advocating for students with disabilities at the school level: Tips for special educators. *Teaching Exceptional Children, 43*(5), 32–39.

White, G. W. (2000). Nonverbal communications: Key to improved teacher effectiveness. *Delta Kappa Gamma Bulletin, 66*(4), 12–16.

Wilder, S. (2014). Effects of parental involvement on academic achievement: A meta-synthesis. *Educational Review, 66*(3), 377–397.

Wilkinson, L. A. (2005). Bridging the research-to-practice gap in school-based consultation: An example using case studies. *Journal of Educational and Psychological Consultation, 16*(3), 175–200.

Will, M. (1986). Educating children with learning problems: A shared responsibility. *Exceptional Children, 52*(5), 411–415.

Williams, J. M., & Martin, S. M. (2001). Implementing the Individuals with Disabilities Education Act of 1997: The consultant's role. *Journal of Educational and Psychological Consultation, 12*(1), 59–81.

Willingham, D., & Daniel, D. (February, 2012). Teaching to what students have in common. *Educational Leadership, 69*(5), 16–21.

Wood, D. Halfon, N., Scarlata, D., Newacheck, P., & Nessim, S. (1993). Impact of family relocation on children's growth, development, school function, and behavior. *Journal of the American Medical Association, 270*(11), 1334–1338.

Working Forum on Inclusive Schools. (1994). *Creating schools for all our students: What 12 schools have to say.* Reston, VA: Council for Exceptional Children.

World Book Dictionary: Volumes 1 and 2. (2003). Chicago: World Book, Inc.

Wormeli, R. (2007). *Differentiation: From planning to practice grades 6–12.* Portland, ME: Stenhouse Publishers, Westerville, OH: National Middle School Association.

Wright, R. E. (2010). LGBT educators' perceptions of school climate. *Kappan, 91*(8), 49–51.

Zabala, J., & Carl, D. (2010, December/2011, January). The AIMing for achievement series: What educators and families need to know about accessible instructional materials. Part Two: Navigating the decision-making process. *Closing the Gap, 29*(5), 12–15.

NAME INDEX

SUBJECT INDEX